OIL RIGS:
LAW AND INSURANCE

(Some Aspects of the Law and Insurance relating
to Offshore Mobile Drilling Units)

AUSTRALIA

The Law Book Company Ltd.
Sydney : Melbourne : Brisbane

CANADA AND U.S.A.

The Carswell Company Ltd.
Agincourt, Ontario

INDIA

N. M. Tripathi Private Ltd.
Bombay
and
Eastern Law House Private Ltd.
Calcutta
M.P.P. House
Bangalore

ISRAEL

Steimatzky's Agency Ltd.
Jerusalem : Tel Aviv : Haifa

MALAYSIA : SINGAPORE : BRUNEI

Malayan Law Journal (Pte.) Ltd.
Singapore

NEW ZEALAND

Sweet and Maxwell (N.Z.) Ltd.
Wellington

PAKISTAN

Pakistan Law House
Karachi

OIL RIGS:
LAW AND INSURANCE

(Some Aspects of the Law and Insurance relating
to Offshore Mobile Drilling Units)

by

MICHAEL SUMMERSKILL

B.C.L., M.A., F.I.Arb. A.C.I.I.

*of Merton College, Oxford and
of the Middle Temple, Barrister*

LONDON
STEVENS & SONS
1979

Published in 1979 by
Stevens and Sons Limited of
11 New Fetter Lane, London and
printed in Great Britain by
The Eastern Press Limited of
London and Reading

ISBN 0 420 44850 0

"Thou by the Indian Ganges' side
Shouldst rubies find: I by the tide
Of Humber would complain."

PREFACE

THE broad title *Oil Rigs: Law and Insurance* needs an explanatory sub-title. In this case it is *Some Aspects of the Law and Insurance relating to Offshore Mobile Drilling Units*. The study does not extend to production platforms nor to the work of the oil industry on land.

In the beginning there is a discussion of the physical aspects of these drilling units, with special reference to the manner in which they are categorised by the major classification societies. Many people ask: Are oil rigs (in this context offshore mobile drilling units) ships? A chapter is therefore devoted to this question, which has its entertaining aspects, as when Lord Justice Scrutton referred to what has been called "the elephant test," by which is meant that though we might not be able to define a ship—or an elephant—we could recognise one when we saw it. Others say that they know what is "essentially" or "really" a ship. The applicability of traditional maritime concepts to drilling units is considered, and the leading English cases on the meaning of the word "ship" are reviewed.

The nature of what, in maritime terms, can be called the hull insurance of a drilling unit is then studied, with particular reference to the London Standard Drilling Barge Form and the Norwegian Hull Form. Although it is appreciated that protecting and indemnity cover can be obtained in a variety of ways, the particular insurances discussed here are those used by the P. & I. clubs generally, and also by the Norwegian P. & I. clubs, which have evolved their own forms.

The relationship between the contractor, as owner of the drilling unit, and the operator of the unit is fundamental to the work of exploration and development. Some typical drilling contracts, including one drafted by the International Association of Drilling Contractors, are therefore considered. The chapter in question deals with the division between the contracting parties of their practical functions, their responsibilities, and their insurance liabilities. The numerous ancillary contracts with tugs, suppliers and others fall outside the scope of this book.

Some of the major liabilities and expenses incurred by the operator are then reviewed. The operator may be liable for pollution. It is necessary to study the terms of a typical policy covering seepage, pollution and contamination; the cover afforded by Oil Insurance Ltd. (O.I.L.); and the liabilities undertaken by the parties to the Offshore Pollution Liability Agreement (OPOL). Some pages are also devoted to a policy covering liability for the removal of debris, and a final chapter deals with the terms of a policy which insures the cost of control. It is appreciated that there are other forms of cover in respect of liabilities and expenses, including policies for comprehensive general liability, workmen's compensation, automobile liability, loss of hire, mobilisation expenses, war risks and so on; but their variety is such that it did not seem appropriate to extend this study to them, particularly as they relate so often to terrestrial as well as to marine risks.

The book concludes with four appendices. These set out the terms of the London Standard Drilling Barge Form and of the "International Daywork Drilling Contract—Offshore" of the International Association of Drilling Contractors. Another appendix discusses the applicability of the Marine Insurance Act 1906 to a policy for the insurance of a drilling unit. The last appendix sets out the story of a minor English constitutional contretemps, which involved discussion as to whether a self-elevating drilling unit was a ship.

There are of course some things which this book is not, and does not purport to be. First, although it is contemplated that those concerned with the multitudinous American aspects of the industry will find the book helpful, it looks at matters largely from an English point of view. It does not claim to state United States law, on which it is for those qualified in that subject to pronounce. Perhaps one day there will be a joint Anglo-American book on the subject. Indeed it is noteworthy that there has been considerable litigation on the subject of drilling units in the United States but an absence of reported cases in the United Kingdom, so far as the subjects discussed here are concerned.

Secondly, the book does not attempt to describe how insurance cover should be assembled for a contractor or an operator. That delicate and complicated task is essentially one for the insurance brokers, who can prescribe for their clients exactly what is needed in a particular situation. The relationships between the various kinds of cover; the relevance of the London market's drilling rig memorandum; the availability of and the need for such things as umbrella policies or bumbershoots; and, with some exceptions, the limitation figures to be sought are therefore not considered.

I have been generously helped by many friends and acquaintances, some of whom I must have tried severely with my second thoughts and requests for clarification. I am of course responsible, however, for all errors or omissions.

Sometimes it is invidious to lay stress on the names of some who have been helpful in such a task; at other times it would be invidious not to single out a few such names. This is one of the latter occasions. I have been particularly helped by and extend my heartfelt thanks to John Westwood of Sedgwick Forbes Marine Ltd., who has not only read and commented on most of the sections on liability and cost of control but also given me many valuable general suggestions. I also owe debts of gratitude to Messrs. Gordon Becker of Exxon Corporation; Theodore G. Dimitry of Messrs. Vinson & Elkins; Leonard D. Goodhill of Messrs. Richards, Hogg International; Taylor Hancock of Global Marine Inc. (and for permission to reproduce parts of his lecture); A. C. Hibbard of Messrs. Middleton Lewis Lawrence Graham; David B. Hill of Lloyd's; John R. Keates of the Offshore Pollution Liability Association Ltd.; H. T. McAdams of Seascope Insurance Ltd.; John C. Magner of Rowan Companies, Inc.; Robin Maxwell-Hyslop, M.P.; Alex. Rein of Messrs. Wikborg, Rein, Ringdal & Waelgaard; Russel F. Sammis of Messrs. Marsh & McLennan, Inc. (and for permission to reproduce parts of his lecture); Peter M. Stone of Messrs. Thos. R. Miller & Son (Insurance); Gr. J. Timagenis, Attorney at Law; E. D. Vickery of Messrs. Royston, Rayzor, Vickery & Williams; and Brian M. Waltham of Messrs. Ince & Co.

Others who have helped me include: Messrs. Robert Ardrey of Amoco (U.K.) Ltd., Stuart N. Beare of Messrs. Richards, Butler & Co. and R. W. Bentham of British Petroleum Co. Ltd.; Dr. Derrick R. Blaikley of Amoco Europe Incorporated; Messrs. G. Bourceau of Bureau Veritas, J. M. Bowen of Shell U.K. Exploration and Production Ltd., Antony Brown of Lloyd's List, August C. Burns of Lamorte, Burns & Co., Inc., John W. Buzbee of Marsh & McLennan, Inc., Clay Carter of Ancon Insurance Co. Ltd., Kenneth B. Charles of BP Petroleum Development Ltd., Robert M. Daniels of J. H. Blades & Co. Inc., Horace G. Davy of the General Council of British Shipping, Fernando de Azqueta of Naviera Vizcaina S.A., and H. E. Denzler Jr., on behalf of the International Association of Drilling Contractors; Captain A. F. Dickson of Shell International and the Oil Companies International Marine Forum; Messrs. Sweeney J. Doehring of Messrs. Fulbright, Crooker and Jaworski, Kenneth G. Elmslie of Messrs. Richards, Butler & Co., James W. Featherstone of the International Petroleum Industry Environmental Conservation Association, Brian Flint of the General Council of British Shipping, and A. Fowler of Shell International; Dr. Thomas F. Gaskell of the Oil Industry International Exploration & Production Forum; Messrs. Peter H. Ghee of Mobil Oil Corporation, C. E. Godsmark of the Home Office, Hans Richard Hansen of Det Norske Veritas, Nicholas J. Healy of Messrs. Healy & Baillie, Charles Hebditch of Messrs. Richards, Hogg International; Lai Herloffson of Assuranceforeningen Gard; Jørgen Højer of the Baltic and International Maritime Conference; Geoffrey Hudson of Messrs. E. R. Lindley & Son; Kjell Jacobsen of Assuranceforeningen Gard, C. A. Janicke of Norsk Boreriggeierforening, Duncan Kent of the Salvage Association, Piraeus, T. A. Lamplough of Lloyd's Register of

Shipping, John G. Maccoy, C.B.E., of Anderson Green & Co. Ltd., Ed McGhee of the International Association of Drilling Contractors, and John C. McHose of Messrs. Lillick, McHose & Charles; Mrs. A. Meldrum of the Inter-Governmental Maritime Consultative Organisation (IMCO); Messrs. Thomas A. Mensah, also of IMCO; Peter N. Miller of Messrs. Thos. R. Miller & Son (Insurance); Sven Moestue of Sven Moestue A/S; and John Oliver of Lloyd's; Dr. Nicos Papadakis of London, Attorney at Law; Messrs. Malcolm C. Pfautz of Gulf Oil Co.-U.S.; Havar Poulsson of Assuranceforeningen Skuld; M. J. Quire of Shell International; Bernard Richardson of Sedgwick Forbes Marine Ltd.; H. J. Russell of Atlantic Richfield Company, Los Angeles; K. Saunders of Continental Oil Company Ltd.; Charles J. L. Schoefer of the American Bureau of Shipping; and Loran Sheffer of Offshore Rig Data Services; the late Mr. George Sherlock of Sedgwick Forbes Marine Ltd.; Messrs. G. R. Smedley of Lloyd's Register of Shipping, Roy R. Smith of Richards, Hogg International; and W. Møller Sørensen of the Baltic and International Maritime Conference; Captain A. T. Thompson of the Oil Companies International Marine Forum; Messrs. Richard E. Towner of Messrs. Richards, Butler & Co., Claude Walder of the Oil Companies International Marine Forum, D. J. Lloyd Watkins of the British Maritime Law Association, and Peter Wingett of the Commercial Union. If I have inadvertently omitted from this list any of those who helped I apologise to them but thank them nevertheless.

I also thank, for permission to quote various definitions, the Bank of Scotland, in respect of its Glossary of Oil Industry Terms, and Kogan Page Ltd., in respect of *An A–Z of Offshore Oil and Gas*, by Mr. Harry Whitehead.

As for my own colleagues of both Messrs. Thos. R. Miller & Son (Bermuda) and Messrs. Thos. R. Miller & Son of London, I would like especially to thank Miss Fiona Pellant and Messrs. Terence G. Coghlin, Stephen J. B. James, Alan H. Maccoy, Michael D. Miller, R. J. Palmer, Vernon J. Parratt and Robin Travis. In addition I thank those from various insurance companies, insurance broking firms, colleges and institutes of insurance, and oil and insurance industry publications who have helped. I thank Mrs. A. Hazan, Mrs. C. Shaylor and Mrs. V. Williams for their help in typing the manuscript, and also Mr. R. Spicer, M.A., Barrister, for his work in preparing the Index. I also greatly appreciate the co-operation and great patience of my publishers Sweet & Maxwell Ltd.

Finally I thank my wife, Audrey, who had the idea.

Kastella, Piraeus, April, 1979.   Michael Summerskill

CONTENTS

Contents

TABLE OF CASES

(Pages on which the facts of a case are set out are indicated in bold type)

Table of Cases

TABLE OF STATUTES

Table of Statutes

CHAPTER 1

PHYSICAL NATURE OF
OFFSHORE MOBILE DRILLING UNITS

THIS chapter discusses the physical nature and the numbers of drill ships, drilling barges, semi-submersible drilling units, submersible drilling units and jack-up drilling units. It also sets out the manner in which three leading classification societies allot such units to their own particular categories of classification.

Drill Ships, or Drilling Ships

A drilling unit may be fashioned from a ship so that the appropriate equipment, known usually as the rig,[1] is incorporated into the structure as a whole. Alternatively a ship-shape structure may be built so as to constitute a drilling unit. In both cases the whole structure is called a drill ship, or sometimes a drilling ship. Such a unit has been defined in the following terms [2]:

> " A ship-shaped, mobile drilling rig, or floater,[3] specially constructed or converted for drilling for oil or gas in deep water."

The American Bureau of Shipping, in its Rules for Building and Classing Offshore Mobile Drilling Units, recognises drill ships for the purpose of its " Classification Notations," including them as a category of " Surface Type Drilling Units." [4] It divides the latter into two groups: (1) " Ship Type Drilling Units "; and (2) " Barge Drilling Units." Of the former, it is said:

> " This category includes seagoing ship-shaped units of the single hull, catamaran or trimaran types which have been designed or converted for drilling operations in the floating condition. Generally these types have propulsion machinery."

The second group, of barge drilling units, is discussed below.[5] In both cases there is a notation in the record to indicate any service limitations, draft and freeboard. The designation is +A1 followed by the words " Surface Type Drilling Unit."

Lloyd's Register of Shipping, in its " Rules for the construction and classification of mobile offshore units," refers to " Ship Units " and " Barge Units." [6] It states, in respect of the former:

---

[1] The complete assembly of hole boring equipment.
[2] *An A–Z of Offshore Oil and Gas*, Whitehead, 1976.
[3] As opposed to a structure sitting on the bottom.
[4] Its other categories are " self-elevating drilling units " (see below, p. 9) and " column stabilised drilling units " (see below, p. 5).
[5] See p. 4.
[6] Its other categories are " Self-elevating units " (see below, p. 10) and " column stabilised units " (see below, p. 5).

1

" Ship Units are self-propelled units of ship-shaped single or multiple hull form designed to operate afloat."

The description " Class 100A1 drilling ship " is

" assigned to sea-going Ship Units built in accordance with these requirements [*i.e.* those set out in the Rules], and the relevant requirements of the Society's Rules and Regulations for the Construction and Classification of Steel Ships."

Det Norske Veritas, in its " Rules for the Construction and Classification of Mobile Offshore Units," does not list a drill ship as a specific category. Instead, after providing for " column stabilised units " and " self-elevating units," it refers to " Other types of offshore units." Under the latter heading it is stated:

" Units which are designed as mobile offshore units, which do not fall into the above-mentioned categories, will be treated on an individual basis and be assigned an appropriate classification designation."

A comparison may be made of the categories established by the American Bureau of Shipping, Lloyd's Register of Shipping, and Det Norske Veritas, in respect of drill ships:

A.B.S. Ship Type Drilling Unit: a form of surface type drilling unit, the other form being the barge drilling unit. The category is not closed because the definition clause begins with the words " This category includes . . . " The units which would in any event qualify are ship-shaped, whether of the single hull, catamaran or trimaran type, designed or converted for drilling operations while in the floating condition, and generally have propulsion machinery.

L.R.S. Ship Unit: a separate category, as distinct from barge units. The requirements are that the unit be ship-shaped, whether in single or multiple hull form, designed to operate afloat, and self-propelled.

D.N.V. No specific category is given in respect of drillships. Under the Rules in respect of mobile offshore units, as quoted above, they fall within the category of units designed as mobile offshore units which do not come into the categories of column stabilised units or self-elevating units.

Drill ships may result, as has been indicated above, from the conversion of other ships, including tankers and bulk carriers. The central part of the ship is cut out so as to permit the installation of a derrick and the other principal elements of a drilling rig,[7] a moon pool,[8] and other essential equipment.

---

[7] For this term see also n. 1, above.

[8] " An exposed area on a drilling rig through which conductor pipe and other equipment are lowered into the sea, and drilling operations are conducted. On a floating rig the moon pool is located at the centre of gravity where vessel motion is least felt, but siting on a jack-up is not critical. Another name for the area is moon well." (*An A–Z of Offshore Oil and Gas*, Whitehead, 1976).

The conversion of existing ships may still occur, but its frequency depends upon demand, and factors such as the depth in which they are required to work. It often proves more economical to arrange for a conversion. A drill ship, whether it is built as such or results from a conversion, is often cheaper to mobilise and to maintain than other types of drilling units. At January 1, 1978, there were 62 drill ships in the world's mobile offshore drilling fleet of 387 units.[9]

The large surface which is exposed to the action of the waves tends to make a drill ship more responsive to such movement than other forms of drilling unit. A turret mooring system consists of a turret mounted in the well of the ship, beneath the derrick, and moored by (say) eight anchor lines which lead from four double drum winches. The ship can then revolve 360 degrees around the turret, by use of its bow and stern thrusters.

Though a turret mooring system helps to reduce heaving and rolling, many drill ships, provided that they were so built and are not conversions, rely solely on dynamic positioning or stationing equipment to keep them in position above the hole. The equipment, which is often controlled by a computer, involves the placing of transducers or acoustic beacons on the sea-bed, and the use of thrusters fitted with controllable pitch propellers. A turret mooring system may be used in support of the dynamic positioning equipment in waters less than 300 metres deep.

Drilling Barges

A drilling unit may resemble a barge rather than a ship, as that term is usually employed, in that it has no propulsion machinery. In other respects it has the same attributes as a drillship.[10] Drilling barges are usually employed in in-shore waters, rivers and estuaries. Such a unit has been defined in the following terms [11]:

> " A term used loosely to describe any type of offshore drilling vessel, but also referring specifically to the early type of unpowered, flat bottomed rig [12] with a ship-shaped hull. The latter are quite small rigs with a displacement in the region of 3,500 tons, although a few of over 10,000 tons have been constructed."

The American Bureau of Shipping, in its " Rules for Building and Classing Offshore Mobile Drilling Units," recognises drilling barges for the purpose of its " Classification Notations," including them as a category of " Surface Type Drilling Units." [13] It divides the latter into two groups:

---

[9] *The Offshore Drilling Register*, 1978, H. Clarkson & Co. Ltd. The Register lists the larger mobile seagoing units, capable of operating in at least 50 feet of water and having an overall drilling depth of at least 3,000 feet.

[10] See above, p. 1.

[11] *An A–Z of Offshore Oil and Gas*, Whitehead, 1976.

[12] See also n. 1, above.

[13] Its other categories are " Self-elevating Drilling Units " (see below, p. 9) and " Column Stabilised Drilling Units " (see below, p. 5).

(1) " Ship Type Drilling Units "; and (2) " Barge Drilling Units." Of the latter, it is said:

> " Barge type hulls are seagoing units designed or converted for drilling operations in the floating condition. These units have no propulsion machinery."

The first group, of ship type drilling units, is discussed above.[14] In both cases there is a notation in the record to indicate any service limitations, draft and freeboard. The designation is $+A1$ followed by the words " Surface Type Drilling Unit."

Lloyd's Register of Shipping, in its " Rules for the construction and classification of mobile offshore units," refers to " Ship Units " and " Barge Units." [15] It states, in respect of barge units:

> " Barge Units are units without primary propelling machinery designed to operate in the floating condition."

The designation " Class OU 100 A1 mobile drilling platform " is " assigned to sea-going self-propelled or non-self-propelled offshore drilling units, other than ship units built in accordance with these requirements."

Det Norske Veritas, in its " Rules for the Construction and Classification of Mobile Offshore Units," does not list a drilling barge as a specific category.[16]

A comparison may be made of the categories established by the American Bureau of Shipping, Lloyd's Register of Shipping, and Det Norske Veritas, in respect of drillships:

A.B.S.   Barge Drilling Unit: a form of Surface Type Drilling Unit, the other form being the Ship Type Drilling Unit. The units are barge typed hulls, designed or converted for drilling operations while in the floating condition, and have no propulsion machinery.

L.R.S.   Barge Unit: a separate category, as distinct from Ship Units. The requirements are that the unit is designed to operate in the floating condition, and has no primary propelling machinery. It is not stated that it should have a barge type hull or otherwise be barge shaped, though this can be implied by the title of barge unit.

D.N.V.   No specific category is given in respect of drilling barges. Under the Rules in respect of mobile offshore units, as quoted above, they fall within the category of units designed as mobile offshore units which do not come into the categories of column stabilised units or self-elevating units.

Drilling barges often resulted from the conversion of barges, including

---

[14] See p. 1, above.

[15] Its other categories are " self-elevating units " (see below, p. 10) and " column stabilised units " (see below, p. 5).

[16] For the nature of its reference to Units other than column stabilised units and self-elevating units see above, p. 2.

surplus U.S. Navy barges.[17] At January 1, 1978, there were 26 drilling barges in the world's mobile offshore drilling fleet of 387 units.[18]

Semi-Submersible Drilling Units

A semi-submersible drilling unit is a unit which floats above the drilling site. Such a unit has been defined and discussed in the following terms [19]:

> " A floating drilling rig consisting of hulls and caissons, carrying a number of vertical stabilising columns, supporting a deck fitted with a derrick and associated drilling equipment. Semi-submersible drilling rigs differ principally in their displacement, hull configuration, and the number of stabilising columns. Most modern types have a rectangular deck, a few are cruciform shaped, others pentagon shaped, while some of the smaller rigs have a triangular deck. The most usual hull arrangement consists of a pair of parallel rectangular pontoons, which may be blunt or rounded, and house thrusters for position-keeping or self-propulsion, although some have individual pontoons or caissons at the foot of each stabilising column or pair of columns. . . ."

The American Bureau of Shipping, in its " Rules for Building and Classing Offshore Mobile Drilling Units," includes semi-submersible drilling units as a kind of " Column Stabilized Drilling Unit " [20] for the purpose of its " Classification Notations." Of Column Stabilised Drilling Units the Rules state:

> " Units of this type are self-contained and are supported by either lower displacement type hulls by means of columns or by large caissons with or without bottom footings. Drilling operations may be carried out in the floating condition, in which condition the unit is defined as a semi-submersible, or when resting on the bottom, in which condition the unit is defined as submersible.[21] A semi-submersible drilling unit may operate either floating or resting on the bottom."

There is a notation in the record to indicate design water depth and wave height for on-bottom condition and design wave height for the afloat condition or both. The load line draft will also be indicated for the afloat condition. The designation is TA1 followed by the words " Column Stabilised Drilling Unit."

Lloyd's Register of Shipping, in its " Rules for the construction and classification of mobile offshore units," refers to " Column Stabilised Units." [22] It states:

> " Column Stabilised Units are working platforms supported on widely spaced buoyant tubular columns. They may be designed to operate when resting on the sea bed, afloat or both. A unit designed for bottom operation

---

[17] For the comparable process of converting ships see above, p. 2.

[18] *The Offshore Drilling Register*, 1978, H. Clarkson & Co. Ltd.

[19] *An A–Z of Offshore Oil and Gas*, Whitehead, 1976.

[20] The other categories are " Self-elevating Drilling Units " (see below, p. 9) and " Surface Type Drilling Units " (see above, p. 1).

[21] See below, p. 8.

[22] Its other categories are " Ship Units " (see above, p. 1), " Barge Units " (see above, p. 4), and " Self-elevating Units (see below, p. 10).

only is described as submersible.[23] A unit which may operate both on bottom or afloat is described as submersible (semi-submersible). The columns are usually attached to a bottom mat or individual buoyant footings which contribute to the buoyancy and provide a larger bearing area for sit-on-bottom conditions. Draught or bearing pressure can be adjusted by ballasting tanks within the columns or footings. Additional primary support for the working platform may be provided by bracing members connected to the columns. Accommodation and storage is also provided in the upper structure, which may comprise several decks."

The designation " Class OU 100 A1 mobile drilling platform " is

" assigned to sea-going self-propelled or non-self-propelled offshore drilling units, other than Ship Units[24] built in accordance with these requirements."

Det Norske Veritas, in its " Rules for the Construction and Classification of Mobile Offshore Units," includes semi-submersible drilling units under " Column stabilised units." [25] Of these it states:

" Units of this type are working platforms supported by either lower displacement type hulls by means of columns or by large caissons with or without bottom footings. A unit designed to operate afloat is described as semi-submersible. A unit designed to operate when resting on the bottom is described as a submersible." [26]

Designations such as "+class 1A1 Column Stabilised " are given to a unit which meets the requirements of the Rules, or a majority of the requirements, if recommendations are made simultaneously that the remaining work is to be completed within a short time, or that new surveys or other measures are to be carried out during a test period.

The platform, on which there is a drilling rig, has flotation chambers, or hulls, underneath it. These chambers, often two in number but sometimes more, below the surface of the water where the action of the waves is less strongly felt, give the unit its necessary buoyancy. It does not depend for its stability on being able to touch the bottom; in that sense it differs from a submersible drilling unit[27] and a self-elevating drilling unit.[28] The flotation chambers support, and are connected to, the platform by a number of vertical columns.

The unit is described as semi-submersible because it can engage in drilling operations without the need for its lowest parts, the flotation chambers, to touch the bottom. It is possible however, if the depth of water is not too great, for them to do so. At such a time the unit is operating in a manner similar to that of a submersible unit.[29] The depth of water would not then be greater than about 35 metres.

When, as is more frequently the case, the semi-submersible unit is not

---

[23] See below, p. 8.

[24] See above, p. 1.

[25] The other categories are " Self-elevating units " see below, p. 10), and " Other types of offshore units " (see above, p. 2).

[26] See below, p. 8.

[27] See below, p. 8.

[28] See below, p. 9.

[29] See below, p. 8.

sitting on the seabed, it will often, in its partially submerged state, be moored by one or more anchors running out from each corner of the platform. The mooring lines may be a kilometre or more in length, the distance depending upon whether they consist of wire or chain or a combination of both. Their function is to keep the unit in its correct position over the well.

In the movement of drilling units out to sea, which is mentioned later when the jack-up or self-elevating drilling unit is discussed,[30] the semi-submersible is the first unit, other than drillships and drilling barges, capable of floating on the water. Its stability is therefore a matter of great importance, as movements of the platform could affect the drilling operations. The anchors ensure that the semi-submersible unit always faces in the same direction. In the cases of the larger and newer semi-submersible units there may also be electrically powered thrusters for help in towing and possibly station keeping.

Accurate dynamic positioning of a semi-submersible unit, by dispensing with the need for anchors, has its own advantages. The existence of anchors, with their lengthy chains, increases the number of points at which a fault can occur in the system, and widens the area of exposure to physical contact, as another craft may contact or otherwise foul one of the anchor lines.[31]

The largest semi-submersible units are constructed so that they can withstand winds of up to 220 km.p.h. and waves of up to 30 metres.

A disadvantage of a semi-submersible unit, however, when compared with a drillship, is that it can carry less weight. This is because the centre of gravity of the semi-submersible unit is relatively high, so that its deck load has to be more restricted. The drillship can stow such items as the drill pipe, the riser pipe and mud below their waterlines, adding to their own stability.

A semi-submersible unit may be up to 100 metres wide and 75 metres long, with an operating draft of 18 to 25 metres.

The expression " semi-submersible " can give rise to misunderstandings. As in the cases of the other types of unit, neither the rig nor its platform is submerged below the sea level. Indeed it is important in all cases that there be adequate clearance between the base of the platform and the sea, with allowance being made for the highest waves which can be anticipated. The parts which are submersible are the stabilised columns and pontoons. In the case of the submersible the lowest parts are on the seabed, whereas in the case of the semi-submersible they are rarely on the seabed.

For short distances a semi-submersible unit may either be towed to its location and from one location to another by large tugs or supply boats or use its own means of self-propulsion.

---

[30] See below p. 9.
[31] See also pp. 111–112, below.

7

At January 1, 1978, there were 118 semi-submersible drilling units, out of 387 offshore mobile drilling units.[32]

A unit which is operating as a semi-submersible can work in waters which are 200 metres deep. Some of these units can work in depths of up to 600 metres. They may drill to a depth of 10,000 metres.

Submersible Drilling Units

A submersible drilling unit has been defined as follows [33]:

> " A type of drilling unit designed to operate close to shore, being an adaptation of the land-based rig. The deck of the rig is supported on a number of vertical or horizontal pontoons which are flooded when the rig is in position for drilling. Hence, the submersible is restricted to drilling in shallow waters, and it is not easily adapted for drilling in different locations."

It must be distinguished from another structure, also used in offshore work, and also known as a submersible. The other structure is an underwater vehicle, with a very small crew, used for a variety of work including inspection and installation of seabed equipment and oceanographic survey.

The American Bureau of Shipping, in its " Rules for Building and Classing Offshore Mobile Drilling Units," includes submersibles as a kind of " Column Stabilised Drilling Units " [34] for the purpose of its " Classification Notations." As to Column Stabilised Drilling Units the Rules state:

> "Units of this type are self-contained and are supported by either lower displacement type hulls by means of columns or by large caissons with or without bottom footings. Drilling operations may be carried out in the floating condition, in which condition the unit is defined as a semi-submersible, or when resting on the bottom, in which condition the unit is defined as submersible. A semi-submersible may operate either floating or resting on the bottom." [35]

Lloyd's Register of Shipping, in its " Rules for the construction and classification of mobile offshore units," refers to " Column Stabilised Units," [36] and says: " A unit designed for bottom operation only is described as submersible."

Det Norske Veritas, in its " Rules for the Construction and Classification of Mobile Offshore Units," also includes submersibles under " Column Stabilised Units," [37] and says: " A unit designed to operate when resting on the bottom is described as a submersible." [38]

---

[32] *The Offshore Drilling Register*, 1978, H. Clarkson & Co. Ltd.

[33] *An A–Z of Offshore Oil and Gas*, Whitehead, 1976.

[34] The other categories are " Self-elevating Drilling Units (see below, p. 9), and " Surface Type Drilling Units " (see above, p. 1).

[35] The nature of the notation in the record and the designation is the same as for semi-submersibles; see above, p. 5.

[36] Its other categories are " Ship Units " (see above, p. 1). " Barge Units " (see above, p. 4), and " Self-elevating Units " (see below, p. 10).

[37] For the exact words used, see above, p. 6. The nature of the designation is also set out on that page.

[38] *Ibid.*

Submersibles originated in the United States and were often used in swampy areas and in shallow bays in the Gulf of Mexico. They floated when the water was blown out of the bottom, and could then be allowed to sink down to the seabed again. One of the first submersibles, built in 1949, consisted essentially of " a drilling platform mounted on a pontoon stabilised compartment type barge." [39] The unit operated in depths of water up to 7 metres but could drill to depths of over 3,000 metres. Most submersibles were limited to water depths of about 25 metres, though some were later designed to operate in greater water depths.

At January 1, 1978, there were 10 submersibles in the world's mobile offshore drilling fleet of 387 units. [40]

Jack-up Drilling Units, or Self-Elevating Drilling Units

A jack-up or self-elevating drilling unit is one which, after being towed, or in some cases propelling itself, to its location, is able to lower its legs so that they rest on the seabed, the deck then being raised above the sea-level. It has been described as follows [41]:

" A type of mobile drilling rig [42] designed to operate in shallow water, generally less than 110 metres deep. Jack-up rigs are very stable drilling platforms as they rest on the sea bed and are not subjected to the heaving motion of the sea as are semi-submersible rigs [43] and drillships. [44] They have a barge-like hull, which may be ship-shaped, triangular, rectangular, or irregularly shaped, supported on a number of lattice or tubular legs. When the rig is under tow to a drilling location the legs are raised, [45] projecting only a few metres below the deck, and the structure behaves like a cumbersome floating box, and so can be towed only in good sea states at a slow speed. On arrival at location the legs are lowered by electric or hydraulic jacks until they rest on the sea bed and the deck is level, some 20 metres or so above the waves. Most jack-up rigs have three, four or five legs, but a few of the earlier models have eight or 10, and one has 14. The legs are either vertical or slightly tilted for better stability. . . ."

The American Bureau of Shipping, in its " Rules for Building and Classing Offshore Mobile Drilling Units," describes these units, in a separate category, [46] as " Self-elevating Drilling Units," for the purpose of its " Classification Notations." Of this category the Rules state:

" These drilling units have barge type hulls with sufficient buoyancy to safely transport the drilling equipment and supplies to the desired location after which the entire unit is raised to a predetermined elevation above the sea surface. Units of this type may have legs which penetrate the sea bed or have legs with enlarged sections at their lower ends to minimise penetration, or be attached to a bottom pad or mat." [47]

---

[39] " Ocean Industry," September 1973.
[40] *The Offshore Drilling Register*, 1978, H. Clarkson & Co. Ltd.
[41] *An A–Z of Offshore Oil and Gas*, Whitehead, 1976.
[42] See above, p. 1.   [43] See above, p. 5.   [44] See above, p. 1.
[45] In some cases the upper sections of the legs are removed.
[46] The other categories are " column stabilised drilling units " (see above, p. 5), " surface type drilling units " (see above, p. 1) and " other types of drilling units."
[47] A " mat-supported jack-up."

9

There is a notation in the record to indicate design water depth and wave height when in the elevated position. In addition, the load line draft is published, and this is valid when the unit is afloat. The designation is +A1 followed by the words " Self-elevating Drilling Unit."

Lloyd's Register of Shipping, in its " Rules for the construction and classification of mobile offshore units," refers to " Self-elevating Units." [48] It states:

> " Self-elevating Units are units having a hull with sufficient buoyancy to permit the safe transport of drilling equipment, supplies, etc., to a desired location. The hull then lifts itself on legs to the required level above the sea surface. The legs may be designed to penetrate the sea bed, or be attached to spuds, or to a mat which rests on the sea bed in the working condition and augments the hull buoyancy in the transit condition."

The designation " class OU 100 A1 mobile drilling platform " is assigned to self-elevating units, and indeed generally " to sea-going self-propelled or non-self-propelled offshore drilling units, other than Ship Units [49] built in accordance with these requirements."

Det Norske Veritas, in its " Rules for the Construction and Classification of Mobile Offshore Units," also refers to " Self-elevating units." [50] Of these it states:

> " A self-elevating unit is defined as a unit which in the normal operating condition rests on the sea bottom by means of legs with the main hull clear of the water. In the transit mode, the unit floats on the sea carrying the legs in lifted position."

Designations such as "+ Class 1A1 Self-elevating Unit " are given to a unit which meets the requirements of the Rules.[51]

The platform has to be jacked up to a safe level above the sea, clear of the heaviest waves. This is the time at which there is the greatest risk of accident. The operation of jacking up and down is a delicate one in which great care has to be exercised.

Historically, in the course of the movement out to sea of drilling units and their operations, the jack-up drilling units were developed from the fixed platforms which worked, with their legs permanently on the bottom, in shallow offshore waters up to a depth of about 30 metres. The first jack-up drilling unit was built in 1954. As a general rule jack-up units are not used for drilling in water more than 90 metres deep though a few can work in about 100 metres of water. The depth at which they work is limited by the length of their legs, which are subject to bending stress. In the North Sea, for example, their employment has been confined to the shallower southern section.

---

[48] Its other categories are " Ship Units " (see above, p. 1), " Barge Units " (see above, p. 4), and " Column Stabilised Units " (see above, p. 5).

[49] See above, p. 1.

[50] Its other categories are " Column stabilised units " (see above, p. 6) and " Other types of Offshore Units."

[51] Or, subject to certain conditions, a majority of the requirements.

Jack-up Drilling Units, or Self-Elevating Drilling Units

Where a jack-up unit is needed for work in deeper waters it is important to ensure that the legs are so constructed that they can take the greater strain thereby involved. In such waters the legs may be built of open fabricated or lattice work, or be of a buttress type. These may be contrasted with the welded-up caisson-like tubes, of a cylindrical nature, of the legs used in shallower waters. It is also possible, where the waters are deep but the weather not too severe, to add sections to the legs to enable the unit to work in such waters. The deep-water jack-up units are more expensive to operate than those which work in shallower waters. They are able to drill up to depths of 7,500 metres.

It is generally not possible to move the unit when it is at sea and on site more than about one and a half to two metres without a risk of damage to the legs. Such a move, even though the legs are down on to the seabed, may be necessary during the periods of breaking out, or uncoupling sections of casing or pipe, and spudding in, or starting a new hole.

At January 1, 1978, there were 171 jack-up drilling units, out of 387 offshore mobile drilling units.[52]

---

[52] *The Offshore Drilling Register*, 1978, H. Clarkson & Co. Ltd.

CHAPTER 2

DRILLING UNITS AS " SHIPS "

(A) Introduction; (B) Applicability of Maritime Concepts; (C) English Cases on " Ships "

(A) INTRODUCTION

ARE drilling units ships? The question is frequently asked both by those connected with drilling units professionally, whether in a commercial, legal or technical capacity, and by those who are outside the industry. This type of question is not new; the application of old and tested categories to new concepts has always caused difficulty, but it is an essential part of the development of language. It is possible to approach the problem by an examination of a dictionary definition, and then by trying to state what elements are common to ships; or in a more abstract way, by seeking to say what is the essence of a ship; or by concluding that there is no answer, except that we must look in each case at the context in which such a question arises. In the sections which follow this introduction this last course is adopted, when the applicability to drilling units of traditional maritime concepts [1] and the approach of the English courts [2] are discussed.

In the discussion which follows we will become particularly aware of the strong desire of most people to put objects into familiar categories by applying a particular label to them. A useful guide to the confusion which can exist when we try to define a term has been provided by Professor Simeon Potter in *Our Language*.[3] We can, he said, distinguish:

Symbol, or counter

Image, or thought

Referent, or thing.

If we bear in mind the word " ship," and this suggested tripartite division, the following passage by this writer [4] is helpful:

> " The study of language would be so much easier for us if we could be assured that the etymology of a word is not only something *real* and *true* (as, indeed, the Greek word *etymon* implies) but also that it is something permanent and that the basic form or *root* of a word has some inherent connection with the thing, quality or action denoted. Primitive peoples still believe that word has power over thing, that somehow the word participates of the nature of the thing. The word [*e.g.* ship] in fact is the symbol and it has no direct or immediate relation with the referent [*e.g.* the Ark, a drilling unit, a floating crane] except through the image [our idea or thought of " ship "] in the mind of the speaker."

---

[1] See p. 16, below.
[2] See p. 58, below.
[3] (Penguin Books, 1950), Chap. IX, " Etymology and Meaning."
[4] *Op. cit.* pp. 105–106. Square brackets indicate author's annotations.

This tripartite division bears some resemblance, and possibly because the minds of people work, consciously or unconsciously, in the way just described, to the trinity of God (symbol, or counter), Spirit (image or thought) and Son (referent, or personification).

The definition given by the dictionary is frequently regarded by lawyers as a useful starting-point, before they proceed to deal with a term in a particular context. Thus the *Concise Oxford Dictionary* gives as its definition of ship: " Vessel with bowsprit and three, four, or five square-rigged masts (*cf.* Barque, Brig, Schooner, Sloop); any sea-going vessel of considerable size. . . ." The term is said to be derived from the old English word scip, and to be comparable with the Dutch word *schif*, and the German word *schiff*. The old Norse was *skipa*. The Greek word for a hull is *skáphos*. A skipper is one who is a sea captain, and especially, according to that dictionary, the master of a small trading vessel.

This definition of a ship contains two elements: (a) a reference to the physical object itself, in that it is described as a " vessel "; and (b) a description of the purpose for which it is used, *i.e.* that it should be " sea-going." [5] The definition of a vessel also involves a reference to its use. The same dictionary defines " vessel " thus: " Hollow receptacle esp. for liquid, *e.g.* cask, cup, pot, bottle, dish; ship, boat, esp. large one. . . ." The term originates from the Old French word *vaissel*, which came from the Latin *vascellum*, a diminutive of *vas*, which itself meant a vessel, or duct. The expression " boat " is, in its turn, often used, sometimes as a synonym for ship or vessel, but rarely in connection with commercial operations. The *Concise Oxford Dictionary* defines a boat as a " Small open oared or sailing vessel, fishing vessel, mail packet, or small steamer . . . . " It follows from this that a boat, like a ship, is a special kind of vessel, but that it may also, according to circumstances, be a kind of ship; the terminology here is not too rigid in its application.

We thus reach the position that a ship is defined as a vessel, subject to certain qualifications, which will be mentioned below, as to the nature and purpose of that vessel; and that a vessel too is defined with some reference to its usage. It has been said [6] that it seems that the term " vessel " designates a variety of maritime craft, while the term "ship" is limited to a few species of the same genus. Though there seem to be good lexicographical reasons for regarding a ship as a species of the genus " vessel," individual statutes can by their wording produce a different result.

It is a characteristic of a vessel used domestically that it should be a container of substances. A jug may properly be called a vessel, as it is used to contain water or some other fluid. When the word is used in connection

---

[5] For a judicial discussion of the meaning of " vessels," see *Edwards* v. *Quickenden & Forester* [1939] P. 261, concerning a Thames collision between a racing skiff and a racing boat.

[6] By George Lazaratos, Attorney-at-Law (Athens), LL.M. (London), on "The Definition of Ship in National and International Law," in *Revue Hellénique du Droit International*, Vol. 22 (1969), at p. 64.

with the sea it does not follow that the object should contain a substance, such as a cargo. The term " passenger vessel " could be and is used almost interchangeably with " passenger ship." It is nonetheless a vessel because it carries only people; but its shape is such that it can be described as a hollow receptacle.

Whether drilling units are drilling ships, semi-submersibles or jack-up units, they usually go to sea, as opposed to remaining in internal waters,[7] or are capable to going to sea. As to whether they are vessels, it is submitted that they do not fail to be so merely because they do not carry cargo. One can speak of a passenger ship or a passenger vessel, which carries only people, as well as fuel, supplies and other necessary equipment; thus it would seem that a drilling unit, carrying people, fuel, supplies and other necessary equipment should not be debarred from being called a ship or vessel. One stumbling block, it may be argued, is that it does not have, except in the case of a drilling ship, the essential shape of a conventional ship or vessel. It does not look like one. It is not, to use the words of the dictionary, a " hollow receptacle," or at least, so far as there are hollow compartments, it is not the type of such receptacle usually encountered at sea.

But what is the significance of these words, "hollow " and "receptacle"? A receptacle is merely an object which may receive or contain some thing or things; and we have seen that a drilling unit does that. As for hollowness, the hollow shape of a conventional ship serves the double purpose of achieving buoyancy and providing somewhere to put the people and objects which are being carried.

A drilling unit has the elements of hollowness necessary to achieve the first of these two objects, that of buoyancy, by virtue of the flotation chambers which form part of it, whether it be a jack-up or a semi-submersible. But the hollowness does not simultaneously constitute the space for the people and things being carried. The space is above and the hollowness below. We have thus moved out of the area of conventional ships, in which the people and things carried are in the hollow area. A simple log raft floats because its specific gravity is less than that of water, and not because it contains a hollow space. It can carry objects, but no hollow space is needed. A raft on floats, however, combines but separates the functions of hollowness, which achieves buoyancy, and carriage. In discussing whether the concept of a " ship " or " vessel " applies to unconventional objects we encounter difficulties. This is because, having tried, by examining conventional modes of sea transport, to arrive at a definition of " ship " we present ourselves with a new object, such as a raft on floats or a drilling unit, and find that the definition does not fit. A decision then has to be made as to whether the definition should be extended because a new form of ship has emerged, or whether the new object is simply not a ship. The

---

[7] It is outside the scope of this work to analyse such concepts as internal waters, territorial waters, continental shelf, high seas or exclusive economic zones.

adoption of the first course may involve a decision either that the earlier definition was inadequate, some essential characteristic of " ship-ness " having been overlooked, or that it was adequate but should now be abandoned. Simeon Potter [8] suggested that some so-called " dictionary definitions " are not really definitions, but are descriptions. He quotes another writer, Michel Bréal, in *Essai de Sémantique* [9]:

> " Language designates things in an incomplete and inaccurate manner: *incomplete*, since we have not exhausted all that can be said of the sun when we have declared it to be shining, or of the horse when we say that it trots; *inaccurate*, since we cannot say of the sun that it shines when it has set, or of the horse that it trots when it is at rest, or when it is wounded or dead."

Another writer, has concluded, in lighter vein, that watertight definitions do not exist, even for ships.[10]

A meticulous listing, or description, of the characteristics of ships can lead, as we have suggested when we are faced with a new object, to a discussion, almost philosophical in its nature, as to what are the inherent qualities of a ship. What, we may ask, is " ship-ness "? Such a discussion is outside the scope of this book; perhaps Thomas à Kempis, however, made an appropriate distinction when he said; " I had rather feel compunction than understand the definition thereof." [11]

Some would say that neither an etymological dissection of the word ship nor a philosophical discussion of the essence of a ship is appropriate. We can adopt a subjective approach, as in the case of a person who says that he cannot define a certain object or concept but can recognise it when he encounters it. This accords with the expression " image," used by Simeon Potter.[12] One writer,[13] in discussing a semi-submersible drilling unit, " Pentagone 84," said: " It is really a ship, and below deck it looks and feels like a ship. But there are differences: the control room, the equivalent of a ship's bridge, is geared to the opposite principle of remaining absolutely stationary . . . ." The emphasis on what is " really a ship," [14] and what it " looks and feels like," is striking, and again suggests that there may be some essential quality of " ship-ness " which can be recognised. As Dr. Lushington said in *A Raft of Timber* [14a]: " This is neither a ship nor sea going vessel; it is simply a raft of timber". Scrutton L.J. spoke in similar terms in *Merchants' Marine Insurance Co. Ltd.* v. *North of England Protecting & Indemnity Association*,[15] referring to the judgment under appeal:

---

[8] *Op. cit.* pp. 104 and 105.

[9] (Paris, Hachette); translated into English as *Semantics; Studies in the Science o, Meaning* (New York, 1900).

[10] H. Meijer, *The Nationality of Ships* (1967), p. 15.

[11] " *Opto magis sentire compunctionen quam scire eius definitionem,*" *Imitation o, Christ*, Chap. 1.

[12] See p. 12, above.

[13] Martin Leighton, in the English newspaper, the *Observer*, on January 29, 1978.

[14] The image; see p. 12, above; and *cf.* " in reality " at p. 73, below.

[14a] (1844) 2 W. Rob. 251.

[15] (1926) 26 Ll.L.R. 201 (C.A.) at p. 203; see also p. 70, below.

" One might possibly take the position of the gentleman who dealt with the elephant by saying that he could not define an elephant but he knew what it was when he saw one, and it may be that this is the foundation of the learned judge's decision, that he cannot define ' ship or vessel ' but he knows that this thing is not a ship or vessel."

We could conclude that a drilling unit lacked the qualities essential to a ship, whether they were those to be found in a dictionary definition, by a more philosophical analysis, or by the adoption of a more subjective approach. We could abandon the attempt to apply a label and say that drilling units were *sui generis*, in a category of their own, though drilling ships, it seems, would have to be excluded from that categorisation. Yet another alternative would be to incorporate drilling units into some other definable category, such as artificial islands.[16] This would involve an analysis of the accepted definitions of an artificial island. These definitions are largely concerned with the extent to which artificial islands can be regarded either as true islands (although they usually lack a natural foundation) with consequent complications as to territorial waters, exclusive economic zones, etc.; or as ships. One view, which can be termed the residual approach, is that they are such man-made structures as are, prima facie, neither islands nor ships in international law. Another approach is that an artificial island should be regarded as *sui generis*, a separate legal category being established for it.[17]

Finally we are left with the question whether, in the case of any particular incident involving the application of certain legal rules normally pertaining to ships, such rules apply to the individual drilling unit. These rules may involve traditional legal concepts, as is the case with general average and salvage; or newly developing ideas, as with conventions relating to oil pollution. The next section is concerned with these problems.

(B) APPLICABILITY OF MARITIME CONCEPTS

The Differing Purposes for which the Definition of " Ship " may be Relevant in the Case of Drilling Units

A drilling unit may be treated as a ship for some but not all purposes. In this section examples are given of the situations in which such a problem might arise. The question, " Is this a ship? " may have to be applied to a drilling unit in a large number of situations. It is probably impossible to give an exhaustive list of such situations. In some cases one has to consider

---

[16] Artificial or floating islands are discussed in Gidel, *Le Droit International Public de la Mer–Le temps de paix* (1932), Vol. 1, pp. 66–68.

[17] A considerable amount of literature exists on this subject. See, among many publications: Gidel, *Le Droit International Public de la Mer* (1934), vol. iii; Professor D. H. N. Johnson, "Artificial Islands" (1961) 41 L.Q.R. 203–215; Colombos, *International Law of the Sea* (6th ed., 1967) pp. 125–127; and *Report on the Legal Status of Artificial Islands built on the High Seas*, by Margue, Council of Europe, Consultative Assembly Doc. 3054, 1971.

whether a drilling unit, or a particular category of unit, is a ship for the purpose of a traditional maritime concept, such as general average or salvage. In other cases we are concerned with the relevance of certain sets of rules which in the usual course are applicable to ships, such as those which govern classification or registration. In yet other cases the relevant law or other source of authority may not employ the word " ship," but a question may arise as to whether it applies to a drilling unit.

In the pages which follow an attempt is made to consider a list of topics with a view to ascertaining how far they concern offshore mobile drilling units. They are:

    (a) Admiralty jurisdiction [1];

    (b) Arrests [2];

    (c) Bills of sale [3];

    (d) Bottomry [4];

    (e) Certificates of fitness [5];

    (f) Classification [6]:

    (g) Collisions [7];

    (h) Flag [8];

    (i) General average [9];

    (j) International Conventions [10];

    (k) Liens [11];

    (l) Limitation of liability [12];

    (m) Load lines [13];

    (n) Mortgages [14];

    (o) Piracy [15];

    (p) Pollution [16];

    (q) Registry [17];

    (r) Safety of life at sea [18];

    (s) Salvage [19];

    (t) Stowaways [20]; and

    (u) Tonnage.[21]

(a) Admiralty jurisdiction

A question may arise as to whether an incident involving a drilling unit should be dealt with by that part of the High Court which deals with Admiralty matters or by some other part of the High Court. Section 1 (1)

---

[1] See this page.   [2] See p. 18, below   [3] See p. 20, below.
[4] See p. 20, below.   [5] See p. 21, below.   [6] See p. 22, below.
[7] See p. 23, below.   [8] See p. 27, below.   [9] See p. 29, below.
[10] See p. 30, below.   [11] See p. 33, below.   [12] See p. 36, below.
[13] See p. 39, below.   [14] See p. 40, below.   [15] See p. 40, below.
[16] See p. 43, below.   [17] See p. 51, below.   [18] See p. 52, below.
[19] See p. 53, below.   [20] See p. 55, below.   [21] See p. 56, below.

of the Administration of Justice Act 1956 sets out the "questions or claims" which fall within the Admiralty jurisdiction of the High Court. They include questions or claims involving possession or ownership of a ship, mortgage of a ship, loss of life or personal injury in relation to a ship, loss of or damage to goods carried in a ship, and other matters. In all the cases listed in the subsection, except for three, there is a specific reference to a ship; the three cases in which the word "ship" is not mentioned concern claims in respect of salvage (s. 1 (1) (*j*)), general average (1 (1) (*q*)) and bottomry (1 (1) (*r*)), all of which would commonly be expected to involve ships.[22] Section 8 (1) of the Act states: ". . . ' ship ' includes any description of vessel used in navigation." This is similar in terms to the definition in section 742 of the Merchant Shipping Act 1894: " ' Ship ' includes every description of vessel used in navigation not propelled by oars." The tests which have been applied in deciding whether a vessel is "used in navigation" appear in certain of the cases decided by the English courts and summarised below.[23] It is to these cases, therefore, that one should refer in order to form a view as to whether a drilling unit is subject to Admiralty jurisdiction. So far as an individual drilling unit can, at the material time, be regarded as a ship, as so defined, it will be subject to Admiralty jurisdiction.

(b) Arrests

1. *The right to arrest*

A right to arrest a ship exists in proceedings undertaken in a court which has Admiralty jurisdiction. The plaintiff thereby enforces his rights *in rem*, *i.e.* against the thing (in this case the ship) in connection with which the claim arose.[24] A plaintiff has first to ascertain whether the cause of action is one which falls within the Admiralty jurisdiction of the High Court, as defined in section 1 (1) of the Administration of Justice Act 1956.[25] Section 3 (1) of that Act states that, subject to certain restrictions which are not relevant here, the Admiralty jurisdiction of the High Court may in all cases be invoked by an action *in personam*. Section 3 (2) says that with respect to certain of the claims and questions set out in section 1 (1) the Admiralty jurisdiction of the High Court may " be invoked by an action *in rem* against the ship or property in question." Section 3 (3) then states that in " any case in which there is a maritime lien or other charge on any ship, aircraft or other property for the amount claimed, the Admiralty

---

[22] See also the references below to salvage (p. 53), general average (p. 29), and bottomry (p. 207).

[23] See pp. 58–85. See also, as to admiralty jurisdiction, such of the cases cited above as refer to the County Courts Admiralty Jurisdiction Acts of 1868 and 1869, *i.e.* those at pp. 65 and 67, below.

[24] For a discussion as to the nature of a maritime lien see Marsden's *The Law of Collisions at Sea* (11th ed. 1961) by McGuffie, Vol. 4 *British Shipping Laws*, at paras. 76 *et seq.*

[25] See also p. 17, above.

jurisdiction of the High Court . . . may be invoked by an action *in rem* against that ship, aircraft or property." Section 8 (1) of the Act contains a definition, as has already been pointed out above in connection with Admiralty jurisdiction [26]: ". . . ' ship ' includes any description of vessel used in navigation." The tests which have been applied in deciding whether a vessel is " used in navigation " appear in certain of the cases decided by the English courts which are summarised below.[27] It is to these cases, therefore, that one should refer in order to form a view as to whether a drilling unit may be arrested. So far as an individual drilling unit, can, at the material time, be regarded as a ship, as so defined, it will be liable to arrest.

2. *The 1952 Convention as to arrests*

The International Convention relating to the Arrest of Seagoing Ships was signed in Brussels on May 10, 1952. The object of the Convention was to agree as to certain uniform rules of law relating to the arrest of sea-going ships; the opening words of Article 2 were, accordingly: " A ship flying the flag of one of the Contracting States may be arrested in the jurisdiction of any of the Contracting States in respect of any maritime claim, but in respect of no other claim. . . ." The expression " maritime claim " was defined in Article 1 as meaning a claim arising out of one or more of a number of incidents, including damage caused by " any ship either in collision or otherwise "; salvage; general average; mortgage or hypothecation; loss of life or personal injury caused by any ship; agreement relating to the use or hire of any ship whether by charterparty or otherwise; loss of or damage to goods including baggage carried in any ship; and disputes as to the title to or ownership of any ship. The subsequent Articles refer to " a ship " and " the ship," but there is no definition of " ship." It would therefore be necessary to examine the relevant municipal law in each case in order to ascertain whether a drilling unit might be arrested.

3. *The draft Off-Shore Mobile Craft Convention*

A draft Convention on off-shore mobile craft [28] was adopted by the Comité Maritime International at Rio de Janeiro in September, 1977, and then transmitted to I.M.C.O. for appropriate action. Article 4, entitled " Arrest," referred to the 1952 Convention. It stated: " A State Party which is also a party to the International Convention for the unification of certain rules relating to the arrest of seagoing ships, dated May 10, 1952, shall apply the rules of that convention to craft [29] to which they otherwise would not apply."

---

[26] See p. 18, above.   [27] See pp. 58–85 below.

[28] For the aims and general provisions of the C.M.I. draft Convention see p. 31, below.

[29] As defined in the C.M.I. draft Convention; see p. 31, below.

(c) Bills of sale

A bill of sale has been defined [30] as a document which procures the assignment of chattels in such a way that the property in such chattels is intended to pass, but without possession of them being given by virtue of the document. A question may arise as to whether the transfer of ownership of a drilling unit requires a bill of sale, or whether the property in a drilling unit can, like that in other chattels, be transferred without a bill of sale. Section 24 (1) of the Merchant Shipping Act 1894 states: " A registered ship or a share therein (when disposed of to a person qualified to own a British ship) shall be transferred by a bill of sale." [31] If a drilling unit is a ship, and is registered, then ownership of the unit, or of any share therein, must be transferred by a bill of sale if the transfer is to a person qualified to own a British ship. For the purpose of the 1894 Act a ship is defined in section 742 thereof [32]; the definition has been discussed in a number of English cases. [33] It is to those cases, therefore, that one should refer to form a view as to whether a drilling unit may be transferred without a bill of sale; the problem would only appear to arise, however, in English law, if the transfer is to a person qualified to own a British ship. The nature of the qualification is set out in section 1 of the 1894 Act, as amended.

(d) Bottomry

Bottomry is a method by which a shipowner borrows money for the purpose of a voyage, using the ship and freight as security, the lender losing the money if the ship is lost. A bottomry bond was defined by Lord Stowell [34] as " a contract by which, in consideration of money advanced for the necessaries of the ship to enable it to proceed on its voyage, the keel or bottom of the ship, *pars pro toto*, is made liable for the repayment of the money in the event of the safe arrival of the ship at its destination." As the owner of a drilling unit does not proceed upon what can be called a voyage in the usual sense of that term, it would seem that the concept of bottomry is inapplicable to drilling units. In any event the financial resources of those involved in these operations are such that the borrowing of money to carry out a voyage or, in this case a movement of the unit, is extremely unlikely. As one authority [35] has said, however: " In practice bottomry is believed to be obsolete."

---

[30] By Lord Esher M.R., *Johnson* v. *Diprose* [1893] 1 Q.B. 512 (C.A.), at p. 515.

[31] For the transfer of a hulk without a bill of sale see *European & Australian Royal Mail Co., Ltd.* v. *Peninsular & Oriental Steam Navigation Co.* (1866) 14 L.T. 704, the decision in which is summarised at p. 59, below.

[32] A ship, according to the section, " includes every description of vessel used in navigation not propelled by oars."

[33] See pp. 58 to 85, below.

[34] In *The Atlas* (1827) 2 Hag.Adm. 48, at p. 53.

[35] Lowndes and Rudolf, *General Average* (10th ed. 1975), Vol. 7, *British Shipping Laws,* para. 374, n. 4.

As for the similar concept of respondentia, where the security is the cargo, the concept is also inapplicable, as the drilling unit does not carry cargo.

(e) Certificates of fitness

Some governments have required offshore operators to have a certificate of fitness in respect of offshore installations. In this connection there is no problem as to whether, for the purpose of such certificates, a drilling unit is or is not to be regarded as a ship, because it will fall within the definition of the structure in question. The definition in the Mineral Workings (Offshore Installations) Act 1971,[36] s. 1 (3) is: " ' offshore installation ' means any installation which is maintained, or is intended to be established, for underwater exploitation or exploration to which this Act applies." Just as it was found appropriate and necessary to legislate for the safety, health and welfare of persons on board ships,[37] so also legislation exists to safeguard the safety, health and welfare of personnel on board offshore installations. The 1971 Act applies to the underwater exploitation and exploration of mineral resources: " (a) in or under the shore or bed of waters to which this Act applies, other than inland waters, and (b) in or under the bed of such inland waters as may for the time being be specified for the purposes of this paragraph by Order in Council." [38] While it is outside the scope of this work to deal with claims to title in respect of territorial and other waters, it is relevant to add that section 1 (2) (a) says that the expression " waters to which this Act applies," contained in section 1 (1) (a), " means the waters in or adjacent to the United Kingdom up to the seaward limits of territorial waters, and the waters in any designated area within the meaning of the Continental Shelf Act 1964." A reference to " territorial waters " in an Act which does not define the extent of these waters can point either to the waters over which the British government claims sovereignty or to such waters as are regarded as territorial by contemporary international usage.[39] The reference to " any designated area" under the 1964 Act is explained by the fact that the Act vests rights to the sea bed and subsoil, with their natural resources, except coal, in the government; the areas within which it can exercise these rights are designated by four Orders, the Continental Shelf (Designation of Areas) Order 1964 [40] and the Continental Shelf (Designation of Additional Areas) Orders 1965, 1968 and 1971.[41]

The 1971 Act, by providing for the safety of offshore installations, and for the health, safety and welfare of those manning them, was designed to

---

[36] This Act is also mentioned in connection with Registry, at p. 51, below.

[37] As, for example, in the Merchant Shipping (Safety Convention) Act 1949, and in the Merchant Shipping (Load Lines) Act 1967.

[38] s. 1 (1).

[39] *R. v. Kent Justices, ex p. Lye* [1967] 2 Q.B. 153.

[40] S.I. 1964 No. 697.

[41] S.I 1965 No. 1531; S.I. 1968 No. 891; and S.I. 1971 No. 594.

implement the primary recommendation of the report of the inquiry into the accident to the drilling unit " Sea Gem." [42] The Offshore Installations (Construction and Survey) Regulations 1974,[43] made by the Secretary of State for Energy, prescribe minimum safety standards for the design and construction of such installations and for the plant and equipment on board; they provide for the appointment of certifying authorities, the carrying out of surveys and the issue and termination of certificates of fitness. With effect from August 31, 1975, no offshore installation could be established or maintained unless there was in force a valid certificate of fitness.

(f) Classification

Ships are put by classification societies into classes, so that all concerned, including especially the insurers, should, by reference to the class, have reliable information as to the standard attained by the hull and the machinery. A classification society sets technical standards of construction and assists, by periodical surveys and recommendations, in the maintenance of those standards. They are also often authorised by governments to carry out surveys with respect to such matters as loadlines,[44] safety [45] and tonnage measurement.[46]

The work of the classification societies is not necessarily confined to ships, for some deal with aircraft and civil engineering. The major classification societies, such as the American Bureau of Shipping, Bureau Veritas, Det Norske Veritas, Germanischer Lloyd and Lloyd's Register of Shipping, have also undertaken the classification of offshore mobile drilling units as well as of fixed production platforms and other structures such as floating storage and tanker-loading systems. In Chapter 1, above, concerning the physical nature of drilling units, the attitudes of some of these societies to the classification of drilling units are described. The approach adopted by the society in question may show that the structures are not treated simply as " ships." Thus the American Bureau of Shipping speaks of " Ship Type Drilling Units " and " Barge Drilling Units "; Det Norske Veritas refers to " column stabilised units," " self-elevating units " and " other types of offshore units "; and Lloyd's Register of Shipping designates the structures as " Ship Units " and " Barge Units."

The existence of differing standards, set by the various national classification societies, of which there are at least 21, can cause problems both for the owners of drilling units and for conventional shipowners. As one book [47] said: " The need for uniformity in standards becomes obvious when the entire problem is examined in the context of international

---

[42] H.M.S.O., Cmnd. Paper 3409.   [43] S.I. 1974 No. 289.
[44] See p. 39, below.   [45] See " Certificates of fitness " at p. 21, above.
[46] See p. 56, below.
[47] Singh and Colinvaux, *Shipowners* (1967), Vol. 13, *British Shipping Laws*, para. 426.

Conventions which regulate merchant shipping . . . the purpose of international regulation would be defeated by the numerous classification societies displaying their numerous standards of enforcement of international Conventions for the building and operation of merchant ships." It is understood to be not uncommon for the owner of an offshore mobile drilling unit to have to spend a substantial sum when moving the unit from one jurisdiction to another, because more stringent requirements have been imposed by the classification society authorised to act in the second jurisdiction than were imposed in the first jurisdiction. Some of the leading classification societies established the International Association of Classification Societies; under its auspices attempts have been made to develop a common approach to the classification of drilling units. The Association, working through one of its member societies, the American Bureau of Shipping, drafted " Unified Requirements for Mobile Offshore Drilling Units and other Similar Units." These were then submitted to the Inter-Governmental Marine Consultative Organisation with a view to their incorporation in the proposed I.M.C.O. Code for Mobile Offshore Drilling Units.

(g) Collisions

1. *Generally*

The word " collision " is generally applied to an accidental contact, usually resulting in damage, between one ship and another ship; some other expression is often used where a ship makes such contact with a fixed object, such as a quay, or a floating object, such as a buoy.[48]

In the case of accidental contact between a drilling unit and a ship, or between two drilling units, it seems appropriate to use the term "collision" to describe the event as such, the applicability of any collision liability insurance cover being a matter for separate consideration. In *Hough* v. *Head*[49] Grove J. said: " ' Collision' appears to me to contemplate the case of a vessel striking another ship or boat, or floating buoy, or other navigable matter—something navigated, and coming into contact with. It, so to speak, imparts, as it were, two things. It may be that one is active and the other is passive, but still, in one sense, they each strike the other. That does not apply to striking on the ground at the bottom."[50]

2. *Collision liability insurance*

Where a drilling unit is insured on the London Standard Drilling Barge Form[51] the relevant clause is clause 6, entitled " Collision Liability."

---

[48] See for example the use of the word " striking " in the discussion as to P. & I. cover for drilling units, at pp. 212 and 235, below.

[49] (1885) 52 L.T. 861 at p. 864. Grove J. appears to have regarded contact with a buoy as a collision.

[50] As had happened in the case before him. The cause of the loss was held not to have been a " collision " for the purpose of a time charterparty off hire clause.

[51] See Chap. 3, and especially pp. 109 *et seq.*, below.

It covers a case in which, as it says, "the Vessel [*i.e.* the drilling unit] shall come into collision with any other ship or vessel." The relevant insurance provision thus uses the term "collision" to describe the contact with "any other ship or vessel." It is thought that where the contact is between two drilling units the words "ship or vessel" would be so construed that such an incident was also covered by the collision clause in the Form.[52] In the case of a conventional ship or a drilling ship insured in accordance with the Institute Time Clauses (Hulls) clause 1 thereof covers a case in which, as it says, "the Vessel hereby insured shall come into collision with any other vessel." [53] It is thought that where a ship insured in that manner comes into contact with a drilling unit, of whatever type, the clause would be so construed that such an incident was covered by the insurance.

There may be a collision between a tug having the drilling unit in tow and a ship or another drilling unit. It was held in *The Niobe*[54] that where only ships are involved this counts as a collision for the purpose of the tow's insurance. It seems that the same principle would apply whether the drilling unit was claiming under the collision liability clause in the London Standard Drilling Barge Form; or the tug (because perhaps of its own negligence combined with an inability for some reason to recover from the tow under the towage contract) was claiming from its own insurers under the Institute Times Clauses (Hulls), and, in either case, whether the aggrieved third party was a conventional ship or a drilling unit.

3. *The* 1910 *Collision Convention and the Maritime Conventions Act* 1911

The International Convention for the Unification of Certain Rules of Law with Respect to Collisions between Vessels was signed in Brussels on September 23, 1910. Article 1 stated: "Where a collision occurs between sea-going vessels or between sea-going vessels and vessels of inland navigation, the compensation due for damages caused to the vessels, or to any things or persons on board thereof, shall be settled in accordance with the following provisions, in whatever waters the collision takes place." There follow a number of Articles, dealing primarily with the apportionment of loss in proportion to the respective degrees of fault, which constitute the "provisions" mentioned. These Articles refer to "the vessels" and to "each vessel," but there is no definition of vessels, sea-going vessels, or vessels of inland navigation.

The Maritime Conventions Act 1911 made the alterations to English law rendered necessary by the Collision Convention and by the Salvage Convention,[55] both having been concluded in 1910. It referred to "vessels"

---

[52] See also the discussion as to P. & I. Club cover at Chaps. 5 and 6, below.

[53] Not "with any other ship or vessel" as in earlier versions of the clause. See for example *Polpen Shipping Co.* v. *Commercial Union Assurance Co.* [1943] 1 K.B. 161 and p. 76, below.

[54] [1891] A.C. 401 (H.L.). Both tug and tow were negligent.

[55] See p. 54, below.

and provided in section 10 that it should " be construed as one with the Merchant Shipping Acts 1894 to 1907." As a result the definition of vessel given in section 742 of the 1894 Act applies; this definition has been discussed in a number of English cases.[56] It is to those cases, therefore, that one should refer to form a view as to whether a drilling unit may fall under the 1911 Act.

4. *The 1952 Collision Conventions*

The International Convention on Certain Rules Concerning Civil Jurisdiction in Matters of Collision and the International Convention for the Unification of Certain Rules Relating to Penal Jurisdiction in Matters of Collision or Other Incidents of Navigation were signed in Brussels on May 10, 1952. The first Convention refers, in Article 1 (1), to an " action for collision occurring between seagoing vessels, or between seagoing vessels and inland navigation craft. . . ." The second Convention refers, in Article 1, to " a collision or any other incident of navigation concerning a seagoing ship. . . ." There are no definitions of vessel or ship in the two Conventions.

The Administration of Justice Act 1956, which implemented the first Convention, refers to ships, and says, at section 8 (1), that a ship " includes any description of vessel used in navigation." [57] The second Convention did not require legislation.

5. *The draft Off-Shore Mobile Craft Convention*

A draft Convention on off-shore mobile craft was adopted by the Comité Maritime International at Rio de Janeiro in September, 1977, and then transmitted to I.M.C.O. for appropriate action.[58] Article 2, entitled " Collisions," referred to the 1910 and to the two 1952 Conventions. It stated: " A State Party which is also a party to:

— the International Covention for the unification of certain rules of law with respect to collision between vessels and Protocol of signature dated September 23, 1910, or to

— the International Convention on certain rules concerning civil jurisdiction in matters of collision dated May 10, 1952, or to

— the International Convention for the unification of certain rules relating to penal jurisdiction in matters of collision or other incidents of navigation dated May 10, 1952,

shall apply the rules of such convention or conventions to craft [59] to which they would not otherwise apply."

---

[56] See pp. 64 *et seq.*, below.

[57] See below, at pp. 58 to 85, the cases in which these or similar words have been considered.

[58] For the aims and general provisions of the C.M.I. draft Convention, see p. 31, below.   [59] As defined in Art. 1 of the C.M.I. draft Convention; see p. 31, below.

6. *The International Regulations for Preventing Collisions at Sea* 1972

The 1972 Regulations were first drafted at the International Conference on Safety of Life at Sea, held in London in 1960. The Convention on the International Regulations for Preventing Collisions at Sea was agreed in London on October 20, 1972. It, and the Regulations, came into effect in 1977.[60] The opening words of the Regulations, in Part A, Rule 1 (*a*), are: " These Rules shall apply to all vessels upon the high seas and in all waters connected therewith navigable by seagoing vessels." Rule 3, containing definitions, states: " For the purpose of these Rules, except where the context otherwise requires: (a) the word ' vessel ' includes every description of water craft, including non-displacement craft and sea-planes, used or capable of being used as a means of transportation on water." A somewhat similar definition [61] in the 1948 International Regulations, which came into force in 1954, had been considered in *The Law of Collisions at Sea*,[62] at para. 649: " Whether a ' vessel ' which is not a ship is strictly speaking bound by the regulations as such is doubtful. . . . The application of the regulations to vessels which are not ships appears to remain a matter of some doubt but it is probable that where a vessel can comply with the regulations she ought to do so as a matter of seamanship. Failure to comply with the rules of good seamanship will in most cases amount to negligence. The point, therefore, may be of no more than academic interest." It seems, nevertheless, that the regulations would apply to a vessel which is not a ship, provided that the structure in question fell within the definition in Rule 3 (*a*). Offshore mobile drilling units, of whatever kind, would seem to be " water craft " in any event; though it might be questioned whether they can properly be described as " used or capable of being used as a means of transportation on water." It does not appear to be essential, in order to satisfy the requirement as to transportation, that commercial cargoes should be carried. A drilling unit can transport, or carry, persons, equipment, specimens of oil, and supplies, and is thus capable of being used as a means of transportation, even if that is not its main task. This view is reinforced by Rule 3 (*g*), which refers to a vessel which is " restricted in her ability to manoeuvre." It sets out the vessels which shall be regarded as restricted in that ability, which include: " (ii) a vessel engaged in dredging, surveying or underwater operations "; and " (vi) a vessel engaged in a towing operation such as renders her unable to deviate from her course."

---

[60] There had been rules of the road at sea, forming part of general maritime law, for many years in England; in 1840 Trinity House introduced regulations to this effect; the Steam Navigation Act 1846 constituted the first British statutory embodiment of such regulations. The 1972 Regulations replaced the 1948 Regulations, which bore the same title.

[61] Rule 1 (*c*) (i): " the word ' vessel ' includes every description of water craft, other than a seaplane on the water, used or capable of being used as a means of transportation on water."

[62] Kenneth C. McGuffie (11th ed., 1961).

26

A further definition, also in Rule 3 (*b*), states: " The term ' power-driven vessel ' means any vessel propelled by machinery." The definition is relevant because many of the Regulations refer specifically to power-driven vessels.

It seems more appropriate here to indicate the nature of the problem than to endeavour to discuss all the permutations which may arise. Each situation would have to be assessed individually. A drilling unit may be on the site, either floating or jacked up, according to its nature; alternatively it may be moving to or from the site, and be either self-propelled or in tow. In each case a question may arise as to the applicability of the Regulations, and whether the drilling unit can be regarded as being propelled by machinery. In any event, as the editor of Marsden has said,[63] the question could be academic, as a court would probably treat failure to comply with the rules of good seamanship as negligence.

7. *The Collision Regulations and English law*

Section 418 (1) of the Merchant Shipping Act 1894, states that the Government may " make regulations for the prevention of collisions at sea, and may thereby regulate the lights to be carried and exhibited, the fog signals to be carried and used, and the steering and sailing rules to be observed, by ships, and these regulations (in this Act referred to as the collision regulations) shall have effect as if enacted in this Act." Section 418 (2) states: " The collision regulations . . . shall be observed by all foreign ships within British jurisdiction. . . ." It has been pointed out [64] that the Collision Regulations refer to vessels, defining them as including " every description of water craft . . . used or capable of being used as a means of transportation on water." The Act, however, refers to " ships," and section 742 defines a ship as including " every description of vessel used in navigation not propelled by oars." [65]

The Order which caused the 1972 Regulations to " have effect as if enacted " in the Act was the Collision Regulations and Distress Signals Order, S.I. 1977 No. 982.

(h) Flag

An offshore mobile drilling unit almost invariably has a flag. The generally accepted view as to flags is expressed in Oppenheim's *International Law* [66]: ". . . every vessel must, in the interest of the order and safety of the open sea, sail under the flag of a State . . . a vessel not sailing under the maritime flag of a State enjoys no protection whatever, for the

---

[63] See p. 27, above.
[64] Temperley, *Merchant Shipping Acts*, (8th ed. 1976), Vol. 11, *British Shipping Laws*, para 310, n. 3. The reference was to the 1948 Regulations, but the material words in the definitions are the same.
[65] See p. 59, below.
[66] Lauterpacht (Ed.) (8th ed. 1955), Vol. 1, pp. 592 and 595.

freedom of navigation on the open sea is freedom for such vessels only as sail under the flag of a State. But a State is absolutely independent in framing the rules concerning the claim of vessels to its flag. It can in particular authorise such vessels to sail under its flag as are the property of foreign subjects: but such foreign vessels sailing under its flag fall thereby under its jurisdiction. The different States have made different rules concerning the sailing of vessels under their flags. Some, like Great Britain, allow only such vessels to sail under their flags as are the exclusive property of their citizens or of corporations established on their territory. Others allow vessels which are the property of foreigners. . . ."

Certain fundamental propositions as to flag are also set out in C. J. Colombos, *International Law of the Sea* [67]: " The Flag which a ship flies is the evidence of her nationality. It is the simplest means of indicating by means of an external sign that the ship has a given nationality. . . . The Flag is, however, only one of the evidences of a ship's nationality; it does not absolutely prove it unless accompanied by the ship's papers showing the regular registration of the ship in one of the ports of her flag-state." A ship without a flag has no nationality and has been said to be unable to " enjoy any protection whatever," [68] just as a stateless person may also lack protection in many respects.

As Oppenheim points out,[69] different states apply different laws, and it is not necessarily the case that a ship or a drilling unit with a certain nationality is owned by a company or by persons with the same nationality. Thus a Liberian ship or drilling unit may be owned by a Panamanian company. Some countries, however, require that there should be a link between the flag and the ownership, but there is disagreement as to what should be the nature and the extent of the link. In the case of British ships, the Merchant Shipping Act, 1894, requires that the British flag can only be used where the ship is entitled to be registered as British,[70] and that such registration can only occur [71] if certain requirements as to ownership are satisfied. The Geneva Convention on the High Seas, 1958,[72] states: " Each State shall fix the conditions for the grant of its nationality to ships, for the registration of ships in its territory, and for the right to fly its flag. Ships have the nationality of the State whose flag they are entitled to fly. There must exist a genuine link between the State and the ship; in particular, the State must effectively exercise its jurisdiction and control in administrative, technical and social matters over ships flying its flag." It is not appropriate here to discuss further the relationship between

---

[67] (6th ed., 1967) p. 291.

[68] See *Naim Molvan* v. *Att.-Gen. for Palestine* [1948] A.C. 351 (P.C.)

[69] See the passage quoted, above.

[70] ss. 69 to 71.

[71] s. 1.

[72] It came into effect on September 30, 1962. It was ratified by some major ship-owning countries, such as Japan, the U.K. and the U.S.A. but not by Liberia and Panama.

ownership and the flag, as the only object of the above comments is to set out, in the simplest terms, the nature of the law and custom affecting flag. In all cases the relevant authorities refer to the flag of a " ship."

The concepts of flags and registry are thus intimately linked, and the flag used is the same flag as that of the country of registry.[73] It is therefore sufficient that a drilling unit should be registered for it to have a flag, and the definition of a ship is not relevant for this purpose.

(i) General average

Rule A of the Rules of Interpretation of the York-Antwerp Rules 1974, states: " There is a general average act when, and only when, any extra-ordinary sacrifice or expenditure is intentionally and reasonably made or incurred for the common safety for the purpose of preserving from peril the property involved in a common maritime adventure." This Rule was carried forward, without amendment, from the York-Antwerp Rules 1950. So far as drilling units are concerned, therefore, there could be a general average act for the purpose of the York-Antwerp Rules if there was " a common maritime adventure." In the rest of the Rules there are references to " the ship " or to " a ship " (Rules C, II to V, VII to XI, XIII, XIV, XVII and XVIII) but there is no definition of a ship or of " a common maritime adventure."

The Marine Insurance Act 1906, s. 66 (2), states: " There is a general average act where any extraordinary sacrifice or expenditure is voluntarily and reasonably made or incurred in time of peril for the purpose of preserving the property imperilled in the common adventure." The words used are thus almost the same as those which appear in Rule A of the York-Antwerp Rules. One relevant difference for our present purpose is that section 66 (2) refers to " the common adventure " whereas Rule A refers to " a common maritime adventure." It does not seem that the difference is significant so far as the applicability or non-applicability of general average to drilling units is concerned. The Marine Insurance Act applies to marine insurance and marine adventures [74]; it is unlikely that the absence of the word " maritime " in section 66 (2) could have the effect of extending the principles of general average to drilling units if they did not in any event apply to them.[75]

It should be borne in mind that even where the York-Antwerp Rules have not been incorporated by the parties to a venture in their contract the principles of general average may still apply. As *Arnould on Marine Insurance* [76] states: " The view best supported by judicial authority in this country [England] is that the right arises not out of contract, but from the old Rhodian laws, and has thence become incorporated in the laws of

---

[73] As to Registry generally, see p. 51, below.
[74] For the relevance of the Act to policies relating to drilling units see Appendix **D**, below, at p. 459.
[75] See s. 2 of the 1906 Act.
[76] (15th ed., 1961), para. 913, n. 9.

England as part of the law maritime." The passage in question adds that this is also the view which has been generally adopted in America.

In *Falcke* v. *Scottish Imperial Insurance Co.*,[77] Bowen L. J. said:

> " With regard to salvage, general average, and contribution, the maritime law differs from the common law. This has been so from the time of the Roman law downwards. The maritime law, for the purposes of public policy and for the advantage of trade, imposes in these cases a liability upon the thing saved, a liability which is a special consequence arising out of the character of mercantile enterprises, the nature of sea perils, and the fact that the thing saved was saved under great stress and exceptional circumstances. No similar doctrine applies to things lost upon land, nor to anything except ships or goods in peril at sea."

In *Lowndes and Rudolf on General Average* (10th ed., 1975), para. 48, a comparison is drawn between (a) a warehouse on land, where, it is said no suggestion has ever been entertained that the owner of goods therein, damaged by water in order to extinguish a fire, would be entitled to a contribution from the owner of the warehouse; and (b) the possibly more doubtful case of goods stored in a ship or hulk used as a floating warehouse, where it is submitted, there is no right of contribution in a similar situation because the ship is not being used in navigation, and there is therefore " no maritime adventure common to her and the goods which she contains. . . ." The editors [78] then say:

> " It is submitted that the doctrine of general average does not extend to aircraft. However, the owners of an oil-rig would, in principle, be entitled to receive and bound to pay general average contribution in respect of events occurring while it was moving or being towed, provided that there was more than one interest involved. But when the rig is stationary and not upon a voyage, it is submitted that there is no maritime adventure."[78a]

(j) International conventions

1. *Conventions generally*

An International convention may be clearly applicable to the various kinds of drilling unit; or it may state that it applies to ships, with or without a definition of ship, so that it is unclear whether it is intended to extend to drilling units; or some other form of words may make it clear, to a greater or less degree, how far drilling units are affected.

In the case of many of the terms discussed in this chapter there exist conventions which deal with the concepts in question. Reference should be made to the following terms, in respect of each of which there is a commentary on the appropriate convention, the full title of which is there given: arrests [79] (the 1952 Convention as to Arrests); collisions [80] (the 1910

---

[77] (1886) 34 Ch.D. 234, at p. 248.

[78] Sir John Donaldson, a High Court Judge, Mr. Christopher Staughton Q.C., and Mr. D. J. Wilson, A.C.I.I., a Member of the Association of Average Adjusters.

[78a] But see p. 85, below.   [79] See p. 18, above.

[80] See p. 23, above.

and 1952 Collision Conventions); flag [81] (the 1958 High Seas Convention); liens [82] (the 1926 and 1967 Conventions); limitation of liability [83] (the 1924, 1957 and 1976 Conventions); load lines [84] (the 1930 and 1966 Conventions); mortgages [85] (the 1926 and 1967 Conventions, dealt with under the same heading as liens); piracy [86] (the 1958 High Seas Convention); pollution [87] (numerous Conventions); safety of life at sea [88] (the 1960 and 1974 Conventions); salvage [89] (the 1910 Convention); stowaways [90] (the 1957 Convention); and tonnage [91] (the 1947 and 1969 Conventions).

2. *The draft Off-Shore Mobile Craft Convention*

In addition, the draft International Convention on Off-Shore Mobile Craft was adopted by the Comité Maritime International (C.M.I.) at Rio de Janeiro in September, 1977.[92] It was envisaged that the Inter-Governmental Maritime Consultative Organisation (I.M.C.O.) might adopt the draft, so that an International Convention might be formally agreed. The basic purpose of the Convention would be to apply the provisions of the existing maritime conventions on arrest, collisions, liens, limitation of liability, mortgages, oil pollution and salvage to such " craft " as are not already covered by them. The word " craft " was defined, in Article 1:

> " In this Convention ' craft ' shall mean any marine structure of whatever nature not permanently fixed into the sea-bed which:
>> (a) is capable of moving or being moved whilst floating in or on water, whether or not attached to the sea-bed during operations, and
>> (b) is used or intended for use in the exploration, exploitation, processing, transport or storage of the mineral resources of the sea-bed or its subsoil or in ancillary activities."

It was thought that drilling units and the other craft which fell within that definition of " craft " shared various maritime aspects with conventional ships, and that it was desirable to regulate those aspects in a Convention. So far as a number of topics, already covered by Conventions, were concerned, it seemed appropriate to treat these craft in the same way as conventional ships, not only because they resembled ships, but because in some countries they were considered to be ships. One solution would have been to spell out in a Convention the complete set of rules in the fields to be covered, and to make them apply to " craft." Another method would have been to provide that in the specified fields the craft should be deemed to be ships and should be treated as such. The third method, which was adopted, was to make the existing Conventions on these subjects applicable to craft to the same extent as they apply to ships.

The Articles of the draft Convention are, so far as they relate to the

---

[81] See p. 27, below. [82] See p. 33, below. [83] See p. 36, below.
[84] See p. 39, below. [85] See p. 40, below. [86] See p. 40, below.
[87] See p. 43, below. [88] See p. 52, below. [89] See p. 53, below.
[90] See p. 55, below. [91] See p. 56, below.
[92] The C.M.I., which was founded in Antwerp in 1897, is a non-governmental body consisting of and supported by the maritime law associations of numerous countries.

individual fields covered, set out in full under those headings, *i.e.* Arrest,[93] Collisions,[94] Liens,[95] Limitation of Liability,[96] Mortgages,[97] Oil Pollution,[98] and Salvage.[99]

The remaining Articles, 8 and 10 to 12 state:

Article 8: *Application of national rules*
 Subject to the provisions contained in Articles 9 and 10, a State Party, in so far as it is not a party to a convention referred to in Articles 2, 3, 4, 5, 6, or 7 shall apply to craft the rules which the State Party applies to vessels, in relation to the subject-matters dealt with in any such convention.
 Nevertheless, a State Party may, when enacting legislation with regard to vessels subsequent to this convention coming into force for that state, exclude craft which are not vessels from the application of such new legislation.

It is understood that proposals had been submitted under which the basic principle would have been that a state was free to apply its own law to craft for the purpose of the matters covered in the existing maritime conventions. This approach was not adopted, however; the draft convention provides that, subject to the provision as to minimum limits of liability for " platforms " (see Art. 9) states which were not parties to the existing conventions were to apply to craft the rules which they apply to ships in respect of matters dealt with by the conventions.

Article 10: *Maritime Lien in Respect of Pollution*
 No maritime lien shall attach to craft in respect of liability for pollution damage of whatever nature other than that imposed by Article 7[1] or similar rules applicable under Article 8.[2]

Article 11: *Nationality*
 If, under any of the conventions applicable pursuant to Articles 2, 3, 4, 5, 6 and 7 or the national rules pursuant to Article 8, nationality is a relevant factor, a craft shall be deemed to have the nationality of the State in which it is registered for title or, if not so registered, the State of its owner.

Article 12: *Savings*
 Nothing in this Convention shall affect the rights or obligations of any person or company in the capacity of concessionaire, licensee or other holder of rights with respect to mineral resources.

3. *The* 1948 *I.M.C.O. Convention*

The Inter-Governmental Maritime Consultative Organisation, or I.M.C.O., was established as a special agency of the United Nations Organisation in 1948. Its objects were set out in the Convention of the Inter-Governmental Maritime Consultative Organisation, signed at Geneva on March 6, 1948. Article 1 of the Convention stated that its purposes were (a) to provide machinery for cooperation in " technical

---

[93] Art. 4; see p. 19.   [94] Art. 2; see p. 25.   [95] Art. 6; see p. 35.
[96] Arts. 5 & 9; see p. 38. [97] Art. 6; see p. 40.   [98] Art. 7; see p. 51.
[99] Art. 3; see p. 55.
[1] Liability for oil pollution; see p. 51.
[2] Application of national rules; see this page, above.

matters of all kinds affecting shipping engaged in international trade " and to encourage " the highest practicable standards in matters concerning maritime safety and efficiency of navigation "; (b) " to encourage the removal of discrimination and unnecessary restrictions by governments affecting shipping engaged in international trade "; (c) to consider " unfair restrictive practices by shipping concerns "; and (d) to provide for " the consideration by the Organisation of any matters concerning shipping that may be referred to it by any organ or specialised agency of the United Nations."

Membership of I.M.C.O. is open to all states, whether or not they have fleets. Other references, direct or indirect, to ships include the provisions that (a) in electing the members of the Council the Assembly shall observe, among other principles, the principle that six members " shall be governments of States with the largest interest in providing international shipping services "; and (b) in the Maritime Safety Committee " Eight members shall be elected from among the ten largest shipowning States." The Convention does not define " shipping " or " shipowning."

It appears to have been accepted by the member governments that I.M.C.O. can and should deal with all technical and related aspects of sea-borne craft used or operated for international commercial purposes.[2a] The International Convention for the Prevention of Pollution from Ships 1973,[2b] concluded at a Conference convened by I.M.C.O., for example, was drafted so that it should apply to off-shore mobile drilling units. Thus it said: " ' Ship ' means a vessel of any type whatsoever operating in the marine environment and includes hydrofoil boats, air-cushion vehicles, submersibles, floating craft and fixed or floating platforms "; but the pollution was limited to pollution from the craft and not from the drilling operations. The Marine Environment Protection Committee of I.M.C.O. is concerned with the implementation of the Convention. Similarly, the Maritime Safety Committee of I.M.C.O. has been concerned with the safe design, construction and equipment of off-shore mobile drilling units.

So also the draft Convention on Off-Shore Mobile Craft, adopted by the Comité Maritime International at Rio de Janeiro in September 1977 [2c] was then referred by the C.M.I. to I.M.C.O. " for appropriate action " by its Legal Committee. The latter Committee, and the I.M.C.O. Council and Assembly, have all stated that they consider such craft to be within the competence of I.M.C.O.

(k) Liens

1. *Admiralty jurisdiction*

Where a collision has been occasioned by a conventional ship or a

---

[2a] The writer is indebted to Dr. Thomas A. Mensah, Director of Legal Affairs and External Relations of I.M.C.O., for much of the information set out here.
[2b] See also p. 45, below. [2c] See also p. 31, above.

drilling ship an aggrieved party has the right to a lien on the ship [3] for the amount of the loss. A lien is a feature of Admiralty jurisdiction, the nature and extent of that jurisdiction being set out in the Administration of Justice Act 1956, at section 1 (1) (*c*), which refers to " any claim in respect of a mortgage of or charge on a ship or any share therein." It would therefore seem that a lien could only arise with respect to a structure which can be described as a " ship," as defined in the Act. Section 8 (1) says that a ship " includes any description of vessel used in navigation." [4] The definition is similar to that in section 742 of the Merchant Shipping Act 1894, which states that a ship " includes every description of vessel used in navigation not propelled by oars."

2. *The* 1926 *Convention*

The International Convention for the Unification of Certain Rules of Law Relating to Maritime Liens and Mortgages, signed at Brussels on April 10, 1926, refers to " Mortgages, hypothecations, and other similar charges upon vessels, duly effected in accordance with the law of the Contracting State to which the vessel belongs. . . ." It provides for their recognition, subject to various provisos, in all other contracting countries. The term " vessels " is not defined in the Convention.

The Convention has not been made a part of English law; there, as the editors of *The Merchant Shipping Acts* put it [5]: " A mortgage of a ship is in general covered by the same principles, legal and equitable, as govern mortgages of other personal chattels, but the peculiar characteristics of ships as securities and the system of registration of ownership, bills of sale, and certificates of sale, have necessitated certain statutory provisions as to registration and transfers of mortgages and certificates of mortgages, which are contained in sections 31 to 38." [6] The provisions relate only to mortgages of British ships. A British drilling unit would be governed by these provisions if it satisfied the definition of a ship in the 1894 Act [7] as including " every description of vessel used in navigation not propelled by oars."

3. *The* 1967 *Conventions*

(a) The International Convention for the Unification of Certain Rules relating to Maritime Liens and Mortgages, signed at Brussels on May 27, 1967, refers to " Mortgages and *hypothèques* on sea-going vessels [9] . . . effected and registered in accordance with the law of the State where the

---

[3] And on the freight which she was engaged in earning, but not on the cargo.
[4] As to the relevance of Admiralty jurisdiction, and the applicability of these words to drilling units, see p. 17, above.
[5] (7th ed., 1976), para. 58.
[6] Of the Merchant Shipping Act 1894.
[7] s. 742.
[8] For the applicability of this definition to drilling units, see pp. 64–85, below.
[9] *Navire* in the equally authentic French text.

vessel is registered." The term "sea-going vessels" is not defined in the Convention.

(b) The International Convention relating to Registration of Rights in respect of Vessels under Construction, signed in Brussels on May 27, 1967, refers in its preamble to the "registration of rights in respect of ships under construction," but in Article 1 to "an official public register . . . of the rights set out in Article 5 [which provides for entry in the register of titles to and mortgages and *hypothèques* on a vessel which is to be or is being constructed] in respect of vessels. . . ." [10] It adds that registration "may be restricted to vessels, which, under the national law of the state of registration, will be of a type and size making them eligible, when completed, for registration as seagoing vessels." [11] There is no definition of the word "vessel" in the Convention.

4. *The draft Off-Shore Mobile Craft Convention*

A draft convention on off-shore mobile craft was adopted by the Comité Maritime International at Rio de Janeiro in September 1977, and then transmitted to I.M.C.O. for appropriate action.[12] Article 6, entitled "Rights in Craft," referred to the 1926 and to the two 1967 Conventions. It stated:

"A State Party which is also a party to:
- the International Convention for the unification of certain rules relating to maritime liens and mortgagees and Protocol of signature dated April 10, 1926, or to
- the International Convention for the unification of certain rules relating to maritime liens and mortgages dated May 27, 1967, or to
- the International Convention relatjng to registration of rights in respect of vessels under construction dated May 27, 1967,

shall, subject to Article 10[13] below, apply the rules of such convention or conventions to craft[14] to which they would not otherwise apply, provided that the State Party has established a system of registration of rights in relation to such craft.

Where such a system permits the registration of ownership of craft, a right so registered in one State Party shall be recognised by the other State parties.

For the purpose of this Article a structure's status as a craft as defined in Article 1 shall be determined in accordance with the law of the State where a title to or a mortgage on such structures is registered."

The proviso, contained in Article 10, entitled "Maritime Lien in Respect of Pollution," was to the effect that no maritime lien should

---

[10] As in the Maritime Liens and Mortgages Convention, the French and English texts are equally authentic. The word used in the French text is *navire*, both in the preamble and in the text itself.
[11] Reference should be made to the discussion of Registry at p. 51, below.
[12] For the aims and general provisions of the C.M.I. draft Convention see p. 31.
[13] For the text of Art. 10 see below, on this page, and p. 36.
[14] As defined in Art. 1 of the C.M.I. draft Convention; see p. 31, above.

attach to craft in respect of liability for pollution damage of whatever nature other than that imposed by Article 7 (liability for oil pollution) or similar rules applicable under Article 8 (application of national rules).

(l) Limitation of liability

1. *Generally*

Successive English statutes have granted to shipowners the right to limit their liability for loss of and damage to property, and for loss of life and personal injury, subject to certain restrictions. There are considered below the relevant international conventions and the Acts which have reflected the provisions of these conventions.

2. *The* 1924 *and* 1927 *Limitation Conventions*

The International Convention for the Unification of Certain Rules relating to the Limitation of the Liability of Owners of Seagoing Vessels was signed in Brussels, on August 25, 1924. Article 1 stated: " The liability of the owner of a seagoing vessel is limited to an amount equal to the value of the vessel, the freight, and the accessories of the vessel. . . ." It went on to set out the matters in respect of which liability could be thus limited, subject to an aggregate limit per ton of the vessel's tonnage in respect of some of these matters. There followed a number of Articles which referred to the " vessel " but there was no definition of a vessel or of a seagoing vessel. For the purpose of tonnage calculations Article II referred first to " steamers and other mechanically propelled vessels," and then to " sailing vessels," as each category was subject to a different method of calculation.

The International Convention relating to the Limitation of the Liability of Owners of Sea-going Ships was signed at Brussels on October 10, 1957. Article 1 (1) stated, in its opening words: " The owner of a sea-going ship may limit his liability in accordance with Article 3 of this Convention " (which set out the applicable limits per ton). There followed the rest of Article 1, and a number of other Articles which referred to " the ship," and to " any ship "; but there was no definition of a ship. For the purpose of tonnage calculations Article 3 (7) referred first to " steamships or other mechanically propelled ships," and then to " all other ships," as each category was subject to a different method of calculation. Under Article 8 each contracting state reserved the right to decide what other classes of ship should be treated in the same manner as sea-going ships for the purpose of the Convention.

3. *The Merchant Shipping (Liability of Shipowners and others) Act* 1958

The main object of the 1958 Act was to incorporate into English law the 1957 Limitation Convention. The limits per ton set to liability in respect of damage to property and life and injury claims in earlier Acts [15] were

---

[15] The Merchant Shipping Acts of 1894, s. 503, and of 1900, s. 2.

increased, from £15 and £8 to 3,100 Gold Francs and 1,000 Gold Francs respectively.[16] The Act said that it was to be construed as one with the Merchant Shipping Acts 1894 to 1954. As a result the definition of ship in section 742 of the 1894 Act, as including " every description of vessel used in navigation not propelled by oars," applied for limitation purposes. This had been extended by the Merchant Shipping Act 1921, s. 1, to cover " lighters, barges, and other like vessels used in navigation in Great Britain, however propelled." The applicability of this definition, and thus of the rules as to limitation, to the various categories of drilling units, must therefore depend upon a study of these cases in the English courts in which the definition has been construed.[17]

The 1958 Act also [18] extended the entitlement to limitation to " any structure, whether completed or in course of completion, launched and intended for use in navigation as a ship or part of a ship." As the extension was linked to the concept of a ship, even though the structure could not yet be called a ship, it did not affect the applicability, or otherwise, of the Act to drilling units.

4. *The* 1976 *Limitation Convention*

The International Convention on Limitation of Liability for Maritime Claims was signed in London, on November 19, 1976. It was intended to replace the 1957 Convention. The concept of " fault or privity," which previously prevented limitation, was replaced by a provision that the right to limit was barred if it was proved that the loss resulted from personal acts or omissions committed with the intent to cause such loss, or recklessly and with the knowledge that such loss would probably result. Limitation was put into two categories: (a) " general limits " (Art. 6), with provisions both for death and personal injury and for property claims; and (b) " Limits for passenger claims " (Art. 7).

Article 1, " Persons entitled to limit liability," states, at subsection 2: " The term shipowner shall mean the owner, charterer, manager and operator of a sea-going ship." The word " ship " was not defined, but Article 15.5 states: " This Convention shall not apply to: (a) air-cushion vehicles; (b) floating platforms constructed for the purpose of exploring or exploiting the natural resources of the sea-bed or the subsoil thereof."

The test is said to lie in the purpose for which the object was constructed. Drilling units other than self-elevating units were constructed for the purposes named and the Convention would not apply.[19] It might also be

---

[16] A Merchant Shipping (Sterling Equivalents) (Various Enactments) Order 1978, made in accordance with authority given by the 1958 Act, fixed the sterling equivalent of these sums (by reference to the Special Drawing Right value of a gold franc) at £134.58 and £43.41, with effect from October 16, 1978.

[17] See pp. 64–85, below.

[18] By s. 4 (1)

[19] So also Tovalop (Tanker Owners' Voluntary Agreement Concerning Liability for Oil Pollution) defines a tanker as " any tank vessel (whether or not self-propelled) designed and *constructed* for the carriage by sea in bulk of crude petroleum [etc.]."

successfully argued that a self-elevating unit was constructed for such purposes although it would not be floating when achieving them. The case of a drilling ship would seem to depend upon whether it was " constructed " for that purpose or adapted from an existing ship. If the latter was the case the Convention would apply.

5. *The draft Off-Shore Mobile Craft Convention*

A draft convention on off-shore mobile craft was adopted by the Comité Maritime International at Rio de Janeiro in September 1977, and then transmitted to I.M.C.O. for appropriate action.[20] Article 5, entitled " Limitation of Liability," referred to the 1924, 1957 and 1976 conventions. It stated:

> " A State Party which is also a party to
> – the International Convention for the unification of certain rules relating to the limitation of the liability of owners of sea-going vessels and Protocol of signature dated August 25, 1924, or to
> – the International Convention relating to the limitation of the liability of owners of sea-going ships and Protocol of signature dated October 10, 1957, or to
> – the Convention on limitation of liability for maritime claims dated November 19, 1976,
> shall, subject to Article 9 [21] below, apply the rules of any such convention to craft to which they would not otherwise apply. In the case of the 1976 Convention, a State Party shall do so notwithstanding the provisions of Article 15, para. 5 of that convention.[22]

Suggestions from some quarters that limitation should rest on a special basis other than tonnage, such as value or a multiple of tonnage measurement, appear to have been resisted. However, a provision was included whereby " craft which are platforms " were deemed to have a minimum tonnage for the purpose of limitation of liability, including liability for pollution. This was achieved by the insertion in Article 5 of the proviso by which the obligation to apply the rules of any of the three earlier conventions was stated to be " subject to Article 9 " of the C.M.I. draft convention. Article 9 stated: " Minimum limits of Liability for Platforms.[23] For the purposes of calculating the limit of liability under Articles 5 [24] and 7,[25] craft which are platforms shall be deemed to be of not less than x tons.[26] The same shall apply to the limit of liability under national law pursuant to Article 8 [27] above if and in so far as such a limit is based on tonnage."

---

[20] For the aims and general provisions of the C.M.I. draft convention see p. 31, above.

[21] For the terms of Art. 9 see the next paragraph.

[22] As to which see p. 37, above.

[23] There is no definition of " platform " in the C.M.I. Convention.

[24] " Limitation of Liability," *i.e.* the Article now under consideration.

[25] " Liability for Oil Pollution "; see p. 51, below.

[26] The minimum figure was left open.

[27] Application of National Rules, see p. 32, above.

(m) Load lines

1. *The* 1930 *and* 1966 *Conventions*

(a) An International Convention Respecting Load Lines was signed in London on July 5, 1930. The preamble referred to the desire of the signatory countries " to promote safety of life and property at sea by establishing in common agreement uniform principles and rules with regard to the limits to which ships on international voyages may be loaded. . . ." Article 2.1 also said that the Convention applied " to all ships engaged on international voyages " with certain exceptions such as ships of war and ships of less than 150 gross registered tons. The term " ship " was not defined. An " international voyage " was defined as " a voyage from a country to which this Convention applies to a port outside such country, or conversely. . . ."

(b) An International Convention on Load-Lines was signed in London on April 5, 1966. It was intended to replace the 1930 Convention. The most important change was a reduction in freeboards for large ships. The preamble referred to the recognition by the signatory countries that " the establishment by international agreement of minimum freeboards for ships engaged on international voyages constitutes a most important contribution to the safety of life and property at sea. . . ." Article 2 did not define ships, but Article 2.4 defined an international voyage as " a sea voyage from a country to which the present Convention applies to a port outside such country, or conversely." [28] This, apart from the insertion of the word " present," was the same as the definition in the 1930 Convention.

In the case of each Convention it would seem inappropriate to say of a drilling unit, whether it was moving to or from the drilling site or was on the site, that it was engaged in an international voyage, if the move was within the " country " in question, by virtue of its laws as to territorial waters or other waters to which its laws extended.

2. *The Merchant Shipping* (*Load Lines*) *Act* 1967

This Act gave effect to the 1966 Convention, which replaced the 1930 Convention, and itself replaced the provisions relating to load lines contained in Part II of the Merchant Shipping (Safety and Load Lines) Conventions Act 1932, and the Merchant Shipping Act 1937. Section 1 states: " This Act applies to all ships except: (a) ships of war; (b) ships engaged solely in fishing; and (c) pleasure yachts." Section 34 (2) provides that the Act " shall be construed as one with the Merchant Shipping Acts 1894 to 1965. . . ." As a result the definition of " ship " for the purpose of the Act is that contained in section 742 of the 1894 Act, *i.e.* that it " includes every description of vessel used in navigation not propelled by oars." [29]

---

[28] The same definition was used in the 1969 Tonnage Convention; see p. 57, below.
[29] As to the applicability of these words to drilling units see pp. 64–85, below.

(n) Mortgages

1. *Generally*

A drilling unit may be the subject of a mortgage, as may a conventional ship. A mortgagee has an insurable interest in the subject-matter insured and may require that the drilling unit be insured in his own name as well as in that of the other interested parties.

2. *The 1926 Convention*

For the International Convention for the Unification of Certain Rules of Law relating to Maritime Liens and Mortgages, signed on April 10, 1926, see the heading " Liens " above.[30]

3. *The 1967 Conventions*

For the International Conventions (a) for the Unification of Certain Rules relating to Maritime Liens and Mortgages, and (b) relating to Registration of Rights in Respect of Vessels under Construction, both signed on May 27, 1967, see also the heading " Liens " above.

4. *Admiralty jurisdiction*

Section 1 (1) of the Administration of Justice Act 1956, in setting out the nature and extent of Admiralty jurisdiction, states that it extends to " (c) any claim in respect of a mortgage of or charge on a ship or any share therein "; Section 8 (1) states, *inter alia*: " ' ship ' includes any description of vessel used in navigation." The definition is similar to that in section 742 of the Merchant Shipping Act 1894, which states that a ship " includes every description of vessel used in navigation not propelled by oars." [31]

5. *The draft Off-Shore Mobile Craft Convention*

For the draft convention on off-shore mobile craft,[32] adopted by the Comité Maritime International at Rio de Janeiro in September 1977, and its provisions as to " Rights in Craft," see the heading " Liens " above.[33]

(o) Piracy

1. *Meaning*

Oppenheim's *International Law* [34] says: " Piracy, in its original and strict meaning, is every unauthorised act of violence committed by a private vessel on the open seas against another vessel with intent to plunder "; but it goes on to say: " If a definition is desired which really covers all such acts as are in practice treated as piratical, piracy must be

---

[30] At p. 34.
[31] For the applicability of these words to drilling units see pp. 64–85, below.
[32] For the aims and general provisions of the C.M.I. draft Convention see p. 31, above.
[33] At p. 35.
[34] Lauterpacht (Ed.) (8th ed., 1955), Vol. 1, pp. 608–609.

defined as every unauthorised act of violence against persons or goods committed on the open sea either by a private vessel against another vessel or by the mutinous crew or passengers against their own vessel." There must, then, be an unauthorised act of violence. It may be committed by a private vessel or, in the wider definition, by a mutinous crew or passengers against their own vessel; in either the action is against a vessel.

An earlier edition of *Halsbury's Laws of England* said [35]: " No authoritative and comprehensive definition exists of piracy *jure gentium*"; and added: " It has been stated that according to international law piracy consists in sailing the sea for private ends without authorisation from the government of any State with the object of committing depredations upon property or acts of violence against persons." [36]

In *Republic of Bolivia* v. *Indemnity Mutual Marine Assurance Co. Ltd.*[37] Kennedy L.J. approved of the definition given in *Carver's Carriage of Goods by Sea* [38]: " Piracy is forcible robbery at sea, whether committed by marauders from outside the ship or by mariners or passengers within it. The essential element is that they violently dispossess the master, and afterwards carry away the ship itself, or any of the goods, with a felonious intent."

For the present purpose it is necessary to discuss not the content of the offence but the places from or against which it is carried out. Thus it could take place: (a) against a ship from the outside, but (i) the second definition cited above [39] refers to " depredations upon property " and did not expressly require that a ship should be attacked though the pirates themselves must be " sailing," and (ii) Carver's definition does not make it essential that the pirates themselves should be on a ship, though the other definitions do impose this requirement; (b) against a ship from within, by crew or passengers, but such an act is no longer piracy *jure gentium* triable as such by British courts.[40]

If outside or internal forces were to commit this act against a drilling unit, it might be necessary to consider whether it could be described as an act of piracy. That in turn would depend upon whether the drilling unit could, in the relevant context, be described as a ship, except where the mere expression " depredations upon property " was regarded as the relevant part of the definition.

2. *The 1958 Geneva Convention on the High Seas*

Article 15 of this Convention, signed at Geneva on April 29, 1958, defined piracy:

---

[35] 3rd ed., Vol. 10, p. 653.

[36] At p. 609.

[37] [1909] 1 K.B. 785 (C.A.) at pp. 802-3.

[38] (4th ed. 1905), para. 94. The wording in the 12th ed., 1971, para. 183, is the same in the first sentence and almost exactly the same in the second sentence.

[39] From a 1927 League of Nations Report, according to Halsbury. See also *Re Piracy Jure Gentium* [1934] A.C. 586 (P.C.), at p. 599.

[40] See p. 42, below.

" Piracy consists of any of the following acts:

(1) Any illegal acts of violence, detention or any act of depredation committed for private ends by the crew or the passengers of a private ship or a private aircraft, and directed:
(a) On the high seas, against another ship or aircraft, or against persons or property on board such ship or aircraft;
(b) Against a ship, aircraft, persons or property in a place outside the jurisdiction of any State;

(2) Any act of voluntary participation in the operation of a ship or of any aircraft with knowledge of facts making it a pirate ship or aircraft;

(3) Any act of inciting or of intentionally facilitating an act described in sub-paragraph (1) or sub-paragraph (2) of this article."

The Convention did not define the term " ship "; one would have to look to the municipal law implementing the Convention to ascertain what meaning was attached to the word by that law.

3. *Municipal law*

Reference should be made to a 1978 Law Commission Report [41] and to the Tokyo Convention Act 1967, which declared that for the purposes of any proceedings the provisions in the Schedule to the Act (which set out the above definition in the 1958 High Seas Convention) should be treated as part of the law of nations.

4. *The* 1965 *agreement on " pirate broadcasting "*

The words " pirate broadcasting " are placed in inverted commas because there is no reference to piracy as such in this agreement, which is entitled the European Agreement for the Prevention of Broadcasts Transmitted from Stations outside National Territories, and was agreed at Strasbourg on January 22, 1965.

The preamble to the Agreement incorporated the words " Considering the desirability of providing for the possibility of preventing the establishment and use of broadcasting stations on objects affixed to or supported by the bed of the sea outside national territories." The Agreement itself states (Art. 1) that it is " concerned with broadcasting stations which are installed or maintained on board ships, aircraft, or any other floating or airborne objects and which, outside national territories, transmit broadcasts within the territory of any Contracting Party, or which causes harmful interference to any radio communication service operating under the authority of the Contracting Party in accordance with the Radio Regulations."

There is a discrepancy between the words in the preamble, " broadcasting stations on objects affixed to or supported by the bed of the sea . . . ," and in Article 1, " broadcasting stations . . . on board ships, aircraft, or any other floating objects." In particular, self-elevating drilling units

---

[41] On the Territorial and Extraterritorial Extent of the Criminal Law 1978.

with their legs down (and production platforms fixed on the seabed, though they are outside the scope of this study) are covered by the pre-amble but not by Article 1. Of course it would be necessary and appro-priate to examine the so-called preparatory work, or *travaux préparatoires* if (though it seems most unlikely) there were any ambiguity here; but in recording their agreement in Article 1 the parties have restricted slightly what they contemplated, or, to use the word therein employed, what they were " Considering . . ." in the preamble. This becomes clear when we consider Article 4 below.

The Convention does not seek to define " ships " or to give examples of " other floating . . . objects." It seems clear, however, that it is expressed in wide enough terms to extend to drilling ships, semi-submersible drilling units and self-elevating units while they are afloat, *e.g.* while they are being towed to or from the drilling site, or preparatory to lowering their legs or just after raising their legs.

Article 4, however, provides: " Nothing in this Agreement shall be deemed to prevent a Contracting Party . . . (b) from also applying the provisions of this Agreement to broadcasting stations installed or main-tained on objects affixed to or supported by the bed of the sea."

When the United Kingdom enacted the Marine, &c., Broadcasting (Offences) Act 1967, the places or objects from which it was made unlawful to make broadcasts were described therein as follows (references to aircraft are omitted here):

> *Section 1 (1).* " a ship . . . while it is in . . . the United Kingdom or external waters . . . a ship registered in the United Kingdom . . . while the ship . . . is elsewhere than in . . . the United Kingdom or external waters. . . ."
> *Section 2 (1).* ". . . (a) a structure in external waters or in tidal waters in the United Kingdom being a structure affixed to, or supported by, the bed of those waters and not being a ship; or (b) any other object in such waters, being neither a structure affixed or supported as aforesaid nor a ship . . ."

In this Act the opportunity has clearly been taken to act with respect to one of the matters which the parties to the 1965 Agreement were " Con-sidering," namely " objects affixed to or supported by the bed of the sea." These words would clearly apply to self-elevating drilling units while their legs were down. The Preamble to the Convention, however, used the words " outside national territories," whereas section 2 (1) of the 1971 Act is restricted to " external waters or . . . tidal waters." In section 9 (1) the term " external waters " is said to mean " the whole of the sea adjacent to the United Kingdom which is within the seaward limits [42] of the territorial waters adjacent thereto."

(p) Pollution

The most important international Conventions relating to pollution are summarised here; in each case it will be possible to consider whether the

---

[42] As determined by reference to the baseline established by the Territorial Waters Order in Council 1964, or any subsequent order.

convention in question applies to drilling units. Such application may arise because it refers to ships, and the definition of ships therein is wide enough to embrace a particular drilling unit, or because its terms of reference are such that irrespective of any reference to ships, drilling units are in any event covered. It is convenient to summarise these Conventions, in some cases with abbreviated titles, as follows:

1. International Convention for the Prevention of Pollution of the Sea by Oil 1954, as amended in 1962, 1969 and 1971; this is considered here [43] in conjunction with the International Convention for the Prevention of Pollution from Ships 1973.[44]
2. International Conventions on Civil Liability 1969, and on International Compensation Fund 1971.[45]
3. International Convention on Intervention 1971.[46]
4. International Conventions as to the Prevention of Dumping 1972.[47]
5. International Convention on Civil Liability for Oil Pollution Damage from Offshore Operations 1975.[48]

1. (a) *International Conventions for the Prevention of Pollution of the Sea by Oil, 1954, as amended in 1962, 1969, and 1971*

The Convention agreed in London on May 12, 1954, prohibits discharges from ships of oil and oily mixtures within certain defined zones upon the high seas. It also provides that ships registered in the contracting states shall be fitted with certain pollution avoidance facilities and that ships shall carry oil record books in which entries of oil discharges must be made.

Article 1 (1) of the Convention states: " ' Ship ' means any sea-going vessel of any type whatsoever, including floating craft, whether self-propelled or towed by another vessel, making a sea-voyage . . . ." The varying kinds of drilling units seem to fall within this definition, but for the closing words, " making a sea-voyage." When a drilling unit is on site, and whether it be a self-elevating unit with its legs down, a submersible or semi-submersible, or a drilling ship, there would seem to be doubt as to whether it can then be described as " making a sea-voyage." If a conventional ship stops in mid-voyage and anchors it can doubtless still be described as making the voyage. A drilling unit, however, has in a sense reached its destination. If the same argument is applied to a conventional ship one would say that the Convention does not apply when it is in port before the voyage begins or after it has ended. This would seem to be the case, because otherwise no meaning would attach to the words " making a sea-voyage," though of course there could be discussion as to what are the exact terminal points of a voyage. The correct conclusion therefore seems to be that a drilling unit is not " making a sea-voyage " for the purpose of

---

[43] pp. 44–45.   [44] See p. 45.   [45] See p. 45.
[46] See p. 47.   [47] See p. 47.   [48] See p. 49.

the Convention when it is on site, but that it is when proceeding to or from the site, whether self-propelled or towed by another vessel.

The Oil in Navigable Waters Acts 1955 to 1971 [49] gave effect in the United Kingdom to the 1954 Convention and certain of the amendments thereto. They refer to the Merchant Shipping Act 1894, in such a way that the definition of ship for the purpose of these Acts is that given by section 742 of the 1894 Act, *i.e.* that it " includes every description of vessel used in navigation not propelled by oars." [50]

1. (*b*) *International Convention for the Prevention of Pollution from Ships* 1973

The International Convention for the Prevention of Pollution from Ships was concluded in London on November 2, 1973, with a view to its replacing the 1954 Convention. The aim of the contracting parties was the elimination of international pollution of the marine environment by oil and other harmful substances which may be discharged operationally, and the minimising of accidental discharges of such substances. A ship was defined, in Article 2 (4), in wide terms, as follows: " ' Ship ' means a vessel of any type whatsoever operating in the marine environment and includes hydro-foil boats, air-cushion vehicles, submersibles, floating craft and fixed or floating platforms." The Convention seems, therefore, clearly to apply to drill ships, semi-submersibles and submersibles. As for self-elevating units they would appear to be covered as floating craft when the legs are not extended and as fixed platforms when the legs are extended.

A discharge was defined in Article 2 (3) (*a*) as follows: " Discharge,' in relation to harmful substances or effluents containing such substances, means any release howsoever caused from a ship and includes any escape, disposal, spilling, leaking, pumping, emitting or emptying." Article 2 (3) (*b*), however, states: " ' Discharge ' does not include: (i) . . . [not relevant here] or (ii) release of harmful substances directly arising from the exploration, exploitation and associated off-shore processing of sea-bed mineral resources; or (iii) . . . [not relevant here]."

The Convention would therefore only apply to offshore mobile drilling units in respect of discharges which do not result directly from the exploration or exploitation of sea-bed mineral resources. If the fuel used by the units, or such substances as garbage, sewage or other waste, were discharged, then the Convention would apply.

2. *International Convention on Civil Liability* 1969, *and on International Compensation Fund*, 1971

(a) The International Convention on Civil Liability for Oil Pollution Damage (or Civil Liability Convention) was agreed in London on

---

[49] These Acts were in turn, with s. 5 of the Continental Shelf Act 1964, consolidated by the Prevention of Oil Pollution Act 1971.
[50] As to the applicability of this definition to drilling units, see pp. 64–85, below.

November 29, 1969, at the International Legal Conference on Marine Pollution Damage.

The Civil Liability Convention imposed strict liability on a shipowner for pollution damage, gave him the benefit of certain defences, set certain maximum limits, and provided for compulsory insurance.[51] Article 1.1 stated: " ' Ship ' means any sea-going vessel and any seaborne craft of any type whatsoever, actually carrying oil in bulk as cargo." It would appear that a drilling unit, of whatever kind, would be excluded from the definition in the Civil Liability Convention, assuming that it could be regarded as a sea-going vessel or seaborne craft, by virtue of the words " actually carrying oil in bulk as cargo."

This Convention is unique among the various pollution Conventions in that it would in any event also apply to drilling units and certain other craft, irrespective of the definition of ship, if the C.M.I. draft convention on off-shore mobile craft, agreed at Rio de Janeiro in September 1977, were to be internationally agreed.[52]

The Civil Liability Convention was incorporated into the law of the United Kingdom by the Merchant Shipping (Oil Pollution) Act 1971. Section 21 (2) provided that the Act was to be " construed as one with the Merchant Shipping Acts 1894 to 1970." As a result the definition of ship for the purpose of the Act is that given in section 742 of the 1894 Act, *i.e.* that it " includes every description of vessel used in navigation not propelled by oars." [53]

(b) The International Convention on the Establishment of an International Fund for Compensation for Oil Pollution Damage (or Fund Convention) was concluded at Brussels on December 18, 1971.

The Fund Convention, which resulted from a resolution at the 1969 International Legal Conference on Marine Pollution Damage, provided for a compensation scheme to give victims full and adequate compensation under a system based on the principle of strict liability, but relieving the shipowner of the additional financial burden imposed by the Civil Liability Convention of 1969.[54] It proposed the establishment of a fund of about $30 million, to be created in part by the cargo interests, to be used where (a) the shipowner was relieved from liability under the Civil Liability Convention *or* (b) the damage exceeded the figure to which liability could be limited.

Article 1.2 provided that the word " ship " was to have the same meaning as that given to it by Article 1.1 of the 1969 Civil Liability Convention. So far as drilling units are concerned, therefore, it can be said in this case as well as in that of the Civil Liability Convention that the Convention is inapplicable because whether or not the drilling unit is

---

[51] And for certification of insurance, normally provided by a P. & I. Club.
[52] See the separate note on this draft Convention at p. 51, below.
[53] As to the applicability of this definition to drilling units, see pp. 64–85, below.
[54] As to which see p. 45, above.

a sea-going vessel or seaborne craft, it is not " carrying oil in bulk as cargo."

The Fund Convention was incorporated into the law of the United Kingdom by the Merchant Shipping Act 1974. Section 23 (1) provided that the Act was to be " construed as one with the Merchant Shipping Acts 1894 to 1971." As a result the definition of ship for the purpose of this Act is that given by section 742 of the 1894 Act *i.e.* that it " includes every description of vessel used in navigation not propelled by oars." [55]

3. *International Convention on Intervention* 1971

The International Convention Relating to Intervention on the High Seas in Cases of Oil Pollution Casualties (or Intervention Convention) was agreed in London on November 29, 1969, at the International Legal Conference on Marine Pollution Damage.

The Intervention Convention [56] authorised the nations which were parties thereto to " take such measures on the high seas as may be necessary to prevent, mitigate or eliminate grave and imminent danger to their coastline or related interests from pollution or threat of pollution of the sea by oil, following upon a maritime casualty or acts related to such a casualty, which may reasonably be expected to result in major harmful consequences."

Article 2.1 stated: " ' Maritime casualty means ' a collision of ships, stranding or other accident of navigation, or other occurrence on board a ship or external to it resulting in material damage or imminent threat of material damage to a ship or cargo."

Article 2.2 stated: " ' Ship ' means: (a) any sea-going vessel of any type whatsoever, and (b) any floating craft, with the exception of an installation or device engaged in the exploration and exploitation of the resources of the sea-bed and the ocean floor and the subsoil thereof."

It would appear that a drilling unit, of whatever kind, would be excluded from the definition in the Intervention Convention, assuming that it could be regarded as a floating craft, by virtue of the exclusion of " an installation or device engaged in the exploration and exploitation of the resources of the sea-bed and the ocean floor and the subsoil thereof." This might not, however, be the case if the incident did not occur during actual exploration or exploitation.

4. *International Conventions as to the Prevention of Dumping* 1972 (*known also as the Oslo and London Dumping Conventions*)

(a) The Convention for the Prevention of Marine Pollution by Dumping from Ships and Aircraft was signed in Oslo on February 15, 1972. It is a regional convention, applicable to the north-east Atlantic Ocean, and to the Arctic and North Seas. It was signed by Belgium, Denmark, the

---

[55] As to the applicability of this definition to drilling units, see pp. 64–85, below.
[56] At Art. 1.1.

Federal Republic of Germany, Finland, France, Iceland, the Netherlands, Norway, Portugal, Spain, Sweden, and the United Kingdom.

Article 1 said that the parties pledged themselves " to take all possible steps to prevent the pollution of the sea by substances that are liable to create hazards to human health, to harm living resources and marine life, to damage amenities or to interfere with other legitimate uses of the sea."

Article 19.1 defined " dumping " as " any deliberate disposal of substances and materials into the sea by or from ships or aircraft other than [there then followed two exceptions relating to discharge related to normal operations and placing of matter for a purpose other than mere disposal]."

Article 19.2 stated: " ' Ship and aircraft ' means sea-going vessels and air-borne craft of any type whatsoever. This expression includes air-cushion craft, floating craft whether self-propelled or not, and fixed or floating platforms." The categories of drilling units falling within the scope of this study, *i.e.* drilling ships, submersibles, semi-submersibles and self-elevating units, would all come within this definition.

(b) The Convention on the Prevention of Marine Pollution by Dumping of Wastes and other Matter was signed in London on December 29, 1972. It follows broadly the format of the Oslo Convention.[57] Its purposes were to ensure adequate control over the dumping of waste and other matter at sea, so as to protect the quality and resources of the sea.

Article III (1) (*a*) defined " Dumping " as:

> " (i) any deliberate disposal at sea of wastes or other matter from vessels, aircraft, platforms, or other man-made structures at sea;
>
> (ii) any deliberate disposal at sea of vessels, aircraft, platforms or other man-made structures at sea." [58]

Article III (2) stated: " Vessels and aircraft means waterborne or airborne craft of any type whatsoever. This expression includes air cushioned craft and floating craft, whether self-propelled or not."

The categories of drilling units falling within the scope of this study would all fall within the expression " vessels . . . platforms or other man-made structures at sea."

A reference in Article VII (i) (*c*), dealing with enforcement, to " vessels . . . and fixed or floating platforms " has been described by Mr. Gr. J. Timagenis, LL.M.,[59] in an article, " International Control of Dumping at Sea," [60] as " a drafting inconsistency in the Convention." The words " fixed or floating " had appeared in an earlier draft of Article III (1) (*a*) (i) at Reykjavik earlier in 1972. They were deleted on the ground that

---

[57] See p. 47, above.

[58] Article III (1) (*b*) contains exceptions to the definition, including " the disposal at sea of wastes or other matter incidental to, or derived from the normal operations of vessels, aircraft, platforms or other man-made structures at sea and their equipment, other than wastes or other matter transported by or to vessels [etc.]."

[59] Attorney-at-Law, Piraeus.

[60] *Anglo-American Law Review*, Volume 2, 1973, at p. 181, n. 168.

the unqualified word " platforms " included both fixed and floating ones. [61]

The Oslo and London Dumping Conventions were incorporated into the law of the United Kingdom by the Dumping at Sea Act 1974. Section 1 (1) provided that no person, except in pursuance of a licence granted by a licensing authority:

> " (a) shall dump substances or articles in United Kingdom waters; or
>
> (b) shall dump substances or articles in the sea outside United Kingdom waters from a British ship, aircraft, hovercraft or marine structure; or
>
> (c) shall load substances or articles on to a ship, aircraft, hovercraft or marine structure in the United Kingdom or United Kingdom waters for dumping in the sea, whether in United Kingdom waters or not;
>
> (d) shall cause or permit substances or articles to be dumped or loaded as mentioned in paragraphs (a) to (c) above."

The relevant words for our present purposes are thus " British ship . . . or marine structure " [62] in (b), and " ship . . . or marine structure " in (c). According to section 12: " ' British marine structure ' means a marine structure owned by or leased to an individual resident in or a body corporate under the law of any part of the United Kingdom "; . . . " ' British ship ' means a vessel registered in the United Kingdom, or a vessel exempted from such registration under the Merchant Shipping Act 1894; . . . ' marine structure ' means a platform or other man-made structure at sea; . . . "

There is no definition of the word " ship." It would seem however that, of the various kind of drilling units, drilling ships would be classed as ships in any event and the other types as ships or marine structures.

5. *International Convention on Civil Liability for Oil Pollution Damage from Offshore Operations* 1975

The Convention on Civil Liability for Oil Pollution Damage Resulting from Exploration and Exploitation of Seabed Mineral Resources was agreed in London on December 17, 1976. It was pointed about above, in connection with the International Convention for the Prevention of Pollution from Ships 1973,[63] that the area described as " the exploration, exploitation [and associated off-shore processing] of sea-bed mineral resources " was exempted when " discharge " was being defined for the purpose of that Convention.

---

[61] See the same article by Mr. Timagenis, p. 177, n. 14.

[62] The expression " marine structure " was also used in the C.M.I. draft convention on off-shore mobile craft, Art. 1, agreed at Rio de Janeiro in September 1977. See p. 31, above.

[63] See p. 45, above.

The object of the Convention is to provide for and regulate the liability of the operator of an installation in respect of pollution damage. We do not have to consider the meaning of the word " ship " here, but the Convention may apply to drilling units. The relevant definitions are:

Article 1.1 (a). " 'Oil' means crude oil and natural gas liquids, whether or not such oil or liquids are mixed with or present in other substances."

Article 1.2. " 'Installation' means:

    (a) any well or other facility, whether fixed or mobile, which is used for the purpose of exploring for, producing, treating, storing or transmitting or regaining control of the flow of crude oil from the seabed or its subsoil.

    (b) any well which has been used for the purpose of exploring for, producing or regaining control of the flow of crude oil from the seabed or its subsoil and which has been abandoned . . . .

    (c) any well which is used for the purpose of exploring for, producing or regaining control of the flow of gas or natural gas liquids from the seabed or its subsoil . . . .

    (d) any well which is used for the purpose of exploring for any mineral resources other than crude oil, gas or natural-gas liquids . . . .

    (e) any facility which is normally used for storing crude oil from the seabed or its subsoil; . .

provided however, that . . . a ship as defined in the International Convention on Civil Liability for Oil Pollution Damage, agreed in Brussels on November 29, 1969, shall not be considered to be an installation."

It can be seen that a drilling unit might fall within the definitions of " Installation " given by Article 1.2 at (a) (" other facility, whether fixed or mobile . . . used for the purpose of exploring ") or, less frequently, at (e) (" any facility which is normally used for storing crude oil "). There is the proviso that a ship as defined in the 1969 Civil Liability Convention shall not be considered to be an installation. The definition of a ship in that Convention [64] was " any sea-going vessel and any seaborne craft of any type whatsoever, actually carrying oil in bulk as cargo." As drilling units do not carry oil in bulk as cargo they would not in any event fall within that definition.

Liability under the 1975 Convention is, by Article 3.1, placed on the operator: " Except as provided in paragraphs 3, 4 and 5 of this Article, the operator of the installation at the time of the incident shall be liable for any pollution damage resulting from the incident . . ." The term " operator " is defined in Article 1.3: " ' Operator ' means the person, whether licensee or not, designated as operator for the purposes of this Convention by the Controlling State or in the absence of such designation the person who is in overall control of the activities carried on at the installation." [65]

---

[64] Art. 1.1; see p. 46, above.

[65] Para. 3 provides for joint and several liability if there is more than one operator. Para. 4 exempts the operator from liability if he proves that the damage resulted from act of war, etc. Para. 5 exempts the operator of an abandoned well from liability in certain circumstances.

6. *The draft Off-Shore Mobile Craft Convention*

A draft convention on off-shore mobile craft was adopted by the Comité Maritime International in September 1977, and then transmitted to I.M.C.O. for appropriate action.[66] Article 7, entitled " Liability for Oil Pollution," referred to the Civil Liability Convention of 1969.[67] It stated:

> " Subject to the succeeding paragraph of this Article, a State Party which is also a party to the International Convention on civil liability for oil pollution damage dated November 29, 1969, shall apply the rules of that convention to the escape or discharge of oil contained in craft,[68] in so far as they would not otherwise apply.
> A State Party shall apply such rules only in the absence of other applicable provisions on liability contained in other International Conventions to which it is a party."

It has been suggested that the provision in Article 7 is defective in that it fails to indicate whether " oil " means oil as defined in the 1969 Convention.

(q) Registry

1. *Generally*

Registry is the method by which a nation maintains a formal record of those ships or vessels which fly its flag.[69] In *Oppenheim's International Law*[70] it is stated, as a principle of international law: " Every State must register the names of all private vessels sailing under its flag, and it must make them bear their names visibly so that every vessel may be identified from a distance. No vessel may be allowed to change her name without permission and fresh registration."

2. *The* 1958 *Geneva Convention on the High Seas*

Article 5 (1) of this Convention, signed at Geneva on April 29, 1958, states: " Each State shall fix the conditions for the grant of its nationality to ships, for the registration of ships in its territory, and for the right to fly its flag." The term " ship " is not defined in the Convention. As a result one must look to the relevant municipal laws as to registration in order to establish whether they apply to the various forms of drilling units.

3. *The Merchant Shipping Acts*

Nearly all British ships have to be registered as a result of section 2 (1) of the Merchant Shipping Act 1894, which states: " Every British ship shall unless exempted [71] from registry be registered under this Act."

---

[66] For the aims and general provisions of the C.M.I. draft Convention see p. 31, above.   [67] See p. 45, above.

[68] As defined in Art. 1 of the C.M.I. draft Convention; see p. 31, above.

[69] As to flag, see p. 27, above.

[70] Lauterpacht (Ed.) (8th ed., 1955), Vol. 1, p. 597.

[71] The ships exempted are certain very small ships of under 15 and 30 net registered tons described in ss. 3 (1) and 3 (2), respectively, of the Act.

Non-registration is not an offence, but its consequence is that the owner does not get the benefits of British ownership, one of which is the entitlement that the ship be described as being of British nationality, and entitled, accordingly, to fly the British flag. The applicability of this provision to the various types of drilling units depends upon the interpretation of the word " ship " which is said by section 742 of the 1894 Act to include " every description of vessel used in navigation not propelled by oars." [72]

4. *Offshore installations*

As a result of the Offshore Installation (Registration) Regulations 1972,[73] made under the Mineral Workings (Offshore Installations) Act 1971,[74] all offshore installations must be registered with the Department of Energy.

Registration is necessary before permission is given to operate in the waters to which the Act applies.[75] The terms " offshore installation " is defined in section 3 (1) of the 1971 Act as meaning " any installation which is maintained, or is intended to be established, for underwater exploitation or exploration to which this Act applies." The Regulations refer, at regulation 2 (1), to a " mobile installation," meaning " an offshore installation which can be moved from place to place without major dismantling or modification, whether or not it has its own motive power "; and to a " fixed installation," meaning " an offshore installation which is not a mobile installation."

The various categories of drilling unit, including a drilling ship, would fall within the definition of " mobile installation." This system of registrations is quite separate from that which applies to ships, as a result of the Merchant Shipping Acts.

(r) Safety of life at sea

1. *The* 1960 *SOLAS Convention*

An International Convention for the Safety of Life at Sea, or SOLAS Convention, was signed in London on June 17, 1960. It replaced the Convention of the same name which had been signed in London on June 10, 1948. It dealt with a wide range of subjects, including surveys, safety certificates, investigation of casualties, construction, life-saving appliances, radiotelegraphy and radiotelephony, safety of navigation, carriage of grain and of dangerous goods and nuclear ships. Its scope of application was shown by regulation 1 (*a*): " Unless expressly provided otherwise, the present Regulations apply only to ships engaged on international voyages."

---

[72] For a discussion of the relevant cases see pp. 64–85, below.

[73] S.I. 1972 No. 702.

[74] This Act is also considered in connection with certificates of fitness, at p. 21, above.

[75] As to the area so covered see p. 21, above.

Regulation 2 (" Definitions ") did not define a ship but stated: " (*f*) A passenger ship is a ship which carries more than 12 passengers. (*g*) A cargo ship is any ship which is not a passenger ship." Regulation 3 (" Exceptions ") stated that the Regulations did not apply to certain types of vessel, including, at Regulation 3 (*a*) (iii), " Ships not propelled by mechanical means."

2. *The* 1974 *SOLAS Convention*

A second International Convention for the Safety of Life at Sea, or SOLAS Convention, was signed in London on November 1, 1974. It replaced the 1960 SOLAS Convention. It dealt with a similar range of subjects. Its regulations 1 (*a*), 2 (*f*) and (*g*), and 3 (*a*) (iii), were in exactly the same terms as those of the 1960 Convention.

Whenever a drilling unit can be regarded as a ship, it could on one view therefore be called a " cargo ship," since such a ship was defined as being " any ship which is not a passenger ship." A drilling unit does not carry cargo, if one assumes that cargo must be goods carried from one place to another, for the commercial purpose of taking them from a shipper to a receiver. On the other hand there are other categories of vessel, which can certainly be regarded as ships, such as tugs, to which the Convention was doubtless intended to apply. An Appendix to Resolution 1 of the International Conference on Safety of Life at Sea, from which the 1974 Convention emerged, stated, as Recommendation 8:

> " 8. *Safety Measures for Certain Types of Ships*
> THE CONFERENCE
>
> TAKING INTO ACCOUNT the development of certain types of ships to which the provisions of the Convention for passenger or cargo ships are not applicable or for which those provisions are not adequate or suitable,
> RECOGNISING the need for future modifications to the Convention in this respect,
> RECOMMENDS that the development and refinement of specific safety requirements for special purpose ships, hovercraft, ships carrying chemicals and liquefied gases in bulk and other new types of ships be continued."

(s) Salvage

1. *Generally*

To find out whether the concept of salvage is applicable to drilling units we must first understand what we mean by the expression. " Salvage, in its simple character, is the service which those who recover property from loss or danger at sea render to the owners, with the responsibility of making restitution, and with a lien for their reward. It is personal, in its primary character at least." [76] This definition refers to recovery " at sea " and is not concerned with the nature of the property. The original jurisdiction of the Admiralty Court extended only to services upon the high seas;

---

[76] Lord Stowell, in *H.M.S. Thetis* (1833) 3 Hagg.Adm. 14.

legislation [77] was needed to extend it to what was traditionally known as the body of a county. The nature of the Admiralty jurisdiction of the High Court was later set out in the Administration of Justice Act 1956, s. 1 (1) (*j*) of which refers to " any claim in the nature of salvage (including any claim arising by virtue of the application, by or under section 51 of the Civil Aviation Act 1949, of the law relating to salvage to aircraft and their apparel and cargo)." Section 1 (4), referring to the preceding provisions of the section, says that they are to apply:

> " (*a*) in relation to all ships or aircraft, whether British or not and whether registered or not and wherever the residence or domicile of their owners may be; (*b*) in relation to all claims, wheresoever arising (including, in the case of cargo or wreck salvage, claims in respect of cargo or wreck found on land)."

We have seen, when considering the applicability of the concept of general average to drilling units,[78] that Bowen L.J.[79] said, in speaking of the maritime law as to salvage and general average: " No similar doctrine applies to things lost upon land, nor to anything except ships or goods in peril at sea." The applicability of the doctrine to the salvage of a drilling unit seems therefore to depend upon whether the particular unit, at the relevant time, can be regarded as a ship or vessel. In Kennedy on *Civil Salvage* [80] it is stated: " Until the enactment of legislation relating to salvage of aircraft the only property which could become the subject of salvage was a vessel, her apparel, cargo, or wreck, and, so far as it may be called property, freight at risk. The Lloyd's standard form of salvage agreement, approved of by the Committee of Lloyd's, refers throughout to the " vessel," and to its cargo and freight.

It therefore seems that one must look to the numerous English decisions as to what is meant by the words " ship " and " vessel "; one may then establish whether the term " salvage " may be properly applied to a case in which a drilling unit is being offered or is actually receiving services of the character described above. The cases in which there were such services, and in which there was discussion as to whether the object in question was a ship and thus susceptible of salvage, are *The Mac*,[81] *Wells* v. *Owners of Gas Float Whitton No. 2*,[82] *and Watson* v. *R.C.A. Victor Co. Inc.*[83]

2. *The* 1910 *Salvage Convention*

The Convention for the Unification of Certain Rules of Law respecting Assistance and Salvage at Sea was signed at Brussels on September 23, 1910. It was agreed [84] that " Assistance and salvage of seagoing vessels in

---

[77] The Judicature Acts 1873–75.　　　　　　　　　　[78] At p. 29, above.
[79] In *Falcke* v. *Scottish Imperial Insurance Co.* (1886) 34 Ch.D. 234, at p. 248.
[80] (ed. Kenneth C. McGuffie) (4th ed., 1958), p. 4.
[81] (1882) 7 P.D. 126 (C.A.); hopper barge was a ship; see p. 60, below.
[82] (1897) A.C. 337 (H.L.); gas float not a ship; see p. 64, below.
[83] (1934) 50 Ll.L.R.77; seaplane not a ship; see p. 73, below.
[84] Art. 1.

danger, of any things on board, of freight and passage money, and also services of the same nature rendered by seagoing vessels to vessels of inland navigation or vice-versa," should be subject to certain provisions, which were then set out. Every such action which had a useful result was to give a right to equitable remuneration; and there were other provisions, relating to such matters as the effect of a prohibition against salvage by the ship in distress and the manner in which the amount of remuneration was to be fixed. In the Convention the word " vessel," rather than " ship" or some other term, was used throughout [85]; it was not defined.

3. *The draft Off-Shore Mobile Craft Convention*

A draft convention on off-shore mobile craft was adopted by the Comité Maritime International at Rio de Janeiro in September 1977, and then transmitted to I.M.C.O. for appropriate action.[86] Article 3, entitled " Salvage," referred to the 1910 Convention and the Convention with Protocol of 1967. It stated:

" A State Party which is also a party to
—the Convention for the unification of certain rules of law relating to assistance and salvage at sea and Protocol signature dated September 23, 1910, or to
—the said Convention with Protocol dated May 27, 1967,[87] shall apply the rules of the said convention or convention with Protocol to craft to which they would not otherwise apply."

(t) Stowaways

1. *Generally*

A stowaway has been defined as a " person getting free passage by hiding aboard ship," [88] and as " A person hiding on a departing vessel, for the purpose of obtaining free passage or passage without authorisation." [89]

2. *The 1957 Convention*

The International Convention Relating to Stowaways was agreed at Brussels on October 10, 1957. The object was to agree uniform rules relating to stowaways. Article 1, defining " stowaway," said that the word " means a person who, at any port or place in the vicinity thereof, secretes himself in a ship without the consent of the shipowner or the Master or

---

[85] Except where it was stated that the Convention did not apply to " ships of war or to Government ships appointed exclusively to a public service."

[86] For the aims and general provisions of the C.M.I. draft Convention see p. 31, above.

[87] The Protocol, amending the 1910 Convention and signed in Brussels, provided that the Convention should " also apply to assistance or salvage services rendered by or to a ship at war or any other ship owned, operated or chartered by a State or Public Authority " (Art. 1, replacing Art. 14 by this and certain related provisions).

[88] *Concise Oxford Dictionary.*

[89] de Kerchove, *International Maritime Dictionary* (2nd ed., 1961).

any other person in charge of the ship and who is on board after the ship has left that port or place." The word " ship " was not defined.

3. *Merchant Shipping Act* 1970

This Act " marked an important stage in the progress towards revising the provisions of the Merchant Shipping Acts so that they were more in accord with modern conditions," [90] but did not incorporate the 1957 Convention into English law. It contained one section, in a group of sections entitled " Offences by Seamen, etc." [91] intended to relate to stowaways:

> " *Offences committed by certain other persons.* 32. Where a person goes to sea in a ship without the consent of the master or any other person authorised to give it or is conveyed in a ship in pursuance of section 62 (5) (*b*) of this Act,[92] sections 27, 29, 30 (*b*) and 30 (*c*) of this Act [93] shall apply as if he were a seaman employed in the ship."

The 1970 Act provided that it was to be construed as one with the Merchant Shipping Acts 1894 to 1967. Section 742 of the 1894 Act stated: " ' Ship ' includes every description of vessel used in navigation not propelled by oars." If one was to consider whether the conduct of a person stowing away on a drilling unit would be covered by section 32 of the 1970 Act, one would have to review the English cases which have interpreted this definition.[94]

(u) Tonnage

1. *Generally*

The word " tonnage " is used in this context to indicate the registered tonnage, which is expressed in tons of 100 cubic feet each. The registered tonnage, whether gross or net, may thus be contrasted with the deadweight tonnage, or deadweight capacity, which is the number of tons which a ship may carry. Systems of tonnage measurement have existed for many centuries, but only since the nineteenth century has there been a general move towards uniformity. Several bilateral treaties, by which countries recognised each other's system of measurement, were then signed.[95]

2. *The Tonnage Conventions of* 1934, 1947 *and* 1969

(a) A Convention Relating to the Tonnage Measurement of Merchant

---

[90] Temperley, *Merchant Shipping Acts* (7th ed., 1976), para. 1341.

[91] *Et al.* seems more appropriate. See Eric Partridge, *Usage and Abusage:* " *et cetera*, etc., meaning ' and other things ' (Latin plural neuter), is insulting when applied to persons." But the draftsmen might say that " etc." referred to " offences."

[92] Under this provision a master of a ship registered in the U. K. may be required to convey a person to a particular place.

[93] The sections dealing with certain offences, *i.e.* misconduct endangering the ship or persons on board the ship, and continued or concerted disobedience, etc.

[94] See pp. 64–85, below.

[95] For a more detailed discussion see Singh, *International Conventions of Merchant Shipping* (2nd. ed., 1973), Chap. 4, pp. 849 to 851.

Ships was agreed in Warsaw on April 16, 1934. It was signed only by four members of the British Commonwealth (Australia, Canada, New Zealand and the U.K.) and by Poland. It is important because it seems to have been the first of the multilateral conventions. The expressions used were " merchant ships " and " ships "; as the Convention related to the recognition of certificates of registry of such vessels, its applicability to drilling units would have depended upon whether such units were registered in the country in question.[96]

(b) A Convention for a Uniform System of Tonnage Measurement of Ships was signed in Oslo on June 10, 1947, by eight European states. It sought to implement the International Regulations for Tonnage Measurement of Ships, issued through the League of Nations in 1939. As for its applicability to the various kinds of drilling units, the same comments apply as in the case of the Warsaw Convention of 1934.

(c) An International Convention on Tonnage Measurement of Ships was signed in London on June 23, 1969. As in the case of the 1947 Convention, the parties asserted their wish to establish uniform principles and rules with respect to the determination of tonnage. The preamble referred to " ships engaged on international voyages." Article 2.3 defined an international voyage as " a sea voyage from a country to which the present Convention applies to a port outside such country, or conversely." [97] The word " ship " was not defined. Article 3.2 provided that the Convention should apply to various types of ships, including new ships, existing ships which undergo alterations, etc., and existing ships if the owner so requests. As for its applicability to various kinds of drilling units, the same comments apply as in the case of the Warsaw Convention of 1934. Recommendation 3 of the Conference, entitled " Uniform Interpretation of Definition of Terms," is interesting because it states:

> " The Conference, recognising that the definitions of certain terms used in the International Convention on Tonnage Measurement of Ships, 1969, such as ' length,' ' breadth,' ' passenger ' and ' weathertight,' are identical to those contained in other conventions of which the Inter-Governmental Maritime Consultative Organisation is depositary, recommends that contracting governments should take steps to ensure that identical definitions of terms used in such conventions are interpreted in a uniform and consistent manner."

Although the word " ship " was not defined, Articles 2.6 and 2.7 defined, respectively, a " new ship " and an " existing ship," but in each case went on to say that it was a certain kind of ship. For example, Article 2.7 said: " ' existing ship ' means a ship which is not a new ship." It might be hoped that it would be regarded as logical for governments, in their municipal legislation, to assist matters by defining the term " ships " itself in a uniform and consistent manner.

---

[96] See " Registry," p. 51, above.
[97] The same definition was used in the 1966 Load Lines Convention; see p. 39, above.

3. *The Merchant Shipping Acts*

The Merchant Shipping Act 1894, contained provisions, at sections 77 to 81, for the measurement of tonnage of ships. By section 82 such tonnage was thenceforth to be deemed to be the tonnage of the ship and to be repeated in every subsequent registry unless it altered or unless an error was discovered. The said sections as to the method of ascertainment were repealed and replaced by the Merchant Shipping Act 1965, s. 1, by which tonnage was to be ascertained in accordance with the regulations of the Department of Trade. Nevertheless only a " ship," itself the subject of registration under the Merchant Shipping Acts, would be subject to such measurement. Section 742 of the 1894 Act had defined a ship as including " every description of vessel used in navigation not propelled by oars." One must therefore look to the cases which have construed this definition [98-99] in order to ascertain whether the various types of drilling unit fall within it.

(C) CASES ON " SHIPS "

We have already discussed the different ways in which the definition of a ship may be approached, so as to help us to decide whether the various kinds of drilling units may be regarded as ships [1]; and we have studied the applicability of the traditional maritime concepts to drilling units.[2] In the following pages there is a review of numerous cases which have been before the English—and in some cases the Scottish—courts and in which the meaning of the word " ship " has been considered. It may not be possible to reach any firm conclusion as to whether drilling units as a genus, or individual types of drilling units, should be regarded as ships, particularly in the absence of decided English cases on the subject. Much will depend upon the context in which the question arises; but some guidance may be obtained from the following review.

A drilling unit may be treated as a ship for some purposes but not for other purposes. So far as modern English case law is concerned, many of the court decisions have involved cases in which the definition of a ship under the Merchant Shipping Act 1854, or its successor in 1894, has been considered. There are other Acts, including other Merchant Shipping Acts, which it will be necessary to examine. It is the main Merchant Shipping Acts,[3] however, which deal with many of the purposes mentioned and which have been the subject of discussion in many cases. In the course of that analysis an endeavour is made to extract the general principles applied by the English courts in their definition of a ship for the purposes of the Merchant Shipping Acts and some other Acts.

[98-99] See pp. 64–85, below.

[1] See above, pp. 12 *et seq.*

[2] See above, pp. 16 *et seq.*

[3] Which can now be cited together as the Merchant Shipping Acts 1894 to 1974.

In the Merchant Shipping Act 1854, section 2 [4] stated: " ' Ship ' shall include every description of vessel used in navigation not propelled by oars." This did not purport to be a comprehensive definition, as those interpreting the Act would have the right to " include " other categories of vessel, though not those propelled by oars. Thus, according to *The Merchant Shipping Acts*,[5] at paragraph 1059, which comments on this definition,

> " The word ' includes ' in an interpretation clause is used by way of extension. Hence it would seem that the present clause does not exclude vessels which are at times propelled by oars, or vessels which are not used in navigation, in cases where, but for the clause, they would be within the term ' ship.' The purpose for which a vessel has been and is being used is material on the question of fact whether she is being used for navigation."

In *European & Australian Royal Mail Co. Ltd.* v. *Peninsular & Oriental Steam Navigation Co.*[6] a vessel, about which there could originally have been no doubt that she was properly called a ship, was for four years used only as a coaling hulk and a workshop, and moored at one of her owners' coaling stations. She had been registered under the then applicable provision of the Merchant Shipping Act 1854.[7] She was transferred, under a written agreement which (as did the invoice) described her as a coal hulk. The sale of a ship would have had to be undertaken by a bill of sale. It was held that the hulk had been so treated and dealt with as, at any rate between the parties, to be no longer a ship for the purposes of the Act; it was thus transferable, like any other chattel, without a bill of sale. The hulk did her only, or at any rate her main, work while she was stationary.

In *Ex p. Ferguson* [8] a steamer on a voyage from Sunderland to Cherbourg was off Saltburn when she ran down a fishing coble,[9] the *Rachel*. Three new members of the coble lost their lives. The coble, which was used in herring fishery, was 24 feet long, with a beam of seven feet, of 10 tons burthen, and drew 18 inches. She had a main mast and a mizzen mast, a jib, mainsail and mizzen sail. The masts and her rudder were removable. She was normally moved by her four oars, but when full of wet nets and fish she was too heavy to be moved by the oars.

The court had to decide whether the coble was a " ship " for the purpose of section 2 of the Merchant Shipping Act 1854. A Board of Trade inquiry had been held in accordance with the Act, but its conclusion, that there had been manslaughter by the mate of the steamer, could be

---

[4] The precursor of s. 742 of the Merchant Shipping Act 1894. For a comparison of the two sections, see below, p. 64.
[5] By Porges and Thomas (6th ed., 1963).
[6] (1866) 14 L.T. 704.
[7] s. 19.
[8] (1871) L.R. 6 Q.B. 280.
[9] " A sea fishing-boat with a flat bottom, square stern, lug-sail, and rudder extending 4 or 5 feet below the bottom; used chiefly on the N.E. coast of England ": *Shorter Oxford English Dictionary*.

annulled if the coble was not a ship, as the Act would be inapplicable.
It was held that this was a ship. Blackburn J. said [10]:

> " The chief argument against that proposition [that it was a ship] is by
> referring to the interpretation clause (s. 2 of 17 & 18 Vict. c. 104 [11]) which
> says, ' " ship " shall include every description of vessel used in navigation
> not propelled by oars.' And the argument against the proposition is one
> which I have heard very frequently, *viz.*, where an Act says certain words
> shall include a certain thing, that the words must apply exclusively to that
> which they are to include. That is not so; the definition given of a ' ship '
> is in order that ' ship ' may have a more extensive meaning. Whether a
> ship is propelled by oars or not, it is still a ship, unless the words ' not
> propelled by oars ' exclude all vessels which are ever propelled by oars.
> Most small vessels rig out something to propel them, and it would be
> monstrous to say that they are not ships. What, then, is the meaning of the
> word ' ship ' in this Act? It is this, that every vessel that substantially goes
> to sea is a ' ship.' I do not mean to say that a little boat going out for a
> mile or two to sea would be a ship; but where it is its business really and
> substantially to go to sea, if it is not propelled by oars,[12] it shall be con-
> sidered a ship for the purpose of this Act. Whenever the vessel does go to
> sea, whether it be decked or not decked, or whether it goes to sea for the
> purpose of fishing or anything else, it would be a ship . . ."

Blackburn J. incorporated the following ideas in his discussion as to the
nature of a ship:

(1) *The means of propulsion.* It was a ship whether it was propelled by
oars or not. The coble was normally but not always moved by oars.
This was because the words " shall include," combined with the
words " not propelled by oars," did not mean that vessels propelled
by oars were excluded.

(2) *Area of work.* It would be a ship if it " substantially goes to sea,"
but not if it was only " a little boat going out for a mile or two."

(3) *Object of work.* It was a ship whether it went to sea " for the
purpose of fishing or anything else."

These three criteria can be followed through the subsequent decisions.

Ten years later, in 1881, the Court of Appeal again considered [13]
section 2 of the Merchant Shipping Act 1854, in order to decide whether a
hopper barge was a ship in distress for the purpose of a salvage award.
A hopper barge is one which carries away mud or other debris. *The Mac*,
with no means of propulsion, was adrift with no one on board, in the
Wash, three miles from Boston, Lincolnshire. The owners of a fishing
smack, which rescued her, applied to the Justices of the Peace, who had
jurisdiction over these matters, for a salvage award in the sum of £1,000,
and were awarded £50. The owners of *The Mac* argued that she was not a

---

[10] At p. 291.
[11] *i.e.* s. 2 of the 1854 Act.
[12] See *Edwards* v. *Quickenden and Forester* [1939] P. 261 for an interesting but
perhaps wrong decision about racing craft.
[13] In *The Mac* (1882) 7 P.D. 126 (C.A.).

ship. If they were right, then salvage awards were inapplicable, as section 458 of the 1854 Act, which referred to a " ship in distress," was not relevant. They said that the decision in *Ex p. Ferguson* [14] was inapplicable, as the hopper barge could not move herself, was not used in navigation, and was employed for dredging purposes only. Though the words " used in navigation " appeared in section 2 of the 1854 Act, the salvors argued that—as Blackburn J. had said in the earlier case—the words were not restrictive, and that, even if they were, they need only be taken to mean " used on the water."

In the trial at first instance [15] Sir Robert Phillimore had held that this was not a ship, saying memorably, in the course of Counsel's argument [16]: " I shall certainly follow *The Leda* [17]." The Court of Appeal, reversing the High Court, decided unanimously that she was a ship [18] and that a salvage award was therefore applicable. As for the means of propulsion Brett L.J. cited the example of a " saloon barge " capable of carrying 200 persons, towed down the Mersey to put passengers on a ship, and said that she would nevertheless be a ship; Cotton L.J. [19] also noted " The question cannot depend upon whether she carries a cargo from port to port. She was propelled by towing, and she carried mud with a crew on board." She was, therefore, propelled but not self-propelled.

The area of work did not play a substantial part in the argument. Brett L.J. said of the word ship [20]: " The word includes anything floating in or upon the water built in a particular form and used for a particular purpose "; and Cotton L.J. said: ". . . a vessel need not be sea-going."

We now come to the third element considered in *Ex p. Ferguson* [21] and then in *The Mac* [22]: the object of the work done by the alleged ship. Clearly the hopper barge was not engaged in conventional cargo-carrying voyages. Thus Cotton L.J. [23]: " The question cannot depend on the circumstance whether she carries a cargo from port to port." Brett L.J., [24] speaking of section 458, [25] said:

". . . the word ' ship ' is not used in the technical sense as denoting a vessel of particular rig. In popular language, ships are of different kinds; barques, brigs, schooners, sloops, cutters. . . . In this case the vessel, if she may be so called, [26] was built for a particular purpose, she was built as a hopper-barge . . . she is used in navigation; for to dredge up and carry away mud and gravel is an act done for the purposes of navigation. . . ."

While the object of the work done by the coble in *Ex p. Ferguson* could have been " fishing or anything else," we see in *The Mac* a greater

---

[14] (1871) L.R. 6 Q.B. 280. See above, p. 59.
[15] (1881) 7 P.D. 38.
[16] *Ibid.* at p. 40.
[17] (1856) Swa. 40; 4 W.R. 322.
[18] (1882) 7 P.D. 126 (C.A.); the decision was followed in *The Mudlark* [1911] P. 116, which also concerned a hopper barge. See below, p. 66.
[19] (1882) 7 P.D. 126, at p. 131.
[20] *Ibid.*, at p. 130.
[21] (1871) L.R. 6 Q.B. 280.
[22] (1882) 7 P.D. 126 (C.A.).
[23] *Ibid.* at p. 131.
[24] *Ibid.* at p. 130.
[25] See on this page, above.
[26] She could certainly be so called; as to vessels see above, p. 13.

concentration upon the purposes to be achieved. The interpretation clause, section 2 of the 1854 Act, contained the words " used in navigation." [27] Brett L.J. seems to have felt obliged to say that a hopper barge was " used for navigation " in that her work made navigation, *i.e.* voyaging by other ships, possible. To use a vessel to make a channel navigable was to use her " for the purposes of navigation," and thus " in navigation." This construction seems strained, and it is noteworthy that his colleagues did not adopt this approach. Lord Coleridge said [28] that it was " immaterial to consider whether the hopper barge was used in navigation." Both the other judges confirmed the view that section 2 was not a restrictive section, and said that the hopper barge was a ship both within and outside the section.

The Judge below,[29] had, as Lord Coleridge put it, failed to deal with the question whether the hopper barge might be considered a " ship " in the ordinary and popular sense of the word. Cotton L.J. added [30] that she was ". . . a ' ship,' both within and without the interpretation clause." He went on to discuss the general meaning of the term in words which have particular relevance to drilling units:

> " ' Ship ' is a general term for artificial structures floating on the water; this is plain upon looking at the meanings given in Johnson's Dictionary; and it is to be observed that one of the meanings of ' boat ' is therein stated to be ' a ship of a small size.' I think that the proper meaning is ' something hollowed out '. . . a vessel need not be sea-going . . ."

The Dictionary definition to which the Judge referred had been summarised by Coleridge C.J.[31] as follows:

> " She falls within the definition cited in Todd's Johnson's Dictionary of the word ship from Horne Tooke, namely *formatum aliquid*,[32] in contradistinction from a raft for the purpose of conveying merchandise, etc., by water, protected from the water and the weather. Although this may not be the definition of Johnson, it is the definition of a great master of language; and I think that it applies to the present case."

We can now reconsider the three elements involved in the definition of a ship, as they may have been amended or refined by the views expressed in *The Mac* [33]:

(1) *The means of propulsion.* It remained irrelevant whether the alleged ship was or was not self-propelled.

(2) *Area of work.* The " little boat " which only went " out for a mile or two " was not considered by the Court of Appeal, though such a geographical restriction would apply to some hopper barges. It remains to be seen, however, whether later cases have some bearing on a situation where a vessel did not go to sea at all.

---

[27] See above, p. 59.
[29] Sir Robert Phillimore; (1882) 7 P.D. 38.
[31] *Ibid.* at pp. 128–9.
[33] (1882) 7 P.D. 126 (C.A.).

[28] (1882) 7 P.D. 126 at p. 128.
[30] (1882) 7 P.D. 126 at p. 131.
[32] *i.e.* anything constructed.

(3) *Object of work.* Since section 2 of the 1854 Act has been clearly held not to be a restrictive section, use in navigation, which is in any event difficult to define, is not the vital test. Presumably, if it has to be defined, the expression imports some degree of movement, in that the definitions of navigable, navigate and navigation [34] refer to " passage " and to " communication." What then must be the function of a ship, if a vessel is to be regarded in law as such? We have the very wide words of Cotton L.J., quoted above. He spoke of the word " ship " as being a general term for " artificial structures floating on the water." The word " floating " may be important.

Some doubt appeared to exist as to whether a ship would have to be sea-going, or indeed whether it might be disqualified if it were only a little one, going out for a mile or two.[35] This problem was considered in *Southport Corporation* v. *Morriss*,[36] where an electrically powered launch, of " three tons burthen," spent its time carrying passengers on pleasure trips round an artificial lake half a mile long and 180 yards wide. The lake, which had been excavated from the sand, was not open to the sea except at the high spring tides. Under section 318 of the Merchant Shipping Act 1854,[37] a " passenger steamer " was subject to a penalty if she plied with any passenger on board without a duplicate of the Board of Trade certificate put up in a conspicuous part of the ship. The Justices of the Peace had convicted the owners under this section, but the Queen's Bench Divisional Court allowed the owners' appeal. Lord Coleridge C.J., in speaking of section 2 of the 1854 Act, with its expression " every description of vessel used in navigation not propelled by oars," said [38]:

" We are therefore reduced to the question whether this launch was a vessel used in navigation. I think that, having regard to the size of the sheet of water on which it was used, it was not. Navigation is a term which, in common parlance, would never be used in connection with a sheet of water half a mile long. The Attorney-General has asked where we are to draw the line. The answer is that it is not necessary to draw it at any precise point. It is enough for us to say that the present case is on the right side of any reasonable line that could be drawn."

Charles J. agreed, saying:

" I agree with my Lord that this launch, used in the place in which it was used, was not a vessel used in navigation within section 2 of the Merchant Shipping Act, 1854.[39] "

---

[34] In, for example, the *Shorter Oxford English Dictionary.*

[35] As Blackburn J. said in *Ex p. Ferguson* (1871) L.R. 6 Q.B. 280 at p. 291; see above, p. 60.

[36] [1893] 1 Q.B. 359.

[37] Later replaced by s. 271 of the Merchant Shipping Act, 1894.

[38] [1893] 1 Q.B. 359 at p. 361.

[39] At p. 362. This decision was distinguished in *Weeks* v. *Ross* [1913] 2 K.B. 229; see below, p. 69.

The crucial words in these judgments, where a small artificial lake was being considered, are " having regard to the size of the sheet of water," and " the place in which it was used." As a result the launch could not be said to be " used in navigation." The Court confined itself here to those words, as set out in section 2, the interpretation clause, and did not look for a wider definition.

Immediately after the *Southport Corporation* decision there came into force the Merchant Shipping Act 1894. As a result section 2 of the 1854 Act was replaced by section 742 of the new Act. So far as the definitions of ship and vessel were concerned, the two relevant words in the two sections stated, respectively:

Section 2 (1854):
" ' Ship ' shall include every description of vessel used in navigation not propelled by oars."

Section 742 (1894):
' Ship ' includes every description of vessel used in navigation not propelled by oars."

Shortly after the 1894 Act the Court of Appeal had to consider all three questions of propulsion, area of work, and object of work. In *Wells* v. *Owners of Gas Float Whitton No. 2* [40] a " gas float," said to be " shaped like a boat," had been moored in tidal waters to give light. It ran aground in a storm, and the question for decision was whether it was a ship, so as to be the subject of a salvage claim under Admiralty jurisdiction. [41] The object, which was 50 feet long and 20 feet broad, had neither oars, mast, nor rudder. It was unmanned and contained a gas cylinder. It came adrift in the Humber, and was salved. The County Court judge made a salvage award for £15, the value of the gas float being about £600. The case went first to the Admiralty Divisional Court, which held [42] that while the float was neither a ship nor a vessel nor a wreck there was jurisdiction as to a salvage claim, since the claim was ". . . in respect of a structure used in connection with navigation and exposed in the ordinary course of its use to the perils of the sea." The Court of Appeal, however, reversed this decision and held that there was no salvage jurisdiction. [43] The House of Lords affirmed the decision of the Court of Appeal. Lord Herschell said [44]:

" It was not constructed for the purpose of being navigated or of conveying cargo or passengers. It was, in truth, a lighted buoy or beacon. The suggestion that the gas stored in the float can be regarded as cargo carried by it is more ingenious than sound."

These three short sentences raise a number of issues.

---

[40] [1897] A.C. 337 (H.L.).
[41] As in *The Mac* (1882) 7 P.D. 126 (C.A.); see above, p. 60.
[42] [1895] P. 301.
[43] [1896] P. 42.
[44] [1897] A.C. 337, at p. 343.

We can consider the three ingredients already studied in connection with the earlier cases:

(1) *Means of propulsion.* The gas float had no means of propulsion, but it had already been established [45] that this did not in itself prevent a structure from qualifying as a ship.

(2) *Area of work.* The gas float was in tidal waters, but clearly at sea, and this was not an issue. [46]

(3) *Object of work.* Lord Herschell's words touched on the purpose of construction, in that he emphasised that the gas float was not built to be navigated or to carry cargo or passengers. Neither the fishing coble in *Ex p. Ferguson* [47] (" whether it goes to sea for the purpose of fishing or anything else "); nor the hopper barge in *The Mac* [48] (" the question cannot depend upon the circumstances whether she carries a cargo from port to port "); carried cargo or passengers but they were held to be ships. But both were built to be navigated in the sense that they were frequently in passage, and carrying out their special tasks during that passage. This could not be said of the gas float, which was navigated only to go to a place and there perform its function. There is a clear parallel with a drilling unit.

In *The Normandy* [49] the Admiralty Divisional Court considered whether " damage by collision " had taken place where a ship struck a pier. The definition of a ship was not an issue, but the case has been mentioned in a later case [50] where that definition was discussed. Section 3 of the County Courts Admiralty Jurisdiction Act 1868 stated that any county court with Admiralty jurisdiction should have jurisdiction to try and determine certain causes, including: " As to any claim for damage to cargo, or damage by collision—any cause in which the amount claimed does not exceed £300." These words had been amended in the following year [51] as follows: " The third section of the County Courts Admiralty Jurisdiction Act 1868 shall extend and apply to all claims for damage to ships, whether by collision or otherwise, when the amount claimed does not exceed £300."

The steamship *Normandy*, being negligently navigated, struck the pier at Ilfracombe, Devon, and damaged it to the extent of £200. A suit was brought in the local county court on behalf of the owner of the pier.[52]

---

[45] In *The Mac* (1882) 7 P.D. 126 (C.A.); see above, p. 60.

[46] In *Ex p. Ferguson* (1871) L.R. 6 Q.B. 280, Blackburn J. said: " I do not mean to say that a little boat going out for a mile or two to sea would be a ship . . ."; see above, p. 60.

[47] (1871) L.R. 6 Q.B. 280; see above, p. 59.

[48] (1882) 7 P.D. 126 (C.A.); see above, p. 60.

[49] [1904] P. 187.

[50] *The Upcerne* [1912] P. 160; see below, p. 67.

[51] By the County Courts Admiralty Jurisdiction Act 1869, s. 4.

[52] He relied on *Mersey Docks & Harbour Board* v. *Turner* (*The Zeta*) [1893] A.C. 468 (H.L.), in which it was decided that the jurisdiction given by the two Acts included a claim for damage to a ship by collision with a pierhead.

The shipowners argued that there had been no damage by collision within the meaning of either of the Acts, and that the county court judge, sitting in Admiralty, had no jurisdiction.[53]

The Admiralty Divisional Court held that damage done to a pier by a ship did not constitute " damage by collision." Gorell Barnes J. said [54]:

> " I may here observe that the true meaning of collision is not a mere striking against, but a striking together; and to me it seems more correct to speak of a vessel stranding, or running, or striking upon or against rocks or the shore, than colliding therewith; and the same to my mind is true when the contact is by a vessel with some structure erected on the rocks or shore, and I notice that the use of the word ' collision ' in sections 418 and 419 of the Merchant Shipping Act 1894 appears to refer only to collisions between ships."

The Judge concluded [55]:

> " Cases of striking something which is not engaged in navigation are very rare, and it is not unreasonable to assume that in using the word ' collision ' the framers of the Act intended to deal with the class of case which forms the ordinary subject of a collision suit."

In 1911 the decision in *The Mac* [56] was followed in *The Mudlark*,[57] where a sea-going steel hopper barge, 90 feet long and $19\frac{1}{2}$ feet wide, without means of propulsion, broke adrift from her moorings at West Hartlepool. She damaged a moored ship, the quay wall, a dry dock caisson and other property. The owners of *The Mudlark* were ready to pay into court an amount calculated on the basis of a limitation figure of £8 per ton, in accordance with the limitation provision (section 503) of the Merchant Shipping Act 1894. Counsel for these owners, Mr. Dawson Miller, relied on section 742 of the 1894 Act, which was an interpretation clause similar to section 2 of the 1854 Act,[58] stating:

> " ' Ship ' includes every description of vessel used in navigation not propelled by oars."

It was held that there was a right to limit. Bargrave Deane J. said [59]:

> " I think I am bound to follow the case of *The Mac* in the Court of Appeal, and hold that *The Mudlark* is a ' ship ' within the meaning of section 742 . . . and that her owners are, therefore, entitled to limit their liability under section 503. . . ."

---

[53] They relied on (among other cases) *Robson* v. *The Owner of the Kate* (1888) 21 Q.B.D. 13, in which a sailing-barge caused damage to an object on the river bank situated above the point reached by the tide, it being held that this was not " damage by collision," so that there was no Admiralty jurisdiction.

[54] [1904] P. 187 at p. 198.

[55] *Ibid.* at p. 201.

[56] (1882) 7 P.D. 126 (C.A.); see above, p. 60.

[57] [1911] P. 116. Meanwhile the Court of Appeal held in *The Craighall* [1910] P. 207, that a landing stage was not a ship in a case involving the interpretation of the Rules of the Supreme Court, Ord. 19, r. 28.

[58] See above, p. 59.

[59] [1911] P. 116 at p. 119.

In 1912 the Admiralty Court considered two cases, both involving collisions, in which the applicability of admiralty jurisdiction depended upon whether two objects, a gas-powered lighting buoy and a dredger, were ships. In both cases it was held that the disputed structures were not ships. The first case was that of *The Upcerne*,[60] which had struck a gas buoy belonging to the River Humber lighting authority. The buoy consisted of a cylindrical steel body with welded joints, which provided the buoyancy and acted as a reservoir for shale-oil gas. A flashing apparatus worked for a period of three to six months. The plaintiffs took out a summons in an admiralty action *in rem* in the Hull County Court for collision damage to their buoy. The County Court held that it had no jurisdiction and the Admiralty Divisional Court upheld that decision. The President, Sir Samuel Evans, said [61]:

> " Now, the particular object injured in the case before us was a gas float, being exactly the same kind of buoy as came under consideration by the House of Lords in the case of *Wells* v. *Owners of Gas Float Whitton No. 2*,[62] where it was decided that an object of this kind cannot be regarded as a ship. Therefore, if the word ' collision ' in section 3 of the County Courts Admiralty Jurisdiction Act 1868 refers to collisions between ships as stated by Sir Gorell Barnes,[63] it cannot apply to this collision, which took place between a ship and a gas float which according to the decision cannot be regarded as if it were a ship. . . . A pierhead [64] is fixed. So in the material sense is a buoy. In one sense it is a floating object, but it is not intended to float here, there and everywhere. It must float in order to be on the surface of the water, but the one purpose of fastening it in a particular place is to enable mariners to see what course to follow, and that purpose cannot be achieved unless the buoy is kept in a particular place, and is in that sense fixed. I therefore see no distinction in principle between an object of this kind, which, though floating, is affixed to the bottom of the sea in order that it may always be approximately in the same spot upon the surface of the water, and a pierhead, which is a more permanently fixed object. In these circumstances I think we should be doing wrong if we did not follow the case of *The Normandy*,[65] and I think the appeal fails."

It was crucial to this decision that the buoy, though floating, did not, in order to achieve its work, move from its position. It was fixed to the bottom of the sea, as was a pierhead, though clearly it would, by the very nature of the sea and its attachment to the bottom, move to a minor extent. So also a drilling unit carries out its work in a fixed position, but the degree of its attachment to the bottom depends upon its nature. A drill ship, for example, is generally accepted as being a ship, although the propositions set out above can be applied to it. It has the additional characteristic, however, that it can be, and sometimes is, used for navigation.

In the second case to be decided in 1912, *The Blow Boat*,[66] the Admiralty

---

[60] [1912] P. 160.
[62] [1897] A.C. 337; see above, p. 64.
[64] As in *The Normandy*.
[66] [1912] P. 217.

[61] *Ibid.*, at p. 166.
[63] In *The Normandy, op. cit.*
[65] *Op. cit.*

Court considered a collision between a dredger and a steam launch. Despite the decisions in *The Mac* [67] and *The Mudlark*,[68] that a hopper barge, used for carrying away mud and other debris, was a ship, the court reached a different conclusion. Whereas the two earlier cases concerned, respectively, the applicability of the concepts of salvage and limitation, this case necessitated a decision as to whether common law or admiralty principles were relevant.

A steam launch, going down the river Stour between Sandwich and the Isle of Thanet, hit a dredger, *The Blow Boat*, the property of the Sandwich town council. The incident had its lighter aspects. As the Judge described it [69]:

> " Accordingly everybody in Sandwich seems to have collected round the place, and one person brought some ropes to lift her [the launch] by, other people manned a crane, and one individual, weighing seventeen stone, sat in the stern of the launch by way of assisting her to go up, with the result that . . . the after sling broke and let not only the launch but the individual weighing seventeen stone down into the mud. . . . Everybody with the greatest good nature lent a hand. . . ."

Each side alleged negligence by the other; the council argued that *The Blow Boat* was not a vessel used in navigation within the definition of a ship in section 742 of the Merchant Shipping Act 1894.[70] If that contention were correct, the case had to be determined on common law and not on admiralty principles, and the contributory negligence of the plaintiffs would deprive them of any right to recovery. It was not until the Law Reform (Contributory Negligence) Act 1945 that there could be an apportionment of blame in a common law case. If, on the other hand, admiralty law applied, and both sides were to blame, the liability for damages would have been equally divided.[71]

The Blow Boat was described by the Admiralty judge, Bargrave Deane J.,[72] who decided that it was a common law action, as " a non-descript craft which was employed in the dredging of the river. . . ." As to its construction, he said, in describing the collision:

> " The plaintiff himself was guilty of negligence because, when he was invited to come on in the river, with this dredger in the way, instead of starting with his launch under command by having her engines moving, he was taken down by the tide on to the after or fore part—I am not sure which is the after and which the fore part—of this square thing, whereby his launch was damaged."

This is all that we learn as to the nature of the craft; there are of course

---

[67] (1882) 7 P.D. 126 (C.A.); see above, p. 60.

[68] [1911] P. 116; see above, p. 66.

[69] [1912] P. 217 at p. 221.

[70] They relied on *The Gas Float Whitton No. 2* [1897] A.C. 337 (H.L.) (see above p. 64) and *The Upcerne* [1912] P. 160 (see above, p. 67).

[71] As, generally, in the U.S.A. until the Supreme Court decision in *U.S.* v. *Reliable Transfer Co. Inc.* in 1975.

[72] [1912] P. 217 at p. 220.

circumstances in which a dredger might be held to be a ship,[73] but much depends on the mobility and the main mode of operation.

While that case did not produce any new law, the next case to be decided, *Weeks* v. *Ross*,[74] concerned the area of work, and came to a different conclusion from that reached in the *Southport Corporation* case.[75] A motor-boat, which took over 12 passengers, was used in a non-tidal part of the River Exe and in a canal leading to double locks which led to tidal waters. She had no Board of Trade certificate as to survey; this was an offence under section 271 (1) (*b*) of the Merchant Shipping Act 1894 [76] in the case of a ship. The Divisional Court held that she was a ship and was " used in navigation " for the purpose of section 742 of the Act.[77] Lord Coleridge J., who had delivered one of the judgments in the *Southport Corporation* case, 20 years earlier, said [78]:

> " I do not think the *Southport Case*, which the magistrates thought bound them, is binding here, because in this case these vessels were proceeding over waters which were used by ships coming from the sea to the docks and back again. Clearly such ships would be held to be navigating these waters on the ground of the nature of the waters they were traversing. If ships coming to and from the sea were clearly navigating these waters, the fact that these particular vessels in question did not proceed to sea does not prevent these waters being navigated by them as they would be by ships going to and from the sea."

The motor-boat, by associating with ships which were " coming from the sea," was therefore a ship although it did not go to that sea. Since ships, truly so called by virtue of the tests which have been applied by the courts, were in the area, it became a place for navigation. As Channell J. put it [79]:

> " Vessels are passing up and down this canal constantly . . . they only go down to the lock to get to the sea when the tide is high. There is navigation there, and it is a place for navigation, and being a place for navigation it is not the less navigation by this launch than by any other craft; the launch is navigating. The grounds upon which the judges decided the *Southport Case* do not in point of fact exist in the present case. No one could say that this place is a place where there could not be navigation when in point of fact there is a very considerable amount of navigation."

In the *Southport Case* the area was an artificial lake, and no other craft appear to have gone there. Certainly there were no craft from the sea. If, however, the motor-boat in *Weeks* v. *Ross* had been a gas float, would the decision have been the same? It seems that it would not, since the

---

[73] As a hopper barge was held to be a ship in *The Mac* (1882) 7 P.D. 126 (C.A.).
[74] [1913] 2 K.B. 229.
[75] [1893] 1 Q.B. 359; see above, p. 63.
[76] s. 271 succeeded s. 318 of the Merchant Shipping Act 1854.
[77] The definitions section.
[78] At pp. 234–235.
[79] *Ibid.* at p. 233.

object of her work would have disqualified her. The gas float in *The Gas Float Whitton* [80] was said not to have been built to be navigated or to carry cargo or passengers.

At this stage the definition of " ship " in the Merchant Shipping Act 1894 was amended, for certain purposes. The Merchant Shipping Act 1921, s. 1, provided that, notwithstanding anything contained in section 742, the 1894 Act should have effect as though in the provisions of Part I (Registry) and Part VII (Limitation of Liability), " ship " included

> " every description of lighter, barge or like vessel used in navigation in Great Britain, however propelled: Provided that a lighter, barge, or like vessel used exclusively in non-tidal waters, other than harbours, shall not, for the purposes of this Act, be deemed to be used in navigation."

Immediately after the last decision the President of the Admiralty Division issued a decree of limitation of liability in respect of a floating crane, in the *Titan*.[81] Its work was done while it was at rest, rather than on a voyage; to this extent it resembled a gas-float [82] or a drilling unit rather than the barges and launches which had so far featured predominantly in the decided cases. The crane had broken adrift from her moorings and moved down the River Tyne, hitting several ships. The owners of one of the ships, the *Benwood*, sued the owners of the *Titan*, who were Swan Hunter & Wigham Richardson Ltd. Hill J., in the High Court,[83] had held the owners of the *Titan* liable, but they then sought to limit their liability to £8 per ton, on a tonnage of 782·14 tons, *i.e.* to £6,257 2s.5d. Their claim was unopposed by the owners of the *Benwood* and a decree was issued, limiting liability.[84] Although this was an agreed order,[85] it can probably be taken to represent the opinions of the Admiralty lawyers concerned, to the effect that a floating crane should be regarded as a ship.

Despite the fact that there had been an agreed order, the last case was mentioned in *Merchants' Marine Insurance Co. Ltd* v. *North of England Protecting & Indemnity Association* [86] in the following terms by Roche J.[87]:

> " I do not rely upon the fact that that claim was unopposed, and that the matter went without argument, because I know how carefully these matters are dealt with in the Admiralty Division."

Roche J. had to deal with a pontoon carrying a crane, as opposed to a floating crane, and he distinguished *The Titan*, holding that in the case before him the pontoon in question was not a ship or vessel for the purpose of the rules of a protecting and indemnity club. An English ship,

---

[80] [1897] A.C. 387. See above, p. 64.
[81] (1923) 14 Ll.L.R. 484.
[82] See *The Gas Float Whitton No. 2* [1897] A.C. 337; and above, p. 64.
[83] (1922) 13 Ll.L.R. 428.
[84] (1923) 14 Ll.L.R. 484.
[85] And the report of the case was later to be described as " very short "; Jones J. in *Cook* v. *Dredging & Construction Co. Ltd* [1958] 1 Lloyd's Rep. 334. See below, p. 81.
[86] (1926) 25 Ll.L.R. 446.
[87] *Ibid.* at p. 448.

the *Fernhill*, when in the River Sevre at the port of La Rochelle, had come into collision with the pontoon. The French name was *ponton mâture*, meaning a pontoon adapted for the lifting of masts. The *Fernhill* damaged both the pontoon and the crane mounted on it, and became liable to the French government, its owners, in a sum of over £12,000. The pontoon, which was built in 1868, was in a naval dockyard, permanently moored to the river bank by six chains, and moored also, fore and aft, to warships. Gangways of a semi-permanent nature had been laid from the pontoon to the shore, and to the warships.

It was possible to move the pontoon, and one witness had seen it being done. It had taken two hours to move her a mile. She was in the shape of a ship or vessel, and adapted by the provision of decks for being inhabited or manned by a staff which was called the crew.

The *Fernhill* was insured by the North of England Protecting & Indemnity Association in respect of certain liabilities, including, under the Association's Rule 2 (b) of Clause 1, liabilities for damages, to the extent of one fourth, " which a member may, in consequence of collision, become liable to pay . . . in respect of loss or damage caused by a steamship entered " in the Association " to any other ship or vessel." Under Rule 2 (e), however, there was cover in full in respect of damages " which the member or owner may become liable to pay . . . in respect of damage done by the steamship " to various named objects, such as docks, piers, quays, works, jetties, erections, or any fixed or movable things, other than ships or vessels.

The question for decision was therefore whether the pontoon was a ship or vessel. If she was, the Association would only be liable as to a quarter of the damages, with the collision liability underwriters, who were the plaintiffs, paying the balance, but if she was not, it would be liable in full.

Counsel for the P. & I. Association, in arguing that the pontoon was a ship or vessel and citing definitions set out in the dictionaries, had said that a vessel was " an artificial structure made and used for the conveyance by water of persons or property." The property to be conveyed, he said, was the crane. That, however, was an incidental use; though the pontoon carried a crane all the time, in the sense that it reposed there, it was not, as a general rule, navigating in order to carry it from one place to another.

Roche J. held that this was not a ship or vessel, saying [88]:

> " In my judgment, having regard to the facts relating to this pontoon, this pontoon is not a ' ship ' or ' vessel ' but is another movable thing within the meaning of sub-rule (e) of Rule 2 of the Association. My reasons for so holding are these: that in my view the primary purpose for which this pontoon is designed and adapted is to float and to lift, and not to navigate. Whatever other qualities are attached to a ship or vessel, the adaptability for navigation, and its use for that purpose, is in my judgment one of the most essential elements. It may be that there are floating cranes, and I think there

---

[88] *Ibid.* at p. 447.

are, which may be ships or vessels within the language of various Acts of Parliament, and which may be ships or vessels within the meaning of this rule, but having regard to the facts of this case, this pontoon is not, in my judgment, such a ship or vessel . . . although fully capable of movement, although it is moved from time to time in order that it may operate elsewhere in the lifting of heavy objects out of ships, yet having regard to its history I am satisfied that movement is the exception in its career and not the rule. . . ."

The crucial elements in this passage are that:

(1) the decision was made on the basis of the rules of the Association but embodies the principles applied in earlier cases;

(2) the primary purpose for which the pontoon was designed and adapted, described as its "adaptability for navigation," was important;

(3) the use to which the pontoon was in fact put, most of the time, described as "its user" for navigation, was important.

It is useful to consider again the three elements which have been the subject of discussion by successive courts:

(1) *The means of propulsion.* It had long been established [89] that it did not matter whether the vessel had independent means of propulsion.

(2) *Area of work.* This was not material in the present case; the *Southport Corporation* case [90] and *Weeks* v. *Ross* [91] dealt with the question of differing types of enclosed, or partly enclosed, areas of water.

(3) *Object of work.* This was the crucial test in the case of the crane-lifting pontoon. In the first case considered above, *Ex p. Ferguson*,[92] it was said [93] that it did not matter whether the coble went to sea "for the purpose of fishing or anything else." In *The Mac* [94] the hopper barge, carrying mud and debris, moved about regularly, as an essential part of her work, even though the pivotal point of the work could be regarded as the task, in a stationary position, of pulling up the mud and debris. She was not carrying cargo. The common factors throughout seem to be that the use itself, whether for fishing, the carriage of cargo, or the collection and disposal of mud, must involve movement. It is not enough that the object can be moved from one place to another to do its work; it must do at least some of that work while in movement. The pontoon in the *Merchants' Marine* case was rarely moved, and then only to enable it to do its work elsewhere. Roche J. was shown a picture of the *Titan*, the floating crane which had been agreed by the parties [95] to the earlier case to be a ship or vessel. He said [96]:

---

[89] For example, in *The Mac* (1882) 7 P.D. 126 (C.A.); see above, p. 60.
[90] [1893] 1 Q.B. 359; see above, p. 63.
[91] [1913] 2 K.B. 229; see above, p. 69.
[92] (1871) L.R. 6 Q.B. 280; see above, p. 59.   [93] *Ibid.* at p. 291.
[94] (1882) 7 P.D. 126 (C.A.); see above, p. 60.
[95] (1923) 14 Ll.L.R. 484; see above, p. 70.
[96] (1926) 25 Ll.L.R. at p. 448.

" The picture shows that although not a very manageable object it was a
boat which seemed to be more capable of guidance and easy movement
than the pontoon with which I am now dealing. The description and terms of
employment seem to point to the same conclusion. . . ."

In these last words the judge was referring to the contract for the *Titan*,
by which payment was made on a time and distance basis. While he
thought that it was right that the floating crane, the *Titan*, should be
regarded as a ship, and right also that the French pontoon, with the crane
mounted on it, should not be treated as a ship, he said [97] that " a floating
crane might under certain circumstances be a ship or vessel " and added:

" . . . my decision was not a decision that no cranes which floated, or that no
objects which transported the cranes, could be ships or vessels, but only that
this pontoon, situated as it was in Rochefort at the time in question, was not
a ship or vessel within the meaning of the rules of the defendant association."

Though both of these structures performed their work in a fixed position,
they fell on opposite sides of the line. One can only speculate as to what
might have been the decision of Sir Henry Duke, the President of the
Admiralty Division in the *Titan*, if the parties had not submitted to him an
agreed Order.

We now turn to a case in which a Scottish court held that a seaplane
was not a ship. Clearly the question of use, and of predominant employment, was of major importance. In *Watson* v. *R.C.A. Victor Co. Inc.*[98] a
privately owned United States seaplane, carrying the pilot, his wife and two
daughters, and a crew of four, on a flight from New York to Europe,
came down in the sea, amid fishing grounds off Cape Dan, Greenland.
The passengers and the seaplane reached a rocky islet surrounded by the
ice pack. A steam trawler, the *Lord Talbot*, recovered cinematographic
equipment with a salved value of £3,000 from the seaplane. The Master of
the *Lord Talbot* as the claimant, or " pursuer," claimed an award of
£300 in the Scottish courts. The Sheriff-Substitute dismissed the claim.
Relying on the judgments of Lord Esher M.R. in the Court of Appeal in
Wells v. *Owners of Gas Float Whitton No. 2*,[99] and of Lord Herschell in
the House of Lords in that case,[1] he said [2]:

" It is common knowledge that a seaplane is in reality only a species of
aircraft, and that although its construction permits of its floating on the sea,
or even being navigated a short distance, its primary function—as illustrated
in this case by the flight from New York to an island off the coast of Greenland—is navigation in the air. Its construction for the purpose of floating or
moving on the water is, I understand, mainly designed for purposes of
safety should it be compelled through stress of weather or mechanical defect
or for other reasons to descend from the air while flying above water. In
short, in popular language no one would I think describe a seaplane as a
ship, or vessel, or boat."

---

[97] *Ibid.* at pp. 448–449.
[98] (1934) 50 Ll.L.R. 77.
[99] [1896] P. 42 (C.A.); see above, p. 64.
[1] [1897] A.C. 337 (H.L.).
[2] *Op. cit.*, at pp. 78–79. As to the words " in reality " *cf.* " really " at p. 15, above.

The judge went on to say that, quite apart from usage of " popular language," a seaplane did not satisfy the definitions or descriptions of a ship or vessel given in either the Merchant Shipping Acts or in the decided cases. As for the Acts, there were the definitions, in section 742 of the Merchant Shipping Act 1894, of " vessel " as including " any ship or boat, or any other description of vessel used in navigation," and of " ship " as including " every description of vessel used in navigation not propelled by oars." It could not be predicated of a seaplane, which was a species of aircraft, that it was " used in navigation " in the sense in which a vessel or a ship was so used. Despite the potentially wider meaning of the word " navigation," [3] it was clear law that it must mean, in contexts such as these, navigation on the water.

As for the decided cases, the Sheriff-Substitute said that they had been fully dealt with in *The Gas Float Whitton No. 2*.[4] The result of the decisions, he said, was that the word " ship " had to be construed in its popular sense, and that the standard to be applied to ascertain whether a structure was a ship for salvage purposes was whether it could " in the broad and popular sense " be regarded as a ship.

There was a conclusive argument against the contention that at common law an aircraft such as a seaplane ought to be regarded as a ship for salvage purposes. This was that the benefit of the law relating to wreck and to salvage of life and property was only extended to aircraft by section 11 of the Air Navigation Act 1920. That section stated:

> " *The law relating to wreck and to salvage of life or property*, and to the duty of rendering assistance to vessels in distress (including the provisions of the Merchant Shipping Acts 1894 to 1916, and any other Act relating to these subjects), *shall apply to aircraft* on or over the sea or tidal waters as it applies to vessels, *and the owner of an aircraft shall be entitled to a reasonable reward for salvage services rendered by the aircraft to any property* or persons in any case where the owner of a ship would be so entitled." [5]

While the first part of the section applies to the law of salvage to aircraft, in general terms, its second part grants an entitlement to a salvage award to " the owner of an aircraft." What, then, was the statutory position so far as concerned salvage services rendered to an aircraft? The section had to be read with the preamble of the Act, which included the words:

> " And whereas it is expedient to make further provisions for controlling and regulating the navigation of aircraft, whether British or foreign, within the limits of His Majesty's jurisdiction as aforesaid, and, in the case of British aircraft, for regulating the navigation thereof both within such jurisdiction and elsewhere."

As a result of these words the British ship in the present case was not entitled to a salvage reward, since this was a foreign seaplane outside the jurisdiction.

---

[3] As in " navigator " of an aircraft; there is, for example, a Livery Company of the City of London called the Guild of Air Pilots and Air Navigators.
[4] [1897] A.C. 337 (H.L.); see above, p. 64.   [5] Italics supplied.

The decision was the subject of an appeal by the Master of the trawler, but it was unsuccessful, Sheriff Morton saying [6] of the Sheriff-Substitute's judgment:

> " I am entirely in agreement with him on the main point of his judgment, viz., that no claim for salvage lies in the circumstances of this case. . . . It [a seaplane] is in my opinion not a ship either according to the authorities or according to the definitions of ' ship ' and ' vessel ' under the Merchant Shipping Acts."

In *The St. Machar* [7] the Scottish Court of Sessions considered a collision between a ship, the *Gwenthills*, which, upon being launched at Aberdeen, struck a steam tug, the *St. Machar*, which had been engaged to take charge of her after the launching. The trial judge considered that both parties were to blame, but counsel for the defendants, who owned the ship which was being launched, contended that the Maritime Conventions Act 1911, with its provisions for apportionment of blame, did not apply to a collision involving a ship being launched. The Act had to be construed with the Merchant Shipping Acts, and section 742 of the 1894 Act defined a vessel as including " any ship or boat, or any other description of vessel used in navigation." The trial judge, Lord Jameson said [8]:

> " It was argued that the *Gwenthills* was not used in navigation. The only authority to which I was referred was the case of *The Blow Boat* [9] . . . where a nondescript square craft used for dredging was held not to fall within the definition. In *Wells* v. *Owners of Gas Float Whitton No. 2* [10] . . . a gas float shaped like a boat was held not to be a ship or vessel in the sense of the same definition in the Merchant Shipping Act 1854."

He quoted Lord Herschell's statement in that case,[11] that the gas float was not constructed for the purpose of being navigated or of conveying cargo or passengers, and added:

> " The *Gwenthills* was constructed for such purposes and to be used in navigation, and in my opinion the Act clearly applies to her. It is not limited to vessels navigating under their own power and would obviously apply to a collision in which a steamer lying at anchor or moored to a quay was involved."

He held the parties equally to blame; his judgment was upheld on appeal,[12] Lord Carmont saying [13]:

> ". . . I am of opinion that the *Gwenthills* was being used in navigation at the time the collision took place. She was waterborne at the time, and I cannot deny to her the character of a vessel merely because she was not capable of

---

[6] (1934) 50 Ll.L.R. 77 at pp. 81–82.
[7] (1939) 64 Ll.L.R. 27; on appeal, (1939) 65 Ll.L.R. 119.
[8] (1939) 64 Ll.L.R. 27 at p. 31.
[9] [1912] P. 217; see above, p. 68. It was held that the dredger was not a ship, so that Admiralty principles did not apply.
[10] [1897] A.C. 337 (H.L.); see above, p. 64.
[11] Set out above, at p. 64.
[12] (1939) 65 Ll.L.Rep. 119.
[13] *Ibid.* at p. 125.

self propulsion, as was suggested, or because she was incapable of self direction, on the assumption that she had no rudder."

A further claim, concerning a flying boat, was considered by the High Court in *Polpen Shipping Co. Ltd.* v. *Commercial Union Assurance Co. Ltd.*[14] The *Polperro* had dragged her anchor and collided with a British government flying boat, which was also at anchor. The owners of the *Polperro* admitted liability, paid £2,263 to the Air Ministry, and then sued the defendants, as one of their insurers, for their proportion of a loss under their time policy of insurance. By Clause 1 of the Institute Time Clauses, which were attached to the policy, it was agreed that if the insured ship

> " shall come into collision with any other ship or vessel and the assured shall in consequence thereof become liable to pay, and shall pay, by way of damages . . . any sum or sums in respect of such collision, the underwriters will pay the assured such proportion of such sum or sums so paid as their respective subscriptions hereto bear to the value of the ship hereby insured. . . ."

The insurers said that they were not liable as the flying boat was not a " ship or vessel." Atkinson J. held that they were right, and that the claim failed. He turned first to the definitions of " vessel " and " ship " in section 742 of the Merchant Shipping Act 1894 [15] and said of them [16]: " It seems to me that the dominant idea is something which is ' used in navigation,' and not merely capable of navigating for the moment." This represents a confirmation of the pattern which had been emerging from the cases (except in *The Titan* [17]) that all or a substantial part of the work done by the alleged ship or vessel should occur while she was engaged in navigation.

Turning to the decided cases, the judge cited with approval extracts from *The Gas Float Whitton No. 2* [18] (the gas float), *Merchants' Marine Insurance Co. Ltd.* v. *North of England Protecting and Indemnity Association* [19] (the pontoon crane), and *Watson* v. *R.C.A. Victor Co. Inc.*[20] (the seaplane), in all of which cases the object had been held not to be a ship or vessel. Of Lord Esher's judgment in *The Gas Float Whitton No. 2* Atkinson J. said [21]:

> " I am satisfied that the dominant idea in Lord Esher's mind [in the Court of Appeal] in considering the attributes of a ship was not merely its ability to be navigated, but whether it could fairly be said to navigate the seas."

As for Lord Herschell's judgment in the House of Lords,[22] which contained [23] the sentence: " It was not constructed for the purpose of being

---

[14] [1943] K.B. 161.   [15] As for the word " ship " see above at p. 64.
[16] [1943] K.B. 161 at p. 164.   [17] See above, p. 70.
[18] [1896] P. 42 (C.A.); see above, p. 64.
[19] (1926) 25 Ll.L.R. 446; see above, p. 70.
[20] (1934) 50 Ll.L.R. 77; see above, p. 73.
[21] [1943] K.B. 161 at p. 165.   [22] [1897] A.C. 337.
[23] *Ibid.* at p. 343.

navigated or of conveying cargo or passengers," Atkinson J. said [24]:
" He seems to me to put his judgment in a nutshell when he says ' for the
purpose of being navigated.' " Despite the stress laid here on the object of
construction, the general emphasis in the cases is more or the current use
than on the original intent of the builders. One could easily envisage a
situation where an object was originally constructed as a sea-going ship,
but, after the passage of time, has ended its days in a truncated, adapted
modified form, moored fast and permanently to the shore, bearing a crane
or some other load, and no longer capable of being described as a ship.
Perhaps the various remarks by the Judges can be reconciled if the changes
inflicted on what was originally built as a ship are regarded as recon-
structions, so that we can then look at the object of that reconstruction.[25]

Atkinson J. then considered the *Merchants' Marine Insurance* decision,
saying [26] of the judgment by Roche J.[27]:

> " I think it is fair to say that again the dominating idea throughout his
> judgment was whether the structure which he was considering had been
> intended to be used for navigation;"

and adding, of the Court of Appeal judgments:

> " The same view was taken in the Court of Appeal. The court were singu-
> larly loth to lay down any principle or any definition. I doubt whether
> Scrutton L.J. was ever so hesitant about stepping in with some clarifying
> remarks, but I think it is clear that all the members of the court thought
> that a floating crane could not be regarded as being built to be ' used in
> navigation.' "

Finally, in reviewing the decision in *Watson v. R.C.A. Victor Co. Inc.*,
the earlier case which concerned a seaplane, Atkinson J. quoted with
approval the judgment of the Sheriff-Substitute [28] but indicated an
important difference in the purposes for which the two aeroplanes had
been constructed. On the one hand, in *Watson*, the Sheriff-Substitute had
said that so far as the seaplane was constructed to float or move on
water it was so built " for purposes of safety should it be compelled
through stress of weather or mechanical defect or for other reasons to
descend from the air while flying above water." Atkinson J. said [29] of
this remark: " That, of course, is not true with regard to the flying boat
with which I am concerned. Its construction is to enable it to land on
water and to take off from water." This seems to involve a distinction

---

[24] [1943] K.B. 161 at p. 165.
[25] In a later case, for example, *Marine Craft Constructors Ltd.* v. *Erland Blomqvist
(Engineers) Ltd.* [1953] 1 Lloyd's Rep. 514 (see below, p. 78), a crane had been removed
from the pontoon to which it had been attached. It was held that, whatever the nature
of the original structure in the special circumstances of the case, where the crane's
swivel ring was being carried from one place to another, the structure could be regarded
as a ship or vessel.
[26] [1943] K.B. 161 at p. 165–166.
[27] See above, pp. 71–72.
[28] See above, pp. 73–74.
[29] [1943] K.B. 161 at p. 166.

between, say, a seaplane, as in the *Watson* case, and a flying boat, as in the *Polpen* case. The *Concise Oxford Dictionary* defines a seaplane as an " aeroplane constructed for rising from and alighting on water "; of a flying boat it says: " Form of seaplane in which a boat serves as both fuselage and float."

So far as there can be such a distinction between a seaplane and flying boat the former would fall more clearly outside the definition of " ship or vessel," since it might only be on the water in the event of some emergency. Nevertheless, Atkinson J. decided that it was impossible to hold that the words " ship or vessel " in the insurance policy included the flying boat. He concluded [30]:

> " I do not want to attempt a definition, but if I had to define ' ship or vessel ' I should say that it was any hollow structure intended to be used in navigation, *i.e.* intended to do its real work on the seas or other waters, and capable of free and ordered movement thereon from one place to another. A flying boat's real work is to fly. It is constructed for that purpose, and its ability to float and navigate short distances is merely incidental to that work. To my mind, that is where the difference lies."

Here the crucial words for the purpose of the decision are " intended to do its real work on the seas or other water," and as that could not be said of the flying boat it followed that it was not a ship or vessel. The sequence of words however, in the expression " intended to be used in navigation, *i.e.* intended to do its real work on the seas or other waters," is open to discussion. The hopper barge, *The Mac*,[31] was held to be a ship; she was intended to be used in navigation, but that was not the real or main nature of her work.[32] The work of a hopper barge consists of the dredging up and the carrying away of mud and gravel. Neither of these tasks can be contemplated without the other. It would be an exaggeration to say that the dredging up was the " real work "; but neither could the carrying away be called the real work, though it is during that part of the work that navigation takes place.

The nature of a pontoon was again considered in *Marine Craft Constructors Ltd.* v. *Erland Blomqvist (Engineers) Ltd.*[33] It will be recalled that a floating crane and a pontoon crane had been the subjects of earlier decisions, in the first of which [34] it had been agreed by the parties that the object was a ship and thus able to limit liability, and in the second of which [35] it was held that it was not a ship or vessel. In the *Marine Craft* case a pontoon had been fitted with a crane, and the structure was known

---

[30] *Ibid.* at p. 167.
[31] (1882) 7 P.D. 126 (C.A.); see above, p. 60.
[32] Unless we accept the view of Brett L.J. in that case that the clearance of mud is for the purpose of navigation, *i.e.* by other ships.
[33] [1953] 1 Lloyd's Rep. 514.
[34] *The Titan* (1923) 14 Ll.L.R. 484; see above, p. 70.
[35] *Merchants' Marine Insurance Co. Ltd.* v. *North of England Protecting & Indemnity Association* (1926) 25 Ll.L.R. 446; see above, p. 70.

as a floating crane. The whole pontoon, which formed its carriage or stage, was about 80 feet long, 50 feet wide, and five feet deep. It was itself made up of two large pontoons, fixed together, in the centre, with four smaller pontoons fixed at either end. There were four towing bollards at each end of the pontoon.

Originally the entire floating crane would, if this were needed, be towed from place to place so that the crane's lifting work could be done. There was to take place however a physical alteration in the nature of this structure. The crane, with the exception of the crane ring or swivel ring, upon which the crane used to rotate, was to be removed from the pontoon. That metal ring, which weighed some three or four tons, had also been detached, but it lay on the top of the pontoon. While it would have been interesting to consider whether the original structure was a ship or vessel, there had occurred a change in construction of such a nature that, as suggested earlier,[36] not only the method of use but also the purpose of the structure had been altered.

The original owners of the entire combined structure of pontoon and crane sold the pontoon to the plaintiffs, Marine Craft, and the crane to the defendants, Erland Blomqvist. While each of these buyers had made further sale arrangements, an immediate problem was the transfer of the structure, from which the crane itself had already been removed, from Cosham, Hampshire, where it lay, to Southampton. The plaintiffs, the buyers of the pontoon, agreed to hire it to the defendants, so that it could be towed to Southampton, where the crane ring could be removed. The owners of the crane ring agreed not only to pay a daily rate of hire but also to insure the plaintiffs' pontoon for £3,000 against total loss and all damage during the hire. That arrangement, it was held, involved also an undertaking by the defendants to be responsible for loss or damage during the time that the pontoon was on hire.

In the course of the journey the pontoon was damaged. Its owners claimed damages from the defendants. The first question which had to be decided by the High Court was whether the pontoon, at the time of the voyage, was a ship or vessel so as to be covered by the Merchant Shipping Acts and the Marine Insurance Act 1906. If the latter Act were applicable there would have been an implied warranty of seaworthiness.

Lynskey J. held that the pontoon was a vessel. He said,[36a] that if he had had to decide the case of a pontoon itself with a crane upon it,[36b] he would have been in great difficulty, because he had no information as to the use of the crane. He would have had to know " whether it was kept at one particular place almost continuously and only moved occasionally in special circumstances, or whether it was in the habit of wandering about

---

[36] See above, p. 77.
[36a] At p. 518.
[36b] As in the *Merchants' Marine* case, op. cit. where a pontoon carrying a crane was held not to be a ship; see p. 70.

from one portion of the docks to another. . . ." In fact the crane had, apart from its ring, been removed:

> " The ring was not attached to the pontoon; it was lying on sleepers, and it is quite plain that the object of this tow from Cosham to Southampton was purely for the carriage of this ring from one port to another to enable it to be lifted off the pontoon. In other words, at the moment, the pontoon was being used to be towed for the carriage of goods through the water and to be navigated for that purpose. She was fitted with bollards for towing, and although she may not have been a vessel when she had a crane on her, it seems to me that, at the time when this arrangement was made, she was to be used as a vessel and was treated as a vessel, at any rate for the purpose of this towing. She was carrying this ring and was within what I should think was a clear definition of a vessel or boat when one bears in mind the many other forms of articles in the water which have been held to be ships and vessels which the ordinary individual would not be likely to have so described in ordinary language. If you have got a dumb barge it can be described as a vessel. It seems to me that a pontoon, particularly a pontoon which is used for the carriage for the time being of goods,[37] must be described as a vessel."

The judge concluded [38] that " there was an implied warranty of seaworthiness for the purpose of this tow." He then found on the evidence that although the seaworthiness required was less for a voyage from Cosham to Southampton than it would be for a voyage from Calais to Dover, the real cause of the damage was the weakness or lack of seaworthiness in the pontoon when she set out. As a result, the defendants were entitled to rely upon the breach by the plaintiffs of the implied warranty of seaworthiness. On the other hand, the defendants had failed to carry out their undertaking to have the pontoon insured. In those circumstances the plaintiffs, having established a breach of contract by the defendants, were entitled to damages, but only to nominal damages, of £1, since even if a contract of insurance had existed there would have been no recovery thereunder.

Lynskey J. referred to the difficulty which he would have had if required to decide the case of a pontoon with a crane upon it. We have already seen that the parties in *The Titan* [39] agreed that a floating crane was a ship, for the purposes of limitation, and that the court held in *Merchants' Marine Insurance Co. Ltd.* v. *North of England Protecting & Indemnity Insurance Association* [40] that a pontoon crane was not a ship. Despite the respectful comments made by Roche J.[41] in the latter case, about the agreement reached in *The Titan*, it seems probable that a pontoon crane can properly

---

[37] Contrast the words of Cotton L.J. in *The Mac* (1882) 7 P.D. 126 (C.A.) at p. 131: " The question cannot depend on the circumstance whether she carries a cargo from port to port. She was propelled by towing, and she carried mud with a crew on board." See above, p. 60.

[38] (1926) 25 Ll.L.R. 446 at p. 519.

[39] (1923) 14 Ll.L.R. 484; see above, p. 70.

[40] (1926) 25 Ll.L.R. 446; see above, p. 70.

[41] *Ibid.* at p. 448: " I know how carefully these matters are dealt with in the Admiralty Division "; see above, p. 70.

be described as a ship or vessel. In the *Marine Craft Constructors* case, however, the conclusive factors were the separation of interests between pontoon and crane ring, and the fact that one was acting as carrier for the other.

The leading decisions as to whether an object was a ship or vessel were reviewed in *Cook* v. *Dredging & Construction Co. Ltd*,[42] which concerned the *Sliedrecht IX*, a blower boat used in reclamation operations, when it removed silt from barges and discharged it to the shore. It was shaped like a ship; it had a deck and hatches, companion ladders, and other equipment characteristic of a ship, but it was flat bottomed, was similarly shaped at each end and had no rudder or means of propulsion. It had been hired from a Dutch company to work in Southampton water. Its work was summarised by Jones J.[43]:

> " It was not used to bring anything up from the bed of a harbour, channel or river—other dredgers did this in Southampton Water at the time in question and discharged the sludge brought up into barges, which we are told are laid alongside this structure. The sludge was not transferred to the structure, but an engine on it forced the sludge from the barge through a pipe that ran on wooden supports from the place where the structure was moored to the shore at that part of Southampton Water, where it was discharged and used for the purpose of reclamation of land. . . . The structure had been moored in this place for 18 months before the day of the plaintiff's accident, but it was not kept permanently in any place: it was moved by tow, from time to time, to any place where it was required."

The accident to which the judge referred occurred when a fireman employed by the defendants, who had hired the dredger, fell into or on to an open hatch. He alleged negligence by the defendants, their servants or agents, in failing to comply with Regulations 12 (a), 12 (c), 37 (a) and 45 of the Dock Regulations 1934 [44]; and in failing to light the hatch adequately and provide fencing and guard rails for it, and to warn the plaintiff that it was there, and open; and in failing generally to provide and maintain safe premises and take proper precautions to guard him against injury. The Dock Regulations 1934 imposed various duties upon the defendants as to lighting, fencing and other matters, but were inapplicable if the structure was not a ship.

Jones J. held that the dredger was a ship. He referred first [45] to the definition in section 742 of the Merchant Shipping Act 1894, to the effect that a ship included " every description of vessel used in navigation not propelled by oars," and continued: "It seems easy to decide that it was a vessel, but less easy to say that it was used in navigation. At the time of the plaintiff's accident, it was being used in a process of dredging and land reclamation. . . ." He then went on to describe the manner of working,

---

[42] [1958] 1 Lloyd's Rep. 334.
[43] *Ibid.* at p. 337.
[44] Made under s. 79 of the Factory and Workshop Act 1901.
[45] [1958] 1 Lloyd's Rep. 334 at 337.

and, in particular, the way in which the engine forced sludge to the shore. The cases to which he referred, albeit briefly, were *The Mac*,[46] where it was held that a hopper barge was a ship; and *The Harlow*,[47] where dumb barges had been held to be ships, though, as he said, " these barges were apparently moved about much more often than this structure would be moved about." The Judge then mentioned *The Gas Float Whitton No. 2*[48] where a gas float, not intended or fitted to be navigated, was held not to be a ship, and *The Titan*,[49] where, as he put it: ". . . a floating crane seems . . . to have been regarded as a ship, but the report of that case is very short." It will be recalled that the claim in the latter case was unopposed.

Jones J. then expressed[50] his conclusion:

> " This structure in some respects is like the gas float and in other respects it is like the floating crane. I think that it should be held that it was used in navigation, as it had been moved often on the sea from place to place as occasion required, and that it should be held to be a ship."

The gas float, which had been held not to be a ship, had done work, but work which was not performed while it was navigating; nor did it navigate often. The floating crane had differed in that it was moved from time to time; but the Judge did not refer to the pontoon, formerly part of a combined pontoon and crane, which had been considered in *Marine Craft Constructors Ltd.* v. *Erland Blomquist (Engineers) Ltd.*[51] and held to be a ship.[52] The latter case, however, can probably be distinguished on its particular facts, although the conclusion was the same, in that a type of " cargo " was being carried by the pontoon, which had, temporarily, changed its function.[53] The Judge, having decided that the structure was a ship, then considered other aspects of the wording of the Docks Regulations 1934, and concluded that they were inapplicable since they only applied if " goods " were being loaded, or if the ship was in a dock, harbour or canal. As for the general question of negligence, he concluded that the accident was due solely to the plaintiff's own negligence.

16 cases were considered above, the first having been decided in 1866 and the last in 1958. In the majority of them the definition in the relevant Merchant Shipping Act had to be applied; in some of the others that definition was considered, although the case in question was not governed by the Act. So far as the structures in question are concerned, we find that the courts held that the following, in their contexts, were not ships

---

[46] (1882) 7 P.D. 126 (C.A.), which, he noted, had been followed in *The Mudlark* [1911] P. 116. For these cases above, pp. 60 and 66 respectively.

[47] [1922] P. 175; they had rudders and were not propelled by oars.

[48] [1897] A.C. 337 (H.L.); see above, p. 64.

[49] (1923) 14 Ll.L.R. 484; see above, p. 70.

[50] [1958] 1 Lloyd's Rep. 334 at p. 338.

[51] [1953] 1 Lloyd's Rep. 514; see above, p. 78.

[52] Nor is the case mentioned in the reported arguments of Counsel.

[53] Similarly, in *The Mac* (1881) 7 P.D. 126 (see above, p. 60) the statement that the hopper barge was used in navigation is one which refers to a special situation, in that the navigation in question was that of other ships.

or vessels: a coal hulk, an electric passenger launch, a gas float (twice) a landing stage, a crane on a pontoon, a seaplane and a flying boat. They held that the following, again in their particular contexts, were ships or vessels: a fishing coble, a hopper barge (twice), a motor-boat, a floating crane (an agreed order), a ship being launched, another floating crane and a blower boat.

Repetition of the following passages from some of the judgments may throw some light on how the courts today might, so far as they followed the views therein expressed, approach any attempt to classify the various kinds of drilling units as " ships " or otherwise.

" What, then, is the meaning of the word ' ship ' in this Act? It is this, that every vessel that substantially goes to sea is a ' ship.' I do not mean to say that a little boat going out for a mile or two to sea would be a ship; but where it is its business really and substantially to go to sea, if it is not propelled by oars, it shall be considered a ship for the purpose of this Act. Whenever the vessel does go to sea, whether it be decked or not decked, or whether it goes to sea for the purpose of fishing or anything else, it would be a ship . . ." (Blackburn J. in 1871 in *Ex p. Ferguson* [54] (the fishing coble)).

" It was not constructed for the purpose of being navigated or of conveying cargo or passengers. It was, in truth, a lighted buoy or beacon." (Lord Herschell in 1897 in *Wells* v. *Owners of Gas Float Whitton No. 2* [55] (a gas float)).

" A pierhead is fixed. So in the material sense is a buoy. In one sense it is a floating object, but it is not intended to float here, there and everywhere. It must float in order to be on the surface of the water, but the one purpose of fastening it in a particular place is to enable mariners to see what course to follow. . . . I therefore see no distinction in principle between an object of this kind, which, though floating, if affixed to the bottom of the sea in order that it may always be approximately in the same spot upon the surface of the water, and a pierhead, which is a more permanently fixed object." (Sir Samuel Evans in 1912 in *The Upcerne* [56] (another gas float)).

". . . the primary purpose for which this pontoon is designed and adapted is to float and to lift, and not to navigate . . . although fully capable of movement, although it is moved from time to time in order that it may operate elsewhere . . . yet having regard to its history I am satisfied that movement is the exception in its career and not the rule." (Roche J. in 1926 in *Merchants' Marine Insurance Co. Ltd.* v. *North of England Protecting and Indemnity Association* [57] (a floating crane)).

" It seems to me that the dominant idea is something which is ' used in navigation,' and not merely capable of navigating for the moment . . . if I had to define ' ship or vessel ' I should say that it was any hollow structure intended to be used in navigation, *i.e.* intended to do its real work on the seas or other waters, and capable of free and ordered movement thereon from one place to another." (Atkinson J. in 1943 in *Polpen Shipping Co. Ltd.* v. *Commercial Union Assurance Co. Ltd.*[58] (the flying boat)).

---

[54] (1871) L.R. 6 Q.B. 280, at p. 291. See p. 59, above.
[55] [1897] A.C. 337, at p. 343. See p. 64, above.
[56] [1912] P. 160, at p. 166. See p. 67, above.
[57] (1926) 25 Ll.L.R. 446, at p. 447. See p. 70, above.
[58] [1943] K.B. 161, at pp. 164 and 167. See p. 76, above.

" I think that it should be held that it was used in navigation, as it had been moved often on the sea from place to place as occasion required, and that it should be held to be a ship." (Jones J. in 1958 in *Cook* v. *Dredging & Construction Co. Ltd.*[59] (the blower boat)).

These passages include comments as to (a) the *reason* for which the object in question was constructed: " It was not constructed for the purpose of being navigated . . ."; " the primary purpose for which this pontoon is designed and adapted is to float and to lift, and not to navigate . . ."; and: " intended to do its real work on the seas or other waters. . . ." The relevant words in the definition of " ship " and " vessel " in the Merchant Shipping Acts, however, " used in navigation," relate to actual use and not the purpose, or main purpose, of the builders. Drilling units have to cross the waters, and thus be navigable, however, and are intended to do their real work on the seas even though at one place at a time. The same could be said of a dredger. (b) The significance of any *attachment* to the seabed: " an object of this kind which, though floating, is affixed to the bottom of the sea in order that it may always be approximately in the same spot upon the surface of the water. . . ." Drilling units use various methods, including thrusters and dynamic positioning equipment, to keep them in the same spot upon the surface of the water, not only approximately but with a remarkable degree of precision. Some go further, resting on the seabed to do their work from time to time or always, in the case of semi-submersibles and submersibles respectively, while the jack-up rigs lower their legs on to the seabed. It is in those various senses that they can be said to be " affixed to the bottom." (c) The extent of any *movement*: " it is moved from time to time in order that it may operate elsewhere . . . yet . . . movement is the exception in its career and not the rule . . ."; and: " it was used in navigation, as it had been moved often on the sea from place to place as occasion required." So also the various kinds of drilling units may spend more time on site than on the move to or from sites or base. They are, however, moved " from time to time." By the very nature of their work they lack that permanence of position which is enjoyed by a production platform, or indeed a gas float.

It is not the task of this work to make a definite forecast, but it would seem quite possible that the English courts would hold that the definition of " ship " in the Merchant Shipping Acts applied to drilling ships, and barges, semi-submersibles and submersibles. They might not be inclined to apply the definition to jack-up rigs in view of their inability to perform their main function without their legs being on the sea bed. On the other hand we have just seen that semi-submersibles, sometimes, and submersibles, all the time, have to be in contact with the bottom to perform their work. This might persuade those responsible for the decision to say that, leaving the drilling ships and barges to one side as being " ships "

---

[59] [1958] 1 Lloyd's Rep. 334, at p. 338. See p. 81, above.

in any event (though even that is not certain when one considers their functions), all the three remaining categories were either ships—or not ships. There would be a certain logic in this approach; on the other hand the line might be drawn between jack-up rigs, as not being " ships," and the other types of drilling units, as being " ships." On being asked where the line should be drawn a court might repeat the words of Lord Coleridge C.J. in *Southport Corporation* v. *Morriss* [60]: " The answer is that it is not necessary to draw it at any precise point. It is enough for us to say that the present case is on the right side of any reasonable line that could be drawn." It is much more probable, however, that a carefully reasoned answer would be given.

It is to be hoped that a court would not adopt the solution, if it could so be called, that a particular drilling unit was a ship during such time as it was moving to or from the drilling site, but not when it had arrived at the site or perhaps when part of the structure (such as the legs in the case of a jack-up rig) was in contact with the seabed. Such a drilling unit would be an indeterminate animal, subject to laws of limitation, salvage and the like at some times and not at others. To adapt the words of Devlin J. in another case [61]: only the most enthusiastic lawyer could watch with satisfaction the spectacle of a drilling unit donning and doffing the guise of a ship as it (or perhaps she, as the case might be) came into or relinquished contact with the sea bed. In the absence of English decisions there is always the possibility that the courts would adopt as persuasive precedents some of the numerous decisions on this subject which have been made by the courts of the United States of America. It is also to be hoped that a definition would eventually be introduced, as a result of which the interests concerned would not be left in doubt, wondering whether a definition formulated well over 100 years ago extended to their own complex and innovative operations. Such a development might take place if there were adopted a Convention similar in its objects to the draft C.M.I. Convention on Off-Shore Craft, adopted at Rio de Janeiro in September 1977.[62] By extending the application of certain leading international maritime Conventions to offshore craft, it would avoid the necessity of deciding in each case whether a drilling unit was a ship or in some other way subject to the Convention (and consequent national legislation) in question.

---

[60] [1893] 1 Q.B. 359, at p. 361. See p. 63, above.

[61] *Pyrene* v. *Scindia Navigation Co. Ltd.* [1954] 2 Q.B. 402, at p. 416: " Only the most enthusiastic lawyer could watch with satisfaction the spectacle of liabilities shifting uneasily as the cargo sways at the end of a derrick across a notional perpendicular projecting from the ship's rail."

[62] See p. 31, above.

CHAPTER 3

THE LONDON STANDARD DRILLING BARGE FORM [1]

Clause 1: The Assured [2]

THE London Standard Drilling Barge Form, at cl. 1, contains the single word " Assured," followed by a blank space.

The Form is generally used for drilling units other than drill ships; the latter are usually covered by the Institute Time Clauses (Hulls) or a similar hull form. The name of the owner of the drilling unit will appear as the party insured. He is thus shown to be the party entitled to be indemnified by the insurers. This is consistent with the requirement of the Marine Insurance Act 1906, and of many countries, that the policy must name the party or for whom it is effected. Thus section 23 states: " A marine policy must specify—(1) The name of the assured, or of some person who effects the insurance on his behalf. . . ."

So far as the Marine Insurance Act 1906 applies,[3] section 1 of that Act sets out the position of the insured in its definition of a contract of marine insurance: " A contract of marine insurance is a contract whereby the insurer undertakes to indemnify the assured, in manner and to the extent thereby agreed, against marine losses, that is to say, the losses incident to marine adventure." The entitlement of the insured to an indemnity under the L.S.D.B. Form is, likewise, subject to the terms of the policy as subsequently set out.

The contractor as insured [4] may have taken out the policy in his own name and in the name of the operator.[5] By being named, the operator would protect himself against an exercise of subrogation rights by under-

---

[1] The Form dated March 1, 1972, is used here as the norm. It is set out in full as Appendix A; see p. 432, below. The Norwegian equivalent is discussed in Chap. 4, below.

[2] cl. 1 of the L.S.D.B. Form.   [3] See Appendix D, below.

[4] It is possible to describe him as the insured or the assured. The term " assurance " is more generally associated with life policies, though the word " assured " is used in the L.S.D.B. Form. In other policies relating to drilling units and to wells, it is more common to find the term " insured."

[5] For the distribution of responsibilities as to insurance see p. 277, below.

86

writers, and be in a better position to give releases to sub-contractors who need to be held blameless in respect of claims for loss of or damage to his drilling unit. A variation of the L.S.D.B. Form contains a clause, after the clause in which the name of the insured is inserted, with the words " For account of themselves. . . ." The names or occupational description of the other parties to the contract may then be inserted. In this context the words " for account of " are used to show that the insured was acting as agent for the addidional parties named, whether or not he was also acting (as the extra words " of themselves " may indicate) for himself. The words in question are not intended to indicate that the additional parties named are the only ones liable to pay the premium. All the insured, including the insured named in the first instance, are jointly and severally liable to the insurers for payment of the premium. If, as is usually the case, a broker is acting for the insured, then he may also be liable for the premium. This is because a policy, if it is subject to the Marine Insurance Act 1906, would be affected by section 53 (1) thereof: " Unless otherwise agreed, where a marine policy is effected on behalf of the assured by a broker, the broker is directly responsible to the insurer for the premium.... "

The insured may also wish, or be required by another party to request, that any payment made under the policy be made to another party. A direction to this effect is contained, in the L.S.D.B. Form and its usual variants, in a Loss Payable clause.[6] In the case of the usual variants that clause may appear immediately after the clause which states for whose account the policy is concluded.

Clause 2: Period of Insurance

PERIOD OF INSURANCE:
" If this insurance expires while an accident or occurrence giving rise to a loss is in progress, Underwriters shall be liable as if the whole loss had occurred during the currency of this insurance." [7]

This standard clause provides for (a) the insertion of the period of insurance and (b) the continued liability of the insurers if the policy expires while an accident or occurrence is in progress,[8] so far as the loss results from the original accident or occurrence, there being no new intervening cause.

A variation of the manner in which the period of insurance is expressed, but also contained in the 1960 version of the L.S.D.B. Form, reads:

" For the term of . . . commencing on the . . . day of . . . 19 . . and ending on the . . . day of . . . 19 . . both days at Noon, Standard Time at the place of the location of the risk or risks insured hereunder as per form and specifications attached."

This variation is more usual in policies concluded in the United States.

---

[6] cl. 18 of this Form; see p. 178, below.
[7] cl. 2 of the L.S.D.B. Form dated March 1, 1972.
[8] For a similar provision in the case of pollution insurance see p. 356, below.

The policy will normally be for a period of 12 months, though at one time three-year policies were issued. This practice reflects that adopted in the case of marine policies generally. That, in its turn, though now a matter of practice, had its origin in the statute law which applied until 1959. The Stamp Act 1891 required that a contract for sea insurance was invalid [9] unless it was expressed in a policy of sea insurance, and that no policy of sea insurance, made on a time basis, could be made for any time exceeding 12 months. So also section 25 (2) of the Marine Insurance Act 1906, now repealed, stated " . . . a time policy which is made for any time exceeding 12 months is invalid." The Finance Act 1959 repealed these provisions of the Stamp Act and the Marine Insurance Act.

The use of the words " both days inclusive " makes it clear that the insurance extends to the whole of each of the two days named. In the absence of such words the cover might run only from the expiry of the former day although it would cover events occurring on the latter day. In *Isaacs* v. *Royal Insurance Co.*[10] the court found to this effect in the case of a fire policy, and it is possible though not certain that the same rule would apply to other types of policy. The words inserted make the matter clear.

If a time on one or both of the days in question is named, it is desirable that the time standard should be stated, as with such words as " Noon, Greenwich Mean Time," or " Noon, Eastern Standard Time." In the absence of such words there may be argument as to whether the cover was in operation, if, for example, an incident which gives rise to a claim occurs at a place other than that at which the insurance was issued. Under English law, combined with insurance practice, it seems that in the case of an insurance policy, issued in England and stating a particular time, Greenwich Mean Time would apply.

In an American case, *Walker* v. *Protection Insurance Co.*,[11] it was held that the time at the place where the contract of insurance was concluded was the relevant time, unless the parties had stipulated otherwise. For example, a contract of insurance in respect of offshore operations in the North Sea may be concluded in Houston, Texas. It might be stated that cover was to begin on January 1, or at a particular time on that day, without any statement as to the applicable time standard. A dispute might arise as to whether a casualty in the North Sea at 0300 local time was covered, since it was then 2100 hours in Houston. It is clearly more satisfactory that a time standard should be indicated.

The main part of the " Period of Insurance " clause [12] in the standard L.S.D.B. Form relates to the continued liability of the insurers if the policy expires while an incident or occurrence is in progress. The wording

---

[9] Other than for risks, in respect of which an owner was able to limit liability; this followed from s. 55 of the Merchant Shipping Act Amendment Act 1862, and s. 506 of the Merchant Shipping Act 1894. [10] (1870) L.R. 5 Ex. 296.

[11] (1849) 29 Maine R. 317. [12] For wording see p. 87, above.

is similar to that of the " Expiry of Policy during Insured Event " clause in a " Seepage, Pollution and Contamination Insurance Policy." [13]

We have seen that a policy will usually be concluded for a period of 12 months.[14] When it expires " an accident or occurrence giving rise to a loss " [15] may be " in progress." Alternatively, in the case of the similar provision in a Seepage, Pollution and Contamination Insurance, " an insured event," which is one of the eventualities set out in the cover clause, may be " in progress." [15a] It is possible that at the time of expiry of the policy part or all of the loss has not occurred, in the case of the L.S.D.B. Form; or that at that time the insured has not become liable to pay the damages, or has not incurred the costs, contemplated by the cover clause in the case of the Seepage, Pollution and Contamination Insurance. This clause ensures that even if the moment at which such events occur is after the expiry of the policy the insurers are liable " as if the loss had occurred during the currency of this insurance," or, in the case of the other policy, " as if the entire loss had occurred prior to the expiration of this insurance." In the absence of such clauses the insured would be unable to recover these sums from the insurers. The extension of the clauses, which are for this purpose only and not so as to cover a new " accident or occurrence " or a new " event," is made " subject to all other terms and conditions of this Policy " in the case of the Seepage, Pollution and Contamination Insurance, though not in the case of the L.S.D.B. Form. This makes it clear that the insured would not, for example, be able to recover by virtue of this clause if a new policy, starting when this policy expired, covered the event in question. It is suggested, however, that such a clause is in any event subject to all the other terms and conditions of the policy, without a provision to this effect, unless it contains some such words as " notwithstanding any other term or condition of this policy to the contrary."

It might be argued that the words " while an accident or occurrence giving rise to a loss is in progress " should be interpreted restrictively, so that at the moment of expiry of the policy at least some of the loss should have already made itself manifest. It would seem that a wider interpretation might be adopted, and that it is enough that the accident or occurrence is one which results in a loss even if such loss occurs after the expiry of the policy.

Clause 3: The Property Insured

The property insured by the L.S.D.B. Form is described in clause 3 thereof, which states:

---

[13] See p. 356, below.

[14] See p. 88, above.

[15] Which would presumably have to be a physical loss (except in the cases of the insurances for collision liability and sue and labour expenses) because the cover clause relates only to " risks of direct physical loss of or damage to the property insured "; see p. 99, below.

[15a] See pp. 356–357, below.

" PROPERTY INSURED HEREUNDER:

This insurance covers the hull and machinery of the drilling barge(s), as scheduled herein, including all their equipment, tools, machinery, caissons, lifting jacks, materials, supplies, appurtenances, drilling rigs and equipment, derrick, drill stem, casing and tubing while aboard the said drilling barge(s) and/or on barges and/or vessels moored alongside or in the vicinity thereof and used in connection therewith (but not such barges and/or vessels themselves), and including drill stem in the well being drilled, and all such property as scheduled herein, owned by or in the care, custody or control of the Assured, except as hereinafter excluded.

Schedule of Property Insured

Description of Drilling Barge	Rate	Insured Value	Hereto Amount

Each deemed to be separately insured.

Any loss paid hereunder shall not reduce the amount of this insurance except in the event of actual or constructive or compromised or arranged total loss."

The initial statement is that the insurance is to cover the " hull and machinery of the drilling barge(s), as scheduled herein," the description of the drilling barge or barges being given in the " Schedule of Property Insured."

The insurance is stated to be in respect of the hull and machinery. The Lloyd's S.G. Policy refers to " the body, tackle, apparel, ordnance, munition, artillery, boat, and other furniture, of and in the good ship or vessel," but not specifically to her hull and machinery. The term " ship " in a policy includes the machinery in the case of a steamship. Thus rule 15 of the Rules for Construction of Policy [16] states:

" The term ' ship ' includes the hull, materials and outfit, stores and provisions for the officers and crew, and, in the case of vessels engaged in a special trade, the ordinary fittings requisite for the trade, and also, in the case of a steamship, the machinery, boilers, and coals and engine stores, if owned by the assured."

In the present case the drilling unit would, where it was self-propelled, be a motor vessel, and not a steamship, but the use of the words " hull and machinery " makes it unnecessary to rely upon rule 15 of the Rules for Construction.

The clause then says that the insurance covers the " drilling barges,"

[16] Sched. 2 to the Marine Insurance Act 1906.

including their equipment, tools and machinery, and the drilling rigs [17] themselves, " while aboard the said drilling barge and/or on barges and/or vessels moored alongside or in the vicinity thereof and used in connection therewith," and then only if the other drilling units so positioned are used in connection with the insured unit. It does not seem necessary that they should be in actual operation at the time to qualify as being so " used." This limitation must, however, be read in conjunction with Clause 4 (b), relating to items separated from the insured property.[18]

The insurance cover is not confined to the items named in these lines, for it is then stated that it extends to " all such property as scheduled herein," *i.e.* in the Schedule which follows.

As for the ownership of all the items in question, the clause speaks, in connection with the drilling units, of " their equipment, tools, machinery," etc., and ends with the words " owned by or in the care, custody or control of the Assured, except as hereinafter excluded." The insurance can thus extend to items which belong to the operator or to other members of the consortium, or to any other person involved in the operation, provided that the insured has care, custody or control thereof. The version of the L.S.D.B. Form often used in the United States ends with the words " the property of the Assured or for which the Assured may be liable, under contract or otherwise, except as hereinafter excluded," instead of the words " and all such property as scheduled herein, owned by or in the care, custody or control of the Assured, except as hereinafter excluded." The effect seems to be the same, in that the act of entrusting property to the insured may involve either a contractual duty, or a duty of care, breach of which would amount to a tort.

The provision in the standard L.S.D.B. Form that each of the drilling units listed in the Schedule is deemed to be separately insured ensures that claims in respect of separate units are dealt with as if there was an insurance policy for each one, with deductibles applying separately. Sometimes there are two insurances: (1) for the hull and machinery and all permanent equipment; and (2) for the movable plant and equipment, consumable stores, supplies, etc.

Clause 4: Navigation Limits

" NAVIGATION LIMITS
(a)

Privilege is granted to be towed within the above Navigation Limits.
Also to cover in port, while going on or off, and while in docks and graving docks and/or wharves, ways, gridirons and pontoons, subject to the terms and conditions of this insurance.
(b) This insurance covers up to 25 per cent. of the scheduled amount of

---

[17] *i.e.* the assemblies of hole-boring equipment on each drilling unit.
[18] See p. 97, below.

insurance hereunder on property insured herein (as described in clause 3 above) [19] when separated from the property insured hereunder whilst in temporary storage at, or in local transit to or from, ports or drilling barges within the Navigation Limits provided in Paragraph (a).[20] It is expressly understood and agreed, however, that this extended coverage is included within and shall not increase the total amount of insurance hereunder." [21]

It is customary for a hull insurance policy to impose trading limits upon a ship. They are usually imposed in order to ensure that the ship does not go to certain areas where the risk of loss or damage is appreciably greater than that to which she would normally be exposed. It is customary for the insurer and the insured to agree that the ship will continue to be covered in the event that she goes to the areas in question, provided that notice is given to the insurer and agreement is reached as to any amendment of the terms of insurance or increase in premium.

In the case of a ship the trading area may be set out in the Institute Warranties, a printed form dated July 1, 1976. The six warranties amount to promises by the assured that the ship will not go to five named and potentially icebound areas and will not, in the case of the sixth warranty, sail with Indian coal at certain times; but it is clearly understood that a breach of any such promise does not bring the cover to an end,[22] provided that agreement is reached as to any required amendment of the terms or increase in premium.

In the case of a breach of any of these warranties, the assured can be held covered in the manner set out in clause 5 of the Institute Time Clauses (Hulls):

" Held covered in case of any breach of warranty as to cargo,[23] trade, locality,[24] towage, salvage services or date of sailing,[25] provided notice be given to the Underwriters immediately after receipt of advices and any amended terms of cover and any additional premium required by them be agreed."

The L.S.D.B. Form deals with " Navigation Limits " in the manner set out above.[26] It begins with a subsection, " (a)," which consists of a vacant space. The extent of the navigation limits is then set out. An operating area, such as the North Sea, may be named; in some cases the underwriters might set a limit of so many hundred miles from a certain place. In both cases the drilling unit would be held covered in the event of a breach. An exception to the practice arises in the case of fully powered drill ships, where the Institute Warranties are usually incorporated.

In a variation of the L.S.D.B. Form often used in the United States [27] the wording corresponding to this part of the standard L.S.D.B. Form is:

---

[19] See p. 90, above.

[20] See p. 91, above.

[21] cl. 4 of the L.S.D.B. Form dated March 1, 1972.

[22] For a discussion as to the status of warranties in an insurance policy, see p. 99, below.

[23] The sixth warranty.

[24] The first five warranties.

[25] The sixth warranty.

[26] At p. 91.

[27] Based on the 1960 L.S.D.B. Form.

Clause 4: Navigation Limits

" NAVIGATION LIMITS:
Warranted confined to the use and navigation of . . . provided that in no case shall the limits for INSHORE DRILLING BARGES extend beyond the Bays, Bayous, marshes and inland waters of Texas, Louisiana, Mississippi, Alabama and Florida but excluding the Atlantic Ocean, not further offshore than the beginning of the Offshore lease-blocks as defined by Lambert Co-Ordinate Grid System, South Zone, with the exception of Breton Sound where the Offshore areas will begin at the lease-blocks seaward of Chandeleur and Breton Islands or the limits for OFFSHORE DRILLING BARGES extend beyond one hundred miles from the coastline of Texas, Louisiana, Mississippi and Florida, but excluding the Atlantic Ocean."

The words " Privilege is granted to be towed within the above Navigation Limits " are also part of subsection (a) in the standard L.S.D.B. Form. The right of the assured to have the drilling unit towed is thus confirmed. If no such sentence were included in the policy, it seems that he would nevertheless have such a right. The list of exclusions, set out in a later clause of the standard L.S.D.B. Form,[28] does not refer to towage. Exclusion (h) [29] excludes " Liabilities to third parties except as specifically covered under the terms of the Collision Liability Clause [30] contained herein." A towage contract creates liabilities on the part of the assured towards the owner of the tug (except so far as the Unfair Contract Terms Act 1977 may apply) and such liabilities would not, as a result of exclusion (h), be recoverable from the insurer unless covered by the " Collision Liability " clause. The latter clause applies where the insured drilling unit has " come into collision with any other ship or vessel, and the Assured or the Surety in consequence of the Vessel being at Fault shall become liable. . . ." If the tug were able to recover for damage to itself (or in respect of its liability to a third party) by either route, the assured being liable in tort and by contract, there would be a right of recovery under the policy. If the assured were made liable under the towage contract, but was not " at Fault," then the " Collision Liability " clause would not apply and there would be no recovery under the " Collision Liability " clause.

The " Privilege " which " is granted to be towed within the above Navigation Limits " thus seems to be a right that would exist in any event. It may be asked whether the existence of such a right might be subject to certain implied limitations. A drilling unit, if it were not self-propelled and using its power, would always be towed when going to the drilling site, being manoeuvred at or in the vicinity of the drilling site, and returning from the drilling site. It would presumably be in the contemplation of the assured and the insurer that towage would occur on these occasions. It might also be necessary for it to occur in the event of an unusual occurrence such as a blowout, or cratering, or damage to the insured drilling unit. These events also would be within the contemplation

---

[28] cl. 8; see p. 127, below.
[30] Discussed at pp. 109–123, below.

[29] See pp. 128 and 131, below.

of the parties to the contract of insurance and it seems that the privilege
" to be towed " would still exist. Indeed, in the case of an unambiguous
express term, such as that set out here in the L.D.S.B. Form, the rule of
construction is that it is assumed that the parties have intended to deal
with the whole of that particular problem, of towage, in those words.
There is thus no room to imply a term. As Lord Denman C.J. said in
Aspdin v. *Austin* [31]: " The presumption is that having expressed some,
they have expressed all the conditions by which they intend to be bound
by that instrument."

The right to be towed, as set out in the L.S.D.B. Form, may be compared with a corresponding provision in the Institute Time Clauses (Hulls).
The S.G. policy itself is silent on the subject of towage but clause 3 (a) of
the I.T.C., often known as the " Tow and Assist " clause, states in part:

> (a) The Vessel is covered subject to the provisions of the Policy at all times
> and has leave . . . to assist and tow vessels or craft in distress, but it is
> warranted that the Vessel shall not be towed, except as is customary or to
> the first safe port or place when in need of assistance, or undertake towage
> or salvage services under a contract previously arranged by the Assured
> and/or Owners and/or Managers and/or Charterers. This clause shall not
> exclude customary towage in connection with loading or discharging."

Towage of the insured ship is thus excluded except where it is customary
or where the ship is in need of assistance. In the case of customary towage
the last sentence makes it clear that such towage " in connection with
loading or discharging " is not excluded. The clause was indeed once
known as the " docking " clause. Where assistance is given to the insured
ship the breach of warranty is only permitted to enable the ship to reach
" the first safe port or place." The cover afforded by the L.S.D.B. Form,
with its granting, or perhaps its recognition,[32] of the " Privilege " of towage, is a reflection of the operations undertaken by drilling units. Towage
is a substantial event in their commercial operation, whereas with a
conventional ship, which is usually engaged in another commercial
operation, namely the carriage of cargo, towage occurs only in connection
with loading or discharging, or when she is in need of assistance. Clause 3
of the I.T.C. would also operate to the benefit of the shipowner where the
ship was towed in order to be dry docked, to be berthed or to change
berths, to bunker, or in the course of a trial trip. In both these cases the
use of tugs is " customary."

By a subsequent provision, clause 5, the Institute Time Clauses (Hulls)
provide protection for an assured where the towage of his ship would
otherwise, as a result of clause 3 (a), not be covered. The relevant words
of clause 5 are:

> " Held covered in case of any breach of warranty as to . . . towage . . . pro-
> vided notice be given to the Underwriters immediately after receipt of

---

[31] (1844) 5 Q.B. 671, at p. 684.
[32] See p. 91, above.

advices and any amended terms of cover and any additional premium required by them be agreed."

The standard L.S.D.B. Form ensures that a drilling unit is covered when in port, being taken to be dry-docked, and in certain other situations, by the use of the succeeding words in its clause 3 (a):

> " Also to cover in port, while going on or off, and while in docks and graving docks and/or wharves, ways, gridirons and pontoons, subject to the terms and conditions of this insurance."

The same wording is used in the variation of the L.S.D.B. Form often adopted in the United States, except that the final words are " subject to the terms and conditions of this certificate or policy." In both cases the closing words are similar to the opening words in clause 3 (a) of the Institute Time Clauses (Hulls): " The Vessel is covered subject to the provisions of this Policy. . . ." They make it clear that any cover reflected in the rest of the clause, whether it represents an extension or a confirmation of the cover already given elsewhere in the contract of insurance, is governed by the remaining provisions of that contract. It is not a separate insurance, and would be governed by, among other provisions, the clauses relating to navigation limits, deductible, exclusions, limit of liability, limitation of action, etc.

The places or operations to which the words apply can be summarised as follows: 1. " in port "; and 2. " while going on or off " and " while in docks and graving docks and/or wharves, ways, gridirons and pontoons." The drilling unit is covered by the policy on such occasions as well as at other times. It seems that this provision is merely declaratory, in that in its absence the insured property would in any event be covered, even though the work for which it was constructed or adapted takes place at sea. What would be the position if on one of these occasions the insured property was outside the navigation limits? Clause 4 of the standard L.S.D.B. Form has the title " Navigation Limits," the limits then being set out at the beginning of subsection (a); the next part of subsection (a) deals with towage within the navigation limits, and subsection (b) [33] also deals with cover within the navigation limits.

The named places visited by the drilling unit, at which the cover is said to continue, are, as stated above:

(a) " *in port* "

It is an established rule of marine insurance law that the term " port " has to be construed in the way in which it is ordinarily understood, in connection with the port in question, in the mercantile world. This mercantile sense may not attach the same limits to the port as would a legal, administrative, fiscal, physical or geographical definition.[34]

---

[33] See p. 97, below.

[34] The same difference arises when, for the purpose of laytime, a question arises as to whether a ship has arrived at a port. Bowen L.J. said in *Sailing-Ship " Garston "*

So in *Constable* v. *Noble* [35] an insurance policy used the terms " port of Carmarthen " and " port of Lyme Regis." A question arose as to whether Llanelly and Bridport, which were legally parts of the two ports respectively, were covered. It was held that the mercantile meaning attached to the terms in the policy extended only to the " town and port of Carmarthen " and the " town and port of Lyme Regis," and not to Llanelly and Bridport.[36]

So also in *Uhde* v. *Waters* [37] mercantile usage prevailed against the views of geographers. The insurance policy provided cover " from London to any port in the Baltic," and the ship sailed to Revel (now Tallinn) in Estonia, which is in the Gulf of Finland and thus, according to geographers, not in the Baltic Sea. It was held that in view of mercantile usage the policy should extend to that area. In *Robertson* v. *Clarke* [38] the court decided that Mauritius was covered by a policy " from Van Diemen's Land to a port or ports of loading in India and the Indian Islands." Although geographers considered Mauritius to be an African island, the court accepted evidence that commercially speaking it was treated as one of " the Indian Islands." In *Royal Exchange Assurance Co.* v. *Tod* [39] a restrictive interpretation was given to the words " from the Pacific," so as to limit the cover to ports on the west coast of South America. Despite the geographical meaning of the words, there was evidence that the assured's policies with the insurers in question, and with other insurers, containing such words, had always been restricted to ships sailing from those ports.

If there is no evidence as to the mercantile practice then the normal rules of construction apply to a policy. In *Birrell* v. *Dryer* [40] a warranty " No St. Lawrence " (between specified dates) was held to refer both to the River St. Lawrence and to the Gulf of St. Lawrence.

b) ". . . *while going on or off, and while in docks and graving docks and/or wharves, ways, gridirons and pontoons.* . . ."

These words show that the cover extends to times when the drilling unit is in the places or objects mentioned and to times when she is " going on or off " them. The latter expression seems to relate to the period during which the drilling unit is moving or being moved on to or off the docks, etc., and while it is there. It is not being used to describe that longer period during which the drilling unit is proceeding towards or moving away from the installations in question. As the sentence as a whole is merely declara-

---

Co. v. *Hickie* (1885) 15 Q.B.D. (C.A.), at p. 596: ". . . you must make up your mind in each particular case as to the sense in which shipowners and charterers would be likely to intend to employ the term ' port.' "

[35] (1810) 2 Taunt. 403.
[36] A similar conclusion was reached in *Payne* v. *Hutchinson* (1810) 2 Taunt. 405.
[37] (1811) 3 Camp. 16.
[38] (1824) 1 Bing. 445.
[39] (1892) 8 T.L.R. 669.
[40] (1884) 9 App.Cas. 345 (H.L.).

tory of the period of cover, and does not add to or detract from it, this restricted interpretation of the words does not mean that cover is excluded during that longer period.

There are expressions in conventional hull policies which are of a similar nature, and where the courts have had to consider the application of insurance cover when a ship is on its way to or from a port, or where there is doubt as to whether she is at a port.[41] The expressions are:

" *at and from.*" These words appear in the first sentence of the S.G. Policy,[42] (which does not of course apply to the L.S.D.B. cover), so that the parties can insert the port or ports. If the ship is not at the named place when the contract is concluded, the risk attaches as soon as she arrives there safely.[43] In the case of the L.S.D.B. Form it is not necessary or appropriate to name a port or ports. The question of a deviation from an authorised voyage does not arise.

" *To touch and stay.*"

> " And it shall be lawful for the said ship, etc., in this voyage, to proceed and sail to and touch and stay at any ports or places whatsoever without prejudice to this insurance."

These words appear in the S.G. Policy. Though they seem to give a wide liberty to the shipowner, rule 6 of the Rules for Construction of Policy [44] says that " In the absence of any further licence or usage, the liberty to touch and stay ' at any port or places whatsoever ' does not authorise the ship to depart from the course of her voyage from the port of departure to the port of destination." The ports in question must therefore, in the absence of evidence elsewhere in the policy to the contrary, lie in the usual course of the voyage. In the L.S.D.B. Form, on the other hand, the wording of clause 4 entitles the drilling unit to be taken anywhere within the named navigation limits. Where there is movement from one area covered by these limits (such as the North Sea) to a different area (such as the Gulf of Mexico), however, it is quite usual for the L.S.D.B. cover to be suspended and for cover to be afforded by a conventional hull policy, with appropriate amendments,[45] for the voyage.

When Insured Property Separated

The second part, or subsection (b), of the clause [46] relating to navigation limits in the standard L.S.D.B. Form provides that the insurance shall so extend that when part of the property insured, as set out in clause 3,[47] is separated from the rest of that property (either while being temporarily stored at, or in local transit to or from, ports or drilling barges in the

---

[41] As to the meaning of " port," see p. 95, above.
[42] Set out in Sched. 1 to the Marine Insurance Act 1906.
[43] r. 3 of the Rules for Construction of Policy, in Sched. 1 to the 1906 Act.
[44] In Sched. 1 to the 1906 Act.
[45] *e.g.* to cover P. & I. and War Risks.
[46] cl. 4.   [47] See p. 90, above.

navigation limits) there is a limit of 25 per cent. to the proportion of the value so insured, and the total insurance is not increased by virtue of the subsection.

The variation of the L.S.D.B. Form customarily used in the United States contains a provision in very similar terms, though it appears there as subsection (b) of its clause 7 entitled " Property Insured Hereunder ":

> " *This insurance* also *covers up to 25 per cent. of the amount of insurance hereunder on property insured herein* (*as described in* paragraph 7 (a) *above*) *when separated from the* drilling barge *insured hereunder*, including property intended to be used aboard or in connection with said drilling barge, wherever located *within the navigation limits* set forth herein or within the Continental limits of the United States of America. *It is expressly understood and agreed, however, that this extended coverage is included within and shall not increase the total amount of insurance hereunder.*" [48]

The words of these clauses envisage a situation in which " property insured herein " (as described in an earlier part of the policy) is separated from " the property insured hereunder." The separated property would consist or one or more out of the list of items set out as part of the property insured after the words " the hull and machinery of the drilling barge(s)." These are their " equipment, tools, machinery, caissons, lifting jacks, materials, supplies, appurtenances, drilling rigs and equipment, derricks, drill stem, casing and tubing and all such property as scheduled herein. . . ." Clause 3 provides that the aforenamed items shall be covered " while aboard the said drilling barge(s) and/or on barges and/or vessels moored alongside or in the vicinity thereof "; but as a result of these words they are also covered while " in temporary storage at, or in local transit to or from, ports or drilling barges," subject to the limitations as to percentage of the insured value represented by these items and as to the navigation limits.

If an accident affected the drilling unit but not the separated items, differing views might be held as to whether a constructive total loss [49] was established. The separated items might, for example, be worth 10 per cent. out of total values of $20 million. Would the cost of repairs to the drilling unit itself have to exceed $18 million or $20 million for a constructive total loss to be established? The test is whether the cost exceeds the actual insured value of the " insured property." The matter is not free from doubt, though it would seem that one has to consider the insured property as a unity, and take the higher figure.

Clause 5: The Cover

The cover provided by the insurers under the L.S.D.B. Form is set out as follows [50]:

---

[48] The words italicised are those which also appear in the L.S.D.B. Form dated March 1, 1972.

[49] See cl. 12 at p. 140, below.

[50] cl. 5.

" COVERAGE:
Subject to its terms, conditions and exclusions this Insurance is against all risks of direct physical loss of or damage to the property insured, provided such loss or damage has not resulted from want of due diligence by the Assured, the Owners or Managers of the property insured, or any of them."

The equivalent clause in the variation on the L.S.D.B. Form often used in the United States [51] states:

" This certificate or policy, subject to its terms and conditions, insures against all risks of direct physical loss or damage to the property insured. Provided such loss or damage has not resulted from want of due diligence by the Assured, the Owners or Managers of the property insured, or any of them."

(a) " *Subject to its terms, conditions and exclusions . . .*"

The " terms " and " conditions " are those set out in the remaining parts of the policy. They relate in particular to the period of the insurance [52]; the property insured [53]; the navigation limits [54]; the deductible [55]; the blowout preventer warranty [56]; the limit of liability [57]; coinsurance [58]; constructive total loss [59]; lay up and cancellation [60]; release agreements and waivers of subrogation [61]; discovery of records [62]; limitation of action [63]; and the party to whom the loss is payable.[64]

The " exclusions " are those set out in that part of the policy [65] so headed, and also in the " Free of Capture and Seizure " clause.[66]

The policy also relates to collision liability [67] and to sue and labour expense.[68] These are mentioned separately here, because in this form of policy, as in the Institute Time Clauses (Hulls), they are looked upon as separate heads of cover, particularly for purposes of limitation on the part of the insurers.[69] Nevertheless the terms and conditions mentioned above are generally applicable to these heads of cover.

The use of the words " terms " and " conditions " in this policy and elsewhere and the use of the word " warranties," which does not appear in this policy,[70] can give rise to some confusion. A " term " in a policy, or in any other contract, is any provision therein, of whatever degree of importance. The provisions of a contract need not all be of equal importance, and the parties to it may indicate, in the contract itself, expressly or by implication, that some provisions are more important than others. In some cases it may be necessary to decide, after the contract has been

---

[51] Based on the 1960 L.S.D.B. Form.
[53] cl. 3; see p. 90, above.
[55] cl. 7; see p. 123, below.
[57] cl. 10; see p. 133, below.
[59] cl. 12; see p. 140, below.
[61] cl. 15; see p. 165, below.
[63] cl. 17; see p. 172, below.
[65] cl. 8; see p. 127, below.
[67] cl. 6; see p. 109, below.
[69] See also p. 133, below.
[70] Though there is a Blowout Preventer Warranty at cl. 9; see p. 133, below.

[52] cl. 2; see p. 87, above.
[54] cl. 4; see p. 91, above.
[56] cl. 9; see p. 133, below.
[58] cl. 11; see p. 139, below.
[60] cl. 14; see p. 155, below.
[62] cl. 16; see p. 171, below.
[64] cl. 18; see p. 178, below.
[66] cl. 19; see p. 178, below.
[68] cl. 13; see p. 154, below.

concluded, which are the more and the less important provisions. Perhaps the most important occasion on which that occurs is when one party alleges that there has been a breach of a term, and it has to be decided whether such a breach would give rise to a right to treat the contract as at an end, or only to a right to damages.

It is in this context that the use of other expressions, less neutral in their meaning than " terms," such as " conditions " and " warranties," may or may not be useful. The word " condition " may mean:

(a) an external fact or state of affairs upon which the existence or otherwise of the contract depends, as in the case of a condition precedent, the satisfaction of which enables the contractual obligations to come into force;

(b) a term of a contract in which all the terms can be described as conditions or warranties,[71] according to their importance, as in the case of a contract for the sale of goods, where a breach of condition would, subject to certain restrictions,[72] entitle the buyer to reject the goods.

It would seem that in the case of the L.S.D.B. Form the word " conditions " is used in the sense set out under (a) above, to contrast it with a term contained in the contract itself.

As for the word " warranty," this is not used in the L.S.D.B. Form (except once, in a special connection, as is shown below), but in marine insurance it has a special significance. It is equivalent, in marine insurance, to a " condition " in the sense set out under (a) above. This is shown by section 33 of the Marine Insurance Act 1906:

" **Nature of warranty**

(1) A warranty, in the following sections relating to warranties,[73] means a promissory warranty, that is to say, a warranty by which the assured undertakes that some particular thing shall or shall not be done, or that some condition shall be fulfilled, or whereby he affirms or negatives the existence of a particular state of facts.

(2) A warranty may be express or implied.

(3) A warranty, as above defined, is a condition which must be exactly complied with, whether it be material to the risk or not. If it be not so complied with, then, subject to any express provision in the policy, the insurer is discharged from liability as from the date of the breach of warranty, but without prejudice to any liability incurred by him before that date."

It can be seen how closely this type of warranty resembles, and is equivalent to, a condition as defined under (a) above. The only use of the word in the L.S.D.B. Form is in clause 9, " Blowout Preventer War-

---

[71] Once known respectively as " dependent covenants " and " independent covenants."

[72] See especially the Sale of Goods Act 1893, s. 11 (1).

[73] *i.e.* ss. 34 to 41.

ranty," [74] where it is " Warranted that the well and/or hole " will have certain equipment. If that warranty is breached then, so far as the Marine Insurance Act 1906 applies to the contract,[75] section 33 (3) would operate to discharge the insurer from further liability.

The word " warranty " may also be used to indicate an exception from a policy. The expression " warranted free of capture, seizure," etc., as in the usual " F. C. & S." clause, does not mean that the assured undertakes that the property will not be captured or seized. It means that if it is captured or seized the policy does not cover a loss resulting from such an incident. Indeed the " Free of Capture and Seizure " clause in the L.S.D.B. Form [76] contains the words ". . . there shall be no liability for any claim caused by, resulting from, or incurred as a consequence of . . ." the items then listed, and does not say that it is " warranted free " of them.

(b) ". . . *this Insurance is against all risks* . . ."

The insurance given by the policy, so far as it is provided in clause 5, is a separate insurance from the insurances given by the same policy in respect of collision liability [77] and for sue and labour expense.[78] This is of particular importance in connection with the limitation of liability available to the insurers. A liability may therefore arise under the " Collision Liability " and " Sue and Labour Expense " clauses and be separate from and additional to a claim under clause 5, even though it arises from the same occurrence. This is reflected by the use of the words " it is further agreed " in the two other clauses. The Institute Time Clauses (Hulls) also provide, in their corresponding clause, that the collision liability is a separate insurance. So also the " Sue and Labour clause, which in the case of marine insurance appears in the Lloyd's S.G. Policy,[79] is stated by section 78 (1) of the Marine Insurance Act 1906, to be " supplementary to the contract of insurance. . . ."

The insurance is said to be " against all risks." [80] This is not the same as saying that the assured can recover, and that the insurer will be liable, whatever may happen to the insured property. Quite apart from the fact that the cover is subject to the " terms, conditions and exclusions " of the insurance, and thus is the subject of certain limitations,[81] it is well established that an all risks policy is subject to certain restrictions. The word " risk " itself may be used in several senses. It may mean the exposure of the insurer, as in the expressions: " The insurer is not yet at risk," or " the

---

[74] See p. 133, below.
[75] See Appendix C, at p. 456, below.
[76] At cl. 19; see p. 178, below.
[77] cl. 6; see p. 109, below.
[78] cl. 13; see p. 164, below.
[79] The reference to suing and labouring in the Institute Time Clauses (Hulls), contained in cl. 9 thereof, is designed not to establish the separate nature of that insurance but to place such expenses on the same basis as general average and salvage.
[80] As in the opening words of cl. 5; see p. 99, above.
[81] The Form itself is sub-titled " All Risks (except as hereinafter excluded)."

attachment of the risk." Alternatively, it may mean the danger incurred by the assured, and the extent of such danger.[82] Finally, it may mean, as in the present context, the perils to which the property is exposed. In the Lloyd's S.G. Policy, for example, these perils are set out specifically, after the words: " Touching the adventures and perils which we, the assurers, are contented to bear and do take us in this voyage: they are of the seas, . . ." etc. These are known as named perils.

The L.S.D.B. Form affords cover in respect of " all risks " and not a list of named perils. A general cover of this nature is often favoured by underwriters, subject to a careful list of exclusions. As one Lloyd's underwriter [83] has said:

> " So far as insuring conditions are concerned regarding both mobile units and fixed structures, I prefer, and it is also favourable to the assured, to give coverage on an all risks of physical loss or damage basis. In the event of a loss, there is a presumption of greater coverage in the assured's favour and the onus is on the insurer to point to and prove that a policy exclusion applies or a policy warranty has not been complied with." [84]

An alternative version of the L.S.D.B. Form, now rarely used, is the " London Standard Drilling Barge Form—Named Perils." The All Risks Form covers all risks of direct physical loss or damage, as described above,[85] subject to certain exclusions.[86] The Named Perils Form covers direct physical loss or damage caused by:

" (a) Perils of the seas or waters designated in the certificate or policy;
(b) Fire, Lightning;
(c) Earthquake;
(d) Jettison, washing overboard;
(e) Tornado, Cyclone, Windstorm, Hurricane, Hail;
(f) Contact with aircraft or with any object falling therefrom;
(g) Loss or damage to the insured property caused by or resulting from raising, lowering, pull in or collapse of the derrick except when such loss or damage is caused by or results from the weight or stress on said derrick being beyond the manufacturer's rated hook load capacity for such derrick."

---

[82] In *Vincentelli & Co.* v. *John Rowlett & Co.* (1911) 16 Com.Cas. 310 the High Court held, on the construction of a particular sale contract, that its insurance provision as to " all risks " referred to the entire quantum of damage, and not to a cover against all causes of accident.

[83] Mr. David B. Hill, in December 1975, as reported in Lloyd's List of December 8, 1975. This has not been the view always expressed. Mr. Harold B. Hill of Lloyd's said, on January 20, 1959: " Requests for ' all risks ' coverage are frequently received and granted by underwriters. Because of the numerous undefined meanings of ' all risks ' in this class of business, I prefer not to grant such cover. . . ." This view was understandable at that time, when the craft involved were mostly new and untried, and the insurance industry had to exercise appropriate caution.

[84] Mr. Harold B. Hill (see n. 83 above) suggested a contributory reason for an all risks cover: " Underwriters have nearly always been wary of granting the fuller policy but because of the demands made by the Banks who, in their wisdom or otherwise, have granted huge loans to the builders and operators, the Banks insisted on such coverage being made available."

[85] See p. 99, above.

[86] See p. 127, below.

In the leading case of *British and Foreign Marine Insurance Co., Ltd.* v. *Gaunt,*[87] Lord Birkenhead said:

" In construing these policies [88] it is important to bear in mind that they cover ' all risk.' These words cannot, of course, be held to cover all damage however caused, for such damage as is inevitable from ordinary wear and tear and inevitable depreciation is not within the policies. There is little authority on the point, but the decision of Walton J. in *Schloss Brothers* v. *Stevens* [89] on a policy in similar terms states the law accurately enough. He said that the words ' all risks by land and water ' as used in the policy then in question ' were intended to cover all losses by any accidental cause of any kind occurring during the transit. . . . There must be a casualty.' Damage, in other words, if it is to be covered by policies such as these, must be due to some fortuitous circumstance or casualty. . . . We are, of course, to give effect to the rule that the plaintiff must establish his case, that he must show that the loss comes within the terms of his policies; but where all risks are covered by the policy and not merely risks of a specified class or classes, the plaintiff discharges his special onus when he has proved that the loss was caused by some event covered by the general expression, and he is not bound to go further and prove the exact nature of the accident or casualty which, in fact, occasioned his loss."

In the case of a marine policy in respect of all risks the assured would not, unless there were words to the contrary, be able to recover where the loss resulted from inherent vice or from mere wear and tear. As Lord Sumner said of the expression [90]:

" It covers a risk, not a certainty; it is something which happens to the subject-matter from without, not the natural behaviour of the subject-matter, being what it is, in the circumstances under which it is carried."

Nor would there be recovery by the assured if the loss resulted from his own act; " for then he has not merely exposed the goods to the chance of injury, he has injured them himself." [91]

1. *Inherent Vice*

In clause 8, the " Exclusions " clause, there are references to matters which may be covered by the term " inherent vice "; clause 8 (f) [92] mentions ". . . gradual deterioration, metal fatigue, machinery breakdown, expansion or contraction due to change in temperature, corrosion, rusting, electrolytic action, error in design . . ." and refers also to the repair and replacement of a part lost, damaged or condemned " by reason of latent defect therein." So far, therefore, as a loss caused by inherent vice is

---

[87] [1921] 2 A.C. 41 (H.L.) at pp. 46 to 47.
[88] For " all risk " of transit of wool from sheep's back in Patagonia by land and by water to Punta Arenas, Chile.
[89] [1906] 2 K.B. 665.
[90] In the *British and Foreign Marine Insurance* case, at p. 57.
[91] In addition, so far as the Marine Insurance Act 1906, applies, s. 41, as to legality, also binds the assured. This is not strictly a warranty because it cannot be waived: see *Arnould on Marine Insurance* (15th ed., 1961) at § 737, n. 1.
[92] See pp. 128 and 131, below. Damages resulting from these conditions (consequential damage) are sometimes covered by an express provision to that effect.

caught by these words it would not be necessary for the insurers to rely on an implied exclusion of inherent vice.

Indeed so far as the Marine Insurance Act 1906 applies, section 55 (2) (c) deals with inherent vice by stating: " Unless the policy otherwise provides, the insurer is not liable for . . . inherent vice or nature of the subject-matter insured. . . ."

2. *Mere Wear and Tear*

Clause 8, the " Exclusions " clause, excludes " wear and tear " at subsection (f). Here also, therefore, it would not be necessary for the insurers to rely on an implied exclusion of wear and tear. Again, section 55 (2) (c) of the Marine Insurance Act 1906 states: " Unless the policy otherwise provides, the insurer is not liable for ordinary wear and tear, ordinary leakage and breakage. . . ."

3. *The Act of the Assured*

Clause 8, the " Exclusions " clause, also excludes the liability of the insurer in respect of a number of named actions of the assured. The three relevant subsections, with their exclusions, are:

" (b) Loss, damage, or expense which arises solely from the intentional sinking of the barge for operational purposes . . .

(c) Loss, damage or expense caused whilst [93] or resulting from drilling a relief well for the purpose of controlling or attempting to control fire blowout or cratering associated with another drilling barge, platform or unit unless immediate notice be given to Underwriters of said use and additional premium paid if required.

(d) Any claim, be it a Sue and Labour Expense or otherwise, for moneys materials or property expended or sacrificed in controlling or attempting to control blowout or cratering or in fighting fire associated with blowout."

So far as the acts of the assured fell within one of these three subsections, (b), (c) and (d), of clause 8, it would not therefore be necessary for the insurers to rely on the rule that they were not liable for his acts. Clause 5 itself, the " Coverage " clause in the L.S.D.B. Form, refers to his omissions, as contrasted with his acts, by including the proviso [94]: " provided such loss or damage has not resulted from want of due diligence by the Assured, the Owners or Managers of the property insured, or any of them."

Does the exclusion of the liability of the insurers for loss or damage in respect of certain acts of the assured lead to the conclusion that they accept liability where loss or damage to the insured property is caused by other acts of the assured? The rule of construction that the expression of one thing implies the exclusion of other things [95] which are of the same

---

[93] This word is often regarded as too stringent, and deleted. The exclusion is then similar to that is the 1960 Form, at cl. 11 (j): " Loss, damage or expense caused by or resulting from . . .," etc.

[94] Considered below at p. 108.   [95] *Expressio unius est exclusio alterius.*

class but are not mentioned has to be applied with great caution. As Wills J. said in *Colquhoun* v. *Brooks* [96]:

"... the method of construction *expressio unius exclusio alterius* is one that certainly requires to be watched. The failure to make the *expressio* complete very often arises from accident, very often from the fact that it never struck the draughtsman that the thing supposed to be excluded needed specific mention of any kind."

The " thing supposed to be excluded," in the present case, is, if one applies the words of Lord Sumner [97] " a loss which the assured brings about by his own act. . . ." The mere existence [98] of exclusions relating to certain acts of the assured would not be sufficient to include the other acts of the assured in the expression " all risks." The exclusion which makes the crucial difference, however, is that contained in the " Coverage " clause,[99] with its exclusion of loss or damage resulting from want of due diligence by the assured (which may include the operator and others), or the owners or managers of the property insured.

It seems that it must follow from this exclusion that it is intended to cover loss or damage caused by other matters even if they fall within the description of acts of the assured. They may be acts of his agents or employees or of independent contractors for whom he is liable provided that none of them falls within the definition of assured; or they may be acts committed by him in the sense that his own head office,[1] the very mind and brain of his organisation, has committed them, provided that due diligence was exercised. There would thus be no cover where the head office had committed a deliberate act which caused the loss or damage.

If the policy is not a marine policy,[2] it is suggested that nevertheless such a conclusion is consistent with the opening words of section 55 (2) (*a*) of the Marine Insurance Act 1906: " The insurer is not liable for any loss attributable to the wilful misconduct of the assured. . . ." It is also consistent with the fact that a marine policy provides cover against loss or damage caused by negligence of certain servants and independent contractors, by the use of the clause,[3] which refers to negligence of master, officers, crew, pilots and repairers, provided that the loss or damage did not result from want of due diligence by the assured or the owners or managers.

The leading exceptions to the cover established by an all risks marine policy, as established at common law,[4] and to some extent set out in the

---

[96] (1887) 19 Q.B.D. 400, at p. 406.

[97] In *British and Foreign Marine Insurance Co.* v. *Gaunt* [1921] 2 A.C. 41 (H.L.), at p. 57.　　　　　　　　　　[98] In cl. 8.　　　　　　　　　　[99] cl. 5.

[1] Assuming that the assured is a company and not an individual.

[2] See Appendix C, at p. 456, below.

[3] cl. 7 of the Institute Time Clauses (Hulls).

[4] Especially in *British and Foreign Marine Insurance Co., Ltd.* v. *Gaunt* [1921] 2 A.C. 41 (H.L.); see p. 103, above.

105

Marine Insurance Act 1906 in sections 41 and 55, have been discussed. These were the exclusions of inherent vice, wear and tear, the act of the assured, and an illegal adventure, or an adventure carried out illegally. These exceptions are covered, to a greater or less degree in each case, except in the case of illegality, by clause 8, the " Exclusions " clause, in the L.S.D.B. Form. Clause 8 sets out a number of other exceptions, which are discussed later.[5] It is convenient to deal with them separately as in nearly every case they relate to matters peculiar to the problems of drilling units.

(c) ". . . (*all risks of*) *direct physical loss of or damage to the property insured . . .*"

This part of clause 5, as to coverage, may be read with clause 8, the " Exclusion " clause, at subsection (e): " Loss, damage or expense caused by or resulting from delay detention or loss of use." In the first place there can only be recovery in respect of " direct physical loss of or damage to the property insured. . . ." The word " direct " in this context may be compared with the word " proximately " which is used in section 55 (1) of the Marine Insurance Act 1906:

> " Subject to the provisions of this Act, and unless the policy otherwise provides, the insurer is liable for any loss proximately caused by a peril insured against, but, subject as aforesaid, he is not liable for any loss which is not proximately caused by a peril insured against."

" Direct physical loss . . . or damage " means loss or damage that is (a) caused directly by a risk rather than indirectly; and (b) physical rather than monetary. The second of these two restrictions means that loss of or damage to the insured property which results in a loss of profit to the assured does not entitle him, unless there are other express provisions to this effect,[6] to recover the lost profit from the insurers. His physical loss or damage has of course to be expressed in monetary terms for the purpose of recovery but that is the limit of his recourse.

The first of the two restrictions is that the loss or damage should be direct; it seems that this is the same as the requirement in section 55 (1) of the 1906 Act, quoted above, that the loss should be " proximately caused " by the insured peril. Just as the word " direct " may be regarded as meaning " proximate," so its opposite, " indirect," may be regarded as being equivalent to " remote," *i.e.* not proximate. The words " indirect " and " remote " do not however appear in clause 5 of the L.S.D.B. Form, or in section 55 (1) of the 1906 Act. The requirement that the physical loss or damage should be direct finds its origin in the legal maxim " *Causa proxima non remota spectatur,*" or " The proximate and not the remote cause is looked at."

---

[5] See p. 127, below.

[6] Such as the " Collision Liability " clause (cl. 6; see p. 109, below) and the " Sue and Labour Expense " clause (cl. 13; see p. 154, below).

The question of causation is one that has, quite apart from its general philosophical implications, troubled lawyers and commercial men for many years. As Francis Bacon said [7]: " It were infinite for the law to judge the causes of causes, and their impulsion one of another; therefore it contenteth itself with the immediate cause." [8] So far as marine insurance policies are concerned the use of the word " proximate " does not mean that the cause of the loss must be the single cause nearest in time to the loss; it will be proximate if it is the dominant or effective cause of the loss, even though it operated at the same time as, or before, another cause. This can be of crucial importance since the other cause may be one which, if it were the sole cause, would preclude the assured from recovery because it was caught by an exclusion cause.

The words in clause 5 of the L.S.D.B. Form differ also from those in section 55 (1) of the 1906 Act, in the sequence of peril and loss or damage which is envisaged. It is necessary to consider whether this makes a difference to the cover provided. The word " risks " is taken, in this all risks policy, to refer to the perils to which the unit is exposed, the occurrence of which may occasion a claim under the policy. The words " all risks *of* direct physical loss of or damage to the property insured " embrace both the perils and the resultant loss or damage. The wording of section 55 (1), on the other hand, speaks of an insured peril which may, or may not, be the proximate cause of a loss. If, as seems more logical and probable, the word " risks " in clause 5 can be taken to be equivalent to " perils," then its wording as a whole can be taken to mean " all risks *resulting directly in* physical loss of or damage to the property insured." Such an interpretation avoids the ambiguity which might otherwise exist in clause 5, and which has been seen to exist where the term " all risks " has been used. In *Vincentelli & Co.* v. *John Rowlett & Co.*[9] a provision in a sale of goods contract on a c.i.f. basis stated: " Insurance to be effected by us [the sellers], all risks." There was a dispute as to whether this meant that the sellers had to cover all risks in the sense of the entire quantum of damage, but under what was known as an all risks insurance, as the sellers contended. The buyers said that the insurance was to be against all causes of accident, such as damage resulting from the breach of the contract of carriage by the shipowners in improperly stowing the goods on deck instead of under deck. Hamilton J. held that the sellers were right, and that the " all risks " policy taken out by them satisfied the provisions of the sale contract even though the buyers had failed to recover from cargo underwriters,[10] because the cargo had been shipped on deck.

[7] In *Maxims of the Law.*
[8] For discussion of the cases as they affect marine policies, see Chalmers, *Marine Insurance Act* (8th ed., 1976), pp. 75–79; *Arnould on Marine Insurance* (15th ed., 1961), §§ 758, 766–769; and Templeman, *Marine Insurance* (4th ed., 1934), pp. 135–141.
[9] (1910) 16 Com.Cas. 310.
[10] *Ibid.* p. 317.

(d) "... *provided such loss or damage has not resulted from want of due diligence by the Assured, the Owners or Managers of the property insured, or any of them*"

If the assured, or the owners or managers of the insured property, fail to exercise due diligence, and if that failure results in the loss or damage which is, prima facie, recoverable, then this proviso exempts the insurer from liability. This is an example not of an act on the part of the assured which disentitles him from recovery,[11] but of a failure, either by him or the owners or managers of the insured property, to act.

A similar proviso appears as the closing words of clause 2, known as the " Inchmaree " clause,[12] of the Institute Time Clauses (Hulls): "... provided such loss or damage has not resulted from want of due diligence by the Assured, Owners or Managers."

Where, in the case of a drilling unit, there is a negligent action committed by an employee of the assured or of one of the contractors for whom he is responsible, or by another person, the assured may nevertheless recover under clause 5, subject to this proviso.

The reference, in the proviso, to " the Assured, the Owners or Managers of the property insured, or any of them " can be compared with the reference in the " Inchmaree " clause to " the Assured, Owners or Managers." It is suggested that the use of the extra words in clause 5 does not alter the meaning which it would otherwise have. A mere reference to " Owners or Managers " would, it seems, have been taken to mean that the persons stood in a relationship of ownership or management towards the property which was the subject of the insurance.[13] Nevertheless the addition of the words " of the property insured " serves to make the position clear.

In both clause 5 and the " Inchmaree " clause the use of the word " Assured," followed by the word " Owners," makes it clear that in some cases the assured may not be the owner of the insured property. He may nevertheless have an insurable interest and wish to be covered by the policy. Thus under section 5 (2) of the Marine Insurance Act 1906, in the case of marine insurances:

> " In particular a person is interested in a marine adventure where he stands in any legal or equitable relation to the adventure or to any insurable property at risk therein, in consequence of which he may benefit by the safety or due arrival of insurable property, or may be prejudiced by its

---

[11] See p. 104, above.

[12] So called after the case of *Thomas and Mersey Insurance Co.* v. *Hamilton* (1887) 12 App.Cas. 484 (H.L) where there was damage to a donkey engine, used in filling the boilers of the " Inchmaree," because a valve was wrongly left open. It was held that the damage was not caused by " perils of the seas " nor covered by the words of the Lloyd's S.G. Policy, "... all other perils, losses, and misfortunes. ..." As a result the " Inchmaree " clause was included in most marine policies. In its form as used in cl. 7 of the I.T.C. (Hulls) it covers more than the matters excluded by the original decision.

[13] See cl. 3 and p. 90, above.

loss, or by damage thereto, or by the detention thereof, or may incur liability in respect thereof."

It seems that a similar principle would apply in the case of the L.S.D.B. Form, so that such persons as a shareholder, a purchaser and others with an insurable interest, can be assured even if they are not owners; mortgagees, though falling within this principle, might deem it more prudent to have a separate policy.

The words " or any of them " appear at the end of the proviso to clause 5, but not at the end of the proviso to the " Inchmaree " clause. There would be a burden of proof upon the insurers, in both cases, to show that the loss or damage resulted from a want of due diligence. The additional words do not appear to give clause 5 a meaning different from that of the " Inchmaree " clause.

Clause 6: Collision Liability

" COLLISION LIABILITY [14]:
And it is further agreed that:
(a) if the Vessel [15] shall come into collision with any other ship or vessel, and the Assured or the Surety in consequence of the Vessel being at fault shall become liable to pay and shall pay by way of damages to any other person or persons any sum or sums in respect of such collision, the Underwriters will pay the Assured or the Surety, whichever shall have paid, such proportion of such sum or sums so paid as their respective subscriptions hereto bear to the Agreed Value provided always that their liability in respect to any one such collision shall not exceed their proportionate part of the Agreed Value;
(b) in cases where, with the consent in writing of a majority (in amount) of Hull Underwriters, the liability of the Vessel has been contested, or proceedings have been taken to limit liability, the Underwriters will also pay a like proportion of the costs which the Assured shall thereby incur or be compelled to pay.

When both vessels are to blame, then, unless the liability of the owners or charterers of one or both such vessels becomes limited by law, claims under the Collision Liability clause shall be settled on the principle of Cross-Liabilities as if the owners or charterers of each vessel had been compelled to pay to the owners or charterers of the other of such vessels such one-half or other proportion of the latter's damages as may have been properly allowed in ascertaining the balance or sum payable by or to the Assured in consequence of such collision.

The principles involved in this clause shall apply to the case where both vessels are the property, in part or in whole, of the same owners or charterers, all questions of responsibility and amount of liability as between the two vessels being left to the decision of a single Arbitrator, if the parties can agree upon a single Arbitrator, or failing such agreement, to the decision of Arbitrators, one to be appointed by the Assured and one to be appointed by the majority (in amount) of Hull Underwriters interested; the two Arbitrators chosen to choose a third Arbitrator before entering upon the

---

[14] cl. 6 of the L.S.D.B. Form, dated March 1, 1972.
[15] Which for this purpose includes semi-submersibles, submersibles and self-elevating units while covered by this Form.

reference, and the decision of such single Arbitrator, or of any two of such three Arbitrators, appointed as above, to be final and binding.

Provided that this clause shall in no case extend to any sum which the Assured or the Surety may become liable to pay or shall pay in consequence of, or with respect to:

(a) removal or disposal of obstructions, wrecks or their cargoes under statutory powers or otherwise pursuant to law;

(b) injury to real or personal property of every description;

(c) the discharge, spillage, emission or leakage of oil, petroleum products, chemicals or other substances of any kind or description whatsoever;

(d) cargo or other property on or the engagements of the Vessel;

(e) loss of life, personal injury or illness.

Provided further that exclusions (b) and (c) above shall not apply to injury to any other vessel with which the Vessel is in collision or to property on such other vessel except to the extent that such injury arises out of any action taken to avoid, minimise or remove any discharge, spillage, emission or leakage described in (c)."

The opening words, " And it is further agreed that: " are similar to the corresponding words in clause 1 of the Institute Time Clauses (Hulls).

The Running Down clause now in the Institute Time Clauses (Hulls) came to be used in conjunction with the Lloyd's S.G. Policy [16] in the nineteenth century. In *De Vaux* v. *Salvador* [17] Lord Denman C.J. had held that an obligation to pay collision damages was not recoverable by a shipowner from his insurers as a particular average loss caused " by the perils of the sea." Two ships had collided in the Hooghly River, each being damaged. In an arbitration it was decided that each ship should bear half the total expenses. The shipowner in question, who was on balance the debtor, claimed against his insurers, but the Court held that his liability was not " a necessary nor a proximate effect of the perils of the sea, but growing out of an arbitrary provision of the law of nations."

In an American case,[18] which was comparable, except that the matter arose in court and not by way of arbitration, the Supreme Court of the United States held that the underwriters were liable, and thus upheld a judgment by Story J. in the Supreme Court of Massachusetts.

Since the introduction of the Running Down clause in the English hull form there has, therefore, been a divergence between the English and the American hull forms. The English form has covered the assured in respect of three-quarters of his collision liability, whereas an assured covered by the American hull form can recover that liability in full. The L.S.D.B. Form follows the American practice in that the collision liability of the owner of the drilling unit is fully recoverable, but the insurance is still described in terms which separate it from the insurance of the hull and machinery. The insurance for collision liability is thus one which is separate from the insurance of the property itself. The significance of this

---

[16] The original Lloyd's policy on ships and goods, set out in its amended form as Sched. 1 to the Marine Insurance Act 1906.

[17] (1836) 4 A. & E. 420.

[18] *Peters* v. *Warren Insurance Co.* (1838) 3 Sumner's Mass.R. 389.

is that there are two separate limits of liability, and that the cover afforded by the Collision Liability clause is not reduced by the extent to which there are claims for a total loss or for particular average, or for other matters covered by the policy.

The separate nature of the insurance in respect of collision liability is expressed in the opening words of clause 10, headed " Limit of Liability " [19]:

> " In no event, except as provided for in the Sue and Labour Expense Clause [20] and Collision Liability Clause herein, shall the Underwriters' liability arising from any one accident or occurrence exceed the amount insured hereunder as set forth in Clause 3 in respect of the items subject to such accident or occurrence. . . ."

It is possible for there to be a single limit. Such a situation exists, for example, in the case of the standard French hull policy for ships, the limit of liability being a single limit in respect of all claims and thus reduced as each of several claims is made in respect of any one incident.

The substantive part of the Collision Liability clause,[21] in which the liability of the insurer to pay is expressed, is contained immediately after the words " And it is further agreed that:," in (a), which states:

> " (a) if the Vessel shall come into collision with any other ship or vessel, and the Assured or the Surety in consequence of the Vessel being at fault shall become liable to pay and shall pay by way of damages to any other person or persons any sum or sums in respect of such collision, the Underwriters will pay the Assured or the Surety, whichever shall have paid, such proportion of such sum or sums so paid as their respective subscriptions hereto bear to the Agreed Value, provided always that their liability in respect to any one such collision shall not exceed their proportionate part of the Agreed Value ";

This provision as to the liability of the insurer can be considered in detail.

1. *" . . . if the Vessel shall come into collision with any other ship or vessel . . ."*

(i) Collision between equipment, etc., of drilling unit and another ship or vessel

These words state that the vessel must come into collision. The insurance is said earlier, in clause 3,[22] to cover " the hull and machinery of the drilling barge(s) . . . including all their equipment, tools, [etc.,] . . . aboard the said drilling barge(s) and/or on barges and/or vessels moored alongside. . . ." What is the position if there is a contact between some part of the equipment, tools, or other items and another ship or vessel? Clearly the subject-matter of the insurance, as described in clause 3, consists not only of the drilling unit but also of the equipment, tools and

---

[19] As to the limit of liability generally, see p. 133, below.
[20] See p. 154, below.
[21] cl. 6. It can be deleted in its entirety, the assured covering itself by a third party liability policy.
[22] See p. 90, above.

other items. It is stated that the insurance " covers the hull and machinery of the drilling barge(s) . . . including all their equipment, tools, [etc.]." On the other hand there is no definition, in the Form, of the term " Vessel " and for the purpose of a claim under the Collision Liability clause a collision involving these additional insured items but not the unit itself might form the subject of a claim. Furthermore this may be looked upon, as we have seen, as a separate insurance.

It has been held that a contact between an insured ship and the anchor of another ship constitutes a collision within the meaning of the " Running Down " clause in the Institute Time Clauses (Hulls).[23] It seems unlikely that a situation could arise in which one of the items (other than the drilling unit) listed as part of the insured property came into contact with another ship or vessel. But if it did; if, for example, the situation in the case of the anchor was reversed, so that a negligent act on the unit caused its anchor to foul an adjacent supply ship, it is not certain that the assured would have a right of recovery against the insurers under clause 6. If unsuccessful he would have to rely on his protecting and indemnity cover.

(ii) Damage to another ship or vessel without contact

There must be physical contact between the insured property and the other ship or vessel. If the other ship or vessel is physically damaged, or suffers damage other than physical, in some way other than by physical contact, for which there is legal liability on the part of the assured, the liability is not covered by this provision. For example, if the drilling unit, as a result of negligence on the part of those responsible for her, breaks away from her position and damage, without contact, results to another ship or vessel because it is taking avoiding action, then clause 6 (a) does not give the assured a right of recovery. As a further example, one may take the situation arising where the insured property is in tow in enclosed waters, and excessive speed on the part of the tug causes the mooring lines of another ship or vessel to be broken. A claim for the cost of replacement of the lines would not be met by this clause. These two examples would also be excluded from a ship's policy with the Institute Time Clauses (Hulls) attached. A ship would normally be able to recover in respect of such liability under its protecting and indemnity cover, of which a typical example is:

> " Loss of or damage to any other ship or any property therein (and costs and expenses incidental thereto) occasioned otherwise than by collision with the entered ship and arising out of the negligent navigation or management of the entered ship or other negligent act or omission on board or in relation to the entered ship. . . ."[24]

---

[23] *Re Margetts & Ocean Accident Guarantee Corporation* [1901] 2 K.B. 792. But contact with fishing nets dragging a mile behind a fishing vessel was held not to be a collision for this purpose; *Bennett S.S. Co, Ltd.* v. *Hull Mutual Steamship Protecting Society Ltd.* [1914] 3 K.B. 57.

[24] r. 34 (15) of the Rules of the United Kingdom Mutual Steam Ship Assurance Association (Bermuda) Ltd.

Clause 8, headed " Exclusions," makes it clear that such matters are not covered by this policy in that it begins with the words: " Notwithstanding anything to the contrary which may be contained in this insurance there shall be no liability under this insurance in respect of: " and then, at (h): " Liabilities to third parties except as specifically covered under the terms of the Collision Liability Clause contained herein."

(iii) Collision between insured drilling unit and a ship (including a drill ship) or a drilling unit (other than a drill ship)

These possibilities are considered later in the course of a discussion as to the position of the protecting and indemnity clubs.[25]

(iv) Similarity to Institute Time Clauses (Hulls) Running Down clause

The opening words of clause 6 (a), " if the vessel shall come into collision with any other ship or vessel," are similar to the opening words of clause 1 of the Institute Time Clauses (Hulls), the Running Down clause: ". . . if the Vessel hereby insured shall come into collision with any other vessel. . . ."

2. "*. . . and the Assured or the Surety in consequence of the Vessel being at fault shall become liable to pay and shall pay by way of damages to any other person or persons any sum or sums in respect of such collision . . .*"

(i) The assured must have paid the damages

This part of the Collision Liability clause sets out the conditions precedent to any recovery by the assured. There must be a fault on the part of the vessel; the assured must become liable to pay damages and must have paid them.

Under the Third Parties (Rights against Insurers) Act 1930, where an insured becomes liable to a third party, and goes into liquidation or becomes bankrupt before making payment, his rights under the policy are transferred to the third party. In such a case the third party can take, as the assured could, direct action against the insurer. Where the liability of the insurer has not been made contingent upon payment of the claim by the assured, then the third party could recover from the insurer even though the insurer had already paid the assured. The insertion of the words " and shall pay " prevents the occurrence of this double liability.

(ii) The Surety

There is a reference to " the Assured or the Surety," whereas the comparable clause in the Institute Time Clauses (Hulls) speaks only of " the assured." The present clause would therefore extend to a situation in which a party makes himself responsible for payment of a sum due from the assured and then pays that sum. Such a situation would arise if after

---

[25] See p. 211, below.

a collision the drilling unit was to be arrested and a surety made himself liable for the claim against the assured. The wording in the following part of this first sentence of clause 6 is to the effect that the underwriters will reimburse the surety in such a case.

3. "*. . . the Underwriters will pay the Assured or the Surety, whichever shall have paid, such proportion of such sum or sums so paid as their respective subscriptions hereto bear to the Agreed Value . . .*"

(i) Payment to assured or surety

This sets out the essential liability of the underwriters, which is that they should pay out to the assured or the surety respectively the sum or sums for which the assured or surety has become liable and has paid. The Institute Time Clauses (Hulls),[26] however, state: ". . . the undersigned will pay the assured," though they also provide [27] for the possibility of assignment of the interest in and the moneys payable under the policy." As for the "Loss Payable" provision in the L.S.D.B. Form,[28] it expressly excepts "claims required to be paid to others under the Collision Liability Clause."

(iii) Proportion to be paid by underwriters

The words used to describe the proportion due from the underwriters are almost identical to those in the Running Down clause of the Institute Time Clauses (Hulls),[29] which refers to "such proportion of three-fourths of such sum or sums so paid as their respective subscriptions hereto bear to the value. . . ." If the total of the "respective subscriptions" of the underwriters is equal to the insured value as set out in clause 3,[30] then they will pay the whole of that value to the assured. If interest is payable by the assured as part of the damages, then it will be included in the amount recoverable from underwriters in such a way that their maximum liability is not exceeded. In arriving at the insured value for the purpose of clause 3, therefore, the assured has to make an allowance for interest, so that the total agreed value will contain one element (the more substantial one) in respect of the collision liability and another element in respect of liability for interest. Costs, however, are dealt with separately by clause 6 (b) of the L.S.D.B. Form.

In addition to the substantive part of the Collision Liability clause [31] the L.S.D.B. Form deals also with costs; the situation arising where both vessels are to blame,[32] or both are in the same ownership [33]; and certain exclusions.[34]

---

[26] cl. 1.
[28] cl. 18; see p. 178, below.
[30] See p. 90, above.
[31] As set out at pp. 109–110, above, and then considered in detail.
[32] See p. 116, below.
[34] See p. 118, below.

[27] cl. 22.
[29] cl. 1.

[33] See p. 116, below.

4. *Costs*

Subsection (b) of clause 6 states:

> " (b) in cases where, with the consent in writing of a majority (in amount) of Hull Underwriters, the liability of the Vessel has been contested, or proceedings have been taken to limit liability, the Underwriters will also pay a like proportion of the costs which the Assured shall thereby incur or be compelled to pay."

This subsection resembles the wording of the Running Down clause in the Institute Time Clauses (Hulls) in that the latter also states:

> ". . . and in cases in which the liability of the Ship has been contested, or proceedings have been taken to limit liability, with the consent in writing of the Undersigned, they will also pay a like proportion of three-fourths of the costs which the Assured shall hereby incur, or be compelled to pay."

(i) A majority (in amount) of hull underwriters

The words " in amount " constitute a reference to the sums or percentages in respect of which the various underwriters have agreed to contribute towards the insured value, and not to the number of individual underwriters.

(ii) Provision as to costs separate from liability for damages

Although this subsection, (b), relating to costs, appears as part of clause 6, dealing with collision liability, the rights of the assured there, under are separate and distinct from his rights under subsection (a)- relating to his third party liability for damages. Before the introduction of the present Running Down clause in the Institute Time Clauses (Hulls), it had been decided that such costs, of defending an action by owners of another ship, could not be recovered from the hull under-writers.[35] The existing Running Down clause, and this subsection in the L.S.D.B. Form, entitle the assured to recover his costs (limited to three-quarters thereof in the Institute Time Clauses (Hulls), from the underwriters. As this is a separate undertaking, the assured's right of recovery is not limited by or related to the agreed value.

(iii) Relationship of 6 (b) to " Sue and Labour Expense " clause [36]

Under clause 6 (b) in the " Collision Liability " clause the assured is given the right to recover from the insurers in respect of costs incurred in contesting or limiting a claim. Clause 13, the " Sue and Labour Expense " clause, is somewhat similar in that the assured is given certain rights " to sue . . . in about the Defence, Safeguard and Recovery of the said property " and to recover the expenses thereof. In both cases, therefore, he is entitled to recover legal expenses from his insurers. Clause 6 (b) however, relates to claims against the assured for collision damage, but clause 13 concerns

---

[35] *Xenos* v. *Fox* (1868) L.R. 3 C.P. 630; 4 C.P. 665; see also p. 116, below.
[36] cl. 13. See p. 154, below.

his costs incurred in connection with the preservation of the insured property, which is the drilling unit. If the latter clause stood on its own, without any such provision as is in clause 6 (b), the assured would not be able to recover costs involved in contesting or limiting collision liability.

Thus in *Xenos* v. *Fox* [37] the assured had incurred expenses in resisting a claim for collision damages. Their hull policy contained a simple Collision Liability clause, which did not, as it now would, refer to costs, and a Sue and Labour Expense clause. It was held that they could not recover from their insurers their costs of resisting the claim, although one object was to save the insurers' money. The main ground of the decision was that the Sue and Labour Expense clause applied only to the perils insured in the main body of the policy and not to the collision liability cover, which for this and certain other purposes [38] constituted a separate insurance.

5. *Both to Blame Provision*

The " Collision Liability" clause [39] of the L.S.D.B. Form, after dealing with the right of the assured to recover in respect of his collision liability and his legal costs, provides for the situation arising when two ships are to blame, and the application of the principle of cross liabilities, in the following manner:

> " When both vessels are to blame, then, unless liability of the owners or charterers of one or both such vessels becomes limited by law, claims under the Collision Liability clause shall be settled on the principle of Cross-Liabilities as if the owners or charterers of each vessel had been compelled to pay to the owners or charterers of the other of such vessels such one-half or other proportion of the latter's damages as may have been properly allowed in ascertaining the balance or sum payable by or to the Assured in consequence of such collision."

As with a number of other provisions in the L.S.D.B. Form, these words are almost exactly the same as the corresponding words of the Running Down clause. The only differences are that the words " or charterers " are added after the word " owners," and that the sentence speaks of claims under " the Collision Liability clause," and not, as in the Running Down clause, of claims under " this clause."

6. *Sister Ships in Collision*

The next part of the " Collision Liability " clause deals with the situation arising where the two ships in collision are the property, in part or in whole, of the same owners or charterers. The principles already set out in the earlier parts of clause 6 are to apply but the questions of responsibility and the amount of liability are to be decided by arbitration. The relevant words are:

---

[37] (1868) L.R. 3 C.P. 630; 4 C.P. 665.
[38] See p. 111, above.
[39] cl. 6.

" The principles involved in this clause shall apply to the case where both vessels are the property, in part of in whole, of the same owners or charterers, all questions of responsibility and amount of liability as between the two vessels being left to the decision of a single Arbitrator, if the parties can agree upon a single Arbitrator, or failing such agreement, to the decision of Arbitrators, one to be appointed by the Assured and one to be appointed by the majority (in amount) of Hull Underwriters interested; the two Arbitrators chosen to choose a third Arbitrator before entering upon the reference, and the decision of such single Arbitrator, or of any two such three Arbitrators, appointed as above, to be final and binding."

As in the case of the both to blame provision,[40] the wording here is similar to that contained in the corresponding passage in the Institute Time Clauses (Hulls).[41] There are three material differences. One difference is that the Institute Time Clauses (Hulls) refer to another vessel belonging " to the same Owners or under the same management " whereas the L.S.D.B. Form speaks of " the same owners or charterers." The second difference is that the Institute Time Clauses (Hulls) clause relates to collision and " salvage services " whereas the present provision is restricted in its application to collisions.

The third difference is that the Institute Time Clauses (Hulls) clause provides only for reference of questions of liability and the amount payable " to a sole arbitrator to be agreed upon between the Underwriters and the Assured." The arbitration provision in the present case is, however, as can be seen, more lengthy, in that it sets out the machinery which should operate in the event that the parties fail to agree upon a single arbitrator. If English law applied to this contract, it seems that even if this part of the clause had been silent as to the procedure, the Arbitration Act 1950 would have the same effect, provided that the parties had agreed that there should be arbitration. Thus, section 6 of the 1950 Act states: " Unless a contrary intention is expressed therein, every arbitration agreement shall, if no other mode of reference is provided, be deemed to include a provision that the reference shall be to a single arbitrator."

If there is failure to agree upon a single arbitrator, section 10 of the 1950 Act applies, if there is no other stipulation as to what should happen in such an event. It provides that in such a case, and in certain other cases,[42] any party may serve the other parties or the arbitrators with a written notice to appoint or to concur in appointing an umpire or third arbitrator, and, if the appointment is not made within seven clear days after the service of the notice, the High Court may appoint an arbitrator, umpire or third arbitrator. The Collision Liability clause in the L.S.D.B. Form, however, provides that if there is such a failure to agree upon a single arbitrator each party shall appoint an arbitrator, and that the two

---

[40] The previous paragraph of the Collision Liability clause; see p. 116, above.
[41] cl. 2.
[42] Refusal of arbitrator to act, or incapability of acting; failure of parties or two arbitrators to appoint umpire or third arbitrator; refusal of umpire or third arbitrator to act, or incapability of acting, or death.

arbitrators shall choose a third arbitrator. In a contract governed by English law section 9 (1) of the 1950 Act would then come into operation.

This subsection states:

" Where an arbitration agreement provides that the reference shall be to three arbitrators, one to be appointed by each party and the third to be appointed by the two appointed by the parties, the agreement shall have effect as if it provided for the appointment of an umpire, and not for the appointment of a third arbitrator, by the two arbitrators appointed by the parties."

7. *Exclusions from " Collision Liability " clause*

The final section of the " Collision Liability " clause [43] in the L.S.D.B. Form consists of a proviso by which certain matters are excluded from the cover otherwise given by the clause. The exclusions are, with one exception, broadly similar to those set out in a comparable proviso to the Running Down clause [44] in the Institute Time Clauses (Hulls). It is useful to compare the two provisos as follows:

Introductory words

L.S.D.B.: " Provided that this clause shall in no case extend to any sum which the Assured or the Surety may become liable to pay or shall pay in consequence of, or with respect to: "

I.T.C.: " Provided always that this clause shall in no case extend or be deemed to extend to any sum which the Assured may become liable to pay or shall pay for or in respect of: "

The L.S.D.B. Form refers to a surety as well as to the assured, whereas the Institute Time Clauses (Hulls) reference is only to the assured. This wording follows that already employed in the earlier words of the respective clauses. The omission in the L.S.D.B. Form of the words " always " and " or be deemed to extend " seems to make no difference to the effect of the proviso.

The addition of the words " in consequence of " in the L.S.D.B. Form appears to widen the exclusion, in that it is not now confined to an exclusion of liabilities or payments " in respect of " the matters stated, but extends to such liabilities or payments " in consequence of, or with respect to " those matters. It might be contended that a certain liability was covered by the clause, and recoverable from the insurers, because it was indirect, or consequential, and thus not " in respect of " (if that phrase refers to a direct result only) the excluded matters. The insertion of the words " in consequence of " may have the effect of rebutting that contention.

The matters excluded in the four subsections set out in the proviso to the Running Down clause in the Institute Time Clauses (Hulls) [45] are

---

[43] cl. 6. [44] cl. 1.

[45] Namely, (*a*) removal of wrecks, etc.; (*b*) real or personal property; (*c*) cargo or property on or the engagements of the insured Vessel; (*d*) loss of life, personal injury or illness.

matters which are usually insured by the shipowner with his protecting and indemnity association. They do not constitute all the matters which can be covered by such an association, but rather those which would have fallen under the substantive provisions of the " Running Down " clause had there not been such an exclusion. The L.S.D.B. Form follows the Institute Time Clauses (Hulls) by setting out a similar list of exclusions.

Subsection (a): wreck removal

> L.S.D.B.: " removal or disposal of obstructions, wrecks or their cargoes under statutory powers or otherwise pursuant to law."
>
> I.T.C.: " removal or disposal, under statutory powers or otherwise, of obstructions, wrecks, cargoes or any other thing whatsoever."

The words of these two provisions are similar. The Institute Time Clauses (Hulls) exclusion, however, is in respect of such removal or disposal " under statutory powers or otherwise," whereas the L.S.D.B. Form exclusion is more limited in that it relates to removal or disposal " under statutory powers or otherwise pursuant to the law." A situation might arise in which an assured becomes liable to pay, or does pay, a sum in consequence of or with respect to removal under a power which is not " pursuant to the law "; there might be an arbitrary order, contrary to the law, by an executive arm of a government. Such a sum would seem not to be caught by the exclusion in the L.S.D.B. Form; it would however be excluded by the wider words of the Institute Time Clauses (Hulls). It does not follow automatically that the event would be covered by the L.S.D.B. Form; it would have to fall within the wording of the opening paragraph of clause 6.[46]

The second verbal difference between the two provisions lies in their references to cargo. The L.S.D.B. Form speaks of " obstructions, wrecks or their cargoes," whereas the Institute Time Clauses (Hulls) exclusion relates to " obstructions, wrecks, cargoes or any other thing whatsoever." A situation in which an assured is liable to pay for the removal or disposal of a cargo is in any event unlikely to arise unless that cargo is in or had been carried by his own drilling unit or the other ship. The difference between the two exclusions is thus slight, since it relates only to cargoes which were not cargoes of the wrecks, *i.e.* " their cargoes." In any event the scope of this exclusion would only be material if the result was that a claim otherwise not covered became recoverable. It seems unlikely, in view of the wording of the opening paragraph of clause 6,[47] that this would be so.

---

[46] In *The North Britain* [1894] P. 77, the Court considered a subsection which referred however, to " statutory powers," without the words " or otherwise." It appeared that the Belgian authorities who had ordered a wreck to be removed had acted within such powers; the insurers were held not to be liable.

[47] At (a); see above, p. 109.

Subsection (*b*): *property*

L.S.D.B.: " injury to real or personal property of every description "
I.T.C.: " any real or personal property or thing whatsoever except other vessels or property on other vessels."

The expression " real or personal property of every description," employed in the L.S.D.B. Form exclusion, could include property on either ship; other property at sea, including property on other ships; property in the air; and property on land. A later exclusion, (d),[48-49] relates specifically to " cargo or other property on . . . the Vessel," [50] *i.e.* the insured unit. Despite the wide scope of the wording, exclusion (b) cannot apply to injury to the other ship with which the insured ship is in collision, nor to property on the other ship.[51] If it were to do so the object of the clause, which is to provide insurance in respect of collision liability, would be defeated. A further proviso to clause 6 [52] states expressly that such liability is not excluded.

A shipowner whose ship is insured by the traditional form of English hull policy usually places cover of this type excluded by (b) with a protecting and indemnity association.[53] Such an association insures a shipowner's liability in respect of " Loss of or damage to any harbour, dock, pier, jetty, land, water or any fixed or moveable thing whatsoever (not being another ship or any property therein or the cargo or other property intended to be or being or having been carried in the entered ship)." [54] A P. & I. association also insures the shipowner against liability for damage to any other ship or any property therein occasioned otherwise than by collision with the insured ship. Such an insurance is primarily in respect of wash damage but it could also extend to damage from fires and explosions.

The Institute Time Clauses (Hulls) provision contains an exception within an exception, in that it refers to " other vessels or property on other vessels." It seems that the omission of these words from the L.S.D.B. Form exclusion makes no difference to the cover given. The opening paragraph of clause 6 [55] refers expressly to a " collision with any other ship or vessel " and to liability " to any other person or persons . . . in respect of such collision." The cover thus extends to liability to other ships and to property on other ships, so that the omission of the extra words which appear in the Institute Time Clauses (Hulls) provision makes no difference to the cover.

[48-49] See p. 121, below.
[50] See below, pp. 121–122.
[51] Except to the extent that the injury arises out of action to avoid, minimise or remove oil, etc.; see below, p. 123.
[52] See below, p. 123.
[53] See below, p. 212.
[54] The wording of r. 34 (14) of the Rules of the United Kingdom Mutual Steam Ship Assurance Association (Bermuda) Ltd.
[55] At (*a*); see above, p. 109.

Clause 6: Collision Liability

Subsection (c): pollution

L.S.D.B.: " the discharge, spillage, emission or leakage of oil, petroleum products, chemicals or other substances of any kind or description whatsoever."

I.T.C.: There is no comparable exclusion in the Running Down Clause.[56] of the standard Institute Time Clauses (Hulls) (cl. 10, October 1, 1970).

The amended version of that clause, however, called " Institute Running Down and Sister Ship Clauses " (cl. 24, October 1, 1971) provides that it " shall in no case extend or be deemed to extend to any sum which the Assured may become liable to pay or shall pay in respect of: . . . (c) pollution or contamination of any real or personal property or thing whatsoever (except other vessels with which the insured vessel is in collision or property on such vessels)." The cover in question would also be subject to exclusion (b),[57] in that a liability, including a liability for pollution, to a third party for " any real or personal property or thing whatsoever " would not be included.

In a comparable situation where the L.S.D.B. Form is used, the assured is also unable to recover. Such a liability would usually be insured by the operator of the drilling unit [58] so far as pollution from the well being drilled was concerned.

Subsection (d): cargo

L.S.D.B.: " cargo or other property on or the engagements of the Vessel "
I.T.C.: " the cargo or other property on or the engagements of the insured Vessel." [59]

The result of these two exceptions is the same, in that the insurers are not liable for any sum which the assured (and, in the case of the L.S.D.B. Form, the surety [60]) becomes liable to pay, or pays, in respect of matters falling under this heading. The liability of a shipowner would traditionally be governed by the Brussels Convention of 1924, so far as its provisions, or similar provisions, governed the contract of carriage for the cargo, either by express incorporation or as a result of the legislation governing that contract. Negligence in navigation is one of the exceptions to liability under that Convention.[61] If he is exempt from liability towards the cargo, as in a case where the negligence of the master caused or contributed to

---

[56] cl. 1.
[57] See above, p. 120.
[58] See below, p. 324.
[59] cl. 1, proviso, exception (c).
[60] See p. 109, above.
[61] For example, as in art. IV, r. 2, of the Schedule to the United Kingdom's Carriage of Goods by Sea Act 1924, which brought into legal effect the Hague Rules of 1921 as amended in 1923 at Brussels. Subs. (a) of r. 2 refers to " Act, neglect, or default of the master, mariner, pilot, or the servants of the carrier in the navigation or in the management of the ship." This provision was not altered by the Carriage of Goods by Sea Act 1971 which repealed the 1924 Act.

the collision, the cargo interests on the culpable ship would claim against the other ship. If, however, he was unable to rely on that or any other exception,[62] then his own cargo interests would claim against him. In such a case the insurers could rely upon the above-mentioned exception in the Institute Time Clauses. The same would apply if his cargo interests sued the other ship and the latter incorporated that liability in a claim against him. In such a case the insurers could rely upon the above-mentioned exception in the Institute Time Clauses, and disclaim liability because the running down clause does not apply where the assured is liable to pay " in respect of . . . cargo . . . on . . . the insured Vessel."

It is virtually certain that a drilling unit would not be carrying cargo which would proceed in this manner. In the most unlikely event of a valid claim by a cargo interest or " other property " against the owners of the drilling unit, the latter would be prevented from making a recovery from the insurers by virtue of this exception.

This sub-paragraph, (d), also has the effect that the " Collision Liability " clause does not extend to any liability of the assured, or the surety, in consequence of or with respect to " the engagements of the Vessel."

Subsection (e): loss of life, injury or illness

> L.S.D.B.: " loss of life, personal injury or illness "
> I.T.C.: " loss of life, personal injury or illness " [63]

This exclusion extends to liability for loss of life, personal injury or illness wherever it may occur and not merely if it occurs, as in the case of the last exception, (d) (as to cargo or other property), on the insured drilling unit. A claim in respect of loss of life, personal injury or illness, may form part of a claim against the assured " in respect of " a collision. In the case of a ship insured under the Institute Time Clauses (Hulls) it would be customary for the shipowners' liability for loss of life, personal injury or illness to be insured by his protecting and indemnity association. Such an insurance would extend to any person in or on board or near the ship, and to any person in or on board any other ship, where the liability arose from the negligent navigation or management of the insured ship or some other negligent act or omission on board or in relation to the entered ship.

In the case of a drilling unit covered by the L.S.D.B. Form the owner would find it necessary to insure such liability elsewhere as a result of this exclusion, where that liability arose in respect of a collision or indeed, though such need does not arise out of this exclusion, where the liability arose otherwise than as the result of a collision.

Proviso as to exclusions

The closing sentence of the exclusions set out at the end of the " Col-

---

[62] As set out in Art. IV, r. 2 of the Schedule to the 1971 Act.
[63] cl. 1, proviso, exception (d).

lision Liability " clause of the L.S.D.B. Form [64] consists of a proviso as to exclusions (b) and (c). The latter relate, respectively,\ to injury to real or personal property [65] and to pollution.[66] The proviso states:

> " Provided further that exclusions (b) and (c) above shall not apply to injury to any other vessel with which the vessel is in collision or to property on such other vessel except to the extent that such injury arises out of any action taken to avoid, minimise or remove any discharge, spillage, emission or leakage described in (c)."

The effect of this proviso is that if there is a collision with another ship, then:

1. The exclusion from the collision liability cover under (b), with respect to claims in respect of " injury to real or personal property of every description," does not apply if the " injury " in question is to the other ship or to property thereon. We have already seen [67] that the main object of the collision liability cover would be defeated if the exclusion as to " property " were to extend to claims in respect of the other ship. This proviso makes that clear; but it also refers to " property on such other vessel," and thus removes from exception (b) claims for injury to property on the other ship. If the owners of such property, or the owners of the other ship (if they have been made liable to the owners of the property), have a good claim against the assured, then he can recover from his insurers by virtue of the " Collision Liability " clause because, to use its words, he has " become liable . . . to any other person or persons . . . in respect of such collision. . . ."

2. The exclusion from the collision liability cover under (c), with respect to claims in respect of " the discharge, spillage, emission or leakage of oil, petroleum products, chemicals or other substances of any kind or description whatsoever " (called " pollution " in the present context for the sake of brevity), does not apply, subject to an exception set out below, if the " injury " in question is to the other ship or to property thereon. As a consequence of exclusion (c) there was to be no cover in respect of pollution liability arising as a result of a collision. As a result of this proviso there is cover in such a case if the pollution claim forms part of the injury to the other ship or property thereon. There is, however, a restraint on this, for there is no reimbursement for liability for expenses incurred to " avoid, minimise or remove " any pollution.

Clause 7: Deductibles

" DEDUCTIBLES [68-69]:
> It is understood and agreed that each claim (including claims under the Sue and Labour Clause [70] and the Collision Liability Clause [71]) shall be

---

[64] cl. 6.
[66] See above, p. 121.
[68-69] cl. 7 of the L.S.D.B. Form, dated March 1, 1972.
[70] cl. 13; see below, p. 154.

[65] See above, p. 120.
[67] See above, p. 120.
[71] cl. 6; see above, p. 109.

reported and adjusted separately and from the amount of each claim the sum of . . . shall be deducted. This clause shall not apply to a claim for actual or constructive or compromised or arranged total loss.[72]

For the purpose of this clause each occurrence shall be treated separately, but it is agreed that a sequence of losses or damages arising from the same occurrence shall be treated as one occurrence."

The comparable clause [73] in the variation on the L.S.D.B. Form often used in the United States reads:

" In consideration of the reduced rate at which this certificate or policy is written, it is understood and agreed that each claim for loss, damage, and expense, if any, other than total or constructive loss hereunder shall be reported and adjusted separately and from the amount of each adjusted loss, when determined, the sum of . . .[74] shall be deducted. For the purpose of this clause each occurrence shall be treated separately, but it is agreed that a sequence of losses or damages arising from the same occurrence shall be treated as one occurrence."

The requirement that the assured shall bear part of the loss has a two-fold effect, in that the insurers are not troubled by very small claims, in respect of which the administrative costs of settlement may be disproportionately large, and that the assured has a financial involvement in every claim, whether or not it falls within the deductible.

The provision for a deductible may be compared with that for a franchise in the case of the Lloyd's S.G. Policy. A franchise resembles a deductible in that it is a requirement that a claim should reach a certain level before it can be treated as a claim under the policy; but it differs from a deductible in that once that level has been reached the insurer is liable for the whole of the claim. The word " excess " is also used in connection with a provision for a deductible. Thus the amount deducted is the deductible, and the amount recovered is the excess. So also an excess reinsurance is one by which the reinsured party is indemnified to the extent that a claim exceeds a certain amount.

The Lloyd's S.G. Policy, in its " Memorandum," employs the following archaic wording,[75] designed largely to deal with cargo claims, but also affecting the assured's right to recovery in respect of claims for loss of or damage to a ship:

" N.B. Corn, fish, salt, fruit, flour, and seed are warranted free from average, unless general, or the ship be stranded—sugar, tobacco, hemp, flax, hides, and skins are warranted free from average, under five pounds per cent., and all other goods, also the ship and freight, are warranted free from average, under three pounds per cent., unless general,[76] or the ship be stranded."

---

[72] See cl. 12 below, at p. 140.
[73] cl. 8 of the 1960 L.S.D.B. Form.
[74] As to the amount see below, p. 126.
[75] The Memorandum first appeared in the policy in 1749.
[76] r. 13 of the Rules for Construction of Policy, in Sched. 1 to the 1906 Act, says that the term " average . . . unless general " means a partial loss other than general average loss and does not include particular charges.

The statement that certain matters are free from average "unless" certain incidents occur or the sum in question is "under" a certain percentage means that in the event that such incidents occur or such percentages are exceeded the whole claim is recoverable, so that this a franchise provision.[77] The wording of this "Memorandum" may be analysed as follows, in order to compare its provisions, so far as ships are concerned, with the "Deductible" clause in the L.S.D.B. Form:

The insurer will be liable in full for any loss or damage if there is a general average situation or a stranding of the ship, whatever the cargo. In the event of a claim, other than in a general average situation or when there is a stranding of the ship,[78] in respect of:

(a) corn, fish, salt, fruit, flour and seed, no claim would lie for partial loss of or damage to any of these especially perishable cargoes[79];

(b) sugar, tobacco, hemp, flax, and skins, no claim would lie in respect of loss of or damage to any of these somewhat less perishable cargoes amounting to less than 5 per cent. of their value;

(c) any other goods, or the ship and freight; no claim would lie for loss or damage, as the case might be, amounting to less than 3 per cent. of the value.

The differences between the effect of clause 7 of the L.S.D.B. Form and the "Memorandum" in the Lloyd's S.G. Policy, so far as concerns a claim for loss of or damage to the insured property, can thus be summarised as follows:

L.S.D.B. Form

(a) Any claim other than one for an actual or constructive or compromised or arranged total loss: there is deducted such sum as may have been agreed, upon the conclusion of the contract of insurance, between the assured and the insurers.

(b) A claim for an actual or constructive or compromised or arranged total loss: no deduction, the claim being recoverable in full[80];

"Memorandum" in Lloyd's S.G. Policy

(a) Any claim other than one arising from a general average situation or as the result of a stranding: in full if it exceeds 3 per cent. of the insured value but otherwise nothing.

---

[77] See Chalmers' *Marine Insurance Act* 1906 (8th ed., 1976), at p. 150.

[78] Despite a conflict as to punctuation between the S.G. Form and Sched. 1 to the 1906 Act it is generally agreed that the closing words, "unless general, or the ship be stranded," apply to both the 5 per cent. and the 3 per cent. categories; see *Arnould on Marine Insurance* (5th ed., 1961), § 35, n. 96.

[79] See p. 180, below for comments on this use of the words "warranted free." This clause was drafted before the days of refrigeration and other improved methods of cargo care.

[80] Subject to the provisions of cl. 10 as to limit of liability (see below, p. 133); and cl. 12 as to constructive total loss (see below, p. 140).

(b) A claim arising from a general average situation or as the result of a stranding: in full.

The wording of Clause 7 of the L.S.D.B. Form analysed

1. " It is understood and agreed that each claim (including claims under the Sue and Labour Clause and the Collision Liability Clause) shall be reported and adjusted separately and from the amount of each claim the sum of . . . shall be deducted."

The effect of these words seems at first to be that an assured might find that if, following the operation of an insured peril, he incurred a number of separate expenses, as for example, for separate items of repair, he would risk the application of several deductibles if each matter were to be the subject of a " claim." It would appear, however, that these would all form the subject of one claim. The " Limit of Liability " clause, clause 10,[81] speaks of " the items subject to claim," and it would appear that, provided that the items all arose from the same accident or occurrence,[82] only one deductible would be applied.

If there are also claims under the " Sue and Labour " and the " Collision Liability " clauses,[83] they are not subject to separate deductibles as they arise from the same accident or occurrence, in spite of the separate nature of the insurances provided by these clauses. The third sentence of the clause [83a] makes this clear.

The deductible is often calculated on the basis of 1 per cent. of the insured value of the drilling unit, with a minimum of U.S. $50,000 and a maximum of U.S. $200,000, but higher deductibles may be negotiated. The actual figure to be used is normally inserted in the policy.

2. " This clause shall not apply to a claim for actual or constructive or compromised or arranged total loss."

This sentence relieves the assured from the obligations both of separate reporting and adjustment and of bearing a deductible in such a case. Despite the use of the general words " This clause . . .," this second sentence is limited in its effect to the first sentence of the clause,[84] which provides for a deductible, and does not apply to the third sentence, which is only relevant to situations in which the deductible applies. It might be better if it began: " This requirement shall not apply . . ."

3. " For the purpose of this clause each occurrence shall be treated separately, but it is agreed that a sequence of losses or damages arising from the same occurrence shall be treated as one occurrence."

The word " occurrence " is not defined in the L.S.D.B. Form. Its

---

[81] See below, p. 133.
[82] See also the third and final sentence of cl. 7, discussed below at pp. 126–127.
[83] cll. 13 and 6 respectively.
[83a] See this page, below.
[84] See this page, above.

ordinary meaning is: " Happening . . .; incident, event." [85] In other parts of the form there are references to " an accident or occurrence " [86], to " any one accident or occurrence " and to " such accident or occurrence." [87] It is common practice for cover to be given in the market with a specified limitation of the liability of the insurers " per any one accident or occurrence." The word " accident," signifying " Event without apparent cause, unexpected . . .; unintentional act, chance, fortune . . ." [88] can be regarded as being more limited in its scope than the word " occurrence." If an " occurrence," such as a storm, occasioned several " accidents," only one deductible and one limitation figure would be applied.

The requirement that " each occurrence shall be treated separately " may be read with the earlier provision in clause 7 that " each claim . . . shall be reported and adjusted separately." It was suggested earlier [89] that the word " claim " should not be restricted for the purpose of applying the deductible to each individual request for reimbursement in respect of an item of payment, but would embrace all such requests, whether made separately or together, in respect of an occurrence.

It is also agreed, in this third sentence of clause 7, that " a sequence of losses or damages arising from the same occurrence shall be treated as one occurrence." The losses or damages caused by a peril may not all manifest themselves at the same time. In such a case, provided that they all arose from the same occurrence, the deductible would only be applied once. The sentence could be clearer. There is one occurrence which gives rise to a sequence of losses or damages. It is not necessary to equate the latter with the occurrence; they are its result. The words should perhaps read: ". . . a sequence of losses or damages arising from the same occurrence shall be treated as giving rise to one claim." This would also be consistent with the wording of the first sentence, which applies the deductible to each claim. In any case there might still be a difference of views as to whether the losses or damages arose from the same occurrence or whether some intervening event interrupted the chain of causation.

Clause 8: Exclusions [90]

" EXCLUSIONS:
Notwithstanding anything to the contrary which may be contained in this insurance there shall be no liability under this insurance in respect of:
(a) Loss, damage or expense caused by or attributable to earthquake or volcanic eruption, or fire and/or explosion and/or tidal wave consequent upon earthquake or volcanic eruption.
(b) Loss, damage or expense which arises solely from the intentional sinking of the barge for operational purposes; such sinking shall not

---

[85] *Concise Oxford Dictionary.* " Occurrence " is defined in the O.I.L. policy (see p. 364, below) as " an event or a continuous or repeated exposure to conditions which commence during the term of this insurance and cause [the matters covered]."
[86] cl. 2 (" Period of Insurance ").   [87] cl. 10 (Limit of Liability).
[88] *Concise Oxford Dictionary.*   [89] See above, p. 126.
[90] cl. 8 of the L.S.D.B. Form, March 1, 1972.

constitute a collision, stranding, sinking or grounding within the meaning of this insurance.

(c) Loss, damage or expense caused whilst or resulting from drilling a relief well for the purpose of controlling or attempting to control fire blowout or cratering associated with another drilling barge, platform or unit unless immediate notice be given to Underwriters of said use and additional premium paid if required.

(d) Any claim, be it a Sue and Labour Expense or otherwise, for moneys materials or property expended or sacrificed in controlling or attempting to control blowout or cratering or in fighting fire associated with blowout.

(e) Loss, damage or expense caused by or resulting from delay detention or loss of use.

(f) Wear and tear, gradual deterioration, metal fatigue, machinery breakdown, expansion or contraction due to change in temperature, corrosion, rusting, electrolytic action, error in design: nor does this insurance cover the cost of repairing or replacing any part which may be lost, damaged, or condemned by reason of any latent defect therein.

(g) Loss of or damage to dynamos, exciters, lamps, motors, switches and other electrical appliances and devices, caused by electrical injury or disturbance, unless the loss or damage be caused by a peril not excluded hereunder originating outside the electrical equipment specified in this clause. Nevertheless this clause shall not exclude claims for physical loss or damage resulting from fire.

(h) Liabilities to third parties except as specifically covered under the terms of the Collision Liability Clause contained herein.

(i) Claims in connection with the removal of property, material, debris or obstruction, whether such removal be required by law, ordinance, statute, regulation or otherwise.

(j) Loss of or damage to drill stem located underground or underwater unless directly resulting from fire, blowout, cratering, or total loss of the Drilling Barge caused by a peril insured hereunder. There shall be no liability in respect of drill stem left in the well and through which an oil or gas well is completed.

Blowout: The term ' Blowout ' shall mean a sudden, accidental, uncontrolled and continuous expulsion from a well and above the surface of the ground of the drilling fluid in an oil or gas well, followed by continuous and uncontrolled flow from a well and above the surface of the ground of oil, gas or water due to encountering subterranean pressures.

Cratering: The term ' Crater ' shall be defined as a basin-like depression in the earth's surface surrounding a well caused by the erosion and eruptive action of oil, gas or water flowing without restriction.

(k) Well(s) and/or hole(s) whilst being drilled or otherwise.

(l) Drilling mud cement chemicals and fuel actually in use, and casing and tubing in the well.

(m) Unrefined oil or gas or other crude product.

(n) Blueprints, plans, specifications or records, personal effects of employees or others.

(o) Scraping or painting the bottom of the hull of the drilling barge."

128

Clause 8: Exclusions

Another version of this form, the L.S.D.B. Form as drafted in 1960, is sometimes used in the United States, but normally only where the assured was covered on that form before the introduction of the 1972 form. It is necessary to set out that version here. The main differences can then be noted before the exclusions themselves are considered in detail. The exclusions clause states:

" 11. NOTWITHSTANDING ANYTHING TO THE CONTRARY WHICH MAY BE CONTAINED IN THESE CLAUSES THERE SHALL BE NO LIABILITY under this certificate or policy in respect of:

(a) Loss, Damage or Expense which arises solely from the intentional sinking of the barge for operational purposes: such sinking shall not constitute a collision, stranding, sinking or grounding within the meaning of this certificate or policy.

(b) Wear and tear, gradual deterioration, metal fatigue, machinery breakdown, changes in temperature, corrosion, rusting, electrolytic action, damage due to or resulting from error in design, nor does this insurance cover the cost of repairing or replacing any part which may be lost or damaged by reason of any latent defect therein.

(c) Loss or damage to drill stem located underground or under water unless resulting from fire, lightning, flood, rising waters, tidal wave, ice, explosion above the surface of the ground, tornado, windstorm, wave action, stress of weather, cyclone, hurricane, earthquake, blowout and/or cratering or collision or loss of drill stem left in the well and through which an oil and/or gas well is completed.

(d) Blueprints, plans, specifications or records, personal effects of employees or others.

(e) Oil and gas, other than fuel in storage on the drilling barge insured hereunder, it being the extent of this paragraph to exclude from coverage hereunder the unprocessed product of the Assured's producing wells.

(f) Drilling mud, cement, chemicals and fuel actually in use, casing and tubing in the well.

(g) Loss or damage to dynamos, exciters, lamps, motors, switches and other electrical appliances and devices caused by electrical injury or disturbance unless fire ensues and then for loss by fire only or unless the damage be caused by a peril not excluded hereunder originating outside the electrical equipment specified in this clause.

(h) Loss or damage caused by or resulting from delay or loss of use, whether resulting from a peril insured against or otherwise.

(i) Liabilities to third parties not otherwise covered hereunder.

(j) Loss, damage or expense caused by or resulting from drilling a relief well for the purpose of controlling or attempting to control fire, blowout or cratering (except in connection with a well in the process of being drilled or completed by the drilling barge insured hereunder) unless notice be given to Underwriters in advance of said use and additional premium paid if required.

(k) Well(s) while being drilled or otherwise.

(l) Use of the insured property to drill a relief well for the purpose of controlling or attempting to control fire, blowout or cratering unless notice be given to Underwriters in advance of said use and any additional premium be agreed.

(m) Negligence of Masters, Mariners, Charterers, Engineers, Pilots, Crew and all Employees of the Assured (including those employees responsible for the operation of the property insured even though they may have interests or titles in the Assured's firm) with respect to loss or damage (except for loss or damages occurring from the other perils insured herein) to drilling rig while actually rigged up at drilling location."

(n) Blueprints, plans, specifications or records, personal effects of employees or others.

(o) Scraping or painting the bottom of the hull of the drilling barge.

The main differences between the exclusions clauses are:

March 1, 1972	1960
1. Loss, etc., resulting from earthquake, volcanic eruption, etc., excluded by (a).	No similar exclusion; but it was customary to add such an exclusion as a separate provision.
2. Loss, etc., arising from sinking for operational purposes, excluded by (b).	The same exclusion, under (a).
3. Loss, etc., caused while or resulting from drilling a relief well to control fire, blowout or cratering associated with another drilling unit, unless notice given to underwriters and additional premium paid if required, excluded by (c).	A similar exclusion, under (j). Instead of the reference to a fire, etc., associated with another drilling unit, the exclusion clause says " except in connection with a well " being drilled or completed by the insured drilling unit.
4. Claims for money materials or property expended or sacrificed in control or attempted control of blowout, cratering or fighting fire associated with blowout, excluded by (d). This is intended to exclude cost of control expenses, which are insured under a separate policy.[91]	A similar exclusion, under clause 17 (b).
5. Loss, etc., caused by or resulting from delay detention or loss of use, excluded by (e).	The same exclusion, under (h), with the addition of the words " whether resulting from a peril insured against or otherwise." The omission of these words in the 1972 Form does not seem to affect the meaning of the exception.

---

[91] See Cp. 9, below.

130

March 1, 1972	1960
(No liability in respect of:)	

6. Wear and tear, etc., and latent defect, excluded by (f).

A similar exclusion, under (b).

Differences

A. " expansion or contraction due to change in temperature "

" changes in temperature "

B. " error in design "

" damage due to or resulting from error in design "

C. " lost, damaged or condemned by reason of any latent defect therein "

" lost or damaged by reason of any latent defect therein "

7. Loss, etc., to dynamos, etc., caused by electrical injury or disturbance, *unless* caused by a peril not excluded hereunder originating outside the electrical equipment specified in this clause. The clause not to exclude " claims for physical loss or damage resulting from fire." Excluded by (g).

A similar exclusion, under (g), *unless* caused by a peril as defined in the 1972 Form *but* with the words " unless fire ensues and then for loss by fire only," instead of the words set out opposite.

8. Liabilities to third parties except as specifically covered under the term of the " Collision Liability " clause,[92] excluded by (h).

A similar exclusion, under (i), which says only " Liabilities to third parties not otherwise covered hereunder."

9. Claims in connection with removal of property, material, debris or obstruction, excluded by (i).

A similar exclusion under clause 17 (b).

10. Loss, etc., to drill stem underground or underwater unless directly resulting from fire, blowout, cratering or total loss of the insured drilling unit, excluded by (j).

Similar exclusion, under (c), *but*
A. several disasters, mostly natural (lightning, flood, rising waters, etc.) added to the list of exceptions;
B. no definitions of blowout and cratering, but these appear elsewhere in 1960 policy, at clause 10.

---

[92] cl. 6; see above, p. 109.

131

March 1, 1972   1960

(No liability in respect of:)

11. Well(s) and/or hole(s) while being drilled or otherwise, excluded by (k).

Similar exclusion, under (k), but confined to well(s).

12. Drilling, mud cement, chemicals and fuel actually in use, and casing and tubing in the well, excluded by (l).

Same exclusion, under (f).

13. Unrefined oil or gas or other crude product, excluded by (m). This seems to express more positively what is, in the 1960 Form, stated to be " the intent " of the corresponding subsection thereunder.

Similar exclusion, under (e), *but* an exclusion of " oil or gas, other than fuel in storage. . . ." It is said to be " the intent of this paragraph to exclude from coverage the unprocessed product of the Assured's producing wells."

14. Blueprints, plans, specifications or records, personal effects of employees or others, excluded under (n).

Same exclusion, under (d).

15. Scraping or painting bottom of hull of drilling unit, excluded by (o).

A similar exclusion, under clause 22.

Of the 15 exceptions, (a) to (o), in the 1972 L.S.D.B. Form, 14, (b) to (o), thus have corresponding exceptions in the 1960 Form, and the other, (a), was customarily added. As for the 1960 Form, it contains one exception, (m), which does not appear in the 1972 Form. This is:

" (m) Negligence of Masters, Mariners, Charterers, Engineers, Pilots, Crew and all Employees of the Assured with respect to loss or damage to drilling unit while actually rigged up at drilling location."

In policies governed by an unamended 1960 L.S.D.B. Form the insurers are not liable in respect of loss or damage resulting from such negligence. In practice (m) was deleted. The absence of this exclusion from the 1972 Form suggests that it is intended that they should be liable for such loss or damage. So far as the Marine Insurance Act 1906, applies to the policy,[93] section 55 (2) (*a*) states:

" The insurer is not liable for any loss attributable to the wilful misconduct of the assured, but, unless the policy otherwise provides, he is liable for any loss proximately caused by a peril insured against, even though the loss would not have happened but for the misconduct or negligence of the master or crew."

---

[93] As to its application see Appendix C, below, at p. 456.

The 1972 Form is not a policy which " otherwise provides," so that section 55 (2) (*a*) applies and the insurer is liable, unless the loss is attributable to the wilful misconduct of the assured.

Clause 9: Blowout Preventer Warranty

" BLOWOUT PREVENTER WARRANTY CLAUSE:
The Assured warrants and agrees that blowout preventers of standard make will be used, same to be installed and tested in accordance with the usual practice."

This is the clause now used in the 1972 L.S.D.B. Form and in the 1960 Form. For some time the 1972 Form contained a more lengthy clause:

" BLOWOUT PREVENTER WARRANTY:
Warranted [94-95] that (a) in all drilling operations, (b) in all operations which require the removal of the Christmas tree the well and/or hole will be equipped with a minimum of three pressure operated blowout preventers, which shall be installed and tested immediately after installation. Two of the aforesaid blowout preventers shall be of the pipe ram and blind ram type and the third shall be of the annular full closing type." [96]

The term " blowout " has already been defined in the L.S.D.B. Form [97] as meaning " a sudden, accidental, uncontrolled and continuous expulsion from a well and above the surface of the ground of the drilling fluid in an oil or gas well; followed by a continuous and uncontrolled flow from a well and above the surface of the ground of oil, gas or water due to encountering subterranean pressures." A blowout preventer has been defined [98] as " A high-pressure valve, usually hydraulically operated, fitted to the top of the casing of a drilling well to prevent an accidental blowout of oil or gas." The " casing " is defined, in its turn, as " the steel lining used to prevent caving of the sides of a well, to exclude unwanted fluids, and to provide means for the control of well pressures and oil and gas production." [99]

Clause 10: Limit of Liability

Clause 10 of the L.S.D.B. Form provides, in its first part, that the insured value of the property insured, as set out in clause 3,[1] shall constitute the maximum amount of the insurers' liability, except in respect of the liability of the insurers under the " Sue and Labour Expense " clause [2] and the " Collision Liability " clause.[3] The second and third parts of clause 10 deal with the cost of repair or replacement [4] and increases in

---

[94-95] As to the meaning of " warranty," see p. 100, above.
[96] cl. 9 of the original L.S.D.B. Form, dated March 1, 1972.
[97] In cl. 8, dealing with exclusions, at (j).
[98] H. Clarkson & Co. Ltd., *The Offshore Drilling Register* (London 1978).
[99] H. Clarkson & Co. Ltd., *ibid.*
[1] See above, p. 90.
[2] cl. 13; see below, p. 154.
[3] cl. 6; see above, p. 109.
[4] See below, p. 136.

the costs of repair or reconstruction resulting from laws or other similar matters affecting such costs.[5]

The first part of clause 10 states:

> " In no event, except as provided for in the Sue and Labour Expense Clause and Collision Liability Clause herein, shall the Underwriters' liability arising from any one accident or occurrence exceed the amount insured hereunder as set forth in Clause 3 in respect of the items subject to claim in such accident or occurrence."

The comparable provision in the 1960 L.S.D.B. Form reads:

> " 23. Limit of Liability.
>
> (a) In no event shall Underwriters be liable in any one accident or occurrence for more than the total amount insured hereunder as set forth in paragraph 4[6] and where several items are separately insured Underwriters shall not be liable in any one accident or occurrence for more than the insured amount in respect of any one item subject, however, to the conditions of paragraph (b) below."

Paragraph (b) enabled underwriters to pay claims for general average, salvage charges and sue and labour expenses in addition to the insured amount but not exceeding 25 per cent. of the amount insured. There is a comparable provision in the 1972 L.S.D.B. Form, so far as sue and labour expenses are concerned, in clause 13 thereof.[7] There is no comparable limitation to 25 per cent. in the Lloyd's S.G. Policy or in the Institute Time Clauses (Hulls); the words of the S.G. Policy permit full recovery, subject to the overall limit.

The wording of this first sentence of clause 10 is such that the insured value would, except in the circumstances stated, represent the maximum amount recoverable. As in the case of ships, the additional 100 per cent. indemnity in respect of collision liability is considered necessary and reasonable. In the case of sue and labour expenses, it can be hard to say whether they were incurred to save the well or the drilling unit. It was thought better to introduce a 25 per cent. limitation.

Section 67 of the Marine Insurance Act 1906, is similar to clause 10 in that it sets out the extent of the liability of the insurer for the loss. Thus section 67 (1) describes the sum recoverable as " the measure of indemnity," by stating:

> " The sum which the assured can recover in respect of a loss on a policy by which he is insured, in the case of an unvalued policy, to the full extent of the insurable value, or, in the case of a valued policy, to the full extent of the value fixed by the policy, is called the measure of indemnity."

The L.S.D.B. policy, is, where the insured value is stated, a valued policy.[8] So far as the 1906 Act applies to the L.S.D.B. Form the sum set out in

---

[5] See below, p. 139.
[6] Which states: " Sum insured hereunder. . . ."
[7] See below, p. 154.
[8] See the wording of cl. 3 at p. 90, above; see also s. 27 of the 1906 Act, as to valued policies.

clause 3 is thus " called the measure of indemnity." It is both convenient and correct to call it the measure of indemnity even in a case of a policy to which the 1906 Act does not apply.[9]

Nevertheless, section 67 (1) of the 1906 Act does not correspond exactly to the first sentence of clause 10 of the L.S.D.B. Form. The subsection serves to define and to introduce the expression " measure of indemnity," which is the title of the group of sections 67 to 78.

The object of the first sentence of clause 10 is to state the maximum liability of the underwriter. Section 67 (2) of the Act has a similar effect:

> " Where there is a loss recoverable under the policy, the insurer, or each insurer if there be more than one, is liable for such proportion of the measure of indemnity as the amount of his subscription bears to the value fixed by the policy, in the case of a valued policy, or to the insurable value, in the case of an unvalued policy."

This subsection sets out the liability of the insurer, stating that his liability shall be related directly to the measure of indemnity (already defined in section 67 (1)), on the basis that he bears the same proportion thereof as his " subscription " bears to the insured value.[10] If the principle were to be applied to the L.S.D.B. Form, then in the case of an insurance by the only insurer or by all the insurers, in respect of an insured value, his or their maximum liability would be that insured value. The effect would thus be the same as that of the first sentence of clause 10. As a result of section 67 (2) an assured who is under-insured will recover less than the measure of indemnity, to the extent and in the proportion that he is under-insured.

" any one accident or occurrence "
" such accident or occurrence "

The expressions " any one accident or occurrence " and " such accident or occurrence " are used in the first sentence of clause 10. The term " an accident or occurrence " was used in clause 2, which deals with the period of insurance [11]; the clause envisaged a situation in which the insurance expired " while an accident or occurrence giving rise to a loss is in progress "; although the whole loss had not in fact occurred, underwriters were to be liable as if it had all occurred during the period of the insurance. An " accident or occurrence " may thus be an instantaneous event, taking place at a moment which can be specified, or a continuing event, of which it may correctly be said that it is " in progress." In clause 7, dealing with deductibles, the word " accident " does not appear. Instead there are references to " each occurrence," " the same occurrence " and " one occurrence." The difference, so far as there may be one, between an " accident " and an " occurrence " is discussed in connection

---

[9] As to the applicability of the Act, see Appendix C, at p. 456, below.
[10] *i.e.* " the value fixed by the policy." See also p. 342, below.
[11] See above, p. 87.

135

with clause 7. There is virtually no discussion in the standard textbooks of terms such as " any one accident or occurrence." [12]

The second sentence of clause 10 deals with the cost of repairs or replacement of the damaged or lost property:

> " In respect of the property insured hereunder Underwriters shall not be liable for more than their proportion of the cost of repairing or replacing the property damaged or lost with materials of like kind and quality to a condition equal to but not superior to or more extensive than its condition prior to the loss; nevertheless in respect of the hull of the Drilling Barge covered hereunder all costs of repair and replacement for which Underwriters may be liable shall be on the basis of new for old with no deduction for depreciation."

The effect of the first part of this sentence is that underwriters have only to pay such an amount as would restore the property (other than the " hull of the drilling barge ") to a condition equal to its previous condition. This could in certain circumstances represent a limitation upon their liability greater than that already imposed by the first sentence of clause 10.[13] Their liability was thereby limited to the amount insured. If it proves possible to repair or replace the property to a condition " equal to " its condition prior to the loss, but at a cost less than the sum insured, then the recovery by the assured will be limited to that cost. In a case of particular average, where there is damage to the insured property, such a restriction presents no unexpected problems. Where there is a total loss of the property, however, the assured might expect to recover in respect of the insured value. If it were shown that the property lost could be replaced " to a condition [14] equal to . . . its condition prior to the loss," but at a cost lower than the insured value, then the underwriters might only be liable for the lesser amount.

Section 69 of the Marine Insurance Act 1906 deals with damage and its repair, and its provisions may be compared with those of the second sentence of clause 10 of the L.S.D.B. Form. Subject to any express provision in the policy, where a ship has been repaired, whether in full [15] or partially,[16] section 69 provides that " the assured is entitled to the reasonable cost of such repairs." In the case of a full repair section 69 (1) says, in respect of the measure of indemnity:

---

[12] There has been some judicial discussion: for example in *South Staffordshire Tramways Co. Ltd.* v. *Sickness and Accident Insurance Ltd.* [1891] 1 Q.B. 402 (C.A.) (" any one accident "); *Allen* v. *London Guarantee and Accident Co.* (1912) 28 T.L.R. 254 (" any one accident or occurrence "); *Australia and New Zealand Banks Ltd.* v. *Colonial and Eagle Wharves Ltd.* [1960] 2 Lloyd's Rep. 241 (" each and every claim "); and *Forney* v. *Dominion Insurance Co. Ltd.* [1969] 1 Lloyd's Rep. 502 (" occurrence "). There is some discussion of such expressions in " Marine Insurance Claims " (Witherby, 1974) by J. Kenneth Goodacre at pp. 644–645.

[13] See above, pp. 133–134.

[14] Taken out of context, the words do not seem to be well expressed; but both words, " repairing " and " replacing," can only relate to this subsequent phrase, " to a condition. . . ."

[15] s. 69 (1).   [16] s. 69 (2).

" Where the ship has been repaired, the assured is entitled to the reasonable cost of repairs, less the customary deductions,[17] but not exceeding the sum insured in respect of any one casualty."

In the case of a partial repair section 69 (2) says:

" Where the ship has been only partially repaired, the assured is entitled to the reasonable cost of such repairs, computed as above,[18] and also to be indemnified for the reasonable depreciation, if any, arising from the unrepaired damage, provided that the aggregate amount shall not exceed the cost of repairing the whole damage, computed as above." [19]

Both subsections refer to " the reasonable cost of repairs," though that dealing with partial repair allows for indemnity also in respect of " the reasonable depreciation." In both subsections a limit is set to the recovery; in the case of the full repair that recovery is limited to the sum insured, and in the case of the partial repair it is limited to the cost of repairing the whole damage. So also in this sentence in clause 10 of the L.S.D.B. Form the recovery is limited by these two considerations. First, though the words " reasonable cost of repairs " are not used, the cost involved is to be that of repair or replacement " with materials of a like kind and quality to a condition equal to but not superior to or more extensive than its condition prior to the loss. . . ." That is one way of setting out, in full, what is meant by a reasonable cost. The meaning of the term " reasonable cost of repairs," for the purpose of a claim on a hull policy, was considered in *Helmville Ltd.* v. *Yorkshire Insurance Co. Ltd.*[20] Roskill J. said [21] that it was a question of fact in each case as to what the phrase included. Similarly, in the case of clause 3 of the L.S.D.B. Form, it must be a question of fact in each case as to whether the costs incurred or to be incurred fall within the scope of the clause.

Secondly, clause 10 limits the extent of recovery by the assured by stating that the underwriters "shall not be liable for more than their proportion of the cost " of repair or replacement. On the assumption, which is usually correct, that there has been a full insurance, so that the underwriters, taken as a group, are responsible as to 100 per cent. of the said cost, the words in question are saying that (a) the recovery is limited to the cost of the repairs, but not exceeding the sum insured; and (b) each individual underwriter is liable only for his own proportion.

" New for old "

It was for many years the practice of insurers to make a deduction from the sums which they paid where the costs claimed were based on the supply of new material to the ship. Their reason was that the new material often replaced material which was old, and that unless some deduction

---

[17] These were the deductions applied to claims in respect of wooden ships, except on their first voyage, of " one third new for old." The deductions were not applicable in the case of iron ships.
[18] The words " computed as above" are a reference to the method of computation set out in s. 69 (1).　　　　　　　　　　　　　　　　　　　[19] *Ibid.*
[20] [1965] 1 Lloyd's Rep. 361. Also known as *The Medina Princess.*
[21] At pp. 518–520.

was made the assured would benefit from the loss or damage. If he were to benefit therefrom, the principle that a contract of insurance was one of indemnity would be lost. It was therefore customary for the insurers to deduct one-third, or sometimes one-sixth, from the sums which they paid. This deduction was not usually made where the repairs did not involve the supply of material to the ship.[22] This practice is not now customary, for clause 10 of the Institute Time Clauses (Hulls) states: " Average payable without deduction new for old, whether the average be particular or general."

Clause 10 of the L.S.D.B. Form follows the customary practice in the hull market by stating, after the above-mentioned words, in its second sentence dealing with the cost of repair or replacement: ". . .nevertheless in respect of the hull of the Drilling Barge covered hereunder all costs of repair and replacement for which Underwriters may be liable shall be on the basis of new for old with no deduction for depreciation." The words in question relate to " the hull of the Drilling Barge " and not to the items of equipment set out at length in clause 3 of the L.S.D.B. Form.[23] Nor do they refer to the machinery; the opening words of clause 3 are: " This insurance covers the hull and machinery of the drilling barge(s), as scheduled below. . . ." Furthermore, the words are expressed in such a way, with the use of the word " nevertheless," as to indicate that they qualify the preceding words which deal with the cost of repair or replacement. If these words are compared with those in clause 10 of the Institute Time Clauses (Hulls), it seems that the three areas of the insurances are dealt with as follows:

	L.S.D.B. Form	I.T.C. (Hulls)
Hull (including the propulsion machinery)	" new for old with no deduction for depreciation "	" Average payable without deduction, new for old. . . ." (clause 10)
Drilling Machinery	" cost of repairing or replacing . . . with materials of like kind and quality to a condition equal to but not superior to or more extensive than its condition prior to the loss "	As above.
Equipment	As for Machinery above.	As above.

---

[22] Rule XIII of the York-Antwerp Rules 1974, entitled " Deductions from Cost of Repairs," sets out the very limited area in which deductions may now be made in respect of " new for old " in adjusting claims for general average. A C.M.I. Assembly in Brussels in 1973 had resolved to introduce a new Rule stating that no deductions " new for old " should be made in any circumstances. This would have been consistent with cl. 10 of the I.T.C. (Hulls) (see below) but the proposal was not adopted in 1974.
[23] See above, p. 90.

The word " equipment " is used above to refer to the items in clause 3 of the L.S.D.B. Form other than the hull and machinery of the drilling unit. In the case of a ship insured in accordance with the Institute Time Clauses (Hulls) the word equipment is also used by way of contrast with the hull and machinery, though the equipment itself is very different in character. The Lloyd's S.G. Policy refers to " the body, tackle, apparel, ordnance, munition, artillery, boat, and other furniture, of and in the good ship or vessel. . . ." Rule 15 of the Rules for Construction of Policy, in Schedule 1 to the Marine Insurance Act 1906, says:

> " The term ' ship ' includes the hull, materials and outfit, stores and provisions for the officers and crew, and, in the case of vessels engaged in a special trade, the ordinary fittings requisite for the trade, and also, in the case of a steamship, the machinery, boilers, and coals and engine stores, if owned by the assured."

The list of items given in the Lloyd's S.G. Policy amounts to a comprehensive but archaic description of the materials constituting and on board a ship. The list in Rule 15 includes items common to ships generally, such as " materials and outfit," and items to be consumed, such as " stores and provisions for the officers and crew." Rule 15 does, however, continue with words which could be applied to the case of a drilling unit, by speaking of vessels engaged in a special trade and " the ordinary fittings requisite for the trade." Clause 3 of the L.S.D.B. Form, on the other hand, after mentioning the hull and machinery, deals with items involved in the drilling operations, but it ends with the words " and all such property as scheduled herein, owned by or in the care custody or control of the Assured."

" In no event shall Underwriters be liable for any increased cost of repair or reconstruction by reason of law, ordinance, regulation, permit or licence regulating construction or repair."

This last sentence of clause 10 of the L.S.D.B. Form might have the effect of excluding any element in the cost of repair or reconstruction which was attributable either (a) to any law, ordinance or regulation whatsoever; or (b) to any permit or licence regulating construction or repair, so that the words " regulating construction or repair " govern only " permit or licence." As a result increased costs by reason of " law, ordinance, regulation " would be excluded whether or not the law, ordinance or regulation related to construction or repair. A more probable interpretation, however, is that the exclusion is not so wide, and the extra costs are only excluded if the relevant law, ordinance or regulation (in addition to any relevant permit or licence) regulated construction or repair. It would not be enough that it only increased the cost.

Clause 11: Coinsurance

COINSURANCE:
" The Assured shall maintain contributing insurance on terms no more

restrictive than this insurance on the property insured hereunder of not less than 100% of the new reproductive cost less a reasonable depreciation. Failing to do so, the Assured shall be an insurer to the extent of such deficit and bear such proportionate part of any claim. If this insurance be divided into two or more items the foregoing conditions shall apply to each item separately." [24]

The comparable clause in the 1960 L.S.D.B. Form, clause 14, states:

" The Assured shall maintain contributing insurance on the property insured hereunder of not less than 100% of the actual sound value thereof, and failing to do so, the Assured shall be an insurer to the extent of such deficit and bear such proportionate part of loss. If this certificate or policy be divided into two or more items, the foregoing conditions shall apply to each item separately."

The object of such clauses is to ensure that there is a full insurance by the assured of both the drilling unit and the equipment. The clause, which is understood to have had its origins in the non-marine policies issued in respect of land rigs, has the effect of ensuring that if only part of the value is covered under this policy there is an insurance elsewhere for the rest of the value. To the extent that the assured does not so insure he bears the risk himself.

Clause 12: Constructive Total Loss

Clause 12 of the L.S.D.B. Form [25] deals with the problem of a constructive total loss. The latter words, and the corresponding expression " actual total loss " must first be defined. A starting point for such a definition [26] is section 56 (1) and (2) of the Marine Insurance Act 1906:

" (1) A loss may be either total or partial. Any loss other than a total loss, as hereinafter defined, is a partial loss.
(2) A total loss may be either an actual total loss, or a constructive total loss."

To the extent that the principles set out in the 1906 Act apply to the L.S.D.B. Form and to other policies concerning drilling units,[27] these subsections are helpful in that they show how the concept of a constructive total loss is treated in the English law of marine insurance. Indeed the idea of a constructive total loss only arises in cases of marine insurance.[28] It is reputed to have been evolved to help the assured where the insured property was captured. In such a case the ship was effectively lost to him though it was not lost physically.[28a] There was the possibility, however remote, that the ship would be recaptured. Lord Atkinson, in *Moore* v. *Evans*, [29] said:

---

[24] cl. 11 of the L.S.D.B. Form dated March 1, 1972.
[25] Set out below, at p. 143.
[26] For the definition itself see s. 60 (1) and below, p. 141.
[27] See Appendix C below, at p. 456.
[28] *Assicurazioni Generali* v. *Bessie Morris Co.* [1892] 2 Q.B. 652, and see Arnould on *Marine Insurance* (15th ed., 1961) at § 7, n. 2.
[28a] See Arnould, *op. cit.* at § 1081.
[29] [1918] A.C. 185 (H.L.), at pp. 193–194.

" One can readily understand that those willing to adventure, who had possessed themselves of expensive but money-making chattels like ships for the purpose of their adventures, should, if they insured, be protected as far as possible from having their capital locked up unprofitably in ships whose fate they were unable actually to ascertain and prove. Hence it was that ships which had sailed and had not been heard of for a length of time were presumed not merely to have been lost, but to have foundered at sea, so that the owner would be at once entitled to recover the full amount under his policy."

Upon notification of abandonment the assured could put himself in the same position as if an actual total loss had occurred. The definition of constructive total loss was widened so that it included cases in which an actual total loss appeared inevitable or could not be avoided without disproportionate expenditure,[30] as well as cases in which the assured was deprived of the possession of the ship [31] and it was also held to include cases in which the cost of repairing damage would exceed the value of the ship when repaired.

The term " constructive total loss " is defined in section 60 (1) of the Marine Insurance Act 1906:

" Subject to any express provision in the policy, there is a constructive total loss where the subject-matter insured is reasonably abandoned on account of its actual total loss appearing to be unavoidable, or because it could not be preserved from actual loss without an expenditure which would exceed its value when the expenditure had been incurred."

If this subsection were applied to the case of a drilling unit, there would be a constructive total loss when the subject-matter, which is the hull and machinery of the unit, was reasonably abandoned because

(a) its actual total loss appeared to be unavoidable; or

(b) it could not be preserved from actual total loss without an expenditure which would exceed its value when the expenditure had been incurred.

The expression " actual total loss " is used in the wording of both alternatives. A reference to section 56 (2) shows that this is one of the two types of total loss. It thus might appear to be unavoidable that the subject-matter insured will be actually lost, in that, for example, it will be destroyed or irretrievably altered by damage or will disappear beneath the sea. There would then be an actual total loss, as defined in section 57 (1) of the 1906 Act: " Where the subject-matter is destroyed, or so damaged as to cease to be a thing of the kind insured, or where the assured is irretrievably deprived thereof, there is an actual total loss."

Alternatively it may be shown, as a matter of fact rather than as a matter of probability, that preservation of the subject-matter from actual total loss would necessitate expenditure which would exceed its value when the expenditure had been incurred. " A man may be said to have

---

[30] See s. 60 (1) of the 1906 Act.
[31] s. 60 (2) (i) of the 1906 Act.

141

lost a shilling when he has dropped it in deep water, though it might be possible, by some very expensive contrivance, to recover it." [32] In marine insurance terms one could say of the shilling, in the words of section 60 (1), that " it could not be preserved from actual total loss without an expenditure which would exceed its value when the expenditure had been incurred." It would be a preservation " from actual total loss," even though the shilling still existed physically, because the definition of actual total loss in section 57 (1) extends to a case in which " the assured is irretrievably deprived " of the subject-matter. A drilling unit may, for example, be severely damaged by fire. If no action is taken, it may fall into the category, to use the words of section 57 (1),[33] of a subject-matter " so damaged as to cease to be a thing of the kind insured " or the assured may as a result be " irretrievably deprived " of it. Expenditure may have to amount to, say, $30 million, in order to preserve it from such actual total loss; but if the value of the drilling unit after the expenditure is incurred will be only $20 million, then there is a constructive total loss.

It is necessary to study also the words of section 60 (2) of the 1906 Act, in order to have a complete picture of what is meant by a constructive total loss in cases where a typical marine policy is involved. It is only then that it is possible to appreciate, by way of contrast, the more restrictive interpretation set out in clause 12 of the L.S.D.B. Form.

Section 60 (2) goes on to state:

" In particular, there is a constructive total loss:
    (i) Where the assured is deprived of the possession of his ship or goods by a peril insured against, and (a) it is unlikely that he can recover the ship or goods as the case may be, or (b) the cost of recovering the ship or goods, as the case may be, would exceed their value when recovered; or
    (ii) In the case of damage to a ship, where she is so damaged by a peril insured against, that the cost of repairing the damage would exceed the value of the ship when repaired. In estimating the cost of repairs, no deduction is to be made in respect of general average contribution to these repairs payable by other interests, but account is to be taken of the expense of future salvage operations and of any future general average contributions to which the ship would be liable if repaired.
    [(iii) Deals with damage to goods and need not be set out here.]

It may seem at first that section 60 (2) constitutes an illustration of the definition of constructive total loss already given in section 60 (1). It has however been said by Lord Wright in *Rickards* v. *Forestal Land, Timber and Railways Co., Ltd* [34] that the subsection is additional, and not by way of illustration: " Subsection (2), as compared with subsection (1) is thus cumulative, not merely illustrative." Indeed, when the wording of section 60 (1) is compared with the wording of section 60 (2), it can be seen that the former relates to cases in which an actual total loss either appears to be

---

[32] Maule J. in *Moss* v. *Smith* (1850) 9 C.B. 103.
[33] Relating to actual total loss.
[34] [1942] A.C. 50 (H.L.), at p. 84.

unavoidable or can only be avoided by disproportionate expenditure; but that the latter relates to cases where the assured is deprived of possession, or where damage repairs would be disproportionately expensive.

If the casualty is not covered by the definition in section 60 (1) it may therefore be covered by section 60 (2) and still rank as a constructive total loss. An example of a situation covered by subsection (2) but not by subsection (1) occurred in *Panamanian Oriental S.S. Corporation* v. *Wright*,[35] where a ship had been seized by customs authorities in South Viet-nam for carrying unmanifested goods. A court ordered her confiscation and the assured failed in his attempts, which endured for some years, to secure her release. It was held that he had been deprived of the possession of his ship by a peril insured against, and that it was " unlikely " that he could recover the ship.

It is against this background of the 1906 Act that it is now possible to examine the wording of clause 12 of the L.S.D.B. Form, which states:

" CONSTRUCTIVE TOTAL LOSS:
There shall be no recovery for a Constructive Total Loss hereunder unless the expense of recovering and repairing the insured property shall exceed the actual insured value.
In no case shall Underwriters be liable for unrepaired damage in addition to a subsequent Total Loss sustained during the period covered by this insurance."

The first sentence does not expressly define a constructive total loss for the purpose of the L.S.D.B. Form. Nor does it exclude the possibility that the definitions given in section 60 (1) and (2) of the 1906 Act may be applied. But its effect is that even where a casualty falls within the wording of one of these definitions, there will be no recovery from the insurers unless the expense of recovery and repair exceeds the actual insured value. Thus it is the insured value and not the repaired value which is the test for the purpose of establishment of a constructive total loss.

This restriction upon recovery can be compared with the provisions of section 60 (1) and (2) by considering various situations, as envisaged in the Act, in order to ascertain whether there would be recovery under the L.S.D.B. Form.

The five situations can be summarised as follows:

1. *The subject-matter insured is reasonably abandoned on account of its actual total loss appearing to be unavoidable.*

2. *The subject-matter is reasonably abandoned because it could not be preserved from actual total loss without an expenditure which would exceed its value when the expenditure had been incurred.*

3. *The assured is deprived of the possession of the subject-matter by a peril insured against, and it is unlikely that he can recover the subject-matter.*

---

[35] [1970] 2 Lloyd's Rep. 365.

4. *The assured is deprived of the possession of the subject-matter by a peril insured against, and the cost of recovering the subject-matter would exceed its value when recovered.*

5. *There is damage to the subject-matter insured, and the cost of repairing the damage would exceed its value when repaired.*

1. *The subject-matter insured is reasonably abandoned on account of its actual total loss appearing to be unavoidable*

In a case to which the principles of the 1906 Act are applicable there would be a constructive total loss as a result of the opening words of section 60 (1). There would however be " no recovery " in the case of a claim under the L.S.D.B. Form unless, in addition, evidence were produced to the effect that the expense of recovery and repair exceeded the actual insured value. It would not, as this wording stands, be enough for the assured to show only that an actual total loss [36] appeared to be unavoidable.

Section 60 (1) uses the words " appearing to be unavoidable." The material time is that at which an action begins or is deemed to begin against the insurer; account is not taken of subsequent events which may make recovery more or less unlikely. As Kennedy L.J. said in *Polurrian S.S. Co. Ltd.* v. *Young*,[37]

> ". . . it is indisputable that according to the law of England in deciding upon the validity of claims of this nature between the assured and the insurer the matters must be considered as they stood on the date of the commencement of the action."

These words are particularly relevant to the validity of the notice of abandonment; the notice must be justified by the facts in existence when it is given and when the action is brought. If underwriters accept notice of abandonment the abandonment is irrevocable and the acceptance of the notice of the loss constitutes a conclusive admission of liability for the loss and of the sufficiency of the notice.[38] As a result the insurer normally refuses to accept abandonment, but it is usual in such a case for insurers to agree to put the assured in the same position as if, on the date on which they refused to accept abandonment,[39] a writ had been issued. This makes it unnecessary for legal proceedings to begin at once.

The *Polurrian* case arose out of a capture during a war between Greece and Turkey. A neutral ship, carrying a cargo of coal and insured against the consequences of hostilities or warlike operations and the risks of capture, seizure and detention and the consequences thereof or any

---

[36] *i.e.* that the subject-matter would be destroyed, or so damaged as to cease to be a thing of the kind insured, or that he would be irretrievably deprived thereof (s. 57 (1)).

[37] [1915] 1 K.B. 922 (C.A.), at pp. 927–928.

[38] s. 62 (6) of the 1906 Act.

[39] As Porter J. said in *Marstrand Fishing Co., Ltd* v. *Beer* (1936) 56 Ll.L.R. 163, at p. 173.

attempt thereat, was captured by Greek men-of-war. Her cargo was removed and used for coaling the Greek fleet, and she was detained for about six weeks. Notice of abandonment was given on October 26, 1912, the day after the capture. Warrington J.[40] said [41]:

> " The fair result of the evidence, in regard to the position on October 26, whether viewed apart from subsequent events, as I think it should be, or by the light of those events, was, in my judgment, one in which her ultimate release from capture was a matter of uncertainty . . . I am of opinion that if the present action had come to be decided before the Marine Insurance Act 1906 had come into force, the plaintiffs would have been held to have been entitled to recover upon the policy of insurance as for a constructive total loss. . . ."

He said that there was a difference between the effects of the words " reasonably abandoned on account of its actual total loss appearing to be unavoidable " in section 60 (1) and the words " it is unlikely that he can recover the ship " in section 60 (2) (i), and that the latter was the less severe test, and added [42]:

> " I think that the statute has modified the pre-existing law to the disadvantage of the assured. One is always afraid of incompleteness in attempting a definition; but I venture to say that the test of ' unlikelihood of recovery ' has now been substituted for ' uncertainty of recovery ' . . . Whence the statute derived the phrase ' unlikely that he can recover ' as expressing a necessary condition of the assured's right to recover for a constructive total loss by capture I do not know. I have referred to many of the reported capture cases, and I have been unable to find it used judicially in any of them; but there it stands in the section of the Act of Parliament; its meaning is quite clear, and therefore in the present case, to enable the plaintiffs to succeed, they must establish fully (1) that at the date of commencement of this action they were deprived of the possession of the *Polurrian;* and (2) that it was not merely quite uncertain whether they would recover her within a reasonable time, but that the balance of probability was that they could not do so."

2. The subject-matter is reasonably abandoned because it could not be preserved from actual total loss without an expenditure which would exceed its value when the expenditure had been incurred

Where the principles of the 1906 Act applied there would be a constructive total loss as a result of the second part of section 60 (1). Both this part of the subsection and clause 12 of the L.S.D.B. Form deal with the expenditure to be incurred. In the case of the subsection it is the expenditure needed to preserve the subject-matter insured from actual total loss, and in the case of clause 12 it is the expense of recovery and repairing the insured property. The express references to the cost of recovery and repair in the 1906 Act are reserved until section 60 (2) thereof. Can it be said

---

[40] Reading and adopting, as did the other member of the Court of Appeal, the judgment of Kennedy L.J., who had died.
[41] At pp. 934–935.
[42] At p. 937.

that expenditure to preserve the subject-matter insured from actual total loss (s. 60 (1)) is in any way different from the expense of recovery and repairing the insured property (cl. 12)?

It does not seem that there is any difference in the effect of these two provisions. In each case a question arises as to how much has to be spent in order to put the insured property into a condition in which it can carry out its task, whether that be a voyage or the work of a drilling unit. As Tindal C.J. said in *Benson* v. *Chapman* [43]:

> "... where the damage to the ship is so great from the perils insured against, that the owner cannot put her in a state of repair necessary for pursuing the voyage insured, except at an expense greater than the value of the ship, he is not bound to incur that expense, but is at liberty to abandon and treat the loss as a total loss."

The motive for the expenditure, or expense, may appear to be somewhat different in these two cases, even though the work done and cost incurred might be the same. In section 60 (1) the expenditure is to preserve the subject-matter " from actual total loss." Section 57 (1) says that there is an actual total loss where the subject-matter is destroyed, or so damaged as to cease to be a thing of the kind insured, or where the assured is irretrievably deprived of the subject-matter. The expenditure under consideration would therefore be that which was needed to preserve the subject-matter from destruction or from being damaged in the manner mentioned or to prevent the assured from being irretrievably deprived of it. Where the aim is recovery and repair, in the case of a drilling unit insured under the L.S.D.B. Form, it seems that the same objects are being pursued.

The expenditure needed, whether to preserve the insured subject-matter from actual total loss (s. 60 (1)) or to recover and repair the insured property (cl. 12), has in each case to be compared with another figure. In the case of section 60 (1) this is " its value when the expenditure had been incurred." Where there is an unvalued policy this means the real value of the ship when repaired. Where there is a valued policy there was in the past some doubt as to whether the insured value must be treated as the value, or whether it was still open to the parties to consider the real value. So far as the 1906 Act is concerned, the parties have a choice. Thus section 27 (4) of the Act states: " Unless the policy otherwise provides, the value fixed by the policy is not conclusive for the purpose of determining whether there has been a constructive total loss." The " value when the expenditure had been incurred " (s. 60 (1)) might not, in the absence of any provision to the contrary, be the same as " the actual insured value " (cl. 12). In practice, however, a different effect is achieved as a result of the application of clause 17 of the Institute Time Clauses (Hulls). This states:

---

[43] (1843) 6 M. & Gr. 792, at p. 810.

Clause 12: Constructive Total Loss

" In ascertaining whether the Vessel is a constructive total loss the insured value shall be taken as the repaired value and nothing in respect of the damaged or break-up value of the Vessel or wreck shall be taken into account. No claim for constructive total loss based upon the cost of recovery and/or repair of the Vessel shall be recoverable hereunder unless such cost would exceed the insured value."

The effect of clause 17 of the Institute Time Clauses (Hulls), the Valuation Clause, is to bring together the expressions " value when the expenditure had been incurred " in section 60 (1) of the 1906 Act, and " the actual insured value," in clause 12 of the L.S.D.B. Form. Consideration of the actual market value after the expenditure is ignored in the case of a ship insured with the Institute Time Clauses (Hulls) attached to the policy. In both cases the yardstick, against which the cost of repairs and replacement is compared, is the insured value. As a result it is easier to say whether there is a constructive total loss than if it were necessary to establish the repaired value. Indeed in the case of a drilling unit it is possible that the parties might encounter special difficulties if it were necessary for them to establish a value. In the case of a property built for or used in a special trade there may not be a market of the type open to one who wishes to sell a ship, though of course different considerations will apply where the ship is highly specialised. The use by the 1906 Act of the word " value " in section 60 (1) rather than the term " market value " may be specially appropriate to such a situation. As Wood V.-C. said in *African Steam Ship Co.* v. *Swanzy* [44]:

" A particular class of ship might be adapted for one particular description of traffic and for that alone, and that description of traffic might be entirely occupied by one company with which it might be hopeless to compete so that there would be no market for a ship of that particular description. If such a case should ever occur, it would be necessary for the court to adopt some other criterion. One, I venture to suggest, might be to ascertain the price given for the ship and the subsequent deterioration."

It may be important to distinguish between the absence of a market and a decline in the quality of the market. If there were an abundance of drilling units or decline in the demand for them, so that the market price dropped severely, only a scrap value being obtainable, then that value would have to be taken as the test. If, however, the drilling unit was very highly specialised and could only be used in one particular area or in one particular way, so that there was not a market in the ordinary sense of the word, an alternative test, such as the purchase price subject to deterioration, or depreciation, would have to be adopted. Where a drilling unit was insured on the L.S.D.B. Form, however, clause 12 would operate so that the criterion would be " the actual insured value." If it were insured in accordance with the Institute Time Clauses (Hulls), clause 17 would cause " the insured value " to be " taken as the repaired value." It is only in the event that the insurance of the drilling unit was not subject to provisions

---

[44] (1856) 2 K. & J. 660, at p. 664.

of this sort, and that there were not a market value available in order to show the true value, that it would be necessary to apply a test of the type indicated above.

3. *The assured is deprived of the possession of the subject-matter by a peril insured against, and it is unlikely that he can recover the subject-matter*

This is the situation envisaged in section 60 (2) (i) of the 1906 Act, as alternative (a). It has been pointed out [45] that an earlier draft of the Marine Insurance Bill contained the word " uncertain " instead of " unlikely." The change to " unlikely " made the task of the assured more difficult. It is harder to show that recovery is " unlikely " than to show that it is " uncertain."

Thus in *Polurrian S.S. Co. Ltd.* v. *Young* [46] it was held that the ship-owners had failed to show, on the balance of probabilities, that the ship would not be recovered in a reasonable time. It was said that the 1906 Act had altered the previously existing common law to the detriment of the assured by the insertion of the word " unlikely." So also in *Marstrand Fishing Co. Ltd.* v. *Beer* [47] the recovery of the ship was uncertain but not unlikely, and the assured failed to establish that there was a constructive total loss.

In that case a fishing ship, the " *Girl Pat*," left Grimsby to fish in the North Sea on April 2, 1936 called at Dover on April 3, and was not heard of for six weeks, when she put in at Corcubion, in Spain, the Master and men having taken possession of her. Meanwhile, on April 28, notice of abandonment had been given to the underwriters, who did not accept it, but agreed to place the owners in the same position as if a writ had been issued on that date. When news was received of the arrival in Spain the owners issued a second notice, purporting to amend the notice of abandonment so that the ship should be treated as abandoned on the ground of the barratry [47a] of the Master. As to whether there had been a constructive total loss at the time of the original notice, Porter J. cited the test set out in *Polurrian S.S. Co. Ltd.* v. *Young*,[48] saying [49] that it was:

> " Is the recovery of the vessel unlikely? It is also, I think, conceded—and at any rate, it has been determined by the *Polurrian* case—that ' unlikely ' means that the balance of probabilities is against the vessel being recovered and also that the person to whom it must appear that the vessel is unlikely to be recovered is not the individual concerned, but is the reasonable man.

---

[45] Chalmers, *Marine Insurance Act* 1906 (8th ed., 1976), p. 86.
[46] (1913) 19 Com.Cas. 143; [1915] 1 K.B. 922 (C.A.); see above, p. 144.
[47] (1936) 56 Ll.L.Rep. 163.
[47a] " The term ' barratry ' includes every wrongful act wilfully committed by the master or crew to the prejudice of the owner, or, as the case may be, of the charterer" ; r. 11, Rules for Construction of Policy, Sched. 1, Marine Insurance Act, 1906. The definition is not exhaustive; see also Arnould, *op. cit.* at § 836.
[48] [1915] 1 K.B. (C.A.), 922; see above, p. 144.
[49] At p. 173.

But that leaves the question: By what information must the person concerned judge? "

He said that the "particular instance" in section 60 (2) of the 1906 Act [50] would seem to point to the true facts being the criterion:

"If that be an accurate view, the word 'appears' is used because the future of the vessel is still unknown and her loss must still be described as appearing unavoidable since certainty can never be predicated of the future."

The example given above, as set out in section 60 (2) (i) of the 1906 Act, as alternative (a), may be compared with the wording of clause 12 of the L.S.D.B. Form. It seems, as a matter of language, that it would not be enough for the owner of the drilling unit to establish only the deprivation of possession and the unlikelihood that he could recover the subject-matter. He may prove both these matters, but the express words of clause 12 are that there shall be no recovery unless the expense of recovery and repair exceed the actual insured value. How are these words to be applied to a situation in which, for example, the drilling unit has stranded, in a place which it is difficult to reach, in such a way that the assured will be unlikely to be able to recover it? It is assumed for the purpose of the example that it cannot be said that he has been "irretrievably deprived" of the drilling unit, because, if he were to be, there would be an actual total loss, as that term is defined in section 57 (1) of the 1906 Act.[51] It may, in the nature of the casualty itself, be impossible to produce evidence as to the "expense of recovering and repairing the insured property." If no tug or helicopter is able to reach her, so as to put on board surveyors and others who can give estimates as to the cost of repairs, the assured may be unable to produce adequate evidence of these matters. On the other hand, it would seem unreasonable that he should be denied the right to recover in respect of such a constructive total loss, the casualty being one which in every respect conforms to the requirements of that part of section 60 (2) (i) which has been quoted.

A solution may be found in the following way. The effect of the relevant part of clause 12 of the L.S.D.B. Form, with its reference to the actual insured value rather than to the repaired value, is the same, as has been shown,[52] as that of the "Valuation" clause [53] in the Institute Time Clauses (Hulls). It is therefore applicable to a situation in which the issue between the assured and the insurers is as to the amount of expenditure which will be involved. In the case of an attempt to establish a constructive total loss, to which the principles of the 1906 Act apply, such

---

[50] As to whether this is a "particular instance" of s. 60 (1) or a separate provision, see above, p. 142.

[51] "Where the subject-matter insured is destroyed, or so damaged as to cease to be a thing of the kind insured, or where the assured is irretrievably deprived thereof, there is an actual total loss."

[52] See above, p. 147.

[53] cl. 17.

consideration of the expenditure which may be incurred is relevant only to certain aspects of a constructive total loss. Part of section 60 (1), part of section 60 (2) (i), and all of section 60 (2) (ii) are concerned with the question of expenditure. The other part of section 60 (1) relates to the apparent unavoidability of an actual total loss, and the other part of section 60 (2) (i) deals with deprivation of possession of the property insured and a resultant unlikelihood that the assured can recover it.

So far as the principles of marine insurance, as set out in the 1906 Act, can be applied here,[54] it seems unlikely, as a matter of construction, that it was intended that the reference to expense in clause 12 of the L.S.D.B. Form was intended to have the effect that it excluded these other methods of establishing that there was a constructive total loss. On the contrary, it seems more likely that it was intended that the words in clause 12 should refer only to the cases mentioned; the possibility of establishing a constructive total loss by other means, where the expense of recovery and repair is not relevant, would then be unaffected. Jenkins L.J., in *Sethia (K.C.) (1944) Ltd.* v. *Partabmull Rameshwar,*[55] said:

> " I do not think that the court will read a term into a contract unless, considering the matter from the point of view of business efficacy, it is clear beyond a peradventure that both parties intended a given term to operate, although they did not include it in so many words."

4. *The assured is deprived of the possession of the subject-matter by a peril insured against, and the cost of recovering the subject-matter would exceed its value when recovered*

This is the situation envisaged in section 60 (2) (i) of the 1906 Act, as alternative (b). If this arose in the case of a drilling unit, and the insurance was subject to clause 12 of the L.S.D.B. Form, then it seems that a similar solution would result, and there would be a constructive total loss. Section 60 (2) (i) has as a criterion the " cost of recovering the ship," and clause 12 refers to the " expense of recovering and repairing the insured property." Although there is no reference to " repairing " in section 60 (2) (i), the word appears in section 60 (2) (ii).[56] The meaning of the expression " value when recovered " in the 1906 Act has been discussed above,[57] when it was also noted that clause 17 [57a] of the Institute Time Clauses (Hulls) provides, where it is being ascertained whether the ship is a constructive total loss, that the insured value should be taken as the repaired value. Indeed the second sentence of clause 17 uses almost the same words as those of clause 12 of the L.S.D.B. Form, in that it says:

---

[54] As to this, see Appendix C below, at p. 456.

[55] [1950] 1 All E.R. 51 (C.A.) at p. 59. The case concerned the export of jute from India to Genoa, and the sellers in Calcutta argued, unsuccessfully, that there should be implied in the sale contract a term that the shipments were " subject to quota," *i.e.* the quota fixed by the Indian government. The House of Lords affirmed the decision; [1951] 2 All E.R. 352.

[56] See above, p. 142.

[57] See p. 147, above.   [57a] Known as the Valuation Clause.

" No claim for constructive total loss based upon the cost of recovery and/or repair of the Vessel shall be recoverable hereunder unless such cost would exceed the insured value."

5. *There is damage to the subject-matter insured, and the cost of repairing the damage would exceed its value when repaired*

This is the situation envisaged in section 60 (2) (ii) of the 1906 Act. It is similar to that set out in the fourth proposition above, [58] except that the prerequisite condition here is that there be damage to the subject-matter rather than that the assured be deprived of possession thereof, and also that this subsection deals with the cost of repair and not the cost of recovery. If these facts occurred in the case of a drilling unit, and the insurance was subject to clause 12 of the L.S.D.B. Form, then the assured would be able to recover in respect of a constructive total loss.

" *In no case shall Underwriters be liable for unrepaired damage in addition to a subsequent Total Loss sustained during the period covered by this insurance.*"

This is the second sentence of clause 12 of the L.S.D.B. Form; it so closely resembles clause 16 of the Institute Time Clauses (Hulls) in dealing with the problem of successive losses that the latter must be quoted here:

" In no case shall the Underwriters be liable for unrepaired damage in addition to a subsequent total loss sustained during the period covered by this Policy or any extension thereof under Clause 4." [59]

The L.S.D.B. Form in this respect therefore excludes certain cover in terms exactly similar to those set out in a policy governed by clause 16 of the Institute Time Clauses (Hulls). Both clauses reflect the principles of common law, as set out in section 77 of the 1906 Act. At common law the insurer was liable for successive losses, even though the total amount of the losses exceeded the sum insured, unless the policy provided to the contrary, or unless there was a partial loss, which had not been repaired or made good, followed by a total loss. As a result section 77 (1) of the Act states: " Unless the policy otherwise provides, and subject to the provisions of this Act, the insurer is liable for successive losses, even though the total amount of such losses may exceed the sum insured." Thus in *Le Cheminant* v. *Pearson* [60] a ship was damaged in port at Jersey, before sailing, and the damage was repaired. Later she was captured; in his action in respect of a total loss by capture the assured claimed for the repair expenses under the sue and labour clause in the policy. It was held that he could recover under both heads.

---

[58] See p. 150, above.

[59] cl. 4 of the Institute Time Clauses (Hulls) provides for a ship to be held covered at a *pro rata* monthly premium to her port of destination if at the expiration of the policy she is at sea or in distress or at a port of refuge or of call, provided that previous notice is given to the underwriters. [60] (1812) 4 Taunt. 367.

As Lord Abinger said in *Brooks* v. *MacDonnell* [61]:

> " It is clear that wherever the underwriter adjusts a partial loss, he still remains liable on the policy, and may go on paying partial losses exceeding in the whole cent. per cent., and may ultimately have to pay a total loss of cent. per cent. Such a case is possible."

The situation is different where the partial loss has not been repaired or otherwise made good. Section 77 (2) of the Act states:

> " Where under the same policy, a partial loss, which has not been repaired or otherwise made good, is followed by a total loss, the assured can only recover in respect of the total loss:
> Provided that nothing in this section shall affect the liability of the insurer under the suing and labouring clause."

The principle that unrepaired damage is merged into a subsequent total loss was established in *Livie* v. *Janson*,[62] where a ship left New York by night in order to escape an American embargo. She stranded on Governor's Island, where the crew deserted, and was seized by the United States government and condemned by it for breach of the embargo. The policy contained an exclusion clause: " warranted free from American condemnation." It was held that the assured could not recover for a total loss for the condemnation as that was excluded by the policy; and that he could not recover for the damage suffered because the damage had become irrelevant, in view of the total loss. The underlying principle, therefore, is that the assured suffered no damage, as he had neither repaired the ship nor suffered a diminution in value.

So also in *The Dora Forster*,[63] where a particular average loss was succeeded by a total loss, the owners were held to be properly indemnified by being paid for the total loss. Damage sustained on an outward voyage was repaired at the loading port, and the underwriters made a payment on account. The charterers had paid for the repairs and obtained from the Master a draft, which they insured, and which pledged the ship for repayment on safe arrival at the port of discharge. After the total loss of the ship on the homeward voyage, and payment for the total loss by the underwriters, the owners claimed against them for the balance of the particular average loss. In rejecting the claim, Gorell Barnes J. held that the shipowners could not recover as they were never personally liable for the cost of the repairs and had sustained no loss, the amount of the draft (on the loss of the ship) having been paid to the charterers by their insurers. He said that the underwriters were entitled to a return of the amount paid on account, and added [64]:

> " . . . the master at the port of shipment, when he was arranging for these repairs to be done, arranged with the parties that they should be liquidated in the same way as the ordinary disbursements were going to be liquidated,

---

61 (1835) 1 Y. & C. 500, at p. 515.
63 [1900] P. 241.
62 (1810) 12 East 648.
64 *Ibid.* at pp. 248 to 250.

and I think he carried out the transaction in such a way that the owners of the ship never became liable to pay for the cost of these repairs . . . there was never a loss for which the owners of this ship could make any claim."

The principle set out in the second sentence of clause 12 of the L.S.D.B. Form is thus the same as that established at common law and set out in section 77 (2) of the 1906 Act. The subsection uses the words " Where under the same policy . . .," so that in the case of policies governed by the 1906 Act, or incorporating clause 16 of the Institute Time Clauses (Hulls) it would be possible for the assured to recover, under different policies, for a partial loss, not repaired or otherwise made good, and a total loss. This would appear to be inconsistent with the underlying theory that the assured should not be able to recover as he has suffered no loss in respect of the partial loss. In *Lidgett* v. *Secretan* [65] an assured had two policies in respect of his ship, one of which covered her from London to Calcutta and the other from Calcutta to London. After being damaged on a reef on the outward voyage she was put into dry dock at Calcutta to be repaired. Some of the repairs had been carried out, and the first policy had expired, when she caught fire and was destroyed. It was held that the assured could recover the full amounts of the partial loss, including the unrepaired element, under the first policy, and of the total loss, under the second policy. The same insurer was, in the event, liable under each policy, but it was held that this was not material. The decision can be reconciled with the general rule that the partial loss is merged with the total loss, because there were two policies. At the expiry of the policy covering the ship from London to Calcutta the liability thereunder could be and had to be determined. As Lord Campbell said in *Knight* v. *Faith* [66]:

" The partial loss must be calculated on the same principles as if she had actually been repaired and proceeded on her voyage, or had foundered at sea without being repaired, soon after the policy expired."

In *Knight* v. *Faith* a ship stranded and was brought into Santa Cruz one week before her insurance expired. She was found to be so badly damaged that the necessary repairs could not be done at Santa Cruz; nor could she be taken to any port where she could prudently have been repaired. She was then sold. It was held that the partial loss by stranding caused an actual prejudice to the assured. That partial loss was not merged in the final loss resulting from the sale, even assuming that to have been a total loss necessarily consequent upon the stranding, since the total loss was one for which the insurers were not liable. As Lord Campbell said [67]:

" The insurers on a ship, if they pay a total loss, certainly are not liable likewise in respect of any prior partial loss which has not been repaired;

---

[65] (1871) L.R. 6 C.P. 616.
[66] (1850) 15 Q.B. 649, at p. 669.

[67] At pp. 668 to 670.

and, if a total loss occurs from which they are exempt, they are not liable for any prior partial loss which in that event does not prove prejudicial to the assured."

Clause 13: Sue and Labour Expense

CLAUSE 13: SUE AND LABOUR EXPENSE

(a) It is further agreed that should the property insured hereunder suffer loss or damage covered under the terms of this insurance, it shall be lawful and necessary for the Assured, their Factors, Servants and Assigns, to sue, labour and travel for, in and about the Defence, Safeguard and Recovery of the said property, or any part thereof, without prejudice to this insurance, and subject always to the terms, conditions, limitations and exclusions of this insurance, the charges thereof shall be borne by the Underwriters. And it is especially declared and agreed that no acts of the Underwriters or Assured in recovering, saving or preserving the property insured shall be considered as a waiver or acceptance of abandonment.

(b) The Underwriters' liability for Sue and Labour Expenses shall not exceed 25 % of the insured value of the item(s) in the Defence, Safeguard or Recovery of which such expense is incurred.

The comparable clause in the 1960 L.S.D.B. Form (cl. 17) states:

(a) In case of loss or damage it shall be lawful and necessary for the Assured, their Factors, Servants and Assigns, to sue, labour and travel for, in, and about the Defence, Safeguard and Recovery of the property insured, or any part thereof, without prejudice to this insurance; such expenses to be borne by Underwriters subject to the terms and conditions of this certificate or policy and it is expressly understood and agreed that no acts of the Underwriters or Assured in recovering, saving or preserving the property insured shall be considered as a waiver or acceptance of abandonment.

(b) In consideration of the rate at which this insurance is written, it is a condition of this insurance that Underwriters shall not be liable for foam solutions nor other fire extinguishing materials, lost, expended, or destroyed in fighting fire, blowout or cratering nor for any other expense incidental to fighting fire, controlling, or attempting to control blowout or cratering.

It is further understood and agreed that the Underwriters shall not be liable for charges incurred by the Assured in connection with removal of material and debris formerly an insured part of the property, whether such removal be required by any valid law or ordinance or otherwise.

The first paragraph in each case is in almost exactly the same terms. The second paragraph in the 1972 L.S.D.B. Form is an innovation. As was stated earlier in connection with the " Limit of Liability " clause, it can be hard to say whether sue and labour expenses were incurred to save the well or the drilling unit. The value of the well may far exceed that of the unit. It was thought prudent to introduce a 25 per cent. limitation. As for the second paragraph in the 1960 Form this contains exceptions, as to (i) materials used to deal with fire, blowout and cratering, and (ii) removal of material and debris, which appear in the 1972 Form list of exclusions, in Clause 8, at (d) and (i) respectively.

Clause 13: Sue and Labour Expense

The Lloyd's S.G. Policy also contains a Sue and Labour Clause:

And in case of any loss or misfortune it shall be lawful to the assured, their factors, servants and assigns, to sue, labour, and travel for, in and about the defence, safeguards, and recovery of the said goods and merchandises, and ship, etc., or any part thereof, without prejudice to this insurance; to the charges whereof we, the assurers, will contribute each one according to the rate and quantity of his sum herein assured.

There is no 25 per cent. limit in the Institute Time Clauses (Hulls), Clause 9 (a) of which states, in part:

In the event of expenses being incurred pursuant to the Suing and Labouring Clause, the liability under this Policy shall not exceed the proportion of such expenses that the amount insured hereunder bears to the value of the Vessel as stated herein, or to the sound value of the Vessel at the time of the occurrence giving rise to the expenditure if the sound value exceeds that value.

So also section 78 (1) of the Marine Insurance Act 1906, states:

Where the policy contains a suing and labouring clause, the engagement thereby entered into is deemed to be supplementary to the contract of insurance, and the assured may recover from the insurer any expenses properly incurred pursuant to the clause, notwithstanding that the insurer may have paid for a total loss, or that the subject-matter may have been warranted free from particular average, either wholly or under a certain percentage.

Clause 14: Lay Up and Cancellation

Time policies usually provide for the assured to receive a return of premium when the insured property is not exposed to risk or is exposed to a lesser degree of risk than would be normal. A minimum period is usually stipulated. A ship is said to lay up, or to be laid up, during such a period.

The L.S.D.B. Form, at clause 14, begins:

" LAY UP AND CANCELLATION:
To return daily pro rata of rates to be agreed by Underwriters for any period of 30 or more consecutive days the vessel may be laid up in port unemployed."

The 1960 L.S.D.B. Form, in its " Lay Up " clause (clause 24), has similar opening words, but sets out the rates of return:

" To return daily pro rata of the following annual rates for any period of 30 or more consecutive days the vessel may be laid up in port unemployed:
(a) . . . per cent. per annum net whilst not under repair.
(b) . . . per cent. per annum whilst under repair.
(c) . . . per cent. per annum whilst under repair (subject to no major repairs involving raising and lowering tests being carried out)."

In the 1972 Form various provisos are then made,[68] and the effect of a laid up return when there are two policies is also considered.[69]

---

[68] See below, p. 158.
[69] See below, p. 162.

The *Concise Oxford Dictionary* defines " lay up " as " put (ship) out of commission." The words " laid up in port " were considered in *North Shipping Co.* v. *Union Marine Insurance Co.*,[70] where a ship spent two months within a port after war broke out but kept steam up and was occasionally shifted so that she could coal British naval ships. The policy stated: " To return . . . for each consecutive 30 days the vessel may be laid up in port " [71] [the rate of return was then stated]. It was held that unless there was a customary meaning to the contrary she was not " laid up in port." Bray J. found that here a customary meaning attached to the words in that insurers were liable generally to make a return while she was loading and discharging, entering dock for repairs and being repaired. He said [72]:

> " It had gone on so long and so continuously that I think it ought to be taken that before April, 1914, these words had a customary meaning, which imposed on them [the underwriters] a legal liability to pay when ships were in port performing these operations in the ordinary way."

He held, however, that such a customary meaning did not extend those words to cover a ship while she was engaged in the hazardous operation of discharging coal into naval ships, and that in this case there was no right to a return. The Court of Appeal affirmed his judgment.[73]

In the case of a drilling unit, therefore, the interpretation thus given of the words " laid up in port " might be thought to allow a return, even where some work was being done, if such a customary meaning were attached to the words. The words do not stand on their own in clause 14, however, for they are followed by the word " unemployed." Whether or not the unit owners were receiving hire, or a reduced rate of hire, there would be no return if the unit was performing any task for the operators while in port. If the unit were shifted, as the ship was shifted in the *North Shipping Co.* case [74] it would not be treated as being laid up, as proviso (d) in clause 14 excludes shifts.[75]

If the drilling unit is laid up in anticipation of its being sold, or after a contract of sale but before delivery, the same rules will govern the right to a return. There are no words in clause 14 which refer to the sale of the unit. In *Hunter* v. *Wright* [76] the time policy allowed " a return of premium if sold or laid up for every uncommenced month." The ship was laid up for several months during the policy year and then re-employed. It was held that in that particular context the words " sold or laid up " had to be read together, so that there was only a return if there was a permanent laying up of the kind which would occur if the ship had been sold.

---

[70] (1918) 24 Com.Cas. 83; and (1919) 24 Com.Cas. 161 (C.A.).
[71] The judge said, at p. 87: " I think the evidence showed that this was an old institute clause, at least 40 or 50 years old. . . ."
[72] At p. 88. [73] (1919) 24 Com.Cas. 161.
[74] See above, on this page. [75] See below, p. 160.
[76] (1830) 10 B. & Cr. 714.

Clause 14: Lay Up and Cancellation

So far as clause 14 of the 1972 L.S.D.B. Form is concerned the rate of return is a matter to be agreed by the insurers. The comparable provision in the Institute Time Clauses (Hulls) is in clause 21, the first part of which states:

> " TO RETURN AS FOLLOWS:
> . . . per cent. for each uncommenced month if this Policy be cancelled by agreement . . . and for each period of 30 consecutive days the Vessel may be laid up in a port or in a lay-up area provided such port or lay-up area is approved by the Underwriters (with special liberties as hereinafter allowed):—
> (a) . . . per cent. net not under repair
> (b) . . . per cent. net under repair.
> If the Vessel is under repair during part only of a period for which a return is claimable, the return payable shall be calculated pro-rata to the number of days under (a) and (b) respectively.[77]

The section of clause 21 of the Institute Time Clauses (Hulls) which deals with laying up thus contains a provision as to a minimum period of 30 days which is similar to that in clause 14 of the 1972 L.S.D.B. Form.[78] Clause 21 refers to the Vessel being laid up " in a port or in a lay-up area," but clause 14 says only " in port." The former words would cover a lay-up in a place other than a port. Such a place might be used at any time for laying up but in times of depression in the shipping industry, when there is considerable demand for places in which to lay up ships, the extended wording is particularly appropriate. In the case of each form of policy the first proviso [79] ensures that the port (and also the place other than a port, in the case of the Institute Time Clauses (Hulls)) should be one which is satisfactory to the insurers.

Clause 14 envisages a situation in which the unit is " laid up in port unemployed." Though the word " unemployed " is not used in the corresponding part of clause 21, proviso (ii) thereof deals with the effect of certain types of work upon the entitlement to a laid-up return:

> " (ii) loading or discharging operations or the presence of cargo on board shall not debar returns but no return shall be allowed for any period during which the Vessel is being used for the storage of cargo."

Such a provision would have been inappropriate in the case of a drilling unit as it is not involved in the operations usually undertaken by most ships, which are the carriage of cargo from one place to another for reward. The proviso has the same effect as the word " unemployed " in clause 14, however, in that the right to a return is lost if the vessel is being used to store cargo. In such a case her owners would normally be receiving remuneration from the cargo interests, and the ship could be said to be employed, if only as a floating warehouse.

---

[77] For the words " and arrival," which appear alongside these words, see p. 160, below.
[78] And to cl. 24 of the 1960 L.S.D.B. Form; see above, p. 155.
[79] See below, p. 159.

Manner of Returns of Premium

Clause 14 of the 1972 L.S.D.B. Form does not provide for the manner in which a laid-up return is to be made.[80] Under the Marine Insurance Act 1906, although the broker is directly liable to the insurer for the payment of the premium, the insurer is under a direct liability to the assured for its return. Section 53 of the Act, which is headed " Policy effected through broker," states, at subsection (1):

> " Unless otherwise agreed, where a marine policy is effected on behalf of the assured by a broker, the broker is directly responsible to the insurer for the premium, and the insurer is directly responsible to the assured for the amount which may be payable in respect of returnable premium."

In similar terms, section 82 of the Act, which is headed " Enforcement of return," states:

> " Where the premium, or a proportionate part thereof, is, by this Act, declared to be returnable,—[81]
> (a) If already paid, it may be recovered by the assured from the insurer; and,
> (b) If unpaid, it may be retained by the assured or his agent."

So far as an insurance of a drilling unit is governed by the Marine Insurance Act 1906, the insurer is both entitled and liable [82] in the absence of an amendment to the L.S.D.B. Form to the contrary, to reimburse or credit the assured direct.

Provisos as to Laid-Up Returns

The provisos to the stipulation for laid-up returns in clause 14 of the L.S.D.B. Form are set out as follows:

> " Provided always that:—
> (a) the location shall be approved by a surveyor appointed by Lloyd's Agent or approved by Underwriters.
> (b) there shall always be a watchman on board.
> (c) no return shall be allowed in the event of the vessel becoming an actual or constructive or compromised or arranged total loss during the currency of this insurance.
> (d) there shall be no shifts during the lay up period.
> (e) there shall be no movement of legs or variation in buoyancy during the lay up period.
> (f) in the event of any amendment of the annual rate, the rates of return shall be adjusted accordingly."

Provisos (a) to (c), but not provisos (d) to (f), appear in the 1960 Form.

---

[80] Addendum 48 to the Drilling Rig Memorandum sets out minimum retentions required by underwriters. These depend upon the area, the type of drilling unit, and the time of year.

[81] As in s. 83, which says that the premium, or, as the case may be, a proportionate part thereof, is returnable where the policy contains a stipulation for the return of the premium, or a proportionate part thereof, on the happening of a certain event, and that event happens; cl. 14 of the L.S.D.B. Form defines the event.

[82] ss. 53 (1) and 82 of the Act.

Proviso (a) " the location shall be approved by a surveyor appointed by Lloyd's Agent or approved by Underwriters " [83]

This proviso is similar in its object to the provision in clause 21 of the Institute Time Clauses (Hulls), that it be a " port or lay-up area approved by the Underwriters (with special liberties as hereinafter allowed)." The location, which, as we have seen,[84] is " in port " in the case of the L.S.D.B. Form, is subject to approval by a surveyor appointed by Lloyd's Agent or approved by underwriters. This is virtually the same as, but somewhat wider than, the approval required in clause 21; in practice there would be no difference as (a) a surveyor appointed by Lloyd's Agent is extremely unlikely to approve of a location of which the insurers would not approve; and (b) the approval by underwriters, to which the Institute Time Clauses (Hulls) is theoretically limited, would in many cases consist of their giving their approval to a place accepted by a Lloyd's Agent's surveyor.

The " special liberties as hereinafter allowed," to which clause 21 of. the Institute Time Clauses (Hulls) refers, are expressed in the words:

> " provided the Underwriters agree that such non-approved lay-up area is deemed to be within the vicinity of the approved port or lay-up area, days during which the Vessel is laid up in such non-approved lay-up area may be added to days in the approved port or lay-up area to calculate a period of 30 consecutive days and a return shall be allowed for the proportion of such period during which the Vessel is actually laid up in the approved port or lay-up area."

The effect of this proviso is that a period in a " non-approved lay-up area " which is agreed by the underwriters to be within the vicinity of an approved port or lay-up area can count towards the minimum of 30 consecutive days needed to entitle the assured to a laid-up return. It does not, however, entitle him to a return in respect of the days in the non-approved area. If, for example, the ship passed 10 days in the non-approved area and then 20 days in the approved port or lay-up area, the entitlement to a return would arise, but only in respect of 20 days.

There are no similar " special liberties " in clause 14 of the L.S.D.B Form, so that no return is due unless there have been 30 consecutive days in a port approved in the manner prescribed.

Proviso (b) " there shall always be a watchman on board " [85]

There is no such requirement in the case of clause 21 of the Institute Time Clauses (Hulls).

---

[83] Proviso 1 to cl. 24 of the 1960 L.S.D.B. Form states: " That the location shall be approved by a surveyor appointed by Lloyd's Agents or approved by Underwriters."

[84] See above, p. 157.

[85] Proviso 2 to cl. 24 of the 1960 L.S.D.B. Form states: "That there shall always be a watchman on board."

Proviso (c) " no return shall be allowed in the event of the vessel becoming an actual or constructive or compromised or arranged total loss during the currency of this insurance " [86]

The expression " actual or constructive or compromised or arranged total loss " is also used in clauses 3 [87] and 7 [88] of the L.S.D.B. Form. The proviso that there shall be no return of premium if such an event occurs " during the currency " of the insurance appears to apply whether or not the loss occurs during the laid up period. Thus a drilling unit might, it seems, be laid up in such a way as to qualify for a return, go back to its area of operations, and then be lost. Provided that the events took place during the currency ot the insurance, which would usually last for 12 months, there would be no entitlement to a laid-up return.

The comparable provision in the Institute Time Clauses (Hulls) is encapsulated in the words " and arrival " set out in the margin, at the side of clause 21 thereof. [89] The effect of those words is that the entitlement to a laid-up return is subject to the proviso that the ship is not totally lost during the currency of the policy, whether the loss results from an insured peril or not. She may be laid up and then lost, as in the example given below; alternatively she may be lost, whether actually or constructively, so that a period elapses between the loss and the time when the policy was to expire. In neither event would there be a return of premium.

The effect of proviso (c) in clause 14 of the L.S.D.B. Form is thus the same as that of the words " and arrival " in clause 21 of the Institute Time Clauses (Hulls), so far as laid-up returns are concerned. A material difference is that proviso (c) relates only to the laid-up returns in respect of the drilling unit, whereas the words " and arrival " apply to laid-up returns and to returns for cancellation by agreement.

Proviso (d) " there shall be no shifts during the lay-up period " [90]

The decision in *North Shipping Co.* v. *Union Marine Insurance Co.* [91] shows that where a ship is shifted it is not treated as being laid up for the purpose of laid-up returns under a marine insurance policy. The insertion of proviso (d) in clause 14 of the L.S.D.B. Form makes clear what might otherwise have to be implied if the insurance was not regarded as covered by the principles of marine insurance. If a drilling unit is shifted during a period in which it is otherwise " laid up in port unemployed," the time

---

[86] Proviso 3 to cl. 24 of the 1960 L.S.D.B. Form states. " No return shall be allowed in the event of vessel becoming a Total Loss, Constructive Total Loss, Arranged or Compromised Total Loss during the currency of this certificate or policy."

[87] Loss paid not to reduce amount of insurance except in the case of such a loss; see above, p. 90.

[88] Deductible not to apply in the case of a loss; see above, p. 124.

[89] See also above, p. 157 and n. 7.

[90] There is no comparable proviso in the 1960 L.S.D.B. Form.

[91] (1918) 24 Com.Cas. 83; and (1919) 24 Com.Cas. 161 (C.A.); the facts are set out above, at p. 156.

taken in shifting would not count as laid-up time, and would have the effect of interrupting what could otherwise count as a " period of 30 or more consecutive days."

Proviso (e) " there shall be no movement of legs or variation in buoyancy during the lay-up period "

Movements of legs and variations in buoyancy are, like shifts, regarded as physical alterations of position which prevent the drilling unit from being treated as laid up.

Proviso (f) " in the event of any amendment of the annual rate, the rates of return shall be adjusted accordingly " [92]

The return due to the assured has been stated, in the opening words of clause 14 of the L.S.D.B. Form, to be " daily pro rata of rates to be agreed." If the drilling unit was laid up for six months and the rate of return was x per cent., then the assured would receive a return in the proportion of $(x \% \times \frac{183}{365})$ of the annual premium. The annual premium may itself be changed as a result of an amendment to the rate charged. If, for example, it is reduced, the insurers would not necessarily wish to give the same return, in view of their own requirements as to such matters as minimum reinsurance and administrative costs. In such a case proviso (f) gives them the right to adjust the rate of return which would otherwise apply.

A similar provision appears in clause 21 of the Institute Time Clauses (Hulls), in proviso (iii): " in the event of a return for special trade or any other reason being recoverable, the above rates of return of premium shall be reduced accordingly." The effect of that proviso is that a reduced rate of return would apply when, for example, the ship was engaged in a special trade. Though the lower rate of return would doubtless be specified, the words in proviso (iii) make it clear that the rates of return set out at the beginning of clause 21 would not apply.

A particular provision for the return applicable where a ship was engaged in a special trade was considered in *Gorsedd S.S. Co. Ltd.* v. *Forbes.*[93] A ship was insured for 12 months at eight guineas per cent., " returning 21s. per cent. should the vessel be employed in the Eastern trade during the whole currency of this policy." The ship was employed only in Eastern trade but became a total loss before the 12 months expired. Though she had not been in the Eastern trade for the whole 12 months, she had satisfied the provision until the moment of loss. It was held that the " whole currency " of the policy ended with the loss and that the return was due. Bigham J. said [94]:

---

[92] There is no comparable provision in the 1960 L.S.D.B. Form.
[93] (1900) 5 Com.Cas. 413.
[94] At pp. 414 to 415.

" The risk no longer exists after the ship is lost; the amount insured is immediately payable, and, being paid, the policy, and all obligations created by it, are at an end; the policy is no longer in any sense current. . . . If the provision was intended to bear the construction contended for by the defendant [the insurer], it would have been simple to have used the words ' during the whole twelve months.' The words ' during the whole currency of this policy ' were, in my opinion, used because it was contemplated that the policy might cease to be current before the twelve months ran out."

In the case of a drilling unit the same principle would doubtless apply, in the absence of words to the contrary, so that it would not be necessary for the full 12 months or other period for which the policy was made to run, for the assured to receive the specified return.

" The return for a laid-up period of 30 or more consecutive days which fall on two policies effected for the same Assured shall be apportioned over both policies on a daily pro rata basis " [95]

This part of clause 14 of the L.S.D.B. Form applies where the assured is covered by two successive policies in respect of the same drilling unit, and would not, in the absence of other words, qualify for a laid-up return by virtue of the minimum period of 30 consecutive days having been achieved in neither case. The period of lay-up may extend over, for example, 30 days of which the first 15 days are covered by the first policy and the second 15 days by the second policy. The assured would in such a case receive a return in an equal amount from each insurer.

The comparable provision in the Institute Time Clauses (Hulls) is set out in greater detail in clause 21 thereof:

" In the event of any return recoverable under this clause being based on 30 consecutive days which fall on successive policies, effected for the same Assured, this Policy shall only be liable for an amount calculated at pro-rata of the period rates (a) and/or (b) above [96] for the number of days which come within the period of this Policy and to which a return is actually applicable.[97] Such overlapping period shall run, at the option of the Assured, either from the first day on which the Vessel is laid up or the first day of a period of 30 consecutive days as provided under (a) or (b) or (i) [98] above."

There is no provision in clause 14 of the L.S.D.B. Form similar to this last sentence in clause 21 of the Institute Time Clauses (Hulls), beginning with the words " Such overlapping period . . .".

Cancellation of the Insurance

Before the relevant sentences in clause 14 of the L.S.D.B. Form and the

---

[95] The same wording is used in cl. 24 of the 1960 L.S.D.B. Form.

[96] These are the periods (a) not under repair and (b) under repair, also in cl. 21.

[97] The predecessor of the present cl. 21 (then cl. 22) said: " . . . this policy shall pay such proportion thereof as the number of days attaching hereto bears to 30."

[98] This is proviso (i) of cl. 21, which refers to returns while a vessel is lying in a place other than an approved lay-up area.

Institute Time Clauses (Hulls) are considered, it is important to establish the general principles which govern a situation in which a party may wish to cancel the policy, and a return of premium may be sought. If the risk is entire and indivisible, and the insurers have been on risk, for however short a time, then, in the absence of agreement to the contrary, the contract cannot be terminated and the assured is not entitled to a return of premium. The converse of this proposition is that where money is received in respect of a consideration which wholly fails, other than as a result of fraud on the part of the party who pays it, the money is returnable. Lord Mansfield, in *Tyrie* v. *Fletcher*,[99] said:

> " There are two general rules applicable to this question: the first is that where the risk has not been begun, whether this be owing to the fault, pleasure, or will, of the assured, or any other cause, the premium shall be returned, because a policy of insurance is a contract of indemnity; the underwriter receives a premium for running the risk of indemnifying the assured, and, to whatever cause it may be owing, if he does not in fact run the risk, the consideration for which the premium was put into his hands fails, and therefore he ought to return it."

If, on the contrary, the risk has begun, then no part of the premium is returnable where a policy is whole and indivisible unless there is an agreement to this effect, either in the original contract of insurance or at a later date.

The contract of insurance set out in the L.S.D.B. Form can, like other contracts, be cancelled by the mutual agreement of the parties, but the latter part of clause 14 also provides for three particular situations in which it may be cancelled:

> " This insurance may be cancelled:—
> (a) by the Assured at any time by written notice subject to a return of premium to be agreed;
> (b) by Underwriters subject to 30 days' written notice in which event a pro rata daily return of premium shall be payable;
> (c) by Underwriters in respect of the perils of strikers locked-out workmen or persons taking part in labour disturbances or riots or civil commotions subject to 7 days' written notice without return of premium.[1]
> Cancellation by either party is subject to the retention by Underwriters of any minimum premium stipulated in the Policy."

The comparable provisions in the 1960 L.S.D.B. Form as to cancellation are set out as a separate clause [2] of that policy:

> " This certificate or policy may be cancelled on the customary short rate basis by the Assured at any time by written notice or by the surrender of the certificate or policy.[3] Cancellation may also be effected by Underwriters or their representatives by sending to the Assured's address not less than 30 days' written notice stating when the cancellation shall be effective,

---

[99] (1777) 2 Cowp. 666.
[1] There is no provision equivalent to (c) in the 1960 L.S.D.B. Form.
[2] cl. 25, " Cancellation."
[3] Equivalent to (a) above, in cl. 14 of the 1972 Form.

163

Underwriters undertaking to refund the paid premium less the earned portion thereof on demand.[4] Cancellation by either party is subject to the rentention by Underwriters of any minimum premium that may have been stipulated." [5]

Both the assured and the underwriters can thus terminate the insurance by written notice, the assured being entitled to do so at any time but the underwriters having to give 30 days' notice. Where the assured terminates the insurance a return of premium has to be agreed, but where the underwriter terminates the return is stated to be payable *pro rata* daily.

The comparable words in clause 21 of the Institute Time Clauses (Hulls) are the opening words " To return as follows: . . . per cent. for each uncommenced month if this Policy be cancelled by agreement. . . ." The L.S.D.B. Form is thus more explicit, in providing for three situations in which the insurance can be cancelled by one of the parties, whereas clause 21 of the Institute Time Clauses (Hulls) does not provide for unilateral cancellation. The latter clause, however, specifies the rate of return payable where there is a mutually agreed cancellation, whereas there is no such provision in the L.S.D.B. Form. The return is to be ". . . per cent. net for each uncommenced month." The words " for each uncommenced month " mean that where, for example, there is a policy for 12 months there is a return for each month left but not for a part of a month. The months in question will be calculated by reference to the termination date in the policy. They will be calendar months and not lunar months.

For example, a policy on a ship may be taken out for 12 months on January 15. It is cancelled by mutual agreement with effect from October 30. There have been nine completed months, the policy being half way through its tenth month, and there is therefore a return at the named net percentage rate for each of the two " uncommenced " months. In the case of a drilling unit insured on the 1972 L.S.D.B. Form it would be necessary for the parties to agree as to the rate of return and as to whether any return should be calculated in relation to the number of uncommenced months.

Clause 14 of the L.S.D.B. Form provides, at (c), that the underwriters may cancel in respect of " the perils of strikers, locked-out workmen or persons taking part in labour disturbances or riots or civil commotions " subject to seven days' written notice and without a return of premium.[6] These " perils " are not excluded in the list of exclusions in clause 8 [7]; and they can exist without amounting to the " Civil war, revolution, rebellion, insurrection, or civil strife arising therefrom, or piracy " set out in (e) of clause 19, the " Free of Capture and Seizure "

---

[4] Equivalent to (b) above, in cl. 14 of the 1972 Form.
[5] Equivalent to the last sentence quoted above, after (c), in cl. 14 of the 1972 Form.
[6] There is no comparable provision in cl. 25 of the 1960 L.S.D.B. Form.
[7] See above, pp. 127–130.

clause.[8] Moreover the latter clause excludes liability for such matters, whereas the provision in question entitles the underwriters to cancel the policy. The word " perils " in this context may be read in conjunction with the wording of clause 5, the " Coverage " clause,[9] which states: ". . . this Insurance is against all risks of direct physical loss of or damage to the property insured. . . ." It seems that in clause 14, at (c), the word " perils " is being used synonymously with " risks," to indicate the dangers to which the insured property may be exposed.[10] It is clearly not limited here, or in the policy generally, to " perils of the sea," whereas the Lloyd's S.G. Policy covers perils " of the seas "; although it then adds " all other perils, losses, and misfortunes. . . ." the latter words have been held to be limited to perils similar in kind to those specified in the policy, in accordance with the *ejusdem generis* rule of construction.[11] Of the word " peril " itself, Lord Halsbury L.C., said in *Hamilton, Fraser & Co.* v. *Pandorf & Co.*[12]:

> " I think the idea of something fortuitous and unexpected is involved in both words, ' peril ' or ' accident '; you could not speak of the danger of a ship's decay; you would know that it must decay, and the destruction of the ship's bottom by vermin is assumed to be one of the natural and certain effects of an unprotected wooden vessel sailing through certain seas."

Though Lord Halsbury's example is now inappropriate, the principle holds good. So, in the present case, which constitutes the only use of the word " perils " in the 1972 L.S.D.B. Form, the underwriters may cancel the policy in respect of such " fortuitous and unexpected " events, that is, the perils of " strikers, locked-out workmen or persons taking part in labour disturbances or riots or civil commotions." It is not necessary that these perils shall have occurred or be imminent. The effect of the cancellation, which can take place at any time, is that the policy would cease to be effective so far as " risks of direct physical loss of or damage to the property insured " arose from such perils. In other respects the cover afforded by the policy would continue.

Clause 15: Release Agreements and Waivers of Subrogation

The assured, whether it be the contractor or the operator, is a party to a number of contracts in the course of the operations involved in drilling and in the movement of the drilling unit. Such contracts frequently involve one or both of the parties thereto in an agreement not to pursue, against the other, a claim to which it would otherwise be entitled. Such entitlement might have arisen at common law, a tort having been committed by the other party; or under the contract, the other party having committed a breach of contract; or by statute, the claiming party having

---

[8] See below, p. 178.   [9] See above, p. 98.
[10] For a discussion of the word " risks," see above, pp. 101–102.
[11] Where a general description follows a particular description it is confined to objects of the same kind as those in the particular description.
[12] (1887) 12 App.Cas. 518 (H.L.), at p. 524.

been vested with certain rights by law. In this context the actions, rights and liabilities of the party can usually be taken to include the actions, rights and liabilities of that party's employees and sub-contractors, and of any other person or company acting on his behalf.

Clause 15 of the 1972 L.S.D.B. Form states:

" RELEASE AGREEMENTS AND WAIVERS OF SUBROGATION:

The Assured may grant release from liability with respect to loss of or damage to property insured hereunder to any person firm or corporation for whom the Assured is operating under specific contract, provided:

(a) the said release is granted prior to the commencement of the operations;

(b) the loss or damage subject to said release arises out of or in connection with such operations.

Underwriters agree to waive their rights of subrogation against such person firm or corporation having been so released from such liability."

The 1960 L.S.D.B. Form contains a similar provision [13]:

" The Underwriters waive right of subrogation against any individual, firm or corporation for whom the Assured may be drilling, but this waiver shall apply only in respect to the specific Contract existing between the Assured and such other individual, firm or corporation, and shall not be construed to be a waiver in respect of other operations of such individual, firm or corporation in which the Assured has no contractual interest."

Under clause 15 of the 1972 L.S.D.B. Form the assured thus has the right to grant a release from liability, with respect to loss of or damage to the insured property, to any person, firm or corporation for whom the assured is operating (as, for example, where the contractor is working for the operator) under a specific contract, subject to the two provisos set out in the clause. Thus, (a) the release must have been granted before the operations under the contract began; and (b) the loss or damage which is the subject of the release must have arisen out of or in connection with those operations. Authority is not given to the assured to grant a release to those working for him.

The grant of the release is usually in the drilling contract, and as a result, will satisfy these two provisos. The assured, as contractor, may be working for the operator (who for this purpose is assumed not to be an assured) and may have released the operator from certain liabilities. In the " International Daywork Drilling Contract—Offshore," [14] for example, clause 1001 states:

". . . each party hereto shall at all times be responsible for and shall hold harmless and indemnify the other party from and against damage to or loss of its own items, regardless of the cause of loss including the negligence of such party and despite the fact that a party's items may be under the control of the other party." [There follow certain exceptions which are not relevant here.]

---

[13] cl. 19.
[14] Issued by the International Association of Drilling Contractors. See Appendix B below, at p. 438.

Clause 15: Release Agreements and Waivers of Subrogation

This clause relates to the party's " own items." Clauses 1003 and 1004 deal with claims by the Contractor's Personnel and the Operator's Personnel, respectively, the Contractor and the Operator each granting a " release from liability " to the other. Thus clause 1003 opens with the words:

> " Contractor agrees to protect, defend, indemnify and save Operator harmless from and against all claims, demands, and causes of action of every kind and character, without limit and without regard to the cause or causes thereof or the negligence of any party, arising in connection herewith in favor of contractor's employees [and certain others] on account of bodily injury, death or damage to their property."

If clause 15 of the L.S.D.B. Form did not give to the assured the right to grant such a release from liability, the assured would be in breach of the contract of insurance when granting that release. Brett L.J. said in *Castellain v. Preston* [15]:

> " As between the underwriter and the assured, the underwriter is entitled to the advantage of every right of the assured, whether such right consists in contract, fulfilled or unfulfilled, or in remedy for tort capable of being insisted on or already insisted on, or in any other right, whether by way of condition or otherwise, legal or equitable, which can be or has been exercised or has accrued, and whether such right could or could not be enforced by the insurer in the name of the assured, by the exercise or acquiring of which right or condition the loss against which the assured is insured, can be, or has been diminished."

The contract of insurance is based on the principle of indemnity, in that the assured can be indemnified only for his loss. Three propositions result from this:

(1) It is contrary to the principle of indemnity that the assured should recover more than once. He cannot, for example, claim or recover under the insurance and also claim against or recover from the third party who caused the loss, without accounting for any recovery to the insurer. As Lord Blackburn said in *Burnand v. Rodocanachi* [16]:

> " The general rule of law (and it is obvious justice) is that where there is a contract of indemnity (it matters not whether it is a marine policy or a policy against fire on land, or any other contract of indemnity [17]) and a loss happens, anything which reduces or diminishes that loss reduces or diminishes the amount which the indemnifier is bound to pay; and if the indemnifier has already paid it, then if anything which diminishes the loss comes into the hands of the person to whom he has paid it, it becomes an equity that the person who has already paid the full indemnity is entitled to be recouped by having that amount back."

(2) There is a corresponding duty on the part of the assured to endeavour to make a recovery, in order to reduce or eliminate the claim against

---

[15] (1883) 11 Q.B.D. 380, at p. 388.
[16] (1882) 7 App.Cas. (H.L.) 333, at p. 339.
[17] This rule therefore applies to all insurances in respect of drilling units, whether or not they are marine policies; see Appendix C below, at p. 456.

insurers, or, alternatively, to reimburse them. Where the claim has been paid, the doctrine of subrogation comes into operation. As Lord Cairns, L.C., said in *Simpson* v. *Thomson*,[18]

> " I know of no foundation for the right of underwriters, except the well-known principle of law, that where one person has agreed to indemnify another, he will, on making good the indemnity, be entitled to succeed to all the ways and means by which the person indemnified might have protected himself against or reimbursed himself for the loss."

(3) So also, before the occurrence of the event which gives rise to a claim, the insurers may be concerned as to whether the assured has agreed to a diminution or an abandonment of the rights which he may be able to exercise on their behalf if a claim arises. In the absence of an express term to such effect in the contract of insurance, however, the assured would seem to be free to enter into a contract by which he granted a release from liability to third parties. The rule that he must not prejudice the insurer's right of subrogation would seem to apply as from the moment at which the assured has already sustained a loss, even though no right of subrogation exists until the insurer pays for the loss, whether it be total or partial. When the right of subrogation comes into existence the insurer is only entitled to such rights and remedies as the assured has against the third party. Although Brett L.J., in the passage cited above,[19] spoke of the entitlement of the underwriter to the advantage of every contractual right of the assured, such entitlement could be subject to restrictions accepted by the assured in such a contract, before or after he concluded his contract of insurance.

He would not be entitled, at common law, however, to accept such restrictions after the occurrence of the event which occasioned a claim by him against his insurer. Such an action would prejudice the insurer's rights of subrogation. In clause 15 of the 1972 L.S.D.B. Form the insurers are agreeing that the assured should grant a release from liability to a person for whom the assured is " operating under specific contract," but only provided that (a) the release is granted prior to the commencement of the operations under the contract in question; and (b) the loss or damage which is the subject of the said release arises out of or in connection with such operations.

The second proviso, by which the loss or damage which is the subject of the release must arise out of the operations in question, ensures that the permission given to the assured does not extend to releases in respect of matters not arising out or or in connection with the operations.

If the assured, in reliance on the permission, has granted a release, what would be the position of the released " person firm or corporation " if, despite the grant given by the insurer, the latter endeavoured to exercise rights of subrogation against that person? He could point to the release

---

[18] (1877) 3 App.Cas. 279 (H.L.), at p. 284.
[19] See p. 167, above.

in the operating contract, but the insurer is not a party to that contract. The answer may be found in section 79 of the Marine Insurance Act 1906, the principles in which, it would seem, govern this situation whether or not the contract of insurance in question is a marine policy. Section 79 states:

> " (1) Where the insurer pays for a total loss either of the whole, or in the case of goods of any apportionable part, of the subject-matter insured, he thereupon becomes entitled to take over the interest of the insured in whatever may remain of the subject-matter so paid for, and he is thereby subrogated to all the rights and remedies of the assured in and in respect of that subject-matter as from the time of the casualty causing the loss.
> (2) Subject to the foregoing provisions, where the insurer pays for a partial loss, he acquires no title to the subject-matter insured, or such part of it as may remain, but he is thereupon subrogated to all rights and remedies of the assured in and in respect of the subject-matter insured as from the time of the casualty causing the loss, in so far as the assured has been indemnified, according to the Act, by such payment for the loss."

As a result of the principles expressed in section 79, the insurer, on proceeding against the person who had been granted a release, would find that he had no more than the " rights and remedies of the assured in and in respect of " the insured subject-matter, " as from the time of the casualty causing the loss." Since the release would, if the assured had complied with the contract of insurance (for otherwise he would have not recovered thereunder), have been granted " prior to the commencement of the operations " it would also have been granted before " the time of the casualty causing the loss." The insurer would therefore find that his rights of subrogation would be limited to the extent that the assured had already reduced his own rights and remedies in and in respect of the subject-matter insured, before " the commencement of the operations."

Nevertheless the second sentence of clause 15 states: " Underwriters agree to waive their rights of subrogation against such person firm or corporation having been so released from such liability." In the circumstances described above it would seem that they are unable to exercise rights against the person so released. They would, in law, apart from this second sentence, be subrogees, but would find that, since the assured had granted a " release from liability " they, too, had no " rights and remedies " against that person. The formal agreement by underwriters, in the second sentence of clause 15, " to waive their rights of subrogation," is a logical consequence of the permission given by them in the first sentence thereof.

Section 79 of the 1906 Act, however, does not only deal with subrogation to the rights and remedies of the assured. It says also, in subsection (1), that the insurer, in the case of a total loss either of the whole, or in the case of goods of any apportionable part, of the subject-matter insured, " becomes entitled to take over the interest of the insured in whatever may remain of the subject-matter so paid for. . . ." It adds that " he is thereby subrogated to all the rights and remedies of the assured."

169

It may be asked whether the waiver by the underwriter, in clause 15 of the L.S.D.B. Form, of his " rights of subrogation " involves also a loss of his entitlement to take over the interest of the insured in whatever may remain of the subject-matter. It seems that the waiver of rights of subrogation in clause 15 is a separate matter and does not affect the right of the insurer to become the owner of the insured property. The rights of subrogation and the right of the insurer in respect of the property itself were distinguished by Lord Blackburn in *Simpson* v. *Thomson* [20]:

> " Where the owners of an assured ship have claimed or been paid as for a total loss, the property in what remains of the ship, and all rights incident to the property, are transferred to the underwriters as from the time of the disaster in respect of which the total loss is claimed for and paid. The right to receive payment of freight accruing due, but not earned, at the time of the disaster, is one of these rights so incident to the property in the ship, and it therefore passes to the underwriters because the ship has become their property, just as it would have passed to a mortgagee of the ship who before the freight was completely earned had taken possession of the ship. . . . But the right of the assured to recover damages from a third person is not one of those rights which are incidental to the property in the ship: it does pass to the underwriters in case of payment for a total loss, but on a different principle. And on this same principle it does pass to the underwriters who have satisfied a claim for a partial loss, though no property in the ship passes."

The rights of subrogation are thus distinct from " the property in what remains of the ship, and all rights incident to the property." Subrogation rights result from the fact that the insurer has indemnified the assured, and they arise whether the loss for which the assured has been reimbursed is total [21] or partial.[22] The distinction made by Lord Blackburn is the same as that made in section 79 (1) of the 1906 Act.[23] The latter subsection sets out the two separate propositions that the insurer, where he pays for a total loss, becomes entitled to take over the interest of the assured in whatever may remain of the subject-matter so paid for, and that he is " thereby " [24-25] subrogated to all the rights and remedies of the assured. Section 79 (2), relating to payment for a partial loss, states that the insurer acquires no title, but is subrogated to all the rights and remedies of the assured.

The agreement by underwriters, in clause 15 of the L.S.D.B. Form, to waive their rights of subrogation does not affect their separate entitlement, in cases where they have paid for a total loss, to take over the interest of the assured in whatever may remain of the subject-matter so paid for.

---

[20] (1877) 3 App.Cas. 279 (H.L.), at p. 292.
[21] As stated in s. 79 (1) of the 1906 Act.
[22] As stated in s. 79 (2) of the 1906 Act.
[23] See above, p. 169.
[24-25] *i.e.* by virtue of the payment.

170

Clause 16: Discovery of Records

" DISCOVERY OF RECORDS:

" During the currency of this insurance or any time thereafter within the period of the time provided for in Clause 17 [26] for bringing suit against these Underwriters, these Underwriters shall have the right of inspecting the Assured's records pertaining to all matters of cost, repairs, income and expenditures of whatsoever nature relating to the properties insured hereunder, such records to be open to a representative of these Underwriters at all reasonable times." [27]

The rights given to the underwriters by clause 16 of the L.S.D.B. Form are greater than those given to insurers by the law as set out in the Marine Insurance Act 1906. Section 17 of the Act, which states that a contract of marine insurance is " a contract based upon the utmost good faith," establishes the general principle that the contract may be avoided by one party in the event that such utmost good faith is not observed by the other party. The obligation set out in the section is not said to be restricted to the period before the contract has been concluded. Section 18, however, requires disclosure by the assured to the insurer of every material circumstance known and deemed to be known by the assured " before the contract is concluded "; section 19, which relates to disclosure by an agent effecting an insurance, is not expressly confined in its application to the period before conclusion of the contract, though the cases involving its application seem to be restricted to that period; and section 20 relates to representations " during the negotiations for the contract, and before the contract is concluded."

The continuing obligation, as set out in the 1906 Act, appears to be that of utmost good faith, as stated in section 17. It does not vest in the insurers a specific right, as is given in clause 16 of the L.S.D.B. Form, to inspect the records of the assured during the currency of the insurance or for some time thereafter.[28] After litigation has begun it is within the jurisdiction of the court, in a case involving a marine insurance policy, to make an order for ship's papers.[29] It is more extensive than an order for discovery in other actions, and it may be made not only against a shipowner and owner of cargo but against mortgagees, and insurers who claim on a reinsurance policy. In confining the application of the order to cases of marine insurance, the court has refused to grant it where the carriage

---

[26] 24 months; see below, p. 172. cl. 17 is entitled " Limitation of Action."

[27] In the 1960 L.S.D.B. Form there is a very similar clause (cl. 27). The only differences are (a) that it refers to " this certificate or policy " and not to " this insurance "; and (b) that the closing words are " during business hours " and not " at all reasonable times."

[28] As specified in cl. 17 of the L.S.D.B. Form.

[29] The origin of the procedure and the scope of the order are discussed in *Arnould*, §§ 1260–1262. " The singular feature about an order for ship's papers is that it is an order on the plaintiff to give discovery of documents before the defendant delivers his defence. . . . But the order should not be made automatically." Lord Denning M.R. in *Probatina Shipping Co. Ltd.* v. *Sun Insurance Office Ltd.* (*The Sageorge*) [1974] 1 Lloyd's Rep. 369 (C.A.).

of goods was inland only, but there have been differing decisions where the transit has been partly by land and partly by sea.

The rights given to the underwriters by clause 16 of the L.S.D.B. Form are, in their turn, wider than those given in the case of an order for ship's papers. The entitlement to inspect the assured's records exists at any time during the currency of the insurance and at any time thereafter within the period of limitation prescribed for the assured to begin a suit or action.[30] The right to inspect records, as given by clause 16, can be exercised at any time, whether or not a suit or action has been begun, but it is wider than an order for discovery, It is, however, restricted to " records pertaining to all matters of cost, repairs, income and expenditures of whatsoever nature relating to the properties insured hereunder."

Clause 17: Limitation of Action [31]

" LIMITATION OF ACTION:
No suit or action on this insurance for the recovery of any claim shall be sustainable in any court of law or equity unless the Assured shall have complied fully with all the requirements of this insurance, and unless commenced within 24 months next after the time a cause of action for the loss accrues, provided, however, that where such limitation of time is prohibited by the law of the State wherein this insurance is issued, then and in that event, no suit or action under this insurance shall be sustained unless commenced within the shortest time limitation permitted under the laws of such State."

By these words clause 17 of the L.S.D.B. Form imposes two obligations on the assured and states that unless, subject to a proviso in the case of one of the obligations, both obligations are discharged by the assured, he shall be unable to sustain a suit or action for the recovery of any claim on the insurance in any court of law or equity.

The expression " suit or action " as used in clause 17, is probably wide enough to cover legal proceedings wherever they may be brought. In particular, the word " suit " is normally used to describe legal proceedings in the U.S.A., while in England the word " action " is normally employed.

The meaning of the term " suit " was discussed in *The Merak*.[32] Bills of lading stated that a voyage was " as per charter dated April 21, 1961," and that a numbered clause of the said voyage charterparty, which was the arbitration clause, was incorporated in the bills. They also contained a clause giving effect to the Hague Rules. Just under 12 months from the final discharge the indorsees of the bills of lading issued a writ. One of

---

[30] cl. 17, see this page, below.
[31] The comparable clause, cl. 28, in the 1960 L.S.D.B. Form is in identical terms except for (a) the use of the words " this certificate or policy " instead of " this insurance "; and (b) the use of the words " or unless commenced " instead of the words " and unless commenced "; as for (b), it would seem that the 1972 Form makes it clearer both that the assured must comply with the requirements *and* that his suit or action against insurers must begin within the 24 months' period.
[32] *Owners of Cargo on Board the Merak* v. *The Merak (Owners)* [1965] P. 223 (C.A.).

their contentions was that the arbitration clause must be rejected because the relevant provision of the Hague Rules, as set out in Article III, rule 6 of the Carriage of Goods by Sea Act 1924, provided for a discharge from liability " unless suit is brought within one year. . . ." In their view the word " suit " meant that arbitration was not appropriate. The shipowners, relying on the arbitration clause, sought to have the action stayed. The Court of Appeal held that the arbitration clause was effectively incorporated in the bills of lading. Article III, rule 6 of the Hague Rules had to be interpreted so as to cover different modes of procedure in different countries and therefore the meaning of " suit " could not be limited to an action in the English courts. Sellers L.J. said [33]:

"... there is nothing to indicate that a step in an arbitration would not be as effective as a writ in an action unless ' suit ' can have only the meaning in our courts of an action. I do not find any authority which requires us so to hold. In their context I think the words mean ' unless proceedings are brought within one year,' and that the commencement of arbitration proceedings would meet the requirement."

Davies L.J.[34] noted:

" The word ' suit ' in English does not appear to have any precise connotation nor does it seem to point at all clearly to an action at law as opposed to an arbitration . . . if ' suit ' excludes arbitration, then the Hague Rules would seem to discourage, if not actually to prevent, the inclusion of an arbitration clause in a bill of lading."

Clause 17 of the L.S.D.B. Form has the title " Limitation of Action." Such an expression is usually taken to refer to the imposition of a time limit upon a claimant, whether that time limit be imposed by statute or by the common law or by agreement. The title of the clause is appropriate to the second obligation imposed by it, which is the duty to begin a suit or action on the insurance within the 24 months' period.[35] It is not a title which, in the usual meaning of the words " limitation of action," is appropriate to the first obligation imposed by the clause, which is the duty to comply fully with all the requirements of the insurance. In the wording of the first obligation, that the assured " shall have complied fully with all the requirements of this insurance," there is no distinction between terms of a greater and a lesser importance or between conditions and warranties.[36] As the clause reads, if the assured has not complied with every requirement of the insurance he is not able to sustain a suit or action on it for the recovery of any claim. The " requirements " are thus given the status of warranties, to the extent that the consequences which result from non-compliance are similar. Section 33 (1) of the Marine Insurance Act 1906, states:

---

[33] At p. 252. These words of Art. III, r. 6 remain the same in the Carriage of Goods by Sea Act 1971, which replaced the 1924 Act.
[34] At p. 257.
[35] See below, p. 177.
[36] Using these words as they are used generally in common law; see above, p. 99.

" A warranty, in the following sections relating to warranties,[37] means a promissory warranty, that is to say, a warranty by which the assured undertakes that some particular thing shall or shall not be done, or that some condition shall be fulfilled, or whereby he affirms or negatives the existence of a particular state of facts."

The meaning of the word " requirements " can be taken to include all these matters, in that in the case of any requirement the assured is, (a) undertaking that a thing shall or shall not be done or that a condition shall be fulfilled, and (b) affirming or negativing the existence of a particular state of facts.

The consequences of a breach of a warranty in a policy governed by the 1906 Act are similar, though not exactly the same, as those which are stated by clause 17 to flow from a breach of a requirement. Those consequences are set out in section 33 (3) of the 1906 Act:

" A warranty, as above defined,[38] is a condition which must be exactly complied with, whether it be material to the risk or not. If it be not so complied with, then, subject to any express provision in the policy, the insurer is discharged from liability as from the date of the breach of warranty, but without prejudice to any liability incurred by him before that date."

The effect of a breach of warranty is thus stated to be that " the insurer is discharged from liability," but only from the date of the breach, and without prejudice to any liability which he has previously incurred. The effect of a breach of a requirement, as set out in clause 17 of the L.S.D.B. Form, is that " No suit or action . . . for the recovery of any claim shall be sustainable. . . ." The exclusion in clause 17 thus seems to be wider, and to extend to suits or actions in respect of claims which arose before there had been a failure, on the part of the assured, to comply with a requirement of the insurance. In particular, clause 17 does not contain a proviso, as it might have done if such a consequence had been intended, that the inability to maintain suit or action does not affect a right to a claim which has accrued before the failure to comply with a requirement of the insurance. Any right to a claim which may have arisen would seem to be extinguished, by virtue of the provision that it is not "sustainable, " where there has been non-compliance with one of the " requirements." What is the position where the failure to comply with a requirement occurs after a suit or action has been begun as, for example, by the issue of a writ? If the words of clause 17 prevent the assured from continuing the legal proceedings, then the expression " shall have complied fully with all the requirements " must be construed as if it read " shall have complied fully before such suit or action and shall have continued to comply fully pending judgment and final order in such suit or action with all the requirements." It is doubtful whether such an implication is necessary to make the words effective. It seems more probable that the words " shall have complied "

---

[37] ss. 34 to 41. [38] See s. 33 (1), as set out above, on this page.

must be taken to mean that the assured, up to the time at which the suit or action is brought, shall have complied with all the requirements of the insurance.

Apart from the preservation of the assured's right of action in respect of accrued liabilities, in cases to which the 1906 Act applies, the consequences imposed by section 33 (3) of the Act and clause 17 of the policy respectively are the same though expressed from the point of view of the insurer in the former case and from that of the assured in the latter case. Section 33 (3) says that the insurer is " discharged from liability," whereas clause 17 says that no suit or action " shall be sustainable." The 1906 Act is more specific, in that it clearly declares that there is no liability. This discharge from liability takes place even if the breach of warranty has no connection with the loss in respect of which the assured makes the claim. In *Overseas Commodities* v. *Style*,[39] where tins of meat were the subject-matter of the insurance, there was a breach of warranty as to the markings of certain tins. It was held that the assured was unable to recover from the insurers, even in respect of the tins which had been correctly marked. In the case of clause 17 of the L.S.D.B. Form the failure to recover would be just as complete, in view of the provision that no suit or action shall be sustainable.

The use in clause 17 of words which say that no suit or action shall be sustainable suggests that, in theory at least, the liability of the insurer continues to exist, although the assured cannot sustain legal proceedings. There is no statement that he is discharged from liability. This gives rise to two interesting questions:

(1) can the assured cure the breach by compliance with the requirements?

(2) in the event of a claim by the insurer against the assured, as, for example, for an outstanding premium, can the assured set up the claim under the policy as a defence or counterclaim even though it would not be " sustainable " as a claim?

(1) It does not seem that the assured can cure a breach of compliance with clause 17 after the breach, whether before or after suit or action is brought. It would be in accordance with the construction of the words " shall be sustainable," as suggested above,[40] that he should have complied with the requirements of the insurance at all times up to the time at which suit or action is brought. Where the 1906 Act applies, section 34 (2) would govern such a case, in that it states: " Where a warranty is broken, the assured cannot avail himself of the defence that the breach has been remedied, and the warranty complied with before loss." In *de Hahn* v. *Hartley* [41] the insurance policy contained a warranty that the ship had " sailed frnm Liverpool with fourteen six-pounders, swivels, small arms, and fifty hands or upwards, copper sheathed." The ship sailed with 46

---

[39] [1958] 1 Lloyd's Rep. 546.
[40] On this page.
[41] (1786) 1 T.R. 343; affirmed, (1787) 2 T.R. 186.

men but remedied the breach within 12 hours by taking on six extra hands at Beaumaris, Anglesey. The court held that in view of the breach the policy was void.[42] The breach had not been remedied, so far as the validity of the policy was concerned, by the acquisition of six extra hands. It seems that the same principle would apply in the interpretation of clause 17 of the L.S.D.B. Form, and that failure by the assured to comply fully with all the requirements of the assurance, at any time, up to the time at which he begins suit or action, must prevent him from sustaining an action.

(2) It is more difficult to be certain as to whether a claim, albeit a suit or action is not sustainable in respect thereof, may have some residual validity, to the extent at least of constituting an effective defence, set-off or counterclaim in an action by the insurer. The considerations involved are similar, though there are numerous differences of detail, to those discussed in *Aries Tanker Corporation* v. *Total Transport Ltd.*[43] Owners claiming freight were met by charterer's claim that they could withhold freight because of a short delivery. Owners succeeded, the Hague Rules having provided that they were " discharged from all liability " unless suit had been brought within one year.

The second obligation imposed upon the assured by clause 17 of the L.S.D.B. Form is that any suit or action on the insurance for the recovery of any claim be " commenced within 24 months next after the time a cause of action for the loss accrues, provided, however, that where such limitation of time is prohibited by the law of the State wherein this insurance is issued, then and in that event, no suit or action under this insurance shall be sustained unless commenced within the shortest time limitation permitted under the laws of such State."

The title given to clause 17, " Limitation of Action," is, as has been stated above,[44] more appropriate to this second part of the clause than to the part which sets out the obligation of the assured to comply fully with all the requirements of the insurance.

As in the case of the first obligation under clause 17, failure to commence a suit or action within 24 months next after the time a cause of action for the loss accrues means that the suit or action is not " sustainable in any court of law or equity." The claim is not said to be void. As with the earlier obligation, it is therefore necessary to consider whether for other purposes, such as the use of the claim by way of defence or counterclaim, the claim can still be said to exist, even where no suit or action has been commenced within the prescribed time. For the reason given above [45] it seems that it must be treated as extinguished.

---

[42] The case is also an authority for the proposition that even if the breach does not prejudice the insurers they can still treat the policy as void, for there was evidence that the ship was as safe with 46 men as with 50.

[43] [1977] 1 Lloyd's Rep. 334 (H.L.).

[44] See p. 173, above.

[45] On this page.

Clause 17: Limitation of Action

The suit or action [46] must be commenced within 24 months next after the time a cause of action for the loss accrues. A cause of action for a loss accrues, so far as the main cover given by the policy is concerned, when there has been " direct physical loss of or damage to the property insured," to use the words of clause 5 of the L.S.D.B. Form.[47] Alternatively, so far as the remaining cover given by the policy is concerned, a cause of action for a loss accrues when (a) under the collision liability clause [48] the assured or the surety has become liable to pay and shall have paid by way of damages any sum or sums in respect of such collisions; or (b) under the sue and labour clause [49] the assured, his factors, servants or assignees has or have incurred charges in suing, labouring and travelling for, in and about the defence, safeguard and recovery of the insured property, or any part thereof.

The Lloyd's S.G. Policy does not specify a period of time within which an action must be brought against the insurer. Nor is any such period specified in the Institute Time Clauses (Hulls) or in the Marine Insurance Act 1906. A claim under a policy governed by English law would therefore be subject to such a period of limitation as applied to other contracts governed by English law. The period is usually six years. This is stipulated by the Limitation Act 1939, section 2 (1) (a) of which provides that an action upon a simple contract shall not be brought after the expiration of six years from the date on which the cause of action accrued. The cause of action is said to accrue when a breach of the contract is committed.

The provisions of clause 17 of the L.S.D.B. Form may now be compared with those applicable to the usual English hull policy. First, the relevant period is two years in the case of the former but six years in the case of the latter by virtue of the 1939 Act.

Secondly, the provisions are similar in that neither states that the claim shall be void in the event that no suit or action is brought within the prescribed period. The suit or action is not " sustainable," in the case of clause 17, and " shall not be brought," in the case of section 2 (1) (a) of the 1939 Act.

Thirdly, clause 17 contains a proviso which is understandably absent from English law. The proviso deals with a situation in which the limitation period of 24 months is " prohibited by the law of the State wherein this insurance is issued." The law of another " State " [50] may merely apply a differing prescription period to contracts governed by the law of that country, in terms similar to those set out in the English Limitation Act of 1939. It may go further, however, by prohibiting the application of a 24 months period; it would presumably do so by stating that its own limitation period, which might be longer than 24 months, must apply to

---

[46] For the difference between these two terms see p. 173, above.
[47] Headed " Coverage "; see p. 99, above.
[48] cl. 6; see p. 109, above.
[49] cl. 13; see above, p. 154.
[50] See below, p. 178.

any insurance issued within that state. In such a case the prescription period for the purpose of clause 17 would be " the shortest time limitation permitted under the laws of such State." There are references to " the law of the State wherein this insurance is issued," and to " the shortest time limitation permitted under the laws of such State." There are no other references in the L.S.D.B. Form to a " State " or to any other governing authority, though there is a reference to " agents of a Sovereign Power " in the F. C. & S. clause.[51] In the case of the L.S.D.B. Form, where it is generally known that the insurance may be issued in the United States of America, it is clear that the word " State " must here be taken to include not only a Sovereign state but one of the member states of the U.S.A.

Clause 18: Loss Payable

The L.S.D.B. Form [52] states at clause 18:

" LOSS PAYABLE:
Loss, if any (except claims required to be paid to others under the Collision Liability Clause), payable to. . . ."

The 1960 L.S.D.B. Form states, at clause 3: " Loss, if any, payable to: . . ." There may be several assured,[53] and it is important that the underwriters should be able to pay one party without being involved in a dispute. By this clause it is agreed between the various assured, on the one hand, and the underwriters, on the other hand, that any loss should be payable to a certain named party. It is possible for that party to be other than one of the assured. In the case of the 1972 L.S.D.B. Form an exception is made for payments under the " Collision Liability " clause,[54] by which the underwriters are to pay, as it says, " the Assured or the Surety, whichever shall have paid."

Clause 19: Free of Capture and Seizure Clause

How the " F. C. & S." clause arose

The Lloyd's form of policy, as set out in Schedule 1 to the Marine Insurance Act 1906, includes, in the named " adventures and perils," " enemies, pirates, rovers, thieves . . . surprisals, takings at sea, arrests, restraints, and detainments of all kings, princes and people. . . ." It thus extends its cover to the assured if control of the subject-matter insured is, in one of more of these ways, assumed by a third party.

It has been customary for many years, in the case of the English hull policy, for the marine insurers to exclude themselves from liability in respect of any claims which result from the taking of the ship, in various specified circumstances, or from hostilities. An early copy of the Lloyd's

---

[51] cl. 19, at (g). See p. 183, below.
[52] Dated March 1, 1972.
[53] See cl. 1 at p. 86, above.
[54] cl. 6; see p. 109, above.

Clause 19: Free of Capture and Seizure Clause

S.G. Policy [55] states: " Warranted free of French, Spanish and American captures, and the consequences of any attempt thereof."

The printed form of the Lloyd's S.G. policy today includes the " Free of Capture and Seizure " clause:

" Warranted free of capture, seizure, arrest, restraint, or detainment, and the consequences thereof or of any attempt thereat; also from the consequences of hostilities and warlike operations whether there be a declaration of war or not; but this warranty shall not exclude collision, contact with any fixed or floating object (other than a mine or torpedo), stranding, heavy weather or fire unless caused directly (and independently of the nature of the voyage or service which the vessel concerned or, in the case of collision, any other vessel involved therein, is performing) by a hostile act by or against a belligerent power; and for the purpose of this warranty ' power ' includes any authority maintaining naval, military or other forces in association with a power. [56]

Further warranted free from the consequences of civil war, revolution, rebellion, insurrection or civil strife arising therefrom, or piracy." [57]

The cover set out in the earlier part of the policy, with its list of " enemies, pirates, rovers, thieves," etc., is thus negatived, to some degree, by this exclusion clause in the same policy. It is not possible to set each of the words of exception against a corresponding word contained in the list of insured adventures and perils. Nor can each word of exception be given a separate definition in such a way that there is no overlapping between the different words. In *Johnston & Co.* v. *Hogg* [58] the subject-matter of the insurance policy, the ship, was warranted " free from capture and seizure, and the consequences of any attempt thereat." Natives took forcible possession of the ship when she ran aground in the Brass River, Nigeria, plundered the cargo and damaged the ship so that she became a constructive total loss. The jury found as a fact that the natives seized the ship to plunder her and not in order to keep her. The defence by underwriters was that the loss was a loss by seizure within the meaning of the warranty; the owners said that for the action to constitute a seizure there would have to be a taking of possession with intent to keep it as one's own, and not merely for the purposes of plunder. It was held that the acts of the natives constituted a " seizure " within the meaning of the warranty, and that the underwriters were not liable. Cave J. considered various definitions, in cases and in books, of capture and seizure, and said [59]:

" The seeming confusion in some of these passages arises from the desire of the authors in question to give a distinct and different meaning to such words as ' capture,' ' seizure,' ' arrest,' ' detention,' ' restraint,' and the impossibility of accomplishing the task is shown by their attempts to

[55] Dated February 26, 1780; this policy is kept at Lloyd's. See Dover, *Handbook to Marine Insurance* (7th ed., 1970), at p. 33. An earlier form of the clause appeared in a policy dated 1739; see *Arnould on Marine Insurance* (15th ed., 1961), § 16, n. 39.
[56] This part of the exclusion may be compared with exception (*h*) below, at p. 184.
[57] This part of the exclusion may be compared with exception (*e*) below, at p. 183.
[58] (1883) 10 Q.B.D. 432.
[59] *Ibid.* at pp. 435 to 436.

distinguish between ' arrest,' ' restraint,' and ' detention.' I have no
doubt that the word ' seizure,' like many other words, is sometimes used
with more general and sometimes with more restricted meaning, and
whether it is used in a particular case with the one meaning or the other
depends not on any general rule but on the context and the circumstances
of the case. . . . Being clearly of opinion that the acts of the natives amounted
to a seizure within the meaning of the warranty, I must direct the verdict
and judgment to be entered for the defendants [the underwriters]."

The passages cited above make it clear that it is impossible " to give a
distinct and different meaning " to words such as " capture," " seizure,"
" arrest," " detention " and " restraint." Whether in the more general
or in the more restricted meaning of each word, there may be an area in
which its meaning is similar to that of another word. In that sense the
words would not be " distinct and different." For example, an intent to
deprive the owner of his property may exist both where there is capture
and where there is seizure, though the two concepts may differ in other
respects. Even if there is some degree of overlapping, it must nevertheless
be possible to give some definitions, whether in a general or in a more
restricted sense, particularly as the words are, in the case of insurance
policies, commonly used in a particular and recognisable context and
circumstances.

F. C. & S. and the L.S.D.B. Form

The L.S.D.B. Form differs from the Lloyd's S.G. Policy in that it it is
stated in its heading to be a cover for " All Risks (except as hereinafter
excluded)." The Lloyd's S.G. Policy, on the other hand, sets out a list of
named " adventures and perils," and although it concludes the list with
the words " all other perils, losses, and misfortunes " these words are
interpreted as referring only to perils of a kind similar to those already
listed. Both the L.S.D.B. Form and the usual Lloyd's S.G. Policy [60] contain, however, a " Free of Capture and Seizure " clause. The Institute
Time Clauses (Hulls) also contains, at clause 23, an " F. C. & S." clause.
This is considered below, where it is compared with clause 19 of the
L.S.D.B. Form.

The 1972 L.S.D.B. Form, however, contains words which may prove
difficult to construe, by referring to " no liability for any claim caused by,
resulting from, or incurred as a consequence of . . ." The comparable
words in the F. C. & S. Clause and the 1960 Form are, respectively,
" Warranted free of . . ." [and " from "]; and " warranted free from any
claim for " [and " from "]. It is not appropriate here to consider in detail
the extensive litigation which has occurred not only with respect to causation generally but in connection with such words as " caused by," " resulting from " or " as a consequence of." An indication of the type of problem
which can arise must suffice here.

---

[60] The current form; the " F.C. & S." clause does not appear in the form set out as
Sched. 1 to the Marine Insurance Act 1906.

Clause 19: Free of Capture and Seizure Clause

" Caused by "

Where these words are used the courts usually look at the immediate or proximate cause. A good example is that of a policy against injuries other than those " caused by or arising from natural disease or weakness ..."; it was held [61] to cover death by drowning, although the insured's fall into the water resulted from an epileptic fit. In another case on a similar policy the judge [62] said that " injury caused by accident " meant that the injury must be immediately caused by the accident. These decisions are examples of the application of the principle expressed by Francis Bacon in " Maxims of the Law ": " It were infinite for the law to judge the causes of causes, and their impulsions one of another; therefore it contenteth itself with the immediate cause, and judgeth of acts by that; without looking to any further degree." It is tempting, therefore, to say that one should always look at the immediate or proximate cause, and ignore other causes earlier in time. That is not always, however, the correct procedure, for adoption of that course would involve the rejection of the conclusion reached by Lord Wright in *Smith, Hogg & Co. Ltd.* v. *Black Sea & Baltic General Insurance Co. Ltd.*[63]: ". . . causes may be regarded not so much as a chain, but as a network. There is always a combination of co-operating causes, out of which the law, employing its empirical or common sense view of causation, will select the one or more which it finds material for its special purpose of deciding the particular case."

" resulting from "

There seems to be little if any judicial authority as to the use of these words. The words " results from " were once considered by the Court of Appeal [64] in the context of a particular Act [65]: ". . . an existing incapacity ' results from ' the original injury if it follows, and is caused by, that injury, and may properly be held so to result even if some supervening cause has aggravated the effects of the original injury and prolonged the period of incapacity. If, however, the existing incapacity ought fairly to be attributed to a new cause which has intervened and ought no longer to be attributed to the original injury, it may properly be held to result from the new cause and not from the original injury, even though, but for the original injury, there would have been no incapacity."

" as a consequence of "

The words " in consequence thereof " were considered in *Hall Brothers S.S. Co. Ltd.* v. *Young.*[66] MacKinnon L.J. said: " It has been a well settled

---

[61] *Winspear* v. *Accident Insurance Co. Ltd.* (1881) 6 Q.B.D. 42 (C.A.).
[62] Huddleston B. in *Isitt* v. *Railway Passengers' Assurance Co.* (1889) 22 Q.B.D. 504, at p. 510.
[63] [1940] A.C. 997 (H.L.), at pp. 1003–1004.
[64] In *Rothwell* v. *Caverswall Stone Co. Ltd.* (1944) 61 T.L.R. 17 (C.A.), *per* du Parcq L.J., at p. 25.   [65] Workmen's Compensation Act 1925, s. 9.
[66] [1939] 1 K.B. 748 (C.A.), at pp. 761–762.

rule for over seventy years, in regard to the construction of marine insurance policies, that where, in an added clause in a policy, there are words like ' in consequence thereof,' you must, in dealing with causation, look at the proximate and not the remote cause."

In the various cases in which the words " caused by," " resulting from " and in " consequence thereof," have been considered, the conclusion has been that one is bound to ascertain the cause of the event, even if it is necessary to add the epithet " proximate." The words " as a consequence of " would have to be considered with care in the event of a claim involving damages which could be called consequential; they might be held to have an effect wider than the two preceding phrases, and to exclude consequential damages particularly in view of the use in Clause 5, the Coverage clause, of the words " all risks of direct physical loss or damage." If there is an intervening act which interrupts the chain of causation, then the court may decide either that it served to cut that chain completely or that the loss or damage was caused partly by the original casualty and partly by the intervening act.[67] It is only appropriate here, however, to indicate the nature of the problem.

The Exclusions in the L.S.D.B. Form " Free of Capture and Seizure " Clause

The " Free of Capture and Seizure " clause is set out in the L.S.D.B. Form as eight separate exceptions, lettered (a) to (h).

" (a) *Capture, seizure, arrest, restraint or detainment, or any attempt thereat; or . . ."* [68]

These words are the same as the opening words of the standard " F. C. & S." clause and of clause 23 of the Institute Time Clauses (Hulls) which, after the words " Warranted free of" stipulates, as the first exclusions, " capture, seizure, arrest, restraint or detainment, and the consequences thereof or of any attempt thereat. . . ."

" (b) *Any taking by requisition or otherwise, whether in time of peace or war and whether lawful or otherwise . . ."*

This exception appears in another form in clause 26 of the 1960 L.S.D.B. Form: " any taking of the property moved by requisition or otherwise, whether in time of peace or war and whether lawful or otherwise." A requisition by a government has been held [69] to constitute a restraint of princes, so that to that extent such a requisition would be excluded by (a) as well as

---

[67] See for example the judgment of Brandon J. in *The Calliope* [1970] P. 172 and the authorities there considered.

[68] The same exclusion appears in the 1960 L.S.D.B. Form, at cl. 26. For a discussion as to the meaning of these words, and references to the cases thereon, see *Arnould on Marine Insurance* (15th ed., 1961) at §§ 820 *et seq.*

[69] *Tamplin S.S. Co.* v. *Anglo-Mexican Petroleum Products Co. Ltd.* [1916] 2 A.C. 397 (H.L.). See also *Arnould on Marine Insurance* (15th ed., 1961), at § 826.

by (b). This exception would also exclude a " taking " other than by way of requisition, whether it was lawful or not.[70]

" (c) *Any mine, bomb, torpedo or other engine of war* "

This exception does not appear in the 1960 L.S.D.B. Form, nor in clause 23 of the Institute Time Clauses (Hulls), or in the standard " F. C. & S." clause. Clause 24 of the Institute Time Clauses (Hulls) refers to " any weapon of war," but that exception has its true parallel in exception (f) of the 1972 L.S.D.B. Form, which is set out below.[71]

" (d) *Any weapon of war employing atomic or nuclear fission and/or fusion or other like reaction or radioactive force or matter* "

This exception appears in clause 26 of the 1960 L.S.D.B. Form: " warranted free, whether in time of peace or war, from all loss or damage caused by any weapon of war employing atomic fission or radioactive force." It also appears in clause 25 of the Institute Time Clauses (Hulls) as: " Warranted free from loss damage liability or expense arising from any weapon of war employing atomic or nuclear fission and/or fusion or other like reaction or radioactive force or matter."

" (e) *Civil war, revolution, rebellion, insurrection, or civil strife arising therefrom, or piracy* "

This exception does not appear in clause 26 of the 1960 L.S.D.B. Form, but clause 10 thereof contains the words " excluding civil war, revolution, rebellion or insurrection, or civil strife arising therefrom." Clause 23 of the Institute Time Clauses (Hulls) states " Further warranted free from the consequences of civil war, revolution, rebellion, insurrection, or civil strife arising therefrom, or piracy," so that it is in exactly the same terms. The same wording appears in the standard " F. C. & S." clause

" (f) (*i*) *the detonation of an explosive*
    (*ii*) *any weapon of war*
    and caused by any person acting maliciously or from a political motive "

This exception does not appear in the 1960 L.S.D.B. Form but Clause 24 of the Institute Time Clauses (Hulls) sets out the same words.

" (g) *Any act for political or terrorist purposes of any person or persons, whether or not agents of a Sovereign Power, and whether the loss, damage or expense resulting therefrom is accidental or intentional:*"

This exception does not appear in the 1960 L.S.D.B. Form, or in the Institute Time Clauses (Hulls).

---

[70] For " takings," which are covered by the Lloyd's S.G. policy, and their exclusion by the words " capture " and " seizure," see *Arnould, supra,* at § 821.
[71] On this page.

" (h) *Hostilities or warlike operations (whether there be a declaration of war or not) but this subparagraph (h) not to exclude collision or contact with aircraft, rockets or similar missiles, or with any fixed or floating object, or stranding, heavy weather, fire or explosion unless caused directly by a hostile act by or against a belligerent power which act is independent of the nature of the voyage or operation which the vessel concerned, or in the case of a collision or contact, any other vessel involved therein, is performing. As used herein, ' power' includes any authority maintaining naval military or air forces in association with a power."*

This exception appears in clause 26 of the 1960 L.S.D.B. Form in a limited sense, in that the clause states: ". . . warranted free . . . from all consequences of hostilities or warlike operations (whether there be a declaration of war or not) . . ." In the Institute Time Clauses (Hulls), however, the exception appears in broadly the same terms, being set out as part of the free of capture and seizure provision, viz.:

" Warranted free [of capture, seizure, etc.] also from the consequences of hostilities or warlike operations, whether there be a declaration of war or not; but this warranty shall not exclude collision, contact with any fixed or floating object (other than a mine or torpedo), stranding, heavy weather or fire unless caused directly (and independently of the nature of the voyage or service which the Vessel concerned or, in the case of a collision, any other vessel involved therein, is performing) by a hostile act by or against a belligerent power; and for the purpose of this warranty ' power ' includes any authority maintaining naval, military or air forces in association with a power."

CHAPTER 4

NORWEGIAN HULL INSURANCE

THE Norwegian Association of Drilling Contractors and the Norsk Olje Forsikringspool (Norwegian Oil Rig Insurance Pool) were responsible for the production of " Norwegian Conditions for Hull Insurance of Drilling Vessels and Insurance of Equipment and Supplies for Drilling Vessels." The form used may be contrasted with the London Standard Drilling Barge Form,[71a] and indeed some comparisons between the two forms are made in this present chapter. A commentary on the Norwegian Conditions has been published, and the summary which follows is a paraphrase thereof, so far as it relates to the hull insurance.

The commentary says, by way of general introduction to the Conditions:

" In the spring of 1973 a Norwegian ' Oil Rig Insurance Pool ' was formed; present (October 1974) [71b] members of this pool are seven insurance companies (Arendal Forsikringsselskab A/S, A/S Haugesund Sjøforsikringsselskap, Forsikringsakjeselskapet Polaris-Norske Sjø, Forsikringsselskapet Neptun A/S, Forsikrings-Aktieselskabet Norden, Storebrand and Forsikringsaktieselskapet Vesta) and the four major mutual hull insurance societies (Skibsassuranceforeningen i Arendal og Christiania, Bergens Skibsassuranceforening, Christiansands Skibsassurance-forening and Skipsassuranceforeningen Unitas). The pool has (as of October 1974) taken over the hull insurances for eight of the nine Norwegian drilling vessels delivered so far.[71c] Members of the pool are liable *pro rata* (as co-insurers) to the insured, but so that altogether they cover the value 100 per cent. A major part of the value is reinsured on the London market under a master-cover. The increasingly large volume of insurance thus offered en bloc for reinsurance cover naturally strengthens the pool's bargaining position."

The new Conditions, known also as DV-kasko, were governed by the Norwegian Marine Insurance Plan of 1964, and were applied to all new covers and renewals in the Norwegian market from June 1975. Some Norwegian critics had found the London Form unsatisfactory. They contended that it had been assembled partly from conditions designed to cover drilling activities in shallow waters in the Gulf of Mexico, and partly from conditions used for the hull insurance of conventional ships, but apparently without any attempt to harmonise or adapt these conditions to the special circumstances of large ocean-going drilling vessels. Some of the conditions, it was argued, were vague; particular reference was made to clause 8 (*f*) of the London Form,[71d] relating to liability for faulty design.[71e]

[71a] See Chap. 3. Hereafter called the London Form.
[71b] In 1978 the Pool consisted of the same companies and societies.
[71c] About 35 were covered by 1978.
[71d] See p. 128, above. There are some differences between the clause numbers used in the Norwegian version of the London Form and those used elsewhere. The numbers in the present chapter are those used in Chap. 3, and in App. A; see also p. 432, below.
[71e] The fact that these criticisms are repeated here does not mean that they are

The group responsible for drafting the Norwegian Conditions consisted of representatives from the Norwegian Association of Drilling Contractors and the Norwegian Oil Insurance Pool, and also of two members who were described as " neutral." These were Dr. jur. Sjur Braekhus [71f] and Mr. Alex. Rein. [71g] The group considered that its main task was to convert the so-called English insurance conditions into conditions more appropriate for Norwegian use. It was also thought that it would be easier to obtain reinsurances on the English market if the new conditions " were more or less equivalent to the English conditions employed hitherto."

General Conditions for Hull Insurance of Drilling Vessels

" 1. NORWEGIAN MARINE INSURANCE PLAN OF 1964

The insurance is governed by the Norwegian Marine Insurance Plan of 1964 (' the Plan ') unless otherwise provided in the policy or in these conditions."

1. The Conditions are intended to be used to cover drilling vessels owned wholly or largely by Norwegian interests. Such vessels will usually be registered in Norway. The insurers are Norwegian companies and the insurances are concluded in Norway. Any disputes as to the insurances would come under Norwegian jurisdiction; consequently it seemed reasonable that they should also be governed by Norwegian law.

2. It was thus natural to base the Conditions on the 1964 Plan. Although it was drawn up with a view to the insurance of conventional ships, there are close parallels between the types of insurance. First, the insured objects are in both cases large, expensive, floating and mobile structures. Secondly, there are similar risks—heavy weather damage, the risk of stranding and collision, and the risk of damage from faulty design, faulty materials, wear and tear, etc. Thirdly, both ships and drilling vessels may require salvage and towage to harbour, may need to be docked as a result of partial damage, and may be totally lost by sinking in deep waters. Fourthly, both categories will need cover for collision liability, wreck removal liability and other third party liabilities. [72]

There are obvious differences in risk. First, drilling operations involve special risks, such as blowouts and cratering. Secondly, drilling vessels are subject to the particular problems which result from remaining stationary at sea for long periods. Thirdly, they can be difficult to handle, not only when being towed but also when self-propelled. These factors necessitate some special clauses, [73] but do not render it difficult to use the Plan as a basis for the cover. There was really no alternative as the rules relating to marine insurance in sections 59 to 76 of the Norwegian Insurance Contracts

---

accepted by the author. It would probably not be a useful exercise, now that the two types of policies are firmly established, to attempt to adjudicate between them.

[71f] Professor at the University of Oslo.

[71g] Attorney of the Supreme Court of Norway and member of the law firm of Wikborg, Rein, Ringdal & Waelgaard. His detailed advice is most gratefully acknowledged.

[72] Many third party liabilities fall under the P. & I. cover; see Chap. 6, below.

[73] For example cl. 5, 6 and 8 of the Conditions.

Act were inappropriate, and the insurance conditions applicable to property on land were also unsuitable.

3. First, part one of the plan, entitled " Provisions common to all types of insurance," applies to the insurance. Secondly, as it is a hull insurance, much of the second part of the Plan (" Hull insurance and similar insurance ") also applies.[74]

The insurance is described in the commentary as having four " levels " of rules with the following priority:

(1) the concluded written agreement as recorded in the individual policy, subject to the insured giving notice without undue delay of any items which have been omitted from or incorrectly set out in the agreement;

(2) the present Conditions;

(3) the rules of the Plan;

(4) Norwegian law, including the Insurance Contracts Act 1930.

4. The 1930 Act contains certain mandatory provisions, but marine insurance differs from insurance of property on land in that the parties can dispense with some of these provisions. The question then arises as to whether this greater freedom of contract applies to the insurance of drilling vessels.[75] Section 59 of the Act defines marine insurance as " insurance against a peril to which an interest is exposed while the ship or cargo to which the interest attaches is on the sea."

The determining factor is thus whether drilling vessels can be regarded as " ships " in the legal sense. The Norwegian commentary says, without further discussion, that if one disregards drilling ships the answer to this question must presumably be in the negative. Consequently, the insurance of drilling vessels cannot be regarded as marine insurance and must therefore be subject to the stricter rules which apply to other insurance. This result, say the commentators, is not very reasonable; the conditions which favour extended freedom of contract in marine insurance have even stronger application as regards the insurance of oil activities in open waters. There may therefore be reason to make the rules relating to marine insurance in the Insurance Contracts Act applicable by analogy.[76] However, it would be better, they conclude, if section 59 of the Act were amended, a question which will no doubt be considered by the Maritime Act Committee in its future work on civil law rules relating to drilling vessels.

5. Any legal action by the assured against the insurer must be brought in

---

[74] See cl. 3 of the Conditions.

[75] See also the comments in Appendix D, below, as to the applicability of the English Marine Insurance Act 1906 to a policy; and Chap. 2, as to the status of drilling units as ships.

[76] This is similar to the approach adopted in the C.M.I. draft Convention on Off-Shore Mobile Craft, agreed at Rio de Janeiro in 1977; it was agreed to extend the rules adopted in various Conventions, by analogy, to drilling units. Legislation was prepared in 1978 in Norway to bring about a similar change.

the place where the insurer has its seat, *i.e.* its registered address. In the case of co-insurance, combined legal action can be brought against all the insurers at the seat of any of them, though a single Norwegian venue may be stipulated.

" 2. DEFINITIONS

In these conditions

    (1) ' drilling vessel ' means drilling ship, jack-up, semi-submersible or any other mobile structure used for off-shore drilling operations,

    (2) ' blowout ' means a sudden, accidental, uncontrolled and continuous expulsion from a well and above the surface of the ground of the drilling fluid in an oil or gas well, followed by continuous and uncontrolled flow from a well and above the surface of the ground of oil, gas or water due to encountering subterranean pressures,

    (3) ' cratering ' means the formation of a basin-like depression in the earth's surface surrounding the well caused by the erosion and eruptive action of oil, gas or water flowing without restriction."

1. The commentary points out that the term " drilling vessel " is not used in the London Form. The term is used in clauses 4 (1), 5 (3) and 10 of the Norwegian Conditions. The definition is of greatest importance in clause 10, since collision liability is covered only in the case of a collision (a) between the insured vessel and a ship or (b) between the insured vessel and another drilling vessel. The definition of " drilling vessel " has four features:

(1) it is a " structure." It may be in the shape of a ship or be a ship, as in the case of a drilling ship; but most drilling vessels will not comply with the ordinary conception of a ship.

(2) The structure must be mobile. This does mean that it must always be mobile. Jack-ups are clearly drilling vessels although during drilling they have their legs lowered on to the sea bed. The same argument applies to submersibles. It is the ability to be moved that is the determining factor. It is irrelevant whether the structure moves under its own power or otherwise. The commentary adds, however, " On the other hand, drilling platforms that are lifted on to specially designed barges and moved by that means, do not come under the definition . . . . " During such a move they would be equivalent to cargo.

(3) The structure must be equipped for offshore drilling operations. Production platforms, submarine storage tanks and floating or fixed structures for offshore loading of oil or for the transport of oil through pipes are not included.

(4) The structure must be used for and not merely intended for such operations. However, a structure being moved to a new drilling site or towed to or from the site must be regarded as being so " used," provided it is to remain in use for drilling. A collision between it and another drilling vessel while it is being moved is therefore covered under clause 10.1.

2. The definition of " blowout " is taken from clause 8 (*j*) of the London Standard Drilling Barge Form.[77] The commentary states:

" This definition of ' blowout ' does not seem very exact. For example it states that the expulsion of drilling fluid shall be ' sudden,' ' accidental ' and ' uncontrolled '; one of these adjectives would probably have sufficed–the other two do not appear to give any further explanation. In the next passage relating to the expulsion of oil, gas or water the expression ' uncontrolled ' has been found adequate. Moreover both passages state that expulsion shall be ' continous,' without imposing any limit as regards duration. The statement that there shall be an ' expulsion ' or ' flow ' from a well and above the surface of the ground can hardly be intended to convey exclusions of leakages of oil or gas through the ground, when this is caused by drilling, *cf.* the Santa Barbara occurrence. Although the definition does not seem explicit, the group did not find it proper to make any alterations. So little information is available concerning these matters that the group is unable to form any independent opinion as to where the borderline should be; it therefore seems better to keep strictly to the existing pattern."

3. The definition of " cratering " is also taken from clause 8 (*j*) of the London Form. In the Conditions the expression is always linked with blowout.

" 3. GENERAL SCOPE OF COVER
The insurance is a hull insurance ' on full conditions ' according to section 151 of the Plan, the provisions of the Plan concerning ' the ship ' to apply correspondingly to the drilling vessel."

1. Section 151 of the Plan, entitled " Insurance ' on full conditions,' " states:

" If not otherwise agreed, the hull insurer is liable for total loss, damage and collision liability in accordance with Chapters 11 to 13." [78] The other possibilities under the Plan are total loss only, total loss and general average only, total loss, general average and collision liability only, and " stranding terms." " Insurance on full conditions " is the most comprehensive of all.

2. Under the Plan the object of the insurance is always a ship. This clause makes it clear that drilling vessels are covered.

" 4. OBJECTS INSURED
Instead of sections 148 and 149 of the Plan the following provisions shall apply:
(1) The insurance includes the drilling vessel scheduled in the policy (' the insured vessel ') with all its machinery and equipment on board, including equipment for the drilling operations on board, above or under water and in hole.
(2) The machinery and equipment mentioned in paragraph (1) is also covered while on board other vessels moored alongside or in the vicinity of the insured vessel and used in connection with that vessel.
(3) The machinery and equipment in paragraphs (1) and (2) is covered irrespective of whether it is owned by the Assured or by a third party provided it is in the care, custody or control of a person whose interests are covered according to clause 15 of these conditions.

---

[77] See p. 128, above.
[78] Chap. 11 is entitled " Total Loss "; Chap. 12 is entitled " Damage "; Chap. 13 is entitled " Assured's liability for collision or striking."

(4) Notwithstanding the provisions of paragraphs (1) to (3) the insurance does not include
>(a) pipes for casing and tubing, drilling mud, cement, chemicals and other materials and supplies intended for consumption in connection with the drilling operations,
>(b) provisions, fuel, engine and deck stores and other similar articles intended for consumption,
>(c) helicopters stationed on board the insured vessel,
>(d) blueprints, plans, specifications and records."

This clause corresponds to clause 3 of the London Form.[79] Sections 148 and 149 of the Plan, which this clause replaces, relate, respectively, to " Objects insured " and " Objects temporarily removed from the ship."

1. The principal assured will be the owner. A number of other persons will nevertheless be co-insured.[80] The Conditions are so formulated that they can be used unaltered if the insurance is effected by a charterer or operator.

Clause 3 of the London Form assumes that more than one vessel may be insured thereunder; space therefore exists for a " Schedule of property insured." It is unlikely, however, according to the commentary, that more than one vessel would be covered by one policy based on the Norwegian Conditions.

2. The proviso in clause 4 (3) that the machinery and equipment in question should be " in the care, custody or control of a person whose interests are covered according to clause 15 " makes no reservation as to whether it is owned by that person. This corresponds to section 148.1 of the Plan, under which the insurance covers, apart from the ship, " equipment on board which belongs to the owners or which they have borrowed, hired or purchased on a hire-purchase agreement, and spare parts on board for the ship or her equipment."

Two matters, however, have been made more explicit in the Conditions:

(1) *The nature of the objects covered*
>On conventional ships the term " equipment " is a relatively firm concept. The equipment usually belongs to the shipowner and constitutes a modest proportion of the value. Drilling vessels will have not only comparable equipment but also drilling equipment. The latter may belong to the owner of the drilling vessel, to the operator, to the charterer, or even to an independent contractor. On a fully equipped semi-submersible the fixed and movable drilling equipment may represent as much as a third of the total values. Clause 3 of the London Form lists the items.[81] The Norwegian group responsible for the Conditions considered that such a list would be

---

[79] See p. 90, above.
[80] See cl. 15, below.
[81] See p. 90, above.

superfluous; and that it would be difficult to give a complete list, as it might be construed as being exhaustive. The reference, in clause 4 (1), to " equipment . . . above or under water and in hole " embraces principally the drill string and blowout preventers, though the cover for the drill string is subject to limitations set out later, in clauses 8 (1) and (2) and 9.1.

(2) *The rights over the equipment*

All the equipment on board owned by, lent to, or hired by the owner, charterer, operator or independent contractor, or any other third party, provided that it is in the care custody or control of a person whose interests are covered according to clause 15,[82] is covered.

3. As in the case of clause 3 of the London Form, clause 4 (2) affords cover for machinery and equipment separated from the drilling vessel but only in the situations set out there. An auxiliary vessel, for example, carrying some equipment, must be " used in connection with " the insured vessel. The commentary says that this means that the auxiliary vessel must be assisting drilling operations, and adds:

" Thus equipment on board a supply ship for transport to or from the insured vessel will not be covered; neither will equipment that has been transferred to a barge while the insured vessel is being repaired—whether the supply ship or barge is moored to or anchored in the vicinity of the insured vessel makes no difference. In both cases the equipment is assumed to be covered under the special equipment insurance, conditions for which have been drawn up by this Group."

4. Clause 4 (*b*) of the London Form [83] provides, as the commentary puts it different and far more extensive cover for equipment separated from the vessel. Such cover is available up to a limit of 25 per cent. of the total insured value while the equipment is " in temporary storage at, or in local transit to or from, ports or drilling barges." The Norwegian Group considered that it was more rational to provide such cover under a separate equipment insurance.[84]

5. Clause 4 (4) sets out certain exclusions from the cover:

(a) Relates to " materials and supplies intended for consumption in connection with the drilling operation." These will be covered under the special equipment insurance.

(b) Relates to articles intended for consumption but connected with the drilling vessel's other operations.

In the case of both (a) and (b) the London form gives combined coverage for hull and equipment and thus includes articles intended for consumption.

---

[82] See p. 205, below.
[83] See p. 97, above.
[84] See below.

(c) Excludes helicopters stationed on the drilling vessel. They would otherwise have been covered by virtue of the reference to equipment in clause 4 (1).

(d) Excludes " blue prints, plans, specifications and records." This corresponds to the exclusion in clause 8 (*n*) of the London Form.

6. The Norwegian Group decided not to exclude certain items which are excluded by the London Form. There are the following exclusions in clause 8 of that form:

(k) " Well(s) and/or hole(s) whilst being drilled or otherwise." It was thought that this exclusion was superfluous because the insured object is defined in clause 4 (1) and does not include the well or hole in any event.

(l) " drilling mud, cement, chemicals and fuel actually in use, and casing and tubing in the well." The Group considered that the exclusion, in the Norwegian Conditions, at clause 4 (4) (*a*) was sufficient to achieve this.

(m) " unrefined oil or gas or other crude product," and

(n) " personal effects of employees or others." It was thought that these exclusions were superfluous for the same reason as that applicable to (k) above.

" 5. PERILS EXCLUDED

The Insurer is not liable for loss caused by perils excluded in the Plan or by

(1) earthquake or volcanic eruption,

(2) the release of atomic energy—disintegration of atomic nuclei (fission) or fusing of atomic nuclei (fusion)—in connection with explosion of atomic weapons and atomic test explosions. If radioactive contamination or other direct influence from an explosion as mentioned in the first paragraph has been a contributive cause of the loss, the whole loss shall be deemed to be caused by such perils. When the insured vessel has been exposed to radioactive contamination the Assured has the burden of proving that the loss is not attributable to circumstances of the nature mentioned above,

(3) the drilling of a relief well performed by the insured vessel for the purpose of controlling or attempting to control a fire, blowout or cratering associated with another drilling vessel or drilling platform.

The Insurer is, however, liable for loss of or damage to the insured vessel resulting from measures taken by state authorities for the purpose of averting or minimising pollution damage. If the risk of the pollution damage has been caused by war perils (s. 16 of the Plan), the liability shall be covered by the war risk insurer; otherwise the insurer against marine perils (s. 15 of the Plan) shall pay."

1. Certain exclusions are set out in the Plan, at §§ 15 to 23, and thus form part of the present policy. These three exclusions are additional. The Plan provides that unless it is otherwise agreed the insurance only extends to marine perils, and not to war perils, and that an insurance against marine perils comprises " all perils to which the interest may be exposed." It is

therefore not necessary to speak of an all risks cover in the Conditions themselves.

2. Marine and war risks coverages are complementary. As a result of § 15 (*b*) of the Plan, however, " measures taken by Norwegian or allied State authorities," *i.e.* all public authorities, are excepted; nor are they insured by the war risks cover. It will be seen from the last paragraph of clause 5, however, that this position is modified somewhat in the case of pollution damage.

The commentary states that the effect of §§ 15 and 16 of the Plan, dealing with marine and war perils respectively, is to restrict coverage in much the same way as the free of capture and seizure clause (cl. 19) in the London Form. So far as there is any difference, it is the same as that existing between the English and Norwegian standard hull insurance conditions for conventional ships.

3. As a result of §§ 150 and 175 of the Plan losses resulting from " ordinary use " and from " Wear and tear, faulty materials, etc." (including " faulty construction ") are excluded. The exclusion would even extend to cases where no blame for the faulty construction attached to the builder—a situation which might well arise in the case of new drilling vessels sent to operate in exposed places. According to the commentary the London Form appeared to exclude all losses arising from faulty design. Part of clause 8 states: " there shall be no liability under this insurance in respect of: . . . (f) . . . error in design. . . ."

In discussing the approach of the Plan to faulty design the commentary concludes that:

(1) Total loss caused by faulty design is covered, as the exception in § 175 is contained in Chapter 12 of the Plan on " Damage " and not in Chapter 11 on " Total Loss."

(2) The exclusion of damage caused by faulty design relates only to the principal damage, *i.e.* " the cost of renewing or repairing such part as was not in a proper condition." Consequential losses, such as resultant damage to other parts of the vessel or cost of towage, are covered. The decisive question is what is meant by a " part " of the vessel.

(3) Insurance under the Plan covers damage due to faulty design if the damage consists of " the fracturing or cracking of a boiler or a part of the main engine." This is so because § 175.2 (*b*) so provides. This principle cannot be clearly applied to drilling vessels because, it is said, no part of the machinery (except presumably in the case of a drill ship) takes the form of a " main engine " and there is not a " boiler." The solution adopted in the Conditions is that one must read clauses 4, 5 and 8 [85] together, and combine them with sections 175 and 176 of the Plan, which are otherwise to apply.

---

[85] See p. 197, below.

4. Chapter 3 of the Plan exempts the insurer partly or wholly from liability where there is blameworthy conduct on the part of the insured. The Conditions do not alter this. Clause 5 of the London Form, however, states that the insurer is not liable for loss which is due to " want of due diligence by the Assured, the owners or Managers of the property insured or any of them." This is contrary to the Norwegian Insurance Contracts Act, s. 20, which says: " It cannot with legal effect be agreed that the company shall wholly or partly be exempted from liability when the occurrence has been caused by negligence on the part of the insured, unless such negligence can be deemed gross negligence." § 56 of the Plan, however, provides that in the event of gross negligence " the decision as to whether, and how much, the insurer shall pay shall be based on the degree of blame and the other circumstances of the case." In the version of the London Form used for Norwegian drilling vessels clause 5 has been altered to conform with § 56 of the Plan.

5. The exclusion in respect of " earthquake or volcanic eruption " in clause 5 (1) is taken from clause 8 (*a*) of the London Form. There is no corresponding exclusion in the hull insurance policies for conventional ships. If the insurance were to apply only to drilling vessels operating in the North Sea, it would hardly be necessary to have this exclusion, as the nearest volcanic region is Iceland. The Conditions, however, are formulated with a view to world-wide cover. Clause 8 (*a*) of the London Form states that there shall be no liability for " fire and/or explosion and/or tidal wave consequent upon earthquake or volcanic eruption." The Group which drafted the Conditions took the view that it was inappropriate to refer to these possible consequential results, as the insurer would be exempt in any event from all direct or indirect results of earthquake or volcanic eruption, except possibly damage which had no foreseeable connection therewith.

6. The exclusion in respect of " the release of atomic energy," in clause 5 (2), is similar in intent to the usual provision in the London Form that the radioactive contamination clause, " physical damage—direct(NMA 1191) " should apply to the insurance.

7. Clause 5 (3) contains an exclusion in respect of perils resulting from the drilling of a relief well by the insured vessel, to assist where there is a fire, blowout or cratering associated with another drilling vessel or drilling platform. There is a close parallel here with attempts at salvage of other ships. Under the Plan a conventional ship is covered in full in respect of the extra risk. As a result of clause 3 of the Conditions, by which a drilling vessel is treated as a ship, such a vessel is also covered in respect of that risk; but it was thought inappropriate to cover the salvage operation involved in drilling a relief well. There is considerable risk and it is in any event primarily the operator's interests that are at stake. The cover can be given by special agreement, however, though possibly with an additional premium.

Clause 8 (*c*) of the London Form,[86] however, covers this risk subject to " immediate notice " being given to the underwriters and an additional premium being paid if required. The view of the commentators is that on the whole the two provisions lead to the same practical result, though under the Norwegian Conditions the underwriters may refuse to give the additional cover.

8. Clause 8 of the London Form contains two exclusions which do not appear in the Norwegian cover: (i) Clause 8 (*b*) [87] excludes liability arising solely from intentional sinking for operational purposes, and says that such sinking shall not constitute a collision, stranding, sinking or grounding within the meaning of the insurance. This provision, which was formulated with reference to early drilling practices in the Gulf of Mexico was, in the view of the commentators, obsolete. Moreover, it might be misconstrued and taken to refer to a jack-up lowering its legs to the bottom. (ii) Clause 8 (*e*) [88] excludes liability for " loss, damage or expense caused by or resulting from delay, detention or loss of use." Such an exclusion was already contained in the Plan, as a result of §§ 63 and 68 2 (*b*), and was therefore superfluous here.

9. The last two sentences of 5 (3) provide that " the Insurer " (of marine risks except where the pollution resulted from war perils) shall be liable for loss or damage to the drilling vessel resulting from measures taken by state authorities to avert or minimise pollution damage. International and national legislation gives such authorities the right of intervention.

> " 6. SAFETY REGULATIONS
>
> In all operations, the well and/or hole shall be equipped with a minimum of three pressure operated blowout preventers of Standard make, installed and tested in accordance with usual practice.[89]
>
> The provisions of the preceding paragraph shall be considered a special safety regulation in relation to section 49 of the Plan."

Blowouts can result in extensive damage. It is important that all reasonable precautions are undertaken to prevent a blowout. The use of blowout preventers is a principal feature of such precautions. The safety regulations laid down by the relevant authorities, which apply in most offshore drilling areas, almost always require the use of blowout preventers. §§ 48 and 49 of the Plan require adherence to the appropriate safety regulations, and relieve the insurer of liability to the extent that non-compliance by the insured brings about the loss. It was nevertheless thought appropriate to insert an express provision in the Conditions as to blowout preventers. In any case there is always the possibility that in the relevant drilling area the appropriate authorities have not issued safety regulations.

---

[86] See p. 128, above.

[87] See p. 127, above.

[88] See p. 128, above.

[89] But there is no great danger of blowouts in the initial stage of the drilling, *i.e.* about the first 250 feet.

An earlier provision as to the number and type of blowout preventers has been simplified to: " blowout preventer of standard make will be used, same to be installed and tested in accordance with the usual practice." Under section 33 (3) of the English Marine Insurance Act 1906 breach of that warranty frees the insurers from liability whether or not the breach brought about the casualty. The Norwegian commentators say that (a) it is not certain whether such an interpretation would be adopted if the policy were judged according to Norwegian law; and (b) the Norwegian Group considers the English rule to be too severe, the underwriters' interests being sufficiently protected by the blowout preventer rules being interpreted as safety regulation.[90]

" 7. Condemnation
An insured vessel is not condemnable under section 163 of the Plan unless the cost of recovering and repairing the vessel shall exceed its insurable value."

The Norwegian title of this clause is *Kondemnasion*, of which the true translation is " Constructive total loss," though the latter is a wider concept; the more direct translation, " Condemnation," was preferred for the official English translation.

The provisions of the Plan as to total loss,[91] which include a paragraph entitled " Condemnation," [92] apply to the hull insurance of drilling vessels, but this clause is more strict than the corresponding paragraph in the Plan. The clause is similar to clause 12 of the London form,[93] which in turn corresponds to the second part of clause 17 of the Institute Time Clauses (Hulls).

There is a departure from the Plan in two respects: (1) Under the Plan a ship is " condemnable " when the cost of repairs " will amount to at least 80 per cent. of the insurable value, or of her value in repaired condition, where this value is higher than the insurable value." In the Conditions, however, the cost of repair has to exceed the insurable value, *i.e.* the assessed value, and it is always in relation to that insurable value. As the Commentary puts it: " If the assessed insurable value is less than the real value of the vessel (undervaluation), the real value will be the governing value according to the Plan, whereas under this clause it will still be the assessed insurable value. Under the Plan the insured is unable to operate with a low value the more easily to secure condemnation. In that respect the arrangement under the Plan is the more advantageous seen from an underwriter's point of view." This Group considers, however, that it would be unreasonable to combine the English 100 per cent. limit with the Norwegian rule of applying the real value of the ship when that is higher

---

[90] See the reference to § 49, above. § 49.2 states: "...negligence by anybody whose duty it is on behalf of the assured to carry out the regulation or to see that it is complied with, is considered equivalent to the negligence of the assured himself."
[91] Chap. 11.
[92] § 163.
[93] See p. 140, above.

than the assessed insurable value. Such a combination would be more restrictive than both the Norwegian and the English rule. (2) Under the Plan [94] the repair costs consist of all the costs of removal and repairs which, when the request for condemnation is made, are anticipated as necessary if the ship is repaired, but not salvage remuneration. Under clause 7 of the Conditions " the cost of recovering . . . the vessel," *i.e.* salvage remuneration, is included; expenses for salvage already effected at the time of the request for condemnation cannot be included.[95] An insured would likewise have, if covered by the Norwegian Conditions, to submit a request for condemnation before the salvage operations if he wanted to have the salvage money included, as it is thought that English practice would be followed.

Clause 17 of the Institute Time Clauses (Hulls) [96] says that the value of the wreck shall not be taken into account when deciding whether a ship is condemnable. Clause 12 of the London Form,[97] however, and clause 7 of the Norwegian Conditions, omit this provision. The Commentary says that this does not mean that it should be taken into account; the value of the wreck is, as stated in the " Motives for the Plan," irrelevant. The same is the position in English law.[98]

> " 8. DAMAGE. To sections 175 and 176 of the Plan
> The insurer is not liable for
> (1) loss of or damage to drill string located underground or underwater, unless directly resulting from fire, blowout or cratering.
> (2) loss of or damage to drill string left in the well and through which an oil gas well is completed
> (3) the scraping and painting of the insured vessel's bottom.
> Otherwise sections 175 and 176 of the Plan shall apply."

The clause adds certain limitations to those imposed by § 175 (" wear and tear, faulty material, etc.") and § 176 (" Loss excluded from insurer's liability ") in Chapter 12 (" Damage ").

Items (1) and (2) correspond to clause 8 (*j*) of the London Form,[99] with an exception mentioned below. The underwriters do not wish to cover this risk, which may arise as a result of lack of skill or diligence by those responsible for the operations; they only wish to cover loss or damage caused by certain clearly demonstrable external hazards, as set out in item (1).

In addition to the three causes of damage to the drill string mentioned above, *i.e.* fire, blowout and cratering, which the Norwegian underwriters are willing to cover, clause 8 (*j*) of the London Form adds " total loss of the Drilling Barge." Thus, the commentators add, the insured sum would be

---

[94] § 163.4
[95] See also s. 60 (2) (ii) of the Marine Insurance Act 1906.
[96] See p. 147, above.
[97] See p. 140, above.
[98] See Chalmers' *Marine Insurance Act* 1906 (7th ed., 1971), pp. 89 to 90.
[99] See p. 128, above.

paid in full in such a case without deduction of the value of the drill string, regardless of whether the total loss were caused by fire, blowout or cratering. Under the system employed in the Norwegian Plan, however, it is not necessary to provide express authority for this.

Item (2) in clause 8 is taken from clause 8 (*j*) of the London Form. It applies where the drill string is left underground for operational reasons, and not where it is abandoned owing to technical difficulties. If it is to serve as a pipeline for gas or oil produced from the well it is no longer part of the drilling equipment and should no longer be covered by the insurance.

Item (3), relating to the scraping and painting of the drilling vessel's bottom, corresponds to clause 8 (*o*) of the London form.

Clause 8 of the London Form contains two exceptions which are not set out in clause 8 of the Norwegian Conditions. They are subsections (h), which excludes:

" Liabilities to third parties except as specifically covered under the terms of the Collision Liability Clause contained herein "

and (*i*) which excludes:

" Claims in connection with the removal of property, material, debris or obstruction, whether such removal be required by law, ordinance, statute, regulation or otherwise."

Both of these items are covered by § 74 of the Norwegian Plan.

As for collision liability, hull insurance is an insurance of property and does not extend to the insured's liabilities to third parties unless there is express provision to this effect, as there is under clause 10 of these Conditions.[1]

As for wreck removal (to use a phrase which summarises the matters set out in clause 8 (*i*) of the London form), this is covered by the P. & I. insurances.[2] Wreck removal liability in respect of war risks falls, as a result of § 167 of the Plan, on the war risks insurers except where they specially provide to the contrary.

" 9. Deductions New For Old
    Loss of or damage to the drill string is recoverable subject to a deduction of 2 per cent. for each month which has elapsed since the commencement of the month in which the objects were taken into use, but not more than 50 per cent.
    Loss of or damage to in-hole equipment and other drilling equipment is recoverable subject to a deduction of 1 per cent. for each month which has elapsed since the commencement of the month in which the objects were taken into use, but not more than 50 per cent.

The modern view is that in most cases the gain made by the shipowner, in connection with repairs of damage, is non-existent or minimal. The Plan does not therefore provide for deductions new for old as part of the normal cover, but it allows for the possibility that there will be an agreement to

---

[1] See p. 199, below.
[2] See Chap. 6, below.

this effect.[3] The Conditions follow the normal practice of the Plan so far as concerns the drilling vessel's hull, machinery or ordinary deck or engine equipment. They provide, however, for deductions as set out above in respect of the drill string, in-hole equipment and other drilling equipment, much of which is extremely expensive. It is subject to heavy wear and needs renewing after a relatively short period of use. If no deduction were made the insured would be unreasonably well rewarded.

" 10. COLLISION LIABILITY. To sections 194 to 196 of the Plan
The Assured's liability is covered only in case of collision between the insured vessel and a ship or between the insured vessel and another drilling vessel.
Liability imposed on the Assured arising from loss caused by cargo on board the colliding vessels or ships and loss through pollution or fire or explosion caused by oil or gas is covered by the Insurer only as far as such loss is caused to the other colliding vessel or ship, its equipment and cargo. Section 194.2, paragraph (*i*), of the Plan to apply correspondingly.
Otherwise sections 194 to 196 of the Plan to apply."

1. Hull insurance contains traditionally an element of liability insurance as within certain limits the underwriters cover collision. This is dealt with in Chapter 13 of the Norwegian Plan, entitled " Assured's liability for collision or striking."
2. The Institute Time Clause (Hulls)[4] cover the liability arising when the insured ship collides with " any other vessel "; the American Institute Time Clauses contain a corresponding clause. § 194 of the Norwegian Plan, however, goes further by covering " liability imposed on the assured for loss caused, through collision or striking by the ship, including equipment and cargo, or by a tug used by the ship." It thus covers liability for collisions (or strikings) with objects other than ships, such as piers, bridges and similar permanent installations, and for collisions between the insured vessel's tug and a third vessel.[5] The Plan also covers collision and strikings where the liability is imposed contractually, as where the tow's liability arises under a towage contract and the only error has been on the part of the tug, if the terms of the contract are customary in the trade concerned. Under the English form this is not covered.[6]

With some exceptions clause 10 of the Norwegian Conditions is based on clause 6 of the London Form, which in turn is based on the collision liability clause in the American hull insurance conditions. Liability for striking permanent installations, such as a pier, and for collision between the insured's tug and a third vessel, is thus not covered.

In two respects the cover under the Norwegian Conditions is wider than

[3] §§ 191 (" Insurance subject to new for old deductions "), 192 (" Calculation of the age "), and 193 (" Amount of the new for old deductions ").
[4] Cl. 1, the running down clause.
[5] For guidance as to whether an English type of policy would afford cover in these latter cases see *The Niobe* [1891] A.C. 401 (H.L.); Arnould on *Marine Insurance* (15th ed., 1961), para. 781, n. 25; and Chalmers' *Marine Insurance Act* (8th ed., 1976), p. 204, n. 6.
[6] See *Furness, Withy & Co.* v. *Duder* [1936] 2 K.B. 461 and Arnould, *loc. cit.* para. 778.

under the London Form. First, there is cover for collision with "another drilling vessel," whether or not it can be regarded as a ship in the legal sense. The commentators have considered whether a drilling unit which carries out work on a well without actually drilling can be regarded as "another drilling vessel" for the purpose of clause 10. They concluded that the use of the words "used for off-shore drilling operations" in the definition in clause 2 (1) clearly meant that a structure is not to be regarded as a drilling vessel only while drilling is being carried out. Furthermore, during shifting, during preparation for drilling and immediately thereafter, and while laid up, it is, they said, a "drilling vessel" if it was designed for offshore drilling. It only fell outside the definition if it was used over lengthy periods, or permanently, for activities which were not drilling operations. Secondly, the insurers cover collision liability based on contract, such as liability under a towage contract for damage to the tug caused by an error on the part of the tug. This follows not from the Conditions as expressed but from § 194 of the Plan, which refers to "liability imposed . . . through collision or striking by the ship, including equipment and cargo, or by a tug used by the ship."

3. Clause 6 of the London Form, which deals with collision liability, excludes, at (c) and (d)[7] of the proviso thereto, liability " in consequence of, or with respect to . . .

(c) the discharge, spillage, emission or leakage of oil, petroleum products, chemicals or other substances of any kind or description whatsoever;

(d) cargo or other property on or the engagements of the vessel ";

Exclusion (c) in the London Form is subject to the provision that it " shall not apply to injury to any other vessel with which the Vessel is in collision or to property on such other vessel except to the extent that such injury arises out of any action taken to avoid, minimise or remove any discharge, spillage, emission or leakage described in (c)."[8] The Norwegian commentators say that there is a parallel to (c) in the Norwegian " Large hull insurance policy (Cefor Form No. 128), clause 1.8, which reads:

" . . . Re section 194, 2nd paragraph of the Plan.
The Insurer is not liable in respect of liability imposed on the assured arising from loss through pollution and/or fire or explosion caused by oil or similar liquid or volatile products and/or liability arising from loss through contamination by radioactive substances. In the event of collision with another vessel the insurer covers the assured's liability for such loss caused to the other vessel, its equipment or cargo.
Section 194, 2nd paragraph (i) of the Plan applied correspondingly."

As for exclusion (d) in the London Form, the commentators say that it would appear to apply only to liability for damage to cargo on board the insured ship, and that it does extend to liability for damage caused by that

---

[7] See p. 110, above.
[8] This is an exception, but it is itself subject to an exception. See also p. 110, above.

cargo to a third party. In the Norwegian Conditions, they say, the more extensive limitation has been selected. This is shown by the second paragraph of clause 10; the underwriter does not cover liability for damage caused by cargo on board the vessels in collision except in the case of damage to the other ship, its equipment or cargo. An example would be pollution caused by oil leakage from a tanker in a collision.

" 11. DEDUCTIBLE. To sections 189 and 197 of the Plan

Loss of or damage to in-hole equipment and underwater equipment whilst not in hole or under water, is covered subject to a deductible of U.S. $5,000 each casualty.

Other loss is covered subject to a single deductible equivalent to one per cent. of the sum insured, but not less than U.S. $50,000 and not more than U.S. $200,000 each casualty.

Damage due to heavy weather, and which has arisen during one stay in port or during one drilling period, counts as one casualty. A drilling period is the period between the insured vessel's departure from port and its departure from the first location where a hole has been drilled (" drilling location "), the period between its departure from one drilling location and its departure from the next drilling location, the period between departure from its last drilling location and the arrival at port, or, in cases where no drilling has been performed en route, the period between departure from one port and arrival at the next port."

As for the sections of the Plan to which the clause refers, § 189 deals with " Franchise " in Chapter 12 (" Damage "); § 197 also deals with " Franchise," but in Chapter 13 (" Assured's liability for collision or striking "); and § 187, in Chapter 12, with " Machinery damage deductions."

1. There are two important departures from the Norwegian Plan in the second paragraph of clause 11: first, there is only one deductible for damage and collision liability arising from the same casualty, whereas under the Plan there is a separate deductible for each; secondly, the deductibles are those applicable under the London Form, and thus higher than under the Plan.

2. The high deductible stipulated in the second paragraph means that the insured will often have no cover for damage sustained by separate components of the drilling vessel or articles of equipment. As a result the Norwegian insurers have, in the first paragraph of clause 11, followed the practice of the insurers who use the London Form. The latter, in a supplementary clause, introduced a special deductible of $5,000 for loss of or damage to in-hole and underwater equipment while not in hole or under water.

3. It may be difficult to say whether damage suffered during rough weather constitutes one or several casualties. The Plan solves the problem by applying one franchise to all such damage " between departure from one port and arrival at the next port." In the Conditions, however, the concept of a " drilling period." as defined in the third paragraph of clause 11, has been used.

The London Form, in the second paragraph of the clause dealing with deductibles,[9] states that " it is agreed that a sequence of losses or damages arising from the same occurrence shall be treated as one occurrence." The Norwegian commentators refer to the difficulty of interpreting the words " arising from," and the need to apply " causation rules—the English-American rules, that is—under which the intervention of a new, unconnected and unexpected incident breaks the ' chain of casuation.' " [10] They felt that this provision could be confusing if the Plan and Norwegian law were to be applied.

4. Under § 189.2 of the Plan no deductible applies to settlement costs and losses connected with measures to avert or minimise the loss. The same rule applies in the case of a collision, as a result of § 197.2, which applies the same rule also to the costs of litigation. In the London Form, however, the deductible is applied to " each claim (including claims under the Sue and Labour Clause and the Collision Liability Clause)."

5. Where the insured has to accept a reduction in his claim as a result of some other provision in the Plan, the full deductible applies after that reduction has been made. For example, if the assured has to bear a 25 per cent. reduction of his claim as a result of § 56 of the Plan,[11] the full deductible is applied to the remaining 75 per cent. payable.

" 12. Loss Through Measures to Avert or Minimise the Loss. To sections 68 to 73 of the Plan.

(1) To sections 80 (*a*) and 196 of the Plan. The Insurer is not liable in excess of the sum insured (s. 79.1 of the Plan), respectively the separate sum insured pursuant to section 196 of the Plan, for loss through measures to avert or minimise the loss.

The Insurer is liable, however, up to the separate sum insured pursuant to section 196 of the Plan, for loss through measures to avert or minimise damage or total loss exceeding the sum insured for such loss, to the extent the separate sum insured is not consumed by liability for collision and for loss through measures to avert or minimise such liability.

(2) Where measures taken to avert or minimise a loss which would have been recoverable from another insurer, have struck an interest covered under this insurance, the Insurer shall be subrogated to the Assured's claim against the other insurer. Section 96 of the Plan shall apply correspondingly.

(3) Loss through measures taken to control or attempting to control blowout or cratering or in fighting fire associated with blowout is not covered under sections 68 to 73 of the Plan."

The references to the Plan made in Clause 12 can be summarised:

§§ 68 to 73 In Chapter 4 (" The insurer's liability "), they constitute Subdivision 2 (" Loss through measures to avert or minimise the loss ").

---

[9] Clause 7; see p. 124, above.

[10] They refer to Buglass on *Marine Insurance and General Average in the United States* (1973), pp. 78–82.

[11] This deals with casualties caused by gross negligence by the assured, and provides for a reduction in the recovery which is dependent upon the degree of blame to be attached to him.

§ 80 (*a*)   § 80, entitled " Liability in excess of the sum insured," refers to certain matters in respect of which the insurer is liable even if the sum insured is exceeded. These include the measures mentioned in §§ 68 to 73.

§ 196   In Chapter 13 (" Assured's liability for collision and striking "), § 196 is entitled " Insurer's maximum liability in respect of one casualty."

§ 79.1   In Chapter 4 (see above), Subdivision 4 (" The sum insured as limit of insurer's liability "), § 79 (" Principal rule ") provides, at 79.1 for the insurer to have a separate liability for third party liabilities arising from collision or striking.

§ 96   In Chapter 5 (" Claims settlement "), Subdivision 3 (" Assured's claim for damages against third party "), § 96 is entitled " Insurer's right of subrogation to the assured's claim for damages against third party."

1. The Plan's rules as to loss prevention measures apply to the Conditions and are equivalent to the Sue and Labour Expense provision in the London Form.[12]

2. Clause 13 of the London Form limits the underwriters' liability for " Sue and Labour Expense " to " 25 per cent. of the insured value of the item(s) in the Defence, Safeguard or Recovery of which such expense is incurred." The Norwegian commentators say that the underwriters' liability might therefore amount to 225 per cent. of the insured sum, *i.e.* total loss of a vessel by collision, collision liability high enough to consume the insured sum for the second time, [13] and on top of that expenses to avert or minimise the loss that exceed 25 per cent. of the insured sum." Under the Norwegian Conditions the insurers' liability would not, they say, exceed twice the insured sum. On the other hand, in the event of a total loss without collision liability the Norwegian cover would afford another 100 per cent. of the insured sum for sue and labour expenses, as compared with 25 per cent. under the London Form.

3. As for clause 12 (2), let us suppose that a vessel is sunk by the authorities to avoid or reduce pollution. The intervention minimised a liability of the owners which would otherwise have fallen on the P. & I. insurers. The owners would also have a claim on their hull insurance.[14] Settlement could then take place between the insurers in accordance with clause 12 (2).

4. Clause 12 (3), based on Clause 8 (*d*) of the London Form,[15] applies unless the measures are intended to save the insured drilling vessel or to minimise the danger to it as a result of the blowout or other matters listed.

---

[12] Cl. 13; see p. 154, above.
[13] Because the collision liability cover constitutes a separate insurance.
[14] See cl. 5, last two sentences, at p. 192, above.
[15] See p. 128, above.

The thought behind this limitation is that these casualties are primarily threats to the oil source itself. It is essentially the operator's affair. Such an exclusion, say the commentators, is also a strong incentive to the owner of the drilling vessel to cover himself through an agreement with the operator that the full costs of measures taken in connection with blowouts, etc. should be borne by the operator.

" 13. RETURN OF PREMIUM. To sections 122–126 of the Plan

If the insured vessel in the course of the period of insurance stays at least 30 consecutive days in a safe port or place approved by the Insurer the Insurer shall return:

70 per cent. of the premium for time in such port or place during which repairs are carried out on the insured vessel,

90 per cent. of the premium for other time in such port or place, provided that

(a) there shall always be a watchman on board,
(b) there shall be no shifts during the lay up period, and
(c) there shall be no movement of legs or variation of buoyancy during the lay up period."

The reference to the Plan made in clause 13 can be summarised:

§§ 122–126   In Chapter 6 (" Premium "), these sections deal (§§ 122–125) with reduction of premium during a stay in port; and (§ 126) with the manner in which a claim therefor should be made.

Clause 13 corresponds to the first three paragraphs of Clause 14 of the London Form,[16] and in both cases the minimum required period for lay up is 30 consecutive days. According to the latter the location has to be " approved by surveyor appointed by Lloyd's Agents or approved by Underwriters." In this clause the requirements are that the location should be " safe " and approved by the insurer.

This clause gives the rates of return whereas the London form refers to a return " daily pro rata of rates to be agreed by Underwriters."

" 14. OTHER INSURANCES AGAINST TOTAL LOSS. To section 160 of the Plan

The Assured shall be permitted to effect hull-interest insurance or gross earnings insurance or any other insurance against total loss of the insured vessel in excess of hull insurance covering 100 per cent. of the insurable value stated in the policy, but the total sum insured under such excess covers must be limited to 25 per cent. of the said insurable value.

If the Assured received any compensations under an insurance effected in breach of the provisions of the preceding paragraph, the Insurer's liability shall be reduced correspondingly."

§ 160 of the Plan, " Reduction of liability in consequence of a hull-interest insurance," states: " Where the assured, as compensation under a hull interest insurance, receive an amount exceeding 25 per cent. of the assessed value applicable to the hull insurance against the same perils, the hull insurer's liability is reduced accordingly."

---

[16] " Lay Up and Cancellation "; see pp. 155 *et seq.*, above.

The London market originally refused to allow total loss coverage in addition to full hull coverage for drilling vessels. It later relaxed its attitude. From 1973 a " gross earnings under contract " insurance in addition to hull insurance was allowed for a sum up to 25 per cent. of the hull value. It is purely a hull interest insurance effected for total loss only. The addendum to the London form dated July 27, 1973, consists of an " Other Insurance Warranty " which forbids additional insurances against total loss only, but makes an exception for 25 per cent. additional coverage with the hull insurers themselves.[17]

Clause 14 of the Norwegian Conditions follows this practice. It is wider in its application than § 160 in that it forbids any form of " against total loss " insurance in excess of the 25 per cent. limit, including freight interest insurances.

The London Form's " Other Insurance Warranty " differs from the Norwegian Conditions in that the term " additional insurance " is said to extend to all total loss insurances " by or for the account of the Assured, Owners, Managers, Operators, Charterers or Mortgagees." The Norwegian view is that this exclusion is too wide, and that such other parties may have an independent insurable interest in the vessel.

" 15. INSURANCE OF THE INTEREST OF THIRD PARTIES. To section 127 of the Plan

This insurance is effected for the benefit of the owners, charterers, drilling contractors and operators of the insured vessel. The Insurer agrees to waive his right of subrogation against these Assureds. The limit stated in section 138, second paragraph of the plan shall be U.S. $500,000."

§ 127 of the Plan appears in Chapter 7 (" Insurance of the interest of third party ") and is entitled " Scope of the rules." It applies five of the later sections (§§ 128 to 132) of the chapter: as to duty of disclosure; loss of assured's rights owing to acts or omissions of the person effecting the insurance; amendments to and termination or cancellation of the contract; settlement of claims; and rights of the insurer against the person effecting the insurance) to insurances effected, wholly or in part, for the benefit of a third party, whether named or not.

As a result of § 127.2 of the Plan the insurance does not cover third party interests in the vessel unless there is express agreement to that effect or unless such cover arises from other provisions in the Plan. Clause 15 constitutes an express agreement to cover certain other interests; and Chapter 8 of the Plan, entitled " Insurance also covering mortgagees' interest " is an example of such cover arising from other provisions of the Plan.

" Charterers, drilling contractors and operators " will, as a result of clause 15, be regarded as co-insured, with the owners, under the policy. " Charterers " include bareboat charterers. Occasionally one of these other parties may have effected the hull insurance; as a result the owners' interest

---

[17] See p. 204, above.

would be co-insured. In discussing the term " contractors " the Norwegian commentators say that while they are the companies who undertake to perform drilling operations with the vessel, the owners themselves may be the contractors [18]; the expression also embraces a " manager " who is not the owner but who manages the drilling operation on behalf of, or in co-operation with the owners. The " operators " are those to whom the petroleum exploration and production licence for the area has been issued·

Co-insurance will be of particular importance:

(1) when the co-insured has a financial interest in the insured object, as, for example, in the drilling equipment. Under clause 4 (1) and (2) of the Conditions [19] such equipment is covered while it is on board the vessel, or is being used for drilling " above or under water and in hole " or is on board another vessel " in the vicinity of the insured vessel and used in connection with this vessel." Under clause 4 (3) it is covered irrespective of ownership when in the " care, custody or control " of a person insured as a result of clause 15;

(2) in that it serves as an indirect insurance of the co-insured persons' liability towards each other, as, for example, where equipment belonging to the owner of the vessel is damaged owing to the negligence of employees of the operator. If the hull insurer pays in the first place he would normally be entitled to recover the amount of the owner's claim from the operator; however, in the drilling contract the owner will in many cases have waived his right to such a claim. Under the Plan the insurer could reduce his payment to the owner to the extent that the latter has debarred him from making such recovery, unless such a waiver is " customary in the trade in question." [20] As a result of clause 15, however, the operator is also an insured and can make a claim under the Norwegian Insurance Contracts Act, s. 20, even if he or his employee was negligent. The same principle applies if the underwriter wishes to exercise a right of subrogation, the owner of the drilling vessel having made the claim. This is a rule of Norwegian law but it is also set out in the second sentence of clause 15. There are some limits to the application of this rule where the party concerned (the operator in this example) has been guilty of gross negligence. [21]

(3) In cases of collision liability. For example, a bareboat charterer of a drilling vessel might incur liability for a collision in his capacity as " owner," *i.e.* as employer of the crew. As a result of clause 15 his liability will be covered by the hull insurance effected by the owner.

Co-insurance of a mortgagee's interest, under Chapter 8 of the Plan, [22] is described by the Norwegian commentators as a dependent co-insurance, in

---

[18] This is the sense in which the term is used elsewhere in this book.
[19] See p. 189, above.   [20] § 97 of the Plan.
[21] § 56 of the Plan.   [22] " Insurance also covering mortgagee's interest."

that the mortgagee's claim against the underwriter cannot be greater than that of the owner.[23] Under Clause 15, however, co-insurance follows Chapter 7 of the Plan[24] and is in principle independent. Thus omissions on the part of one insured resulting in his losing all or part of his claim against the underwriter do not usually affect the claims of the other persons insured. There are some important exceptions which are relevant to drilling vessels. For example, § 129 of the Plan, in Chapter 7,[25] states:

" Where the subject-matter insured is in the custody of the person effecting the insurance or has been left with somebody holding it on his behalf, the rules concerning the assured's loss of rights against the insurer shall apply correspondingly to acts and omissions of the persons effecting the insurance, even if no blame attaches to the assured."

Furthermore, certain sanctions, as, for example, against the omission of information required according to the rules of the Plan[25] also affect an insured who did not place the insurance.

---

[23] § 134.1 of the Plan, the relevant words of which are " . . . the mortgagee's rights against the insurer shall not exceed the rights of the owner."

[24] " Insurance of the interest of third party."

[25] §§ 24 *et seq.* (Duty of disclosure, fraud and dishonesty, etc.).

CHAPTER 5

PROTECTING AND INDEMNITY COVER—GENERALLY

PROTECTING and indemnity cover has its origin in the third party liability insurance given to shipowners by the mutual clubs which arose in England during the first half of the nineteenth century. The most distinctive feature of P. & I. cover is to be found in the system of calls; members pay an advance call, usually representing a substantial part of the total estimated call, in the first part of the policy year; they then, after the policy year has ended, pay a supplementary call. The total of the supplementary calls needed from the members as a whole depends upon the experience of the Club in that year, as represented by the amount needed for claims paid and outstanding estimates. The supplementary call is usually expressed, for all members, as a percentage of the advance call. It is the same percentage, payable by all [1] irrespective of their individual records in that year; in that fact lies the mutuality of a Club, each contributing to the losses of the others.

Although there are usually between 30 and 40 heads of cover in a P. & I. Club's Rules, the main groups may be categorised as follows:

A. Loss of Life, Personal Injury, Illness, etc. [2]
B. Statutory and Contractual Obligations towards Employees [3]
C. Liability to Ships and Other Property [4]
D. Excess Collision Insurance [5]
E. Liability under Contracts [6]
F. Removal of Wreck [7]
G. Property of Others on the Insured Vessel [8]
H. Various Other Matters—Life Salvage, Quarantine Expenses, Fines, etc. [9]
I. Legal and Associated Expenses [10]

The protecting and indemnity clubs now insure virtually all the world's ocean-going tonnage, though it is possible to obtain some protecting and indemnity cover elsewhere in the insurance market. Such cover outside the clubs, which is rarely sought in the case of ocean-going ships, may be needed for temporary purposes such as a break-up voyage or for certain port movements where full club cover for 12 months is inappropriate. So far as drilling units are concerned there are also the two same sources of cover, though the proportion of drilling units insured on the market, as

---

[1] Apart from a small category on a fixed premium basis.
[2] See p. 209, below.
[3] See p. 210, below.
[4] See p. 211, below.
[5] See p. 214, below.
[6] See p. 214, below.
[7] See p. 216, below.
[8] See p. 217, below.
[9] See p. 218, below.
[10] See p. 220, below.

opposed to being insured with the P. & I. Clubs, is much more substantial than in the case of conventional ships.

A distinction has to be made between the cover afforded by the P. & I. Clubs generally, other than two Norwegian Clubs; and the two Norwegian Clubs, *i.e.* Assuranceforeningen Gard, or Gard, and Assuranceforeningen Skuld, or Skuld. The basic difference is that the P. & I. Clubs provide cover for drilling units by means of their own coventional policies, or sets of Rules, as used for ships generally, subject to specific terms and exclusions applicable to drilling units, but that the Norwegian Clubs have separate forms of policies for use in respect of drilling units only.[11] The wording of the cover given by each P. & I. Club to its members is almost exactly the same in every case. So far as individual heads of cover are quoted below they are taken from the Rules of one particular P. & I. Club, however,[12] and may differ slightly from the wording adopted by other Clubs.

Cover Given by the P. & I. Clubs Generally

In the case of the P. & I. Clubs generally, Club cover is given in respect of the matters normally covered by their Rules, subject to certain terms and exclusions. Some of these terms and exclusions are contained in the form of cover applicable to conventional ships; others are peculiar to drilling units, and are set out below.

In the following commentary the words " drilling unit " have been inserted wherever the word " ship " appears in the Club cover. The P. & I. Clubs under consideration normally accept as members the owner of the drilling unit, *i.e.* the contractor, and any of its subsidiaries, including the management firm, but not the operator.

A. Loss of Life, Personal Injury, Illness, Etc.

This cover is in respect of damages or compensation for which the owner is liable towards

(a) any person, other than a person referred to in (b) hereunder, or in Section B, below (including hospital, medical or funeral expenses) in respect of loss of life, personal injury or illness or loss of or damage to personal effects, if the liability arose out of a negligent act or omission on board or in relation to the entered drilling unit. A proviso to this head of cover states that where the liability arises under the terms of any indemnity or contract and would not have arisen but for such terms, such liability shall not be recoverable under this head but may be recoverable under a later category dealing with indemnities. The P. & I. Club cover for conventional ships refer also to negligence in relation to the handling of cargo and to persons engaged in the handling of cargo; although, as has been explained above, the usual P. & I. Rules are incorporated in the cover for

---

[11] See Chap. 6, below.
[12] The United Kingdom Mutual Steam Ship Assurance Association (Bermuda) Ltd.

drilling units a reference to cargo is clearly inapplicable in the present case.

(b) any person in or on board any other ship or vessel (which includes a drilling unit) caused by the negligent navigation or management of the entered drilling unit or other negligent act or omission on board or in relation to the entered drilling unit.

B. Statutory and Contractual Obligations Towards Employees

Protection is afforded to the owner of the drilling unit in respect of various special liabilities towards the unit's personnel. They may be on or proceeding to or from the drilling unit. The drilling contract would usually provide that the contractor and the operator are each responsible for their own personnel, their rights of recourse against each other being waived.

The Club insures the liabilities of a member in respect of damages, compensations or expenses arising from:

(a) Loss of life, personal injury or illness of any employee on the entered drilling unit or proceeding to or from it arising by statute or under any employment agreement or other contract of service, provided that such agreement shall previously have been approved on behalf of the Club.

(b) Repatriation as a statutory obligation or under the terms of any agreement or contract of service or employment in respect of any personnel, subject to the proviso in (a) above. No such expenses are recoverable if they arise out of or ensue upon the termination of any agreement either in accordance with its terms or by mutual consent, or out of the sale of the drilling unit or any other act of the member.

(c) Sending out substitutes or securing, engaging, repatriating or deporting a substitute engaged abroad, to replace an employee on board the entered drilling unit who shall have died, or shall have been left ashore in consequence of injury, illness, desertion or in any other case in which the Directors shall determine that such expenses were reasonably incurred. No such expenses are recoverable if they arise out of or ensue upon the termination of any agreement either in accordance with its terms or by mutual consent, or out of the breach by the assured of any statutory or contractual obligations to drilling unit personnel. Wages are only recoverable as part of such expenses when payable to substitutes engaged abroad, while awaiting and during repatriation.

(d) Payments to personnel for loss of effects by marine perils, if incurred under statutory or other legal obligation or any crew agreement or other contract of service or employment, subject to the proviso in (a) above.

(e) Wages or other compensation payable to any employee under statutory obligation or under the terms of any crew agreement or other contract of service or employment, in consequence of the actual or constructive total loss of an entered drilling unit, subject to the provision in (a) above. In the case of conventional ships this is known as shipwreck unemployment indemnity.

(f) Landing or disposing of stowaways or refugees or landing or securing treatment for an injured or sick person being carried in an entered drilling unit, being port charges and the net loss to the member in respect of fuel, insurance, wages, stores and provisions incurred for such purpose or while awaiting a substitute for such person. These have also been called port and deviation expenses, or, alternatively, deviation expenses. It would seem improbable that a person could successfully become a stowaway on something as restricted in its accommodation as a drilling unit, though the possibility cannot be excluded. The reference to refugees was added by the P. & I. Clubs to the earlier wording as a result of the experiences of ships in South-East Asian waters, when refugees in small boats asked to be taken on board.

C. Liability to Ships and Other Property

(1) *Collisions with ships and other drilling units*

(a) *Collisions with conventional and drilling ships.* A typical P. &. I. Club cover in respect of collision liability is expressed in such terms as " One fourth of an Owner's liability, with costs incidental thereto, for damage done by collision with any other ship or vessel including the one fourth liability which is not covered under the usual Lloyd's Policy on Hull and Machinery with Running Down Clause attached and which may not be covered under other forms of Hull Policy approved by the Managers; if the Hull Policies exclude a less fraction than one fourth, the fraction so excluded." There is also a provision in P. & I. Club Rules to the effect that the Club shall not cover any of the liabilities, costs and expenses against which an owner would be insured if the entered ship were fully insured for its full value under hull policies on terms not less wide than those of the usual Lloyd's policy with Institute Time Clauses (Hulls), including the Running Down Clause, attached.

If a drilling unit is insured on the London Standard Drilling Barge Form, and by a P. & I. Club, its cover in respect of liability for collision with another ship will be provided by the L.S.D.B. policy, so that the Club collision liability policy will not be needed. This is because the L.S.D.B. collision clause applies " if the Vessel shall come into collision with any other ship or vessel." If, however, the drilling unit is a drilling ship, and is covered by the Institute Time Clauses, then it would, if also entered in a P. & I. Club, have to recover one-fourth of its collision liability from the Club.

(b) *Collisions with other drilling units.* A collision may take place between a drilling unit and another drilling unit, other than a drilling ship. One would examine first the hull insurance policy to see whether any liability was insured thereunder. In the case of the London Standard Drilling Barge Form, and some other policies commonly used to insure the hulls of the drilling units themselves, the collision cover extends [13] to liability " if

---

[13] See p. 109, above.

the Vessel shall come into collision with any other ship or vessel." Where a drilling unit, of whatever nature, entered in the P. & I. Club, has a hull insurance in such terms, its owner need not look to the P. & I. Club as the liability is covered by the hull insurer, provided that the hull insurer agrees to treat the other drilling unit as a " ship or vessel." If that other drilling unit is a drilling ship this would clearly be the case; it is understood that even if it falls under one of the other categories of drilling unit the incident will also be treated as constituting a collision with another " ship or vessel " for the purpose of the policy.

The drilling unit might, on the other hand, as in the case of a drilling ship, be insured under the usual Lloyd's policy, as described above, with the Running Down Clause attached. The Running Down Clause in the Lloyd's policy then responds to as three-quarters of the collision liability " if the Vessel hereby insured shall come into collision with any other vessel and the Assured shall in consequence thereof become liable to pay and shall pay by way of damages " [etc.] to the other side. In the present case we have assumed that the drilling unit entered in the P. & I. Club is a drilling ship and that the collision is with another drilling unit. There are then two possibilities. First, the collision may be with another drilling unit which is also a drilling ship. If so the other drilling unit clearly falls within the words " any other vessel " used in the Running Down Clause and the hull underwriters would respond as to three-quarters of the collision liability. The other possibility is that the collision may be with another drilling unit which is not a drilling ship. It is understood that in such a case the incident would be treated as constituting a collision with an " other vessel " for the purpose of the policy. As a result, the hull underwriters would in this case also respond as to three-quarters of the collision liability.

(2) *Liability to objects other than ships*

Where there is a liability towards the owner of an object other than another ship or vessel the P. & I. Club generally covers the liability incurred. If, however, the hull insurance policy of the owner entered in the Club extended to cover such liabilities, then that policy would apply and the Club cover would be inapplicable. In the case of a drilling unit covered by the London Standard Drilling Barge Form there is no cover in respect of liability towards fixed and floating objects, other than ships or vessels, so that the P. & I. Club cover would operate. Liability of this nature, where, as often, there is a contact between the ship and an object, is sometimes described as " striking," to distinguish it from a collision.[14] The P. & I. Club cover is expressed in such away that it extends to liability for loss of or damages to any fixed or floating object, provided that the liability was imposed by statute or arose out of negligence on the part of or on board or in relation to the entered drilling unit. The fixed or floating

---

[14] See, for example, the description of the cover given by the Norwegian P. & I. Clubs in this respect, at p. 234, below.

objects in question include harbours, docks, piers, jetties, buoys, land itself, water, or any property thereon, and indeed any fixed or movable thing whatsoever other than another ship or vessel. Liability to another drilling unit (which was not a drilling ship) could therefore also theoretically be included under this head. We have, however, considered this above, in discussing what happens when either a drilling ship or a drilling unit other than a drilling ship comes into collision with a drilling unit other than a drilling ship.[15] In the latter event the owner of the drilling unit at fault, and entered in the Club, would have to look to his hull policy to see whether he was covered under its collision liability terms.

(3) *Damage to ships other than by collision*

Protecting and Indemnity Club cover extends to liability for loss or damage to any ship or any property therein occasioned otherwise than by collision with the insured drilling unit, and arising out of the negligent navigation or management of the unit or other negligent act or omission on board or in relation to the entered unit. This provision usually forms the basis of recovery by a P. & I. Club member when he is liable for wash damage, the entered ship having been navigated at such a speed or in such a manner that another ship has suffered loss or damage, often by its moorings being broken, or by being made to range against a third ship or a quay or a jetty. A drilling unit, for example, whether under tow or self-propelled, might go at too great a speed through an enclosed area, such as a harbour, and cause wash damage to another ship, which for this purpose includes a drilling ship, by causing it to range against a jetty or to break its mooring lines. The owner of a drilling unit, if made liable, could recover that liability from his P. & I. Club.

(4) *Pollution*

Protecting and Indemnity Club cover extends to the owner of an insured drilling unit in respect of liability for pollution only where the pollution does not consist of oil pollution or other pollution from holes and/or wells which are being or have been drilled by the insured drilling unit.[16] An escape from the drilling unit itself, however, in the case of an outflow of bunkers, or from a sample tank, would be covered. This part of the P. & I. Club cover also extends, in the case of owners of tankers, to any loss or damage or expense for which he is liable as a party to any agreement which relates to the cost of cleaning up pollution caused by oil which escapes from a tanker, including the expense which the owner incurs in performing obligations under such agreement. These words were introduced to deal with the contractual liability of an insured tanker owner under Tovalop, *i.e.* the Tanker Owners' Voluntary Agreement in respect of Liability for Oil Pollution. A comparable agreement, in the case of drilling operations, is the Offshore Pollution Liability Agreement, referred

---

[15] See C (1) (b), at p. 211.   [16] For exclusions generally, see p. 221, below.

to as OPOL.[17] It is not relevant to the P. & I. Club cover given to contractors, because the parties to OPOL are operators and not contractors. Their liability would therefore be insured by way of other insurance and not by the P. & I. Clubs.

D. Excess Collision Insurance

A P. & I. Club usually covers a member in respect of collision liability, with costs and expenses incidental thereto, to the extent that such liability, costs and expenses are not recoverable under the Club collision liability cover or under the hull policies. There is a proviso to the effect that the Directors of the Club may, for the purpose of assessing any sum recoverable, determine the proper value at which the entered ship should have been insured under the hull policies, so that the Club shall pay only the excess, if any, of the amount which would have been recoverable under the hull policies if the entered ship had been insured thereunder at such value. It is understood that in the case of drilling units the same principles would apply.

E. Liability Under Contracts

Protecting and Indemnity Clubs provide cover for their members in respect of certain contractual liabilities. One category thereof, that of towage contract liabilities, has existed for many years and can, in the case of coventional ships, be clearly defined. The other category, that of liabilities under other contracts of indemnity, is wider in its scope and more difficult to define.

(1) *Towage contracts*

In the case of conventional ships the P.& I. Club cover extends to:

(1) loss or damage arising out of or during the course of customary towage of an entered ship in the ordinary course of trading for which the owner may become liable under the terms of the towage contract but only to the extent to which such liability is not recoverable under the hull policies. " Customary towage " is defined as meaning (i) towage for the purpose of entering or leaving port or manoeuvring within the port during the ordinary course of trading or (ii) towage of such entered ships (*e.g.* barges) as are habitually towed in the ordinary course of their trading. Special cover may be granted, on agreed terms, in the case of towage other than customary towage as so defined.

(2) loss or damage arising out of or by reason of any agreement or contract for the towage by the entered ship of any other ship or object, subject to the decision of the Directors of the P. & I. Club that, having regard to all the circumstances of the case, the particular claim falls within the scope of the cover.

---

[17] See p. 377, below.

Under both (1) and (2) there is usually a proviso to the effect that a claim may be rejected or reduced if the Directors decide that it was unreasonable to perform the particular towage or to enter into the particular contract of towage.

We will consider the first heading, (1), here, as it may concern the towage of a drilling unit entered in a P. & I. Club. In the case of a conventional ship its owner would enter into a strict form of contract, as exemplified by the United Kingdom Towage Conditions. Under such a contract he has, subject only to a few exceptions, to indemnify or hold harmless the owner of the tug in respect of a wide range of matters, including any damage suffered by the tug or by the property of third parties, even if it resulted from negligent navigation on the part of the tug.

As we have pointed out, the Club cover is normally only given in respect of customary towage; this is defined to mean either towage near or within a port in the ordinary course of trading or towage of an entered ship such as a barge which is habitually towed in the ordinary course of trading.

In the case of a drilling unit entered in a P. & I. Club there is an exclusion [18] as to " Contractual towage liability."

As expressed this exclusion is entire, but it is understood that the essential intention is that there should be a prima facie exclusion of liability in the case of ocean towage, as, for example, from the U.S. Gulf to the North Sea. If requested, a P. & I. Club would normally cover customary port towage, as in the case of conventional ships, and movements on site. In addition, but for an appropriate additional premium, it would cover towage to and from the site.

(2) *Contracts other than towage contracts*

The second category of cover in respect of the contractual liability of a P. & I. Club member relates to liabilities under indemnities and other contracts. The cover extends to loss, damage or injury to persons (including loss of life and illness) or to any property whatsoever (other than the entered ship or cargo intended to be or being or having been carried in the entered ship) for which an owner may be liable under the terms of any indemnity or contract given or made by him, or by the Club at his request, in consideration of the provision of any facilities afforded or to be afforded to or in connection with the entered ship. The Club is not under any liability to its member unless

   (i) the terms of the indemnity or contract were approved in writing by the managers; or

  (ii) the Club Directors had previously directed that the specified class or description of indemnity or contract should not thereafter require the approval of the managers; or

 (iii) the Club Directors in their absolute discretion should otherwise determine.

---

[18] For a full list of exclusions see p. 221, below.

A typical example of such a contract in respect of a conventional ship, for which a Club member might seek approval, would be a contract submitted by a repair yard. The contract might require the shipowner to accept strict liability for any damage to the property of the yard and for any loss of life or injury to the yard's employees or the employees of its contractors, while the ship was under repair.

In the case of a drilling unit the P. & I. Club usually excludes " Contractual liability (other than those liabilities normal to drilling) and care, custody and control liability, but not excluding liabilities under the drilling contract submitted to the Association [*i.e.* the P. & I. Club] and agreed." The P. & I. Club managers examine the drilling contract when an application for insurance is made, primarily to enable them to assess the nature and extent of the risk involved for underwriting purposes. If the owner of the drilling unit has entered into a contract by which it has to indemnify, for example, a repair yard or a port authority, its liabilities thereunder are therefore excluded. This exclusion does not apply, however, to any of its liabilities, even though they may relate to the same incident and the same loss or damage, if it incurs such liabilities under the drilling contract. If, for example, the P. & I. Club has approved of the terms of the drilling contract, and the contractor has as a result to indemnify the operator in respect of such a liability, then the Club cover will apply.

F. Removal of Wreck

The leaseblock holder may be obliged by statute law or by virtue of the leasing agreement to remove both the wreck of the drilling unit, whether from the drilling site or some other place on the way to or from the site, and any debris produced by the drilling operations. The operator may, as a member of the consortium, have to discharge these liabilities. In addition the drilling contract, in dealing with such obligations, usually refers both to the wreck of the unit and to the other debris. Liability for removal is imposed upon the operator in such terms as: " Operator shall be liable for the cost of regaining control of any wild well, as well as the cost of removal of debris, and shall indemnify the Contractor for any such cost regardless of the cause thereof, including, but not limited to, the negligence of Contractor, its agents, employees or subcontractors." [19]

The cover provided by a P. & I. Club in the case of conventional ships extends to the liability of its member for removal of wreck.[20] The Rules state that the member is covered in respect of costs and expenses of or incidental to the raising, removal, destruction, lighting or marking of the wreck of an entered ship " when such raising, removal, destruction, lighting or marking is compulsory by law or the costs thereof are legally recoverable from the Owner." In the case of drilling units, however, the cover is subject to an important exception. This exception will usually be

---

[19] International Daywork Drilling Contract—Offshore, Art. 1006. See p. 267, below.
[20] For the terms see p. 389, below.

to the effect that the removal of wreck or removal of debris is excluded from the P. & I. cover " so far as it arises from the blow-out or cratering " or, alternatively, " so far as it arises from the drilling operations." The drilling unit may sink in a busy estuary on the way to the drilling site, and the responsible authority may order its removal. In such a case the P. & I. Club cover would operate to protect the assured. This would be the case even if the second exception quoted, as to claims arising from drilling operations, were to apply. The claim would not have arisen but for the fact that the drilling operations were in contemplation, but it did not arise out of them, and would not be regarded as having done so even if the drilling unit were on its way back from such operations.

As a general rule the liabilities envisaged by the words " compulsory by law " and " legally recoverable " are also imposed by statute. It is understood, however, that if there were a statutory obligation as a result of the leaseblock agreement, and if that obligation were to be passed on to the contractor (rather than the operator) under the drilling contract, then that contractual liability would be recoverable from the P. & I. Club.

G. Property of Others on the Insured Vessel

Under the drilling contract the contractor may have certain obligations in respect of the property of others on the drilling unit. The usual P. & I. Club provisions as to the liability of a member in respect of " cargo or other property " (to cite the words often employed) are not appropriate for such obligations. The words of one typical P. & I. cover, for example, refer to " Damage to or responsibility in respect of cargo or other property intended to be or being or having been carried in an entered ship arising out of any breach by the Owner or by any person for whose acts, neglect or default he may be legally liable of his obligation or duty *as a carrier by sea* properly to load, handle, stow, carry, keep, care for, discharge and deliver such cargo or property, or out of unseaworthiness or unfitness of the entered ship." [21]

The words used refer to " other property " and thus could extend to property other than cargo; but the use also of the words " as a carrier by sea " make it clear that liability to property which is on the drilling unit would not be covered.

Such liabilities of the owner of the drilling unit are covered by the P. & I. Club though not, for the reasons stated, by the heads of cover dealing with cargo liability. There is a head of cover, often spoken of as " the fixed and floating object rule." It refers to loss of or damage to any " harbour, dock, pier, jetty, land, water or any fixed or movable thing whatsoever (not being another ship or any property therein)," where the liability arises by statute or out of the negligent navigation or management of an entered ship or other negligent act or omission on board or in relation to an entered ship.

---

[21] In this case the words " drilling unit " can be deemed to have been used.

So far as the owner of the drilling unit may have a liability in respect of the property of others on the entered drilling unit it is understood that cover would be afforded by this provision. In some cases of course, he might be under no liability, because the drilling contract may provide that each party must bear responsibility for any loss of or damage to the property owned or controlled by itself or by its employees, sub-contractors, or sub-contractors' employees.[22]

H. Various other matters

(1) *Life Salvage*

Protecting and Indemnity Clubs usually provide for recovery in respect of the member's liability for life salvage in such terms as: " Life salvage shall be recoverable to the extent only that the same is not recoverable from hull underwriters on the entered ship or from cargo owners or underwriters." We assume here that the concept of salvage, and liability therefor, is applicable to drilling units.[23]

The common law, as demonstrated by the decisions of the Admiralty courts, was that there was no right to life salvage where lives only were saved. The main reason was that some part of the property concerned, *i.e.* the ship, cargo or freight, had to be saved so as to constitute a res to which the claim could attach.[24] The position was summarised by Brett M.R. in " *The Renpor* "[25]: ". . . there must be something saved more than life, which will form a fund from which the salvage may be paid, in other words, for the saving of life alone without the saving of ship, freight or cargo, salvage is not recoverable in the Admiralty Court." The position was altered by statute, however, in 1854, and is now represented by the successor to that statutory provision, section 544 (1) of the Merchant Shipping Act 1894: " Where services are rendered wholly or in part within British waters in saving life from any British or foreign vessel, or elsewhere in saving life from any British vessel, there shall be payable to the salvor by the owner of the vessel, cargo, or apparel saved, a reasonable amount of salvage . . . . "

This alteration had the effect that persons who had saved only life, or very little property, could be awarded life salvage; but some part of the ship, cargo or freight must have been saved as well. Nevertheless, a person who was only the life salvor did not save the *res*; or, if he was salvor both of *res* and life, his life salvage work could be said not to have referred to the *res*. As McNair J. said in *The Bosworth No. 3*[25a]: " It needs possibly a little stretching of the language to say that a salvage award in so far as it reflects an element of life salvage gives rise to a charge incurred in preventing a loss by perils insured against. I think the answer to that is that by

---

[22] See p. 260, below.   [23] See the discussion at p. 53, above.
[24] *The Fusilier* (1865) Brown & Lush, 341, at p. 344.
[25] (1883) 8 P.D. 115 (C.A.) at p. 117.
[25a] [1962] 1 Lloyd's Rep. 483 at p. 490.

the practice of the Admiralty Court an award made in these circumstances is treated as being, and is in fact, an award for services rendered to the ship and cargo."

So far we have considered how and when life salvage may be recoverable from the ship or other interests. What then is the situation in which life salvage, having been awarded, is either wholly or partly unrecoverable from underwriters, and thus recoverable from the P. &. I. Club? If a salvage award reflects an element of life salvage and either there is no separate life salvage award or the award itself does not state that part of it is in respect of life salvage, the insured is customarily able to recover under the hull policy. There therefore can be and indeed there have been situations in which life salvage would be recoverable from a P. & I. Club.

(2) *Quarantine expenses*

P. & I. Clubs usually provide for recovery in respect of the member's liability for quarantine expenses as follows:

" Quarantine expenses and extraordinary expenses incident to the outbreak of infectious disease upon an entered ship incurred for or by way of:

(a) The disinfection of the entered vessel or of persons on board her under Quarantine or Public Health Enactments, Regulations or Orders, including the cost of taking in fuel in Quarantine, and of loading and discharging cargo and of the victualling of the crew and passengers after deducting the ordinary expenses of loading, discharging and victualling;

(b) Fuel consumed or towage in proceeding to and from and lying at a special Station or place in accordance with such Enactments, Regulations or Orders; and

(c) Expenses directly consequent upon bearing up for, or putting into, a port or place of refuge and resuming the voyage thereafter by reason solely of the outbreak of infectious or contagious disease upon an entered ship

PROVIDED ALWAYS that:

There shall be no recovery under this Rule if the entered ship was, at the times such expenses were incurred, chartered to proceed to or under orders from the Owner to proceed to a port at which it was known or should in the determination of the Directors have reasonably been anticipated that she would be quarantined."

So far as such a situation may arise in the case of a drilling unit, the contractor is able to recover these expenses from the P. & I. Club.

(3) *Fines*

P. & I. Clubs usually provide for recovery in respect of the members' liability for all fines other than fines for overloading. Fines for overloading are excluded in view of the risk of loss of life if a ship is overloaded with cargo. Such fines would not arise in respect of a drilling unit as it does not load cargo. The categories of fines in respect of which a P. & I. Club reimburses its members may be listed as follows:

(a) Fines imposed upon an owner in respect of an entered ship [26] by any court, tribunal or authority of competent jurisdiction for failure to maintain safe working conditions in respect of an entered ship under the provisions of the Factories Acts or similar statutes, decrees or regulations of any country.

(b) Fines imposed upon an owner in respect of an entered ship by any court, tribunal or authority of competent jurisdiction for short or over delivery of cargo, or for failure to comply with regulations relating to declaration of goods or to documentation of the ship or cargo.

(c) Fines or any other penalties imposed upon an owner in respect of an entered ship by any court, tribunal or authority of competent jurisdiction:

(i) For smuggling by the Master, Officers or Crew of the ship or other servant or agent of the owner or person for whom the owner may be held responsible; or

(ii) For any infringement of any Customs Law or Regulation relating to the construction, adaptation, alteration or fitment of the entered ship.

(d) Fines imposed upon an owner in respect of an entered ship by any court, tribunal or authority of competent jurisdiction for breach of any matter relating to immigration.

(e) Fines other than those specified above imposed upon an owner by any court, tribunal or authority of competent jurisdiction for any neglect or default of the Master, Officers or crew or other servant or agent of the owner in respect of an entered ship.

So far as such fines may be imposed upon the owner of the drilling unit they are recoverable from the P. & I. Club.

I. Legal and Associated Expenses

It is usual for a P. & I. Club to insure its members in respect of (a) legal and other expenses associated with such matters as are covered by the Club; and (b) certain other categories of general expense to which the member may be exposed. These categories of cover may be expressed as follows:

(1) *Legal and other expenses*

" Costs and expenses, including legal costs and charges, which an owner may incur in respect of (or in avoiding or attempting to avoid) any liability or expenditure against which he is wholly or, by reason of a deductible, partly insured by the Association;

PROVIDED ALWAYS that:

No such costs or expenses shall be recoverable unless either (a) the same have been incurred with the prior consent in writing of the Managers, or (b) the Directors shall determine that such costs or expenses were reasonably incurred."

---

[26] The Club definition of " ship " is wide enough to include drilling units.

(2) *Certain other categories of general expenses*

(a) Enquiry Expenses

" Costs and expenses incurred by an owner in defending himself or in protecting his interest before a formal enquiry into the loss of or a casualty to an entered ship, but only to such extent and/or on such conditions as the Directors in their absolute discretion may determine."

(b) Expenses arising from interference by local authorities

" Costs and expenses incurred with the authority of the Directors in the defence of or obtaining redress for an owner in cases of interference by any lawful authority of any country, which the Directors shall decide to be unwarranted or to require investigation."

(c) Expenses incidental to shipowning

" Liabilities, costs and expenses incidental to the business of owning, operating or managing ships which the Directors may decide to be within the scope of the Association. Claims under this paragraph shall be recoverable to such extent only as the Directors may determine."

This does not include liabilities, costs and expenses which are expressly excepted in the Rules.

(d) Expenses incurred by direction of the Association

" Costs, expenses and loss which an owner may incur by special direction of the Association in cases in which the Directors consider that the interests of the Members of the Association are or may be affected."

So far as such expenses may be incurred by the owner of the entered drilling unit they are recoverable from the P. & I. Club, provided that they do not fall under the exclusions applicable to drilling units.

Exclusions from P. & I. Club Cover

In the preceding pages the nature of the cover afforded by the P. & I. Clubs, other than the Norwegian Clubs,[27] has been set out. Certain exceptions to that cover have been mentioned, in the course of that description, to show where these heads of cover do not apply. When this P. & I. Club cover is given it is usually expressed as being an insurance in accordance with the P. & I. Club's Rules, but with the following exceptions, some of which have already appeared above:

(a) *Liability for loss of hole and in-hole equipment.* So far as the contractor incurs a liability, which would be towards the operator, in respect of the loss of the hole, there is no Club cover. If the contractor is liable to any party in respect of loss of or damage to in-hole equipment, then such liability is not covered by the P. & I. Club.

(b) *Cost of control.*[28] The cost of controlling a well when there has been a blowout, seepage, pollution, or some other incident, will normally fall on

---

[27] As for which see Chap. 6, below.
[28] For insurance in respect of the cost of control, see Chap. 9, below.

the operator in the first instance. Even were the operator able to pass such liability on to the owner of the drilling unit, the latter would be unable to recover that liability from the P. & I. Club in which the drilling unit is entered. The exclusion extends to the cost of drilling relief wells.

(c) *Products liability.* Liability in respect of the manufacture, sale or the putting into circulation of a product may be imposed upon a defendant. Where liability is established the damages awarded may be considerable, particularly in the United States. Insurance is often taken out in respect of such a liability, but, as it is of a highly specialised nature, an exclusion of this cover is found in most insurance policies.

(d) *Contractual liabilities (other than those normal to drilling) and care custody and control liability, but not excluding liabilities under the drilling contract submitted to the P. & I. Club and agreed.* Cover may be provided in respect of this type of liability, however, subject to (a) prior advice being given to the Club and (b) payment of any additional premium required. The contract in question would have to be submitted to the Club for its approval.

(e) *Contractual towage liability.* Club cover may, however, be agreed, for an additional premium, in respect of (a) a tow between the base and the drilling site and (b) movements within the site. The effect is that ocean tows are excluded.[29]

(f) *Oil pollution or other pollution from holes and/or wells, which are being or have been drilled by the insured drilling unit.* An escape from the unit itself, however, as in the case of an outflow of bunkers, or from a sample tank, would be covered.

(g) *Automobile liability.* The liabilities insured by a P. & I. Club in the case of coventional ships would in any event be unlikely to include a liability of a member or member's employee arising out of driving a motor-car. The range of operations conducted by drilling unit contractors is, however, considerable, and would include the arrangement of various forms of transportation on land. As motor insurance, like product liability insurance, constitutes a specialised area of insurance, it is usual, in this as in many other types of insurance policy, to exclude "automobile liability."

(h) *Claims arising out of the operation of*: Submarines or mini-submarines; diving bells; divers while engaged in diving operations but not excluding liabilities arising from the negligence of divers forming part of the crew of a salvage tug engaged in salvage operations and for which the tug owner is liable.

---

[29] See also the reference to towage contract liability cover at p. 214, above.

CHAPTER 6

NORWEGIAN PROTECTING AND INDEMNITY COVER

THE Norwegian P. & I. Clubs, Assuranceforeningen Gard (" Gard ") and Assuranceforeningen Skuld (" Skuld "), use a form of insurance policy [1] for drilling units which differs in form from those provided by them for ships generally. Other P. & I. Clubs usually, however, employ their normal policies, adding any necessary adaptations, or exclusions, for the purpose of the cover to be given for drilling units, by way of additional terms.[2] The only commentary on the approach of the Norwegian P. & I. Clubs to this matter is contained in a booklet, " Insurance Conditions for P. & I. Insurance of Drilling Vessels with Commentary," [3] by Dr. jur. Sjur Braekhus and Mr. Alex. Rein.[4]

The commentators say, by way of general introduction to the Conditions:

" By drilling vessel [5] is meant a movable, floating structure for drilling for deposits of petroleum (oil or gas) under the seabed. This does not only mean a structure which is kept afloat during the drilling operation (the so-called drill-ship which looks like a conventional ship, and the semi-submersible platform), but also a structure which is afloat when being moved from one place to another, although it rests on the seabed during the drilling operation ('jack-up')."

They add that by their Statutes the two Norwegian Clubs are authorised to insure both mobile structures and stationary structures (such as production platforms) which are not " vessels." [6]

The Norwegian drilling units being operated before 1973 were mostly insured in the London market. In that year some Norwegian marine insurance companies and mutual hull clubs prepared to offer hull insurance to these drilling-units through the Norsk Oljeforsikringspool (Norwegian Oil Insurance Pool). The Pool and the Norsk Boreriggeierforening (the Norwegian Association of Drilling Rig Owners) prepared, in English, a policy called General Conditions for Hull Insurance of Drilling Vessels,

---

[1] Or " Rules," as they are known in P. & I. Club parlance. The form was drafted by Dr. jur. Sjur Braekhus, Professor at the University of Oslo, and Mr. Alex. Rein, attorney of the Supreme Court of Norway and member of the law firm of Wikborg, Rein, Ringdal & Waelgaard. The advice of Mr. Rein is most gratefully acknowledged.

[2] See Chap. 5, above.

[3] The only printed version is one issued by Gard, in English, in 1976, but the commentary applied to both the Gard and Skuld policies.

[4] The summary which follows is a paraphrase of their booklet; it has been submitted to Mr. Rein, who, subject to some modifications, nearly all of which have been incorporated, approved of it.

[5] Or drilling unit; the Norwegian terminology is applied here.

[6] A " ship," in the Rules of the United Kingdom P. & I. Club, means " ship, boat, hovercraft or other description of vessel or structure . . . used or intended to be used for any purpose whatsoever in navigation or otherwise on, under, over or in water."

known also as DV-kasko. These Conditions, based on the Norwegian Marine Insurance Plan of 1964,[7] were applied to all new covers and renewals in the Norwegian market from June, 1975.

As a result Gard and Skuld decided to make an equivalent offer by way of P. & I. cover, by insuring independently but reinsuring their own retentions with each other. A certain excess was reinsured in the Norwegian Oil Insurance Pool, and a further excess in the London market. As the commentators put it: " The insurance conditions which were used were not an amended form of the clubs' own general P. & I. conditions for ships, but conditions which had been ' scissored together ' from various English and American clauses." The usual P. & I. conditions of the Clubs were, nevertheless, incorporated as supplementary terms.

It was then decided that it would be preferable to have a form of cover which would be in the Norwegian style and clearly complementary to the DV-kasko conditions. The DV-kasko conditions differed from the general Norwegian hull conditions for ships in some respects, so as to ensure that they were similar in substance to the London Standard Drilling Barge Form, and thus acceptable in the London market. As a result the new Norwegian P. & I. conditions reflect, in their turn, the DV-kasko conditions, expanding the P. & I. cover where the hull cover contracts. In respect of collision liability, for example, the hull insurer covers collision liability in the narrow sense but not liability for striking, such as a contact with a jetty.[8] On the other hand the collision liability is covered in full, and not only as to one fourth, as is the case with the running down clause in the Institute Time Clauses (Hulls).

In general the Conditions are much shorter than those contained in the conventional Rules of the Norwegian P. &. I Clubs. This is mainly because certain types of liability do not arise or do not need to be covered, even where they might arise. This includes especially liability is respect of cargo and fines.

The Insurance Conditions are in four groups, comprising 20 sections:

A.   General Rules (sections 1 to 6)

B.   The Scope of the Cover (sections 7 to 12)

C.   Limitation of the Liability of the Association (sections 13 to 18)

D.   Insurance of the Interest of a Third Party (sections 19 and 20)

The Conditions are first set out below in full, and then repeated separately, with a summary of the Commentary placed after each Condition.

"A.   General Rules

Section 1.   Membership in the Association[9]
By the entry of the drilling vessel the owner becomes a member of the Association with the rights and duties which this entails. The provision in

---

[7] See also p. 229, below.   [8] See also p. 235, below.
[9] See p. 229, below.

224

the bye-laws of the Association empowering the Committee in the particular case to compensate losses which are not covered by the insurance conditions, shall not apply.

Section 2. *Norwegian Marine Insurance Plan of* 1964 [10]
The insurance is governed by Part One of the Norwegian Marine Insurance Plan of 1964 ('the Plan') unless otherwise provided in these Insurance Conditions ('the Conditions').

Section 3. *The General Rule on the Scope of Cover* [11]
The Association shall cover liability and other loss of the nature enumerated in sections 7–12 of the Conditions, provided that the loss has occurred:

(a) in direct connection with the operation of the drilling vessel entered,
(b) in connection with the activity at one or more supply bases provided that the activity is in direct connection with the operation of the drilling vessel,
(c) in direct connection with transport between the drilling vessel and a supply base or a port or airport in the vicinity of the base.

Section 4. *Perils insured against* [12]
The insurance shall not comprise loss caused by war perils, see § 16 [13] of the Plan.

Section 5. *Sum Insured* [14]
1. *Global limitation.* When the assured is entitled to limit his liability pursuant to the rules of Chapter 10 of the Norwegian Maritime Code; the British Merchant Shipping Act (1894), section 503 with later amendments; U.S. Code, Title 46, Chapter 8; or equivalent rules in the law of other countries, the sum insured (§ 79 of the Plan) is the amount to which the assured may limit his liability. The second paragraph of §79 of the Plan shall not apply.

2. *Further limitation.* In any case, the liability of the Association for loss caused by one single casualty shall be limited to the sum insured set out in the policy. The second paragraph of § 79 and § 80 (a) of the Plan shall not apply.

Section 6. *Regulations* [15]
1. *Safety regulations.* The Association may at any time issue general or special directions concerning measures for the prevention of liability or other loss covered by the Association, see § 48 of the Plan.

2. *Notice of regulations.* The Association shall notify the assured immediately of regulations issued pursuant to 1 or to § 51 of the Plan and of the time of their coming into force.

A complete list of all current regulations shall be sent to the assured at least once a year.

B. The Scope of the Cover

Section 7. *Liability for personal injury, etc.*[16]
The Association shall cover the assured's liability:

---

[10] See p. 229, below.   [11] See p. 229, below.   [12] See p. 231, below.
[13] The sign " § " is used in Norwegian legal texts to indicate " paragrafer " or provisions; it is used here for the purpose of reference to the Norwegian Marine Insurance Plan.
[14] See p. 232, below.
[15] See p. 233, below.
[16] See p. 233, below.

(a) in consequence of personal injury or loss of life,

(b) for salvage monies awarded for life saving, provided that the monies have been awarded for the saving of life only or together for the saving of life and salvage of goods of relatively insignificant value.

Liability which is covered under sections 11 or 12 of the Conditions shall not be covered under this section.

Section 8. *Liability for Property Damage* [17]

The Association shall cover the assured's liability in consequence of damage to or loss of objects not belonging to the assured himself. Excepted herefrom are:

(a) liability for damage to or loss of the entered drilling vessel, its equipment, outfit or supplies, on board or outside the drilling vessel,

(b) liability for damage to or loss of hole which is being drilled by the entered drilling vessel.

Liability which is covered under section 12 of the Conditions shall not be covered under this section.

Section 9. *Excess of Loss through Measures to Avert or Mininise Loss under the Hull Insurance* [18]

The Association shall cover that part of the assured's loss through measures as mentioned in §§ 68–73 of the Plan, which, by its nature but not with the sufficient amount, could have been covered by the assured under the general hull insurance conditions in the country whose hull conditions form the basis for the hull cover of the drilling vessel, provided that the sum insured is at least equivalent to the full value of the drilling vessel.

Section 10. *Liability for Obstructions and Wreck Removal* [19]

The Association shall cover the assured's liability for the removal of wreck and liability to owners of harbours, canals and similar structures and liability to owners of other vessels for loss caused where the entered drilling vessel as a result of a casualty has caused an obstruction to the free passage.

Section 11. *Statutory Obligations in Respect of Master and Crew* [20]

The Association shall cover the assured's liability to the drilling vessel's master and crew according to statutory law and collective wages agreements governing the contracts of employment, for:

(a) nursing and maintenance of master and crew ashore in case of illness or injury,

(b) master's and crew's expenses including maintenance for travelling to their places of residence in cases of illness or injury or after shipwreck,

(c) funeral expenses and the cost of sending home urn of ashes or coffin and the effects of the deceased.

Section 12. *Liability for Wages and Effects* [21]

The Association shall cover the assured's liability to the drilling vessel's master and crew according to statutory law and collective wages agreements governing the contracts of employment for:

(a) wages in respect of the time after the termination of the employment and wages to their dependants, where the employment has been terminated as a result of shipwreck, illness, injury or death,

---

[17] See p. 234, below. [18] See p. 236, below. [19] See p. 237, below.
[20] See p. 238, below. [21] See p. 238, below.

(b) damage to or loss of effects belonging to the ship's complement or other persons carried in the ship and employed on board.

C. Limitation of the Liability of the Association

Section 13. Limitation Owing to Other Insurance [22]

The Association shall not cover:

(a) loss which by its nature can be insured by the assured under the general hull insurance conditions for drilling vessels in the country whose hull insurance conditions form the basis for the ship's hull insurance,

(b) loss which is covered under the Norwegian Folketrygd or which is or should have been covered under equivalent obligatory insurance system in a country to which the operation of the entered drilling vessel has a natural connection,

(c) liability which by its nature may be covered by customary hull insurance, P. & I. insurance or other liability insurance of other vessels, motor vehicles or aircraft of which the assured is the owner, lessee or charterer,

(d) loss as mentioned in § 77 of the Plan, provided that it could have been covered by hull insurance, cargo insurance, fire insurance or other customary insurance against damage to property.

The Association shall, however, cover such part of the assured's liability for collision and striking which exceeds the amount which is covered under the drilling vessel's hull insurance, or which could have been covered under a hull insurance on conditions as mentioned under (a) in the preceding paragraph with a sum insured equivalent to the full value of the vessel. As regards loss as mentioned in § 77 of the Plan, deduction shall also be made for loss which is covered by freight insurance, or could have been covered by another insurance as mentioned in the preceding paragraph.

Section 14. Privity of the Assured [23]

The Association shall not cover loss caused by the assured by a grossly negligent act or omission.

Where the loss is a consequence of defects in the drilling vessel or its equipment which may impair her safety or expose human lives to danger or of equivalent defects in moorings or supervision while the vessel is laid up, the Association is not liable if the assured was, or ought to have been, aware of the defects and has omitted to remedy them to the best of his ability. The same applies if the assured knew or should have known that recommendations had been issued in respect of the drilling vessel by a classification society or a public maritime safety authority and he has omitted to comply with them to the best of his ability.

Section 15. Amounts Saved to the Assured [24]

Where the assured, through circumstances involving loss for him, has obtained extra revenue, saved expenses or avoided liability which would otherwise have been incurred and which would not have been covered by the Association, the latter may deduct from the compensation an amount corresponding to the benefit obtained.

Section 16. Liability for Loss through Measures to Avert or Minimise Loss [25]

Where measures taken to avert or minimise loss which would have been

---

[22] See p. 239, below.   [23] See p. 241, below.   [24] See p. 242, below.
[25] See p. 242, below.

recoverable from another insurer have resulted in liability for the Association, the Association shall be subrogated to the assured's claim against the other insurer. § 96 of the Plan shall have equivalent application.

The items enumerated below are in no case recoverable as loss through measures to avert or minimise the loss in accordance with § 68 of the Plan:

(a) costs of measures that have been or could have been accomplished by the crew or by reasonable use of the drilling vessel or her equipment,

(b) assured's liability for non-fulfilment, or delay in fulfilment, of a drilling contract or of an agreement for the sale of the drilling vessel,

(c) cost of regaining control of the oil or gas well on which the drilling vessel is working.

Section 17. Blow-out Damage, etc.[26]

The Association shall not cover:

(a) loss resulting from pollution and measures taken to avert or minimise such loss,

(b) loss resulting from sub-surface oil or gas having been damaged or lost,

(c) loss as a result of damage to property by cratering, reduced buoyancy or similar occurrence,

provided that the loss is occasioned by uncontrolled flow from the well which is being drilled by the entered drilling vessel, whether resulting from blow-out or other causes.

Section 18. Deductible[27]

For each single casualty the amount set out in the policy shall be deducted.

D. Insurance of the Interest of a Third Party

Section 19. Insurance of the Interest of the Lessee, Drilling Contractor or Operator[28]

Where it is set out in the policy that the insurance has been effected in favour of a person who has leased the entered drilling vessel or who employs it in his activities as drilling contractor or operator, the following rules shall apply:

1. The Association shall have no recourse against the assured or third party covered unless such person has caused the loss by his own fault as mentioned in section 14 of the Conditions.

2. The Association shall cover the loss of the nature enumerated under subdivision B, see also A and C, of the Conditions, to the extent the loss is incurred by the third party in his capacity as lessee, drilling contractor or operator as above mentioned.

Section 20. Insurance of the Interests of the Mortgagee (Chapter 8 of the Plan)[29]

1. The period of advance notice set out in the second paragraph of § 135 of the Plan shall be extended from seven to 21 days, provided that the mortgagee has guaranteed payment of premiums earned from the time such notice is received by him until expiry of the insurance, but not beyond the expiry of the period of notice.

2. The limit set out in the second paragraph of § 138 of the Plan shall be raised to U.S. $500,000."

---

[26] See p. 243, below.
[28] See p. 244, below.

[27] See p. 244, below.
[29] See p. 245, below.

The Cover Considered in Detail

A. General rules

"Section 1 Membership in the Association
By the entry of the drilling vessel the owner becomes a member of the Association with the rights and duties which this entails. The provision in the bye-laws of the Association empowering the Committee in the particular case to compensate losses which are not covered by the insurance conditions shall not apply."

It is by virtue of the inception of the insurance that the owner of the drilling vessel becomes a member of the Association, or Club. The lessee, the drilling contractor (who may not always be the owner) or the operator, may be insured under the owner's policy,[30] but they do not thereby become members.

The Clubs, in common with other P. & I. Clubs, have an " omnibus clause " under which the directors may grant compensation although the insured is not specifically covered. It does not, as a result of the second sentence in section 1, apply to drilling units. It was felt that those providing reinsurance for the two Clubs in question would be less accustomed to such payments than is the case with the traditional reinsurers of the P. & I. Clubs.

"Section 2. Norwegian Marine Insurance Plan of 1964
The insurance is governed by Part One of the Norwegian Marine Insurance Plan of 1964 ('the Plan') unless otherwise provided in these Insurance Conditions ('the Conditions')."

Part One of the Plan is entitled " Provisions common to all types of insurance." It also applied to the earlier P. & I. conditions for drilling units, as the Club Rules, which had been incorporated as supplementary terms,[31] incorporated the Plan by reference. The Plan is issued and occasionally revised by Norske Veritas, the Norwegian classification society; it results from negotiations between owners, underwriters and other interested parties. It is more comprehensive in its nature than the laws of marine insurance, but incorporates the mandatory part of such legislation. It is used almost without exception in the insurance of Norwegian ships and drilling units.

Parts Two and Three of the Plan deal, respectively, with hull insurance and P. & I. Insurance. Gard does not incorporate Part Three in its P. & I. Rules for ships, but uses its own conditions. Skuld uses Part Three for Norwegian ships but with modifications. The Gard drilling unit Conditions are not based on Part Three; their only link with the Plan is by the incorporation of Part One.

"Section 3. The General Rule on the Scope of Cover
The Association shall cover liability and other loss of the nature enumerated in sections 7–12 of the Conditions, provided that the loss has occurred:

---

[30] See s. 19, and the comments thereon, at p. 244, below.
[31] See p. 224, above.

(a) in direct connection with the operation of the drilling vessel entered,
(b) in connection with the activity at one or more supply bases provided that the activity is in direct connection with the operation of the drilling vessel,
(c) in direct connection with transport between the drilling vessel and a supply base or a port or airport in the vicinity of the base."

The commentators point out that the three parts of the proviso " are alternative and may be overlapping." They add: " Although P. & I. insurance is liability insurance it is not a general liability cover. Only liabilities which have been expressly mentioned are covered. In addition to liabilities certain types of other losses have been positively indicated, see for instance section 9[32] of the Conditions."

" *(a) in direct connection with the operation of the drilling vessel entered.*" This is the formula used by Gard and Skuld with respect to P. & I. insurance of conventional ships. It is stated: " Because of the special purposes of drilling vessels this entails a certain extension as compared with the cover for conventional ships The operation of a drilling vessel includes all operations which the vessel is intended to perform, including drilling and all activities in connection therewith."

" *(b) in connection with the activity at one or more supply bases, provided that the activity is in direct connection with the operation of the drilling vessel.*" A loss under (b) may also be covered under (a), as, for example, when the drilling vessel is lying at the base and liability arises for damage during loading of equipment. The commentators state: " The essential point is, however, that this sub-paragraph establishes an insurance cover of activities away from the vessel; the loss may occur while the vessel is situated far away from the base." Damage may be inflicted on the property of a third party during movement of equipment at the base. The member, or another insured, such as the operator,[33] may become liable for the damage. The loss has occurred during an activity in direct connection with the operation of the drilling vessel if the equipment was destined for that vessel; but, say the commentators: " Activities in connection with the base activities at large, for instance transport of fuel for use at the base or repair work on the base, fall outside. The same applies to activities which are directly connected with the operation of other drilling vessels which are being served at the base . . . ."

A supply base is one from which the drilling vessel is regularly supplied and which serves as the regular terminal when crews are changed. A base so used only occasionally is not deemed to be the entered vessel's supply base.

" *(c) in direct connection with transport between the drilling vessel and a supply base or a port or airport in the vicinity of the base.*"
The sub-paragraph is intended to cover loss for which the assured may

---

[32] s. 9 is entitled " Excess of loss through measures to avert or minimize loss under the hull insurance." See p. 236, below.
[33] As to who may be the insured see p. 229, above.

become liable whether or not the transport in its turn has a direct connection with the operation of the vessel. Thus the proviso contained in sub-paragraph (b) does not appear here.

The transport may be effected not by the assured but by another party, such as a shipowner or a helicopter owner. The assured may not have a liability in such a case. If he does, however, as he may where he has given an indemnity, the Plan makes a special provision (§ 76) as to such liability, which is of a contractual rather than a tortious nature. The Plan says that the insurer (in this case the Club) is not liable where the liability of the insured arises from his:

(a) having entered into a contract that results in a greater liability than that which follows from the ordinary rules of maritime law, unless such terms may be considered customary in the trade concerned

(b) having used or omitted to use terms of contract which the insurer in accordance with § 51 [of the Plan] has prohibited or prescribed." It is anticipated that, under (a), certain customary terms [34] may emerge and that, under (b), the insurers will issue special regulations.

Supplies might go from a port or airport not in the vicinity of the base, *e.g.* from Hull to a vessel whose base is at Stavanger. Such transport is said to be in a border area between " base transports," to which sub-paragraph (c) is intended to apply, and the ordinary carriage of cargo; it is difficult, however, to make a distinction which is both clear and fair.

"*Section 4. Perils Insured Against*
The insurance shall not comprise loss caused by war perils, see § 16 of the Plan."

It has been pointed out above [35] that Part One of the Plan, entitled " Provision common to all types of insurance," is incorporated into this cover by section 2, though Part Three, dealing with P. & I. insurance, is not incorporated. Clause 16 of the Plan, to which section 4 refers, is entitled " Perils comprised by an insurance against war perils," and defines these perils as follows:

"An insurance against war perils comprises:
(a) perils attributable to war or war-like conditions, or to the use of arms or other implements of war in the course of military manoeuvres in time of peace or during armed neutrality,
(b) capture at sea, condemnation in prize, confiscation, requisition for title or use and other similar measures taken by alien State authorities. By alien State authorities is understood authorities of State with whom Norway is not allied, and persons and organisations who unlawfully pretend to be exercising public or inter-governmental authority,
(c) civil commotions, strikes, lock-out, sabotage and the like,
(d) piracy and mutiny.

---

[34] See the reference to towage contracts at p. 235, below.
[35] At p. 229.

231

The insurance does not comprise insolvency.

Where the subject-matter to which the interest attaches is temporarily seized or requisitioned for use by alien State authorities, the insurance also covers those perils which according to § 15 are comprised by an insurance against marine perils."

Despite its positive heading, " Perils insured against," the object of section 4 is thus to state that the insurance shall not extend to loss caused by war perils, as defined by Clause 16 of the Plan. It is not strictly necessary for this statement to be made; the insurance in any event incorporates other features of that Part of the Plan, and in particular: (a) Clause 15 thereof, which defines marine perils and says that they do not include war perils as defined by Clause 16; and (b) Clause 17 thereof, which says that unless otherwise agreed the insurance only extends to marine perils. The P. & I. drilling vessel cover is thus consistent with the Norwegian hull conditions for drilling vessels (DV-kasko), which except perils excluded by the Plan.

"Section 5. Sum Insured

1. *Global limitation.* When the assured is entitled to limit his liability pursuant to the rules of Chapter 10 of the Norwegian Maritime Code; the British Merchant Shipping Act (1894), section 503 with later amendments; U.S. Code, Title 46, Chapter 8; or equivalent rules in the law of other countries, the sum insured (§ 79 of the Plan) is the amount to which the assured may limit his liability. The second paragraph of § 79 of the Plan shall not apply.

2. *Further limitation.* In any case, the liability of the Association for loss caused by one single casualty shall be limited to the sum insured set out in the policy. The second paragraph of § 79 and § 80 (a) of the Plan shall not apply."

1. *Global limitations.* Although most P. & I. cover is given without limits, P. & I. cover for drilling vessels was from its inception subject to limitation, particularly because the question of the right of drilling vessels to invoke the rules of limitation of liability might be a disputed one. The first sentence of paragraph 1 of this section is intended to make it clear that the P. & I. Club should not, as a result of direct action against it by a third party, be held liable for an amount greater than the one to which the assured can limit its liability. This will be the case even if the sum insured, as set out in the policy, is greater than the limitation figure. Under the second paragraph of clause 79 an insurer is liable for collision liability up to a separate sum insured. It is provided that the paragraph is inapplicable here to make it clear that the insured's additional liability for collision (the excess cover under the proviso to s. 13) and striking (s. 8) does not constitute a separate fund in addition to the general global limitation fund for third party liabilities.

2. *Further limitation.* The sum insured, set out elsewhere in each policy, is in any event to represent the limit of liability of the Association for loss

232

caused by one single casualty.[36] In 1977 the amount varied between $25 and $30 million.

Under § 80 (a) of the Plan an insurer would be liable, even if the sum insured is exceeded, for certain supplementary costs such as those of preventive measures and litigation. The Norwegian P. & I. Clubs do not accept this as a liability towards the assured in the case of drilling vessels, unless the sum involved is within the insured sum.[37] Where, however, the sum in question is incurred by the Club on a direct basis it is not taken into account in the limitation figure.

"Section 6. Regulations

1. *Safety regulations.* The Association may at any time issue general or special directions concerning measures for the prevention of liability or other loss covered by the Association, see § 48 of the Plan.

2. *Notice of regulations.* The Association shall notify the assured immediately of regulations issued pursuant to 1 or to § 51 of the Plan and of the time of their coming into force.

A complete list of all current regulations shall be sent to the assured at least once a year."

1. *Safety regulations.* Clause 48 of the Plan, entitled " Safety Regulations," defines these as being " directions concerning measures for the prevention of loss, issued by public authorities, stipulated in the insurance contract, prescribed by the insurer under the insurance contract, or issued by the classification society if, at the conclusion of the contract, it is an implied condition that the ship shall be classed in such society."

Clause 49 of the Plan provides that in the event of a violation of a safety regulation the insurer is liable only to the extent that it is proved that the loss is not a consequence of the violation or that the violation cannot be imputed to the assured.

2. *Notice of regulations.* Clause 51 of the Plan provides that " the insurer may stipulate that at the conclusion of contracts concerning the trading of the insured ship certain special terms of contract are to be used or that certain special terms of contract are not to be used . . . ." This could doubtless apply, subject to appropriate modifications, to the contracts concluded in respect of a drilling vessel.

B. The scope of the cover

"Section 7. Liability for personal injury, etc.

The Association shall cover the assured's liability:

    (a) in consequence of personal injury or loss of life,
    (b) for salvage monies awarded for lifesaving, provided that the monies have been awarded for the saving of life only or together for the saving of life and salvage of goods of relatively insignificant value.

---

[36] See also the reference above, at p. 134, to the words " any one accident any one occurrence," in the London Standard Drilling Barge Form. The original Norwegian Club conditions referred to " any one accident or series of accidents arising out of the same event."   [37] See also p. 238, below.

Liability which is covered under sections 11 or 12 of the Conditions shall not be covered under this section."

(a) *Personal injury or loss of life.* Provided that the liability arose in connection with activities covered by the insurance,[38] it is covered without regard to how or where it arose and regardless of the identity of the victim. Liability under section 11[39] (" Statutory obligations in respect of master and crew ") and section 12 [40] (" Liability for wages and effects ") is not, however, recoverable under section 7, although the wording of this section would otherwise permit such recovery. As a result sections 11 and 12 may be excluded from the cover, as, for example, when the assured wishes to have a higher deductible or to bear such a risk himself, and there will be no question of such liability being recoverable under section 7.

(b) *Life salvage.* Though it is doubtful how far the rules of law relating to ships generally apply to drilling vessels, so far as they are not conventional ships, it has to be assumed in this section that the usual rules of salvage will apply.[41] Life salvage can only be claimed if there has also been salvage, even by another salvor, of some part of the property (ship, cargo or freight) concerned. Norwegian P. & I. insurers, in common with other P. & I. insurers, cover liability for life salvage to the extent that it is not recoverable from the hull or cargo insurers. In addition, where the property is of " relatively insignificant value " the present conditions also allow for recovery of the whole salvage liability, so as to avoid the necessity for an invidious determination as to the value of the lives involved. One salvor may save the passengers and crew and the lifeboat in which they have taken refuge, while another salvor saves the ship. The Club would pay out in respect of the whole of the award made to the former salvor.

"*Section 8. Liability for Property Damage*
The Association shall cover the assured's liability in consequence of damage to or loss of objects not belonging to the assured himself.
Excepted herefrom are:
- (a) liability for damage to or loss of the entered drilling vessel, its equipment, outfit or supplies, on board or outside the drilling vessel.
- (b) liability for damage to or loss of hole which is being drilled by the entered drilling vessel.

Liability which is covered under section 12 of the Conditions shall not be covered under this section,"

1. *Introductory words.* The commentators state that this section constitutes the most comprehensive and important provision in the list of matters covered. Losses suffered by the assured because his own property is damaged or lost are not covered, subject to what is said under note 5, below.[42] If the assured is made liable to a mortgagee or a lessee who suffered loss, as a result of damage to the property of the assured, he can-

---

[38] See s. 3, at p. 229–231, above. [39] See p. 238, below.
[40] See p. 238, below. [41] See also p. 53, above.
[42] At p. 236.

not recover under the P. & I. policy. On the other hand a party other than the owner of the drilling vessel, such as a lessee, might be a co-assured.[43] If that party damages an object belonging to the owner of the drilling vessel or to another co-assured the liability is covered because the object does not belong to " the assured himself," *i.e.* to the particular assured who has incurred the liability.

2. *Damage to or loss of " objects."* An " object " is said to mean a physical thing of any kind whether real estate or a chattel. Where the object is damaged physically the insurance extends not only to liability for loss of value, but to liability for consequential losses such as loss of time or profit.

3. *Contractual liability.* Certain types of contractual liability for " damage to or loss of objects," which are common in the case of conventional ships, rarely if ever occur in the case of drilling vessels. These include cargo liability and liability for passengers' luggage. There may, however, be liability to tugs under towage contracts which oblige the owner of the drilling vessel to hold the tug harmless for damage to the tug or damage to property belonging to third parties. Collision liability which arises during the towage is not contractual and is covered by the DV-kasko policy. Nor would the assured be able to recover if the terms of the towage of the contract were not customary; this follows from clause 76 of the Plan, which was mentioned above in connection with section 3.[44]

4. *Liability other than contractual liability.* Liability for collision with a ship or another drilling vessel and liability for striking a fixed or floating object are worthy of special mention. The words of section 8 itself extend to such liabilities (whether the actual damage was done by the drilling vessel or by a tug employed by it), subject to the important qualification, resulting from section 13 of the cover,[45] that the Norwegian P. & I. Clubs do not cover liability which can be covered by the ordinary hull insurance of the drilling vessel. The English market cover is restricted usually to three-fourths of the collision liability, with the balance of the collision liability, and the whole of the liability for striking a fixed or floating object, being absorbed by the P. & I. Club. The Norwegian drilling vessel hull conditions (DV-kasko), however, cover only collision liability, although they cover the whole of that liability; as a result a drilling vessel covered by DV-kasko would recover from its Norwegian Club its liability for striking a fixed or floating object which was not a ship or a drilling vessel, including for instance a production platform.

This section also extends to liability for oil pollution, subject to the exception set out in section 17 [46] in respect of loss occasioned by uncontrolled flow from the well being drilled.

---

[43] See s. 19, at p. 244, below.
[44] See p. 231, above.
[45] For s. 13, entitled " Limitation Owing to Other Insurance," see p. 239, below.
[46] Entitled " Blow-out damage, etc."; see p. 243, below.

5. *Damage to the assured's own property.* Section 8 deals only with the liability of the assured for property damage, and he cannot be liable for damage to his own property. The exception in (a) serves to exclude Club liability where the property in question does not belong to the assured, and should be covered by its own insurance, as in the case of a ship on demise to the assured. It is true that § 77 of the Plan [47] provides that there can be a recovery if the loss or damage occurs under such circumstances that the assured would have become liable if the object had belonged to a third party, but that paragraph itself is subject to an exception in respect of loss of or damage to the insured ship, her provisions, stores and outfit.

6. *Damage to or loss of the entered drilling vessel, its equipment, outfit or supplies (exception (a)).* Damage to or loss of the vessel is excluded, so far as its owner is concerned, by the opening words " objects not belonging to the assured himself." If the assured is other than the owner, as, for example in the case of a mortgagee, there would still be no liability on the P. & I. Club by virtue of exception (a), excluding damage to or loss of the vessel in any event.

As for the equipment, outfit or supplies, there is no cover if the assured in question is the owner of the drilling vessel, because of exception (a); if the interests of other assureds are in issue, there would be no cover either because of exception (a), or if they were the owners of the equipment, etc., by virtue of the exclusion in the opening words of section 8, by which the assured's property is excluded.

7. *Liability for damage to or loss of the hole which is being drilled by the vessel (exception (b)).* Liability in respect of the hole will almost invariably be apportioned in the drilling contract between the owner of the drilling vessel and the operator.[48] Damage to the hole can include damage to equipment, such as tubing, which has became part of the hole; damage to or loss of other equipment, such as the drilling vessel's drill string, is excluded by exception (a).

"*Section 9. Excess of Loss through Measures to Avert or Minimise Loss under the Hull Insurance*

The Association shall cover that part of the assured's loss through measures as mentioned in § 68–73 of the Plan, which, by its nature but not with the sufficient amount, could have been covered by the assured under the general hull insurance conditions in the country whose hull conditions form the basis for the hull cover of the drilling vessel, provided that the sum insured is at least equivalent to the full value of the drilling vessel."

The liability of the hull insurer in respect of loss through measures to avert or minimise a loss is not to exceed a total of (a) the sum for which the hull is insured plus (b) the separate sum insured in respect of preventive measures. He is liable up to the separate sum insured under (b) to the extent

[47] Known as the sister ship clause, though its application is not limited to sister ships.
[48] See p. 266, below.

that it is not consumed by liability for collision or striking and for loss through measures taken to avert or minimise such liability. The same commentators have given two examples in connection with the conventional P. & I. cover for ships, but the same principles apply in the case of drilling vessels:

"(1) The entered ship with a sum insured of Kr. 50 million is grounded. Its own hull damage amounts to Kr. 20 million. In order to salvage the ship costs of preventive measures, inter alia in the form of pollution damage, are incurred in the amount of Kr. 82 million. The hull insurers cover the hull damage out of the sum insured. The balance of the sum insured (Kr. 30 million) together with the total of the sum insured for liability (§ 196 of the Plan) is consumed in covering the cost of preventive measures up to Kr. 80 million. The deficit, Kr. 2 million, must be borne by the assured (or his P. & I. insurer).

(2) The entered ship with a sum insured of Kr. 50 million comes into collision with another ship and is solely to blame. Its own hull damage is Kr. 20 million and its liability to the other ship Kr. 10 million while the cost of endeavouring to minimise that liability runs into Kr. 42 million. The aggregate of the collision liability and the cost of the preventive measures exceeds the sum insured for liability by Kr. 2 million. This amount is not recoverable by the assured; it is not covered out of the Kr. 30 million which are left of the sum insured for hull damage."

"Section 10. *Liability for Obstructions and Wreck Removal*
The Association shall cover the assured's liability for the removal of wreck and liability to owners of harbours, canals and similar structures and liability to owners of other vessels for loss caused where the entered drilling vessel as a result of a casualty has caused an obstruction to the free passage."

1. *Wreck liability.* This section affords general cover in respect of liability for the removal of wreck, provided that the liability has the necessary connection with the entered drilling vessel.[49] The liability may be for the removal of the wreck of the entered vessel, which is not covered by the hull insurer, even where it results from a collision; or it may be for the removal of the wreck of another drilling vessel or a ship which, for example, has sunk as a result of an explosion in the entered vessel. It is immaterial whether the liability flows from the ordinary law of tort or arises because a public authority or anyone else has a legal right to require removal of the wreck.

If the assured is liable for removal of wreck as the result of damage to objects, then the liability would be recoverable in any event under section 8.[50] If the liability is for removal of the wreck of a ship with which the insured drilling vessel has been in collision it is covered by the hull insurer and only the excess liability is the concern of the P. & I. cover, under the second part of section 13.[51]

2. *Liability for obstructions.* Section 8[52] would cover the liability of the assured for obstructions to the free passage of other ships, as, for example,

---
[49] See Section 3, at p. 229, above. [50] See p. 234, above.
[51] See p. 240, below. [52] " Liability for property damage "; see p. 234, above.

237

where the drilling vessel causes a bridge to collapse and block the fairway. Section 10 provides a wider basis of recovery, as there need not be property damage. The drilling vessel may merely have run aground or had a machinery breakdown, and be blocking the fairway.

The commentators say that the " other vessels " may be conventional ships or other drillings vessels.

"*Section* 11. *Statutory obligations in respect of master and crew*

The Association shall cover the assured's liability to the drilling vessel's master and crew according to statutory law and collective wages agreements governing the contracts of employment, for:

(a) nursing and maintenance of master and crew ashore in case of illness or injury,

(b) master's and crew's expenses including maintenance for travelling to their places of residence in cases of illness or injury or after shipwreck,

(c) funeral expenses and the cost of sending home urn of ashes or coffin and the effects of the deceased."

This Section mainly repeats the equivalent provision in the ordinary Norwegian P. & I. cover for conventional ships. The cover provided by section 11 may be excluded; that is why section 7 [53] provides that it does not cover liability covered under section 11 (and s. 12). If section 11 is retained it is advisable to give a more specific description of the cover by listing the liabilities involved.

"*Section* 12. *Liability for wages and effects*

The Association shall cover the assured's liability to the drilling vessel's master and crew according to statutory law and collective wages agreements governing the contracts of employment for:

(a) wages in respect of the time after the termination of the employment and wages to their dependants, where the employment has been terminated as a result of shipwreck, illness, injury or death,

(b) damage to or loss of effects belonging to the ship's complement or other persons carried in the ship and employed on board."

This section. like section 11, mainly repeats the equivalent P. & I. provision for conventional ships, and the same comments apply.

Cover supplementary to Part B

In connection with section 5 [54] it was pointed out that under § 80 (a) of the Plan an insurer would generally cover certain supplementary matters such as the costs of preventive measures and of litigation, even if the sum insured is exceeded. As a result of section 5.2 this is not the case under the present conditions, so that they are subject to the limitation imposed by the sum insured. The following are the main matters to which the restrictions in section 5.2 apply:

---

[53] " Liability for personal injury, etc."; see p. 233, above.
[54] " Sum insured "; see at p. 233, above.

The Cover Considered in Detail

1. Costs of averting or minimising the loss

This cover is available as a result of § 68 (" Particular measures to avert or minimise the loss ") and § 69 (" Loss through measures relating to several interests ") of the Plan. It is equivalent to a sue and labour clause.

2. Costs of providing security

Under the Plan the insurer has no duty to provide security for the assured's third party liability, but in practice P. & I. Clubs do so if the matter falls within the cover, but without prejudice to the liability of the Club. The Club would in any event be liable, under § 95 of the Plan, for reasonable costs incurred by the assured in giving security.

Costs of litigation

This cover is available as a result of § 65 of the Plan (" Costs of litigation ") if (a) the litigation concerns the loss covered; and (b) the steps taken are approved by the insurer or must, after they have been taken, be regarded as justifiable.

4. Settlement costs

This cover is available as a result of § 66 of the Plan (" Costs in connection with the settlement of claims "). It extends to (a) " the necessary costs for the ascertainment of the loss and the calculation of the claim," where the insurer is liable for the loss; and (b) the necessary expenses of sending out the assured's own surveyor, if he has reasonable grounds to do so.

C. Limitations of the liability of the association

This group of sections imposes certain restrictions and exceptions, rather than financial limitations, upon the cover given by sections 7 to 12.

"*Section* 13. *Limitation Owing to Other Insurance*

The Association shall not cover:

(a) loss which by its nature can be insured by the assured under the general hull insurance conditions for drilling vessels in the country whose hull insurance conditions form the basis for the ship's hull insurance,

(b) loss which is covered under the Norwegian Folketrygd or which is or should have been covered under equivalent obligatory insurance system in a country to which the operation of the entered drilling vessel has a natural connection,

(c) liability which by its nature may be covered by customary hull insurance, P. & I. insurance or other liability insurance of other vessels, motor vehicles or aircraft of which the assured is the owner, lessee or charterer,

(d) loss as mentioned in § 77 of the Plan, provided that it could have been covered by hull insurance, cargo insurance, fire insurance or other customary insurance against damage to property.

The Association shall, however, cover such part of the assured's liability for collision and striking which exceeds the amount which is covered under the drilling vessel's hull insurance, or which could have been covered under a

239

a hull insurance on conditions as mentioned under (a) in the preceding paragraph with a sum insured equivalent to the full value of the vessel. As regards loss as mentioned in § 77 of the Plan, deduction shall also be made for loss which is covered by freight insurance, or could have been covered by another insurance as mentioned in the preceding paragraph."

1. *General remarks on the relationship to hull insurance.* The placing of the demarcation line between P. & I. and hull cover is of great importance. Paragraph (a) is the main provision is this respect. It emphasises that the P. & I. cover is complementary to the general hull insurance in the country whose hull conditions form the basis for the drilling vessel's hull insurance. If, for example, the drilling vessel is insured for hull risks on the Norwegian terms, the full cover given by DV-kasko is the relevant one. If it is insured on English terms, the relevant conditions are the full English conditions for drilling vessels. If one-fourth of the collision liability has been specially excluded from the Norwegian terms, the cover is nevertheless deemed to have been on such terms, and the one fourth liability does not become recoverable from the P. & I. insurers.

2. *Cover of the assured's collision liability.* This is the area in which overlapping between the hull and the P. & I. insurances is most likely to occur.

Under the Plan the hull insurer covers the assured's liability for collision with another ship and for striking a fixed or floating object.[55] Under DV-kasko, however, only collision (with a ship or drilling vessel) is covered. Paragraph (a) of section 13 thus excludes such liability from the P. & I. cover. The P. & I. cover extends to liabilities not excluded by paragraph (a) provided that they are positively included in the cover section, 7 to 12. Broadly speaking, it thus extends to liabilities in respect of:

(i) Personal injury (section 7) in all cases and property damage (section 8) where the entered drilling vessel strikes an object other than a ship or another drilling vessel.

(ii) a collision between the entered drilling vessel and a ship or another drilling vessel where liability is excluded from the hull cover, *e.g.* by DV-kasko.

The second paragraph of section 13, however, makes it clear that the P. & I. cover will extend to liability which by its nature is included in the hull insurance but which exceeds the amount payable by the hull insurer, *i.e.* the excess collision liability. This is so if the amount in question would in principle be payable by the hull insurers or would have been payable by them if there had been hull cover under the standard conditions (as set out in paragraph (a)) with a sum insured equivalent to the full value of the vessel. The " full value " means, according to the commentators, the market value, regardless of contractual encumbrances which reduce the value.

---

[55] See also the comments on s. 8 at p. 235, above.

3. *The relationship to social insurances.* Paragraph (b) excludes from the P. & I. cover liability for loss covered by the Norwegian Folketrygd or which is or should have been covered under equivalent compulsory insurance in a country with which the operation of the entered drilling vessel has a natural connection. The Norwegian " Lov om Folketrygd " (Social Security Act) of June 17, 1966, No. 12, and subsequent amendments, provides for social security insurance for persons residing in Norway and Norwegian subjects employed on Norwegian ships. Foreign subjects employed on such ships are covered by the Act with respect to compensation for death and injury suffered in the course of employment. The Folketrygd institution has no recourse against a tortfeasor unless the injury was caused wilfully.

The paragraph refers to loss which " is covered " under the Folketrygd or " is or should have been covered " under other schemes. Where the liability " is covered " the situation is the same whichever scheme is involved. The words " should have been covered " refer to other schemes where membership is obligatory but steps have to be taken to effect entry.

The commentators explain that the words " a country to which the operation . . . has a natural connection " mean:

(a) the country of the flag, *i.e.* the country where the drilling vessel is registered, or the " home country " if it is not registered; and
(b) the countries on the territory or continental shelf of which the drilling vessel is operating.

4. *The relationship to insurances of the assured's other means of transport.* Liability may arise from the use of a means of transport (*e.g.* a supply ship, a motor car, an aircraft) which the assured owns, leases or charters. He will normally be insured in respect of such liability by a separate liability insurance. The other insurances and the P. & I. insurance should complement each other; paragraph (c) provides that the decisive consideration should be not whether such insurances have been taken out, but whether it is customary to do so.

5. *The relationship to object insurance of the assured's own property.* The P. & I. insurers are liable in certain cases for damage to the assured's own own property.[56] It follows from paragraph (d) of section 13 that the sistership rule (§ 77 of the Plan) is complementary to the other insurances listed in (d).

"*Section* 14. *Privity of the Assured*

The Association shall not cover loss caused by the assured by a grossly negligent act or omission.

Where the loss is a consequence of defects in the drilling vessel or its equipment which may impair her safety or expose human lives to danger or of equivalent defects in moorings or supervision while the vessel is laid up, the Association is not liable if the assured was, or ought to have been, aware

---

[56] s. 8, n. 5; see p. 236, above and the reference to the sister ship rule.

of the defects and has omitted to remedy them to the best of his ability. The same applies if the assured knew or should have known that recommendations had been issued in respect of the drilling vessel by a classification society or a public maritime safety authority and he has omitted to comply with them to the best of his ability."

The commentators say that the reference to " a grossly negligent act or omission " constitutes, indirectly, and as a result of § 55 of the Plan, a statement that the P. & I. cover does not extend to a loss which the assured has caused wilfully. However, an act or omission may be " grossly negligent " where it results from a considerable lack of diligence, but it is not necessary that there should have been a " wilful " lack of diligence, equivalent to the " wilful misconduct " to which the English and American legal systems often refer.

The paragraph refers to " defects in the drilling vessel or its equipment," without mentioning unseaworthiness. It is however assumed that the provisions of Norwegian law [57] which forfeit cover if damage is caused by unseaworthiness, of which the assured knew or ought to have known, apply by analogy to drilling vessels which are not ships.

"Section 15. Amounts Saved to the Assured
Where the assured, through circumstances involving loss for him, has obtained extra revenue, saved expenses or avoided liability which would otherwise have been incurred and which would not have been covered by the Association, the latter may deduct from the compensation an amount corresponding to the benefit obtained."

This section is identical to a provision in the Gard and Skuld P. & I. cover in respect of conventional ships and to § 241 of the Plan.

"Section 16. Liability for Loss through Measures to Avert or Minimise Loss
Where measures taken to avert or minimise loss which would have been recoverable from another insurer have resulted in liability for the Association, the Association shall be subrogated to the assured's claim against the other insurer. § 96 of the Plan shall have equivalent application. The items enumerated below are in no case recoverable as loss through measures to avert or minimise the loss in accordance with § 68 of the Plan:
(a) costs of measures that have been or could have been accomplished by the crew or by reasonable use of the drilling vessel or her equipment,
(b) assured's liability for non-fulfilment, or delay in fulfilment, of a drilling contract or of an agreement for the sale of the drilling vessel,
(c) cost of regaining control of the oil or gas well on which the drilling vessel is working."

The object of the first paragraph is to resolve the problem of double insurance where the P. & I. Club is primarily liable, as in the case of oil pollution, but the liability has been incurred in the interest of another insurer, such as the hull insurer, to avert or minimise his loss. The assured is fully covered by the club, which bears the burden of a recourse action against the other insurer.

---

[57] In the Insurance Contracts Act of June 6, 1930, No. 20.

The second paragraph sets out certain exceptions to the rules of the Plan as to costs of preventive measures.

Sub-paragraphs (a) and (b) correspond to provisions in the Gard and Skuld P. & I. cover. Sub-paragraph (c), however, is a special rule for drilling vessels. The loss resulting from loss of control of a well affects primarily the interest of the operator. The provision has to be read in conjunction with the proviso to section 17.[58]

> "*Section 17. Blow-out Damage, etc.*
> The Association shall not cover:
>   (a) loss resulting from pollution and measures taken to avert or minimise such loss,
>   (b) loss resulting from sub-surface oil or gas having been damaged or lost,
>   (c) loss as a result of damage to property by cratering, reduced buoyancy or similar occurrence,
>
> provided that the loss is occasioned by uncontrolled flow from the well which is being drilled by the entered drilling vessel, whether resulting from blow-out or other causes."

The object is that certain types of loss resulting from an uncontrolled flow from the well being drilled by the entered vessel should properly be covered by the operator by a separate insurance the benefit of which would also extend to the owner of the drilling vessel. The P. & I. insurer would, however, cover losses resulting from a flow from another well, *e.g.* where the insured vessel, while shifting, collides with a production platform.

The exceptions do not apply where the well is under control but a mistake has occasioned a limited spillage. The flow will usually be of oil or gas but the section applies to all flows, including a flow of drilling mud.

Paragraph (a) deals with loss resulting from pollution. The commentators say; " pollution includes contamination."[59] There is no general exclusion of liability for oil pollution. To the extent that the Association is not liable for loss from pollution it has no liability for the cost of preventive measures. The commentators say that although the words " and measures taken to avert or minimise such loss " are superfluous in most cases, the assured may have a duty to take such measures, although he has no primary liability for pollution. The measures may include clean-up operations or operations to arrest a flow by drilling a relief well. Costs of control are generally excluded by section 16(c)[60] even if incurred to avert or minimise a loss of a type not listed in the present section.

Paragraph (b) excludes the liability of the Norwegian P. & I. insurers in respect of loss resulting from damage to or loss of sub-surface oil or gas. As a result the assured may be liable to the owner of the well without the right of recovery under his liability insurance.

---

[58] "Blow-out damage, etc.," see this page, below.
[59] For a definition of pollution see pp. 333–334, below.
[60] See p. 242, above.

Paragraph (c) excludes the liability of the P. & I. insurers in respect of loss resulting from damage to property by cratering, reduced buoyancy or a similar occurrence. There may be a reduction of buoyancy in the case of nearby ships or drilling vessels if gas escapes from the well in such a way as to reduce the density of the sea water.

> "*Section* 18. *Deductible*
> For each single casualty the amount set out in the policy shall be deducted."

The amount of the deductible is to be set out in each individual policy, as there is not a standard deductible applicable to all entries. The deductible applies, as the limitation of liability of the P. & I. insurers to the sum insured also applies,[61] to " each single casualty." It also applies to the ancillary covers such as the costs of preventive measures.

D. Insurance of the interest of a third party

> "*Section* 19. *Insurance of the Interest of the Lessee, Drilling Contractor or Operator*
>
> Where it is set out in the policy that the insurance has been effected in favour of a person who has leased the entered drilling vessel or who employs it in his activities as drilling contractor or operator, the following rules shall apply:
> 1. The Association shall have no recourse against the assured or third party covered unless such person has caused the loss by his own fault as mentioned in section 14 of the Conditions.
> 2. The Association shall cover the loss of the nature enumerated under subdivision B, see also A and C, of the Conditions, to the extent the loss is incurred by the third party in his capacity as lessee, drilling contractor or operator as above mentioned."

1. *General remarks.* An insurance on normal Plan conditions does not, unless it is expressly agreed, include the interest of a third party. It is presumed that the owner of the drilling vessel is the person effecting the insurance and the principal assured and a member of the Association.[62] The additional parties who may be insured under the present conditions are the " lessee," or bareboat charterer; the " drilling contractor," who in this context is described as " the party performing the drilling operations " but the term may also include a " manager " who performs such operations on behalf of the owner (of the drilling vessel); and " the operator," who is described as " the party who has the permit to exploit the petroleum deposits at the place where the vessel is operating." [63] Each co-insured is covered in his own right.

2. *Waiver of subrogation.* As a general rule the Association acquires rights of subrogation from the assured in respect of his claim for redress

---

[61] See s. 5.2 at p. 232, above.
[62] See s. 1, at p. 229, above.
[63] The terminology differs from that employed elsewhere in this book; see especially p. 247, below.

from other parties, when it has compensated the assured. The owner of a drilling vessel often has, as a result of his drilling contract or otherwise, to waive his claims of recourse against the lessee, the drilling contractor or the operator, but the waiver does not necessarily bind the P. & I. insurer, which may wish to reduce its compensation accordingly, unless (in accordance with a provision to this effect in the Plan) the waiver is deemed to be customary in the trade.

The most simple form of insurance of the interest of such third parties consists of a waiver by the Association of claims for redress against them where they have caused a loss for which the assured receives compensation.

It is not intended, however, that the third party should obtain better cover that is available to the assured where he has caused the loss.[64] Nevertheless, a judgment as to whether the third party was grossly negligent, or had shown a lack of due diligence, is made on the basis of what he knew or ought to have known, and not on the basis of the knowledge of the principal assured, and vice versa.

3. *Full insurance of third party.* Where a third party is fully insured he is covered in respect of the matters mentioned in group B,[65] consisting of sections 7 to 12, and subject to the terms of groups A [66] and C.[67] The cover is an independent one, and applies even where no loss is incurred by the principal assured. There is one insurance only, however, and the Association is liable only up to one insured sum per casualty, subject to one deductible, even though the loss is incurred by several assureds.

"*Section* 20. *Insurance or the Interest of the Mortgagee* (*Chapter* 8 *of the Plan*)

1. The period of advance notice set out in the second paragraph of § 135 of the Plan shall be extended from seven to 21 days, provided that the mortgagee has guaranteed payment of premium earned from the time such notice is received by him until the expiry of the insurance, but not beyond the expiry of the period of notice.

2. The limit set out in the second paragraph of § 138 of the Plan shall be raised to U.S. $500,000."

§ 134 of the Plan provides for the interest of the mortgagee to be automatically insured. If, however, the Association has not been notified of the mortgage the principal assured has the power, by agreement with the insurer, to make dispositions which may be to the detriment of the mortgagee. The rights of the mortgagee are not to exceed those of the owner; if the owner has neglected his duty of disclosure or caused the casualty by his own fault, the mortgagee will suffer to the same extent as the owner.

§ 135 of the Plan,[68] to which section 20.1 refers, provides that where the insurer gives notice of termination the mortgagee is entitled to be notified

---

[64] See s. 14 (" Privity of the Assured ") at p. 241, above.
[65] p. 233, above.
[66] p. 229, above.
[67] p. 239, above.
[68] Entitled "Notices of termination and other dispositions concerning the insurance."

with the same period of notice as the owner, but that this period should not be less than seven days. Section 20 modifies this by extending the period to 21 days, subject to the proviso in section 20.1.

Clause 138 of the Plan, to which section 20.2 refers, provides: " . . . A claim for damage which, in respect of one single casualty, exceeds 5 per cent. of the sum insured or Kr. 200.000,[69] must not, without the consent of the mortgagee, be settled by the insurer except against a receipted bill for repairs effected. . . ." Section 20.2 raises the limit to $500,000. With respect to P. & I. insurance, payment of compensation for property damage to the mortgagee is rare.

---

[69] About $41,000 at February, 1979 rates.

CHAPTER 7

DRILLING CONTRACTS

DIVISION OF FUNCTIONS, LIABILITIES AND INSURANCES

1. Introduction

THE relationship between the owner of the drilling unit, or contractor, and the operator, is governed by the drilling contract. In each contract there is a division as to those matters which can properly be said to appertain, respectively, to the contractor and the operator. In the broadest sense, the operator is, as his name implies, conducting the operation, and the use in French contracts of the expression *maître de l'ouvrage*, or " master of the undertaking, is a striking indication of the importance of his position. An operator has a series of contracts, of which the first in time is frequently the lease for a block with a government. His contract with the contractor is in some respects analogous to a time charterparty, in that he hires the drilling unit from the contractor, paying on the basis of time, for a specified or, where it is not specified, an ascertainable period.

The contract exists in order to record the arrangements between the contractor, as owner of the drilling unit, and the operator. It sets out the nature of the task to be achieved; the functions to be performed by each party, as far as the provision of equipment and personnel is concerned [1]; the responsibilities and expenses which are to be assumed by each party [2]; and their respective responsibilities for the insurances. [3]

The preamble to the International Daywork Drilling Contract—Offshore [4] shows how the contracting parties may describe the nature of the task to be achieved:

" WHEREAS, Operator desires to have offshore wells drilled in the Operating Area and to have performed or carried out all auxiliary operations and services as detailed in the Appendices hereto [5] or as Operator may require; and WHEREAS, Contractor is willing to furnish the drilling vessel complete

---

[1] See below, p. 251.
[3] See below, p. 277.
[2] See below, p. 258.

[4] Revised June 1975; an Offshore International Contract approved by the International Association of Drilling Contractors. For the contract in full see Appendix B to this book. In this chapter it is called the I.A.D.C. contract.

[5] Appendix A, the " Equipment, Materials, Services and Personnel List "; Appendix B, " Insurance Requirements "; and Appendix C, " Depreciation Schedule Contractor's Equipment.

with drilling and other equipment (hereinafter called the " Drilling Unit "), insurances and personnel, all as detailed in the Appendices hereto for the purpose of drilling the said wells and performing the said auxiliary operations and services for Operator."

A form of contract sometimes used by a major oil company [6] contains a similar preamble:

" WHEREAS Company [the operator] desires to have wells drilled in the Offshore Concession Areas of Company in . . . and all auxiliary operations carried out and services performed as detailed hereinafter in connection with such operations or as Company may require; and WHEREAS Contractor is engaged in the business of drilling, testing and completing, working over, and deepening of wells; represents that it has adequate resources and equipment in good working order and fully trained personnel capable of efficiently operating such equipment; and is ready, willing and able to drill the said wells and carry out the said auxiliary operations and services for the Company and to furnish the drilling unit with the drilling and other equipment and personnel, as detailed in the Appendix ' A ' hereto, [7] for this purpose: "

The relationship between the contractor and the operator, in which the latter can give instructions to the former, is exemplified by the following provisions in the I.A.D.C. contract:

" 504 COMPLIANCE WITH OPERATOR'S INSTRUCTIONS. Contractor shall comply with all instructions of Operator consistent with the provisions of this Contract including, without limitation, drilling, well control and safety instructions. Such instructions shall, if Contractor so requires, be confirmed in writing by the authorized representative of Operator. However, Operator shall not issue any instructions which would be inconsistent with Contractor's rules, policies or procedures pertaining to the safety of its personnel, equipment or the Drilling Unit.

701 INSTRUCTIONS TO CONTRACTOR. Operator may, from time to time, through its authorized representative or representatives, issue written or oral instructions to Contractor covering operations hereunder. Operator's instructions may be general or may deal with specific matters relating to operations hereunder including, without limitation, instructions to stop operations, as to safety and well control, and drilling instructions, but Operator may not require Contractor to drill deeper than . . . feet unless Contractor agrees."

In a contract used by a major oil company there are similar provisions:

" Contractor shall without prejudice to the provisions of Clause [see below] comply with all instructions of the Company consistent with the provisions of this contract which may from time to time be given by Company. Such instructions will be confirmed in writing by Company [8] and may include instructions as to drilling methods or stoppage of operations in progress."; and

---

[6] Reference will be made to several such contracts, as well as to the I.A.D.C. contract, in the following pages.

[7] Entitled " Equipment, Supplies, Personnel and Services to be furnished by Contractor in accordance with Clause 2 " (a clause dealing with the provision of equipment and personnel).

[8] Not, as in the I.A.D.C. contract, " shall, if Contractor so requires, be confirmed in writing. . . ."

" In the performance of its work hereunder, Contractor shall be an independent contractor with the authority to control and direct the performance of the detail of its work, subject to Company's rights to give instructions and of inspection and supervision as laid down in this contract. The presence of and the inspection and supervision by Company's representative at the site of the work shall not relieve Contractor from Contractor's obligations and responsibilities."

and, on the subject of well depth, which is mentioned in the extract from the I.A.D.C. contract cited above:

" Wells shall be drilled to a depth to be specified in each case by Company, *PROVIDED* that for drilling wells to a greater depth than . . . feet or in water depth greater than . . . feet Contractor's consent shall be required. Company shall have the right to complete or abandon the well at any depth; Company shall make every reasonable effort to keep Contractor duly informed with as much advance notice as practicable in this respect."; and

" Company shall be entitled in emergency, at its own discretion, to take over the operation of the drilling unit and to direct its personnel in the event that Company's interests will demand so. In such case Company will notify Contractor of its action and within three days confirm such notice in writing, setting forth the reasons for its action."

This chapter discusses the distribution, between the contractor and the operator, of functions; of responsibilities and expenses; of the duties to undertake insurances, so far as these matters are set out in the drilling contract; other sections of the drilling contract, with particular reference to payments, legal and formal provisions, etc.[9]; and indemnities and subrogation rights. Although there are many references to the I.A.D.C. contract in this chapter, we rarely find a contract executed on a standard form, except in the cases of some low risk ventures or contracts between parties of unequal bargaining strengths. Occasionally, inland waterway or close offshore and shallow wells may be drilled under an I.A.D.C. form with very little modification. Furthermore, virtually every significant operating oil company or offshore drilling contractor has what it considers to be its own form of contract. These forms, however, frequently serve as nothing more than the basis for a request for a bid or an offer of services. Once interest is generated actual contractual negotiations may occupy several weeks and the final contract may bear little resemblance to the original form. The factors which govern these developments include the identity of the negotiating parties, the area of the world in which the contract is to be performed, the type of equipment required (jack-up, semi-submersible or drill ship) and, most importantly, the current supply and demand in respect of that particular type of equipment.

A. *Functions* [10]

The drilling contract sets out the tasks to be undertaken by each party to the drilling operation. These include more general obligations, such as

---

[9] See below, p. 284.   [10] See below, p. 251.

the duty of the contractor to provide a drilling unit and to comply with the operator's instructions; and more specific obligations, such as each party's duty to provide certain personnel and items of equipment, and to maintain stocks and to carry out repairs. Though each party is under a " liability " to undertake these tasks, it seems more appropriate to deal with them in a separate section, because they constitute functions of the operation, as opposed to liabilities or responsibilities consequent upon, or flowing from, the operation itself.

B. *Responsibilities and Expenses Generally* [11]

As a result of the drilling operation either party may find itself involved in legal liabilities or financial consequences; the drilling contract sets out the manner in which these results should be adjusted, as between the parties. Although a legal liability, as, for example, towards a third party or under the law, may fall in the first instance upon one party the contract may provide that, as between the parties, the other party should assume that liability. So also in the case of a financial consequence, such as the expense involved in cleaning up oil which has escaped from the well, the contract may provide that one or the other party should be responsible for that expense. The placing of that obligation will usually depend upon whether the source of the leak or spill is above or below the rotary table.[12]

C. *Insurances* [13]

It is in the interest of each party not only to maintain certain insurances itself but to be aware as to what insurances are maintained by the other party. The drilling contract usually sets out the respective responsibilities of the contractor for the maintenance of its insurances. Mr. Russel F. Sammis [14] has said:

> " My own observation over the years is that the insurance section of many drilling contracts is in reality a primer for the design of an insurance program for the contractor. We should first consider the reason for the Operator's interest in the drilling contractor's insurance program. If the reason is concern that an uninsured loss could seriously affect the contractor's ability to perform, a detailed insurance program should be described and required. If, as is more likely, the contractor is considered able to respond to his financial obligations, a brief insurance section is indicated."

The description of the insurance section as a " primer for the design of an insurance program for the contractor " is correct. It does not purport to set out the whole of the contractor's insurance scheme; and it

---

[11] See below, p. 258.

[12] " A heavy piece of machinery fitted into the derrick floor as a means of rotating the drill string, and at the same time allowing the kelly to be lowered or raised through it so that pipe can be added or removed "; Whitehead, *An A-Z of Offshore Oil & Gas.*

[13] See below, p. 277.

[14] Senior Vice-President of Marsh & McLennan Inc., Houston, Texas, in a lecture delivered in Denver, Colorado, in November 1975.

usually imposes no obligations as to the insurances to be undertaken by the operator. This pattern may vary, however, according to the relative financial strengths of the contractor and the operator.

2. The Differing Functions of the Contractor and the Operator

The functions of the contractor and the operator are considered here, so far as they concern the provision of material, equipment and personnel; these functions are clearly different; they are set out in the drilling contract and, because they separate the areas of work, some indication is thereby afforded as to how the assumption of responsibilities and expenses will be spread between the parties. In another part of the contract the division of risk is set out in express terms.

The basic obligations imposed on the two parties, to provide material, equipment and personnel, are exemplified by the following provisions in the I.A.D.C. contract.[15]

" ARTICLE III—CONTRACTOR'S PERSONNEL
302. Providing Personnel
    Contractor shall have its personnel available at the proper Operations Base or at a mutually agreed place ready to conduct operations hereunder."

" ARTICLE IV—CONTRACTOR'S ITEMS
401. Obligation to Supply
    Contractor shall provide Contractor's items and personnel and perform the services to be provided or performed by it according to the Appendices.[16] Operator shall move or pay the cost of moving Contractor's items, personnel and their personal effects between Operations Bases."

" ARTICLE VI—OPERATOR'S OBLIGATIONS
601. Equipment and Personnel
    Operator shall at its cost provide Operator's Items and personnel and perform the services to be provided or performed by it according to the Appendices.[16] . . .'"

The differing functions of the contractor and the operator can be expressed with reference to the following matters with which the drilling contract usually deals:

I. Material and Equipment
    A. Material provided by the Contractor
        (a) The Unit
        (b) The Equipment on the Unit
    B. Equipment and Materials supplied by the Operator.
II. Personnel and Services
    A. Personnel and Services provided by the Contractor
        (a) Marine Crew
        (b) Drilling Crew
        (c) Catering Personnel
    B. Personnel and Services provided by the Operator

---

[15] See n. 4, above.   [16] Appendices A and B; see n. 5, above.

Drilling Contracts

I. Material and Equipment

A. Material provided by the contractor

(a) *The Unit.* The main item is the drilling unit itself. This is provided by the contractor. The nature of the specifications, as set out in the contract, varies according to which type of unit is to be employed. The unit will have to be inspected by Lloyds, the American Bureau of Shipping, Norske Veritas, or some other acceptable classification society [17] and put in class. The contract states the dimensions, such as the overall length, the beam, the overall height to main deck, the draft, the maximum loads in drilling condition and in tow or transit condition, and the displacement at normal draft. The sizes of the ship's diving well and of the drilling well are also stated. As for the drilling unit's performance, the contract sets out the total horsepower and speed which can be developed, It will have to be able to withstand specified sea and weather conditions up to certain anticipated maxima in terms of wind speed, maximum wave height, significant wave period, surface current speed, etc. The term " variable deck load " is frequently used to refer to the weight of material or equipment which can be placed on deck without adversely affecting the stability of the drilling unit.

The storage capacity of the drilling unit is of considerable importance, since it has to be able to accommodate the individual items of equipment which are listed later. The relevant items include the storage capacities, expressed in volume or weight, and the fuel, drilling water or ballast, and drinking water capacities, usually expressed in barrels.

(b) *The Equipment on the Unit.* The contract may stipulate that the contractor shall provide equipment and spare parts as listed in the same part of the contract or in an appendix to the contract. He may also be liable for the replenishment of those items which constitute surface equipment, at his expense, and for maintaining adequate stock levels. The operator may have a corresponding liability in respect of in-hole equipment. The contractor may also be made liable to provide at his expense any items of equipment or spare parts which are not listed, but which are required for normal drilling operations according to good oilfield practice. Use of sub-contractors will not, according to the terms of the contracts mostly used, relieve the contractor from any liability under the contract. In particular, anything said in respect of the equipment and spare parts to be supplied by the contractor would likewise apply to any property of a sub-contractor as if it were the property of the contractor. In the I.A.D.C. contract Article 402 states:

" Maintain Stocks
Contractor shall be responsible, at its cost, for maintaining adequate stock levels of Contractor's items and replenishing as necessary."

---

[17] Classification is also discussed at p. 22, above.

This provision has been described [18] as " One of the highest potential points of conflict in this area of the Contract." The speaker added that it was not necessarily practical, however, to include a complete list of inventory items as a part of the contract, though it is important to describe adequately the contractor's items. Some people think, however, that this provision does not often give rise to problems except in remote areas or with items which are hard to replace.

There are listed, in the body of the contract or in an appendix thereto,[19] the individual items of equipment and supplies, with specifications, which are to be provided by the contractor. These may include: (i) The derrick [20] and sub-structure;

> *Example:* " One derrick or mast, at least 150 ft. high and with a 45 ft. wide base, to have a gross nominal capacity of at least 1,000,000 lbs., to be of the all-welded type, and capable of withstanding the dynamic loads imposed by the motions of the floating unit while under tow or the same loads with 15,000 ft. of 5″ drill pipe racked in the derrick or mast while in drilling position unless the pipe is racked on the pipe rack outside the derrick during normal round trips."

(ii) the draw works [21];

> *Example*: " One electric draw works, of at least 2,000–2,500 horsepower rating, driven by at least two electric motors of 750 HP each continuous rating and 1,000 HP intermittent.
>
> Complete with sandreel assembly, Lebus grooving for $1\frac{3}{8}″-1\frac{1}{2}″$ wire line, make-up and breakout catheads, Elmagco Model 7838 electric brake and Crown-O-Matic device. The draw works and electric brake shall have a separate fresh water cooling system of adequate capacity.

(iii) the drilling line and the sand line;

> *Examples*: " One drilling line, $1\frac{3}{8}″-1\frac{1}{2}″$, 6×19 I.P.S. with wire rope core of at least 7,500 ft. length spooled on a steel reel."
> and: " One sand line $\frac{9}{16}″-\frac{5}{8}″$, 6×7 I.P.S. with fibre or plastic core, 20,000 ft. long."

(iv) the pumping equipment;

> *Example:* " Pumps. Two duplex, alternatively triplex single-acting each equipped with an independently driven centrifugal charging pump, power slush pumps [22] of 1,500–1,700 HP rating, with forged steel fluid ends and quick change cylinder and valve covers. Each pump driven by two 800-HP electric motors and equipped with lube oil systems for the chain drive and piston rods; counter balanced eccentrics; a Hydril K20-5,000 psi pulsation dampener, a Cameron 3″ type ' B ' reset relief valve and cumulative pump stroke counter."

---

[18] By Mr. Taylor Hancock, of Global Marine Inc., in a lecture on " The Marine International Drilling Contract."

[19] As in Pt. I of Appendix A to the above-mentioned I.A.D.C. contract, the Equipment, Materials, Services and Personnel List.

[20] " The steel structure, used to support the drill pipe and other equipment which has to be raised or lowered during well-drilling operations." *Bank of Scotland Glossary.*

[21] " The hoisting winch for handling drill pipe, casing and tubing "; *ibid.*

[22] Slush pump: " Pump used in rotary drilling for circulating the drilling fluid," *ibid.*

(v) the power plant; The contract will probably stipulate that D.C. power and A.C. power should be available. The D.C. power would have to be sufficient to control and power simultaneously one slush pump and rotary table [23] at full load and the draw works at half load with at least one diesel engine operator as a stand-by. The A.C. power might have to consist of two generator sets of 500 to 1,000 kilowatts, one set being capable of taking the peak demand with the second as a stand-by. There could also be provision for an independent emergency generator set, with its own switchboard and wiring.

(vi) Mud [24] facilities; these could include: (a) the mud treating equipment, *i.e.* a specified number of main mud tanks, a settling tank, a pill tank and a chemical mixing tank; centrifugal mud mixing pumps; a de-sander; a de-silter; a shale shaker [25] and a de-gasser; and
(b) a dry mud and cement storage and transfer system, comprising pressure storage tanks, possibly with space heaters, dry mud surge tanks, a cement surge tank and a compressor unit.

(vii) air compressors; *i.e.* a fixed number of electrically driven water-cooled air compressors for the rig air and ship service air supply; an electrically driven air compressor to deliver starting air for the diesel engines if they require higher than rig air pressure, a hand-started diesel engine-driven air compressor for the initial start-up; air receivers; and chemical or refrigerating air drying units to dry the compressed air.

(viii) handling equipment; including revolving cranes with certain specifications, especially as to lifting capacity and hoisting speeds; and hoses, sufficiently long to reach down to the supply ship, for loading and unloading water, fuel, dry mud, cement, etc.

(ix) various lines and other connections relating to the well testing equipment; although the operator is responsible for the supply of the equipment itself [26]; these will include working pressure lines, gas lines, oil lines, water lines and air lines, and burner booms.

(x) crown block [27] and travelling block, the tonnage capacity for each being specified;

(xi) multiple anchors;

Example: " Dead line anchor. One National type ' E ' wire line anchor."

---

[23] " Chain or gear-driven circular unit, mounted in the derrick floor which rotates the drill pipe and bit," *ibid.* See also n. 61, below, for another definition.
[24] Mud is also known as drilling fluid, *i.e.* " Fluid, commonly consisting of clay suspended in water, used in drilling wells. It is pumped down through the drill-string to the bottom of the bore-hole, whence it rises to the surface through the space between drill-string and bore-hole wall," *ibid.*
[25] " Vibrating screen over which the drilling fluid is conducted. The drill cuttings are retained on the screen, while the fluid passes through the meshes," *ibid.*
[26] See below, p. 255.
[27] " Assembly of sheaves at the top of a derrick over which the wire line is reeved," *Bank of Scotland Glossary.*

(xii) rotary table [28];

> *Example*: " One rotary table having at least a 37½″ table opening driven by a 600–800 HP electric motor through a two-speed gear, alternatively driven from draw works.[29] Complete with master bushing and pin type kelly [30] drive bushing."

(xiii) cementing unit; it is usually necessary to fill part of the space between the casing [31] and the bore-hole wall with cement slurry. This keeps the casing stationary and prevents leakage from or to other strata which have been drilled.[32]

> *Example:* " One twin skid-mounted cementing unit, Halliburton HT-400 or equivalent, each pump driven by a 600–800 HP electric motor, through a 3-speed Cotta transmission, complete with low-pressure centrifugal mixing pump driven by a 60 HP electric motor, low-pressure hopper and Martin Decker, 15,000 psi pressure recorder-indicator."

(xiv) Blowout preventer [33] control units and inside blowout preventers;

> *Examples:* " One 3,000 psi W.P. automatic pump accumulator unit with control manifold, three air driven pumps (50:1 ratio), one 20-HP electrically driven pump, and fluid reservoir. The unit to be capable of closing and opening all preventers and closing again the bag type and one ram type preventer without reloading and holding them closed against rated working pressure of the preventers . . ." and:

> " Two inside B.O.P. each for 5″ and 3½″ drill pipe. Two Hydril drop-in valves complete with subs for both 5″ and 3½″ string [34] and all drill collar [35] sizes in use."

Some offshore units have three or more blowout preventers of 5,000 to 10,000 psi each.

(xv) safety equipment, including life-saving, emergency fire-fighting, first aid and any other equipment required under the safety regulations.

B. *Equipment and materials supplied by the operator*

There have been listed above [36] the items of equipment supplied by the contractor. The contract will also stipulate the items of equipment

---

[28] For one definition see n. 23, above.   [29] For definition see n. 21, above.

[30] " Kelly. Hollow, 40 foot long, square or hexagonal pipe attached [to] the top of the drill-string and turned by the rotary table during drilling. It is used to transmit the torque or twisting moment from the rotary machinery to the drill-string and thus to the bit." *Bank of Scotland Glossary.*

[31] " Steel lining used to prevent caving of the sides of a well, to exclude unwanted fluids, and to provide means for the control of well pressures and oil and gas production," *ibid.*

[32] See also the definition of " Cement/Cementing of Wells," *ibid.*

[33] " Blow-out preventer. High pressure valve, usually hydraulically operated, fitted to the top of the casing of a drilling well to prevent an accidental blow-out of oil or gas," *ibid.*

[34] " Drill-string. The column of drill pipe and drill collars screwed together, at the end of which the bit is screwed," *ibid.*

[35] " Drill Collar. Length of extra-heavy pipe, several of which are placed directly above the drilling bit. They serve to concentrate part of the weight of the drill-string near the bottom of the hole and to exert the necessary pressure on the bit, thereby preventing buckling of the upper part of the string," *ibid.*   [36] At pp. 252–255.

and materials to be supplied by the operator.[37] It may do so by stating that he shall provide, in addition to two fundamental items which are "Offshore drilling permit(s)" and "Drilling site, surveyed, and marked and cleared of obstructions":

(a) the equipment needed for geological surveillance of the wells;
(b) supply and stand-by boats for supplies and safety, respectively;
(c) radio apparatus for operator's special frequencies;
(d) a shore base with office space and warehouse for contractor;
(e) spools and their connections to the blowout preventer system provided by the contractor (see (xiv) above);
(f) main towing line for moves between locations;
(g) special equipment such as tubing, production equipment, fishing equipment, setting tools, etc.;
(h) various expendable items such as drilling tools, coring bits, casing and accessories, mud products and plugging agents, cement, casing protectors, spares for stabilisers, and special grease for the casings;
(i) fuel for operating the drilling unit and other facilities related to the unit;
(j) underwater television equipment, if required;
(k) industrial and drinking water;
(l) other necessary equipment for operations, so far as it is not set out above or to be provided by the contractor.

In the I.A.D.C. contract Article 601 deals with this matter by stating: "Operator shall at its cost provide Operator's items . . . In addition to providing the initial supply of Operator's items, Operator shall be responsible, at its cost, for maintaining adequate stock levels and replenishing as necessary." This Article is the counterpart to Article 401 "with the change," as the speaker mentioned above [38] has said:

"that Operator at any time or from time to time may request Contractor to furnish equipment, personnel or services that Operator is obligated to furnish under the Contract. As compensation for furnishing such items, Contractor is to be reimbursed for all costs plus a certain percentage handling charge; this handling charge usually varies somewhere between 5 per cent. and 10 per cent. depending upon the location and conditions."

II. *Personnel and Services*

A. *Personnel and services provided by the contractor*

Though certain specialised personnel are provided by the operator, the contractor provides the bulk of the personnel needed to operate the drilling unit and its equipment.[39]

[37] As in Pt. III of Appendix A to the above-mentioned I.A.D.C. contract, the Equipment, Materials, Services and Personnel List.
[38] Mr. Taylor Hancock, of Global Marine Inc., in a lecture entitled "The Marine International Drilling Contract."
[39] As in Pt. II of Appendix A to the above mentioned I.A.D.C. contract, the Equipment, Materials, Services and Personnel List.

(a) Marine crew. These are usually a few men only, such as the Captain, the First Mate, an Engineer, a Radio Officer and four or five ordinary seamen. The crew will be larger when the drilling unit is self-propelled than when it has to be towed.

(b) Drilling crew. Although most of the geological experts associated with the drilling are, as may be expected, provided by the operator, the people who actually drill the well are provided by the contractor. These may include a Chief Mechanic and a Chief Electrician, and their assistants, a tool pusher, drillers and assistant drillers, derrick men, welders, crane operators and so-called roughnecks. A tool pusher is the drilling supervisor, or foreman in charge of the operation; roughnecks, sometimes called floormen, are members of the unit crew who set the slips to hold the drill pipe, handle the tongs and generally handle the equipment around the floor.

(c) Catering personnel.

The contract may also set out various restrictions imposed upon the contractor in respect of his personnel. He might have to limit the number of expatriate personnel, *i.e.* personnel from a country other than that in whose waters, or near whose waters, the drilling unit is working. He may be obliged to replace personnel who are incompetent, upon due notice from the operator, and to ensure that they respect local law and customs, and that they follow the technical and safety instructions given by the operator. It would also be the duty of the contractor to maintain general discipline on the drilling unit.

The contractor will also provide a number of services. These may include [40]: transfer on to and from the drilling unit of any and all materials, equipment and personnel of contractor and of operator; accommodation of contractor's personnel and their families on shore; medical services for contractor's personnel and their families and first aid medical attention for all persons aboard the drilling unit; accommodation, housekeeping services and supplies and messing on board the drilling unit for contractor's personnel and up to a fixed number of operator's personnel, operator's visitors, and operator's service personnel; the toolpusher's office; if possible, operator's petroleum engineer's office; drill pipe inspection; and assistance in all services performed by service companies used in the operations so far as that can be done with contractor's personnel during the regular working hours except in case of emergencies.

B. *Personnel and services provided by the operator*

(a) towing services for towing between locations and from last location to nearest suitable port, the contractor being given the right to inspect and approve towing contracts with respect to the drilling unit;

---

[40] The examples are taken from " Part II of Appendix A to the above mentioned I.A.D.C. contract; see n. 39.

(b) anchor handling vessels and crews for handling mooring and anchors;

(c) marine and air transportation of contractor's and operator's items and personnel between shore bases and drilling unit;

(d) rig positioning, diving, weather forecasting and seabed survey services;

(e) cementing, mudlogging and geological services;

(f) any specialised personnel either not specified as being supplied by the contractor or needed for the operation of equipment other than the equipment provided by the contractor.

3. Division of Responsibilities and Expenses Generally

The drilling contract vests in the operator the right to direct the operations and to give instructions to the contractor. Thus, the I.A.D.C. contract states at Article 504, as quoted in the Introduction above:

" COMPLIANCE WITH OPERATOR'S INSTRUCTIONS
Contractor shall comply with all instructions of Operator consistent with the provisions of the Contract including, without limitation, drilling, well control and safety instructions. Such instructions shall, if Contractor so requires, be confirmed in writing by the authorised representative of Operator. However, Operator shall not issue any instructions which would be inconsistent with Contractor's rules, policies or procedures pertaining to the safety of its personnel, equipment or the Drilling Unit."

In addition, it describes the respective duties of the contractor and the operator as to provision of the drilling unit, the equipment and the personnel and services. These duties were discussed in the last section.[41] The performance by either of the two parties, or by one or more sub-contractors on behalf of either of them, may involve them in certain responsibilities and expenses. Such responsibilities and expenses may result from an act by one party which may or may not constitute a breach of contract towards the other party, or a breach of a duty to a third party; alternatively they may result from an external action, by a third party or by a natural force.

It seems more suitable to refer to responsibilities than to liabilities in this context. It is usual to talk of liabilities when there is a legal duty to another. The events which have now to be contemplated do not necessarily result in one of the parties to the contract being made liable to the other or to a third party. Sometimes an event results in a direct responsibility for an expense which falls upon a party in the first instance; it does so because it occurs in the course of the operations, is a normal operating or commercial expense, and there is no recourse against anyone else.[42]

The distribution of responsibilities found in drilling contracts can be

---

[41] See above, pp. 251–258.
[42] As, for example, in the case of a blowout, where the cost of control expenses, unless the terms of the drilling contract provide otherwise, fall upon the operator; see below, p. 394.

approached by a consideration of the matters usually mentioned in these contracts. They can be classified as follows:

(a) physical objects, such as the drilling unit itself, and equipment belonging to the contractor or the operator, or their sub-contractors;

(b) liabilities, whether created by laws or by contract or resulting from a tort, including liability for removal of debris, for compensation to personnel for loss of effects, or for pollution.[43]

(c) expenses, such as the cost of control of a well if there has been a blowout.

At other stages in this book, when the relevant insurance policies are discussed, the above sequence is adopted. There are, therefore, Chapters devoted to insurance of the drilling unit,[44] and to insurance of certain liabilities [45] and expenses.[46]

The division of responsibilities may be set out in a drilling contract in varying ways, but a convenient one is as follows:

1. Drilling unit, equipment and materials (subject to 2, below).[47]
2. Contractor's equipment and materials when in-hole and operating below the rotary table, and its underwater drilling equipment, when operating below the spider deck.[48]
3. Loss of hole and cost of control.[49]
4. Claims by third parties, *i.e.* any persons other than the other party to the drilling contract.[50]

It is possible to present these matters in various forms, provided that all possible categories of loss are covered. One oil company contract, for example, divides its section on responsibilities into responsibilities towards (1) administrations; (2) third parties; (3) the personnel and equipment of the contracting parties. The formal structures of the contracts vary considerably but in practice the result is often the same. It is when liability for negligence is moved from one party to the other, or when one party does not indemnify the other in respect of certain matters, or when one party has to bear a particular franchise, that the substantive differences arise.

I. *Drilling Unit, Equipment and Materials* (subject to II below)

There will be included among the drilling unit, equipment and materials any property belonging to or under the control of both the contractor and the operator. The contractor's property comprises the drilling unit and its own equipment, of which the former constitutes the most expensive

---

[43] Liability for such an incident may be created in more than one way. For example, a liability for pollution may arise by virtue of a statute, a contract, or because pollution may constitute the tort of negligence.　　[44] Chaps. 3 and 4.
[45] Chap. 8.　　　　　　　[46] Chap. 9.　　　　　　[47] See below, pp. 259–263.
[48] See below, pp. 263–266.　　[49] See below, pp. 266–267.　　[50] See below, pp. 267–277.

property in the venture. The operator will have property of its own on the unit. This will include mud, casing and drill pipe and other equipment.[51]

It is usually stipulated that, except where there is express provision elsewhere to the contrary, the contractor and operator is each to bear the risk of loss of or damage to its own property (subject to what is said in II, below), howsoever such loss or damage may be caused. This would mean that the loss would remain where it fell, whether it was caused by a third party or by the other party to the contract, even if at the material time the property was under the control of a temporary custodian, including the other party.

In the I.A.D.C. contract,[52] for example, Article 1001 states:

" LIABILITY FOR EQUIPMENT AND THE HOLE.

Except as specifically provided herein to the contrary, each party hereto shall at all times be responsible for and shall hold harmless and indemnify the other party from and against damage to or loss of its own items, regardless of the cause of loss including the negligence of such party and despite the fact that a party's items may be under the control of the other party, except that. . . ." [There follow three exceptions to this general rule, which are set out below.]

The general rule is expressed in terms by which each party shall " be responsible for and shall hold harmless and indemnify the other " so far as " its own items " are concerned. For example, the drilling unit itself may be lost. In the first place the contractor is to " be responsible for " this loss of one " of its own items." The loss therefore lies where it falls and there is no recourse. The loss may, however, have resulted from an act of negligence on the part of the operator. If so it must still fall on the contractor, because he is to " hold harmless and indemnify " the operator from such a loss, despite the negligence of the operator.

There is a similar provision in one of the drilling contracts used by a major oil company:

" (a) Company [the operator] shall in no circumstances ever be liable for damage to, loss or destruction of Contractor's drilling unit or other property of Contractor and Contractor will hold Company harmless in respect of any expense, loss or claim related to or resulting from such damage, loss or destruction. (b) Contractor shall not be liable for damage to or destruction of Company's equipment, property or materials involved in the operations and Company will likewise hold Contractor harmless for any such loss."

Both the I.A.D.C. contract and the oil company contract contain certain exceptions to the general rule that each party is responsible for its own property. The exceptions to the general rule as set out in Article 1001 of the I.A.D.C. contract concern (a) loss caused by corrosive or other destructive elements; (b) damage to or loss of contractor's drill

---

[51] See list of equipment, etc., provided by operator, at p. 256, above.
[52] Approved by the International Association of Drilling Contractors (I.A.D.C.).

string and certain " subsea " items; and (c) loss of or damage to the hole. The first two are expressed as follows:

". . . except that:

(a) Operator shall, to the extent Contractor's insurance does not compensate Contractor therefor, be responsible at all times for damage to or destruction of Contractor's equipment caused by exposure to unusually corrosive or otherwise destructive elements, including those which are introduced into the drilling fluid from subsurface formations or the use of corrosive additives in the fluid.

(b) Operator shall, to the extent Contractor's insurance does not compensate Contractor therefor, be responsible for damage to or loss of Contractor's drill string, as well as Contractor's subsea equipment and subsea mooring gear,[53] and shall reimburse Contractor for such damage or loss at the CIF replacement cost of the item so lost or damaged."

In the case of a jack-up unit the I.A.D.C. contract revises Article 1001 (b) to read:

" Operator shall, to the extent Contractor's insurance does not compensate Contractor therefor, be responsible for all Contractor's in-hole equipment, including the drill string while in the hole."

There is an exception in similar terms in the major oil company contract mentioned above. It provides for the operator to reimburse the contractor in respect of damage to or loss of the contractor's in-hole equipment (while operating below the rotary table) and underwater drilling equipment (while operating below the spider deck). This liability is qualified in the event that the contractor's negligence caused the damage or loss.[54]

" (c) In the event the hole should be lost or damaged, Operator shall be solely responsible for such damage or loss to the hole,[55] including the casing therein, regardless of whether such loss or damage was caused by the negligence of Contractor, or its employees, agents or subcontractors."

In the case of a jack-up rig the I.A.D.C. contract revises Art. 1001 (c) to read:

" Operator's responsibility for loss of or damage to Contractor's drill string is limited to Contractor's CIF replacement cost less depreciation of 25 per cent. per year. Depreciation will be deemed to have commenced on Commencement Date or on date of first use hereunder, whichever is later."

Again there is an exception in similar terms in the major oil company contract mentioned above. It provides that the contractor shall not be responsible for damage to or loss of the hole or casing therein or for any cost of regaining control of a wild well, and that the operator shall hold the contractor harmless for such loss or expense, except where the contractor's negligence caused the loss or damage.[56]

The passages cited above show that the question of negligence can be dealt with in differing ways. The I.A.D.C. contract begins by stating that

---

[53] See also below, p. 263.   [54] See also below, p. 264.
[55] For responsibility as to loss of hole see below, p. 266.
[56] *Ibid.*

each party is to be responsible for damage to or loss of its own items, " regardless of the cause of loss including the negligence of such party . . ."; the exceptions to that rule place responsibility upon the operator whether or not the contractor is negligent. Only exception (c) says expressly " regardless of whether such loss or damage was caused by the negligence of Contractor," but it seems that in all three cases the operator would have to accept responsibility. In the case of the major oil company contract the main provision as to responsibility does not refer to negligence, but the exceptions to the rule state that they are inapplicable if the contractor's negligence caused the damage or loss.

It is usual to provide that the contractor shall inspect the equipment and materials to be used by the operator. Thus the I.A.D.C. contract states, at Article 1002:

> " INSPECTION OF MATERIALS FURNISHED BY OPERATOR.
>
> Contractor agrees to visually inspect all materials furnished by Operator before using same and to notify Operator of any apparent defects therein. Contractor shall not be liable for any loss or damage resulting from the use of materials furnished by Operator."

So also a contract used by a major oil company states:

> " COMPANY'S MATERIALS. Contractor shall visually inspect all equipment and materials furnished by Company [the operator] before using same and shall notify Company forthwith of any apparent defect therein in order to permit replacement or repair of the defective item at once; Contractor shall exercise the correct care, maintenance and manipulation of Company-furnished equipment and will carry out maintenance and repair of this equipment on board the drilling unit, provided, however, that Company shall, at its costs, provide all spare parts and materials required to maintain or repair Company's items. Upon termination of contract Contractor shall return to Company any Company items which are at that time in Contractor's possession."

The general intent of these two clauses is the same, in that the contractor is to inspect the equipment and materials, or, as one clause puts it, the materials,[57] and to notify the operator of any apparent defects therein. The wide I.A.D.C. provision that the contractor shall not be liable for any loss or damage resulting from the use of materials furnished by the operator is not echoed in the corresponding clause, as quoted above, in the major oil company's contract. The latter contract relies instead upon a division of liabilities, in this and other clauses, which does not link liability with the provision of equipment and materials.

Though it is provided that responsibility for loss of or damage to its own property shall fall upon the contractor or upon the operator, the parties may make a similar agreement with respect not only to property owned by them but also to property of their respective employees and invitees or

---

[57] It would seem that the word is used in such a way that all of what is sometimes known as the " equipment and materials " is included.

their sub-contractors, or their employees. Such a result may be achieved by an indemnity clause, as in the following in favour of the operator [58]:

> " CONTRACTOR'S PERSONNEL.
>
> " Contractor agrees to protect, defend, indemnify and save Operator harmless from and against all claims, demands, and causes of action of every kind and character, without limit and without regard to the cause or causes thereof or the negligence of any party, arising in connection herewith in favour of Contractor's employees, Contractor's subcontractors or their employees, or Contractor's invitees, on account of bodily injury, death or damage to their property."

and the following, in the same terms, in favour of the contractor [59]:

> " Operator agrees to protect, defend, indemnify and save Contractor harmless from and against all claims, demands and causes of action of every kind and character, without limit and without regard to the cause or causes thereof or the negligence of any party, arising in connection herewith in favor of Operator's employees, Operator's contractors or their employees (other than those identified in Clause 1003 above) or Operator's invitees, on account of bodily injury, death or damage to their property."

So far as these clauses deal with claims for death and injury they are discussed below.[60] Their relevance here is that they relate to the employees, sub-contractors or their employees, and invitees of the party who gives the indemnity; and that they relate to damage (though there is no reference to loss) of their property, as well as to bodily injury and death. As a result the general responsibility of each party for its own items, with its corresponding duty to hold harmless and indemnify the other party, is extended to the property of the other named persons. Some words of warning are necessary; the language used may not be sufficiently wide or specific to meet the requirements which the courts, especially in the United States, apply when considering whether a party should be indemnified in respect of its own negligence.

II. *Contractor's Equipment and Materials, when in-hole and operating below the Rotary Table,[61] and its Underwater Drilling Equipment, when operating below the Spider Deck* [62]

Loss of or damage to the contractor's equipment and materials, when in-hole and operating below the rotary table, and its underwater drilling equipment, when operating below the spider deck, constitutes an exception

---

[58] Art. 1003 of the I.A.D.C. contract.

[59] Art. 1004 of the I.A.D.C. contract.

[60] See pp. 268–269.

[61] The piece of machinery fitted into the derrick floor as a means of rotating the drill string, and at the same time allowing the kelly to be lowered or raised through it so that pipe can be added or removed. (*An A–Z of Offshore Oil and Gas* (Whitehead, 1976).) For another definition see n. 23, above.

[62] The substructure beneath the main deck of a semi-submersible drilling unit; the equivalent of the cellar deck of a jack-up unit.

to the general rule that each party is to bear the risk of loss of or damage to its own property. The existence of this exception has been noted earlier.[63] As set out in Article 1001 of the International Daywork Drilling Contract —Offshore, exception (b) is so expressed that the operator is to " be responsible for damage to or loss of Contractor's drill string, as well as Contractor's subsea equipment and subsea mooring gear." The major oil company contract mentioned earlier refers to damage to or loss of " Contractor's in-hole equipment, while operating with such equipment below the rotary table," and to " Contractor's drilling equipment . . . while operating with such equipment below the spider deck."

The operator is usually to bear the risk of loss of or damage to these items when in the situations described except in those cases where the contractor has to bear: (a) a deductible amount in any event; or (b) the cost of such loss or damage as was occasioned by his own negligence. Negligence may be stated to include, without being limited to, the failure of the contractor to replace worn-out material in time at his own cost. Such a casualty is more closely related to the drilling operations, and less able to be averted by the contractor, than other cases of loss or damage to its equipment. In the first place the general rule as to responsibility does not apply, and the contract usually states that loss of or damage to the contractor's sub-surface equipment while it is in-hole and operating below the rotary table will be borne by the operator. The amount of reimbursement by the operator may be limited to a written-down value based on, say, a three-year life for underwater equipment. It could, alternatively, be expressed as a percentage of its replacement value per calendar month. Such a clause gives to the parties a method of calculation which would not be so easily available to them if the contractor were merely to be entitled to the reasonable cost of replacement or repairs. Section 69 of the Marine Insurance Act 1906, for example, deals with the measure of indemnity where a ship is damaged, but not totally lost, subject to any express provision in the policy:

> " (1) Where the ship has been repaired, the assured is entitled to the reason-
> able cost of the repairs, less the customary deductions, but not exceeding
> the sum insured in respect of any one casualty."

The " customary deductions " applied to wooden ships, where there was a deduction of one-third, " new for old," from the cost of repairs. They do not apply to other ships, particularly where the Institute Time Clauses (Hulls) apply, as clause 10 states: " Average payable without deduction, new for old, whether the average be particular or general." The provision in the drilling contract as to the written down value therefore has an effect, as between the parties to the contract, similar to that of the old one-third new for old clause, which applied as between the assured and the insurers.

---

[63] See above, p. 260.

The major oil company contract which was mentioned earlier deals with this problem in the following terms:

" CONTRACTOR'S IN-HOLE AND UNDERWATER DRILLING EQUIPMENT

(a) Damage to or loss of Contractor's in-hole equipment, while operating with such equipment below the rotary table, excluding, however, damages or losses due to Contractor's negligence, will be reimbursed by Company at the written-down value based on a three-year life period [64] for such in-hole equipment.

In each instance, however, Company's liability shall only cover the excess over U.S.$5,000 of the amount of loss or damage.

(b) Damage to or loss of Contractor's underwater drilling equipment is covered by Contractor's Marine Hull insurance, which insurance provides for a deductible of U.S. $. . . .

Such damage or loss, while operating with such equipment below the spider deck, excluding, however, damages or losses due to Contractor's negligence, [65] will be reimbursed by Company at the written-down value based on a three-year life period, [64] but in no case in excess of the above deductible.

In each instance, however, Company's liability shall only cover the excess over U.S. $5,000 of the amount of loss or damage.

(c) In this respect Contractor's negligence referred to under (a) and (b) above will include but not be limited to Contractor not having replaced worn-out material in time at its own cost.

(Normal wear and tear on the above-mentioned equipment will not be classified as damage.) "

Loss of or damage to the equipment of the contractor while it is " subsea," or in the hole and operating below the rotary table thus constitutes an exception to the general rule as to responsibility for loss or damage, which is that the owner of the equipment bears that risk.[66] Such loss or damage also constitutes an exception to the general rule [67] that negligence is not relevant. Where it has arisen as a result of negligence by the contractor, the general rule as to responsibility applies, and the contractor has to accept responsibility. This could, alternatively, be viewed as an exception within an exception. If so, the proposition can be stated as follows: responsibility for loss of or damage to equipment shall fall upon the owner of that equipment, irrespective of negligence, *except that* where the loss or damage is to the contractor's equipment and materials while subsea or in-hole and operating below the rotary table, such responsibility shall fall upon the operator *except* where the loss or damage resulted from the negligence of the contractor. This last exception constitutes a bargaining point and the result will vary as between one contract and another.

Special wear suffered by contractor's in-hole and other equipment. It is often provided that in the event of wear of an excessive nature to the contractor's equipment while it is in the hole, and caused by corrosive

---

[64] Or some other period, such as five years.
[65] See above, p. 264.
[66] See above, p. 260.
[67] See above, p. 260.

elements, the operator will be under a particular liability to compensate the contractor. This obligation may be distinguished from the operator's general liability for loss or damage. A provision to this effect may state:

> " Operator will suitably compensate Contractor for a rate of wear appreciably in excess of the normal rate, if established by Contractor to Operator's satisfaction, caused by Hydrogen Sulphide to Contractor's in-hole equipment or choke [68] manifold," or alternatively [69]:

> " Operator shall, to the extent Contractor's insurance does not compensate Contractor therefor,[70] be responsible at all times for damage to or destruction of Contractor's equipment caused by exposure to unusually corrosive or otherwise destructive elements, including those which are introduced into the drilling fluid from subsurface formations or the use of corrosive additives in the fluid."

III. *Loss of Hole and Cost of Control*

The contract may provide that the contractor should not be responsible for loss of or damage to the hole or casing,[71] or for any cost of regaining control of the well [72] except to a limited extent where the loss or damage was occasioned by the negligence of the contractor.[73] As one authority [74] has put it:

> " The Operator usually retains liability for loss of the hole, with the provision in some cases that, if the hole is lost as a result of the negligence of the contractor, the contractor will redrill to the point of loss at a reduced rate, such as the force majeure rate."

The " *force majeure* rate " is usually the rate payable during any period in which operations are not being carried on because of *force majeure*, other than adverse sea or weather conditions.

The major oil company contract which was mentioned earlier provides:

> " THE HOLE OR WELL AND THE RESERVOIR
> Contractor shall not be responsible for damage to or loss of the hole or casing therein or for any cost of regaining control of a wild well [75]; Company will hold contractor harmless for any such loss or expense, except where the particular loss or damage is caused by or results from Contractor's negligence in which event Contractor shall be responsible

---

[68] The " choke " is a " Removable nipple inserted, for example, in the flow line of a well to control oil or gas flow": *Bank of Scotland Glossary.*

[69] Exception (a) in Art. 1001 of the I.A.D.C. contract, see above, p. 261.

[70] As to the relevance of the contractor's insurance, see below, p. 277.

[71] " The thick-walled steel pipe placed inside the borehole as a lining to secure the hole and prevent the walls from collapsing " (*An A–Z of Offshore Oil and Gas* (Whitehead, 1976).

[72] For cost of control insurance, see below, Chap. 9.

[73] The contractor may also suffer loss in the event of his negligence by being paid at a lower rate during the period of repair and replacement; see p. 290, below, as to the reduced day rate.

[74] Mr. Russel F. Sammis, Senior Vice-President of Marsh & McLennan Inc., of Houston, Texas, in Denver, Colorado, in November, 1975.

[75] A well which is out of control because of a blowout; cost of control is discussed below, at Chap. 9.

therefor; in any event the extent of Contractor's liability as to the hole and to regaining control of a wild well shall be limited to the repair or replacement of the hole so damaged or lost; during such repairs/replacements Contractor will be paid in accordance with Clause . . .[76] Contractor shall never be liable for damage to any underground reservoir."

It is more common, on the other hand, for the parties to agree that the operator shall assume responsibility for damage to the hole, including the casing therein, whether or not there has been negligence on the part of the contractor. Thus the I.A.D.C. contract states at Article 1001 (c):

" In the event the hole should be lost or damaged, Operator shall be solely responsible for such damage or loss to the hole, including the casing therein, regardless of whether such loss or damage was caused by the negligence of Contractor, or its employees, agents or subcontractors."

The same contract deals in similar terms with responsibility for the cost of control at Article 1006:

" LIABILITY FOR THE WELL
Operator shall be liable for the cost of regaining control of any wild well, as well as the cost of removal of debris,[77] and shall indemnify Contractor for any such cost regardless of the cause thereof, including,[78] but not limited to, the negligence of Contractor, its agents, employees or subcontractors."

IV. Claims by Third Parties, i.e. Any Persons other than the Other Party to the Drilling Contract

It is possible, for the purpose of the apportionment of liabilities under the drilling contract, to divide these claims into three categories, two of which are expressed in terms of the persons who make the claims, and a third which is expressed in terms of the type of claim being made. These categories are:

A. Claims for injury or death by or on behalf of the personnel of the operator and the contractor;
B. Claims by third parties other than the claims set out in A above, and other than in respect of pollution;
C. Claims in respect of pollution.

So far as United States law is concerned, it is understood that indemnity provisions by which one party is called upon to hold harmless a second party or indemnify him for the second party's own negligence have been the subject of substantial litigation in recent years. Those provisions are like to be unenforceable under that law unless they specifically require indemnity whether or not a casualty is " caused or contributed to, in whole or in part, by the sole or concurrent negligence of the indemnitee."

---

[76] A clause providing for a " reduced day rate " in the event of negligence by the contractor.
[77] For the insurance of such costs, see below, p. 388.
[78] As to the meaning of " includes " see p. 59, above.

Many other countries are not so strict in their interpretations of indemnity provisions.

A. *Claims for injury or death by or on behalf of the personnel of the operator and the contractor*

The word " personnel " is used in this context so as to include not only the employees of each party but also the employees of that party's sub-contractors. The drilling contract may provide that neither party shall be liable for injury to or death of the other party's personnel, howsoever caused; or it may contain provisions that achieve the same result, stating that each will hold the other harmless from and indemnified against any claim in respect of such injury or death.

An example of such a provision, with an equal balance between the parties, appears in the I.A.D.C. contract at Articles 1003 and 1004, so far quoted only with respect to their reference to damage to property.[79]

> " 1003. CONTRACTOR'S PERSONNEL
> Contractor agrees to protect, defend, indemnify and save Operator harmless from and against all claims, demands, and causes of action of every kind and character, without limit and without regard to the cause or causes thereof or the negligence of any party, arising in connection herewith in favor of Contractor's employees, Contractor's subcontractors or their employees, or Contractor's invitees, on account of bodily injury, death or damage to their property."

> " 1004. OPERATOR'S PERSONNEL
> Operator agrees to protect, defend, indemnify and save Contractor harmless from and against all claims, demands and causes of action of every kind and character, without limit and without regard to the cause or causes thereof or the negligence of any party, arising in connection herewith in favor of Operator's employees, Operator's contractors, or their employees (other than those identified in Clause 1003 above [80]) or Operator's invitees, on account of bodily injury, death or damage to their property."

Many contracts deal only with the status of the people involved and avoid references to negligence which may occasion conflicts of evidence. It is possible for the balance to be tipped in favour of the operator. Thus the contract might include a provision by which he is indemnified and held harmless in respect of injury to or death of the contractor's personnel, howsoever caused. It might also, however, indemnify the operator in respect of any liability which he might have for injury to or death of his own personnel, so far as such injury or death arises out of or relates to the contractor's operations under the contract, and whether or not the contractor is negligent.

One major oil company's contract contains a clause in which the

---

[79] See above, p. 263.

[80] These words of exception prevent the clause from indemnifying the owner of the drilling unit himself, *i.e.* the contractor; it is only intended that it should apply to those who have contracted with the operator other than by way of the drilling contract itself.

balance is shifted in this way. The contract deals first with the contractor's personnel:

> " PERSONNEL OF CONTRACTOR
> Company [*i.e.* the operator] shall not be liable for injury to or death of Contractor's personnel however caused, and Contractor will hold Company harmless from and indemnified against any claim in respect of such injury or death."

This provision exempts the operator from the liabilities set out and obliges the contractor to hold harmless and to indemnify the operator. It is similar in effect to the above-mentioned Article 1003 of the I.A.D.C. Contract. The contract then goes on to deal with the operator's personnel:

> " THIRD PARTIES, PERSONNEL OF COMPANY
> Contractor shall indemnify and hold Company harmless from and against any and all claims, demands or judgements, including costs and attorney's fees, which may be filed or rendered against Company during the term of this contract or thereafter on account of loss, damage or personal injury or death suffered by any person, including Company's personnel arising out of or relating to the Contractor's operations under this contract, whether or not such loss or damage arises out of or results from faults or negligent performance on the part of Contractor and/or its agents or personnel. This Clause . . . is without prejudice to Clause . . . above." [81]

This provision, taken with the provision immediately preceding it, ensures that the contractor is liable to indemnify and to hold the operator harmless, not only where its personnel are concerned, but also where the operator's personnel are involved, provided that the claim is one " arising out of or relating to " the contractor's operations, and whether or not there was negligence by or on behalf of the contractor.

B. *Claims by third parties other than the claims set out in* A *above,*[82] *and other than in respect of pollution*

In this context the expression " third parties " is used to mean all parties whatsoever other than the parties to the drilling contract and the personnel of those parties or of their sub-contractors. For the present purpose, therefore, the expression includes public authorities. The latter expression is used here so as to include: (a) governments, whether national (or federal) or local (or state) and (b) bodies constituted by such governments or pursuant to their laws, which are in a position of authority in relationship to the public or to special classes of the public. These authorities will usually have certain powers, enabling them to enforce laws, bye-laws and other regulations.

As a general rule where the contractor or the operator incurs a liability to a third party it has no right of recourse against the other party to the contract. This result is often achieved by the fact that the contract is

---

[81] *i.e.* the clause headed " Personnel of Contractor."

[82] That is, other than in respect of claims for injury or death by or on behalf of the personnel of the parties.

silent on the point, so that the loss falls on one party and remains there. The contract, may, however, deal with the matter expressly, as in the case of one oil company contract:

> " Generally speaking, each party shall bear fully all direct or indirect financial charges for civil liability, resulting from the application of common law, or from any physical accident or damage to property caused to a third party when performing operations under this contract."

The liability is usually for damages as a result of a claim under the relevant civil law for physical or financial damage suffered by the third party; there may also be liability for fines or other penalties of a criminal or quasi-criminal nature. If the contractor or the operator or their personnel is found to be in breach of official regulations as to navigation, fishing, maintenance of equipment, and pollution arising other than from the drilling, for example, it or they will probably have to bear the consequent civil or criminal liability, or other penalty.

Five categories of exceptions to this general rule can be said to exist:
1. Action not that of party made liable
2. Liability for underground damage
3. Removal of debris
4. Claims covered by insurance
5. Other specified claims.

1. *Action not that of party made liable.* It is possible that the action in respect of which the third party claimed, successfully, against one party, was one which had been carried out by the other party. The relevant law may have given the third party the right to claim against one of the parties. In such an event one party may be given a right of recourse, under the contract, against the other party. A contract may thus provide that one party will indemnify and hold the other party harmless from and against any and all claims so far as they arise out of the first party's operations, whether or not the claim in question arises out of negligence.

This concept is closely linked to the proposition that, as a general rule, each party should accept its liability to third parties without recourse to the other party. This result may be achieved, as we have seen,[83] by the contract remaining silent on this point or by an express provision in the contract to that effect. The contract may also state, as does one oil company contract, after saying that each party shall take responsibility for third party claims resulting from its own operations: " As a result the party liable for such damage will hold safe and harmless the other against all claims by a third party."

It is possible that an error or omission on the part of the contractor may arise in respect of a task which it is his duty to perform, but which he has been ordered by the operator to carry out in a certain way. Such a situation

---

[83] See bottom of p. 269.

is similar to that which may arise in a charterparty where, for example, the relevant clause states: " charterers are to load, stow and trim the cargo at their expense under the supervision of the captain." In such a case, the task is allotted to one party but to be under the supervision of a representative of the other party. It has been held [84] that a shipowner, in the absence of proof that the Master had actively intervened in the method of stowage, could recover from the charterer in respect of damage to the cargo by bad stowage for which the shipowner had been made liable to the receiver.

So also in the case of a drilling contract a particular task may be allotted to the contractor, but a question may arise as to whether some consequent liability to a third party arose merely from the performance or nonperformance of that task, or from some intervention by the operator. The situation is similar, though there is a reversal of roles, to that in the case of the above charterparty, in that the active intervention may come from the operator, who is in some ways equivalent to a charterer. It would seem that the contractor can, in the absence of other clauses to the contrary hold the operator liable for the consequences.

2. *Liability for underground damage.* The operator may agree to indemnify the contractor for claims against the latter which result from operations on account of loss of or damage to underground property.[85] The I.A.D.C. contract provides [86]:

" LIABILITY FOR UNDERGROUND DAMAGE
 Operator agrees to defend and indemnify Contractor for any and all claims including, but not limited to, claims arising as a result of the negligence of Contractor, its agents, employees or subcontractors against Contractor resulting from operations under this Contract on account of injury to, destruction of, or loss or impairment of any property right in or to oil, gas, or other mineral substance or water, if at the time of the act or omission causing such injury, destruction, loss or impairment, said substance had not been reduced to physical possession above the seabed, and for any loss or damage to any formation, strata, or reservoir beneath the seabed."

Another contract has expressed the same concept, but without any concession in respect of the negligence of the contractor:

" Operator shall indemnify, save and hold harmless Contractor from and against any risk or loss or liability arising out of claims asserted or imposed against Contractor for loss of underground formation, zone, or reservoir unless caused by Contractor's negligence or wilful act or omission."

3. *Removal of debris.* The contractor may be made liable for the removal of debris. In such a case the contract usually provides that the operator should indemnify the contractor. Thus the I.A.D.C. contract states [87]:

---

[84] In *Canadian Transport Co.* v. *Court Line* [1940] A.C. 934 (P.C.).
[85] For comment as to the reason for this see below, p. 273.
[86] Art. 1007.   [87] Art. 1006.

" LIABILITY FOR THE WELL
Operator shall be liable for the cost of regaining control of any wild well, as well as the cost of removal of debris, and shall indemnify the Contractor for any such cost regardless of the cause thereof, including, but not limited to, the negligence of Contractor, its agents, employees or subcontractors."

An oil company contract puts it as follows:

" Contractor shall never be liable for . . . removal of debris if required by the Governments concerned or by Company itself and Company will hold harmless Contractor in this regard."

It would seem more prudent, from the point of view of the contractor, for the exclusion of contractor's negligence to be expressly stated. The word " never " might be strong enough to exculpate the contractor in some jurisdictions, but this is unlikely to be so in the United States. The contractor may be made liable by a third party for removal of the wreck or debris other than on the site. It may therefore be prudent, in case he has no right of indemnity against the operator, to take out separate cover for this liability. The terms of such a policy are discussed in Part 2 of Chapter 7, below.

4. *Claims covered by insurance.* An operator often seeks to take advantage of insurances concluded by the contractor. In one oil company contract the respective liabilities of the parties are first set out; and there then appears the following clause:

" Notwithstanding anything said in the conditions of the contract, Company shall never be liable for any loss, damage, cost, expense, injury or death referred to therein which is covered by any of Contractor's insurances; Contractor shall keep Company indemnified and held harmless against liability for the same to the extent that any loss, damage, cost or injury is covered by such insurance."

5. *Other specified claims.* There have been set out so far [88] four categories of exception to the general rule that claims by third parties have to be borne by the contracting party who is made liable in the first instance. The list does not purport to be exhaustive, for other exceptions to this rule may appear in drilling contracts. One contract, for example, states:

" Operator shall indemnify, save and hold harmless Contractor from and against . . . any claim, suit, action or expense in connection with an alleged infringement of patent held by any third party resulting from the use of equipment furnished by Operator and/or resulting from use of any combination of equipment furnished in part by Contractor . . . provided, that, Operator shall have the benefit of all patents owned or controlled by Contractor or its employees. . . ."

C *Claims in respect of pollution*
Responsibility for pollution is the subject of careful apportionment between the parties to the drilling contract but as a matter of principle

---

[88] At pp. 270–272.

the operator is generally liable for pollution from the well. As one authority [89] has put it:

" In practically all cases, the Operator has total responsibility for all pollution liability and clean-up and containment expenses following blow-out or cratering. Operational pollution, such as fuel or garbage spills, is normally that of the drilling contractor if it results from his negligence."

Another authority [90] has considered the reason for this attribution of liability:

" There are, of course, many areas in which insurance is either not available or is prohibitively expensive, such as damage to underground reservoirs, [91] pollution, and the like. In these areas there are two theories, each of which seems to lead toward the same conclusion. One theory is along the line discussed above that in most cases one or other of the parties will be more in control of the situation by way of site selection, selection of rig, selection of personnel, or whatever the risk might be; and it is this over-all controlling party who should bear the ultimate risk; the other somewhat concurrent theory is that in those instances of potential vast exposure (damage to underground reservoir, control of a wild well, blow out damage, and the like) the risk should follow the reward."

Responsibility for pollution may be divided between the contractor and the operator in such terms as the following, set out in Article 1005 of the I.A.D.C. contract:

" POLLUTION AND CONTAMINATION

Notwithstanding anything to the contrary contained herein, it is understood and agreed by and between the Contractor and Operator that the responsibility for pollution or contamination shall be as follows:

(a) The Contractor shall assume all responsibility for cleaning up and containing pollution or contamination which originates above the surface of the water from spills of fuels, lubricants, motor oils, normal water base drilling fluid [92] and attendant cuttings, pipe dope, [93] paints, solvents, ballast, bilge and garbage wholly in Contractor's possession and control and directly associated with Contractor's equipment and facilities.

(b) Operator shall assume all responsibility for (including control and removal of the pollutant involved) and shall protect, defend and save the Contractor harmless from and against all claims, demands, and causes of action of every kind and character arising from all pollution or contamination, other than that described in subclause (a) above, which may occur from the negligence of Contractor or otherwise during the term of this Contract or as a result of operations hereunder, including but not limited to, that which may result from fire, blowout, cratering, seepage or any other uncontrolled flow of oil, gas, water or other substance, as well as the

---

[89] Mr. Russel F. Sammis, Senior Vice-President of Marsh McLennan Inc., Houston, Texas, speaking in Denver, Colorado, in November, 1975.

[90] Mr. Taylor Hancock of Global Marine Inc., in his lecture on " The Marine International Drilling Contract."

[91] See above, p. 271.

[92] Drilling Fluid: "The stream of gases, liquids, liquids and solids suspended in liquid, with additives, which circulates through the drill string and the annulus [the space between the drill pipe and the bare wall] at high pressure . . ." (*An A–Z of Offshore Oil & Gas* (Whitehead, 1976)).

[93] The thick grease used to treat the threads of the drill pipe.

use or disposition of oil emulsion, oil base or chemically treated drilling fluids, contaminated cuttings or cavings, lost circulation and fish recovery materials and fluids.

(c) In the event a third party commits an act or omission which results in pollution or contamination for which either the Contractor or Operator, for whom such party is performing work, is held to be legally liable, the responsibility therefor shall be considered, as between the Contractor and Operator, to be the same as if the party for whom the work was performed had performed the same and all of the obligations respecting defense, indemnity, holding harmless and limitation of responsibility and liability, as set forth in (a) and (b) above, shall be specifically applied."

By way of summary the responsibility for pollution and contamination is divided, as a result of these three subclauses, as follows:

(a) the contractor is responsible for cleaning up and containment where pollution and contamination originates above the water surface from a number of items (but not the oil being extracted) wholly in his possession and control;

(b) In this, the most important subsection, the operator is stated to be responsible for and bound to hold the contractor harmless in respect of claims for pollution and contamination (other than in (a)) arising from the contractor's negligence or otherwise, including, but not limited to, pollution and contamination resulting from fire, blowout, cratering, seepage, etc.;

(c) if the act or omission of a third party working for the contractor or the operator results in pollution or contamination for which either party is held to be legally liable, then the responsibility of each shall be the same as if the one for whom the work was being done had done that work, and the distribution of responsibilities, etc., set out in (a) and (b) applies.

As a contrast we consider a corresponding clause in the drilling contract, quoted earlier, used by a major oil company:

" POLLUTION/OBSTACLES

Contractor shall take all reasonable steps to prevent pollution of surrounding sea waters including adjacent beaches and to keep the sea bottom free of obstacles which could cause damage to third parties or hamper the installation of production facilities. Unless such pollution/obstacle is attributable to Contractor's negligence Contractor shall not be liable for said pollution/obstacles. Contractor shall, however, never be liable for pollution resulting from a blowout or uncontrolled flow from the well and Company will hold Contractor harmless from any claims resulting from such pollution. However, in the event of negligence on the part of Contractor resulting in a blowout or uncontrolled flow from the well Contractor will be liable for third party claims up to the amount of U.S.\$100,000. However, Contractor shall always remove at its own costs the drilling unit, or part thereof, in the event that the drilling unit is lost, or damaged beyond repair, from Company's concession area, if so required by law or governmental authority, or if interfering with Company's operations."

The responsibility for pollution and obstacles is here divided as follows:

(a) the contractor is to take reasonable steps to prevent pollution and to keep the sea bottom free of obstacles [94];

(b) the contractor is only liable for any pollution or obstacles resulting from his negligence;

(c) in this, the most important subsection, the contractor is said not to be liable for pollution resulting from a blowout or uncontrolled flow from the well and the operator will hold him harmless for such pollution, except that if it resulted from his negligence he is liable for third party claims up to U.S. $100,000;

(d) the contractor must remove his drilling unit (or part of it) if it is lost or damaged beyond repair from the operator's concession area, if he is required to do so by law or if the unit is interfering with the operator's operations.

The I.A.D.C. contract and the last-mentioned contract have approached the distribution of responsibility for pollution by different routes, but they have some provisions in common. In both cases the operator accepts responsibility for pollution resulting from a blowout, even if the pollution resulted from the contractor's negligence, except that in the case of the oil company contract the contractor's negligence results in his being liable for the first U.S. $100,000 of any third party claim. Some contracts require the contractor, where pollution results from his negligence, to pay up to the available limits of his insurance, the operator then paying the balance.

Relief from responsibilities in certain events

It is customary to insert various clauses in the contract by which each party is excused from compliance with some or all of its terms in certain specified events. The clauses which are discussed here, and which are set out in the I.A.D.C. contract, are entitled:

1. *Force Majeure* (Art. 1404). This is set out in full below, and discussed, in connection with the same contract's provision as to a Force Majeure Rate.

2. *Expropriation, Confiscation, Nationalization and War Risks* (*Art.* 1409).

" 1409. EXPROPRIATION, CONFISCATION, NATIONALIZATION AND WAR RISKS
(a) In the event the Drilling Unit or any or all of Contractor's equipment, spare parts and/or supplies directly associated therewith (i) cannot lawfully be exported from the country in which it was operating following termination of drilling operations under this Contract because Contractor cannot obtain an export license or permit or because of other governmental restrictions; or (ii) are lost to Contractor through confiscation, expropriation, nationalization or governmental seizure; or (iii) are seized or damaged or destroyed as a result of insurrection, terrorist acts, riot or war (declared or undeclared) or other similar occurrences during the term of this Contract,

---

[94] This part concerns removal of debris and not pollution but obstacles are dealt with in this part of the contract.

Operator will within sixty (60) days following the occurrence of any such event pay to Contractor the value (as set out in Appendix C) of all such property so restricted, confiscated, expropriated, nationalized, seized, damaged or destroyed, from which value shall be subtracted the total of the following:

(1) any amount paid Contractor by such governmental unit or body;
(2) any amount paid Contractor from insurance;
(3) depreciation in accordance with the schedule attached hereto as Appendix C, but not to exceed 30 per cent. of said value. Depreciation shall be computed commencing with the date upon which each component of Contractor's equipment is placed into service under this Contract.

Following the payment by Operator for Contractor's property under the conditions set forth (which shall be made in the currency in which the original purchase thereof was made) and payment of all other moneys then due Contractor, Operator shall have no obligation thereafter to make payments to Contractor and at the time of such payments, Operator shall have the option to require Contractor to immediately assign all of its right, title and interest in the Drilling Unit to Operator.

(b) Should a change of political or other condition occur which would enable Contractor again to assume possession of the Drilling Unit and/or its equipment, spare parts and supplies directly associated therewith, Contractor agrees to repay to Operator such amounts as Operator may have paid to Contractor under this Clause 1409, less such amounts, if any, as may be required to restore the Drilling Unit, equipment, spare parts and supplies directly associated therewith to the same condition they were in at the time of suspension of drilling operations, and also less such amount (to be agreed upon by Operator and Contractor) as shall equitably compensate Contractor for deterioration, and/or depreciation thereof during the period of nonuse resulting from the causes set forth in this Clause 1409. In the event of such resumption of possession of the Drilling Unit by Contractor, if Operator has previously received title to said Drilling Unit, Operator shall reassign all of its right, title and interest in said Drilling Unit to Contractor as of the time of such resumption of possession.

(c) All costs and other charges provided for in this Clause 1409 are subject to adjustment after audit.

(d) If requested by Operator in writing, Contractor agrees to obtain to the extent then and thereafter available, insurance covering all or such portion of the risks specified in this Clause 1409 as Operator may direct.

Operator shall be named as an additional assured in any such policy or policies of insurance, which shall provide for the payment of losses thereunder in United States dollars. The provisions of such insurance and the cost thereof shall be subject to Operator's approval prior to the issuance thereof."

In the case of any of the events specified under subsection (a), *i.e.* (i) inability to export owing to a licence or permit being unobtainable or because of other governmental restrictions; (ii) loss through confiscation, expropriation, nationalisation or governmental seizure; (iii) seizure or damage as a result of various causes including insurrection, terrorist acts, riot or war, the operator has to pay to the contractor the value [95] of the

---

[95] As set out in Appendix C to the contract, entitled " Depreciation Schedule Contractor's Equipment." It shows each item, its value as of commencement date

property in question. That value is subject to the three types of deduction set out, which include any amount paid to the contractor from his insurance. Where there is " a change of political or other condition " which enables the contractor to assume possession of the property, the contractor has, as a result of subsection (b), to repay to the operator the amounts paid by the operator, less certain amounts. Mr. Russel F. Sammis [96] has summarised the position: " The most important exceptions to the contractor being responsible for the drilling equipment are the exceptions dealing with war and political risks. It is customary for the Operator to be totally responsible for the risks of war and such political risks as confiscation, nationalisation or expropriation. Insurance is generally available for the perils of war, confiscation, nationalisation and expropriation, but there are termination provisions of these policies which must be thoroughly understood."

4. Division of Responsibilities for Insurance

As a general rule the contractor and the operator take out various insurances, in respect of the drilling unit itself, equipment and liabilities, so far as the contractor is concerned, and in respect of liabilities and equipment, so far as the operator is concerned.[97] The drilling contract obliges the contractor to conclude certain insurances. It does not usually require the operator to undertake insurances, though it often refers to such insurances,[98] and to such matters as the operator's insurers' rights of recourse, and the entitlement of the contractor to the benefit of the insurances.

In the I.A.D.C. contract, for example, Article 1101 states:

" CONTRACTOR'S INSURANCE
Contractor shall carry and maintain the insurance shown in Appendix B.[99] Contractor may from time to time with the approval of Operator change the insurance it carries. Contractor will increase its insurance beyond the limits provided for herein or will change its insurance if required by Operator, but any additional cost will be paid by Operator."

These contractual insurance requirements are expressed in a wide variety of ways. The needs of a small operator are usually set out in considerable detail, with references to particular standard forms of policies. Larger operators, using their own forms of contract, refer in more general terms to the kind of cover required.

In the major oil company contract which has been mentioned earlier

---

(arrival of drilling unit at the designated or other mutually agreeable place), and the depreciation rate.

[96] Senior Vice-President of Marsh & McLennan Inc.

[97] As to the addition of the operator's name as an assured when the drilling unit is insured see p. 86, above.

[98] See below, pp. 278–284.

[99] Appendix A is the " Equipment, Materials, Services and Personnel List "; see above, pp. 247 and 253.

the provision as to the contractor's insurance, corresponding to Article 1101 of the I.A.D.C. contract, reads:

" INSURANCE SCHEME

Contractor shall adopt and maintain insurances as indicated in Appendix B [1-2] (which Appendix shall be deemed to be part hereof and which hereinafter shall be referred to as Appendix B). Contractor may from time to time make changes in its insurances but not without the express approval of the Company.

If the Company requires the Contractor to increase its insurance beyond the coverage provided for in this contract, any additional cost will be at the expense of the Company."

The effect of this clause is the same as that of Article 1101; each has three provisions, so that (a) the contractor is to maintain the insurances set out in a later appendix; (b) the contractor can alter the insurances with the approval of the operator; and (c) if the operator requires an increase or a change in the insurance, it must pay for any extra cost thereby incurred.

Appendix B, to which Article 1101 of the I.A.D.C. contract refers, is entitled " Insurance Requirements " and contains the following headings:

A. Insurance for Personnel
B. Comprehensive General Liability
C. Automobile Liability
D. Marine Hull Insurance
E. Other [*i.e.* other insurance requirements, *e.g.* adequate insurance on contractor's shore-based property, etc.].

The Appendix B to which the oil company contract refers is also entitled " Insurance Requirements," which expression is followed by the words " Limits—not less than those stipulated." It contains the following headings, which are similar to those in the I.A.D.C. contract:

A. Insurance for Personnel
B. Comprehensive General Liability
C. Automobile Liability
D. Marine Hull Insurance
E. War Risk Insurance
F. Adequate insurance on Contractor's shore-based property [etc.].

I. *Insurance for Personnel*

The stipulations under this heading, in Appendix B to each of the contracts, the I.A.D.C. contract and the above-mentioned oil company contract, are exactly the same. The contractor must carry and maintain the following insurance in respect of insurance for personnel:

[1-2] Appendix A is entitled " Equipment, Supplies, Personnel and Services to be furnished by Contractor. . . ."

" Any insurance covering personnel in accordance with the governing law of the jurisdiction where the work is performed or in accordance with applicable laws of other countries, covering those persons employed by Contractor or its subcontractors for work to be performed hereunder whose employment may be subject to such laws, during the period such persons are so engaged."

This obligation to insure relates only to the persons employed by the contractor or its subcontractors. The nature of the contractor's liabilities in respect of those persons, as between the contractor and the operator, was set out earlier in the two contracts. In the case of the I.A.D.C. contract the liabilities were described in Article 1003,[3] and in the case of the oil company contract they were described in the clause called " Personnel of Contractor." [4] The insurance provision set out above does not, however, speak of the liabilities of the contractor towards its personnel. Instead it refers to " insurance covering personnel " and to such insurance as is " in accordance with " either (a) the governing law of the jurisdiction where the work is performed, or (b) the applicable laws of " other countries, covering persons employed . . . whose employment may be subject to such laws. . . ." It seems that the contractor must take into consideration (a) the law which governs the jurisdiction where the work is performed and (b) the " applicable " laws which cover the employees specified, the question of whether their employment is subject to such laws being perhaps the same question as whether those laws are applicable. Any insurance which the contractor then concludes must be " in accordance with " those various laws. Clearly this must mean that it should not in any way contravene those laws; it is less clear whether the contractor can discharge his obligation by taking out only the insurances which those laws make compulsory, or whether the contractor must take out all such insurances as would afford cover in respect of any liability to employees arising under those laws, though perhaps the latter is intended.

A duty of this nature is probably more clearly established when expressed in greater detail, so as to leave little or no doubt as to what insurances should be undertaken by the contractor. It is not practicable to do this unless information is available as to the relevant jurisdiction. In one United States contract the contractor is obliged to conclude certain minimum insurance coverages in respect of personnel; those coverages, summarised briefly, are stated to be for workmen's compensation insurance for statutory requirements and employer's liability insurance with limits of not less than $5,000,000 for injuries to or death of any one person and not less than $5,000,000 for injuries to or death of more than one person resulting from any one accident covering location of all work places involved. The insurance coverage is to include (1) protection for liability under the Federal Longshoremen's and Harbor

---

[3] See above, pp. 263 and 268.
[4] See above, p. 269.

Workers' Compensation Act, as amended, including protection with respect to the extension of the Act under the Outer Continental Shelf Lands Act; (2) coverage for liability under the Jones Act, Death on the High Seas Act, and the general maritime law for all employees or all employees except crew members if the vessels are covered in full for crew liabilities under the protecting and indemnity policies; (3) coverage amended so that a claim *in rem* is treated as a claim against the employer; (4) protection against liability of the employer to provide transportation, wages and maintenance for any maritime employees.

There has been a tendency to express these contractual requirements in broad terms. There might be a general reference to employer's liability and Workmen's Compensation Insurances, to the extent required by the country or state in which the contractor qualifies as an employer and where the operations are to be performed; to this there may be added appropriate endorsements in respect of such matters as the Longshoremen's and Harbor Workers' Compensation Act, including the Outer Continental Shelf Lands Act, and general third party liability and property damage insurance.

II. *Comprehensive General Liability*

The stipulation under this heading in Appendix B [5] to the I.A.D.C. contract reads:

> " Comprehensive General Liability insurance with the watercraft exclusion deleted covering all operations of Contractor, including, among other risks, the contractual liability herein assumed by Contractor, with a combined single limit of $10,000,000 for bodily injury and property damage liability in any one occurrence. (Protection and Indemnity Insurance may, at Contractor's option, be substituted for this coverage of marine liabilities.) "

The corresponding stipulation under the same heading in Appendix B to the oil company contract is in similar terms and reads:

> " Comprehensive General Liability insurance covering all operations of Contractor including, among other risks, the contractual liability herein assumed by Contractor, [6] with a combined single limit of not less than $5,000,000 for bodily injury and property damage liability in any one occurrence.
> It will be evident from this policy that Company's employees will be considered as ' third party persons.' "

The clauses both provided that there shall be a comprehensive liability insurance " covering all operations " of the contractor, including the contractual liability assumed by the contractor. This contractual liability, so far as it arises between contractor and operator, is set out earlier in the drilling contract. [7] A combined single limit of liability for bodily

---

[5] " Insurance Requirements."

[6] One contract contains the words " including Contractor's Contingent Liability with respect to subcontractors."

[7] For example, Art. 1101 of the I.A.D.C. contract.

injury and property damage liability is then given. The material differences between the two clauses are that the clause in Appendix B of the I.A.D.C. contract states that: (a) the watercraft exclusion is to be deleted from the Comprehensive General liability insurance; and (b) "Protection and Indemnity Insurance" may, at the contractor's option, be substituted for this coverage of marine liabilities. There is no reference to P. & I. insurance under the Comprehensive General Liability heading to Appendix B to the oil company contract; but the Marine Hull Insurance heading in Appendix B to the latter contract obliges the contractor to have P. & I. insurance on the drilling unit and its equipment.

III. *Automobile Liability*

The stipulations under this heading, in Appendix B to each of the contracts, the I.A.D.C. contract and the above-mentioned oil company contract, are almost exactly the same. They begin with the same words:

> "Automobile Liability Insurance in accordance with any local legislation on all owned, non-owned and hired vehicles used in connection with the work hereunder . . ." and continue:
> [I.A.D.C.] ". . . with limit of U.S. $250,000 for any one occurrence"
> [oil company] "Minimum insured limit U.S. $250,000 for any one occurrence."

IV. *Marine Hull Insurance* [8-12]

The stipulation under this heading in Appendix B of the I.A.D.C. contract reads:

> "Marine Hull Insurance on the Drilling Unit and its equipment during all operations under this Contract including moves within the Operating Area."

The corresponding stipulation under the same heading in Appendix B of the above-mentioned oil company contract reads:

> "Marine Hull Insurance including P. & I. risks on the drilling unit and its equipment to its extent of value during all operations under this contract including moves within the area of operations."

The section dealing with the distribution of liabilities in the same contract [13] states that damage to or loss of the contractor's underwater drilling equipment is covered by the "Contractor's Marine Hull insurance, which insurance provides for a deductible of U.S. $. . . ."

Another contract requires:

> "Hull insurance to the full value of the drilling unit, insured on the London Standard all risks drilling form [14] then in use while being used in connection with work to be performed under this Agreement and subject to a deductible

---

[8-12] The covers given by the London Standard Drilling Barge Form and by the Norwegian Conditions for Hull Insurance of Drilling Vessels are discussed in Chaps. 3 and 4, above.

[13] See above, p. 265.

[14] See p. 86.

of $25,000. Subject to the deductible, such policy covers the loss of or damage to Contractor's equipment in the hole and anchors and anchor lines if such loss or damage is caused by any of the perils insured against. But specifically excludes the BOP [blowout preventer], riser [15] and related equipment."

V. *Protecting and Indemnity Insurance* [16]

The I.A.D.C. contract does not require the contractor to maintain protecting and indemnity insurance on the drilling unit and its equipment. Under the Comprehensive General Liability heading, however,[17] Appendix B to the I.A.D.C. contract allows the contractor to substitute P. & I. insurance for a comprehensive general liability insurance. As we have also seen above, one of the major oil company contracts requires the contractor to have " Marine Hull Insurance including P. & I. Risks." Other contracts specify P. & I. insurance as a requirement separate from the hull insurance. One United States contract speaks of " Protecting and Indemnity Insurance including Collision Liability with Sistership Clause unamended on the standard ocean form or comparable form."

VI. *Insurance on Contractor's Shore-based Property*

There are stipulations, in Appendix B to each of the contracts, the I.A.D.C. contract and the above-mentioned oil company contract, which are exactly the same:

> " Adequate insurance on Contractor's shore-based property, including housing, offices, stores, materials and equipment, including coverage during transportation of materials and equipment to and from the Drilling Unit."

This requirement, which occurs in most drilling contracts, may be considered in conjunction with earlier provisions as to the distribution of responsibilities between the parties.[18-19] Those provisions, while placing some liabilities upon the operator, assume that the contractor has undertaken certain insurances. Thus in the I.A.D.C. contract the clause which deals with liability for equipment and the hole [20] states that the operator shall be responsible for damage to or destruction of the contractor's equipment caused by exposure to unusually corrosive or otherwise destructive elements, but only " to the extent Contractor's insurance does not compensate Contractor therefor." The same proviso appears later in the same clause, in relation to the operator's responsibility for damage to or loss of the contractor's drill string, subsea equipment and subsea mooring gear. The stipulation as to insurance which is quoted above, however, refers to " shore-based property"; although it extends to coverage

---

[15] " A flowline carrying oil or gas from the base of a production platform to the processing plant on the deck " (*An A–Z of Offshore Oil and Gas* (Whitehead, 1976)).

[16] The nature of P. & I. Club cover is set out above, at Chaps. 5 and 6.

[17] See above, p. 280.

[18-19] See above, p. 258.

[20] Art. 1001 and see above, p. 260.

" during transportation of materials and equipment to and from the Drilling Unit," the type of incident contemplated in the clause which deals with liability would not normally fall within its scope. For example, damage to the contractor's equipment by exposure to an unusually corrosive element introduced into the drilling fluid from a sub-surface formation would not be expected to occur during transportation of that equipment to the drilling unit. Damage to the contractor's subsea equipment (to take an example from the latter part of the above-mentioned I.A.D.C. clause), on the other hand, might occur during its transportation to the drilling unit. If any of these damages occurred, the liability of the operator to the contractor would appear to be reduced to the extent that the contractor's insurance does not compensate the contractor therefor. The insurance to be taken out by the contractor, however, is described, in the opening words of the relevant insurance requirement, as " insurance on Contractor's shore-based property, including . . . materials and equipment. . . ." If damage of the types mentioned above were to take place, the operator would only benefit from the contractor's insurance if the materials and equipment could be correctly described as " shore-based."

VII. Other Insurance Requirements

A. *War risks insurance*

The oil company contract mentioned above, and some other drilling contracts, require the contractor to take out " war risk insurance on the drilling unit and the equipment to the extent available on the open market."

In the case of the I.A.D.C. contract, Article 1409, entitled " Expropriation, Confiscation, Nationalisation and War Risks," states, at subsection (d):

> " If requested by Operator in writing, Contractor agrees to obtain to the extent then and hereafter available, insurance covering all or such portion of the risks specified in this Clause 1409 as Operator may direct.
>
> Operator shall be named as additional insured in any such policy or policies of insurance, which shall provide for the payment of losses thereunder in United States dollars. The provisions of such insurance and the cost thereof shall be subject to Operator's approval prior to the issuance thereof."

[Art. 1409 is set out in full in Appendix B to this book].

B. *Other vessels*

The I.A.D.C. contract [21] and the above-mentioned oil company contract both deal with the case of vessels used by the contractor:

> " Should Contractor at any time put in service in connection with these operations any vessels which are either owned by it, or chartered from third parties, Contractor will carry or require to be carried adequate hull and protection and indemnity insurance on such vessels and will name Operator as an additional insured."

---

[21] At Appendix B thereof, " Insurance Requirements."

This reference is clearly to " vessels " other than the drilling unit itself, which is covered by the requirement as to marine hull insurance.[22] If, as a result of some action by or on behalf of these additional vessels, a liability falls on the contractor or the operator, both will be covered by such liability provisions as fall within the hull insurance, and by the protecting and indemnity insurance.

C. *Cost of insurance*

The section dealing with insurance requirements may also state [23]:

> " Costs of all insurance as listed above are included in the rates unless specifically stated otherwise in this contract."

The " rates " to which this provision refers include the operating rate, the standby or reduced day rate, the rate during repair, the *force majeure* rate, any special rate, and any variant of these rates. These variations may be occasioned by changes in the contractor's costs as a result of alterations in such matters as its labour costs, a change in the location of the operations base, a new law, the cost of catering, and some other matters. In addition, it may be provided that the contractor's rates may be varied as a result of a change in insurance costs. Such a variation may occur " if the cost of insurance premiums varies by more than five per cent."; alternatively, the contract may state that the rates should be adjusted:

> " To the extent of any increase or decrease in the costs of hull insurance under this contract from a . . . % rate or for any additional insurance which Contractor may be required to carry as a consequence of drilling under this contract."

The contract may also provide that the operator shall pay for any extra insurances which it requires the contractor to undertake.

5. Payments, Legal and Formal Provisions, etc.

I. *Payments*

A drilling contract makes provision for payment by the operator to the contractor. The most important rate is the operating rate, as this gives rise to the largest payment which will be made, and reflects the market conditions prevalent at the time of the conclusion of the contract. There are other provisions for payment, however, some of which represent variations in the rate, while others constitute lump sum payments without reference to a daily rate. The drilling contracts employ various terms to describe the payments to be made. The provisions as to payments can be summarised as follows:

    A.   Mobilisation Fee [24]
    B.   Operating Rate [25]

---

[22] See above, p. 281.
[23] As in Appendix B of the I.A.D.C. contract.
[24] See below, p. 285.   [25] See below, p. 286.

C. Standby Rate [26]
D. Rate During Repair [27]
E. Force Majeure Rate [28]
F. Demobilisation Fee [29]
G. Additional Payments [30]
H. Variation of Rates [31]

A. *Mobilisation fee*

The mobilisation fee, or rate, is the sum paid by the operator to the contractor in consideration of the contractor moving the drilling unit with its equipment, supplies and personnel, to a place nominated by the operator. One definition [32] states:

> " Mobilization rate. The charge levied by a drilling contractor to muster a rig, equipment and crew, to a drilling location. Thereafter, the drilling contractor supports his crew and rig, and charges the operating company either daywork or footage rates."

The place to which the unit goes may be an operating base or a drilling location. The sum named has to cover the cost to the contractor of the physical transfer of the drilling unit, equipment, supplies and personnel; it usually has to cover also the cost of the establishment of an office if an operating base has been named, and other consequential items. Any cost of registering to do business at the operating base will also have to be borne by the contractor out of the operating fee, though in some cases the contract will provide that this and other similar items should be borne by the operator. The cost of fuel has also to be considered. A contract may provide that the contractor should bear this cost during mobilisation and demobilisation, and that the operator should bear it during the operating period after mobilisation and before demobilisation. Many contracts, however, provide that the operator shall provide fuel throughout the whole time from the beginning of mobilisation until after demobilisation.

The I.A.D.C. contract states, at Article 802:

> " MOBILIZATION FEE
> Operator shall pay Contractor a mobilization fee of $ . . . which shall be payable on the date the Drilling Unit departs for the Operating Area." [33]

The moment of payment is that at which the drilling unit departs for the operating area; the process of mobilisation will already have begun, and the unit may already have been taken by the contractor to the operating base.

---

[26] See below, p. 287.   [27] See below, p. 290.   [28] See below, p. 292.
[29] See below, p. 297.   [30] See below, p. 298.   [31] See below, p. 300.
[32] In *A–Z of Offshore Oil and Gas* (Whitehead, 1976).
[33] Defined in Art. 101 as follows: "'Operating Area' means those areas of the seabed and subsoil beneath the waters offshore . . . in which Operator may from time to time be entitled to conduct drilling operations."

The list of equipment, materials and services to be furnished by the operator, as set out in Part 3 of Appendix A to the same contract, includes:

> " All diesel fuel for the use on the Drilling Unit." and
> " Shore base with office space and warehouse for Contractor, including basic furnishings."

To the extent that these constitute part of the task of mobilisation the cost and responsibility thereof is moved from the contractor to the operator.

Two other examples of contractual provisions for a mobilisation fee, taken from other drilling contracts, are as follows:

> " A lump sum mobilization payment of . . . to be paid by Company to Contractor on the ' Commencement Date.' " [34] and:

> " Mobilization—$100,000 upon commencement of the operational term."

The first of these contracts states that the operator shall supply " All diesel fuel for use on the drilling unit only " but it does not oblige the operator to provide office space and a warehouse at the shore base for the contractor. The second contract obliges the operator to provide both " Fuel (diesel oil) for drilling unit " and " Land Base for Operator and Contractor, heliport, office and means for movement of equipment to dock site."

B. *Operating rate*

This is the basic rate payable from the time when the drilling unit reaches its first drilling location. It is sometimes known as the daywork rate, which has been defined [35] as " The daily rate charged by a drilling contractor for operating his rig and crew on behalf of an exploration or operating company." The rate applies unless a state of affairs arises which causes one of the rates set out below to apply. The I.A.D.C. contract states, at Article 804:

> " OPERATING RATE
> The Operating Rate will be $ . . . per 24-hour day and will first become payable from the moment when the Drilling Unit is properly positioned at the first drilling location and ready to commence operations. The Operating Rate shall continue to be payable except as herein otherwise provided."

In the case of a jack-up rig, however, Article 804 states:

> " The Operating Rate will be $ . . . per 24-hour day and will first become payable from the moment when the legs are pinned at the first drilling location and the Unit begins jacking operations. The Operating Rate shall continue to be payable except as herein otherwise provided."

In two other contracts the comparable clause reads:

---

[34] Defined in that contract as " the moment the drilling unit has arrived and is properly anchored at the first drilling location designated by Company."
[35] *An A–Z of Offshore Oil and Gas* (Whitehead, 1976).

" The Operating Rate will be . . . per 24 hour day and is payable from the Commencement Date [36] onwards, unless superseded by one of the other rates (including no rate whatsoever) contained in this contract, and will continue during the term of this contract." and:

" Operating Rate—$ . . . per day each day during the operational term, excepting only those days that other rates, as set forth herein, are applicable."

As the relevant word is " rate," it follows that there should be a *pro rata* apportionment in respect of any part of a day, at the beginning or end of the operational term, or, during the operational term, when a different rate (or no rate at all) becomes applicable. The apportionment in the case of the I.A.D.C. contract is to the nearest hour. This is provided in Article 901, concerning monthly invoices,[37] which contains the words " calculated to the nearest hour." One oil company contract states:

" CALCULATION OF PAYMENT

Payment of the rates shall be calculated on the basis of time to the nearest hour." Another contract says:

" All compensation stated at a rate per day is based upon a twenty-four hour day with full crews and shall be prorated to the nearest hour."

It does not seem that the use of the words " per 24-hour day," as opposed to " per day," make any difference to the calculations. Perhaps they serve to emphasise that the broken periods are dealt with separately, on a *pro rata* basis, and that the full operating rate then applies to each whole period of 24 hours starting at midnight. If the operating period began at noon on the first day, for example, the calculations would not be cast in such a way that a new day began every day thereafter at noon.

The moment from which the payment becomes due is variously expressed as " when the Drilling Unit is properly positioned at the first drilling location and ready to commence operations "; or " from the Commencement Date," *i.e.* from " the moment the Drilling Unit has arrived and is properly anchored at the first drilling location "; or " during the operational term," which is not defined in the contract in question, but which appears to begin when the drilling unit is at the first location; or " when the first anchor is positioned at the drilling location "; or " when drilling begins."

Perhaps the first of all these examples is the most precise, since it states that the unit must be properly positioned, which would include its being properly anchored, and ready to commence operations. All of them may become bargaining counters in the negotiations.

3. Standby rate

There are occasions on which the contractor is not working but is awaiting orders from the operator. As one authority [38] has put it:

---

[36] For definition, see n. 34, above.
[37] Set out in full in Appendix B to this book, at p. 438.
[38] Mr. Taylor Hancock of Global Marine Inc., in his lecture, " The Marine International Drilling Contract."

" Traditionally in all Drilling Contracts, the standby rate originated [in] and still applies to cover those periods of time when the Drilling Contractor is ' standing by,' waiting for the Operator to do something, such as giving further orders, deciding whether or not to proceed, waiting for cement to harden, or the like. The concept has been considerably expanded over the years, and particularly in Marine Drilling Contracts."

The I.A.D.C. contract states, at Article 805:

" STANDBY RATE

The Standby Rate will be $ . . . per 24-hour day and will be payable:

(a) during any period of delay when Contractor is unable to proceed because of adverse sea or weather conditions or as a direct result of an act or omission of Operator including, without limitation, the failure of any of Operator's Items,[39] or the failure of Operator to issue instructions, provide Operator Items or furnish services; or

(b) from the Commencement Date [40] until the moment when the Operating Rate first becomes payable; or

(c) during any period after Commencement Date that the Drilling Unit is under tow, or under way, provided that if, at the termination of this Contract, the Drilling Unit does not go to . . . or the nearest port as agreed, the period shall not exceed the reasonable estimated time required to go to that harbor."

These periods are examples of downtime, which has been defined [41] and then discussed, in the following terms:

" The period during which any piece of equipment is inactive or unfit for use, on account of repair or overhaul, or due to bad weather. Jack-up drilling units, once they are jacked up, experience little downtime due to bad weather, unlike semi-submersibles which often have to stop drilling when heavy seas are running. Downtime can be of great significance in areas such as the North Sea."

The authority cited above has commented on this Article 805, with reference to subsection (a) above:

" You will note in the I.A.D.C.[42] form that the rate applies during periods of delay when the Contractor is unable to proceed because of adverse sea or weather conditions: incidentally, there is an area of possible misunderstanding or disagreement here that should be covered under the Contract: there have been instances in which an Operator has felt that the lower standby rate should commence at the moment that normal operations for the drilling of the well cease and shutting down for adverse weather begins, with the lower rate continuing until the bit is back on bottom and all operations are again functioning. Naturally, I speak through the prejudiced mind of a Drilling Contractor's representative, but, from the Drilling Contractor's point of view, the rig and the people are, if anything, working harder during the shutting down operations and during the starting up operations than at any other time: it is therefore logical (through the

---

[39] Defined in Art. 101, at (b), as "the equipment, material and services which are listed in the Appendices that are to be provided by or at expense of Operator."
[40] For definition see n. 34, above.
[41] *An A–Z of Offshore Oil and Gas* (Whitehead, 1976).
[42] International Association of Drilling Contractors.

aforesaid prejudiced mind) that the Operating Rate should continue until the vessel is actually completely shut down and really ' standing by '; and the lower rate should apply only during the true ' standing by ' period of time. This is the type of item that should be in any event ' on the table ' at the time of Contract negotiations. If, for some reason, the Operator would insist that the lower Standby Rate should apply at all times that drilling operations are not actually going forward, there would of necessity be an adjustment in the rate structure as presented by the Drilling Contractor."

The fact that the contractor's drilling unit and employees are " if anything working harder during the shutting down operations and during the starting up operations " cannot alter whatever meaning correctly attaches to the words in subsection (a). The argument that the standby rate should not apply until the unit " is actually completely shut down and really ' standing by ' " is an attractive one and probably correct. The parties to the contract have agreed that the lower rate is to apply " during any period of delay when Contractor is unable to proceed." With what must he be unable to proceed? The answer must be: the operations which the operator has instructed him to perform. The two situations which must be contrasted are, first, that in which work has come to a stop and, secondly, that in which some delay is being experienced but work has not yet stopped. If work has come to a stop, through no fault of the contractor, then the standby rate applies. If there is drilling at a slower rate, whether because there is heavy weather or unavailability of items to be provided by the operator; or if some work required by the operator, such as closing down, is taking place, it seems that the contractor is able to proceed and is not subject to the standby rate.

If the contractor wishes to ensure that the rate should only apply when no work at all is being done, and that it should not apply during the shutting down and starting up operations, then it is necessary for such a provision to be inserted in the contract when it is being concluded.

Subsection (b) of Article 805 applies the standby rate " from the Commencement Date until the moment when the Operating Rate first becomes payable." The definition of " Commencement Date " in Article 101 (a) is " the point in time that the Drilling Unit arrives at the place in or near the Operating Area designated by Operator, or at a mutually agreeable place in or near the Operating Area, or on arrival at the first drilling location, whichever event occurs earliest." The " Operating Area " is, in its turn, defined in Article 101 (e): " ' Operating Area ' means those areas of the seabed and subsoil beneath the waters offshore . . . in which Operator may from time to time be entitled to conduct drilling operations." It is important for both parties that this area be clearly defined; where a country is named attention should be paid to the fact that it may have more than one coastline, so that it is helpful if a particular coastline is named. The operating rate becomes payable, according to Article 804,[42a]

[42a] Subject to the amendment as to jack-up rigs; see p. 286, above

" from the moment when the drilling unit is properly positioned at the first drilling location and ready to commence operations." If the " earliest " event under Article 101 (a) is the arrival at a designated or agreed place in or near the operating area, the standby rate applies from then until the unit is also properly positioned at the first drilling location and ready to operate. If the earliest event is arrival at the first drilling location, then it only applies until the unit is also properly positioned and ready to operate.

Other drilling contracts contain comparable provisions for standby rates. In one contract, the rate, called a reduced day rate,[43] is payable during " any period while operations are suspended due to adverse weather or sea conditions " and " when waiting for Company orders or for Company furnished items or services, unless during such waiting periods Contractor's drill string is being employed in the hole either for round tripping,[44] circulating or rotating operations." This provision is comparable to Article 805 (a) in the I.A.D.C. contract. The other contract in which this provision appears also states that its reduced day rate shall apply in situations similar to those foreseen in Article 805 (c), namely during:

> " all moving operations from one location to the other designated by Company, as from the moment when the first anchor is started to be pulled prior to a move and shall continue until the moment the last anchor is in position to moor the unit on the next location on completion of the move."

The parties to the contract may also agree that a standby or reduced day rate should apply in other situations as, for example, during electric logging operations,[45] production testing [46] and suspension of operations during public holidays.

D. *Rate during repair*

The drilling contract may state that a lower rate is to apply while operations are suspended for a certain period for the purpose of repairs and related matters, and an even lower rate after the end of that period.

---

[43] In that contract the rate payable when *force majeure* suspends operations is also called the reduced day rate; see below, p. 296.

[44] *An A–Z of Offshore Oil & Gas* (Whitehead, 1976) says, of " tripping ": " The action of drilling hole. Thus, to spud is also to start a trip. Round tripping involves tripping out, or pulling-out (removing the string from the hole), and running back (lowering the string to the bottom again)."

[45] The electric log: " Known also as an E-log, a method of determining porosity [the volume of interconnected free space in a rock available for retention of fluid], permeability [the rate at which fluid will flow through the pore spaces of a rock due to an external pressure] and fluid content of formation rocks. An electrode, or several electrodes, are lowered down the hole before casing is run, to collect and transmit information about the resistivity, conductivity and spontaneous potential of the strata "; *An A–Z of Offshore Oil & Gas, op. cit.*

[46] " Verification of the capabilities of a commercial well to produce hydrocarbons after the well has been completed, as opposed to formation testing before completion," *An A–Z of Offshore Oil & Gas, op. cit.*

This is an example of downtime.[47] There are many variations in the wording of these clauses, and much may depend upon the bargaining position of the parties. The I.A.D.C. contract states, at Article 806:

" RATE DURING REPAIR

The Repair Rate will be $ . . . per 24-hour day and will be payable for any period in excess of . . . days during which operations are suspended to permit necessary replacement, inspection, repair or maintenance of Contractor's Items [48]; provided, however, that should said suspension continue for a period of more than 75 days, Contractor's rate of pay shall after the seventy-fifth day be reduced to . . . percent of the Repair Rate. Contractor will use due diligence in effecting such repairs, replacements or inspection in a good workmanlike manner and will use its best efforts to familiarize itself with the location of rentable replacements for Contractor's Items."

There are thus three relevant periods:

1. An initial period during which the repair rate does not apply even though operations are suspended for one or more of the reasons mentioned;

2. A period of 75 days, including what may be called the deductible or franchise period in 1, during which the repair rate is payable for the period in excess of the deductible or franchise period;

3. The period after the expiry of the said 75 days, during which the payment rate is reduced to an agreed percentage of the repair rate.

The authority mentioned earlier [49] has said:

" Some of the variations that you will run across in actual Drilling Contracts will be a cumulative number of hours or days each month or during each 30-day period of the Contract during which the full operating rate will continue to apply prior to dropping down to the lower Repair Rate. Another variation is that there will be no drop in rate, or a very small drop in rate, for repairs to sub-sea equipment, as contrasted to repairs to surface equipment. Typically, repairs to sub-sea equipment will be handled under the Standby Rate."

Another example of a repair rate appears in a passage from a clause used by one oil company and headed " Payment of rates during repairs/inspection/maintenance." The clause opens with the words:

" In case of suspension of normal operations to be performed by Contractor due to inspection, necessary replacement, repairs or maintenance, etc. [the words used in Article 806 above] of the drilling unit and all other items for which Contractor is responsible, the rates as mentioned hereunder will apply."

There is then a division into two categories of delay:

" (a) For periods when normal operations cannot be carried out due to damage to, loss, failure, maintenance, and inspection of Contractor's equipment from or for any cause, the Reduced Rate [50] will be payable to

---

[47] See above, p. 288.

[48] Defined in Art. 101 (c) as " the equipment, material and services which are listed in the Appendices that are to be provided by or at expense of Contractor."

[49] Mr. Taylor Hancock of Global Marine Inc.; see above, p. 287, n. 38.

[50] The reduced day rate, equivalent to a standby rate, mentioned above, at p. 290.

Contractor, provided, however, that if operations cannot be resumed after twelve hours for any one occurrence, the Special Rate will be paid for the period in excess of twelve hours."

[The special rate mentioned in the closing words of (a) is mentioned in the section dealing with rates of payment: "The Special Rate will be . . . per 24 hour day and is payable during the periods as specifically described in this contract." The periods thus "specifically described" are this repair period and the period after the twenty-first day of suspension owing to *force majeure*.[51]]

and

" (b) If operations cannot be carried out after a cumulative period of seventy-two hours for one or several occurrences during a calendar month, Contractor will not be entitled to any compensation during any further suspension of normal operations occurring during the remainder of that calendar month."

This is an example of the situation contemplated in the clause in that contract which said that the operating rate should apply unless superseded by one of the other rates " including no rate whatsoever " included in the contract.

E. *Force majeure rate*

The *force majeure* rate is, generally speaking, the rate which applies when *force majeure* prevents operations from being carried on. One dictionary definition [52] of *force majeure* is " Irresistible compulsion, coercion diplomatically recognised as irresistible; war, strike, act of God, &c., excusing fulfilment of contract." There must be some external power which prevents and so excuses the performance of the contractual obligations. Not all external powers are sufficient to bring the exception into operation. Bad weather, for example, is often excluded, either because it is considered as a matter of general principle not to constitute *force majeure* or because the particular definition of *force majeure* in the contract under consideration excludes it. In the following section some consideration is given first to the general approach of the courts and then to the manner in which the parties to drilling contracts have sought to attach a precise definition to the term.

In *Yrazu* v. *Astral Shipping Co.*[53] a contract for the shipment of live-stock stated: " The vessel . . . not to call at any port or ports before landing her livestock except in case of *force majeure*." Walton, J. said: [54]

" The words in question appear to me to amount to an absolute under-taking by the shipowners that the vessel should not before landing her live-stock call at any port, whether in or out of the ordinary course of the voyage, except in case of *force majeure*. I think that this undertaking is

---

[51] See below, p. 296.
[52] *Concise Oxford Dictionary*.
[53] (1904) 20 T.L.R. 153.
[54] *Ibid*. at pp. 154–5.

made subject to one exception and one exception only, which is, the case of *force majeure*. What, then, is the meaning of *force majeure*? The vessel might be seized and carried into some port by her captors. This would be a plain, though unusual, case of *force majeure*. A more ordinary case would be where, in consequence of some casualty occurring in the course of the voyage, the master is compelled to put into a port for the safety of the ship or cargo, or of both . . . I think that if the steamer ran short of coals, not in consequence of any casualty, but simply because by some mistake she had not when she left Buenos Aires sufficient coals for the voyage to St. Vincent, there was no case of *force majeure*."

An act of God was given as an example in the dictionary definition set out above; one English judge has discussed the relationship between the two terms. Thus Bailhache, J. in *Matsoukis* v. *Priestman & Co.*[55] said:

" The words '*force majeure*' are not words which we generally find in an English contract. They are taken from the *Code Napoléon*. . . . I cannot accept the argument that the words are interchangeable with ' *vis major* ' or ' act of God'. I am not going to attempt to give any definition of the words '*force majeure*', but I am satisfied that I ought to give them a more extensive meaning than ' act of God ' or ' *vis major*'. The difficulty is to say how much more extensive . . . I think that the complete dislocation of business in the north of England as a consequence of the universal coal strike . . . did come within the reasonable meaning of the words '*force majeure*' . . . So far as the shipwrights' strike is concerned it comes within the very words of the exceptions clause. As to delay due to breakdown of machinery it comes within the words '*force majeure*', which certainly cover accidents to machinery. The term '*force majeure*' cannot, however, in any view, be extended to cover bad weather,[56] football matches, or a funeral. These are the usual incidents interrupting work. . . ."

It is often said that the incident must not be one which could have been prevented by the party seeking to rely on this exception. In the first of the two cases cited above the court mentioned a possible shortage of coals, " not in consequence of any casualty," but because of a mistake, in not taking on sufficient coals; that would not constitute *force majeure*. In the second case the court referred to " delay due to breakdown of machinery," and said that it came within the term *force majeure*, " which certainly covers accidents to machinery." A situation in which such a breakdown resulted from a mistake, in not carrying out necessary repairs, would seem to combine elements of both situations, so that there might be a difference of opinion as to whether there was a *force majeure*.

An example of an act of omission which did not constitute *force majeure* is to be found in the Privy Council decision in *The Concadoro*[57]:

". . . it was argued that the inability of the master to procure the necessary funds for his voyage brought the *Concadoro* under art. 2 [of the Hague Convention No. VI of 1907], and that she was unable to leave the enemy

---

[55] [1915] 1 K.B. 681, at pp. 685–7.
[56] See the reference at p. 294 below to Art. 807 of the I.A.D.C. contract.
[57] [1916] 2 A.C. 199 (P.C.), at p. 202.

port within the days of grace '*par suite de circonstances de force majeure*'. In their Lordships' opinion, this contention cannot be maintained. The '*force majeure*' contemplated in the article is one which renders the vessel unable to leave the port, and cannot be construed to include the circumstance that the master has not been provided by the owners with sufficient financial resources to continue his voyage."

These and other decisions make it clear that it is desirable to define *force majeure* when that concept is employed in a contract. One English judge dealt with a case [58] in which a local authority was bound to supply energy to premises, and in default was liable to a penalty unless the default was caused by inevitable accident or *force majeure*. He said:

" I regret the introduction of foreign words into English statutes and Orders without any definition of them being given. In my view *force majeure* in this case means some physical or material restraint, and does not include a reasonable fear or apprehension of such a restraint."

Whatever language is used, it is often helpful if it is defined. Virtually all contracts concluded by experienced companies contain a carefully worded definition of *force majeure*. The I.A.D.C. contract states, at Article 807:

" FORCE MAJEURE RATE
The Force Majeure Rate will be $ . . . per 24-hour day and will be payable during any period in which operations are not being carried on because of force majeure, other than adverse sea or weather conditions."

The exception in respect of adverse sea or weather conditions is necessary because in such conditions the standby rate [59] is applicable; as we have seen above, bad weather does not, in any event, usually form part of *force majeure*.

The same contract contains a clause, Article 1404, setting out the circumstances in which each party to the contract is excused from complying with the terms of the contract:

" FORCE MAJEURE
Except as otherwise provided in this Clause 1404, each party to this Contract shall be excused from complying with the terms of this Contract, except for the payment of moneys then due, if and for so long as such compliance is hindered or prevented by riots, strikes, wars (declared or undeclared), insurrections, rebellions, terrorist acts, civil disturbances, dispositions or orders of governmental authority, whether such authority be actual or assumed, acts of God (other than adverse sea or weather conditions), inability to obtain equipment, supplies or fuel, or by act or cause which is reasonably beyond the control of such party, such causes being herein sometimes called ' Force Majeure '. If any failure to comply is occasioned by a governmental law, rule, regulation, disposition or order as aforesaid and the affected party is operating in accordance with good oilfield practice in the area of operations and is making reasonable effort to comply with such law, rule, regulation, disposition or order, the matter

---

[58] *Hackney Borough Council* v. *Dore* [1922] 1 K.B. 431; the comments were made by Sankey J. at p. 437.
[59] See p. 287, above.

shall be deemed beyond the control of the affected party. In the event that either party hereto is rendered unable, wholly or in part, by any of these causes to carry out its obligation under this Contract, it is agreed that such party shall give notice and details of Force Majeure in writing to the other party as promptly as possible after its occurrence. In such cases, the obligations of the party giving the notice shall be suspended during the continuance of any inability so caused except that Operator shall be obligated to pay to Contractor the Force Majeure Rate provided for in Article 807 (Force Majeure Rate)."

The principles set out in the above four sentences in Article 1404, defining *force majeure*, can be paraphrased as follows:

1. Each party is excused from complying with the terms of the contract, except for the payment of moneys then due, if and for so long as compliance is hindered or prevented by the various matters listed, or by an "act or cause which is reasonably beyond the control of such party" (as to which see 2, below). In the case of acts of God an exception is made in the case of adverse sea or weather conditions, because these are dealt with separately by Article 805 (a) which provides that in those cases the standby rate should apply.

2. If there is a failure to comply which is occasioned by a governmental law or other similar provisions, and the affected party is both operating in accordance with good oilfield practice and is making a reasonable effort to comply with that law or other similar provisions, the matter shall be deemed to be beyond the control of that party. In such a case the failure to comply excuses the party from compliance in accordance with 1, above.

[There could be a failure to comply of the type contemplated, but the party would not be excused from compliance unless it satisfied the two conditions set out, *i.e.* that it had been operating in accordance with good oilfield practice and was making a reasonable effort to comply with the law or other similar provisions. This could result in its being unable to rely on the *force majeure* clause if, for example, it had not been operating in accordance with good oilfield practice, even if that failure so to operate had not occasioned its non-compliance with the terms of the contract.]

3. If either party is rendered wholly or partially unable by any of the causes set out in 1 or 2, above, to carry out its contractual obligation it shall give written notice and details of the *force majeure* to the other party as promptly as possible.

4. In such cases the obligations of the party giving the notice are suspended during the continuance of the inability except that the operator must pay the *force majeure* rate provided for in Article 807.

The Article in which *force majeure* is defined is effective (1) to define the circumstances in which each party to the contract is excused from complying with its terms, except for the payment of moneys then due, for so long as compliance is hindered or prevented by the circumstances set out; (2) to cause the *force majeure* rate to come into operation during the period when the obligations of the party giving the notice are suspended. The list set out in Article 1404 ends with the words " or by act or cause which is reasonably beyond the control of such party, such causes [*i.e.* all the situations set out in the Article] being herein sometimes called ' *Force Majeure*.' " The situations listed cannot be said to fall into a particular genus, so that the closing words open the definition, for the purpose of the contract, to any act or cause reasonably [60] beyond control.

In another contract, used by an oil company, there is provision for *force majeure* in the following terms:

" PAYMENT OF RATES DURING FORCE MAJEURE CIRCUMSTANCES

In the event of suspension of normal operations due to circumstances as referred to in Clause [the *Force Majeure* Clause below] hereof, the Reduced Day Rate will be payable by Company, less any savings realised by Contractor by releasing part or all of its crew as mutually to be agreed between Contractor and Company and other savings realised under such circumstances (including operation for a third party), but with the understanding that as from the twenty-first day, the payment by Company calculated as hereinbefore mentioned will not exceed the Special Rate." and:

" FORCE MAJEURE

Neither party to this contract shall be responsible for any failure to fulfil any of its obligations hereunder if fulfilment has been delayed, hindered or prevented by any circumstance of whatsoever nature which is not within the control of the party concerned and is not preventable by reasonable diligence on its part or by compliance by that party with any order or request from any national, port or local authority or any body or persons purporting to be or to act for such authority; provided that Contractor shall have the benefit of this provision only if Contractor maintains as far as possible its relevant insurance cover and takes all reasonable precautions to protect the well against damages or destruction as may result from blowout, bad weather, collision with marine vessels, etc. In this case either party shall have the right to terminate this contract by notice given in writing so as to take effect at any time after the thirtieth day since the first day of the failure to fulfil the contractual obligations unless explicitly stipulated otherwise in this contract."

In both the I.A.D.C. contract and this last mentioned oil company contract the crucial provision is that a different rate is to apply in the event of operations not being carried on because of *force majeure*. In the latter contract, however, there is not a separate *force majeure* rate; instead the operator is to pay the " Reduced Day Rate," less certain savings, and in any event after 21 days a rate not exceeding the " Special Rate." The reduced day rate, in that contract,[61] is the rate equivalent to, and applicable in the same circumstances as, what is often known as the standby rate.

Mr. Taylor Hancock [62] has discussed the variations which may occur in the *force majeure* provisions:

" I would say that most Drilling Contracts contain a somewhat broader definition of the operational features of the application of the Force Majeure

---

[60] It is doubtful whether the addition of the word "reasonably" adds anything to the meaning of the phrase.   [61] See above, p. 290.

[62] Vice-President of Global Marine Inc.

Rate than the I.A.D.C. form. One of these variations is: in order to take care of a prolonged force majeure period, the Force Majeure Rate will be a rate without any factor for labor costs in it, but with a provision that the Operator will pay the direct cost of supplying whatever minimum amount of labor is necessary to maintain the drilling rig during the force majeure period; and the Operator will pay for returning employees and their families to their point of origin, and bringing them back when the force majeure cause is over, so that operations may recommence. Another variation is to provide that the Operator must give a specific period of notice, such as three days, to the Contractor before placing the Contractor on the lower Force Majeure Rate; still another variation is to allow the operator to place the Contractor on the Force Majeure Rate literally at any time whether or not there be a force majeure, provided that the drilling unit is back in a safe harbor or anchorage during such time."

It may be asked whether *force majeure*, as defined in these two contracts, differs from frustration. Comparing the two concepts, one writer has said: " Suffice it to say that few of the instances of *force majeure* relied on in most *force majeure* clauses would discharge the seller from performance under the frustration doctrine." [62a] A contract is discharged by frustration if an event occurs to make its performance " illegal, impossible or commercially sterile." [62b] Alternatively one may speak of frustration of the common venture instead of commercial sterility. The clauses quoted above come into operation where " compliance is hindered or prevented " (the I.A.D.C. contract) or where " fulfilment has been delayed, hindered or prevented " in the situations listed or envisaged. This would seem to cover illegality or impossibility but there may be some doubt as to whether commercial sterility, or frustration of the common venture, would be held to amount to *force majeure* under the clauses in question. If it was so held then there would be no problem. If not, the appropriate tribunal would have to decide whether the general law as to frustration would permit one or the other party to treat itself as discharged from liability to perform. It should be noted that the I.A.D.C. contract says that in the event of *force majeure* a party is " excused from complying with the terms . . . if and for so long as such compliance is hindered or prevented . . ." The oil company contract, on the other hand, expresses the result in broader terms, saying: " Neither party shall be responsible for any failure to fulfil any of its obligations if fulfilment has been delayed, hindered or prevented. . . . In this case either party shall have the right to terminate this contract. . . ."

F. Demobilisation fee

The I.A.D.C. contract provides for a demobilisation fee in the following terms, in Article 803:

[62a] Bernard J. Cartoon, B.A., LL.B., LL.M., Attorney of the Supreme Court of South Africa, on " Drafting an Acceptable Force Majeure Clause " (The *Journal of Business Law*, July 1978, at p. 231).
[62b] G. H. Treitel, *The Law of Contract* (4th ed., 1975) p. 583.

" DEMOBILIZATION FEE

Operator shall pay Contractor a demobilization fee of $ . . . which may be invoiced on the date of termination of this Contract except that no demobilization fee shall be due if this Contract is terminated pursuant to Clause 202 (a) (Duration)." [63]

The demobilisation fee is comparable to the mobilisation fee,[64] a charge made by the contractor for the work involved in concluding the operation and taking the steps necessary to disperse the equipment and crew. Where this contract applies, however, the standby rate will also be payable, under Article 805 (c),[65] during the period that the unit is under tow, or under way.

G. *Additional payments*

The I.A.D.C. contract provides, at Article 808:

" ADDITIONAL PAYMENTS

Operator shall, in addition, pay to Contractor:

(a) the cost of any overtime paid by Contractor to Contractor's personnel in respect of the maintenance or repair on board the Drilling Unit of Operator's Items or other overtime required by Operator; and

(b) Contractor's costs associated with waiting on Operator-furnished transportation or for time in excess of . . . hours in transit to or from the Drilling Unit."

These payments are in addition to those which are set out in the section dealing with " Rates of Payment," and which are the mobilisation fee,[66] the operating rate,[67] the standby rate,[68] the rate during repair,[69] the *force majeure* rate [70] and the demobilisation fee.[71] The form in which this provision is expressed does not mean that the operator will not be liable for other payments under the contract. Article 801 states, with respect to the above-mentioned items: " No other payment shall be due from Operator unless specifically provided for in this Contract, or agreed to in writing by Operator." There is provision in this contract, and there usually is provision in other contracts, for other payments by the operator to the contractor. These include, apart from those set out in connection with " Variation of Rates " below,[72] the costs of or pertaining to:

1. Moving contractor's items, personnel and their personal effects between Operations Bases (Art. 401).

2. Reimbursement for damage to the drilling unit by obstructions at or within the anchoring area at the drill site, to the extent that such damage is not covered by the contractor's insurance (Art. 607).

3. Reimbursement of amounts paid by the contractor of taxes levied

---

[63] cl. 202 (a) provides that the contract shall terminate immediately if the drilling unit becomes an actual or constructive total loss.

[64] See above, p. 287.   [65] See above, p. 288.   [66] See above, p. 285.
[67] See above, p. 286.   [68] See above, p. 287.   [69] See above, p. 290.
[70] See above, p. 292.   [71] See above, p. 297.   [72] At p. 300, below.

by the government of the area where the drilling unit operates, where the taxes pertain to performance by the contractor under the contract (Art. 608).

4. Liabilities incurred by the operator towards the contractor in accordance with the general provisions as to liabilities (Arts. 1001 to 1008).[73]

5. Increases or changes in the contractor's insurances (Art. 1101).

6. Attorney's fees and costs, as the operator agrees that if the contract is placed in the hands of an attorney for collection of any sums due thereunder, or suit is brought on the same, or if sums due thereunder are collected through bankruptcy or arbitration proceedings, those fees and costs shall be added to the amount due (Art. 1403).

7. Liabilities incurred by the operator towards the contractor in accordance with the general provisions as to expropriation, confiscation, nationalisation and war risks (Art. 1409).[74]

The above items may form the subject of payments by the operator to the contractor, and are set out in the I.A.D.C. contract; the list may, however, be continued by the addition of other items, which may or may not have been paid for by the contractor in the first instance.

8. Customs and excise duties, port charges, pilot fees, docking fees (partly covered by Art. 606). Article 606 states: " CUSTOM OR EXCISE DUTIES. Operator shall pay all import or export charges or customs or excise duties including, without limitation, local sales taxes, added value taxes, clearing agents' fees, or other similar taxes or fees that are levied on Contractor's and/or Operator's items."

Mr. Taylor Hancock [75] has said:

"... it is the practice of the industry for customs duties and excise taxes to be for the account of Operator. Prudent Operators typically negotiate a protective clause into their concession, permit, production-sharing contract, or whatever, under which the Operator and parties that are under Contract with the Operator are permitted to import drilling equipment and supplies into the country of operations free of customs duties, excise taxes, added value taxes, and the like."

9. Materials and equipment bought, transported, or stored on shore at operator's request, at invoice cost to contractor plus an agreed percentage.

10. Third party services obtained by the contractor at the operator's request, at invoice cost to contractor plus an agreed percentage.

11. Import duties, local rates and registration fees imposed by governments and governmental bodies.

12. Licences, permits, and authorities required to be obtained by the contractor to perform the operator's drilling programme.

This list is not intended to include items in respect of which the responsibility for payment falls in any event upon the operator without the

---

[73] See above, pp. 260 *et seq.*
[74] As to war risks insurance, see p. 283, above. [75] See n. 49.

contractor having paid for such items and requiring to be reimbursed by the operator. These include the costs of providing spare parts and materials required to maintain or repair operator's items (Art. 403 of the I.A.D.C. contract); of providing operator's items and personnel (Art. 601); and of maintaining the repairing operator's items on the drilling unit which the contractor is not qualified to or cannot maintain or repair (Art. 602).

H. *Variation of rates*

The I.A.D.C. contract provides, in Article 809, for certain variations in the rates set out elsewhere in that contract:

" VARIATION OF RATES

The rates and/or payments herein set forth shall be revised by the actual amount of the change in Contractor's cost if an event as described below occurs or if the cost of any of the items hereinafter listed shall vary by more than the amount indicated below from Contractor's cost thereof on . . . or by the same amount after the date of any revision pursuant to this clause:

(a) if labor costs, including all benefits and the cost of foreign income taxes paid by Contractor for its expatriate employees, vary by more than five per cent;

(b) if Operator requires Contractor to increase the number of Contractor's personnel [76];

(c) if it becomes necessary for Contractor to change the work schedule of its personnel or change the location of its operations base;

(d) in the event described in Clause 1202 (Assignment) [77];

(e) if there is any change in legislation (other than Corporate tax legislation) by the country granting Operator the concession in which Contractor is working that alters Contractor's financial burden;

(f) if the cost of insurance premiums varies by more than five per cent;

(g) if the cost of catering varies by more than five per cent;

(h) if Contractor's interest rate varies by more than one-half of one per cent;

(i) the rates listed herein shall be increased or decreased for costs other than those listed above on the Commencement Date and at three month intervals thereafter based on changes in the Bureau of Labor Statistics Oilfield Drilling Machinery and Equipment Wholesale Price Index (Code No. 1191–02) as published by the U.S. Department of Labor from that reported for the month of . . . Said rates shall be increased or decreased (proportionately and on a pro rata basis) . . . % for each change of five per cent (5%) in said Index."

It is a condition of any revision that one of the listed events shall have occurred or that the cost of any of the listed items shall have varied to the

---

[76] Art. 304 states: "Operator may, at any time, with Contractor's approval require Contractor to increase the number of Contractor's personnel and the day rates provided herein shall be adjusted accordingly."

[77] The assignment clause, after dealing with the conditions for assignment, states: " If any assignment is made that alters Contractor's financial burden, Contractor's compensation shall be adjusted to give effect to any increase or decrease in Contractor's operating costs or in taxes in the new operating area." See also below, p. 307.

extent stated. When that condition is satisfied the "rates and/or payments" are to be revised by the actual amount of the change in the contractor's cost. This would seem to mean that the mobilisation and demobilisation fees are not affected, because they are not categorised as rates or payments, although of course they constitute payments in the usual sense of that word.

Mr. Taylor Hancock [78] has commented on this section of the contract:

"Ten years ago the only rate adjustment provided for in the typical Drilling Contract was a provision for a change of rate based upon a general increase or decrease in labor costs. Now, in almost every Drilling Contract, domestic or international, you will find a provision similar to Item 809 of the IADC form providing for an adjustment of rates for a variety of causes—the intention being to protect the Contractor for those changes in the Contractor's cost and expenses which are beyond the Contractor's control. You may wish to pay special attention to Item 809 Sub sec. (i) in which what might be termed the operating costs factor is covered by reference to the United States Bureau of Labor Statistics Oilfield Drilling Machinery and Equipment Wholesale Price Index. It is important here to tie down the base month, which typically would be the time or date that the rate is fixed, which might be the date of the Contract, or conceivably could be a date considerably earlier. A typical ratio is 1 per cent change in the total day rate for each change of 5 per cent in the index, on a pro-rated basis."

II. *Other Provisions Connected with Payment and Monetary Adjustments*

A drilling contract contains a number of sections which enumerate the payments to be made by the operator to the contractor or on behalf of the contractor, and the payments which are in any event to be borne by the operator, usually because they arise out of and relate to services, equipment and personnel provided by the operator. Certain other sections of a contract deal with ancillary arrangements as to payment. There are set out below several of these provisions, as extracted both from the I.A.D.C. contract (the number of the relevant Article being given) and some other drilling contracts.

They can be summarised as follows:

A. Currency
B. Invoices
C. Time and Manner of Payment
D. Accounts.

A. *Currency*

The rates and sums of money listed may or may not be preceded by a clear reference to the currency of account. The contract may state:

"CURRENCY
In this Contract, all amounts expressed in dollars are United States dollar amounts" (Art. 102).

[78] Vice-President of Global Marine Inc.

The provision as to payment in local currency does not, it will be seen, apply to the rates, such as the operating rate, but only to disbursements. It is important that the parties should consider the currency and exchange provisions of the country where, or in the adjacent waters of which, the operations are to be conducted, as some countries operate two-tier or three-tier exchange rates.

In some cases the sums debited by the contractor have been expended in a local currency. The contract may deal with this possibility:

" All payments due by Operator to Contractor hereunder shall be made in United States dollars at Contractor's bank which is . . .; with the understanding, however, that either Operator or Contractor shall have the right to specify that Operator shall pay Contractor in the currency of the country where the Drilling Unit operates in amounts equal to Contractor's local currency expenditures (including those expenditures incurred locally by Contractor for the account of Operator) and as needed by Contractor. All amounts of local currency so paid Contractor during the month shall be credited against Contractor's U.S. Dollar monthly invoice for that month at the rate of exchange of U.S. Dollars for the local currency in effect on . . . as published in the Wall Street Journal " [79] (Art. 903).

2. *Invoices*

There may be provision for monthly invoices:

" MONTHLY INVOICES

Contractor shall bill Operator at the end of each month for all daily charges earned by Contractor during the month. Other charges shall be billed as earned. Billings for daily charges will reflect details of the time spent (calculated to the nearest hour [80]) and the rate charged for that time; billings for other charges will be accompanied by invoices supporting costs incurred for Operator or other substantiation as required " (Art. 901), or as follows:

" Contractor shall invoice Operator as of the 1st day of each month at the appropriate rate or rates for services rendered during the immediately preceding month. Reimbursable items will be billed as incurred, but no less than monthly. Payment of undisputed invoiced amounts shall be made by Operator within twenty days following receipt of Contractor's invoice by check payable in U.S. currency." or:

" Contractor shall bill Company on or before the tenth day of each calendar month in respect of expenses incurred, items provided, operations carried out and services rendered during the previous month. All billings shall be accompanied by time sheets with regard to the applied rates and by all invoices and other documentary evidence of costs incurred and to be charged to Company. Contractor will use its best endeavours to render invoices as they become due."

In some contracts the monthly invoice clause provides that an operator shall pay automatically on presentation of a provisional invoice based on a minimum rate, such as the standby rate. An adjustment is made on presentation of the final invoice.

---

[79] It is important to ensure that the relevant country has its rates published in the *Wall Street Journal*.

[80] See also above, p. 287.

Mr. Taylor Hancock [81] has described the general procedure:

". . . in actual practice, the procedure is for the operating manager of the Drilling Contractor to prepare a tentative monthly invoice at or near the end of the current month, and to review this tentative invoice with his counterpart, the field representative of the Oil Operator, to the end and effect that an invoice agreed upon in the field by both parties can be submitted to the home office of the Oil Operator for payment within the first few days of the month ensuing the month that is covered by the invoice."

3. *Time and manner of payment*

The invoices are usually made monthly, so far at any rate as the rates of payment, such as the operating rate, are concerned. The contract may then state:

" PAYMENT

Operator shall pay by telegraphic transfer all billings within thirty days after the receipt thereof except that if Operator disputes an item billed, Operator shall within twenty days after receipt of the bill notify Contractor of the item disputed, specifying the reason therefor, and payment of the disputed item shall be withheld until settlement of the dispute, but payment shall be made of any undisputed portion. Any sums (including amounts ultimately paid with respect to a disputed invoice) not paid within thirty days after receipt of invoice shall bear interest at the rate of . . . per cent. per annum or pro rata thereof from the due date until paid. If Operator refuses to pay undisputed items, Contractor shall have the right to terminate this contract " (Art. 902); or:

" TIME AND MANNER OF PAYMENT

(a) Company shall pay or cause to be paid the invoices, within twenty days after receipt, into the account of Contractor with the Bank of . . .

(b) In the event of Company disputing an item billed, Company shall within twenty days notify Contractor of the item under dispute specifying Company's complaint and payment of that item shall be withheld until settlement of the dispute, either by mutual agreement or in accordance with the provisions of [the arbitration clause] of this contract. The undisputed amount, however, shall be paid without delay."

" FAILURES OF PAYMENTS

Contractor may terminate this contract for failure to receive payment of undisputed amounts in accordance with the provisions of [the above Clause], giving 30 days' written notice, provided that such termination shall become ineffective by Company's payment of such undisputed amount within said 30 days."

The above clauses, dealing with the time and manner of payment, have the following features:

1. The operator is to pay the invoices within a certain period after it receives them.

2. If the operator disputes an item billed it must notify the contractor of the disputed item within a certain period, specifying the reason for the dispute.

---

[81] Vice-President of Global Marine Inc.

3. In such an event the operator may withhold payment of the disputed item until the dispute is settled but it must pay any undisputed amount.

4. (in one contract only). Interest must be paid on sums not paid within the period fixed under 1. above, even where the sums were the subject of dispute.

5. The contractor can terminate the contract in the event of failure by the operator to pay undisputed items. In the case of the first contract such a right of termination is automatic and comes into operation by virtue of the expiry of the period fixed under 1. above. In the case of the second contract the right of termination is somewhat less strictly expressed in that it enures only if the contractor gives 30 days' notice—presumably drawing attention to that provision and/or to its intention to terminate—and the operator fails to pay within that period.

4. *Accounts*

It is essential that the contractor should keep records not only of the operations themselves but also of expenditures. Thus:

> " RIGHT TO AUDIT
> Contractor shall keep proper books, records and accounts of operations hereunder and shall permit Operator at all reasonable times to inspect the portions thereof related to any variation of the rates hereunder " (Art. 1405).

The variations of the rates are those changes which occur when, owing to a change in circumstances such as adverse wind or weather, or the need to carry out repairs, the standard operating rate is replaced by one of the other rates specified in the contract.

III. *Legal, Formal and Associated Provisions*

These can be summarised as follows:

    A.   Definitions
    B.   Governing Law
    C.   Arbitration
    D.   Assignment
    E.   Notices
    F.   Waiver
    G.   Term of Contract

A. *Definitions*

A drilling contract often sets out a number of definitions of terms used in the contract. The I.A.D.C. contract, for example, gives definitions, in Article 101,[82] of Commencement Date, Operator's Items, Contractor's Items, Contractor's Personnel, Operating Area, Operations Base and Affiliated Company.[82]

---

[82] Set out in full in Appendix B to this book, at p. 438.

B. *Governing Law*

If a contract is silent as to the law which should be applied, it may become necessary to reach a decision as to what is the applicable, or proper, law of the contract. This may be especially difficult if the contracting parties are of different nationalities, the companies in question being located in different countries, and if the operations are to be carried out in territorial waters, exclusive economic zone or continental shelf of another country or other countries, or on the high seas. In such cases the law of a different, or neutral country, is often chosen.

The I.A.D.C. contract states, at Article 107:

" GOVERNING LAW
This Contract shall be construed and the relations between the parties determined in accordance with the law of . . ., not including, however, any of its conflicts of law rules which would direct or refer to the laws of another jurisdiction."

Another contract states, more briefly:

" GOVERNING LAW
This contract shall be governed by and interpreted in accordance with . . . Law."

The I.A.D.C. contract is clearer, because the expression " Ruritanian law " for example, is ambiguous. It may mean domestic Ruritanian laws or all the rules, including those of the conflict of laws, which the Ruritanian courts apply.

The space to be completed in both these clauses may be filled by reference to a country, or nation state, or by reference to a member state or province of such a country or nation state. The latter would more frequently be the case where a confederation or federation was involved, since the individual laws of its constituent parts might differ. An example of such a provision is: " This Agreement will be construed under the laws of the State of California." Some contracts refer to the " general maritime law of the United States, supplemented when necessary, and not when contradictory, by the law of the State of . . ."

C. *Arbitration*

In many commercial contracts the parties provide for arbitration. In the absence of such a provision any disputes which they found themselves unable to resolve would go to court, unless, after the dispute arose, they entered into a separate arbitration agreement, or submission, as such a separate and subsequent agreement is often known. The parties may prefer to agree to arbitration because the proceedings are confidential to the parties, and not a matter of public report as is usually the case in the proceedings in court; because the arbitration award represents the end of the matter in most jurisdictions, with no appeal to the courts, either because there is no legal provision to that effect or because, in practice, the parties do not wish to take the matter further; and, finally, because an arbitration award often has some procedural advantages in terms of enforcement in foreign countries.

The arbitration clause in the I.A.D.C. contract (Article 1402) states:

> " ARBITRATION
>
> As between the parties, any claims, disputes or controversies arising under or in connection with this Contract which cannot be adjusted by mutual agreement will be decided by the Courts of . . . to whose jurisdiction the parties hereto agree, whatever their domicile may be; provided that either party prior to its having filed a complaint or petition in any court of law, may elect to have any such claim, dispute or controversy referred to arbitration in . . . in accordance with the provisions of the . . . Arbitration Act or any statutory modifications or reenactment thereof for the time being in force."

Such a clause is somewhat unusual in commercial contracts, which usually contain a simple provision that the parties agree to the arbitration of their disputes in a particular country. This clause has the effect that, prima facie, there shall be adjudication by the courts, but that at any time before suit is commenced therein a party may elect to have the matter referred to arbitration. The party in question would normally be the party on whose behalf the claim, dispute or controversy arose; the wording of the clause is such, however, that even where the substantive claim is about to be made by one party the other party may, if it has a " claim, dispute or controversy," elect to have that matter (namely, its own claim, dispute or controversy) referred to arbitration. In practice it might then follow that the other party also agreed to arbitrate, but it would seem that in law it could say that it had not made such an election, and it could ask the courts to adjudicate. A question might then arise as to whether, particularly if the disputes were fundamentally concerned with the same issue, there should be a stay of arbitration, but that would have to be decided by the appropriate court.

Another form of arbitration agreement, as set out in another drilling contract, states:

> " ARBITRATION
>
> All disputes arising in connection with the present contract whether arising during its term or thereafter shall be finally settled by arbitration under the Rules of Conciliation and Arbitration of the International Chamber of Commerce in . . . [83] by one or more arbitrators appointed in accordance with the said Rules. A dispute shall be deemed to have arisen when either party notifies the other party in writing to that effect."

The International Chamber of Commerce, whose headquarters are in Paris, provides facilities, as the terms of this arbitration clause indicate, for both conciliation and arbitration. The Chamber has an Administrative Commission consisting of one member from each country whose business organisations are affiliated to the Chamber. The Commission may hear the parties and try to conciliate, though the parties have the right to

---

[83] Town, city, state or country to be inserted.

proceed direct to arbitration. If an attempt to conciliate fails the matter is submitted to the Court of Arbitration.

D. *Assignment*

Market conditions, changes in beneficial ownership of companies, and other factors, may result in one of the parties wishing to assign to a third party the rights and duties which it has assumed under the drilling contract. The I.A.D.C. contract states, at Article 1202:

> " ASSIGNMENT
> Neither party may assign this Contract to anyone other than an affiliated company without the prior written consent of the other, and prompt notice of any such intent to assign shall be given to the other party. In the event of such assignment, the assigning party shall remain liable to the other party as a guarantor of the performance by the assignee of the terms of this Contract. If any assignment is made that alters Contractor's financial burden, Contractor's compensation shall be adjusted to give effect to any increase or decrease in Contractor's operating costs or in taxes in the new operating area."

The general rules of English law as to the assignment by a party of its rights and duties under a contract are:

1. The benefits of a contract may be transferred to a third party and the consent of the other party is not necessary. Where the assignment is made in accordance with the requirements of section 136 (1) of the Law of Property Act 1925, it is not necessary for the third party-assignee, when wishing to sue the debtor, to join the assignor as plaintiff, or if the assignor does not wish to be joined, as defendant.[84] Under the Act a party may assign his rights by an absolute and written assignment of which express written notice has been given to the other party.

2. The liabilities under a contract may not be transferred to a third party without the agreement of the other party.

The terms of Article 1202 differ from the provisions of English law, as set out above, in that they expressly prohibit assignment, except to an affiliated company, without prior written consent of the other party, though both the Article and the 1925 Act provide for notice to be given to the other party. The Article does not, in the general statement in its first sentence as to assignments, distinguish between the assignment of rights and the assignment of duties. The second sentence, however, has the effect that the assignor remains liable " as a guarantor " for the performance of any duties which have been the subject of assignment. A guarantee is a promise to perform if another person fails to do so. It is thus agreed by the parties that the assignee assumes a primary liability in respect of the duties. This, taken with the need of the assignor to obtain prior consent from the other party, is consistent with the requirements of English law as to the assignment of liabilities.

---

[84] See Halsbury's *Laws of England* (3rd ed.), Vol. 8, pp. 258–261.

The words " an affiliated company " would usually be taken to mean a company which formed part of the same group as the original contracting party; there would usually be a link in the form of shareholding, directly between the companies or through some other company or companies. It seems arguable that other links, such as a service or management or agency contract, could also constitute affiliation for the purpose of this clause.

The third and final sentence of Article 1202 refers to an assignment which " alters Contractor's financial burden," it being made clear that such an alteration must result in an adjustment to the contractor's compensation whether the alteration is favourable or unfavourable. The opening words, with their reference to an alteration in the financial burden, are of a general nature and open the way to an adjustment in the compensation. The adjustment, however, is to give effect to any increase or decrease in the contractor's operating costs or in taxes in the new operating area. These words could limit the scope of the adjustment; a situation might, in theory, arise, in which the contractor's financial burden was altered, upwards or downwards, in a manner which did not involve an alteration in its operating costs or in its taxes in a new operating area. In such a case there would, it seems, be no entitlement to an adjustment.

E. *Notices*

Many contracts which create rights and duties of a continuing nature make provision for the manner in which the parties shall give notices to each other. The I.A.D.C. contract, for example, states, at Article 1301:

" NOTICES

Notices, reports and other communications required or permitted by this Contract to be given or sent by one party to the other shall be delivered by hand, mailed, telexed, or telegraphed to:

Operator's address:

Contractor's address:

as the case may be. Either party may by notice to the other party change its address."

Examples of notices " required or permitted " by the contract are the notice of termination from the operator [85] and notice of intent to assign. Reports and other communications include the record of work performed and formations drilled to be kept by the contractor, the instructions given by the operator to the contractor as to the operations, and the provision by the contractor to the operator, if requested, of certificates of all its insurance policies relating to the contractor's operations.

Another notice clause reads as follows:

---

[85] See the discussion of the term of the contract below, at p. 310.

" ADDRESSES FOR NOTICES

Any notification under this contract shall be well and sufficiently served on the party concerned when received by telex, telegram or registered mail at the following addresses:

Contractor:

Company:

In the event of a change of address, prompt notice shall be given by the party concerned."

A party may purport to give a notice to the other party in some other manner as, for example, by sending the notice to a branch office or an agency and not to the stipulated address. This would be contrary to the provision in the I.A.D.C. contract that a notice " shall be " despatched to the address given. Despite this breach the notifying party might show that the other party had received the notice, because it had been passed on; or it might argue that whether it was passed on or not the other party must be deemed to have knowledge of it, in accordance with the rule that the knowledge of the agents is imputed to the principal.

The second notice clause cited above is less strictly expressed. Whereas the first clause says simply that notices " shall be " sent to the addresses stated, the second clause says that notices to the addresses given " shall be well and sufficiently served on the party concerned when received . . . at the following addresses." The implication, however, is that they are not " well and sufficiently served " if sent elsewhere, so that the practical effect may be the same as that of the first clause. The second clause does however state that the service is effective " when received." In the case of acceptance of an offer, the general rule in English law is that acceptance is complete when the letter of acceptance is posted. The theory is that the postal service acts for this purpose as the agent of the offeror, so that the action of posting concludes the contract. This general rule only applies if it is reasonable to use the postal system to indicate acceptance—the circumstances of the offer may be such that an acceptance by telephone, in person, by telegram or by telex is required.[86]

F. *Waiver*

Where a contract provides for the performance of a number of actions by both parties over a period of time one party or both parties may fail to perform a particular action, either once or several times. A typical and important example is that of late payment of the monthly invoice. This is comparable to late payment of hire under a time charterparty. The other party may forbear, by not calling him to task for that breach, but a time may arrive when he wishes to do so. Sometimes that step is met by a claim by the other party that the breach of contract has already been

---

[86] For a helpful discussion of this subject see G. H. Treitel, *The Law of Contract* (4th ed., 1975), pp. 17 to 23.

waived, because the complaining party has failed to complain on an earlier occasion. Except in the cases where the waiver amounts to a dissolution of the contract, or a variation of a term of the contract, it cannot be said that the contract has been terminated or altered. Nevertheless the complaining party may find itself unable to refuse to accept the altered method of performance.

The parties may seek to avoid this difficulty, at the time of the contract, by the insertion of a clause such as the following, which appears as Article 1406 in the I.A.D.C. contract:

> " WAIVERS
> It is fully understood and agreed that none of the requirements of the Contract shall be considered as waived by either party unless the same is done in writing, and then only by the persons executing this Contract, or other duly authorized agent or representative of the party."

Another contract states:

> " WAIVER IN WRITING
> None of the requirements in this contract shall be considered waived unless waived in writing by the party concerned or its representative."

Nevertheless a difficulty might still arise if it were argued that the transaction was not a waiver, evidencing a permanent intention to abandon contractual rights, but a mere forbearance, reserving the right to retract, and not covered by such a clause.[87]

G. *Term of the contract*

It is normal for one section of the drilling contract to state the date at which the contractual liabilities begin and the circumstances in which the contract may terminate.

Commencement. In the I.A.D.C. contract, Article 201 states:

> " EFFECTIVE DATE
> The parties shall be bound by this Contract when each of them has executed it."

Another contract says:

> " This Agreement shall be effective as of . . . at 1200 hours . . . time."

In the absence of such a provision a drilling contract would be effective when the parties had reached final agreement; the existence of an offer and an acceptance, an intention to create legal relations, and certainty and finality as to the terms are the usual requirements in such a case. Unless the parties had inserted a term by which the contractual obligations were not to apply until a certain event, the obligation would exist when that final agreement had been achieved. Nor is it strictly necessary, in the absence of a condition precedent or some other agreement to that effect, for the contract to be reduced to writing. The commencement of the

---

[87] G. H. Treitel, *op. cit.*, pp. 75–77.

obligations may depend upon the contract having been put into writing; or upon each party having " executed it "; or upon a provision that it shall not be effective until a certain time. In each case the intention of the parties is the relevant factor. The law as it applies to charterparties, which also applies here, has been stated in *Scrutton on Charterparties* [88]:

> " A charterparty is usually signed before any steps are taken under the contract it contains, but its main provisions are almost always agreed in advance by correspondence, telex, or oral negotiation. Whether the parties are bound before the charter is signed will depend on (i) whether they are *ad idem* and (ii) whether on the true construction of the language used in the negotiations, including the use of such phrases as ' subject to contract ' or ' subject to signature of charterparty,' it was the intention of the parties that they should be bound before signature of the formal document."

The point of time at which the legal obligations begin is not necessarily that at which the obligation of the operator to make payments arises. The incidence and nature of these obligations is usually set out in a separate section of the contract. The operating rate,[88a] for example, may not become payable until the drilling unit is at the drilling location and ready to begin work. The standby rate [89] may not become payable until the commencement date, which may be defined as the time when the unit arrives in or near the operating area.

Duration. The I.A.D.C. contract states, at Article 202:

> " DURATION
>
> This contract shall terminate:
> (a) immediately if the Drilling Unit becomes an actual or constructive total loss;
> (b) . . . months after receipt by Contractor of notice of termination from Operator, but Operator may not give such notice until at least . . . months after the Commencement Date, (or, if operations are then being conducted on a well, as soon thereafter as such operations are completed) and the Drilling Unit has arrived at . . ., unless some other port is mutually agreed;
> (c) on the . . . anniversary of the Commencement Date (or, if operations are then being conducted on a well, as soon thereafter as such operations are completed) and the Drilling Unit has arrived at . . ., unless some other port is mutually agreed."

Some contracts refer to the time required for completion, to the operator's satisfaction, of an agreed number of wells.

As for the provision as to a total loss in Article 202 (a), a contract may deal with this situation at greater length:

> " In the event that the drilling unit becomes a total loss (which term will include a constructive, arranged and/or compromised total loss), the

---

[88] 18th ed., (1974), p. 3.
[88a] See above, p. 286.
[89] See above, p. 287.

contract will be considered as terminated, without notice, as from the moment the incident directly leading to that loss occurred and no payment whatsoever shall become due by Company to Contractor as from that moment."

Section 56 (2) of the Marine Insurance Act 1906 states: " A total loss may be either an actual total loss, or a constructive total loss." The addition, in the second contract quoted above, of the concept of an " arranged and/or compromised total loss " has the effect of extending the number of situations in which the contract shall terminate. This is because the additional words cover a situation where the casualty does not fall within the definitions of actual or constructive total loss, but where it is agreed with the insurers to treat the casualty in a similar way, though the insured may not receive the same amount by way of settlement.

The wordings of Article 202 (b) and 202 (c) differ in that the former provides for notice of termination, though by the operator only, whereas the latter provides for automatic termination after a named period. In both cases there is a proviso that the termination shall not be effective, if operations are being conducted on a well, until those operations are completed. One commentator [90] has said of these two possibilities:

> " The basic issue that frequently has to be thrashed out between parties during the Contract negotiation is the ' Contract Term '; the first question here is whether the effective term shall be for a specified number of wells (which frequently is the choice of the Operator), or on the other hand whether the term shall be for a specified number of months or years (which is usually the choice of the Drilling Contractor). Typically, the Operator has a specified number of wells to drill, and wishes to contract to meet this requirement; on the other hand, the Drilling Contractor needs to be able to plan the use of his drilling rigs in such a way that there will be no down time, or a minimum of down time, and therefore wishes to know the date at which a particular Contract term will end, in order that the further use of the rig may be properly scheduled."

As a result of Article 202 (b) the operator is able to bring the contract to an end when its operations make that appropriate, although the subsection does not specify the number of wells. Article 202 (c), on the other hand, helps the contractor by stating a specific period at the end of which the contract shall terminate.

Termination of obligations. The termination of the contract is usually associated with the end of the drilling operations for one of the reasons set out in Article 202 of the I.A.D.C. contract.[91] There may nevertheless remain in existence certain obligations which must be discharged by one or both of the parties. To that extent there has not been a true termination of the contract in the sense of a mutual release from all liabilities. The above-mentioned drilling contract therefore provides, at Article 203:

> " CONTINUING OBLIGATIONS
> Notwithstanding the termination of this Contract, the parties shall

---

[90] Mr. Taylor Hancock, Vice-President of Global Marine Inc.
[91] See above, p. 311.

continue to be bound by the provisions of this Contract that reasonably require some action or forbearance after the cessation of the day rates provided for hereinafter."

An example of such necessary action is contained in the immediately succeeding provision, Article 204:

" RETURN OF OPERATOR'S ITEMS

Upon termination of this Contract, Contractor shall return to Operator any of Operator's Items which are at the time in Contractor's possession."

6. Indemnities, Subrogation Rights, Benefits of the Insurance, etc.

The drilling contract may deal with such matters, possibly in ascending order of efficacy and completeness, and in relation to property losses and to liabilities, as (a) the bearing by each party of its own losses, each agreeing not to claim against the other; (b) the indemnification or holding harmless by each party of the other if such losses are suffered by that other in the first instance; (c) the waiver by the underwriters of each party of its rights of subrogation against the other party; and (d) the naming of one party on the relevant insurance policy or policies of the other.

The drilling contract frequently contains provisions by which the parties oblige themselves to procure from their respective insurers agreements which parallel or supplement the indemnity agreements in that contract. These agreements to procure specific insurance terms are important because the indemnity agreements only oblige the contractor or operator to hold harmless and defend the other from and against certain property losses and liabilities. Those undertakings in the contract do not themselves affect the rights or obligations of the respective insurers of the operator and the contractor.

The insurer, in the case of a policy which covers property, is obliged to pay for losses to that property caused by insured perils. In the case of a liability policy, the insurer is obliged to pay for or indemnify its assured for the cost of defence against a claim made by, as well as a judgment awarded in favour of, a party who claims to have suffered loss resulting from an insured peril. Accordingly, an operator who insists upon being named as an additional assured on a policy which insures only the contractor's interest in certain property may gain little, if anything. An operator through whose fault a contractor loses or sustains damage to insured property acquires the protection which he needs by making certain that the contractor's insurers have waived their right to subrogate or to make a claim against the operator for having caused the loss, if the operator also has severed the contractor's right of recourse by an appropriate and enforceable hold harmless or indemnity agreement.

However, an operator would usually wish to be named as an additional assured in a policy of insurance which protects against liability to third parties since that liability might arise not only out of the contractor's activities, but as a result of those of the operator as well. Having an insurer obliged to bear the cost of investigation and defence is frequently as worthwhile as having it obliged to pay a judgment. A contractor has a similar interest in the operator's insurance and would wish to make certain that the operator's policies reflect the indemnity provisions or other risk allocation portion of the drilling contract.

The insurance section of the drilling contract may state [92]: " BENEFIT. Contractor's insurance hereunder shall be endorsed to provide that the underwriters waive their right of recourse against Operator. Operator will, as well, cause its insurer to waive subrogation against Contractor." In the case of a contract used by a major oil company, the corresponding clause reads: " Any insurance, taken out by Contractor . . . shall be endorsed to provide that the underwriters waive their rights of recourse on Company (the operator)." The effectiveness of these and other provisions (especially as to indemnities, where negligence may be involved) will vary in different jurisdictions. Under the general law of the United States, for example, much will depend upon the current interpretation of such cases as *Bisso* v. *Inland Waterways Corporation* [93] and *M/S Bremen* v. *Zapata Offshore Co.*[94] and subsequent decisions.

It is a fundamental rule of marine insurance that when an insurer has paid a claim he is thereupon subrogated [95] to all the rights and remedies of the assured in and in respect of the subject-matter insured. This principle applies whether the claim is in respect of an object belonging to or under the control of the assured or in respect of a liability or expense incurred by the assured. By such contractual provisions as are set out above the contractor promises the operator that it (the operator) will agree with its underwriters that they will abandon the right, which they would otherwise have, of recourse [96] against the operator. The operator enters into a similar undertaking so far as its own insurer's rights of subrogation are concerned. If one contracting party giving such an undertaking fails to make the necessary arrangements with its insurer, with the result that the insurer exercises rights of subrogation against the other contracting party, then the first contracting party has breached its contractual undertaking and the second party would have a right to claim against the first party. The claim would be for an amount equal to that for which the second party has been made liable.

It is important to emphasise that this agreement to procure an abandonment by the underwriters of their rights of subrogation is not the same as an agreement to have the other party named as an additional assured in the policy, or, as is sometimes said, to " give the benefits " of the insurance policy to the other party. In the I.A.D.C. contract, for example, it is provided in Appendix B (Insurance Requirements) that where the con-

---

[92] I.A.D.C. contract, Art. 1103.
[93] (1955) 349 U.S. 85.
[94] (1972) 407 U.S. 1.
[95] See, for example, s. 79 of the Marine Insurance Act 1906.
[96] That is, the right to be subrogated to the contractor's rights and remedies.

tractor puts other vessels into service it will arrange hull and protecting and indemnity insurances " and will name Operator as an additional insured." So also the oil company drilling contract to which reference has been made earlier states, somewhat loosely: " Any insurance taken out by Contractor shall be to the benefit of Contractor and Company and shall be endorsed to provide that the underwriters waive their rights of recourse on Company." It is submitted that the words " benefit " and " recourse " do not clearly express the obligations of the parties and may invite litigation.

The importance of the distinction between, on the one hand, the abandonment of the right of subrogation by the insurers, and, on the other hand, the naming of a party as an additional insured or a provision that it should have the benefit of the insurance, is a well recognised one. Mr. Russel F. Sammis [97] in his lecture on " Risk and Insurance Provisions of Offshore Operations Agreements " said:

" It is not uncommon to have the Operator require that the Operator be named as an additional insured on the drilling or service contractor's policies and to include owner's property. There are good reasons why this is a questionable practice. We will explore property coverages, workmen's compensation, and employers' liability and third party liability separately. . . ." [98] Then, referring particularly to property coverages and the insurance of the drilling unit, he said: " Being named as an insured on the drilling contractor's insurance policies does not necessarily relieve the Operator of liability to the underwriter unless there is also a waiver of subrogation. If the drilling or service contract requires a waiver of subrogation, or there is no right to subrogation because the drilling or service contract has given up the contractor's right, why is it necessary for the Operator to be named as an additional insured on the property insurance coverage? " Of course, there may well be a valid reason for the operator to be named as an additional insured if the insurance form chosen to insure property also extends to the insurance of liabilities, such as collision liability and removal of debris.

We have seen that in the case of the I.A.D.C. contract each party agrees to cause its insurers to waive their rights of subrogation against the other party, and that this agreement is of a general nature so far as insurances prescribed by the contract are concerned; it is not restricted to particular types or branches of the insurances [99]; but only in the case of other vessels put into service by the contractor is there a provision that one party, the contractor, will name the other, the operator, as an additional insured. In the case of the major oil company drilling contract to which reference has been made earlier, it is only the contractor who has to arrange for its

---

[97] Senior Vice-President of Messrs. Marsh & McLennan Inc.

[98] These headings correspond to those set out above (see p. 278) respectively, as: D. Marine Hull Insurance; A. Insurance for Personnel (*i.e.* workmen's compensation and employers' liability); and B. Comprehensive General Liability.

[99] Art. 1103; see p. 314, above.

insurers to waive their rights of recourse against the operator. In addition, the contractor's marine hull insurance has to provide that the insurers waive their rights of recourse against any party designated by the operator with whom the operator has entered into a hold harmless agreement. As in the case of the I.A.D.C. contract, the only case in which the operator is to be named as an additional insured is where other vessels are put in service by the contractor. It should be remembered that such contract forms are frequently used in connection with offers to do business, and do not necessarily embody the final commitments of the parties. In practice it would be unusual to find a knowledgeable contractor willing to conclude a contract without some reciprocal agreements from the operator. The existence of obligations that one party should arrange for its insurers to waive rights of subrogation against the other party, and have the other party named as an additional insured in respect of one or more policies, depends in practice upon the state of the market and the relevant bargaining powers of the parties as well as upon local conditions in the area of the world where drilling is contemplated.

From a legal point of view however, the consequences may be significant. In this respect it is helpful to consider, as Mr. Russel F. Sammis [1] has done, the various insurance requirements in turn.[2]

I. *Insurance for Personnel*

The contractor must usually agree to indemnify the operator in respect of any claims brought, irrespective of the negligence of any party, against the operator by any personnel employed by the contractor or his subcontractors. Such an indemnity is given, for example, in the case of the I.A.D.C. contract.[3] As for the operator's personnel, a liability towards them will arise either (a) on the part of the operator, by virtue of their being its employees, in which case it would look to its own modified Workmen's Compensation and Employees' Liability policy; or (b) on the part of the contractor, by virtue of a third party liability towards them, in which case it (the contractor) would look to its modified Comprehensive General Liability policy or Protecting and Indemnity policy. Mr. Russel F. Sammis [4] has summarised the position as follows:

" A request to name the Operator on the [contractor's] Workmen's Compensation and Employers' Liability policy is technically not permitted and is always undesirable. Except in the case of a claim brought on the basis of being a borrowed servant, the Operator has no direct interest in the Workmen's Compensation and Employers' Liability coverage of the drilling contractor or service contractors. A waiver of subrogation may be

---

[1] See p. 315 and n. 98, above.
[2] The same sequence is adopted as that employed earlier when these requirements were considered.
[3] Art. 1003; see p. 268, above.
[4] *Op. cit.* at pp. 10–14 of his lecture.

requested, but an enforceable indemnity agreement is a more desirable solution." Although it is beyond the scope of this book generally to discuss in detail matters which are peculiar to the law of the United States or of some American states, it is appropriate to make some comments as to the enforceability of such indemnity agreements.[5]

In the continuing development of the law of the United States, the Federal Longshoremen and Harborworkers' Compensation Act and the law of some states create doubt as to the enforceability of some indemnity agreements. In addition, many drilling operations frequently involve the participation of employees of sub-contractors of either the operator or the contractor; these lead to much litigation over the status, either as seamen or as other categories of employee, of those third party employees who are injured. These claimants, who are strangers to the contract between the operator and the contractor, are not individually bound by its terms. They may pursue recovery of statutory workmen's compensation benefits from their employers and simultaneously seek recovery of damages in tort from whichever other defendants are available. Where indemnity agreements are of questionable enforceability, a limited source of protection for an operator against such claims may be the waiver of subrogation by the respective sub-contractors' Employers Liability and Workmen's Compensation insurers. This is not altogether satisfactory as it affects only the insurers' rights and not those of the injured employee. The latter's pursuit of both statutory compensation and relief in tort simultaneously may raise the possibility of double recovery from the same injury. Whether or not the respective insurers may set off one recovery against the other under the circumstances is an issue frequently litigated and not yet settled.

II. *Comprehensive General Liability*

The drilling contract normally requires the contractor to take out a Comprehensive General Liability policy [6]; the policy has to include all the contractor's operations including its contractual liabilities under the drilling contract. Although the contract usually requires the contractor to arrange that its insurers waive any rights of recourse against the operator, it is unusual for it to state also that the operator should become an additional insured on the contractor's policy. Mr. Russel F. Sammis [7] has said: " A request of the Operator to be named as an additional insured on the third party liability coverages of a drilling contractor can present real coverage problems, create confusion, and increase costs. Before making a request of a contractor to include the Operator as an additional insured

---

[5] The author is indebted to Mr. Theodore G. Dimitry of Messrs. Vinson & Elkins, Attorneys at Law, of Houston, Texas, for the substance of the paragraph which follows, and for other invaluable contributions to and comments on this entire section.

[6] See p. 280, above.

[7] *Op. cit.* at p. 15.

under liability coverages, the Operator should carefully consider his objective. If the objective is to have the contractor arrange all of the insurance for a given venture, this should be made clear to all parties so that there is no question of the intent of the contractor's underwriters. The exposure of a contractor can be distinguished from that of an Operator and the insurance underwriter who is to protect both, not one or the other, is entitled to price his product accordingly. If the purpose is, in effect, to get something for nothing, the effort will probably fail. The capital commitment required to be an offshore drilling or service contractor today requires a sophisticated business organisation capable of understanding all facets of risk and insurance. A request to provide insurance for an Operator will undoubtedly be reflected in the day rate. If the request is made for the contractor to provide insurance for both parties, or conceivably for all parties connected with the venture, this fact should be clearly set forth in the insurance of the contractor, the Operator and any other interested parties. If one insurance contract is not clearly made primary, the result easily could be contribution by the liability insurers for all parties and massive confusion."

When a decision is being made as to whether the operator should be named as an additional insured on the contractor's policy there will have to be taken into account the vicarious liability which an operator may have for certain matters which are properly those of the contractor and intended to be covered by the latter's Comprehensive General Liability policy. As plaintiffs frequently name the operator as an additional defendant when they sue the contractor the costs incurred can be significantly increased if the operator has to provide its separate defence and investigation. This will be inappropriate if the contractor's insurer has ultimately to respond to a judgment against the contractor and waive subrogation rights against the operator.

Both operator and contractor should consider carefully, and in advance, the risks likely to be encountered in the specific drilling venture proposed, and determine virtually on a well-to-well basis whether the operator should be named as an additional assured and, if not, whether the contractor's Comprehensive General Liability policy should be endorsed to expand the coverage afforded without actually naming the operator as an additional insured. This coverage may be purchased separately or as an additional cover in either the Comprehensive General Liability or Marine Hull insurance policies. One problem which has to be thoroughly considered in this connection is that of the nature and extent of coverage in respect of liability for removal of wreck or debris. The cover, when added to a Comprehensive General Liability or to a hull policy, may refer to liability which is " compulsory by law." This might be inadequate if the liability was contractual (either between the operator and the contractor under the drilling contract or upon the operator by virtue of the lease) or was arbitrarily imposed by a government.

III. *Automobile Liability* [8]

It is customary for each party to the drilling contract to arrange for its own automobile liability insurances. The insurance requirements in the contract include the requirement that the contractor shall carry and maintain this category of insurance. The reciprocal agreement by which each party is to arrange that its insurer waives its right of recourse against the other applies to these insurances; but there would be no requirement that one should be named on the policy of the other.

IV. *Marine Hull Insurance* [9]

The contractor has, as a result of the insurance requirements in the drilling contract, to carry and maintain insurance [10] on the drilling unit and its equipment during all operations under the contract, including moves within the operating area. It also has to arrange that its insurers waive their right of recourse against the operator. It is not usual for the contract to provide that the operator should be named as an additional insured, although this requirement may be made, as we have seen, in the case of insurances taken out by the contractor for other vessels which he puts in service in connection with the drilling operations.

Mr. Russel F. Sammis [11] has dealt at some length with the problem raised: " In the area of property, the drilling rig, be it a mobile or platform type, is one of the major values involved and certainly is an area of interest for the Operator. The Operator is paying the premium for rig insurance in the sense that rig insurance cost is part of the make-up of the daily rate of the drilling unit. The drilling unit can be lost as a result of negligence on the part of the Operator or agents of the Operator and, therefore, the Operator has a legitimate interest in being released from responsibility to the drilling contractor's or service contractor's underwriters. Being named as an insured on the drilling contractor's insurance policies does not necessarily relieve the Operator of liability to the underwriter unless there is also a waiver of subrogation. If the drilling or service contract requires a waiver of subrogation, or there is no right to subrogation because the drilling or service contract has given up the contractor's right, why is it necessary for the Operator to be named as an additional insured on the property insurance coverage?

" There are specific areas where the Operator has a very real and direct interest in the insurance coverages. We refer specifically to subsea gear, in the case of semi-submersibles and ship-shapes and in-hole drilling equipment on all types of drilling equipment. Customarily the Operator is responsible for subsea gear on semis and ship-shapes and on all types of

---

[8] For the requirement, so far as the contractor is concerned, see p. 281, above.
[9] For the requirement, so far as the contractor is concerned, see p. 281, above.
[10] Which is sometimes specifically stated to include protecting and indemnity cover.
[11] *Op. cit.* at pp. 10–10 to 10–14.

rigs for in-hole equipment lost while in use.[12] The subsea gear on semis and ship-shapes is covered under the normal rig insurance, subject to policy deductibles, and the Operator would seem to be entitled to benefit from this coverage. In-hole equipment is insured against named perils, specifically blowout, cratering and fire, and the Operator has a justifiable interest in these coverages."

Here Mr. Sammis has referred to the responsibility placed upon the operator for subsea gear and in-hole drilling equipment, saying that the former is covered under the normal rig insurance and the latter against named perils such as blowout, cratering and fire. We have seen,[13] in connection with the distribution of liabilities between the parties, that the operator may be responsible for loss of or damage to the contractor's in-hole and underwater drilling equipment, to the extent that the contractor's insurance does not compensate the contractor therefor. As for the con-tractor's in-hole equipment, when being operated below the rotary table, this responsibility on the part of the operator may be excluded, in some contracts, where the loss or damage resulted from the contractor's negligence. As for the contractor's underwater drilling equipment, when being operated below the spider deck, the contract may state that it is covered by the contractor's marine hull insurance, but that the operator is to be responsible for the loss or damage except so far as it resulted from the contractor's negligence. All of these provisions may then be modified, in their turn, by general statement that in any event the operator is not to be liable for any loss or damage covered under any of the contractor's insurances. The same lecturer proceeds to deal with this possibility, but he mentions first certain of the disadvantages which may attach to the name of the operator being included in the contractor's policy: " From the contractor's standpoint, there is a definite disadvantage to having the Operator named for his limited interest, as underwriters will require that all proofs of loss and loss drafts include the Operator, if he is named as an additional insured. This is not only an inconvenience, but, in some cases, considering the geographical location of Operators and contractors, there could be a considerable length of time involved in having proper signatures affixed to proofs and loss drafts." He then mentions the pro-vision found in some contracts, by which the operator is not to be named in the contractor's insurance but is, indirectly, to receive a benefit there-from: " A solution can be found in the drilling or service contract to satisfy the Operator's legitimate interest in subsea gear and in-hole equipment to the extent they are insured under the contractor's insurance. A clause could be inserted which would provide that, to the extent the drilling or service contractor is protected by insurance the Operator is relieved of his responsibilities under the contract for loss or damage to

---

[12] See pp. 263–265, above.
[13] See p. 266, above.

subsea gear or in-hole equipment. Since the contractor might have reason not to pursue a claim against his underwriters if he had a valid claim against the Operator, the drilling or service contract might go further and provide for a form of due diligence clause as respects the contractor's efforts to recover the loss from his underwriters. To protect against a claim by the contractor or his underwriters for any other damage, the contract should clearly release the Operator from all claims except as provided elsewhere."

Operator's supplies and equipment

The general provisions of the drilling contract as to liability, as opposed to the specific exception of the type just considered, result, as we have already seen,[14] in each contracting party taking responsibility for its own items. The problems of recourse, of subrogation, and of naming the other party on a policy, do not therefore apply in the case of these items. Mr. Sammis, for example, was able to comment, in relation to the operator's own supplies and equipment: "Operator's supplies and equipment on the drilling unit present a somewhat different problem and should be approached separately from the area of liability of the Operator for loss of or damage to subsea gear and in-hole equipment. While the contractor's rig insurance can be used to cover owner's equipment and supplies, it is necessary for the contractor to amend the amount of insurance to protect against inadequacy of insurance in the event of total loss of the unit and all equipment on board. If the contractor's insurance is to be used as the vehicle to protect Operator's property, the question of who is to assume the deductible must be answered. The value of Operator's supplies and equipment on board a drilling unit fluctuates, and if the Operator desires insurance—and many do not—it is easier for the Operator to arrange his own on terms and deductibles to his own satisfaction."

Service contractors' supplies and equipment

Again the comments made by Mr. Sammis are helpful: " The property of service contractors does not usually run to the substantial values of property as does the drilling contractor's, but if the value is large enough to warrant consideration. In the case of specialty contractors, it is not uncommon to find the Operator or drilling contractor assume total responsibility for equipment of the specialty contractors. In this event, the assumed liability should be treated the same as exposure to loss of property of the Operator or drilling contractor. If the contractor's insurance is to be used as the vehicle for protection, or if it is to be the owner's insurance, the amount required should be to the value of the actual owner's or drilling contractor's property plus the values assumed under contract."

---

[14] See p. 260, above.

V. *Protecting and Indemnity*

Protecting and indemnity insurance may or may not be required. This will depend upon the type of drilling unit involved.

The contractor's Comprehensive General Liability policy is frequently expanded sufficiently to embrace such exposures as are of concern to the operator. On the other hand some forms of cover, such as the Norwegian hull insurance for drilling vessels,[15] may merely refer to the corresponding protecting and indemnity insurance.

---

[15] See Chap. 4.

CHAPTER 8

LIABILITIES

THE categories of liability in respect of which one or both of the parties may insure include, though there may be overlapping between some of these headings: Pollution Liability (the expression used in the policies and clauses is usually " seepage, pollution and contamination," but, for the sake of brevity, the single word "pollution" is used here); Removal of Debris Liability; Employer's Liability; Third Party Liability; Protecting (sometimes called Protection) and Indemnity Liability, a cover which may embrace some or all of the categories above; Products Liability; and Automobile Liability. In this Chapter there is discussion of liability insurance in respect of pollution and removal of debris. Chapters 5 and 6 gave consideration to the problems of P. & I. liabilities with particular reference to the cover given by the P. & I. Clubs. The remaining categories are not dealt with in this work; though it is important that a prospective assured should consider their applicability with his brokers, they are to some extent less directly related, as policies, to the day-to-day work of offshore mobile drilling units, and have much in common with policies of a non-marine nature.

PART 1. POLLUTION

A. POLLUTION GENERALLY

A liability for pollution [1] is a liability which may fall upon the operator or the contractor as a result of

(a) a law or other regulation imposed by a duly authorised body such as a government;

(b) a contract, such as the operating contract or a contract between the contractor or the operator and a third party;

(c) a general duty imposed by the civil law, and of a nature other than that set out at (a) and (b) above [2]; and

(d) in the case of the operator, under the licensing agreement.

---

[1] The meanings of the terms seepage, pollution and contamination are discussed below, at pp. 333–335.

[2] The way in which this liability may arise is set out in greater detail below, at p. 330 where it is shown how liabilities in general may fall upon the contractor or the operator.

Pollution may occur as a result of some unexpected situation in the oil well itself, such as oil being found under very high pressure. Alternatively, there may be a failure in the normal working system or on the drilling unit, as when the blowout preventer fails to operate, or there is an act of negligence in management by employees. Finally, some outside event may occasion the pollution; the drilling unit or the pipeline may be damaged, either negligently by a ship or another drilling unit which has broken loose, or maliciously, as, for example, by a terrorist.

We have seen earlier [3] that the drilling contract usually deals with the question of responsibility for pollution. The broad distribution of risks is often that the operator is responsible for all pollution liability (and clean up and containment costs) following a blowout or a cratering; and that the contractor is liable for operational spills, such as spills of fuel and garbage, if they result from the operator's negligence. The contract may thus provide that:

1. the contractor shall assume responsibility (and hold the operator harmless) for loss or damage arising from pollution originating above the surface of the water from negligent spills of items other than oil from the well [4] and which are wholly in the contractor's possession and control,

but that

2. the operator shall assume responsibility (and hold the contractor harmless) for loss or damage arising from pollution other than that described above, and including but not limited to pollution resulting from fire, blowout, cratering, seepage or any other uncontrolled flow of oil, gas, water or other substance during the drilling operations.

From this form of words it is clear that the operator is liable for pollution by " oil, gas, water or other substance during the drilling operations." It also follows, as a result of such words as " other than that described above, and including but not limited to pollution," that the operator is liable for spills of items other than oil [5] where they originate above the surface, provided that the contractor has not been negligent, and even where these items are wholly in the contractor's possession and control.

The responsibility assumed by the operator as a result of 2 is qualified in some cases by such words as " unless caused by contractor's negligence or wilful act or omission." Alternatively the responsibility of the operator may be modified in extent by a requirement that a certain amount be paid by the contractor in the first instance. Thus the contractor may have to bear, for example, the first $100,000 or $250,000 of any one claim by a

---

[3] See Chap. 7.
[4] For example, fuels, lubricants, motor oil, pipe dope, paints, solvents, ballast, bilge, garbage and drilling fluid.
[5] See n 4.

third party. This requirement may be an absolute one, or it may be stated as one to be applied only if there was negligence on the part of the contractor or a party for whom he was responsible.

In some contracts, however, the responsibility assumed by the operator is unqualified; and it is then irrelevant that the contractor may have been negligent or that the operator, irrespective of the contractor's negligence, is asked to pay the whole of the claim. Thus the International Daywork Drilling Contract—Offshore [6] provides, at clause 1005, that the operator shall assume responsibility for the matters set out above " which may occur from the negligence of Contractor or otherwise. . . ." This is consistent with the approach adopted in this widely used contract, and in some other contracts, by which certain areas of liability depend upon and are related to the activities undertaken by the respective parties, irrespective of negligence. If an action by the contractor has occasioned the pollution then the provisions in the drilling contract for down time, or a reduced payment to him by way of operating rate, may in any event result in his suffering a penalty to that extent, whether or not he has been negligent.[7]

By way of summary it can thus be said that the operator would usually bear responsibility for pollution resulting from the drilling operations, subject, in the case of some drilling contracts, to the contractor having to bear either (1) all that liability if the contractor or those for whom he was responsible had been negligent or (2) part of that liability, if there had been such negligence or in any event.

It is customary for the operator rather than the contractor to take out pollution insurance. From the point of view of the insurers of this potentially very substantial liability it is desirable that there be no duplication of cover, with the attendant danger that the insurers might be liable, in respect of any one incident, for more than the sum which the market felt able to bear. After the occurrence of substantial pollution from wells in the Santa Barbara Channel off California, on and after January 28, 1969, it was usual in the London market for any insurance cover given to contractors and indeed any party other than an operator to exclude pollution,[8] so that only the operators, or, as they were often described for this purpose, the leaseblock holders, could obtain such insurance. The insurers thus limited their loss per accident while at the same time giving the maximum cover which they felt able to give.

The main reason for the selection of the operators was that the countries which grant licences usually impose liabilities for pollution and clean up either upon the licensees as a whole, to whom the leases are granted, or upon the operators, as the managing firm agreed by the other licensees. The parties thus made liable must then obtain such recourse as they deem

---

[6] Drafted for the International Association of Drilling Contractors (I.A.D.C.), see p. 273, above.

[7] See above, pp. 288 and 290.　　　　　　[8] And the cost of clean-up.

appropriate from the contractors, and from other parties with whom they have contracts by an indemnity clause in the drilling or other contract; alternatively, they can protect the contractors and others by a hold harmless agreement.[9] This imposition of liability upon the licensees or the operators, in effect in consideration for the grant of the licence, need not constitute the sole basis for any claim in respect of pollution. As was said earlier,[10] a claim may arise as a result of: (a) a law or other regulation; (b) a contract; or (c) a general duty imposed by the civil law, and of a nature other than that set out in (a) and (b).

These developments also encouraged the use, in some cases, of the clauses in the drilling contract by which the operator required the contractor to bear some responsibility, either for a fixed amount or in the event of negligence.[11] It also encouraged a number of oil companies to develop their own mutual insurance company, Oil Insurance Ltd, or O.I.L., to cover a number of risks including that of oil pollution.[12]

The endeavours by insurers to ensure that liability for pollution should reach them only by certain routes, such as, in the case of wells, the operating companies, led to the development of standard exclusion clauses. One such clause is the Seepage, Pollution and Contamination Exclusion Clause No. 2,[13] approved by Lloyd's Underwriters' Non-Marine Association:

"This insurance does not cover any liablility for:
(1) Personal Injury or Bodily Injury or loss of, damage to, or loss of use of property directly or indirectly caused by seepage, pollution or contamination.
(2) The cost of removing, nullifying or cleaning-up seeping, polluting or contaminating substances.
(3) Loss of, damage to, or loss of use of property directly or indirectly resulting from subsidence caused by sub-surface operations of the Assured.
(4) Removal of, loss of or damage to sub-surface oil, gas or any other substance, the property of others.
(5) Fines, penalties, punitive or exemplary damages."

The first two subsections, (1) and (2), refer to seepage, pollution or contamination, and the next two subsections, (3) and (4), refer to sub-surface operations and substances. The last subsection, (5), however, excludes all fines, penalties, and punitive or exemplary damages. In some cases the policy has adopted the approved clause but there has been added, in (5), after the word " damages," the words " in connection with matters provided for in items 1, 2, 3 and 4 of this Pollution and Contamination Exclusion Clause."

The above Seepage, Pollution and Contamination Exclusion Clause is issued as a separate clause for incorporation in insurance policies where such incorporation is appropriate. We have seen earlier [14] that clause 6

---

[9] See above, p. 313.
[11] See above, p. 274.
[13] Dated January 22, 1970; N.M.A. 1684.

[10] See p. 323.
[12] See below, p. 357.
[14] In Chap. 3, at p. 121.

(Collision Liability) of the London Standard Drilling Barge Form also contains an exclusion relating to pollution:

"Provided that this clause shall in no case extend to any sum which the Assured or the Surety may become liable to pay or shall pay in consequence of, or with respect to: . . .

(c) the discharge, spillage, emission or leakage of oil, petroleum products, chemicals or other substances of any kind or description whatsoever; . . .

Provided further that exclusions [(b) and (c)] shall not apply to injury to any other vessel with which the Vessel is in collision or to property on such other vessel except to the extent that such injury arises out of any action taken to avoid, minimise or remove any discharge, spillage, emission or leakage described in (c)."

B. SEEPAGE, POLLUTION AND CONTAMINATION INSURANCE

The cover afforded in one standard clause is expressed in the following terms:

" *Insuring Agreements*

Whereas the Insured [15] has agreed to pay the premium as stated in the Schedule,[16] Underwriters, subject to the limitations, terms and conditions of this policy,[17] agree to indemnify the Insured against or pay on behalf of the Insured:

(a) all sums which the Insured shall by law be liable to pay as damages for bodily injury (fatal or non-fatal) and/or loss of, damage to or loss of use of property caused by or alleged to have been caused directly or indirectly by seepage, pollution or contamination arising out of the operations stated in the Schedule,[18]

(b) the cost of removing, nullifying or cleaning up seepage, polluting or contaminating substances emanating from the operations stated in the Schedule,[19] including the cost of preventing the substances reaching the shore.

Provided always that such seepage, pollution or contamination results in a claim being made during the period of Policy as stated in the Schedule and of which immediate notice has been given in accordance with Clause 5 hereof [20] except that any claim subsequently arising out of the circumstances referred to in such notice shall for the purpose of this Policy be deemed to have been made during the currency of this Policy."

The structure of the clause is that there is (1) a recital of an agreement by the insured to pay the premium, followed by (2) a statement that the underwriters agree to indemnify him, or to pay on his behalf (3) (a) specified sums and (b) a specified cost. There is then (4) a proviso to the effect that the incident has to result in a claim being made during the period of the policy, with immediate notice in accordance with the clause

---

[15] See p. 332.
[17] See pp. 228–357, below.
[19] See p. 340.

[16] See p. 339.
[18] See below, p. 339.
[20] See below, p. 344.

which relates to notice of loss; but (5) an exception that a claim arising later, but out of the circumstances referred to in the immediate notice, shall be regarded as having been made during the currency of the policy.

(1) The Agreement by the Insured to Pay the Premium

This agreement constitutes the consideration which moves from the insured, and which is necessary, in the case of each of the parties, if a contract governed by English law (except in the case of a contract under seal) is to be enforceable. Although the traditional view of consideration is that it should involve some detriment to the promisee, or some benefit to the promisor, it is not necessary, if the contract is to be upheld, that the action promised should already have taken place. In the present case, for example, it is stated that the insured has agreed to pay the premium. That is regarded as consideration, in that the giving of such a promise is regarded as involving some detriment to him. It would have to be a promise which, when performed, itself also involved him in some detriment. A promise to receive a gift, for example, would not of itself constitute a detriment.[21]

The statement that the assured has agreed to pay the premium may be compared with the words in the Lloyd's S.G. Policy, so far as they relate to the payment of the premium: " And so we, the assurers . . . confessing ourselves paid the consideration due unto us for this assurance by the assured. . . ." The seepage, pollution and contamination insurance (called here " the pollution insurance ") speaks of the agreement to pay, whereas the Lloyd's S.G. Policy speaks neither of an agreement to pay, nor payment in fact, but says that the insurers are " confessing " themselves paid. This can be regarded as an attempt to treat the situation as if the payment constituted the consideration, or alternatively as if payment had been made, even though this were not the case. If the broker fails to hand on the premium, for example, the assured would be protected by this provision.[22] As we have seen, however, a promise to pay can constitute consideration. In addition, by section 52 of the Marine Insurance Act 1906, ". . . the insurer is not bound to issue the policy until payment or tender of the premium." [23] In the case of this pollution insurance the policy itself makes it clear that consideration has moved from the assured, even though he may not yet have paid the premium, and whether or not the insurers yet have a duty to issue the policy.

(2) The Statement that the Underwriters Agree to Indemnify the Assured, or to Pay on his Behalf

Here we find the consideration which moves from the insurers, who, in return for the agreement by the assured pay the premium, agree to

---

[21] The cases on this subject are considered in Pollock, *Principles of Contract* (13th ed., 1950), p. 133; in Cheshire & Fifoot on *The Law of Contract* (9th ed., 1976), p 72; and in Treitel, *Law of Contract* (4th ed., 1975), p. 3.
[22] Many insurance company policies do not contain this Clause, and so do not acknowledge that the premium has been paid.   [23] Section headed "When premium payable."

indemnify or to pay. Their agreement is said to be " subject to the limitations, terms and conditions of this Policy." The word " limitations " could be taken in a general sense, as meaning the extent of the cover set out in the policy. Perhaps it is better taken in a specialised sense, as referring to the financial measure of recovery, which is set out in such clauses as those relating to the limit of liability,[24] and the retention to be carried by the assured.[25] The meaning of the expression " terms and conditions " has been discussed earlier.[26]

Insurance is often described as a contract of indemnity. This means that the assured can, subject to other provisions in the contract of insurance, be expected to be placed in a position equivalent to that which he would have occupied, in relation to the subject-matter of the insurance, if the event against which the insurance policy was concluded had not occurred. The indemnity is sometimes said to be an imperfect one. The court said in *Irving* v. *Manning* [27]:

> " . . . a policy of insurance is not a perfect contract of indemnity. It must be taken with this qualification, that the parties may agree beforehand in estimating the value of the subject assured, by way of liquidated damages, as, indeed, they may in any other contract to indemnify."

This pollution insurance provides that the insurers should indemnify the assured against, or pay on his behalf, the sums and the cost then set out. Where a contract of insurance states alternative courses of action in this manner, the general rule is that the option is one which is open to the insurer, and not one which is offered to the assured. In practice no such choice may be necessary. If he is indemnified, then he would be reimbursed in respect of the sums for which he was liable and which he had paid out, or the clean-up cost which he had incurred, for this would be the course by which he would be made whole. If he has not made such payments, then the insurers may " pay on behalf of the Insured " the said sums or clean-up costs.

As the loss suffered by the assured would be financial, the indemnity to the assured would, like the action to be taken " on his behalf," which would involve the insurers in acting as his agents, consist of a payment. The policy then goes on to state the matters in respect of which the insurers will pay.

(3) The Sums and the Cost in Respect of which the Assured is Insured

The assured is insured in respect of (a) his liability resulting from seepage, pollution or contamination [28]; and (b) the cost of removing, nullifying or cleaning up (described hereafter as " cost of cleaning up ") seepage, polluting or contaminating substances. This provision for the cost of cleaning up, in addition to the insurance of the liability, is similar to, and

---

[24] See below, p. 341.
[25] See below, p. 343.
[26] See above, p. 99.
[27] (1847) 1 H.L.Cas. 287, at p. 307.
[28] See below, p. 333.

329

arises out of, the general principle that an assured may and should use all reasonable efforts to avert or to minimise a loss.

(a) *Legal Liability*

The obligations of the insurers are in respect of all sums which the assured is liable by law to pay " as damages " for:

(i) " bodily injury (fatal or non-fatal) "; and/or

(ii) " loss of, damage to or loss of use of property "

where those damages were caused by or alleged to have been caused directly or indirectly by seepage, pollution or contamination arising out of the operations stated in the Schedule.

The assured must be liable " by law " to pay the sums as damages. In such a context the " law " is generally taken to mean the general law, and thus the general duty of the assured as expressed in the law relating to tort, or civil wrong, and the public laws contained in statutes, byelaws, and the like. Such an interpretation would not include a liability of the assured which arose solely by virtue of a contract between himself and another by which he accepted responsibility for seepage, pollution or contamination. If that contractual liability arose, as it might, for example, between an operator and a contractor, it would not form the basis of a claim against the insurers. So also in the case of collision liability insurance, as set out in the Running Down Clause of the Institute Time Clauses (Hulls), at clause 1, the obligation of the insurers in respect of the liability of the assured to pay damages does not extend to a contractual liability. Thus in *Furness Withy & Co. Ltd.* v. *Duder* [29] a shipowner in hiring a tug had agreed that he would be liable for all damage to the tug, however caused. The tug, as a result of its own negligent navigation, collided with the ship. It was held that the liability of the shipowner under the contract was not covered by the Running Down Clause. [30]

The policy does not state that the assured shall be liable to pay, and shall have paid, the damages in question. It is enough, so far as these words are concerned, that the liability exists even though the sums in question have not been paid. [31] This wording thus differs from that contained in another liability insurance, the Running Down Clause, [32] in the Institute Time Clauses (Hulls). In the latter the liability of the insurers to pay the assured is said to arise if, following a collision, the assured " shall in consequence thereof become liable to pay and shall pay by way of damages . . . any sum or sums in respect of such collision . . ." of the type

---

[29] [1936] 2 K.B. 461.

[30] So also in *Hall Brothers S.S. Co. Ltd.* v. *Young* [1939] 1 K.B. 748 (C.A.) it was held that where a shipowner, who had not been negligent, paid an indemnity under French law to a pilot boat, the payment was not " by way of damages."

[31] See also p. 329, above.

[32] See above, p. 109, for a discussion of this type of liability as it appears in the London Standard Drilling Barge Form.

then set out. In the case of this pollution insurance, however, so far as it is a contract of indemnity, it could be argued that the insurers would not be liable to make a payment to the assured where he had only incurred a liability but had not discharged that liability. The liability to indemnify the assured, it might be contended, is a liability to indemnify him in respect of the financial loss suffered by him, and not to indemnify him in respect of the liability, except for the provision that the insurers may make payment on his behalf. If this were so he would not therefore be able to recover payment from the insurers himself unless he had made such payment to a third party. On the other hand, and in contradiction to these arguments, the principle enunciated in the Marine Insurance Act 1906 as section 74 is:

> " Liabilities to third parties. Where the assured has effected an insurance in express terms against any liability to a third party, the measure of indemnity, subject to any express provision in the policy,[33] is the amount paid *or payable* by him to such third party in respect of such liability."

Although the 1906 Act does not govern this policy, perhaps similar principles apply in this context; thus, in the absence of words in the policy to the contrary, we can speak of an indemnity to the assured, and his entitlement to an indemnity, even where he has not made a payment to the third party.

We come now to the nature of the injury, loss, or damage, for which the assured may be liable, and proceed then to the causes of that injury, loss or damage. The policy refers to sums which by law he is liable to pay as damages " for bodily injury (fatal or non-fatal) and/or loss of, damage to or loss of use of property." There is no restriction here, or in the exclusion clauses, upon the expression " bodily injury," so that there is insurance for liability " by law " to all persons, whether they be at or near or far away from the operations, and whether they be employees of the operator or of the contractor, or of anyone else, or have some other or indeed no legal relationship with the parties to the operations. Provided that there is a liability towards them " by law " the policy extends to their claims. As a result of the interpretation given to words such as these [34] by the courts, however, a liability of the assured which arose solely by virtue of a contract would probably not be covered. This would be the position whether the contract which imposed that liability was between the assured and the person injured or one between the assured and another party in which the assured agreed to undertake such a liability. If there is such a contract, but the assured would have been liable in any event, without there being such a contract, as a result, for example, of his negligence or the application of a government regulation, then the policy would apply.

The assured is also covered by the policy in respect of sums which he is

---

[33] Such as the words " and shall pay " in the Running Down Clause; see above, p. 113.   [34] See above, p. 330.

liable, " by law," to pay as damages for " loss of, damage to or loss of use of property." In this case the exclusions clause in the policy [35] is relevant, because it states: " The Policy does not cover loss of, damage to, loss of use or the cost of clean-up of property belonging to the Insured or in the Insured's care, custody or control."

The effect of the clause, so far as it gives cover to the assured, is that he is insured in respect of his liability, other than liability arising solely out of a contract, towards the owners of property. The term " property " can refer to real or personal property, and thus to land or chattels. It would seem that in these contexts the term is restricted to physical property; thus it does not extend to property in the widest sense of the word, when it can describe every interest which a person can have, including rights of action.

The insurance does not extend only to loss of and damage to property, but also to the liability of the assured for " loss of use of property." For example, seepage, pollution or contamination [36] may result in the owners of a pipelaying barge being unable to use it for some time, if it has to be cleaned or is otherwise immobilized. If the assured is under a legal liability towards those owners for their claim for loss of use, then he is entitled to reimbursement by his insurers. The existence of such a liability will of course depend upon the terms of any contract between the operator and the owners of the pipelaying barge.

The exclusion quoted above [37] results in the assured being unable to recover under the policy in respect of property which belongs to him or is in his care, custody or control. Where a person owns property he would not be capable of having a legal liability towards that property, as a person cannot be liable to himself. The policy may list those who are insured, however, in the following manner:

" *INSURED*
(a) [a vacant space in which the name of the operator and others may be inserted]
(b) The Contractors and/or Sub-Contractors of the Named Insured and/or any parties whom the Named Insured has agreed to hold harmless in respect of liability for bodily injury and for loss of, damage to or loss of use of property or clean-up costs pursuant to operating agreements with such parties."

When the cover itself, other than any relevant exclusion, is considered, it therefore follows that any of the " insured " would be covered for their liability to the owner of property. The insured are (at (a) above) the named insured and (at (b)) his contractors and sub-contractors, and anyone whom he has agreed to hold harmless [38] in respect of liability towards property, under operating agreements.

This last class of persons, who have been held harmless, could include the owners of helicopters, supply boats, and pipelaying barges with whom

---

[35] See below, p. 346.
[36] For the meaning of these terms see pp. 333–335, below   [37] On this page.
[38] For " hold harmless " agreements and indemnities, see above, p. 313.

the operator has concluded operating agreements. They are thus not only held harmless but brought into the policy, with the operator, its contractors and sub-contractors, as insured persons. Any one, or more, of them might incur liability towards property. That liability is covered by the insurance policy except where the exclusion applies. The exclusion, as we have seen, relates to " property belonging to the Insured or in the Insured's care, custody or control."

". . . caused by or alleged to have been caused directly or indirectly by . . ."

The damages which the insured is, by law, liable to pay must be in respect of bodily injury and/or loss of, damage to or loss of use of property which has been caused by or alleged to have been caused directly or indirectly by seepage, pollution or contamination.

The words " or alleged to have been caused " mean that as between the insurers and the insured the question of the correctness of the allegation cannot be raised. It may, for example, be alleged, against the insured, that bodily injury or property damage was caused by seepage, pollution or contamination. He may deny the allegation, arguing that such damage did not occur at all, or that, if it did occur, it was not caused by the seepage, pollution or contamination. He may nevertheless be held liable in law to pay damages. His denial, even if it may seem to be more justifiable than the allegation against him, does not prevent him from making a successful claim against the insurers. Nor does his denial entitle them to contend that the seepage, pollution or contamination were not the real cause of the bodily injury or the loss of, damage to or loss of use of property.

The words " caused directly or indirectly " indicate that the seepage, pollution or contamination may be the direct cause or the indirect cause of the bodily injury or the loss of, damage to or loss of use of property. A direct cause, as opposed to an indirect cause, is one which has produced a result without there being another cause or some event, either of which may do something to make the cause itself become other than a direct cause of the incident in question. The other cause or event need not be subsequent in time to the cause itself.[39]

". . . seepage, pollution or contamination "

These terms are not usually defined in a seepage, pollution and contamination insurance policy. It is necessary to look to the usual meanings of these words, especially as shown by their dictionary definitions, and to such definitions as have been set out in laws, judicial decisions, conventions and contracts, with the proviso that these must all be considered in the context of the situation with which they are dealing.

Among the dictionary [40] definitions which lead to an understanding of the words seepage, pollution and contamination are the following:

---

[39] Causation is discussed in more detail at p. 181, above.
[40] *Concise Oxford Dictionary.*

Seepage   To seep: " Ooze out, percolate slowly. . . . Hence -age. . . ."
Pollution   To pollute: " Destroy the purity or sanctity of; make (water etc.) foul or filthy. So pollution."

The Tanker Owners' Voluntary Agreement Covering Liability for Oil Pollution, or " Tovalop ",[41] defines " Damage by Pollution " as follows: " ' Damage by Pollution ' means physical contamination damage to Coast Lines resulting directly from a Discharge of Oil, and does not include damage from fire or explosion, consequential damage, or ecological impairment." For the present purpose the part of the definition which says what is not included can be ignored, as it is peculiar to the Tovalop agreement. The relevant words are " physical contamination damage." Neither the Tovalop definition nor those contained in the many pollution conventions [42] are binding here, but the comparison is interesting.

Contamination   To contaminate: " Pollute, infect. So contamination."

There is clearly a considerable similarity and a degree of overlapping between the meanings of pollution and contamination. If there was pollution there would usually be contamination, and vice versa, even if one term rather than the other might seem more appropriate on the occasion in question.

The word " seepage " is, in the sense in which it has been defined here, different in quality from the words " pollution " and " contamination." It relates to and describes the process by which the damaging substance emerges from its source; the other words concern damage itself and not the manner in which the polluting or contaminating agent was released. In the first case, of " seepage," the policy refers to bodily injury and loss of, damage to or loss of use of property caused by a particular form of escape. In the other two cases, of " pollution " and " contamination," the policy speaks of those consequences, and of their having been caused by pollution or contamination. Pollution and contamination, however, are, strictly speaking, the particular forms which the consequence assumes, or, to take an earlier stage, the processes by which the consequence is produced, rather than the originating process.

This interpretation of the word " seepage," however, although it seems to be in accordance with its true meaning, has to be modified as a result of the way in which the word is used later in the same clause. As we shall see below,[43] one of the two succeeding sentences refers to: ". . . the cost of removing, nullifying or cleaning up seepage, polluting or contaminating substances . . ." and the other states: " Provided always that such seepage, pollution or contamination results in a claim being made . . ." (etc.).

From this use of the word seepage, and particularly in the case of the first sentence quoted, it seems that the term should in this context be

---

[41] At cl. 1 (h).
[42] See pp. 43–51, above.
[43] See p. 335.

regarded as being descriptive of the effect of the damage, rather than the method by which the incident occurred.

There can be seepage even though the oil does not enter into the sea. Thus drilling by the insured party might cause oil to move from the insured well into a reservoir controlled by another operator, causing damage to it. The second operator would then have a claim against the insured party, which would recover under its insurance.

(b) *The Cost of Removing, Nullifying or Cleaning Up Seepage, Polluting or Contaminating Substances*

This part of the cover represents a clear contrast to the part which refers to the liability of the insured, by law, to pay damages. Where the assured incurs this cost it is possible that his action will result in a claim for damages (as set out in (a) above) [44] not being made, or, if it is made, being made for a lower sum or resulting in lower damages being awarded than would otherwise have been the case. In the Lloyd's S.G. Policy the sue and labour clause states that it is " lawful to the assured . . . to sue, labour, and travel for, in and about the defence, safeguards, and recovery of the said goods and merchandises, and ship, etc. . . ." The present clause in the seepage, pollution and contamination insurance policy gives a similar right to the assured, and entitles him to recover the cost involved.

The right of recovery under this heading would, like a claim in respect of legal liability, be subject to the retention provision by which the insured is to bear the first part of any claim and/or series of claims arising out of one event. [45]

Does recovery under the clean-up clause depend upon the existence of legal liability?

The obligation of the insurers to indemnify the insured against, or to pay on his behalf,[46] the cost of removing, nullifying or cleaning up seepage, polluting or contaminating substances is not stated, in the cover subsection itself, to be dependent upon there being a responsibility upon the insured to pay that cost. He may of course have such a responsibility as a result of a local law or a contract.

As an example of a local law, the Continental Shelf Act 1964 provides in section 5 (1) that where there is a discharge or escape of oil otherwise than from a ship " as the result of any operations for the exploration of the sea bed and subsoil or the exploitation of their natural resources in a designated area " then " the person carrying on the operations shall be guilty of an offence unless he proves . . . in the case of an escape . . . that as soon as practicable after it was discovered all reasonable steps were taken for stopping or reducing it." The existence of this potential criminal

---

[44] See p. 330.
[45] See below, p. 343.
[46] See also p. 327, above.

liability and of the defence made available results effectively in the person carrying on the operations having a responsibility, though it would not be described as a legal liability, to take " all reasonable steps . . . for stopping or reducing " the escape.

An example of a responsibility resulting from a contract may be found in the Offshore Pollution Liability Agreement, or OPOL.[47] Under this Agreement many operators agreed among themselves to accept liability to claims for escapes or discharges of oil from offshore facilities situated within the jurisdiction of certain states.[48] The claims may be in respect of pollution damage and in respect of " remedial measures." The latter are defined as being " reasonable measures . . . to prevent, mitigate or eliminate pollution damage following such discharge of oil [*i.e.* from an offshore facility] or to remove or neutralise the oil involved in such discharge. . . ." This contractual liability would result in the operator taking such remedial measures.

In the examples given the " reasonable steps," in the case of the Continental Shelf Act 1964, and the " remedial measures," in the case of OPOL, would usually involve, in the words of the policy, removal, nullifying and cleaning up the seepage, polluting or contaminating substances. As a result the insured would be able to recover the cost from the insurers even though it has been under no legal liability (other than a contractual liability in the second case) to incur that cost.

The examples given are ones in which the insured was motivated by a type of responsibility which could be expressed in legal terms, such as the avoidance of a criminal liability in the case of the 1964 Act, and the performance of a contractual liability in the case of OPOL. The cover subsection is so worded, however, that the mere fact that the insured has incurred the cost, as defined there, is sufficient to enable him to recover that cost from the insurers. His motive is not relevant. The answer to the question posed earlier, therefore, is that the right of the insured to recover under the clean-up clause does not depend upon the existence of a legal liability.

The " seepage, polluting or contaminating substances " must be ones which emanate from the operations stated in the schedule to the policy.[49] This is a necessary limitation, as it is not intended that the insured should, in respect either of liability for damages [50] or of the cost of clean-up, be insured for seepage, pollution or contamination from other operations.

In the case of the liability for damages, it is unlikely that a situation would arise in which the insured was made liable except in respect of damages arising out of his own operations. To that extent the addition of the words " arising out of the operations stated in the Schedule " is

---

[47] Dated September 4, 1974; see also below, p. 377.
[48] Denmark, France, German Federal Republic, Ireland, Netherlands, Norway, United Kingdom.
[49] See below, p. 339.
[50] See above, p. 330.

unnecessary. In the case of the cover subsection dealing with the cost of removing, nullifying or cleaning up, however, there is, as we have seen,[51] no need for there to be any legal liability upon the insured to take these measures. In the absence of limiting words, therefore, he would be able to incur the cost of such measures in respect of seepage, polluting or contaminating substances which were present in the area of his operations but had emanated from other operations. The insertion of the words " emanating from the operations stated in the Schedule " makes certain that his recovery is restricted to matters arising from these operations. It is the responsibility of other operators to conclude the insurances which they need to deal with matters arising from their own operations.

This cover subsection concludes with the words " including [52] the cost of preventing the substances reaching the shore." Such expenditure might clearly help the insured, and thus the insurers, to avoid the cost of legal liability for shore pollution. The words " removing, nullifying or cleaning up seepage, polluting or contaminating substances " would not necessarily, despite the use of the word " nullifying," include a step, such as the establishment of a protective boom round the area. which was designed to prevent the substances reaching the shore. The addition of these words makes it clear that the cost of such action is covered. The use of the words " the substances " makes it necessary to consider what substances are the subject of this reference. The words used in the first part of the sentence are " removing, nullifying or cleaning up seepage, polluting or contaminating substances." We have seen earlier [53] that although by a strict definition the word " seepage " refers to the manner of escape rather than to the result of such escape, it is probably better in the present context to look upon the escaping matter itself as constituting " seepage." If so, it is much easier to look upon each of the three actions, of removing, nullifying and cleaning up, as capable of applying to each, or to any combination of, the three matters named, *i.e.* the " seepage, polluting or contaminating substances." The final words, however, concern " the cost of preventing the substances reaching the shore." They seem to refer only to the " polluting or contaminating substances," as opposed to the " seepage." This would be an acceptable interpretation if one regarded the seepage as constituting the escaping matter at an early stage, before it constituted a polluting or contaminating substance. If the insured incurred expenditure in preventing the " seepage," as opposed to the polluting or contaminating substances, from reaching the shore, it is conceivable that there would be no cover under the policy. Despite the verbal distinction which is possible, however, it seems that in practice any preventive expenditure could not be regarded as being limited to the polluting or contaminating substances.

---

[51] Above, p. 335.
[52] As to the meaning of " includes " see above, p. 59.
[53] See above, pp. 334–335.

(4) Proviso to the Cover Clause and (5) Exception

The proviso to the cover clause appears to apply to the subsections dealing with legal liability [54] and the cost of clean up.[55] It states:

"Provided always that such seepage, pollution or contamination results in a claim being made during the period of Policy as stated in the Schedule and of which immediate notice has been given in accordance with Clause 5 hereof [56] except that any claim subsequently arising out of the circumstances referred to in such notice shall for the purpose of this Policy be deemed to have been made during the currency of this Policy."

A question may arise as to whether a "claim" means a claim by the assured against the insurers, or by a third party against the assured. It is helpful to consider the use of the word "claim" elsewhere in the policy. For example: (a) the limit of liability clause [57] refers to the insurers' limit of liability for "any one claim and/or series of claims"; (b) the retention clause [58] provides for the assured to bear a certain amount "of any claim and/or series of claims"; (c) the definition of ultimate net loss, an expression used in the limit of liability clause, refers to "the sums paid in the settlement of claims covered by this Policy"; to "costs and expenses incurred in the defence of any claim or claims"; and to "Costs and expenses of litigation awarded to any claimant against the Insured"; (d) the notice of loss clause [59] refers to "any event likely to give rise to a claim hereunder"; (e) the cost and appeals clause, referring to and echoing the words of the retention Clause, speaks of "any claim and/or series of claims"; and (f) the discovery clause [60] refers to an extension of cover "in respect of any claim or claims which may be made against the Insured."

It seems that in the proviso the expressions "a claim" and "any claim" refer to a claim against the assured by a third party. The words "a claim . . . of which immediate notice has been given in accordance with Clause 5 hereof" must be read with those in clause 5, the notice of loss clause, "any event likely to give rise to a claim hereunder." Where the policy intends to refer to a claim by a third party there are usually clear words to that effect, as in the extension of cover clause,[61] and its reference to any claim or claims "against the insured."

It follows from this conclusion that the proviso makes recovery under the cover clause conditional upon (a) the assured making his claim against the insurers within the period of the policy as stated in the Schedule [62]; and (b) by virtue of the reference to the notice of loss clause, the assured having given immediate written notice to the insurers of any event likely

---

[54] See above, p. 330.
[55] See above, p. 335.
[56] As to the need to give immediate written notice to the insurers of any event likely to give rise to a claim under the policy, see below, p. 344.
[57] See below, p. 341.   [58] See below, p. 343.   [59] See below, p. 344.
[60] See below, p. 355.   [61] See below, p. 355.
[62] Usually, therefore, before the period of 12 months has expired; see also, p. 340, below.

to give rise to a claim under the policy. If, on the other hand, the word " claim " in this context had meant a claim by a third party against the assured, then the cover afforded under the clean-up clause would have been dependent upon such a claim being made; in fact, as we have seen,[63] it is an integral part of that aspect of the insurance that the assured should be engaged in an operation of removing, nullifying and cleaning up, not only to mitigate but also to avoid a claim being made.

The proviso concludes with an exception. This is to the effect that a claim (against the insurers) which arises later than the period of the policy but out of the circumstances referred to in the immediate written notice shall be deemed to have been made during the currency of the policy.

Other Provisions of the Seepage, Pollution and Contamination Insurance Policy

The following pages deal with provisions of the seepage, pollution and contamination insurance policy other than the fundamental provisions as to cover.

The remaining provisions of the policy usually relate to or appear under the following titles:

1. Schedule.
2. Limit of Liability.
3. Retention (or Deductible)
4. Definitions.
5. Notice of Loss.
6. Salvages, Recoveries, Repayments.
7. Calculation of Premium.
8. Exclusions.
9. Costs, settlements, and Appeals against Judgments.
10. Inspection and Audit.
11. Assignment.
12. Bankruptcy.
13. Extension of Cover.
14. Warranties.
15. Expiry of Policy during Insured Event.

1. Schedule

The Schedule to the policy usually contains the following headings:

" (A) *Insured* (a) . . . [Name or names inserted here]

(b) The Contractors and/or Sub-Contractors of the Named Insured and/or any partners whom the Named Insured has agreed to hold harmless in respect of liability for bodily injury and for loss of, damage to or loss of use of property or clean-up costs pursuant to operating agreements with such parties."

---

[63] See above, p. 337.

A recital that a certain person is or that certain persons are the insured in a policy is consistent with section 23 of the Marine Insurance Act 1906, which states: " A marine policy must specify—(1) The name of the assured, or of some person who effects the insurance on his behalf. . . ." Where other parties as well as the named insured are interested, subsection (b) serves to introduce them, if they fall into either of the stated categories, which are: (i) the contractors and/or sub-contractors of the named insured; and (ii) any parties whom the named insured has agreed to hold harmless in respect of liability for the matters then mentioned.[64] These matters are those which are set out in the cover clause, or the insuring agreements, in the policy. This extension of the cover to other parties is similar to, though more restrictive than, the wording at the opening of the Lloyd's S.G. Policy: " Be it known that . . . as well in . . . own name as for and in the name and names of all and every other person or persons to whom the same doth, may, or shall appertain, in part or in all doth make assurance. . . ."

This description of the insured does not prohibit the application of the principle that one who had no original interest, *i.e.* at the time at which the insurance was concluded, may acquire an interest or, subject to the clause as to assignment of the insured's interest, have the interest assigned to him.

" (B) *Address of Insured* "

" (C) *Period of Policy*:

From:

To:

both days inclusive."

" (D) *Minimum and Deposit Premium*
　　　Basis of adjustment "

A later clause, concerning " Premium Computation and Adjustment," [65] states that the premium on the policy is a " Minimum and Deposit Premium " based on the number and categories of wells declared to the insurers at the inception of the policy.

" (E) *Operations* "

[Here the area and the nature of the operations are inserted.]

---

[64] As for the effect of hold harmless agreements, etc., see above, p. 313.
[65] See below, pp. 345–346.

2. Limit of Liability

The policy invariably contains a provision by which the liability of the insurers is limited to a specific amount. A typical clause reads:

" *Limit of Liability*

The Underwriters' limit of liability hereunder shall be . . . Ultimate Net Loss in respect of any one claim and/or series of claims arising out of one event."

The term " Ultimate Net Loss " may appear in the list of definitions [66]:

" The term ' Ultimate Net Loss ' shall be understood to mean the sums paid in the settlement of claims covered by this Policy (and after making deductions for all recoveries, salvages and other insurance [67]) and shall include Costs and expenses incurred in the defence of any claim or claims, and also Costs and expenses of litigation awarded to any claimant against the Insured." [68]

A figure, which may be of the order of $20 m.,[69] is inserted before the words " Ultimate Net Loss."

There must first be taken the amount paid in the settlement of " any one claim and/or series of claims arising out of one event." [70] Deductions are made from that amount for all recoveries, salvages and other insurance, although it is made clear by the " Application of Salvage " clause [71] that ascertainment of the Ultimate Net Loss in this way should not mean that losses are not recoverable until then. The amount is to include the costs and expenses incurred in defending any claim or claims. Such costs and expenses are thus not the subject of a separate head of claim against the insurers, but are included in and subject to the limitation figure which applies to the settlement itself. The amount, as calculated, has also to include the costs and expenses of litigation awarded to any claimant against the insured.

When the " Ultimate Net Loss " has been calculated in this manner the insurers' limit of liability is known. It is a limit in the sense that the insurers can in no circumstances be liable to pay more than that sum; but the insured could find that he is only able to recover a smaller sum, because the retention clause [72] may require the insured to bear a fixed amount or a proportion of that " Ultimate Net Loss."

The limit of liability is stated to be " in respect of any one claim and/or series of claims arising out of one event." This wording is intended to ensure that if more than one claim against the insured arises out of an

---

[66] Otherwise set out below, p. 343.
[67] For the provision as to " Salvages, Recoveries, Repayments," see below, p. 344.
[68] For the provision as to " Costs, Settlements, and Appeals against Judgments," see below, p. 352.
[69] A typical figure in 1978.
[70] Similar words are considered below, p. 352.
[71] See below, p. 344.
[72] See below, p. 343.

event the insured cannot recover the full limitation figure in respect of each such claim. It would avoid the situation which arose in *South Staffordshire Tramways Co. Ltd.* v. *Sickness and Accident Insurance Association Ltd.*,[73] where a tramcar company was insured against claims for third party liabilities, the policy stating: ". . . the Association shall pay the assured the sum of £250 in respect of any one accident." A tramcar overturned and 39 passengers were injured. The question was whether there had been one or 39 accidents for the purpose of the clause. The Court of Appeal held that there had been 39 accidents. Although there had been a " tramcar accident," the words used referred to the accident suffered by each person.

The words " any one accident or occurrence " were used in *Allen* v. *London Guarantee and Accident Co.*[74] Two people were injured in a cart accident; it was held that although there were two accidents there was only one " occurrence." In *Forney* v. *Dominion Insurance Co. Ltd.*[75] the words used in a solicitor's professional negligence policy were " any one claim or number of claims arising out of the same occurrence." These words bear a close resemblance to those used in the present clause. The High Court held that where one act of negligence had occasioned loss to several clients there had only been one " occurrence." Mr. Justice Donaldson said [76]:

> " ' Occurrences ' like accidents can be looked at from the point of view of the tortfeasor [*i.e.* the Assured] or of the victim. . . . However, the provision of the policy which limits the indemnity contemplates the possibility that a number of claims may arise out of one occurrence. This seems to me to indicate that a number may be injured by a single act of negligence—in other words that ' occurrence ' in this context is looked at from the point of view of the insured."

It is helpful to take an example. The limitation figure for the " Ultimate Net Loss " is, say, $20 m. " in respect of any one claim and/or series of claims arising out of one event." The insured is liable to pay for two separate pollution claims, of $10 m. each, and he has incurred $20 m. in respect of clean up expenses, constituting $40 m. in all. The principles to be applied seem to be that (a) the " claims " are those made by the insured against the insurers, and not by the third parties against the insured; (b) the " event," like an occurrence in the *Forney* case,[77] is looked at from the point of view of the insured. The insured has a series of three claims arising out of " seepage, pollution or contamination," *i.e.* from one, two or all of these. The two resultant pollutions and the cleaning up may have occurred in chronological succession, but if they can be regarded as having arisen out of one event, then the single limit of $20 m. will apply to, and reduce, the insured's claims for $40 m.

---

73 [1891] 1 Q.B. 402 (C.A.).
74 (1921) 28 T.L.R. 254. See also p. 135, above.
75 [1969] 1 Lloyd's Rep. 502.
76 *Ibid.* at p. 508.
77 See above on this page.

3. Retention (or Deductible)

The policy usually contains a provision by which the insured has to bear a fixed amount or a percentage of the Ultimate Net Loss [78] otherwise recoverable from the insurers.

Such a provision may read as follows:

" *Retention of the Insured*

It is understood and agreed that the Insured shall bear the first . . . Ultimate Net Loss of any claim and/or series of claims arising out of one event."

4. Definitions

It is usual for a seepage, pollution and contamination insurance policy to define certain of its terms.

(a) " *Insured* "

" The unqualified word 'Insured' includes the Named Insured, and any partner, executive officer, director or stockholder or employee thereof while acting within the scope of his duties as such."

The Schedule to the policy [79] itself provides for the insured to consist of (a) the named insured; and (b) the contractors and/or sub-contractors of the named insured and any parties whom the named insured has agreed to hold harmless under the operating agreements. This definition of " Insured " does not affect category (b) of the part of the Schedule just cited. It affects category (a), and other references to the " Insured " in the policy, by extending the rights and duties affecting the named insured to " any partner, executive officer, director or stockholder, or employee thereof," but only while acting " within the scope of his duties as such." A law might, for example, impose liability not only upon the operator itself who might be the named insured, but also upon other persons falling within the categories set out in this definition, and acting within the scope of their duties. If so, they also would have the right to recover from the insurers in respect of their liability. The reference to their acting within the scope of their duties means that if, for example, there were an act of negligence, occasioning their legal liability for oil pollution, but committed outside the scope of their duties, there would be no recovery from the insurers by them. A question would arise as to whether the named insured would be liable to the third party claimant. In such a case, where the other person was acting outside the scope of his duties, the employer is not liable for the act of negligence. As a result there would be no liability upon the insurers. The expression " the scope of his duties " must be taken to mean the same as " the scope of his employment," so far as the persons named are employees of the named insured.

---

[78] For the definition of Ultimate Net Loss see above, p. 341.
[79] See above, p. 339.

(b) " Ultimate Net Loss "

This term, which is usually included in the list of definitions, has already been discussed above in connection with the insurers' limit of liability.

(c) " Costs "

" The word ' Costs ' shall be understood to mean interest on judgments, investigation, adjustment and legal expenses (excluding, however, all expenses for salaried employees and retained counsel of and all office expenses of the Insured)."

It is necessary to define the word " Costs " because it is used elsewhere in this policy. In particular, it appears in (a) the definition of " Ultimate Net Loss," [80] which is said to include " Costs and expenses " incurred in defending claims and " Cost and expenses " of litigation awarded to the insured; (b) the Costs and Appeals Clause, with its reference to the need to obtain the consent of the insurers to the incurring of costs. The effect of the exclusion is that the insured has to bear certain costs which he would have had to incur in any event. If, for example, a salaried employee were to devote a part of his time to the claims in question, the insured could not, as a result of this exclusion, recover from the insurers a proportion of his salary. The same principle applies to a counsel, or lawyer, who is not a full-time employee but is on a retainer from the insured. The expenditure would have been incurred by the insured in any event. So also the office expenses of the insured are excluded, though they may have been augmented by virtue of the event. It is conceivable that a situation could arise in which the insured might, as a result, find it to be in his interest to incur outside legal expenses, rather than to devote the services of his retained counsel to the problem. The costs, however, would usually form a relatively small proportion of the sums in issue.

5. Notice of Loss

The clause by which the insured is obliged to give notice to the insurers of a possible claim may read as follows:

" *Notice of Loss*:
The Insured upon knowledge of any event likely to give rise to a claim hereunder shall give immediate written notice thereof to Underwriters."

6. Salvages, Recoveries, Repayments

The insurance policy may provide that the insured should give credit to the insurers for any sums received by or credited to him after the loss has been settled by the insurers. The following clause may be used:

" *Application of Salvage*
All salvages, recoveries or repayments recovered or received subsequent to a loss settlement under this Policy, shall be applied as if recovered or

---

[80] See above, p. 341.

received prior to such settlement, and all necessary adjustments shall then be made between the Insured and Underwriters, provided always that nothing in this clause shall be construed to mean that losses under this Policy are not recoverable until the Insured's Ultimate Net Loss [81] has been fully ascertained."

The insured is entitled to recover from the insurers the loss which he has suffered in accordance with the cover clause, or the insuring agreements,[82] when he has suffered them. After the settlement of his loss the insured may recover or receive " salvages, recoveries or repayments." In the context of this insurance the word " salvages " does not at first seem apt. One can take it to refer to financial or physical benefits accruing from the expenditure which he has incurred. The cost of a boom might form part of his claim for sue and labour expenses, but he now has it for possible future use. Such an item might fall under this heading. The word " recoveries " includes recoveries which the insured has been able to make from other parties who were partly or wholly liable for the event which caused the loss. The word " repayments " includes repayments of money by virtue of any adjustments which might be made with others, such as those engaged in clean up operations, who received money from the insured.

All such recoveries or receipts have to be taken into account as if they had been recovered or received before the loss settlement, and the necessary adjustments are then made between the insured and the insurers.

The clause can be viewed as an application of the underlying principle of indemnity and its corollary of subrogation which are fundamental to a contract of insurance. As Bowen L.J. said in *Castellain* v. *Preston* [83]:

" What is the principle which must be applied? It is a corollary of the great law of indemnity, and is to the following effect: That a person who wishes to recover for and is paid by the insurers as for a total loss, cannot take with both hands. If he has a means of diminishing the loss, the result of the use of those means belongs to the underwriters. If he does diminish the loss, he he must account for the diminution to the underwriters."

The insured will therefore take the recoveries or receipts as trustee for the insurers, subject to deduction only of such sums as were necessarily expended by him in order to achieve these recoveries or receipts.

7. Calculation of Premium

The basis of adjustment of the premium is set out in the Schedule to the policy.[84] The premium is, as we have seen, based upon the number and categories of wells declared. The " Premium Computation and Adjustment " clause sets out the method used:

---

[81] For a definition of Ultimate Net Loss see above, p. 341.
[82] See above, p. 327.
[83] (1883) 11 Q.B.D. 380 (C.A.), at p. 388.
[84] See above, p. 339.

" Premium Computation and Adjustment

The premium hereon is a Minimum and Deposit Premium [84] based on the number and categories of wells declared to Underwriters at inception. If during the period of this Policy the Insured drills any additional wells, Underwriters agree to cover such additional wells subject full details being given to Underwriters prior to the commencement of drilling and the payment of any additional premium as may be required by Underwriters. Upon expiration of this Policy the Insured shall furnish Underwriters with a statement of the number and categories of wells covered hereunder and the actual earned premium shall be computed thereon at the premium stipulated in the schedule. If the actual earned premium is more than the minimum and deposit premium the Insured shall pay the difference to Underwriters."

The provisions for an additional premium, in the event that the insured drills any additional wells, are that full details should be given to the insurers and that the insured must pay " any additional premium as may be required." This may be contrasted with section 31 (2) of the Marine Insurance Act 1906:

" Where an insurance is effected on the terms that an additional premium is to be arranged in a given event, and that event happens but no arrangement is made, then a reasonable additional premium is payable."

In the present case the insured has not to pay an arranged additional premium, which would be a reasonable additional premium if no arrangement or agreement were reached, but such additional premium " as may be required." It is arguable that this could involve an objective test as to what was, as an actuarial problem, needed by the insurers; or even that it enables the insurers to state and to obtain a sum assessed by them without the necessity to show that it is objectively necessary. It is more probable that the clause should be regarded as containing an implied term that the additional premium must be, like the premium to be arranged (but not arranged) under section 31 (2), a reasonable premium.

8. Exclusions

Certain exclusions are usually inserted in the seepage, pollution and contamination insurance policy. They may be expressed in the following manner:

(a) Fines and Penalties

" No liability shall attach to Underwriters hereunder in respect of any fines or penalties, which shall be deemed to include but not restricted to punitive or exemplary damages, imposed under the laws of any state or country."

The provision in the cover clause, or insuring agreements,[85] that the insurers would indemnify the insured in respect of all sums which the insured " shall by law be liable to pay as damages " for matters arising out of the operations stated in the Schedule might be taken to include fines or

---

[85] See above, p. 327.

penalties. Under some systems of law there is a clear distinction between (a) civil damages payable to a third party, including a government, for breach of a duty established by the common law of tort or by law created by the government or other authority; and (b) fines and penalties imposed by a part of the law identifiable as relating to criminal offences and similar contraventions. The distinction is not always clear, however, and this exclusion clause makes clear that which might not otherwise be clear from the cover clause. Fines and penalties imposed on the insured under the laws of any state [86] or country are not recoverable from the insurers. " Punitive or exemplary damages " are usually damages assessed in excess of the actual damages suffered so as to express the sense of outrage felt by the court; to punish the offender; and to deter others by the example given. Where the court or other body imposing the fine or penalty uses its powers to order that the insured should pay punitive or exemplary damages, then they also are excluded from the cover. Apart from any penal proceedings, however, there may be a civil action in which the court awards such damages. This clause seems to preclude him from recovery under the policy, even if he argued that part of the damages would have been awarded in any event.

(b) Double Insurance

The exclusion clause may state:

> " This Policy does not cover any liability which is insured by or would, but for the existence of this Policy, be insured by any other existing insurance(s) except in respect of any excess beyond the amount which would have been payable under such other insurance(s) had this Policy not been effected."

There may be another insurance policy which, on its face, covers the insured in respect of the same matters. It may therefore be possible to speak, in the words used above, of a liability " which is insured by . . . any other existing insurance(s)." That other policy may itself, however, contain a similar clause by which its own cover is not to apply if another policy exists. Such a possibility accounts for the words ". . . or would, but for the existence of this Policy, be insured by any other existing insurance(s). . . ." In neither event does the existing policy cover the insured. In the first case the other policy would assume the liability. In the second case it seems that neither policy would do so and the insured would be left uncovered. If so he could not be said to be doubly insured, or insured at all.

Double insurance is defined in section 43 (1) of the Marine Insurance Act 1906:

> " Where two or more policies are effected by or on behalf of the assured on the same adventure and interest or any part thereof and the sums insured exceed the indemnity allowed by this Act, the assured is said to be over-insured by double insurance."

---

[86] This can mean a sovereign state, in which case it is synonymous with the word " country " as used here; alternatively, in the U.S.A. for example, it may mean one of the constituent states.

The Act allows for the possibility that the situation so arising may be dealt with by an agreement in the policy, for section 32 (2) states:

> " Where the assured is over-insured by double insurance—(a) The assured, unless the policy otherwise provides, may claim payment from the insurers in such order as he may think fit, provided that he is not entitled to receive any sum in excess of the indemnity allowed by this Act."

In the present case " the policy otherwise provides," because it says that apart from the excess it does not cover this liability. It would not therefore be open to the insured to include this insurer among those against whom he claims " in such order as he may think fit."

(c) Insured's Property

> " The Policy does not cover loss of, damage to, loss of use or the cost of clean-up of property belonging to the Insured or in the Insured's care, custody or control."

This typical clause excludes from the insurance any liability of the insurers which might otherwise arise under the cover clause, or insuring agreements, so far as these agreements extend to (a) loss or damage to, loss of use of property belonging to, or in the care, custody or control of the insured; and (b) clean up of such property.

The clause has been set out, in these last lines, in this form, to reflect the two parts, (a) and (b), of the cover clause itself.[87] It then becomes easier to ascertain how far this exclusion affects that cover.

The first part, (a), of the cover clause, extends to such liability of the insured not only towards property but also for bodily injury, whether fatal or non-fatal. An individual could not have a liability towards his own property, because an individual, not being able to sue himself, cannot be liable towards himself. As there is usually more than one insured, however, an insured might incur a legal liability towards another of the insured in respect of property belonging to the latter. That liability is not covered. It is as if the clause referred to property belonging to " an insured." A similar exclusion applies in respect of property which does not belong to an insured but is in his care, custody or control.[88] Such property may belong to one of the contractors or sub-contractors of the named insured, or to one of the parties whom the named insured has agreed to hold harmless in respect of the liabilities set out in the cover clause. If so, the owners of the property would in any event be an insured by virtue of the description of the insured at (A) (b) in the Schedule,[89] and excluded from recovery in any event by the exclusion relating to property of the insured.

The second part, (b), of the cover clause, extends to the cost of removing, nullifying or cleaning up seepage, polluting or contaminating substances.[90]

---

[87] See above p. 327.
[88] Often abbreviated to " c.c.c."
[89] See above, p. 339.
[90] See above, p. 335.

The exclusion clause removes from the cover " the cost of clean up of property belonging to the Insured or in the Insured's care, custody or control." So far as the clean-up of " seepage,[91] polluting or contaminating substances " is not clean-up of such property then the cover clause remains effective. There may, for example, be an escape of oil, as a result of which costs are incurred in cleaning up the surrounding waters, a support boat, a supply ship, the nets of some nearby fishermen and the unit itself. The cover under the policy continues, unaffected, in respect of such of these items of property as do not belong to, or are not in the care, custody or control of an assured. In the example given only the clean-up costs in respect of the waters and the nets might be covered.

The other matters covered under part (b), which are the costs of " removing " and " nullifying " the seepage, polluting or contaminating substances, are not removed from the cover by the exclusion clause, the words of which relate only to the cost of " clean up." It is not always easy to distinguish a cost of clean up from costs of removing and nullifying. In a colloquial sense of the expression a " clean up " might be regarded as including the whole operation of " removing, nullifying or cleaning up." If that were the correct legal interpretation then the exclusion clause would relate to, and suspend the insurers' liability for, everything under part (b) of the cover clause so far as concerns property belonging to or in the care, custody or control of the insured. That is not, however, what is said.

(d) Cost of Control

" This Policy does not cover any of the cost of controlling a well nor the cost of drilling relief wells whether or not the relief well be successful."

It is possible that some of the costs incurred under part (b) of the cover clause, or insuring agreements, in removing, nullifying or cleaning up seepage, polluting or contaminating substances, could also be described as costs of controlling a well or of drilling a relief well. The same action which occasioned the expense may result, for example, in both nullifying the seepage and controlling the well, as the outflow of oil would be brought to an end. This exclusion is designed to ensure that such expenditure, where two objects are achieved, would not be covered by this policy. They would fall instead under the cost of control insurance policy, which provides for the reimbursement of the insured for the expenses of regaining control of a well.[92]

The exclusion also extends to " the cost of drilling relief wells whether or not the relief well be successful," though the cost might otherwise qualify as a " cost of removing, nullifying or cleaning up seepage, polluting or contaminating substances." In this case also the cost of drilling relief wells will usually be recoverable under the cost of control insurance policy,[93]

---

[91] As to the meaning of seepage, see pp. 333–335, above.
[92] See below, Chap. 9.
[93] See below, p. 427.

so far as that cost is part of the cost of regaining control of the well or wells declared under that policy.

(e) *War, Invasion, etc.*

" This Policy does not cover any claims directly or indirectly happening through or in consequence of war, invasion, act of foreign enemies, hostilities (whether war be declared or not), civil war, rebellion, revolution, insurrection or military or usurped power."

The claims thus excluded are those " directly or indirectly happening through or in consequence of " the nine matters then mentioned. There is a general resemblance between this clause, the Free of Capture and Seizure Clause in the London Standard Drilling Barge Form,[94] and the similar exclusion clause in the cost of control insurance policy.[95]

(f) *Intentional or Illegal Seepage, Pollution or Contamination*

" This Policy does not cover any claims arising directly or indirectly from seepage, pollution or contamination if such seepage, pollution or contamination
(i) is intended from the standpoint of the Insured or any other person or organisation acting for or on behalf of the Insured, or
(ii) results directly from any condition in violation of or non-compliance with any governmental rule, regulation or law applicable thereto."

This exclusion affects both part (a) of the cover clause, or insuring agreements, which deals with legal liability, and part (b) thereof, which deals with the cost of removing, nullifying or cleaning up seepage, polluting or contaminating substances. In both cases there are excluded claims arising from seepage, pollution or contamination where the latter (i) is intended, subject to certain limitations or (ii) results " from any condition in violation of or non-compliance with " certain legal requirements.

As for (i), above, the insured is unable to recover, as a result of this exclusion, if the seepage, pollution or contamination is " intended." So far as the law presumes that a person intends the natural consequences of his actions, this exclusion might be thought to affect any pollution resulting from an action of the assured, though this is not presumably the intention of the parties.

If this were a policy to which the Marine Insurance Act 1906 applied, the event which gives rise to a possible claim might be one excluded from the cover if it fell within the words of section 55 (2) (a):

" The insurer is not liable for any loss attributable to the wilful misconduct of the assured but, unless the policy otherwise provides, he is liable for any loss proximately caused by a peril insured against, even though the loss would not have happened but for the misconduct or negligence of the master or crew ";

The test there is whether there was wilful misconduct by the assured.

---

[94] See above, Chap. 3.   [95] See above, p. 408.

The exception clause speaks of seepage, pollution or contamination which " is intended from the standpoint of the Insured or any other person or organisation acting for or on behalf of the Insured." A situation might arise in which it is argued that " intended from the standpoint of . . ." has a different meaning from " intended by. . . ." In practice the two expressions seem to have the same meaning. It is a matter for consideration whether the exception should be restricted to cases in which there was action akin to wilful misconduct by the assured; or where there was actual fault or privity [96-97]; or whether the principle that he was presumed to intend the natural consequences of his actions should be modified.

As for (ii) above, the insured is unable to recover, as a result of this exclusion, if the seepage, pollution or contamination results directly " from any condition in violation of or non-compliance with any governmental rule, regulation or law applicable thereto." A condition, in this context, means the state of affairs, or the situation, or the circumstances. Where the condition is in violation of or non-compliance with the matters mentioned, the exclusion applies. For example, there may be a breach of governmental rules as to safety. A claim which would otherwise arise is excluded by this provision. The word " governmental " means that the rules, regulations and laws not only of central governmental but also of local governments are affected by this exclusion. In the U.S.A. the word " government " includes federal, state and county authorities. In the United Kingdom the word includes the central government and the local authorities, whether they be counties, boroughs or other authorities.

(g) *Carriage of Oil, etc., by Watercraft*

" This Policy does not cover any claims arising directly out of the transportation of oil or other similar substances by watercraft."

The effect of this exclusion is that an escape or spillage of " oil or other similar substances " being carried by watercraft is not covered by the policy. The seepage, pollution or contamination must arise " out of the operations stated in the Schedule." [98] The operations are defined in the manner stated above,[99] but this exclusion prevents recovery by the insured in respect of the matters stated. A claim against one of the insured may arise out of such transportation. It might arise against him if he was the owner of the watercraft, and also one of the insured under this policy, as a contractor and/or sub-contractor of the named insured.[1] As a result of this exclusion he would have to look elsewhere for reimbursement. He might have a right of indemnity against the operator [2] or, alternatively, a claim under his own insurance.

[96-97] To use the term employed in s. 503 of the Merchant Shipping Act 1894, where a shipowner is given certain rights of limitation of liability where various casualties occur without his actual fault or privity.

[98] See the cover clause, above, p. 327.   [99] At p. 340.

[1] See the comments on the Sched. above, p. 339.   [2] See above, p. 272.

9. Costs, Settlements, and Appeals Against Judgments

The policy may provide for the insurers to have some control over expenditure on costs, where their interests are likely to be affected; over any settlement; and over any appeal. A typical clause reads:

> " In the event of any claim and/or series of claims arising out of one event where the Ultimate Net Loss is likely to exceed the retention of the Insured, no Costs [3] shall be incurred on behalf of Underwriters without the consent of Underwriters, and if such consent is given, Underwriters shall consider such Costs as part of the Ultimate Net Loss. No settlement of losses by agreement shall be effected by the Insured where the Ultimate Net Loss will exceed the retention of the Insured without the consent of Underwriters.
>
> In the event that the Insured elects not to appeal against a judgment in excess of the retention of the Insured, Underwriters may elect to conduct such appeal at their own cost and expense, and shall be liable for the taxable cost and interest incidental thereto, but in no event shall the liability of Underwriters for Ultimate Net Loss exceed the limit of liability stated in Clause 2 [4] hereof and in addition the costs and expense of such appeal."

It follows from the first sentence of this clause that the insured can incur costs where the ultimate net loss is not likely to exceed the retention of the insured. If, either upon the occurrence of a claim or at any later date, that loss is likely to exceed the retention the insured must obtain the consent of the insurers if the costs to be incurred will be on behalf of the insurers, in the sense that the insured wishes to recover those costs from them. If and when the insurers agree, then the costs form part of the ultimate net loss. Thus they do not form a separate category of claim but are included in the assessment of the ultimate net loss and in the processes by which the retention of the insured [5] and the limit of liability of the insurers [6] are calculated.

The second sentence of the clause, relating to the settlement of losses by agreement (*i.e.* otherwise than by a decision of the court or of arbitrators) provides that the insured must obtain the consent of the insurers if " the Ultimate Net Loss will exceed the retention of the Insured."

The third sentence of the clause relates to an appeal against a judgment given for a sum in excess of the retention of the insured. It would seem that for this purpose a " judgment " includes a decision of a court and of an arbitration tribunal. If the insured elects to appeal against the judgment, the further costs which may be incurred would be caught by the wording of the first sentence, so that he would have to obtain the consent of the insurers. If he elects not to appeal, the sentence empowers the insurers to " elect to conduct such appeal at their own cost and expense." They are in consequence also to be liable " for the taxable cost and interest incidental thereto. . . ." The taxation of costs is the process by which an official of

---

[3] See definition above at p. 344.
[4] See above, p. 341.
[5] See above, p. 343.
[6] See above, p. 341.

the court, after a decision or an agreement as to which party or parties are to bear the costs, may, in the absence of agreement between the parties, assess the costs and decide how much is properly recoverable, bearing in mind how much it was reasonable to expend. In addition the insurers are to bear any interest incidental to the appeal, if they elect to proceed with the appeal. This will be the interest which attaches to any amount awarded against the insured, and which may have been increased as a result of the extra time involved in the appeal.

The final words of the third sentence, ". . . and in addition the costs and expense of such appeal," mean that the costs and expense of the appeal will be borne by the insurers as a separate item, apart from the limit set out in the limit of liability clause.[7]

10. Inspection and Audit

The insurers are usually given certain powers of inspection of the insured's premises and other related areas and items, and of examination of the insured's books. These powers are sometimes expressed as follows:

> " Underwriters shall be permitted at all reasonable times during the period of this Policy, to inspect the premises, plants, works, machinery and appliances used in connection with the Insured's trade, business or work, and to examine the Insured's books at any time during the currency hereof and within one year after the expiration of this Policy so far as they relate to the subject-matter of this Policy."

11. Assignment

It is usual to provide that the rights of the insured under this policy are those of the insured alone and that no purported transfer of interest from the insured is effective unless the insurers agree thereto in the manner prescribed in the policy. A clause to this effect may read as follows:

> " Nothing herein contained shall give any rights against Underwriters to any person or persons other than the Insured, and Underwriters shall not be bound by any trust assignment transfer or devolution of interest of the Insured, unless and until Underwriters shall by endorsement declare the insurance to be continued for the benefit of other person or persons."

This provision is more restrictive so far as the rights of the insured are concerned than that which is envisaged by section 50 (1) of the Marine Insurance Act 1906 in the case of marine policies:

> " A marine policy is assignable unless it contains terms expressly prohibiting assignment. It may be assigned either before or after loss."

and by the opening words of section 50 (2) thereof:

> " Where a marine policy has been assigned so as to pass the beneficial interest in such policy, the assignee of the policy is entitled to sue thereon in his own name . . ."

---

[7] See above, p. 341.

By an assignment the insured by a positive action purports to vest his rights in the assignee. The present clause relates not only to a mere assignment but also to a trust, transfer or devolution (as, for example, in the case of a liquidation [8]) of the interest of the insured. The condition for the effectiveness of such a passing of rights is that the insurers should " by endorsement " declare the insurance to be continued for the benefit of another or others. This need for the insurers to express their consent constitutes an exception to the general rule, though some American policies require the agreement of the insurers to any assignment. The words used in Arnould on *Marine Insurance* [9] in this connection are:

> " Unless the policy (as is usually the case in policies issued to their members by mutual insurance associations [10]) imposes such a condition, the consent of the underwriter is never necessary to the validity of an assignment of it."

Section 50 (3) of the 1906 Act refers to endorsement, by stating:

> " A marine policy may be assigned by endorsement thereon or in any other customary manner ";

but the endorsement there contemplated is one which it is for the assignor (the insured) rather than the insurers, as in the case of the present clause, to endorse on the policy.

There is a comparable provision in the Institute Time Clauses (Hulls),[11] by which " No assignment of or interest in [the policy] . . . is to be binding on or recognised by the Underwriters unless a dated notice of such assignment of interest signed by the Assured, and by the assignor in the case of subsequent assignment, is endorsed on this policy. . . ." It is thus the endorsement by the insured, and subsequent assignors, which is necessary in such a case, and not that of the insurers, as in the case of the seepage, pollution and contamination insurance.

12. Bankruptcy

A typical clause states:

> " It is expressly agreed that in the event of bankruptcy or insolvency of the Insured Underwriters shall not be relieved of the payment of such indemnity as would have been payable but for such bankruptcy or insolvency."

This provision may be read in conjunction with that which relates to the assignment of rights.[12] By that clause the endorsement of the insurers was necessary before they were bound by, among other things, any

---

[8] As to bankruptcy, see below, on this page.

[9] (15th ed., 1961), para. 236.

[10] " No insurance given by the Association and no interest arising under these Rules or under any contract between the Association and any Owner may be assigned without the written consent of the Managers who shall have the right in their absolute discretion to give or refuse such consent . . ."; rule 10 (A) of the Rules of the United Kingdom Mutual Steam Ship Assurance Association (Bermuda) Ltd.

[11] cl. 22.

[12] See above, p. 353.

" transfer or devolution of interest of the Insured." The insured or one of the insured may have a valid claim for an indemnity under the policy, but may have become bankrupt or insolvent. The fact that he is bankrupt or insolvent would not of itself preclude the insured from his right to an indemnity, but this clause makes it clear that the liability of the insurers continues. If the bankruptcy or the insolvency had proceeded to the stage at which the liquidator of the insured had succeeded to the insured's rights, this provision would presumably override the one in the assignment clause by which an endorsement by the insurers is necessary if the insurers are to be bound by a " devolution."

13. Extension of Cover

The policy may provide for an extension of cover in the event of non-renewal of the policy, so that the insured may be protected, but the extension is limited to incidents which occurred before the policy period ended. Thus:

> " In the event of non-renewal of this Policy either by the Underwriters or the Insured, the Insured shall have the right to an extension of the cover granted by this Policy, in respect of any claim or claims which may be made against the Insured during the period of 90 days after the date upon which the Policy period ends, but only in respect of any incident that occurred before such date."

It is necessary to consider what would have been the position in the absence of such a clause, and in the event that a claim was made after the end of the policy period but in respect of an incident which occurred before that date. Under the cover clause [13] a claim must, to be recoverable, be one which is made during the period of the policy and of which immediate notice had been given; except that any claim arising thereafter out of the circumstances referred to in the notice shall be deemed to have been made during the currency of the policy. It was suggested, in the discussion of that clause,[14] that the word " claim " in that context meant a claim by a third party against the insured, and not a claim by the insured against the insurers.

Let us suppose, then, that the policy has expired. If a claim had been made during the period of the policy, immediate notice having also been given of the event likely to give rise to the claim,[15] then the cover is unaffected. If a claim is made after the period of the policy, the cover is also unaffected, provided that it arises out of the circumstances referred to in the immediate notice. That claim, so far as the cover clause is concerned, may be made at any time, *i.e.* before or after the expiry of 90 days from the end of the policy period, provided that the immediate notice had been given.

---

[13] See above, p. 327.
[14] See above, p. 338.
[15] See the notice of loss clause, above, p. 344.

14. Warranties

Certain express warranties,[16] relating to the duty of the insured to avoid or to minimise a claim, may be included in the policy. Thus:

> " It is warranted that the Insured will use every endeavour to ensure that they and or their Contractors comply with all regulations and requirements in respect of fitting blow-out preventers, storm chokes and other equipment to minimise damage or pollution.
>
> It is also warranted that in the event of a blow-out or other escape of oil, the Insured will use every endeavour to control well or stop the escape."

The insured is not under an absolute obligation to ensure that he and/or his contractors do the things mentioned, but he must " use every endeavour " to do so. The reference to " all regulations and requirements " appears to embrace not only the regulations imposed by law but also requirements imposed by authorities other than governments and other similarly established bodies. Thus the appropriate registry [17] may impose requirements as to the maintenance of the drilling unit. So also, apart from such formalised requirements which may be common to all drilling units of a certain type, the insured and/or his contractors may be subject, by contract, to obligations in respect of the matters mentioned. The contractor may have warranted, as for example under the London Standard Drilling Barge Form, that the well or hole will be equipped with " a minimum of three pressure operated blowout preventers." This and other contracted liabilities may amount to " requirements " for the purpose of this clause.

The second part of the clause relates to the duty of the insured in the event of a blowout [18] or other escape of oil. He must then use every endeavour to control the well or stop the escape.

These requirements are consistent with the obligation set out in section 78 (4) of the Marine Insurance Act 1906, which applies to marine policies.[19] The subsection states: " It is the duty of the assured and his agents, in all cases, to take such measures as may be reasonable for the purpose of averting or minimising a loss." The clause, by its references first to compliance with regulations and requirements and then to the control of the well and stopping the escape, embraces the concepts both of " averting " and of " minimising " the loss.

15. Expiry of Policy during Insured Event

It is usual for the policy to provide for the possibility that it will expire while the seepage, pollution or contamination is occurring, or while costs are being incurred for removing, nullifying or cleaning up seepage, polluting or contaminating substances.[20] It may do so in the following words:

---

[16] As to the significance of a warranty, see above, p. 99.
[17] As to registry, see above, p. 51.   [18] For a definition see above, p. 128.
[19] As to this problem see Appendix C to this book, at p. 456.
[20] See the cover clause above, p. 327.

" If this Policy should expire while an insured event is in progress, it is understood and agreed that Underwriters, subject to all other terms and conditions of this Policy, are responsible as if the entire loss had occurred prior to the expiration of this insurance."

This wording is similar to that contained in the Period of Insurance Clause in the London Standard Drilling Barge Form.[21] The differences are that the present clause uses the words (a) " while an insured event is in progress "; and the L.S.D.B. Form states: " while an accident or occurrence giving rise to a loss is in progress "; (b) " Underwriters, subject to all other terms and conditions of this Policy, are responsible as if the entire loss had occurred prior to the expiration of this insurance "; and the L.S.D.B. Form states: " Underwriters shall be liable as if the whole loss had occurred during the currency of this insurance."

The effect of the two provisions is, however, the same, and the reader is referred to the earlier discussion of these words.[22]

C. OIL INSURANCE LTD. (O.I.L.)

This mutual insurance company was established in Bermuda in 1970 [22a] by over 30 companies constituting or representing oil company interests. The Recital to the shareholders' agreement stated:

" The Company was formed because there was no longer available to petroleum companies on terms consistent with sound business practice commercial insurance covering substantial risks including catastrophe coverage for on-shore and off-shore property, pollution, and bringing under control wild oil or gas wells or extinguishing oil or gas well fires. In view of the magnitude of these risks in the petroleum industry, the Company was formed as a mutual type insurance company to provide reasonable and effective insurance and reinsurance coverage."

It will be recalled that the Santa Barbara Channel pollution had occurred in the previous year [22b]; as a result conditions in the insurance markets had become more stringent in a number of ways. In the following pages the nature of the cover afforded by O.I.L. is discussed. The policy extends not only to pollution but also to the cost of removal of debris and the cost of control. Although these last two matters, so far as they are covered by insurance policies generally, are discussed elsewhere,[22c] it is more appropriate in the case of O.I.L. to deal with all the heads of cover together. The policy states, as Condition S: " This policy shall be interpreted and construed under the laws of the State of New York "; but any disputes between the assured and the underwriter are to be determined in London under the provisions of the Arbitration Act 1950, as amended, by a board of three arbitrators.

---

[21] See above, p. 87.   [22] See above, pp. 87–88.
[22a] The circumstances in which its founders felt that such a step was appropriate are set out at p. 325, above.
[22b] See also p. 325, above.
[22c] Removal of debris at p. 388; cost of control at p. 394.

O.I.L.

The nature of the indemnity provided by O.I.L. to its assureds is shown in its insurance policy, which states the three categories of risk in respect of which cover is given. The material words, for the purpose of the indemnity itself, are set out under the heading of " Insuring Agreements ":

> " In consideration of the premium stated herein, the Underwriter [O.I.L.] does hereby agree with the Policyholder [*i.e.* the company or companies named in the policy] and its non-consolidated subsidiaries and affiliates included for coverage under paragraphs 2, 3, and 4 above,[23] both independently and as participants in joint ventures with others (hereinafter called the ' Assured ')."

There then follow three numbered sections, each beginning with the words " To indemnify." They may be summarised as follows:

1. An indemnity in respect of all risks of direct physical loss or damage to property.[24]

2. An indemnity in respect of:
   (a) sue and labour expenses;
   (b) cost of control expenses;
   (c) removal of debris expenses.[25]

3. An indemnity (or an agreement to pay on behalf of the assured) in respect of the liability of the assured, arising from the law generally or by contract, and out of seepage, pollution or contamination.[26]

1. Physical Loss or Damage to Property [26a]

The first undertaking, by way of indemnity, is in the following terms:

> " To indemnify the Assured for all risks of direct physical loss or damage, caused by an occurrence, to property of any kind or description wherever located, owned by the Assured, or to non-owned property in which the Assured has an insurable interest. An insurable interest for the purposes of this provision shall be deemed to exist with respect to leases, security agreements and other contractual arrangements under which the Assured has the use or actual or constructive possession of property or has assumed the liability for loss to property or has the obligation to insure property. . . [There follow two further sentences dealing with the exclusion of ' non-owned property ' from the insurance.[27]] "

The liability of O.I.L. is thus at the outset, in the first sentence of this section, stated to be a liability to indemnify the assured. This is consistent with the basic principle of a contract of marine insurance,[28] as set out in the Marine Insurance Act 1906 at section 1, that it is " a contract whereby the

---

[23] In a section entitled " Named Insured."
[24] See below, pp. 358–360.
[25] For these see below, p. 365.
[26] See below, p. 367.
[26a] As to the application or non-application of the insurance to drilling units see below under " Exclusion of ships from basic O.I.L. cover," at p. 368.
[27] These are set out below, at p. 360.
[28] As to which see Appendix C to this book, at p. 456.

insurer undertakes to indemnify the assured. . . ." The assured being entitled to an indemnity, it follows that a person with no interest in the property insured would not be one who needed, or would be entitled, to an indemnity, because he could not suffer a loss. Indeed the 1906 Act at section 4 declares void any contract of marine insurance if the assured has not an insurable interest and the contract was entered into with no expectation of such an interest being acquired. It achieves this result by the statements at section 4 (2) (*a*) that such a contract " is deemed to be a gaming or wagering contract " and at section 4 (1) that: " Every contract of marine insurance by way of gaming or wagering is void."

The first sentence of this first section then goes on to state that cover is afforded to the assured in respect of his owned property, or property not owned by him but in which he has an insurable interest.

The second sentence of the section then stipulates certain situations in which an insurable interest should be deemed to exist. These situations, such as the one in which the assured is the lessee of property, are ones in which he is not the owner. The first sentence has already stated that, provided that he has an insurable interest in the property, he need not be the owner. The words used in the second sentence do not constitute a definition of an insurable interest but instead make it clear that in certain situations, where an insurable interest would not have existed or where there might otherwise have been doubt, there is an insurable interest. In the Marine Insurance Act 1906, which forms a useful standard of comparison, the term " insurable interest " is dealt with in section 5, which states:

> " (1) Subject to the provisions of this Act, every person has an insurable interest who is interested in a marine adventure.
> (2) In particular a person is interested in a marine adventure where he stands in any legal or equitable relation to the adventure or to any insurable property at risk therein, in consequence of which he may benefit by the safety or due arrival of insurable property, or may be prejudiced by its loss, or by damage thereto, or by the detention thereof, or may incur liability in respect thereof."

How far does the requirement in the O.I.L. policy that there should be an insurable interest, which is then amplified by words which set out certain cases in which an insurable interest " shall be deemed to exist," resemble the definition of insurable interest set out in section 5 (2) of the 1906 Act? The basic requirement in the O.I.L. policy as to an insurable interest is the same as that in a marine policy. The second sentence first refers to the existence of leases, security agreements and other contractual arrangements and, secondly, refers to the assured having as a result either (a) the use or actual or constructive possession of property or (b) assumed either the liability for the loss of property or the obligation to insure property. It seems that the wording of section 5 (2) of the 1906 Act would in any event be wide enough to cover any situation in which the assured had the use or actual or constructive possession of property, *i.e.*

(a) above, as a result of such leases, agreements and other contractual arrangements. This would be so because the benefit or prejudice, or liability, specified in section 5 (2) could arise. It also seems that the wording of section 5 (2) would be wide enough to cover a situation in which the assured had assumed the liability for the loss of property or the obligation to insure property. This would be so because the liability specified in section 5 (2) could arise.

The last two sentences of this first section provide for the exclusion from the insurance of " non-owned property ". They state:

> " By a written notice to the Underwriter specifying the property and its actual cash value, the Assured may elect to have excluded from the insurance provided for in this insuring agreement any non-owned property. Any such election may be rescinded only with the consent of the Underwriter."

2. (a) Sue and Labour Expenses; (b) Cost of Control Expenses; (c) Removal of Debris Expenses

The second undertaking, or insuring agreement, as to the indemnity of the assured by O.I.L. is in respect of sue and labour expenses, cost of control expenses, and removal of debris expenses.

(a) Sue and Labour Expenses

The undertaking, so far as it relates to sue and labour expenses, is in the following terms:

> " 2. To indemnify or pay on behalf of the Assured any sum or sums which the Assured may be obligated to pay or incurs as expenses, on account of
>   a. Sue and Labor Expense arising from an occurrence [29] covered hereunder."

The term " Sue and Labor Expenses " is also mentioned in a later part of the O.I.L. policy, under " Conditions," where Condition B reads:

> " In case of loss or damage or imminent loss or damage hereunder, it shall be lawful and necessary for the Assured, his, its or their factors, servants and assigns to sue labor and travel for, in and about the defense, safeguard and recovery of the insured property, or any part thereof without prejudice to this insurance, nor shall the act of the Assured or the Underwriter in recovering, saving and/or preserving the insured property in case of disaster be considered a waiver or an acceptance of abandonment.[30]

Condition B both entitles and obliges (" it shall be lawful and necessary ") the assured to take steps to defend, safeguard and recover the insured property, or any part of it. It differs in an important respect from the Sue and Labour clause in the Lloyd's S.G. Policy which it resembles in other respects. The Lloyd's S.G. Policy clause and the O.I.L. clauses can be compared as follows:

---

[29] For this term see p. 364.

[30] For a comparable clause in the London Standard Drilling Barge Form, see p. 154, above. As the American spelling (*e.g.* labor, defense) appears in the policy it is also used here where the clauses themselves are quoted, but not in the text generally.

(1)   *Lloyd's*   *O.I.L.*
" *And in case of any loss or misfortune*   " *In case of loss or damage or imminent*
. . ."   *loss or damage hereunder . . .*"

The essential difference here is that the more general expression, " any loss or misfortune," is replaced by the more precise words "loss or damage or imminent loss or damage." In both cases, however, it is clear that the Sue and Labour clause only applies when the insured subject-matter is exposed to a risk which, if it caused loss or damage, would be the subject of recovery under the policy. This is also stated in the Marine Insurance Act 1906, at section 78 (3):

> " Expenses incurred for the purpose of averting or diminishing any loss not covered by the policy are not recoverable under the suing and labouring clause."

If, for example, the assured had made the election, available to him under the O.I.L. policy, to exclude from the insurance any non-owned property,[31] then expenses of a Sue and Labour nature, but concerning the safeguarding of the non-owned property, would not be recoverable. The position would be the same as that arising under a marine insurance policy in respect of a ship, if the insurance was warranted free of particular average, and expenses were incurred by the assured to reduce or to minimise particular average. In such a case, however, sue and labour expenses are recoverable if as a result a total loss is avoided. In *Kidston* v. *Empire Insurance Co.*,[32] for example, an insurance on chartered freight was warranted free of particular average. As a result of sea damage the ship became a constructive total loss, and the shipowner incurred expenses in forwarding the cargo to its destination, so as to earn, in full, the insured chartered freight. It was held that he could recover the expenses under the Sue and Labour clause.

2)   *Lloyd's*   *O.I.L.*
". . . *it shall be lawful to the assured*   ". . . *it shall be lawful and necessary for*
[*and others*] "   *the Assured* [*and others*] "

The addition, in the O.I.L. policy, of the words "and necessary" place an express duty on the assured to take these actions. The view has been expressed, however,[33] that although the language of the Lloyd's S.G. policy itself is only permissive, " it has long been settled that it is a clear duty of the assured so to labour for the recovery and restitution of the detained or damaged property." A duty of this nature is set out in the Marine Insurance Act 1906, at section 78 (4):

---

[31] See above, p. 360.
[32] (1866) L.R. 1 C.P. 535; affirmed (1867) L.R. 2 C.P. 357.
[33] In Arnould on *Marine Insurance* (15th ed., 1961), at para. 32. This was also the view of Arnould himself, *i.e.* in the two editions which he wrote. See the 1st ed. (1848) vol. 1, p. 35.

" It is the duty of the assured and his agents, in all cases, to take such measures as may be reasonable for the purpose of averting or minimising a loss."

The duty arises after the occurrence which may give rise to a claim. This proposition is supported by section 78 (3):

" Expenses incurred for the purpose of averting or diminishing any loss not covered by the policy are not recoverable under the suing and labouring clause."

So far as the provision in the O.I.L. policy concerns an obligation to take protective steps in respect of the property, it does not alter the duty which would apply in the case of a marine insurance policy.

(3) *Lloyd's*	*O.I.L.*
" the assured, their factors,[34] servants, and assigns,"	" the Assured, his, its or their factors, servants and assigns "

The categories of person who have the right and the duty to sue and labour are the same in each case, the only difference being the added care in the use of the possessive pronoun, *i.e.* " his, its or their " instead of merely " their."

(4) *Lloyd's*	*O.I.L.*
" to sue, labour, and travel, for, in and about the defence, safeguards, and Recovery of the said Goods and merchandises, and ship, etc., or any part thereof, ..."	" to sue, labor and travel for, in and about the defense, safeguard and recovery of the insured property, or any part thereof. . . ."

The wording is identical, those drafting the O.I.L. policy having clearly decided to adopt words which have been the subject of interpretation by the English courts for many years, with the exception of course of the subject-matter insured, which is described merely as " the insured property."

(5) *Lloyd's*	*O.I.L.*
". . . without prejudice to this insurance; [there follow words relating to the amount of contribution by the insurers [35]] And it is especially declared and agreed that no acts of the insurer or insured in recovering, saving, or preserving the property insured shall be considered as a waiver, or acceptance of abandonment."	" without prejudice to this insurance, nor shall the act of the Assured or the Underwriter in recovering, saving and/or preserving the insured property in case of disaster be considered a waiver or an acceptance of abandonment."

It was once thought that the assured might, if he took measures to rescue or repair the insured property, prejudice his right to abandon the property.

---

[34] A factor is defined in the *Concise Oxford Dictionary* as " Agent, deputy; merchant buying & selling on commission. . . ."   [35] See below, p. 363.

At that stage it might of course be too soon for him to be able to forecast whether the property might eventually have to be abandoned. To ensure that he could and would take these preventive or remedial actions, the words " without prejudice to this insurance " were inserted in the Lloyd's policy. In the O.I.L. policy the same words are used. In both cases the two sentences in question represent the conclusions set out above, so that the assured shall not be regarded as waiving the right to abandonment, nor O.I.L. be regarded as accepting abandonment. There is no material difference between the respective sentences in the two policies dealing with this situation. In both cases there is a reference to acts of the insurer or the insured; in both cases the acts are said to be in respect of recovering, saving or preserving the property [36]; and in both cases it is provided that such action shall not be considered to be a waiver or an acceptance of abandonment. The O.I.L. policy inserts the proviso " in case of disaster."

In the above section [37] it has been possible to analyse the condition [38] in the O.I.L. policy relating to sue and labour expenses, and to compare it with the similar provision in the Lloyd's policy. The assured's right to recovery in respect of " *Sue and Labor Expense arising from an occurrence covered hereunder . . .*" and the corresponding right to recover, in the case of the Lloyd's policy, are contained in the words which follow " without prejudice to this insurance "; and which are: ". . . *to the charges whereof we, the assurers, will contribute each one according to the rate and quantity of his sum herein assured.*"

(b) Cost of Control Expenses [39]

The undertaking, so far as it relates to cost of control expenses, is in the following terms:

> " 2. To indemnify or pay on behalf of the Assured any sum or sums which the Assured may be liable to pay or incurs as expenses, on account of: . . .
> b. Bringing under control an oil or gas well that is out of control, where such circumstance arises from an occurrence, or extinguishing an oil or gas well fire where such fire arises from an occurrence. These expenses include, but are not limited to, the value of materials and supplies consumed in the operation, rental of equipment, fees of individuals, firms, or corporations specialising in fire fighting and/or the control of oil or gas wells, and cost of drilling direction relief well(s) necessary to bring the well(s) under control or to extinguish the fire. This shall further include any expenses incurred in respect of fighting a fire endangering or involving property insured hereunder."

This is a type of cover which is not comparable to anything in the Lloyd's S.G. Policy and Institute Time Clauses. The insurer is agreeing to pay certain expenses incurred by the assured, but they are not incurred in

---

[36] Though the O.I.L. policy employs the words " and/or," *i.e.* " recovering, saving and/or preserving."

[37] pp. 360–363. [38] Condition B.

[39] For a form of words used on the market see Chap. 9, below.

order to replace or repair an insured property, and are therefore not akin to the moneys payable when there is a total loss of or particular average to the insured property. Nor are they sue and labour expenses, because they are incurred not in order to avoid or minimise damage to an insured property, but, essentially, to control the well or to extinguish a fire. The expenses may as an incidental result protect an insured property; if so, it would be immaterial whether, in the course of making a claim, the assured were to designate them as sue and labour or as cost of control expenses. Indeed the closing words of 2b confirm this view by stating that this head of cover includes expenses incurred in fighting a fire endangering or involving insured property.

Although it is not necessary that there should be loss of or damage to an insured property, or, necessarily, expenses incurred to avoid such loss or damage, the loss of control or the fire must have arisen from " an occurrence." All the insuring agreements have this in common, in that " an occurrence " is a necessary condition for recovery from the insurer. According to condition C: " The word ' occurrence '. . . means an event or a continuous or repeated exposure to conditions which commence during the term of this insurance and cause personal injury or bodily injury or loss or damage to property, or a condition covered by insuring agreement 2b or 2c, that is neither expected nor intended by the Assured." The references to " personal injury or bodily injury or loss or damage to property " relate to the first and third insuring agreements, which deal, respectively, with property loss or damage " caused by an occurrence " and with personal injury or bodily injury " caused by an occurrence." As for cost of control expenses, under 2b, the relevant words of the definition thus appear to be: " The word ' occurrence '. . . means . . . a condition covered by insuring agreement 2b. . . ." The effect of the reference in 2b itself to " an occurrence " makes this definition at first seem to be somewhat circular. In practice, by limiting cost of control expenses to those occasioned by an occurrence it also restricts them in certain other ways set out in condition C, which defines " occurrence." These restrictions include the requirement that the occurrence be neither expected nor intended by the assured and that a series of losses attributable to one accident, event or cause should be added together and treated as one occurrence.

Although there are several exclusions in the policy, the majority of which apply to all three insuring agreements, exclusion 14 deals specifically with cost of control expenses. It excludes: " With respect to insuring agreement 2b, bodily injury, damage to property of others, loss of hole, and all expense of conditioning well(s) to resume drilling operations." These words thus relate to two categories of liability and two categories of expense. The two latter categories are clearly regarded as being of a commercial nature and thus more properly to be borne by the assured himself.

Sue and Labour Expenses

(c) Removal of Debris Expenses [40]

The undertaking, so far as it relates to removal of debris expenses, is in the following terms:

> " 2. To indemnify or pay on behalf of the Assured any sum or sums which the Assured may be liable to pay or incurs as expenses, on account of: . . .
> c. Removal of Debris of property covered hereunder or which the Assured is legally obligated to remove, where such Debris arises from an occurrence, including expenses incurred for the purpose of complying with laws, regulations or orders of any governmental authority or agency or instrumentality thereof specifically including but not limited to the United States Coast Guard."

The liability must be in respect of the property insured, or, if the property is not insured by the policy, there must be a legal liability upon the assured to remove the debris. Those responsible for the wording clearly envisaged a situation in which the assured had not insured the property " hereunder," but nevertheless had an obligation to remove the debris thereof. Such an obligation could be imposed by a law or other regulation, created by a public authority, or by a contract. In the latter case the contract would usually be the operating contract, the operator having undertaken, towards the contractor, the responsibility for removal of the debris,[41] or the leasing agreement. As the word " debris " is not defined in the O.I.L. policy, it can be taken in its common sense, to mean the " Scattered fragments, wreckage, drifted accumulation " [42] of the property. It could thus mean part or all of the property.

The pre-condition for recovery is that the presence of the debris should have arisen " from an occurrence." As in the case of the cost of control expenses,[43] condition C is helpful in so far as it defines occurrence to mean " a condition covered by insuring agreement . . . 2c. . . ." In other words it refers back to Insuring Agreement 2c, which contains the agreement to indemnify in respect of removal of debris expenses.

Insuring agreement 2c itself refers expressly to " Removal." The comparable provision in a Protecting and Indemnity Club cover would refer to

> " Costs and expenses of or incidental to the raising, removal, destruction, lighting or marking of the wreck of an entered ship, when such raising, removal, destruction, lighting or marking is compulsory by law or the costs thereof are legally recoverable from the Owner. . . ." [44]

In the cases both of the O.I.L. policy and the P. and I. Club cover the assured is covered in respect of the expenses of removal itself, whether incurred by him or by others, if he is liable for them. In both cases also

---

[40] For a form of words used on the market see p. 388, below.
[41] See for example, p. 271, above.
[42] *Concise Oxford Dictionary.*
[43] See above, p. 364.
[44] Rule 34 (18) " Removal of Wreck," of the Rules of the United Kingdom Mutual Steam Ship Assurance Association (Bermuda) Ltd.

he is covered whether the obligation arises by law or is otherwise legally recoverable from him. The difference between the two covers appears at first to be in respect of expenses relating to the insured property, and not incurred in respect of the removal itself, but in respect of other matters, of which destruction, lighting and marking are those specified in the P. and I. cover.

However, Insuring Agreement 2c continues by stating that the sums which the assured may be obligated to pay or incurs as expenses include " expenses incurred for the purpose of complying with laws, regulations or orders of any governmental authority or agency or instrumentality thereof. . . ." If such laws, regulations or orders require the assured to incur expenses in respect of the destruction, lighting or marking of the debris, would those expenses be recoverable from O.I.L. even though they were not incurred in the course of removal of the debris? It would seem that they would not be recoverable, if the word " including " is used only to introduce examples of matters which would in any event be covered by 2c in the absence of those examples.

It is arguable, however, that the word " including " may be taken to indicate that the words following it serve to define, rather than to exemplify, the term " Removal of Debris." If this is so, then the O.I.L. policy covers the assured in respect of such expenses as the expenses of destruction, lighting or marking of the debris. It would indeed include any expenses incurred if they were for the purpose of complying with such laws, etc., provided, it would seem, that the expenses were occasioned by the existence of the debris itself. Such an interpretation would not only afford the assured cover similar to that given to a shipowner or other assured in the case of a wreck; it would also be consistent with the obligation incurred by law and by contract, so far as the operator is concerned, in so far as he is liable to destroy, light or mark the debris.

The addition of the words " specifically including but not limited to the United States Coast Guard " makes it clear that it should, if there were any doubt as to the matter, be regarded as a " governmental authority or agency or instrumentality."

The insuring agreement refers, as has been pointed out above, to sums which the assured has agreed in writing to assume, provided that they were incurred in the manner set out. The Offshore Pollution Liability Agreement, or OPOL,[44a] may be regarded as such an agreement. There is however a specific Opol Endorsement (Endorsement No. 3) to the O.I.L. policy. Its material words are :

> " Notwithstanding any other provision of this policy but subject to the applicable annual aggregate and deductible provisions and Conditions H and I hereof, the Underwriter agrees to indemnify or pay on behalf of the Named Insured any sum or sums the Assured is required, directly or indirectly, to pay pursuant to the provisions of the Offshore Pollution

---

[44a] See p. 377, below.

Liability Agreement or the Articles of Association of the Offshore Pollution Liability Association Limited as such are in effect from time to time: provided, however, that no change in such Agreement or Articles made after September 12, 1975, shall operate to enlarge the liability of the Underwriter hereunder; provided, however, that a change made solely to increase the territorial application of such Agreement or Articles shall not be deemed to enlarge the liability of the Underwriters. . . . ''

3. Seepage, Pollution or Contamination Liability [45]

The third undertaking, or insuring agreement, as to the indemnity of the assured by O.I.L. is in respect of liability arising out of seepage, pollution or contamination. The undertaking is in the following terms:

" 3. To indemnify or pay on behalf of the Assured any sum or sums for which the Assured may be legally liable, or has agreed in writing prior to a loss to assume for the benefit of others, excluding subsidiaries and affiliates, as a result of personal injury or bodily injury, including death, or loss of or damage to, including loss of use thereof, property of any kind or description other than property insured under insuring agreement 1 arising out of seepage, pollution or contamination caused by an occurrence, provided, however, coverage under this insuring agreement shall be in excess of the limits of all other of the Assured's insurance policies, which are then in force to insure its liability for seepage, pollution or contamination."

The liability of the assured may arise " legally," *i.e.* as a result of a law, regulation or order of a public authority. Alternatively his liability may result from his having " agreed in writing," as, for example, by contract, to assume a liability for the benefit of others. The latter expression does not seem to exclude a unilateral promise to undertake a liability, even though a contract is not concluded, provided that the promise is in writing and it is made before the loss.

The sum or sums for which the assured may be liable, or which he has agreed in writing to assume,[46] must be " a result of personal injury or bodily injury, including death, or loss of or damage to, including loss of use thereof, property. . . ." The injury, loss or damage must, in their turn, be matters " arising out of seepage, pollution or contamination," and the contamination must be " caused by an occurrence." This chain of causation, therefore, with the original cause given first, and the links being given as arrows, can be set out as follows: "an occurrence"——→"seepage, pollution or contamination " (caused by the occurrence)——→injury, loss or damage (" arising out of " the seepage, pollution or contamination)——→liability for a sum or sums (" a result of " the injury, loss, or damage).

The proviso at the end of Insuring Agreement 3 has the effect that account must be taken of all the other insurance policies which the

---

[45] For a form of words used on the market see p. 327, above.

[46] It seems that the Insuring Agreement is saying that the assured is " to assume " the sum or sums, though the wording is not entirely clear at this point. It may have been the intention that it should state that he assumes *liability* for such sums.

assured may have in respect of liability for seepage, pollution and contamination. The coverage given by Insuring Agreement 3 is to be in respect of such amounts as are in excess of the cover given by such other policies.

Exclusion of ships from basic O.I.L. cover

Insuring Agreement 1 refers to loss of or damage to " property of any kind or description . . . owned by the Assured," and Insuring Agreement 3 refers to the liability of the assured arising out of seepage, pollution or contamination. On the face of these Insuring Agreements, therefore, it would be possible for the assured to expect that the O.I.L. policy would cover him in respect of loss of or damage to his ship, and liability for seepage, pollution or contamination caused by his ships. So also under Insuring Agreement 2c, dealing with removal of debris, it might be assumed that there was cover for liability for removal of the wreck of a ship owned by the assured.

Exclusion 1 makes it clear that it was not the object of the O.I.L. policy, as such,[47] to afford cover in respect of ships owned by the assured. Exclusion 1a, referring to Insuring Agreements 1 (property owned by the assured) and 2 (sue and labour expenses, cost of control expenses, and removal of debris expenses), excludes " With respect to insuring agreements 1 and 2, watercraft (vessels) owned, chartered or used by the Assured, excepting watercraft used in oil, gas and other mineral exploration, drilling and producing operations." Only such watercraft as were engaged in the operations of exploration, drilling and producing could be covered by the O.I.L. policy. Others, engaged in normal commercial operations, would have to be covered by other means for such matters as hull insurance and wreck removal.

Similarly, exclusion 1b, referring to Insuring Agreement 3 (liability for seepage, pollution or contamination), excludes

> " With respect to insuring agreement 3, any liability of the Assured as an owner, operating agent of an owner,or bareboat charterer of:
> (1) watercraft classified as a tank vessel designed and constructed for the carriage by sea in bulk of crude petroleum and hydrocarbon fuels and oils derived therefrom; and
> (2) vessels enrolled or eligible for enrolment in TOVALOP.[48] "

The effect of exclusion 1b is to exclude from the seepage, pollution or contamination cover afforded by the O.I.L. policy any shipowner's liability (or liability as an operating agent or bareboat charterer) of the assured, so

---

[47] Endorsement No. 4, Watercraft (Vessel) Endorsement, provides that for an additional premium, and notwithstanding exclusion 1a, watercraft, *i.e.* vessels, of the assured may be insured. The assured provides an annual schedule which " must include all Vessels owned by or under bareboat charter to the Assured, except towboats and barges."

[48] Tanker Owners' Voluntary Agreement Concerning Liability For Oil Pollution.

far as his tankers, as therein defined, are concerned. The description given under (1) may be compared with the definition of " Tanker " given in Tovalop. The latter agreement states, under " Definitions ":

> " ' Tanker ' means any sea-going vessel and any sea-borne craft of any type whatsoever, designed and constructed for carrying Oil in bulk as cargo, whether or not it is actually so carrying Oil."

The agreement also defines " Oil ": " ' Oil ' means any persistent hydrocarbon mineral oil such as crude oil, fuel oil, heavy diesel oil and lubricating oil whether or not carried as cargo."

Other exclusions from the O.I.L. policy

Certain categories of loss are excluded from the whole of the O.I.L. policy. These exclusions are in addition to the exclusion of water-craft, other than those used in oil, gas and other mineral exploration, drilling and producing operations, by exclusion 1a, and tankers by exclusion 1b.[49] The remaining 17 exclusions may be summarised in the following categories:

(a) Loss resulting from actions by governments, armed forces, and other similar bodies or individuals.

(b) Crude oil, natural gas, or other minerals in situ, prior to initial recovery.

(c) Loss of hire.

(d) Inherent defect, wear and tear, deterioration, expansion or contraction, and defects in design, workmanship and material.

(e) Failure to save and preserve the property.

(f) Use and occupancy or business interruption loss.

(g) Confiscation and expropriation.

(h) Waste products.

(i) Fines and penalties.

(*a*)[50] *Loss resulting from actions by governments, armed forces, and other similar bodies or individuals.*

Such loss may be incurred in respect of (i) *offshore*[51] *properties* or (ii) *onshore properties*[50] of the assured.

(*i*) *Offshore properties.* So far as these properties are concerned, the exclusion (exclusion 2) set out in the O.I.L. policy is similar to that contained in the Free of Capture and Seizure clause in the Institute Time Clauses (Hulls).[52-53] Exclusion 2 excludes:

---

[49] See p. 368, above.
[50] See p. 374, below.
[51] See pp. 369–374.
[52-53] Clause 23.

Liabilities

" Loss, damage or expense in respect of ' Offshore ' properties (including hulls *and cargoes*) of the Assured caused by or resulting from: capture, seizure, arrest, restraint or detainment, or the consequences thereof or of any attempt thereat, or any taking of the vessel or property, by requisition or otherwise, whether in time of peace or war and whether lawful or otherwise, by or under the order of any government (whether civil, military or de facto) or public or local authority; also from all consequences of hostilities or warlike operations (whether there be a declaration of war or not), but the foregoing shall not exclude collision or contact with aircraft, rockets or similar missiles, or with any fixed or floating object, stranding, heavy weather, fire or explosion unless caused directly (and independently of the nature of the voyage or service which the vessel concerned or, in the case of a collision, any other vessel involved therein, is performing) by a hostile act by or against a belligerent power, and for the purpose of this policy ' power ' includes any authority maintaining naval, military or air forces in association with a power; also whether in time of peace or war—from all loss, damage or expense caused by any weapon of war employing atomic or nuclear fission and/or fusion or other reaction or radioactive force or matter, or from the consequences of civil war, revolution, rebellion, in-surrection, or civil strife arising therefrom. Nothing contained in this Exclusion 2 shall be held to exclude loss caused by any act or acts com-mitted by one or more persons, whether or not agents of a sovereign Power, for political or terrorist or other purposes and whether the loss or damage resulting therefrom is accidental or intentional, provided that: (i) such person or persons are not acting on behalf of a Government, governmental authority or power (usurped or otherwise) which exercises de facto juris-diction over part or all of the populated land area of the country in which the described property is situated; and (ii) if such person or persons are acting as an agent or agents of any government recognised de jure by a majority of Belgium, Canada, France, Italy, the United Kingdom and the United States, such person or persons are acting secretly and not in connection with the operation of regular military or naval armed forces in the country where the described property is situated."

By contrast, clauses 23 to 25 of the Institute Time Clauses (Hulls) state:

" 23. Warranted free of capture, seizure, arrest, restraint or detainment, and the consequences thereof or of any attempt thereat; also from the conse-quences of hostilities or warlike operations, whether there be a declaration of war or not; but this warranty shall not exclude collision, contact with any fixed or floating object (other than a mine or torpedo), stranding, heavy weather or fire unless caused directly (and independently of the nature of the voyage or service which the Vessel concerned or, in the case of a collision, any other vessel involved therein, is performing) by a hostile act by or against a belligerent power; and for the purpose of this warranty ' power ' includes any authority maintaining naval, military or air forces in association with a power.
Further warranted free from the consequences of civil war, revolution, rebellion, insurrection, or civil strife arising therefrom, or piracy.
24. Warranted free from loss damage liability or expense arising from:
    (a) the detonation of an explosive
    (b) any weapon of war and caused by any person acting maliciously or from a political motive.

370

" 25. Warranted free from loss damage liability or expense arising from any weapon of war employing atomic or nuclear fission &/or fusion or other like reaction or radioactive force or matter."

The exclusions in exclusion 2 and in clauses 23 to 25 of the Institute Time Clauses (Hulls) are broadly similar. The material differences are that:

1. Exclusion 2 also excludes

" any taking of the vessel or property, by requisition or otherwise, whether in time of peace or war and whether lawful or otherwise, by or under the order of any government (whether civil, military or de facto) or public or local authority. . . ."

The expression " taking " is also to be found in the Lloyd's S.G. Policy, where among the matters covered are " takings at sea." This term includes situations in which a ship is taken into port for examination. This would usually occur in wartime, when a neutral ship would be examined for contraband. It could also take place in peacetime if a government were so minded. The Lloyd's policy cannot be considered on its own, however, because the Free of Capture and Seizure clause, appearing as clause 23 of the Institute Time Clauses (Hulls) is normally added; the cover given by the word " taking " is thus modified or removed by the words " Warranted free of capture, seizure, arrest, restraint or detainment. . . ."

The effect of the Free of Capture and Seizure clause on the Lloyd's policy is not necessarily the same as that of the exclusion of " taking " on the O.I.L. policy. There may be a taking which does not constitute a capture. This is because the term " capture " may mean only belligerent capture.[54] If there was a peaceful " taking " with no intent to deprive the owner of his property, then the Lloyd's policy might well cover the consequent loss, whereas the O.I.L. policy would not cover it, as a result of the exclusion of " taking."

2. Exclusion 2, in referring to the vessel or property, and the consequences of hostilities or warlike operations, states that such references " shall not exclude collision or contact with aircraft, rockets or similar missiles, or with any fixed or floating object. . . ." The comparable wording in clause 23 of the Institute Time Clauses (Hulls) is: " shall not exclude collision, contact with any fixed or floating object (other than a mine or torpedo). . . ." Mines and torpedoes are thus excluded from clause 23, which would otherwise admit them as a result of the words " shall not exclude." They are not, however, excluded by comparable words in exclusion 2. As for " aircraft, rockets or similar missiles " these are admitted by the express words of exclusion 2, but not admitted by clause 23, since the latter only opens its exception to take in " any fixed or floating object (other than a mine or torpedo)."

---

[54] *Mauran* v. *Insurance Co.* (1767) 6 Wall. 1.

3. Exclusion 2 excludes " the consequences of civil war, revolution, rebellion, insurrection or civil strife arising therefrom." The comparable words of exclusion in clause 23 of the Institute Time Clauses (Hulls) (the Free of Capture and Seizure clause) are: " the consequences of civil war, revolution, rebellion, insurrection, or civil strife arising therefrom, or piracy." The insertion of the words " or piracy " serves to remove the cover otherwise given in the Lloyd's S.G. Policy, where the list of insured perils includes piracy, in the expression: ". . . they are of the seas, men of war, fire, enemies, pirates, rovers, thieves. . . ."

Rule 8 of the Marine Insurance Act 1906 [55] states: " The term ' pirates ' includes passengers who mutiny and rioters who attack the ship from the shore." This is not an exhaustive definition; it is possible to envisage an act of piracy which is not necessarily committed by those who fall within this definition, so that the exclusion of piracy in clause 23 does more than exclude acts by those defined in rule 8. Losses from piracy, being excluded generally from marine policies, are normally only recoverable under war risks policies.

The O.I.L. policy, by not excluding piracy, makes possible a recovery by the assured in respect of loss, damages or expense caused by or resulting from piracy, provided that the said loss, damage or expense fell within the cover afforded by one of the three Insuring Agreements.[56]

4. The last sentence in exclusion 2 [57] says that nothing in the exclusion " shall be held to exclude loss caused by any act or acts committed by one or more persons, whether or not agents of a sovereign power, for political or terrorist or other purposes and whether the loss or damage resulting therefrom is accidental or intentional. . . ." The proviso thereto [58] is to the effect that the exclusions in exclusion 2 may still apply if (i) such persons are acting on behalf of a government, governmental authority or power exercising *de facto* jurisdiction over part or all of the populated land area of the country in which the described property is situated [59]; and (ii) if such person or persons are acting as an agent or agents of any government recognised de jure by a majority of Belgium, Canada, France, Italy, the United Kingdom and the United States (*i.e.* four out of the six), they are acting secretly and not in connection with

---

[55] Contained in the " Rules for Construction of Policy," in the First Schedule to the Act.

[56] See above, p. 358.

[57] See above, p. 370.

[58] See above, p. 370.

[59] Exclusion 2 relates to offshore properties, so that this can raise a question of law as to whether the offshore mobile drilling unit concerned is " situated " in the country in question.

the regular forces in the country where the described property is situated.

Loss caused for " political or terrorist or other purposes " is thus covered by the O.I.L. policy, if it falls within one of the three Insuring Agreements and is not occasioned by those acting for a government, as defined in the proviso.

Clause 24 of the Institute Time Clauses (Hulls), on the other hand, excludes " loss damage liability or expense arising from: (a) the detonation of an explosive (b) any weapon of war and caused by any person acting maliciously or from a political motive." Loss caused " for political or terrorist or other purposes," to use the description of the acts admitted by exclusion 2, would almost certainly be excluded by a policy to which clause 24 was attached. An act by a terrorist or another person, even if for some reason it was not political, would almost certainly be regarded as having been done " maliciously." Even if he had an honest belief in his cause, whether it were that of a group or his own personal campaign, it seems that an act such as the detonation of an explosive or the use of a weapon of war would almost certainly be held to be malicious. To that extent the use of the word " maliciously " might be thought to be superfluous, but a rare situation might arise in which " loss damage liability or expense " might arise from one of these two causes, but not be caused maliciously. The words in exclusion 2, however, in admitting that there is cover for acts of a political nature, say merely that the acts should be " for political or terrorist or other purposes." They need not be malicious. If the act is committed as part of the campaign waged by or on behalf of an individual, it might still be regarded as " political " if its aim was to influence the actions of a government, as, for example, by releasing an individual. There is also the possibility that the terrorist was merely negligent.

5. Exclusion 2 excludes, whether in time of peace or war, loss, damage or expense " caused by any weapon of war employing atomic or nuclear fission and/or fusion or other reaction or radioactive force or matter. . . ." This must be distinguished from the usual nuclear exclusion clauses, which exclude loss, damage or expense caused by nuclear reaction or radiation and other related matters.[60]

The comparable provision in the Institute Time Clauses (Hulls) is that contained in clause 25, stating: " Warranted free from loss damage liability or expense arising from any weapon of war employing atomic or nuclear fission and/or fusion or other like reaction or radioactive force or matter."

---

[60] As in exclusion 4b.

Apart from the omission in exclusion 2 of the word " like " before the word " reaction," the exclusions are in the same terms. The omission is unlikely to make any difference since the words " or other reaction," following immediately the words " nuclear fission and/or fusion," are likely to be construed in accordance with the *ejusdem generis* principle; this requires that where there is a particular description, followed by general words, the scope of the latter will be confined to matters of the same class, or genus, as that to which the preceding items belong.

(*ii*) *Onshore properties.* These properties are outside the scope of this work. It is sufficient therefore to say that exclusion 3 of the O.I.L. policy excludes from the cover loss in respect of onshore properties caused directly or indirectly by (1) enemy attack by armed forces; (2) invasion; (3) insurrection; (4) rebellion; (5) revolution; (6) civil war; (7) usurped power; (8) any discharge, explosion or use of any weapon of war employing atomic fission, fusion or radioactive force.

(*b*) [61] *Crude oil, natural gas, or other minerals in situ, prior to initial recovery*

The O.I.L. policy does not, as a result of exclusion 5, apply to " Crude oil, natural gas, or other minerals *in situ,* prior to initial recovery above ground." Insuring Agreement 1,[62] for example, with its cover in respect of loss or damage of property of the assured, does not extend to a loss of crude oil belonging to the assured if it has not yet appeared above the ground. So also Insuring Agreement 3,[63] with its cover in respect of liability as a result of damage to property arising out of seepage, pollution or contamination, does not extend to such seepage, pollution or contamination by crude oil which has not yet appeared above the ground.

(*c*) *Loss of hire*

The O.I.L. policy does not, as a result of exclusion 7, apply to " Any loss of hire of vessels, aircraft or vehicles." The assured can lose hire as the result of an otherwise insured loss in that he either (a) ceases for a period to be able to let out a vessel, aircraft or vehicle as a result of an otherwise insured loss, and consequently fails to receive hire; or (b) continues to be bound to pay hire, for a period, to the owner of a vessel, aircraft or vehicle, and consequently achieves nothing in return for his expenditure of hire money. It is arguable that both categories are covered.

Where a shipowner insures " Time Charter Hire or Charter Hire for Series of Voyages," as a permitted additional insurance under clause 20 (4) of the Institute Time Clauses (Hulls), he is insured only in respect of hire which he does not receive as a result of the operation of the insured peril.

---

[61] For (*a*), see above, p. 369.
[62] See above, p. 358.
[63] See above, p. 367.

(*d*) *Inherent defect, wear and tear, deterioration, expansion or contraction, and defects in design, workmanship and material*

   (i) The O.I.L. policy does not, as a result of exclusion 8, apply to

   " Any loss, damage, or expense caused by or resulting from inherent defect, wear and tear, gradual deterioration or expansion or contraction due to changes of temperature, unless resulting in the collapse of the property or a material part thereof, but not excluding resultant physical loss or damage to the remaining property or to other property insured hereunder."

   If loss is suffered as a result of an inherent defect, for example, it would not be covered unless the property as a whole, or a material part of it, collapsed. It would appear that where there is a collapse of the property, or of a material part thereof, the exception to the exclusion does not apply unless the other property affected was insured. It would, for example, not be possible, where the assured was covered by Insuring Agreements 2 and 3, and not by Insuring Agreement 1 in respect of property, for him to recover under those Agreements merely because there had been such a collapse.

   In the Institute Time Clauses (Hulls), clause 7, the Inchmaree clause, extends the insurance, by subsection (a) thereof, to include loss of or damage to the subject-matter insured directly caused by, among other matters, " bursting of boilers breakage of shafts or any latent defect in the machinery or hull," provided that such loss or damage has not resulted from want of due diligence by the assured or the owners or managers.

   (ii) The O.I.L. policy does not, as a result of exclusion 9, apply to " cost of repairing or replacing that portion of property which is defective in design, workmanship, or material."

   It has been pointed out [64] that in the case of ships covered by the Institute Time Clauses (Hulls) the Inchmaree clause covers " any latent defect in the machinery or hull." Nevertheless it is settled law that the insurers thereunder are not liable for the cost of replacing any part of the machinery or hull which may have broken or become unserviceable owing to a latent defect unless the defect arose during the currency of the policy. Their liability is then to meet the cost of the damage caused, and not the cost of remedying the defect itself.[64]

(*e*) *Failure to save and preserve the property*

   The O.I.L. policy does not, as a result of exclusion 10, apply to

   " Loss or damage to property caused by or resulting from the neglect of the Assured to use reasonable means to save and preserve the property at the time of and after any disaster or peril insured against."

   This exclusion may be compared with the provision in section 78 (4) of the Marine Insurance Act 1906: " It is the duty of the assured and his agents, in all cases, to take such measures as may be reasonable for the

---

[64] *Scindia Steamships (London) Ltd.* v. *London Assurance* [1937] 1 K.B. 639.

purpose of averting or minimising a loss." The reference to reasonable measures is similar to that contained in exclusion 10, and the object, which is to avert and to minimise a loss, is also similar to that set out in exclusion 10, namely to save and preserve the property. Exclusion 10, in this exposition of the usual construction of the Sue and Labour clause, also makes it clear that this duty arises " at the time of and after any disaster or peril insured against." [65]

(f) Use and occupancy or business interruption loss

The O.I.L. policy does not, as a result of exclusion 11, apply to " Any Use and Occupancy or Business Interruption Loss or extra expense in connection therewith sustained by the Assured."

(g) Confiscation and expropriation

The O.I.L. policy does not, as a result of exclusion 12, apply to " Any loss or damage arising directly or indirectly from confiscation or expropriation." This exclusion has some resemblances to exclusion 2,[66] which excluded cover for loss, damage or expense caused by or resulting from a number of actions by governments or public or local authorities.

(h) Waste products

The O.I.L. policy does not, as a result of exclusion 13, apply to:

" Injury to or destruction of property, including the loss of use thereof, caused by the intentional or wilful introduction of waste products, other than in accordance with industry practice, into any soil or inland or tidal waters or atmosphere, unless such injury to or destruction of such property or the loss of use thereof is caused by accident."

The injury or destruction or loss of use will therefore be covered if, and only if, the introduction of the waste products was either (a) in accordance with industry practice; or (b) accidental.

(i) Fines and penalties

The O.I.L. policy does not, as a result of exclusion 15, apply to:

" Liability for fines and penalties imposed under any laws of any country or any political subdivision thereof, excluding, however, civil fines or penalties imposed to pay or reimburse others for loss, damage or expense resulting from an occurrence to the extent that the amount of the civil fine or penalty is measured by but does not exceed the actual loss, damage and/or expense incurred."

The two words " fines and penalties " differ in meaning in that the word " fine " is that more usually employed to describe an amount imposed with a threat of the sanction of the criminal law by a court for an offence against the law, whereas the word " penalty " has a connotation of a less pejorative nature. A fine is also a penalty and indeed it has

---

[65] See also above, p. 154.
[66] See above, p. 369.

been defined [67] as a ". . . sum of money fixed as penalty for offence." The word " penalty " may also be used to describe the infliction of a monetary sanction by some body other than a court, as for example, a port authority. If a penalty is imposed by such a body, it would not be recoverable under the O.I.L. policy if it could properly be described as a penalty imposed under the " laws of any country or any political sub-division thereof. . . ." What is the position in the unlikely, or rare, situation where a penalty is imposed by, for example a port authority, but not under such laws? It might have its own system of penalties, created independently of any laws. The penalties might be enforceable, even if not made " under " the law. The ability of the assured to recover under the O.I.L. policy would then depend, since recovery was not excluded by exclusion 15, upon whether the claim fell under one of the three insuring agreements. If it did so, as, for example, in the case of a penalty imposed for causing a death (see the wording of Insuring Agreement 3 [68]) then it seems that it would be recoverable.

There is an exception to exclusion 15, in that civil fines or penalties imposed to pay or reimburse others in respect of an occurrence may be covered, so far as they fall within one of the Insuring Agreements. The amount imposed may be measured by but must not exceed the actual loss, damage and/or expense incurred.

D. OFFSHORE POLLUTION LIABILITY AGREEMENT (OPOL)

It is possible for operators to accept voluntarily, as between themselves, certain minimum standards of liability. This was done, in the case of the Offshore Pollution Liability Agreement, or OPOL, to ensure that, in the event of a spillage or escape of oil, claims for pollution damage are met and the cost of remedial measures reimbursed. The Agreement does not itself constitute a contract of insurance, though in some rare circumstances the organisation which administers the agreement, the Offshore Pollution Liability Association Ltd., of London, accepts certain financial liabilities.[69-73]

OPOL, dated September 4, 1974, came into effect on May 1, 1975, and was amended on September 12, 1975, March 23 and December 14, 1976, May 5, 1977, and May 22, 1978. It was established by a number of companies who were the operators of, or who intended to become the operators of, offshore facilities used in connection with the exploration for or the production of oil and gas. By this agreement they accepted strict liability, with certain exceptions, up to a maximum of $25 m. per incident. This sum is made up of $12\frac{1}{2}$ m. to cover pollution damage claims and $12\frac{1}{2}$ m. for remedial measures. There is a measure of overlapping between these two categories, however; when all the claims in one category have

---

[67] *Concise Oxford Dictionary.*
[68] See above, p. 367.
[69-73] See below, p. 383.

been met, any surplus can be used to meet unsatisfied claims in the other category. Thus in the event of there being pollution damage claims amounting to $6¼ m. and remedial measures amounting to $18¾ m. it would be possible for both the sums in question to be paid, as the total of $25 m. would not have been exceeded. So also if the total claims exceed the sums available, then the compensation is distributed proportionately among the claimants. Thus pollution damage claims for $15 m. and claims in respect of remedial measures for $15 m. would be reduced so that the two categories were limited to payments of $12½ m. and $12½ m. respectively.

The Introduction to the Agreement, after referring to the possibility that an accident could give rise to an escape of oil, says: "... the oil industry has therefore voluntarily developed an Agreement to ensure that, in the event of a spillage or escape of oil, claims for pollution damage are met and the cost of remedial measures reimbursed." The 16 parties signing the contract, which as drafted applied initially to United Kingdom waters, were operators who were associated with many of the world's major oil companies. The oil companies represented [74] were: BP, Shell, Esso (or Exxon), Gulf, Mobil, Texaco, Amoco, Burmah, Total, Conoco, Phillips, Signal, Hamilton, Siebens, Cluff and Sun Oil.

The parties have to prove, to the satisfaction of the body which they set up to administer the affairs of OPOL, the Offshore Pollution Liability Association Ltd., a company established in London, that each of them has the ability to meet the claims for which they have agreed to accept liability. This process, which is described as the establishment of " Financial responsibility," can be achieved by the production of evidence of in-surance, self-insurance, or other means satisfactory to the administering company.

The guarantee that claims will be met, up to the maximum of $25 m. per incident mentioned above, operates in two directions. First, it is a contract by the parties with each other; secondly, it is an undertaking by each and all of the parties towards potential claimants. These claimants may be public authorities or private individuals. We now turn to the two categories of " claims for pollution damage " and " the cost of remedial measures." Anyone, whether a public authority or a private individual, may make a claim for compensation for pollution damage. This is defined [75] as " direct loss or damage (other than loss of or damage to the designated Offshore Facility involved), by contamination which results from a Discharge of Oil. A discharge of oil is defined [76] as " any escape or discharge of oil into the sea from a Designated Offshore Facility."

The term offshore facility is said to mean:

" A. any well and any installation or portion thereof of any kind, fixed or mobile, used for the purpose of exploring for, producing, treating or transporting crude oil from the seabed or its subsoil; and

---

[74] The names by which they are generally known are used here.
[75] Cl. I, definition 12.   [76] Cl. I, definition 11.

B. any well used for the purpose of exploring for or recovering gas or natural gas liquids from the seabed or its subsoil during the period that any such well is being drilled (including completion), recompleted or worked upon (except for normal work-over operations);

which is located within the jurisdiction of a Designated State to the extent that it is to seaward of the low-water line along the coast as marked on large scale charts officially recognized by the Government of such Designated State:

provided however that none of the following shall be considered an Offshore Facility:—

(i) any abandoned well, or

(ii) any ship, barge or other craft not being used for the storage of crude oil, commencing at the loading manifold thereof." [77]

Since one of the objects of OPOL is to encourage immediate remedial action, and not only to provide compensation after pollution damage has taken place, it is understandable that it should also make provision for reimbursement, within certain limits, of parties who incur expense when taking such remedial action. The parties so entitled are public authorities and the operator of the offshore facility from which the escape or discharge of oil occurred. A public authority may claim in respect of remedial measures which it has taken to prevent, mitigate or eliminate pollution damage, or to remove or neutralise the oil following an escape or discharge.

OPOL only applies in the event of a spillage or escape of oil from offshore facilities situated within the jurisdiction of any state specified in the Agreement. It applied initially only to United Kingdom waters, but it was subsequently extended [78] by the parties to Denmark, France, the German Federal Republic, Ireland, the Netherlands, and Norway. It can be extended to any other state by agreement between the parties and consequential amendment of OPOL.

If the places where the pollution damage occurred or where the remedial measures were taken were outside the jurisdiction of the state in question, the Agreement still applies, provided that the offshore facilities in question are within those waters.

OPOL was drafted so that it could have regional or world-wide application. Clause I, which sets out a number of definitions, lists the said seven countries as Designated States and adds the words " and any other State recognised as such under international law or custom which the Parties by appropriate amendment hereto under Clause X [79] may so denominate."

The parties to OPOL are the operators themselves, and those who intend to become operators, rather than the licensees of blocks, since it was considered that the operators were more directly involved, and in a better

[77] Cl. I, definition 7.

[78] By the amendments of September 12, 1975, which, among other matters, extended the definition of " Designated State " in cl. 1 to include the six additional countries.

[79] Entitled " Amendments," and providing for the contract to be amended by resolution adopted at a general meeting of the members upon a vote in which at least 75 per cent. of the votes cast are in favour of the resolution, save that a simple majority of the votes cast can adopt an amendment with respect to the denomination of a state as a designated state.

position to assume the obligations under the Agreement.[80-81] Many facilities, such as pipeline systems, could serve a number of different licensees, but would only have a single operator whose responsibility is defined in an operating agreement.

The categories of potential claimants in respect of pollution damage and the cost of remedial measures are set out in the Agreement. Anyone, including a public authority, may claim compensation for pollution damage. The original agreement spoke of " states " in this connection, but the amended agreement introduced the expression " Public Authority," which it defines as follows:

> " ' Public Authority ' means the Government of any State recognised as such under international law or custom and any public body or authority (municipal, local or otherwise) within such State competent under the municipal law of such State to carry out Remedial Measures."

As for remedial measures, a distinction is made, in respect of potential claimants, between the types of remedial measure involved. Public authorities may claim in respect of remedial measures taken to prevent, mitigate or eliminate pollution damage, or to remove or neutralise the oil following an escape or discharge. The party who is the operator of the facility is also entitled to claim in respect of remedial measures, except for the cost of well control measures, or any measures taken to protect, repair or replace the facility. The cost of remedial measures by the operator may be set off against the total amount of compensation that would otherwise be available to meet the claims of the public authorities.

A claim by any person, including a public authority, or indeed another operator, whether or not he is a party to the agreement, must be made directly against the operator concerned, and must be filed within one year of the date of the incident which resulted in the escape or discharge of the oil.

The nature of the liability accepted by the parties to OPOL is, so far as the Agreement itself is concerned, a contractual one, stated as constituting a duty on the part of each operator to all the other operators who are parties to the Agreement. For this purpose the crucial Clause in the Agreement is Clause IVA, and the material words are:

> " If a Discharge of Oil occurs from a Designated Offshore Facility, and if, as a result, any Public Authority or Public Authorities take Remedial Measures and/or any Person sustains Pollution Damage, then *the Party hereto who was the Operator* of said designated Offshore Facility at the time of the Discharge of Oil *shall reimburse the cost of said Remedial Measures and pay compensation for said Pollution Damage* up to an overall maximum of U.S. $25,000,000 per Incident. . . ."[82]

The parties are thus not entering into an undertaking with the " Public Authority or Public Authorities " or with " any Person." That would in any case be impracticable because the authorities or persons who might

---

[80-81] And, in particular, best able to insure these obligations; see above, p. 325.
[82] Italics supplied.

benefit cannot be identified in advance of the incident in question, except possibly where the public authority is a sovereign state. In addition the operators may have a legal liability which results from the provisions of a national or local law, with provisions for compensation to governments and to private individuals, an obligation to clean up, and exposure to a fine. This is a separate liability, and one of a different nature, which the operators cannot of course avoid by their agreement as set out in OPOL. In the event of a discharge of oil both types of liability may attach to the operator. Offshore Pollution Liability Association Ltd. has stated, in its " Information for Prospective Participants in OPOL " [83]: " This acceptance of strict liability cannot supplant legal liability, but it does provide a means of dealing with claims that is simpler and more satisfactory both to the claimant and to the operator."

The area in which the discharge of oil took place may be either one in which no law of any public authority applies, or one where the relevant law is one which requires less of an operator than is required of him under OPOL. For example, the limit of liability per incident may be less; the nature of the liability may be less strict, with more defences being made available to the operator than are available under OPOL; or the time limit for claims may be less than the one year given under OPOL.[84] In all these cases it would be true to say that the " means of dealing with claims " was " more satisfactory . . . to the claimant."

The operators have, as has been stated above,[85] a contractual right, as between themselves, to ensure that they perform the duties set out in OPOL. This corresponds to and is correlative with the liabilities which each has assumed. In assuming these duties have they, in addition, given legal rights to third parties? The third parties in question are the public authorities, in respect of both remedial measures and pollution damage, and other persons than public authorities, in respect of pollution damage.

The ability of a third party to sue under a contract which states that it is conferring a benefit upon him is one which varies according to different systems of law. The leading English case on the subject is *Tweddle* v. *Atkinson*.[86] A marriage was to take place; as a result a contract was made between the fathers of the engaged couple, each promising to pay money to the bridegroom. The bride's father failed to pay the money. He then died, and the husband sued his executors. His claim was rejected, the Judge [87] saying: ". . . it is now established that no stranger to the consideration can

---

[83] As published with the text of the Agreement.

[84] Cl. VI—" Time for Filing Claim: No Party hereto shall have any obligation under this Contract with respect to any Claims filed over one year from the date of the Incident which resulted in the Pollution Damage or the taking of the Remedial Measures in question." If the time limit in the area in question was longer than one year, the third party would then be left to his remedy under civil law.

[85] At p. 378.

[86] (1861) 1 B. & S. 393.

[87] Wightman, J. at p. 397.

take advantage of a contract, although made for his benefit." This principle does not necessarily apply in other systems of law. In French law for example, the concept of *stipulations pour autrui*, or promises for another, is accepted by the Civil Code.

The strict rule of English law has been found inconvenient in commercial transactions.[88] In *Walford's Case* [89] brokers negotiated a time charterparty under which they were to receive three per cent. commission on the signing of the charterparty (ship lost or not lost), the commission being based on the estimated gross amount of hire. The ship was requisitioned and as a result the charterparty was cancelled. The House of Lords held that in such a case charterers could, as trustees on behalf of the brokers, sue the shipowners. The effect of this decision and of such a provision as to commission has been summarised as follows [90]:

> " Such a clause does not make the broker a party to the charter, but the charterer is entitled, and can be compelled by the broker, to sue, as trustee for the broker, upon the covenant by the shipowner in the charter to pay commission to the broker."

It may therefore be the case that two results follow from the obligation undertaken by the parties in Clause IVA of OPOL, [91-94] *i.e.*:

(1) an operator is entitled to go to arbitration under the terms of OPOL against another operator, if both are parties to OPOL, upon the latter's promises to reimburse and to pay compensation;

(2) a public authority or any other person can compel any of the operators, other than the operator in breach, to go to arbitration against the operator in breach upon his promises. It is possible, however, that direct proceedings may be available against the operator in breach.

The parties to OPOL accept strict liability, in the sense that they are liable to meet claims unless they can bring themselves within one of the following four exceptions:

(a) if the incident resulted from an act of war, hostilities, civil war, insurrection, or a natural phenomenon of an exceptional, inevitable and irresistible character;

(b) if the incident was wholly caused by an act or omission done by a third party with intent to cause damage;

(c) if the incident was wholly caused by the negligence or other wrongful act of any state or other authority, or resulted from compliance with conditions or instructions given by the licensing state;

(d) if the incident resulted wholly or partially either from an act or

---

[88] For a discussion see G. H. Treitel, *The Law of Contract* (4th ed., 1975), pp. 437 to 443.

[89] *Les Affréteurs Réunis S.A.* v. *Walford* [1919] A.C. 801 (H.L.).

[90] In Scrutton on *Charterparties* (18th ed., 1974), at p. 39.

[91-94] See p. 380, above.

omission of the claimant done with intent to cause damage, or from the negligence of that claimant, in which case the liability is proportionately reduced.

As has been stated above, OPOL is not a contract of insurance. The parties to OPOL undertake, however, to establish and to maintain their financial responsibility to meet their contractual obligations. They can do so by means of insurance [95], self-insurance, the issuance of a surety bond, or by obtaining a guarantee. They may arrange any combination of these methods in order to ensure that they could satisfy a liability of not less than the limit of $25 m. for any one occurrence and $50 m. in the annual aggregate.

The parties to OPOL agree that the Association shall guarantee the payment of claims due from a party which fails to meet its obligations. Each of the remaining parties who are operating offshore facilities must pay its share of any claims which the Association has to meet. The contribution for which the parties are thus liable are calculated in proportion to the number of certain offshore facilities which they operate and to which they have made OPOL applicable at the time of the incident.

Each operator must produce evidence of its financial responsibility to the Offshore Pollution Liability Association Ltd., the British company which is responsible for the administration of the agreement. Such evidence may be provided wholly by the operator or partially by the operator and partially by any or all non-operators in a venture. Where the operator relies on its insurance policies as evidence of financial responsibility it has to produce a certificate of insurance, in a form specified by the Association, from an insurance company or from an insurance broker or agent acceptable to the Association.[96] A maximum deductible of $1 m. per incident is permitted.

Whether the verification of insurance is given by an insurance company or by an insurance broker or agent the certificate of insurance states that a policy of insurance has been issued to the operator, and " that the policy covers the Insured's liability for claims for Remedial Measures and/or Pollution Damage arising out of or resulting from an Incident, as those terms are defined in the Offshore Pollution Liability Agreement dated September 4, 1974 (hereinafter referred to as " OPOL "), occurring during the period the policy is in effect, regardless of whether the Insured is the Operator under OPOL or a non-operating participant. . . ." [97] The insurance company or insurance broker or agent also has to certify

" that the coverage afforded by said policy will not be cancelled or materially changed until notice in writing has been given to the Insured and to the

---

[95] This may be on the market; but it was noted at p. 366, above, that by an " OPOL Endorsement " O.I.L. may indemnify its assured in respect of sums payable under an OPOL obligation.

[96] Rule 1 of the Rules for Establishment of Financial Responsibility.

[97] See below, p. 385, as to the situation in which a person other than an Operator will give evidence of financial responsibility.

Association at ... [address stated] ... furthermore, that such cancellation and/or change shall not become effective until after the expiration of 30 days from the date the notice is received by the Association, or until substitute evidence of financial responsibility as required by OPOL has been filed with and accepted by the Association, whichever occurs first."

The verification of insurance, whether given by an insurance company or by an insurance broker or agent, sets out other material details of the policy. These are its number, the times and dates at which it becomes effective and expires, the limit per incident, the aggregate per policy year and the deductible per incident. It also sets out the subject-matter to which the policy applies, and gives the " Description and location of Designated Licences." By way of precaution, and protection to the insurers, it concludes with the words:

" The issuance of this document does not make the Association [*i.e.* the Offshore Pollution Liability Association Ltd.] an additional insured, nor does it modify in any manner the contract of insurance between the Insured and the Insurers."

Where the operator is self-insured, it must demonstrate financial responsibility by providing its latest audited financial statement [98] certified by a recognised independent public accounting firm, and meeting the following criteria:

" (a) Ratio of sum of net income and depreciation, depletion and amortisation to the sum of interest expense and retirement of long-term debt must be at least 1·5 to 1.
(b) Ratio of either (i) current assets to current liabilities or (ii) current assets plus unused committed lines of credit to current liabilities plus self-insured limit must be at least 1·25 to 1.
(c) Interest expense must not exceed $33\frac{1}{3}$ per cent. of the sum of the net income before extraordinary items and depreciation, depletion and amortisation.
(d) The ratio of total capitalisation, *i.e.* shareholders' funds and long-term debt to long-term debt must be at least 2·5 to 1.
(e) The amount self-assumed in the annual aggregate must not exceed 10 per cent. of the net income before extraordinary items, plus depreciation, depletion and amortisation.
If the company is a subsidiary of another Corporation it may utilise the consolidated financial statements of its parent company to demonstrate financial responsibility, provided the parent company executes an Acknowledgement of Commitment of Subsidiary.[99]

The qualifications for being a self-insurer are, understandably, set out in considerable detail, in order to protect the intended beneficiaries of the Agreement, *i.e.* the persons, including states, who may claim compensation, and the states and operators who may claim in respect of remedial measures. Major enterprises, and particularly multi-national companies, frequently have arrangements for self-insurance or for a large measure of

---

[98] Rule 4.
[99] On one of the Association's standard forms.

self-insurance, subject to certain overall covers in the event of catastrophes. It was thought necessary, nevertheless, for the Association responsible for the administration to set out the above criteria, so as to ensure that there is proper evidence of financial responsibility. The Directors may accept a company as self-insured for a sum not in excess of $500,000 any one occurrence.

Where the operator wishes to rely on the issuance of a surety bond or to obtain a guarantee, in order to demonstrate his financial responsibility, he has to produce an " Operator's Surety Bond " in a specified form, issued by a surety company acceptable to the Association, or an " Operator's Guaranty," also in a specified form, issued by a guarantor acceptable to the Association.

An " Operator's Surety Bond " provides that the operator, who is a member of the Association, as principal, and the surety,

> " are held and firmly bound unto The Offshore Pollution Liability Association Limited (hereinafter called " Obligee ") and to the Claimants [*i.e.* the claimants under OPOL] . . . in the sum of U.S. $ . . . [1] for the payment of which sum well and truly to be made we, the said Principal and the said Surety, bind ourselves, our heirs, executors, administrators, successors and assigns, jointly and severally, firmly by these presents."

The obligation of a surety, both in ordinary parlance and in the wording of this bond, is a secondary obligation, in that it is effective only in the event of a breach of his obligations under OPOL by the operator. The term " surety " has been defined [2] as: ". . . person who makes himself responsible for another's appearance in court or payment of sum or performance of engagement. . . ." The bond itself confirms the secondary character of the undertaking when it goes on to state

> ". . . the condition of this obligation is such, that if the said Principal [the operator] shall truly, faithfully and promptly perform all the obligations assumed by Principal in the [Agreement] in accordance with the provisions of said Agreement, which is by reference made a part hereof, then this obligation to be null and void; otherwise to remain in full force and effect."

This undertaking of suretyship is similar in nature to a guarantee, and is of a collateral or supportive nature, though none the less binding. It can be contrasted with an indemnity, where the obligation is a direct one, irrespective of the fact that the supported party has an additional con-tracted liability. In the case of a suretyship there is no obligation if the principal carries out his own obligations.

The Operator's Surety Bond, which is signed by both operator and surety, is stated to be effective at 0001 hours Greenwich Mean Time on a named date, and to continue in force until terminated by either of them giving written notice to the Association, " such termination to become effective

---

[1] $25 million if the Operator is providing evidence of financial responsibility for the entire venture, but a lesser sum if a part of that evidence is provided in some other form, or if non-operators are providing a share.

[2] *Concise Oxford Dictionary.*

thirty (30) days after actual receipt of said notice by the Obligee," *i.e.* by the Association. The termination does not affect any liability of the surety in respect of events giving rise to claims under the bond occurring prior to the effective date of termination. If, for example, the surety is a bank or, as is often the case in the U.S.A., a bonding company, a situation may arise in which there is a failure by the operator to pay interest or bonding charges. Though the surety may give prompt notice to the Association, he will still be exposed to liability under the bond in respect of a claim under OPOL for 30 days after the Association receives notice of termination. The surety himself will of course have a measure of protection from this exposure, in that he will almost invariably have secured a counter-guarantee from the operator. Indeed it has been said [3] that where a person acts as surety at the request of another, there is an implied contract to indemnify the surety, so that strictly speaking the latter could be protected even where he has failed or been unable to obtain the necessary counter-guarantee from the operator.

An " Operator's Guaranty " is the fourth and remaining method [4] by which an operator may provide the Association with acceptable evidence of financial responsibility to meet the obligations which he has assumed under OPOL. A guarantor, like a surety, accepts a secondary or supportive obligation. Thus the " Operator's Guaranty," after saying that the guarantor " is agreeable to assisting Operator to establish its financial responsibility," states: ". . . the undersigned Guarantor hereby guarantees to the Association to discharge Operator's liability under OPOL *in the event and to the extent such liability has not been discharged by Operator*." [5] There is a difference of emphasis here, when the document is compared with the Operator's Surety Bond. Under the Surety Bond, if the operator carries out his obligations under OPOL, the obligation of the surety ceases. Under the Guaranty, the obligations of the guarantor are said to exist so far as there is a failure by the operator. This point of view is supported by subsequent words in the Guaranty, which are: " Guarantor's liability under this Guaranty shall attach *only* in respect of Incidents occurring during the period the Guaranty is in force. In no event shall Guarantor's liability hereunder exceed the amount of Operator's liability under OPOL." [6]

The Operator's Guaranty, which is signed by the guarantor only, is stated to be effective at 0001 hours Greenwich Mean Time on a named date. It can, as in the case of the Operator's Surety Bond, be brought to an end by written notice; here, however, it is only the guarantor, and not the operator, who can give such notice, and the notice becomes effective 60 days, rather than 30 days, after it has been received by the Association.

---

[3] In Halsbury's *Laws of England* (3rd ed., 1957), Vol. 18 at p. 475.
[4] For the methods generally, see above, p. 383.
[5] Italics added.
[6] Italics added.

The Guaranty also comes to an end if the operator ceases to be a party to OPOL, or if substitute, *i.e.* alternative, evidence of financial responsibility is accepted by the Association. Termination is in each case at 2400 hours G.M.T. on the date in question.

The Rules for Establishment of Financial Responsibility also state:

" Where a part of the evidence is to be provided by a Non-Operator in place of the Operator, it is the responsibility of the Operator to obtain and submit to the Association a Non-Operator's Undertaking on Form FR-5 (Rev) [7] with evidence of financial responsibility."

This paragraph envisages a situation in which a member or members of the leasing company or consortium other than the Operator himself give the necessary evidence of financial responsibility. He is still treated as an Operator for the purpose of the Agreement, and they, the " Non-Operators," assume the burden of producing the evidence. They have the same choice open to them as that available to an operator, in that they can show evidence of insurance, or self-insurance, or produce a surety bond or a guarantee.

The non-operator, in his undertaking, certifies to the Association that it also is a participant in a joint operating contract relating to offshore facilities which are operated by the operator. Details of the licence authorising the operation are given, and the non-operator " Warrants it will pay as per the joint operating contract its proportionate share of all amounts said operator is obliged to pay under OPOL." It is thus necessary to obtain such undertakings from all those non-operators in respect of whose interest the operator is not providing evidence of financial responsibility. The certification given by the non-operator is stated to be given " in consideration of the payment of One Dollar ($1.00) and other good and valuable consideration, receipt of which is hereby acknowledged. . . ." This is in accordance with the doctrine of consideration applicable in the English law of contract. A simple promise, except where it is in the form of a deed, is usually unenforceable unless some corresponding promise of action is undertaken by the promisee, though the benefits of the latter promise or action need not necessarily be directed towards the promisor. Where no such promise or action would otherwise be contemplated it is usual to provide that there be a nominal consideration, as in this case by the payment of a dollar.

As was stated earlier,[8] the non-operator may submit evidence of financial responsibility; he has the same range of choice, in that he may show evidence of insurance, or self-insurance, or produce a surety bond or a guarentee. The requirements for the verification of insurance and self-insurance are the same as those in the case of the operator.[9] The non-operator's surety bond is also in terms similar to those of the operator's

---

[7] One of the Association's standard forms.
[8] Above, p. 383.
[9] See above, pp. 383–385.

surety bond.[10] The surety files the bond to demonstrate the financial responsibility of " the Principal," who in this case is the non-operator who is liable under a non-operator's undertaking. So also the non-operator's guaranty is in terms similar to those of the operator's guaranty,[11] the guarantor giving a guarantee to the Association to discharge the non-operator's liability under the latter's undertaking so far as such liability is not discharged by the non-operator.

PART 2. REMOVAL OF DEBRIS

The responsibility for removal of debris of any property or equipment used in carrying out the drilling operations is usually apportioned to one of the parties to the drilling contract, and then insured by that one, although sometimes both parties might conclude such an insurance. When the words " debris " and " wreck " (the word used more frequently in connection with conventional ships) are used in the following pages, it is important to bear in mind that they refer, in this connection, to any property or equipment. Furthermore, the use of the word debris,[12] as distinguished from the word wreck, serves to emphasise that there need not necessarily have been a catastrophe in respect of the drilling unit and/or its equipment. The drilling operations may result in such a catastrophe and a liability for removal; but, alternatively, the termination of the operations in the normal manner may be combined with a previous requirement by the relevant authorities, including the grantors of the lease, that the operator should leave the area clean and free of obstructions within one year from the termination of his activities. A drilling contract could be worded so that this type of clearance, not resulting from a catastrophe or other loss, became the responsibility of the operator; and so that removal of the drilling unit itself, or part thereof, or of its equipment, resulting from a catastrophe or other loss, became the responsibility of the contractor. In such a case the definition of debris and wreck would be such that the operator would be liable in respect of the former and the contractor in respect of the latter.

We have seen earlier [13] that the London Standard Drilling Barge form excludes the insurers from liability for removal of debris, by the words [14]:

> " Notwithstanding anything to the contrary which may be contained in this insurance there shall be no liability under this insurance in respect of: . . .
> (i) Claims in connection with the removal of property, material, debris or obstruction, whether such removal be required by law, ordinance, statute, regulation or otherwise."

---

[10] See above, p. 385.
[11] See above, p. 386.
[12] Defined in the *Concise Oxford Dictionary* as " Scattered fragments, wreckage, drifted accumulation."
[13] See above, p. 128.
[14] In cl. 8 [Exclusions].

There is also an exclusion in respect of this type of liability in the Collision Liability clause (clause 6) of the L.S.D.B. Form:

" Provided that this clause shall in no case extend to any sum which the Assured or the Surety may become liable to pay or shall pay in consequence of, or with respect to: (a) removal or disposal of obstructions, wrecks or their cargoes under statutory powers or otherwise pursuant to law; . . ."

So also the Institute Time Clauses (Hulls) state, in a proviso to clause 1 (the collision clause):

" Provided always that this clause shall in no case extend or be deemed to extend to any sum which the Assured may become liable to pay or shall pay for in respect of: (a) removal or disposal, under statutory powers or otherwise, of obstructions, wrecks, cargoes or any other thing whatsoever. . . ."

In the case of conventional ships it has long been customary for governments to take upon themselves statutory powers to remove wrecks when these wrecks have been likely to impede or to constitute a hazard to navigation. Under the Merchant Shipping Act 1894, section 530,[15] for example, states:

" Where any vessel [16] is sunk, stranded, or abandoned in any harbour or tidal water under the control of a harbour or conservancy authority, or is or near any approach thereto, in such manner as in the opinion of the authority to be, or be likely to become, an obstruction or danger to navigation or to lifeboats engaged in lifeboat service in that harbour or water or in any approach thereto, that authority may—
 (a) take possession of, and raise, remove, or destroy the whole or any part of the vessel; and
 (b) light or buoy any such vessel or part until the raising, removal, or destruction thereof; and
 (c) sell, in such manner as they think fit, any vessel or part so raised or removed, and also any other property recovered in the exercise of their powers under this section, and the authority shall hold the surplus, if any, of the proceeds in trust for the persons entitled thereto . . ."

A shipowner will usually be covered in respect of this liability, whether it arises under English law or some other law by his protecting and indemnity club. The cover [17] will be in respect of:

" Costs and expenses of or incidental to the raising, removal, destruction, lighting or marking of the wreck of an entered ship when such raising, removal, destruction, lighting or marking is compulsory by law or the costs thereof are legally recoverable from the Owner.
PROVIDED ALWAYS that:
(a) The value of all stores and materials saved, as well as of the wreck itself, shall first be deducted from such costs charges and expenses, and only the balance thereof, if any, shall be recoverable from the Association.
(b) Nothing shall be recoverable from the Association under paragraph (18)

---

[15] The case law on this provision and on similar provisions in the legislation is discussed in *The Merchant Shipping Acts* (7th. ed., 1976) at paras 477–8.

[16] As defined in s. 742; see above, p. 64.

[17] The example is taken from the Rules of the United Kingdom Mutual Steam Ship Assurance Association (Bermuda) Ltd., rule 34 (18).

of this Rule if the Owner shall, without the consent of the Managers in writing, have transferred his interest in the wreck, otherwise than by abandonment, prior to the raising, removal, destruction, lighting or marking of the wreck."

Liability to remove part or all of the wreck of a drilling unit may be imposed upon either party by the drilling contract though at one time many contracts were silent on this subject; by the terms of the lease; and by a governmental law. The contractual liability may be imposed upon the operator [18]; in the International Daywork Drilling Contract—Offshore,[19] for example, clause 1006 (" Liability for the Well ") states:

" Operator shall be liable for the cost of regaining control of any wild well, as well as the cost of removal of debris, and shall indemnify Contractor for any such cost regardless of the cause thereof, including, but not limited to the negligence of Contractor, its agents, employees or subcontractors."

Another contract, however, used by a major oil company, states:

" However,[20] Contractor shall always remove at its own costs the drilling unit, or part thereof, in the event that the drilling unit is lost, or damaged beyond repair, from Company's concession area, if so required by law or governmental authority, or if interfering with Company's operations."

Although the contracts differ in that they place responsibility for the cost of " removal of debris " (or of " the drilling unit or part thereof ") in one case upon the operator and in the other case upon the contractor, they resemble each other in that the insurance requirements in each case are that the contractor is to take out marine hull insurance; this may, in one case, and must, in the other case, include P. & I. insurance. The latter insurance is normally taken to include insurance of liability for the removal of wreck. In the case of the I.A.D.C. contract, where the operator is liable for the removal of wreck, he would be protected against any recourse from the contractor's underwriters by the provision that the contractor's insurance shall be endorsed to provide that the underwriters waive their right of recourse against the operator; but it seems that he would be liable, apart from the question of the contractor's insurance, for a simple claim by the contractor, under the contract, that he was liable for the removal.

Secondly, liability for removal of debris, at any rate on site, may be imposed by the lease granted to the consortium by the licensing authority. When a licence or drilling permit is granted in the United States, for example, its terms may provide that the U.S. Corps of Engineers, as the body dealing with the administration of U.S. navigable waters, can require the leaseholder to remove wreck or debris down to or below the waterline at his own expense; in addition, or alternatively, the Corps of Engineers

---

[18] See above, p. 388.

[19] Drafted for the International Association of Drilling Contractors (I.A.D.C.), Revised June, 1975. See Appendix B to this book, at p. 438.

[20] This is a reference to an immediately preceding sentence by which the contractor was to be liable for third party claims where there was a blowout or uncontrolled flow up to $100,000 if they were occasioned by the contractor's negligence.

may have the right to undertake this task at its own expense and to recover the cost from the leaseholder.

A lease may be revocable in the event of failure to comply with these requirements. So also in the case of North Sea leases the operator is obliged to remove debris of property of all types, if the relevant law so requires. As for the contractor, it has been said [21]:

> " The liability of a drilling contractor is less clear, as they have no contractual relationship with the U.S. government nor the government of lands bordering the North Sea. In the case of the drilling contractor, his liability might be to mark the wreck or remove it to a point where it is no longer a menace to navigation. This latter case could well be short of the action required of the leaseholder."

Thirdly, liability for removal of debris may be imposed by a governmental law. So far as the Merchant Shipping Act 1894 is concerned, we have seen [22] that its section 530 empowers a harbour or conservancy authority to take certain steps. Where a drilling unit falls under the description of " any vessel " for the purpose of the Act [23] its owners would be affected by this provision, if the sinking, stranding or abandonment to which the Act refers occurred " in any harbour or tidal water " under the control of such an authority. It may be asked whether the effect of the Act is (a) to make the authority liable to remove, etc., the wreck; and (b) to impose any liability upon the owner of the wreck in respect of (i) expenses of removal or (ii) the removal itself. As for (a), the position is not free from doubt. In one case [24] a Court of Appeal judge thought that the power was obligatory. In another case [25] the court declined to follow this view but held the authority liable for damage caused by a wreck, negligently left unbuoyed by them, on the ground that their receipt of funds, under a special Act, for such purpose, obliged them to undertake the removal and to exercise reasonable care in so doing. As for (b) (i), and the expenses of removal, the Act does not give the authority a personal remedy against the owner for the expenses of removal, etc., although in certain circumstances [26] the authority may have a claim against the owner on the ground of negligence or of public nuisance. As for (b) (ii), and the liability for removal, etc., this Act does not impose an obligation on the owner. Where such a liability arises, however, under any relevant law, it may be insured by one of the methods set out below, and it may in its turn, as we have seen, form the subject of a contractual agreement, between contractor and operator, as to which of them should bear the cost of such work.

Insurance of liability for removal of debris may be obtained by a specific

---

[21] By Mr. Russel F. Sammis, Senior Vice-President of Marsh & McLennan, Inc., of Houston, Texas.   [22] Above, p. 389.   [23] See above, p. 64.
[24] *The Douglas* (1882) 7 P.D. 151 (C.A.) *per* Cotton L.J., but *obiter*, at p. 160. See also *The Merchant Shipping Acts* (7th ed. 1976), para. 477 and the cases there cited.
[25] *Dormont* v. *Furness Rly. Co.* (1883) 11 Q.B.D. 496.
[26] *The Merchant Shipping Acts, op. cit.*, para. 85, n. 8.

cover to that effect; as part of a P. & I. policy (other than a P. & I. Club policy); or by insurance with Oil Insurance Ltd. (O.I.L.).

(a) *Specific covers*

A specific cover in respect of liability for the removal of debris may be in such terms as the following:

" 1. In consideration of the Premium charged Underwriters agree to reimburse the Assured for expense incurred in removal of ' Debris.' It being specifically understood and agreed that reimbursement under this Certificate shall apply only to removal of ' Debris ' caused by a peril listed below and consisting of materials making up a platform installation and equipment mounted thereon owned by the Assured or for which the Assured may be liable and at the location and for the specified amounts at each location listed below.

2. If caused by a peril(s) listed below:
   (a) Fire, Lightning;
   (b) Tornado, cyclone, windstorm, hurricane, hail;
   (c) Explosion above the surface of the ground (except as hereinafter excluded);
   (d) Collision of any vessel or object with the property hereby insured;
   (e) Blowout, Cratering (as hereinafter defined);
   (f) Earthquake;
   (g) Stress of weather;
   (h) Rising Water.

3. At the following locations and for the amount specified at each location:....

4. Such claim for reimbursement under each item shall be reported and adjusted separately, and from the amount of each adjusted loss, under each item, when determined, the sum of £........ shall be deducted.

All other terms and conditions remain unchanged."

Some brokers have designed linked forms which insure operators in respect of removal of debris in conjunction with cost of control and pollution liabilities, including clean up expenses. One such combination form is described as an " operator's extra expense indemnity." The relevant wording in one of these covers is:

" The Underwriters shall also indemnify the Assured for the following costs, liabilities and expenses, necessarily incurred by contract or otherwise in respect to the property and wells as scheduled. . . .
   (a) [Cost of Control]
   (b) [Cost of extinction of a well fire]
   (c) To remove debris of offshore property provided removal is required by a legal or contractual obligation of the Assured. . . ."

This cover is distinctive in that it specifically refers to the " contractual obligation " of the operator to remove debris.

(b) *P. & I. cover*

Cover for liability in respect of removal, etc., of wreck may be provided as part of a protecting and indemnity policy [27] in such terms as the following:

---

[27] As to P. & I. Club cover, see Chap. 5, above, at pp. 216–217.

" The Assurer hereby undertakes to make good to the Assured or the Assured's executors, administrators and/or successors, all such loss and/or damage and/or expense as the Assured shall as owners of the vessel named herein have become liable to pay and shall pay on account of the liabilities, risks, events and/or happenings herein set forth: . . .

Liability for cost or expenses of, or incidental to, the removal of the wreck of the vessel named herein when such removal is compulsory by law, provided, however, that:

(a) There shall be deducted from such claim for cost or expenses, the value of any salvage from or which might have been insured, to the benefit of the Assured.

(b) The Assurer shall not be liable for such costs or expenses which would be covered by full insurance under the .... or claims arising out of hostilities or war-like operations, whether before or after declaration of war."

The cover set out here relates to cases " when such removal is compulsory by law ". It would not seem to cover liability assumed under the drilling contract even though finally the law enforces a contract; it would have to be covered by a suitable amendment of the policy.

(c) *O.I.L. cover*

Cover for removal of wreck, or debris as it is called in that context, may also be provided as part of the cover afforded by Oil Insurance Ltd. (O.I.L.) [28] in the following terms:

". . . the Underwriter does hereby agree with the Policyholder and its non-consolidated subsidiaries and affiliates . . . both independently and as participants in joint ventures with others (hereinafter called the " Assured ").
. . .
2. To indemnify or pay on behalf of the Assured any sum or sums which the Assured may be obligated to pay or incurs as expenses, on account of:
. . .
c. Removal of Debris of property covered hereunder or which the Assured is legally obligated to remove, where such Debris arises from an occurrence, including expenses incurred for the purpose of complying with laws, regulations or orders of any governmental authority or agency or instrumentality thereof specifically including but not limited to the United States Coast Guard."

This cover, like that afforded by the P. & I. cover described above, does not appear to extend the liability assumed by the insured party under the drilling contract, because it refers only to removal of debris which it " is legally obligated to remove." Furthermore, the examples given, after the word " including " (a word which does not exclude other possibilities) are of laws, etc. of the government and similar authorities. On the other hand, the insured is " legally obligated " to observe the requirements of a contract, so that it could be argued, though it may not have been intended, that contractual liabilities are covered.

---

[28] As to the scope of the O.I.L. cover see above, p. 357.

CHAPTER 9

COST OF CONTROL

Introduction

THE object of cost of control insurance is that the operator, who is usually
the assured, though the contractor and others may also be included
on the policy, should be reimbursed in respect of the expenses which he
incurs in order to regain control of a well. Loss of control occurs when
pressure within the well is strong enough to breach the safety devices with
which the well is equipped. The weight of drilling mud or fluid in the well
normally produces a downward pressure which exceeds the upward
pressure from within the well. If the upward pressure exceeds the downward pressure, the blowout preventer and other safety devices are used to
control the upward flow. If they fail to do so then an uncontrolled flow
from the well is likely. An insurance policy in respect of the cost of control
may be used both offshore and on land; and it may relate both to exploration and to production activities.

The two most important conditions precedent to any right of recovery
by the assured under a cost of control insurance are that

(1) a well shall have become out of control, and

(2) he shall have incurred expenses in regaining control.

Various forms of words are used to provide this cover. The following
definitions of loss of control are taken from forms in common use:

A.[1]

" *Well Out of Control.* A well(s) shall be deemed out of control only so long
as there is a continuous flow of drilling fluid,[2] oil, gas or water above the
surface of the ground which is uncontrollable."

B.[3]

" A well(s) shall be deemed out of control when there is a continuous flow
of drilling fluid, oil, gas or water above the surface of the ground (or

---

[1] Definition 1 in a list of definitions set out in a policy called " Cost of Control of
Well Insurance," as amended in December, 1972, and described hereafter as policy "A."
The cost of control can also be insured with Oil Insurance Ltd.; see Chap. 8, p. 357,
above.

[2] " The stream of gases, liquids, liquids and solids suspended in liquid, with additives,
which circulates through the drill string and the anulus at high pressure, and is an
essential requirement for all rotary drilling operations " (*An A-Z of Offshore Oil & Gas*
(Whitehead, 1976)).

[3] Cl. 6 (c) in a policy called " Cost of Control Insurance," dated 1973, and described
hereafter as policy " B."

water-bottom in the case of a well(s) located in water) which is uncontrollable."

These definitions are almost exactly the same, the material difference being that " A " uses only the words " above the surface of the ground " whereas in " B " there is a clear contemplation of the fact that an offshore drilling unit (or indeed a fixed platform when drilling has been completed) may be involved, so that the words " or water-bottom in the case of a well(s) located in water " are added.

There must be " a continuous flow of drilling fluid, oil, gas or water." A temporary flow of one or more of these elements, sometimes called a " kick," would not entitle the assured to say that the well was out of control.

In both policies the well is deemed to be " out of control " so long as, or when, there is a continuous flow, of the elements listed, " which is uncontrollable." Mere underground loss of control is not covered. The object of such a policy, however, is to insure the assured in respect of costs incurred in regaining control. At first sight there would seem to be a contradiction in terms, in that a policy should refer to the expenses incurred in regaining control of a well but should provide that it cannot be regarded as being out of control unless the continuous flow is uncontrollable.

The description of the continuous flow as " uncontrollable " means that the flow cannot be controlled by the methods normally employed by those on the drilling unit to ensure that drilling fluid, oil, gas and water are mechanically contained or flow only in the directions and for the purposes contemplated in the course of the normal operations of the drilling unit.

Recovery of Expenses of Regaining Control

The basic responsibility of the insurers can be expressed in words such as the following, taken from two forms in common use [4]:

A.

> " 3b. To cover expenses as hereinafter defined [5] incurred by the Assured in regaining control of producing and/or non-producing oil or gas well(s) including well(s) being drilled and tested, directly arising from fire, lightning, explosion, blow-out, cratering and any other well or hole that gets out of control as a direct result of a well insured under this policy getting out of control."

and:

B.

> " 6 (a). The Underwriters shall reimburse the Assured under this Policy for expenses as hereinafter defined,[6] incurred by the Assured in regaining control of oil or gas well(s) covered hereunder, and/or any other well(s) which get out of control, during the period from the beginning of drilling,

---

[4] See above, p. 394.
[5] See below, p. 398.
[6] See below, p. 399.

recompletion, completion, reworking, testing, cleaning out, repairing, reconditioning operations or other operations of any nature on well(s) of Assured or in which Assured owns an interest, until completion or abandonment of such operations as set forth in Paragraph 7 [7] of this form, and other coverages as set out in Paragraph 6 (e) [8] below."

The two clauses quoted here have in common the statement that the assured shall be covered or reimbursed in respect of expenses which are defined elsewhere in the form of insurance.[9] The risk is that a well should get " out of control." If this occurs, and the assured incurs expenses " in regaining control," such expenses, as defined elsewhere in the form of insurance, are recoverable from the insurers. If the operation is unsuccessful, and the well continues to be out of control, it seems that the expenses reasonably incurred, up to the point at which it became unreasonable to continue, would be recoverable, even though on one view they could not be said to have been incurred " in regaining control." It would seem that it is enough that they should have been incurred in an attempt to regain control.

The fact that a storm, for example, made it impossible for operations to be conducted, would not mean that the well was out of control. One form of cost of control insurance deals with this problem, as can be seen in " A " above,[10] by its reference to ". . . expenses . . . incurred . . . in regaining control . . . directly arising from fire, lightning, explosion, blow-out, cratering . . . ." It seems clear that the loss of control must have been caused by " fire, lightning, explosion, blow-out, cratering." As the words stand, the words " directly arising " have as their subject the " expenses ", *i.e.* " expenses . . . directly arising from fire," etc. The missing words, which could reasonably be implied, can, it is suggested, be inserted in the following manner: ". . . expenses . . . incurred . . . in regaining control . . . *in the event of loss of control* directly arising from fire," etc. The words in " B " above are more satisfactory and cover expenses in trying to regain control, however that control was lost, subject to any policy exclusions.

Which Wells are Covered?

The cover provision quoted above [11] in the case of " A " refers to the regaining of control of " producing and/or non-producing oil or gas well(s) including well(s) being drilled and tested . . . and any other well or hole that gets out of control as a direct result of a well insured under this policy getting out of control." Provided, therefore, that a well insured under the policy gets out of control, and as a direct result another " well or hole " gets out of control, the assured is also reimbursed in respect of

---

[7] Dealing with attachment and termination of cover; see below, p. 404.

[8] Specifying that the cover applies to other wells, such as a shut-in well or a well temporarily abandoned; see below, pp. 397 and 398.

[9] See below, pp. 398 and 399.

[10] At p. 395.

[11] At p. 395.

the cost of control of that other well or hole. It is not provided that the assured should have been under any liability to the party interested in the other well or hole, even if in practice those involved would be contemplating only wells in the same ownership. In the case of the other provision, " B," quoted above,[12] the cover extends to expenses in regaining control of " oil or gas well(s) covered hereunder, and/or any other well(s) which get out of control . . . ." The quoted provision does not state that the loss of control of the wells not covered should have resulted from the loss of control of the covered wells. A later clause in " B," however,[13] states:

> " It is understood and agreed that coverage afforded by this Policy also applies to: (1) a producing well . . . (2) a shut-in well or a well temporarily abandoned . . . and any other well or hole that gets out of control as a direct result of a well insured under this Policy getting out of control."

In the case of policy " A," there are the following references to the wells themselves, so far as the provision of cover is concerned, other than that already quoted from Clause 3b [14]:

> " 1. All Wells to be declared. . . ."

> " 3a. It is agreed that coverage afforded by this policy applies to:
> 1 The well being drilled.
> 2 The well being reconditioned to make multiple completion.
> 3 The well being reconditioned to restore production.
> 4 The producing well.
> 5 The shut in well."

> " 5. Termination of Coverage
> [(a) provides that the insurance is to apply only during the course of drilling operations or temporary cessations thereof]
> (b) If producing well covered herein [see 3a above, at (4)], Clause 5(a) above does not apply."

The comparable provisions in the case of policy " B " refer to the wells themselves, other than that already quoted from clause 6 (a) [15]:

> " 5. The Underwriters agree, subject to the terms and conditions of this Policy to reimburse the Assured for expenses incurred by Assured in regaining control of all well(s) covered by this Policy located within the areas specified in the attached schedule." [16]

[This provision is similar in general intent to the cover provision, clause 6 (a) of policy " B ", set out at page 395, above, in that it expresses the liability of underwriters to reimburse the assured, but it is relevant in the present context because it makes provision as to the wells covered.]

> " 6 . . . (e) [17] It is understood and agreed that coverage afforded by this Policy also applies to:

---

[12] At p. 395.   [13] Cl. 6 (e).
[14] See above, p. 395.   [15] See above, pp. 395–396.
[16] Entitled " Schedule of Areas and Rates."
[17] Already cited (this page, above) to show that in the case of policy " B ", as in policy " A " the cost of control of wells other than those insured may be covered.

(1) a producing well

(2) a shut-in well or a well temporarily abandoned

and any other well or hole that gets out of control as a direct result of a well insured under this Policy getting out of control."

There are exclusions in respect of relief wells in both policies. Thus, in policy " A ":

" 7. Exclusions . . .

(b) Absolutely no coverage is provided hereunder on relief well except the cost of drilling a relief well as so provided under this policy."

This is similar in terms to the exclusion in respect of relief wells in the case of clause 13 of policy " B ":

" 13. Relief Wells.

Absolutely no coverage is provided hereunder on Relief Wells except the cost of drilling a Relief Well as provided elsewhere herein; any wells insured under the Continuation Clause [18] (if any) of the expiring Policy are also excluded."

The cost of drilling a relief well would include the premium for cost of control insurance in respect of that well.

Nature of Expenses Recoverable

The extent of the costs incurred " in regaining control " [19] will vary according to the nature of the problem involved and the conclusion reached by the assured as to how that problem should be handled. In the case of policy " A " " Expenses " are included in the list of definitions:

" *Expenses*: In the event that the well(s) insured gets out of control the Underwriters will reimburse the Assured for the costs of materials and supplies required, the services of individuals or firms specializing in controlling wells including directional drilling and similar operations necessary to bring the well(s) under control.

In any circumstances Underwriters' liability for expenses of regaining control of well(s) shall cease when the well(s) is controlled above the surface of the ground or water-bottom if located in waters."

This definition is linked directly to the cover provision [20] which referred to cover in respect of " expenses as hereinafter defined." The definition thus extends to the costs of materials and supplies, and of services, provided that the latter are the services of individuals or firms specialising in the control of wells. [21] The liability of the underwriters for such expenses is

---

[18] A clause providing that operations begun during the policy period are covered, irrespective of the expiry date of the insurance, until the operation is complete or the well is abandoned.

[19] To quote the words used in policies " A " and " B " above; see pp. 395 and 395–396 respectively.

[20] See above, p. 395.

[21] This constitutes a restriction upon the assured, though it is clearly intended to ensure that he does not endanger the chances of " regaining control " by the use of others than specialists. He might, however, need to use ordinary labour for some simple task involved in the operation. It seems that the words " specialising in controlling wells " would have to apply to " individuals " as well as to " firms." To this extent the

said to cease when the well is controlled, but the location, and thus the extent, of that control is specified. The clause uses the words " in any circumstances Underwriters' liability for expenses of regaining control of well(s) shall cease . . ." The intention is not, strictly speaking, that the underwriters shall be released from their liability for the expenses which have already been defined, but that they should have no liability for expenses incurred after the well has been brought under control. The words would, no doubt, be construed as if they read:

> " In any circumstances Underwriters shall not be liable in respect of expenses of regaining control of well(s) so far as such expenses are incurred after the well(s) is controlled above the surface of the ground or waterbottom if located in water."

As the clause stands the cessation of liability occurs upon the achievement of control (to take the two alternatives in the reverse order):

(a) if the well is located in water, above the waterbottom;

(b) if the well is not located in water, above the surface of the ground.

A comparable definition of expenses is set out at clause 6 (b) of policy " B ":

> " In the event the well(s) insured gets out of control the Underwriters will reimburse the Assured for the costs of materials and supplies required, contractors' equipment and services, and equipment and services of individuals or firms specialising in controlling wells, including directional drilling, and other operations necessary to bring the well(s) under control."

This definition thus also extends to the costs of materials and supplies, the wording being virtually identical to that contained in the corresponding provision of policy " A." [22] Having dealt with the costs of materials and supplies, it then goes on to refer to the equipment and services of those giving help, whereas the earlier provision, in policy " A," refers solely to their services; it is, presumably, taken for granted in the earlier case that the equipment, from whichever source it might have come, is covered by the reference to the costs of materials and supplies required.

The clause ends with a reference to " other operations necessary to bring the well(s) under control." These words can be taken in conjunction with the words " costs of . . ." earlier in the clause; the assured is thus not strictly limited in his recovery to the costs of the materials, services and equipment as set out in the earlier words, but can incur other costs if the operations were needed to bring the well under control.

The liability of the underwriters for such expenses is said to cease, as in the case of policy " A," [23] when the well is under control, in words almost

---

corresponding provision in policy " B " (see this page, above), with its reference to contractors' services, gives the assured a greater right of recovery. As both clauses end with the words " and other operations necessary to bring the well(s) under control," however, this difference may be irrelevant.

[22] See above, p. 398.

[23] See this page, above, and the comments there as to the wording of the cessation provision.

the same as those used in the earlier policy. Clause 6 (d) of policy " B " thus states:

> " In any circumstances Underwriters' liability for expenses of regaining control of well(s) shall cease when the well(s) is controlled above the surface of the ground (or water-bottom in the case of a well located in water) and no action or further action is required by regulatory authority(ies) to ensure permanent control."

Other Provisions of Cost of Control Insurance

The circumstances in which a well shall be considered to be out of control,[24] the right of the assured to recover from the insurers the expenses incurred in regaining control,[25] the extent to which the insurance affects wells which are not the subject of the policy,[26] and the nature of the expenses recoverable,[27] have been discussed in earlier pages. The other usual provisions of a cost of control insurance policy concern:

1. Period of Insurance
2. Co-Ventures
3. Limits of Liability
4. Attachment and Termination of Cover
5. Deductibles
6. Coinsurance
7. Exclusions
8. General Conditions of the Policy
9. Definitions
10. Premium
11. Continuation Clause
12. Relief Wells
13. Areas and Rates

1. *Period of Insurance*

It is usual for the cover to be placed for not more than 12 months at a time, subject to the continuation clause, so that a clause might read: " Period of Insurance. For and during the space of 12 calendar months commencing at [28]... and ending at ...," or more succinctly: " Period of Insurance. From ... to...." The exploratory programme of a drilling compan,y as operator, might be completed in less than 12 months. The policy could be worded, and cover would cease, accordingly.

2. *Co-Ventures*

The operator may [29] be one of several who have joined together in a

---

[24] See above, p. 394. [25] See above, p. 398.
[26] See above, p. 396. [27] See above, p. 398.
[28] As to commencement of cover in respect of individual wells, see the comments on attachment and termination of cover below, p. 404.
[29] See above, p. 325.

consortium to which a lease has been granted. Any or all of the other parties to the arrangement may also have an insurable interest.[30]

The policy will usually state that its cover extends to such other interests as additional assureds. In the case of one policy, described here as policy " A," [31] the provision states:

> " *CO-VENTURES.* In consideration of the premium charged, it is hereby understood and agreed that this insurance, subject to its terms and conditions, is extended to cover as additional assureds all co-ventures arising out of Mining Partnerships [32] and/or Joint Ventures provided, however, that for the purpose of this Insurance the terms ' Mining Partnerships and/or Joint Ventures ' shall be construed to mean only those partnerships and/or joint ventures in connection with the operations insured hereunder."

The introductory words, " In consideration of the premium charged ..." show that consideration, a necessary attribute of a contract, exists between the insurers and the additional assureds. As between the original assured and the insurers, the former promises to pay a premium, and to abide by the other terms of the contract of insurance, and the latter, in return, agrees to insure the former. The Lloyd's S.G. policy (which of course is not used here) includes the statement:

> " And so we, the assurers, are contented, and do hereby promise and bind ourselves, each one for his own part . . . to the assured . . . for the true performance of the promises, confessing ourselves paid the consideration due unto us for this assurance by the assured. . . ."

The insurers are thus agreeing that they have been paid. Some marine insurance policies use such words as " in consideration of the assured paying," to make it clear that the cover depends upon the payment. The latter is consistent with the wording of section 52 of the Marine Insurance Act 1906:

> " Unless otherwise agreed, the duty of the assured or his agent to pay the premium, and the duty of the insurer to issue the policy to the assured or his agent, are concurrent conditions, and the insurer is not bound to issue the policy until payment or tender of the premium."

The cost of control of well insurance now being discussed, however, opens with the words " In consideration of the premium charged. . . ."

A separate promise by the insurer to the additional assureds, that he would insure them, without any return, or consideration, moving from them, would be unenforceable. In the present case the agreement to cover them has been included in the original and only contract of insurance. Although they do not accept responsibility for payment of the premium they become co-assureds. Do the insurers have a liability towards them and

---

[30] Although s. 5 (2) of the Marine Insurance Act 1906 defines an insurable interest it seems that this is not a contract of insurance against marine losses, *i.e.* the losses incident to a marine adventure as defined in s. 3 of the Act. See Appendix C to this book.
[31] See above, p. 394, n. 1.
[32] A term which appears to have arisen in the early years of land drilling in the U.S.A.

do they have a right to claim under the policy? Would that liability and that right arise (1) because a premium was charged to the original assured; or

(2) because the policy stated that they were insured in consideration of that premium being charged; or

(3) because, by virtue of the words " subject to its terms and conditions," the additional assureds themselves could be said to be giving consideration?

This last proposition seems to be correct. In practice, it is understood, the brokers would look for payment of the premium to the person who asked them to arrange the insurance; this would usually be the operator.

The existence and number of any additional assureds, it should be added, is to some extent determined by the operating agreement between the partners or by separate agreements between the operator and one or some of the partners. The operator may agree to provide certain insurances, including cost of control insurance, for some or all of the partners. In so doing he would accept responsibility to pay the premium, and might become an agent of the other insuring partners. An operator is often a member of several consortia, whose memberships are subject to alteration; as a result it may be impossible to name all the other assureds at the outset.

It seems to be established that the insurers have a liability towards the co-assured and that the co-assured has a right to claim under the policy. The Lloyd's S.G. Policy, for example, though not used for the present purpose, states that the insurance is by the person who concludes it, ". . . as well in (his) own name as for and in the name and names of all and every other person or persons to whom the same doth, may, or shall appertain, in part or in all. . . ." In Arnould on *Marine Insurance* [33] the editors say, as to this last passage:

> " Questions have been raised as to the parties who may avail themselves of these very broad and comprehensive terms . . . it must be shown that the person effecting the insurance either intended it for their benefit, or at all events did not intend it exclusively for the benefit of others having a conflicting or inconsistent interest, but meant it to apply generally, so as to cover the interests of those who should ultimately appear concerned. . . ."

This statement is relevant to the additional assureds to which this cost of control of well insurance refers, although the policy is not subject to the Marine Insurance Act 1906.[34] Indeed it goes further, by its reference to those whose interest may appear later.

A similar provision as to co-assureds appears in another cost of control insurance [35]:

> " CO-VENTURES. It is understood and agreed that this Insurance shall be deemed to insure the interest of the Named Assured and of any or all non-operators, co-venturers, co-owners, mining partners, partners, or other

---

[33] (15th ed., 1961), at para. 227.
[34] See n. 30, above.
[35] Described here as policy " B "; see above, p. 394, n. 3.

party/ies (all hereinafter referred to as ' Co-Venturer(s) ') for whom the Named Assured is responsible to provide insurance, in the expenses hereinafter defined. The cover granted under the immediate preceding paragraph in respect of Co-Venturers shall be limited to those wells in which a Co-Venturer has a common interest with the Named Assured(s) and shall be subject in all respects to the terms, conditions and rates specified herein. A Co-venturer shall be deemed to be named as an additional Assured hereunder for the period(s) of time that their interest is insured hereunder."

Under this provision, as in the comparable provision in policy " A," [36] the other interested parties, if falling into the categories listed, are given the benefit of the insurance. They are also bound by it, in view of the words " subject in all respects to the terms, conditions and rates specified herein." The words " for whom the Named Assured is responsible to provide insurance " reflect provisions to this effect in the contract between the participants in the venture.

3. *Limits of Liability*

It is normal for insurers to limit their liability to a named sum for any one accident. In policy " A," for example, there appear the words [37]:

" *LIMITS OF LIABILITY.* It is understood and agreed that the maximum limit of liability hereunder shall not exceed . . . in any loss or occurrence, subject to co-insurance [38] and deductible." [39]

Similarly, in policy " B," a comparable provision [40] states:

" *LIMIT OF LIABILITY.* It is the intent of this Policy to make available to the Assured(s) insurance up to but not exceeding \$ . . . any one occurrence subject to deductible as Paragraph 10 and co-insurance as Paragraph 11."

These provisions set limits upon the expenses recoverable under the policy. It is natural to enquire whether they can be compared to the provisions in a hull policy, but the valuation clause in the Lloyd's S.G. Policy [41] is one which places a value upon the ship. In the present case the policy is intended to insure the assured in respect of expenses. To that extent the insurance resembles an insurance for suing and labouring, under which " the assured may recover from the insurer any expenses properly incurred." [42]

In addition to the provision for a maximum limit for any one loss or occurrence, there is usually a provision that any loss shall not reduce that limitation figure. For example:

" It is understood and agreed that any loss hereunder shall not reduce the limits of liability as set forth in Paragraph No. 4 of this Form." [43]

---

[36] See above, p. 401. [37] Cl. 4. [38] See below, p. 406.
[39] See below, p. 406. [40] Cl. 8.
[41] " The said ship, etc., goods and merchandises, etc., for so much as concerns the assured by agreement between the assured and assurers in this policy, are and shall be valued at. . . ."
[42] s. 78 (1) of the Marine Insurance Act 1906.
[43] Policy " A," condition G, para. No. 4, as set out above. The provision in policy " B," general condition F, is in the same words, referring to para. No. 8 of that form; see also above.

During the period of the insurance the assured may incur expenses of the type insured on more than one occasion, so as to entitle him to make more than one claim against the insurers. It has been stated in the policy that the limitation figure is in respect of any one loss or occurrence. That figure, however, is also described in one case as " the maximum limit of liability hereunder " and in the other case the opening words are: " It is the intent of this Policy to make available to the Assured(s) insurance up to but not exceeding. . . ." On one reading, therefore, the limitation provision might be construed as setting a limit in respect of not only the loss or occurrence but also the policy as a whole. The condition now quoted makes it clear that the limitation figure is not reduced because of the occurrence of an event giving rise to a claim. The full figure will be available for each later claim.

So also section 77 (1) of the Marine Insurance Act 1906 states: " Unless the policy otherwise provides, and subject to the provisions of this Act, the insurer is liable for successive losses, even though the total amount of such losses may exceed the sum insured." A ship may have been damaged and repaired, and then totally lost, during the period of cover under the time policy. Despite the valuation clause in the Lloyd's S.G. Policy,[44] the ship-owner may recover from the insurers in respect of both the cost of repairs, if he had been personally liable to pay for them,[45] and the total loss, although the total amount so recovered exceeded the valuation in the policy.

4. *Attachment and Termination of Cover*

(a) Attachment of cover

The time at which the insurance begins is stated in the clause dealing with the period of insurance.[46] At that time, however, the wells which are the subject of the insurance, and which have all to be declared, may not all have come into existence. It is essential to make it clear when the insurance begins in respect of these new wells. As part of the clause dealing with the period of insurance, therefore, policy " A " states [47]:

" All wells to be declared.
    (a) When being drilled—at time of spudding in.
    (b) When idle/producing
        (1) Commencement of Policy period
        (2) At time of attachment of Assured's interest."

A comparable provision in policy " B " [48] states:
" Such Insurance as is provided hereunder shall attach on new wells at the

---

[44] See above, p. 90.
[45] In *The Dora Forster* [1900] P. 241, the ship was pledged by the charterer s in respect of the cost of repairs, but the shipowner was not made personally liable for the cost. She later became a total loss. It was held that the insurers were liable only in respect of the total loss.
[46] See above, p. 400.
[47] Cl. 1.
[48] Part of cl. 7, " Attachment and Termination of Coverage."

time of ' spudding-in ' and on all other wells not otherwise insured here-under upon the commencement of deepening, reworking, reconditioning or other similar operations."

In the case of new wells, therefore, the policy attaches at the time of spud-ding-in. As for wells which are already in existence they may, at the beginning of the policy period as provided in the period of insurance clause, be either idle or in production. In the case of a well which is idle, it seems that cover would attach, or re-attach if it had already been in existence, when work began again, whether that work were to be described as reworking, deepening, reconditioning " or other similar operations."

(b) Termination of cover

Although the period of insurance clause [49] nominates a date at which the insurance shall end, the policy usually provides for cover to cease in certain events. Thus, in policy " A " [50]:

" *TERMINATION OF COVERAGE*:
   (a) Such insurance as is provided hereunder shall apply only during the course of drilling operations or temporary cessations thereof and shall cease upon either total and complete abandonment or completion of the well(s) which shall include the setting of the ' Christmas Tree ' [51] pumping equipment or well head equipment or the dismantling and removal of the drilling equipment from the location whichever shall first occur.
   (b) If producing wells covered herein, Clause 5 (a) above does not apply."

In similar words, policy " B " states [52]:

" Except in respect to completed wells insured hereunder, the Insurance as is provided hereunder shall terminate upon either total and/or complete abandonment or completion of the wells, which shall include the setting of ' Christmas Tree ' pumping equipment or well head equipment or the dismantling or removal of the drilling equipment from the location which-ever shall first occur."

In the case of policy " A " there are additional words in this termination clause to the effect that the insurance " shall apply only during the course of drilling operations or temporary cessations thereof. ...." In a clause which is designed to deal with termination of coverage, it would perhaps have been inadequate to state that the insurance " shall apply only " in certain cases. These earlier words are introductory, and, as has been seen, are not included in policy " B." Despite some differences and obscurities in wording, the effect of these two clauses is similar. The insurance is to cease upon (a) total or complete abandonment of the well(s) or (b) completion of the well(s), which, shall include:

---

[49] See above, p. 400.
[50] cl. 5.
[51] " The complex of valves and pipes installed at the well-head to control the flow of high pressure oil or gas, so called because the pipes form several branches and are festooned with valves and control mechanisms ..." (*An A-Z of Offshore Oil & Gas*, Whitehead, 1976).
[52] Cl. 7.

405

(i) the setting of the Christmas Tree, pumping equipment or well head equipment, or

(ii) the dismantling or (" and " in " B ") removal of the drilling equipment from the location, whichever of (i) or (ii) shall first occur.

5. *Deductibles*

A deductible is a sum which has to be deducted from the amount suffered as a loss by the assured, the loss being in all other respects one which would qualify for recovery under the insurance, so as to arrive at the net sum which he may recover. It may be distinguished from a franchise, which is a sum or percentage, and which, if it is exceeded, results in the whole of the claim being recoverable from the insurers.

The deductibles in cost of control insurance policies may depend upon the area in which the drilling unit is working and, in individual cases, the requirements of the assured or of the underwriters. The areas [53] are usually listed in a schedule to the policy and named and defined, often with specified limits of latitude and longitude. These areas are also relevant for purposes of rating.

The provisions for deductibles are expressed in such words as:

" *DEDUCTIBLES*
(A) *Areas* 1 *and* 2
(i) Policy for Cost of Control Only: Assured to bear the first $25,000 of any claim.
(ii) Policies for Cost of Control and clean up and containment combined: assured to bear the first $75,000 of any claim.
(B) *Areas* 3 *and* 4
(i) Policy for Cost of Control Only: Assured to bear the first $50,000 of any claim.
(ii) Policy for Cost of Control and clean up and containment combined: assured to bear the first $100,000 of any claim."

or:

" *DEDUCTIBLE CLAUSE*
Areas 1 *and* 2
Assured to bear the first $25,000 of each claim.
Areas 3 *and* 4
Assured to bear the first $50,000 of each claim."

6. *Coinsurance*

Taken literally, the word " coinsurance " means insurance together, and thus refers to a situation in which two or more parties are insured together in respect of the same risks. In that sense the parties in question could be joint assureds and both named in the policy.[54] In the case of a cost of control of well insurance, however, the provision as to coinsurance has the effect that the insurers and the assured share the loss although it

---

[53] See below, p. 428. The areas are also relevant in connection with coinsurance; see below, pp. 406–407.

[54] See the discussion of co-ventures above, p. 400.

exceeds the deductible. Such a provision is designed to involve the assured more closely in the venture and to encourage him to be even more interested in ensuring that the cost of control expenses are kept as low as possible. [55]

One such provision states [56]:

> " *COINSURANCE*
> It is a condition of this insurance that the assured shall be a coinsurer with underwriters as follows:
> (A) Areas 1 and 2 [57]—15% coinsurance
> (B) Areas 3 and 4—20% coinsurance.
> It is further a condition that this Coinsurance remains uninsured."

Let us take a claim for $1,000,000 under Area 3 or Area 4. The underwriter pays 80 per cent. less 80 per cent. of the deductible, *i.e.* $800,000 less $40,000, *i.e.* $760,000. The assured is regarded as having " paid," as coinsurer $200,000 less 20 per cent. of the deductible, *i.e.* $10,000, namely $190,000.

7. *Exclusions*

The cost of control of well insurance policies normally include a list of matters excluded from the cover. These matters may either be covered by some other form of insurance or not be covered at all. The categories of exclusion commonly found, with examples of the provisions used, are as follows:

A. Personal injury, death, etc.

> " The Underwriters shall have no liability for expense in connection with Bodily injury, illness, disease, death, workmen's compensation. . . ." [58]

The cover itself in the cost of control of well insurance is in respect of expenses incurred by the assured in regaining control of the well, the expenses themselves also being defined in the policy.[59] If the assured incurs a liability for bodily injury or the other matters mentioned in the course of and as a result of trying to regain control, and incurs expenses in order to discharge such liability, those expenses are excluded from the cover. Liabilities of the type mentioned here are usually covered elsewhere.

B. Loss of hole and certain other expenses of an operational nature

> " The Underwriters shall have no liability for expenses in connection with . . . loss of hole, loss of drill stem, damage to any part of contractors' drilling equipment, loss of or damage to property, loss of production, all fishing costs, all expenses of conditioning well(s) to resume drilling operations." [60]

---

[55] As to the duty of the assured to take such measures as may be reasonable to avert or minimise a loss, see below, p. 416.
[56] In policy " A " at cl. 6 and in policy " B " at cl. 11; see above, p. 394, nn. 1 and 3.
[57] As to Areas see above, p. 406 and below, p. 428.
[58] As in policy " A," cl. 7 (a) and policy " B," cl. 12 (a).
[59] See above, pp. 398 and 399.
[60] As in policy " A," cl. 7 (a), and policy " B," cl. 12 (a).

C. Relief Wells

" Absolutely no coverage is provided hereunder on relief well except the cost of drilling a relief well as so provided under this policy." [61]

A relief well is a well which serves to relieve the insured well or wells, so that control of that well, or those wells, can be regained. It has been defined [62] as " A deviated well drilled into a structure for the purpose of relieving pressure in an adjacent well which has suffered a blowout."

The aim of the exclusion clause quoted here is to ensure that the cost of control of well insurance does not extend to the relief well in addition to the insured well or wells. A blowout may alter the pressures encountered below ground so that the drilling of a relief well is more hazardous than normal exploration or production drilling. If the relief well gets out of control the expenses incurred in regaining control of it are not covered. This exclusion applies even if control is lost of the relief well as a result of the original loss of control of an insured well. Such cover might otherwise exist, but for the exclusion, as a result of the general cover afforded by a cost of control of well insurance, under which cover extends to other wells which get out of control. [63] The question of cover in respect of the expense of drilling a relief well is discussed below. [64]

D. Hostile or warlike actions

Just as the Institute Time Clauses (Hulls) provides [65] that the cover is " Warranted free . . . from the consequences of hostilities or warlike operations, whether there be a declaration of war or not," so also a cost of control of well insurance excludes the insurers from liabilities of a similar nature. Thus one policy [66] states:

" Excluding claim for expenses resulting from:
(1) Hostile or warlike action in time of peace or war, including action in hindering, combating or defending against an actual, impending or expected attack, by any Government or Sovereign power (*de jure* or *de facto*) or by any authority maintaining or using military, naval or air forces or by military, naval or air forces or by an agent of any such government, power, authority or forces."

The basis of this clause is similar to that in the Institute Time Clauses (Hulls), in that the exclusion relates to matters, which would otherwise be covered, resulting from " hostile or warlike action in time of peace or war." The words " warlike action " seem to be wider in their effect than the words " warlike operations," and might serve to embrace a single action, as, for example, by one submarine or aircraft, which might not be equivalent to " operations." So also the words " in time of peace or war "

---

[61] As in policy " A," cl. 7 (b).
[62] In *A-Z of Offshore Oil & Gas, op. cit.*
[63] See above, p. 396.
[64] See below, at p. 427.
[65] At cl. 23.
[66] Policy " A " at cl. 7; and policy " B " at cl. 12 (c) (1).

may be more exhaustive than the words " whether there be a declaration of war or not." They make it more clear that one is dealing not only with a situation in which a state of hostilities or of war may exist, but there has been no declaration of war. That is now a common enough situation. It is apparent, in view of the words " in time of peace or war," that it is not necessary that a warlike situation should exist, provided that there is a " Hostile or warlike action."

After what has been described above as the basis of the clause, which is the reference to " hostile or warlike action in time of peace or war," the word " including " [67] introduces various categories of action which fall within that description. They can be categorised thus, as including: —action in hindering, combating or defending against an actual, impending or expected attack by

(1) any government or Sovereign power (*de jure* or *de facto*); or by
(2) any authority maintaining or using military, naval or air forces; or by
(3) military, naval or air forces; or by
(4) an agent of any such government, power, authority or forces.

As a result of these words there is excluded from the control of well insurance not only (a) the cost of control of a well which has become out of control as a direct result of the hostile or warlike action of another, but also (b) the expenses resulting from steps taken against such an action. As for the first of these two heads of expense, or (a), if there were a hostile and warlike action against a drilling unit, and that attack resulted in loss of control of the well, and expenses being incurred by the assured to regain control, those expenses would be excluded by this provision.

We now turn to the second of these two heads of expense, or (b), which are those resulting from steps taken against such an action. In the analysis set out above items (2) and (3) are separately defined in such a way that it seems that " an agent," under item (4), could be a representative of a force under (3). That force need not be one which was maintained or used by an " authority," because the latter words appear only under (2). If so, this would mean that even an isolated act by an agent, provided that he was acting on behalf of, say, a military force, would be excluded, even though the force was not maintained or used by an " authority."

E. Atomic and radioactive weapons

The Institute Time Clauses (Hulls), at clause 25, state: " Warranted free from loss damage liability or expense arising from any weapon of war employing atomic or nuclear fission &/or fusion or other like reaction or radioactive force or matter." In similar terms, a cost of control of well insurance may contain such an exclusion [68]:

---

[67] As to the meaning of " includes," see above, p. 59.
[68] As in policy " A " at cl. 7 (2); and in policy " B " at cl. 12 (c) (2).

" Excluding claim for expenses resulting from . . .
    (2) any weapon of war employing atomic fission or radioactive force whether in time of peace or war."

The exclusion is less comprehensive than that contained in the I.T.C. (Hulls), in that the words " or nuclear fission and/or fusion or other like reaction " are omitted. As a result in the unlikely event that cost of control expenses resulted from the use of a weapon of war employing " nuclear fission and/or fusion or other like reaction," and not merely " atomic fission," the assured would not be excluded from recovering such expenses. So also the words " or matter " appear after " radioactive force " in the I.T.C. (Hulls) but are omitted from the passage quoted from the cost of control of well insurance. Again, in the unlikely event that cost of control expenses resulted from the use of a weapon of war employing " radioactive . . . matter," and not merely " radioactive force," the assured would not be precluded from recovering such expenses.

F. Insurrection, etc., destruction and confiscation

The cost of control of well insurance may also contain such an exclusion provision as the following [69]:

" Excluding claim for expenses resulting from . . .
(3) Insurrection, rebellion, revolution, civil war, usurped power, or action taken by governmental authority in hindering, combating or defending against such an occurrence, destruction under quarantine or Customs regulations, confiscation by order of any government or public authority, or trade."

The clause may be analysed as follows, as excluding expenses resulting from three distinct categories of event:
  (1) Insurrection, rebellion, revolution, civil war, usurped power, or action taken by governmental authority in hindering, combating or defending against such an occurrence;
  (2) destruction under quarantine or Customs regulations;
  (3) confiscation by order of any government or public authority or trade.

Provisos to D. *Hostile or Warlike actions* (*p.* 408)

    E. *Atomic and radioactive weapons* (*p.* 409)

    F. *Insurrection, etc., destruction and confiscation* (*p.* 410)

The cost of control of well insurance policies, having excluded claims for expenses resulting from actions falling within the above three categories, D, E and F, then contain a proviso which relates to the actions of certain individuals [70]:

" Notwithstanding the above this insurance shall cover loss directly caused by acts committed by an agent of any government, party or faction engaged

---

[69] Policy " A," cl. 7 (3).
[70] Policy " A," proviso to cl. 7 (3), and policy " B," proviso to cl. 12 (c).

in war hostilities or other warlike operations, provided such agent is acting secretly and not in connection with any operation of the armed forces (whether military, naval or air forces) in the country where the property is situated."

There had been an earlier reference to the acts of an agent under category D above.[71] The exclusion in question had the effect of denying to the assured the right to recover expenses of " action in hindering, combating or defending against an actual, impending or expected attack ... by an agent. ..." By its reference to an agent who is (a) acting secretly and (b) not in connection with any operation of the armed forces in the country where the property is situated, the proviso appears to admit, as recoverable, those expenses which would otherwise be excluded by the earlier reference to an agent.

A second proviso to the three categories D, E and F reaffirms the effectiveness of the exclusion, by category E, in respect of atomic and radioactive weapons. The proviso, which by its terms would seem to refer to the first proviso, makes it especially clear that the cover extended in the case of certain agents does not affect the exclusion in respect of such weapons. Thus:

" Nothing in the foregoing shall be construed to include any loss or expenses caused by or resulting from any of the risks or perils excluded above [72] excepting only the acts of certain agents expressly covered herein [73] but in no event shall this insurance include any loss of expense caused by or resulting from any weapon of war employing atomic fission or radioactive force whether in time of peace or war."

The last words in particular, and the proviso as a whole, thus serve to emphasise that no detraction from the exclusion as to atomic and radioactive weapons is intended.

G. Natural Catastrophes

A further exclusion clause in the cost of control of well insurance is worded as follows [74]:

" (4) Notwithstanding anything to the contrary contained herein, this policy does not cover loss damage or expense caused by or attributable to earthquake or volcanic eruption; nor to fire and/or explosion and/or tidal wave consequent upon earthquake or volcanic eruption."

This clause can be deleted in areas not subject to earthquakes, or, in certain fringe areas, deleted subject to an additional premium.

---

[71] Hostile or warlike operations; see above, p. 408.
[72] *i.e.* A. Personal injury, death, etc. (p. 407); B. Loss of hole and certain other expenses of an operational nature (p. 407); C. Relief Wells (p. 408); D. Hostile or warlike actions (p. 408); E. Atomic and radioactive weapons (p. 409); F. Insurrection, etc., destruction and confiscation (p. 410).
[73] As a result of the first proviso; see above, p. 410.
[74] Policy " A," cl. 7 (4); policy " B," earthquake risks exclusion clause.

H. Wells under continuation clause

An additional exclusion clause in the cost of control of well insurance is worded as follows [75]:

> " Any wells insured under the Continuation Clause (if any) of the expiry Policy are excluded."

The continuation clause [76] provides for continuation of cover in respect of drilling and other work begun during the period of the policy, irrespective of the expiry date of the insurance. The reference in the exclusion clause to wells insured under the continuation clause of the expiry policy ensures that such continuation cover is confined to the expiring policy, and is not adopted by the new policy. If there was no expiring policy, or if it existed but had no continuation clause, all wells insured under the current policy would be fully covered from its inception.

8. *General Conditions of the Policy*

A cost of control insurance policy will, in addition to the provisions set out in the preceding pages, contain a number of other general conditions. Those discussed below are entitled, or relate to:

A. Blowout preventer.
B. Inspection of records.
C. Abandonment.
D. Recovery of loss from other insurers.
E. Duty of assured to minimise loss.
F. Notification to insurers.
G. Arbitration.
H. Time limit as to claims.
I. Assignment to insurers.
J. Release from liability.
K. Cancellation.

A. Blowout preventer

It may be provided that a blowout preventer must be employed:

> " It is made a condition [77] of this insurance that a blowout preventer of standard make will be set on the surface casing of the well being drilled, same to be installed and tested in accordance with the usual drilling practice " [or " the usual practice "].

A definition of blowout sometimes appears in the policy:

> " *BLOWOUT.* The term ' Blowout ' shall mean a sudden, accidental, uncontrolled and continuous expulsion from the well and above the surface of the ground of the drilling field in an oil or gas well, followed by continuous

---

[75] Policy " B," cl. 12 (b); the words are repeated in cl. 13 of the same policy which deals with Relief Wells.
[76] See below, p. 427.
[77] As to the significance of this term see p. 100, above.

and uncontrolled flow from the well and above the surface of the ground of oil, gas or water due to encountering subterranean pressures during the drilling or reworking of such well."

B. Inspection of records

The insurers are given the right to inspect the records of the assured, so far as they may be relevant to the computation of premium,[78] and the assured is under a duty to keep such records. Thus, for example [79]:

> "The Assured shall maintain records of the information necessary for premium computation on the basis stated in the schedule above,[80] and the Underwriters or their duly authorised representatives shall be permitted to examine and audit the Assured's books and records at any time during the Policy or Certificate period and any extension of the Policy or Certificate period and within three years after the final termination of the Policy or Certificate as far as they relate to the premium basis on the subject-matter of this insurance."

In most cases the contractor instals the blowout preventer, though the assured is the operator.

So also in another policy [81]:

> "Any of the Underwriters or their authorised representatives shall have the right and opportunity, wherever the Underwriters so desire, to inspect and examine any books or records so far as they relate to the premium computation hereon."

The latter clause, granting to the insurers a right of inspection, is similar to the second half of the earlier clause, the insurers having access to the assured's books and records as far as they relate to the premium basis or computation. A material difference is that no time limit is expressed in the latter clause, whereas the earlier clause enables the right to be exercised only up to three years after the final termination of the policy or certificate. If a dispute arose, however, it does not seem that this clause would preclude the insurers from exercising the rights of discovery of documents which are incidental to a civil action, and granted by the court, even though three years had elapsed since the final termination of the policy or certificate. Such a right would be one which was incidental to the action rather than to the contract.

C. Abandonment

The cost of control of insurance policy may contain the following provision [82]:

> "There can be no abandonment to the Underwriters of any property."

---

[78] As to premium generally see p. 427, below.
[79] Policy " A," condition B.
[80] A schedule as to the calculation of premium.
[81] Policy " B," general condition B.
[82] Policy " A," condition C; policy " B," general condition C.

The word " abandonment " can be used in several senses. In its strict definition abandonment arises only in the case of a constructive total loss, and

> " means the voluntary cession by the assured to the insurer of all that remains of the subject-matter insured, which must take place before a claim for a total loss is made, and this is the sense in which it is used in sections 61, 62 and 63 [83] of the Marine Insurance Act 1906." [84]

Such a cession would also give to the insurer all proprietary rights and remedies in respect of the subject-matter insured.

The proposition in a cost of control of insurance policy that there can be no abandonment to the underwriters of any property seems at first to be difficult to apply, because the concept of abandonment, in its strict sense, is relevant only where there is a constructive total loss. In its turn, a constructive total loss occurs, to quote section 60 (1) of the Marine Insurance Act 1906, [85]

> " Where the subject-matter insured is reasonably abandoned on account of its total loss appearing to be unavoidable, or because it could not be preserved from actual total loss without an expenditure which would exceed its value when the expenditure had been incurred."

In a cost of control of insurance policy what is the subject-matter insured? The policy refers to the "control of oil or gas well(s) covered hereunder" [86] and "the well(s) insured," [87] and the insurers agree to "reimburse the Assured for the costs . . ." of regaining control. [88] It might be argued that the well is to be regarded as the subject-matter of the insurance. So also, under the Institute Time Clauses (Hulls), the ship is the subject-matter of the insurance not only as to the insurance against its loss or damage but also as to the separate insurance thereunder in respect of sue and labour expenses. But in the case of the Institute Time Clauses (Hulls) there are two separate insurances, for the ship and for the sue and labour expenses. In a cost of control insurance policy the well itself is not insured, even though the policy refers to " the well(s) insured." It seems permissible to describe it as the subject-matter of the policy only in the sense that all depends upon its fortunes. Unless control of the well is lost the assured does not have to incur expenses and the loss has not occurred.

The insurance is in respect of the costs of regaining control, and those costs do not, for the purpose of the insurance, stand in any particular relationship to the total loss or the value of the well. If the concept of constructive total loss is inapplicable, then it follows that there is no question of that voluntary cession to the insurers, of all that remains of the

---

[83] Dealing, respectively, with "Effect of constructive total loss," " Notice of abandonment," and " Effect of abandonment."

[84] These are the words used in Arnould on *Marine Insurance* (15th ed., 1961), at para. 1084.

[85] As to the relevance of the 1906 Act, see Appendix C to this book, at p. 456.

[86] See above, p. 395.

[87] See above, p. 398.

[88] See above, p. 398.

subject-matter insured, which constitutes abandonment.[89] The insurers will not become responsible for the property in the vicinity or for liabilities in respect thereof. Although they are obliged to pay or may have made a payment in respect of the expenses incurred in regaining control, they do not have that sort of interest in the well which would have arisen by virtue of the doctrine of subrogation.

The distinction made here arises because of the fundamental difference between abandonment and subrogation. Lord Blackburn, in *Simpson* v. *Thomson*,[90] said:

> " Where the owners of an assured ship have claimed or been paid as for a total loss, the property in what remains of the ship, and all rights incident to the property, are transferred to the underwriters as from the time of the disaster in respect of which the total loss is claimed for and paid . . . But the right of the assured to recover damages from a third person is not one of those rights which are incidental to the property in the ship; it does pass to the underwriters in case of payment for a total loss, but on a different principle. . . . The right . . . could only arise, and did only arise, from the fact that the underwriters had paid an indemnity, and were so subrogated for the person whom they had indemnified in his personal rights from the time of the payment of the indemnity."

If there was no provision in a cost of control insurance policy as to abandonment, it seems that the concept of abandonment would be inapplicable for the reasons just given. Nevertheless the express exclusion of abandonment " of any property," which thus includes not only the well but the drilling unit and its equipment, so far as the assured had any rights to dispose of them, makes the position clear.

D. Recovery of loss from other insurers

An assured may, usually by inadvertence, be insured in such a way that the policies seem to entitle him to recover more than any individual underwriter had intended should represent his limit of recovery.

Cost of control insurance policies may as a result contain such clauses as the following:

> " No loss shall be paid hereunder if the Assured has collected the same from others." [91]

and:

> " It is a condition that no additional Cost of Control policy is placed." [92]

or:

> " *Other Insurance.* Warranted no additional Control of Well Insurance in existence on the wells insured hereunder during the currency of this Insurance for the account of the Assured, unless the Underwriters hereon agree thereto in writing " [93]

An oil company might be the operator in one operation but at the same

---

[89] See above, pp. 143–144.
[90] (1877) 3 App.Cas. 279 (H.L.) at p. 292.
[91] Policy " A," condition D; Policy " B," general condition D.
[92] Policy " A," one of the exclusions.
[93] Policy " B," cl. 18.

time have a partial but not an operating interest in, say, 50 other wells. It might insure all 51 wells under the same policy; but the operators of the other 50 wells might also have insured them with or without the first operator's knowledge. The underwriters would be concerned with the possibility that one cost of control insurance would operate in addition to, *i.e.* in excess of, another. For example an assured may have spent $50 million on control expenses and have two policies each with a limit of $5 million. If he tried to collect under both policies the above provisions would disentitle him from doing so. This sort of provision is especially necessary in the case of a liability policy, where the limit imposed is unrelated to the value of any property.

E. Duty of assured to minimise loss

A cost of control insurance policy may provide:

> "It is the duty of the Assured and his agents, in all cases, to take such measures as may be reasonable for the purpose of averting or minimising a loss." [94]

In similar terms section 78 (4) of the Marine Insurance Act [95] states: " It is the duty of the assured and his agents, in all cases, to take such measures as may be reasonable for the purpose of averting or minimising a loss."

In the case of a policy governed by the Marine Insurance Act 1906, s. 78 (4) has to be read in the context of the other sub-sections of section 78, which relates to the suing and labouring clause. [96] That clause deals with the right of the assured to take steps to protect the insured subject-matter and to recover the expenses thus incurred from the insurers. Section 78 (4) makes it clear that it is also his duty to take reasonable measures to avert or to minimise a loss after the occurrrence of a casualty. [97]

In the case of a cost of control insurance policy, the assured must take reasonable measures to avert or minimise a loss. There is not, at least in the two policies from which examples are being taken in the course of the present discussion, a separate provision that such sue and labour expenses are recoverable under the policy. In such situations, however, the object of the insurance itself is to cover the expenses incurred to regain control. The clause quoted states the duty of the assured to minimise a loss when it has occurred. At first it would seem that the word " averting," as opposed to the word " minimising," could refer to (a) the avoidance of the loss in the first place; and (b) the avoidance of further loss, once some loss had occurred, but there are contrary views.

---

[94] Policy " A," condition F; policy " B," general condition E.

[95] s. 78 is headed " suing and labouring clause."

[96] As for the suing and labouring clause in the London Standard Drilling Barge Form, see above, p. 154.

[97] As is stated in Arnould on *Marine Insurance* (15th ed. 1961), para. 788: " The duty imposed in s. 78 (4) can only arise after the occurrence of a casualty has created a potential loss—this the assured must minimise if he can. Failure to distinguish these essentially different matters has undoubtedly led to confusion in the past."

The loss may have occurred as a result of an action or omission on the part of someone ultimately answerable to the operator. The drilling superintendent employed by the contractor may have been negligent. It does not seem that this would be imputed to the operator so as to preclude recovery under the policy. In this respect the situation would be similar to that set out in section 55 (2) (*a*) of the 1906 Act [98]:

> " The insurer is not liable for any loss attributable to the wilful misconduct of the assured, but, unless the policy otherwise provides, he is liable for any loss proximately caused by a peril insured against, even though the loss would not have happened but for the misconduct or negligence of the master or crew."

F. Notification to insurers

It is usually provided in a cost of control insurance policy, as in other insurance policies, that there shall be prompt notice to the insurers of any event likely to give rise to a claim. For example:

> " The Assured upon knowledge of an accident or occurrence likely to give rise to a claim hereunder, shall give, as soon as practicable, immediate written notice thereof to: . . . [99] [for transmittal to Underwriters.]" [1]

This is not a provision, therefore, which deals with advice as to the claim itself. It is enough that there should be an accident or occurrence which is " likely to give rise to a claim."

It seems that not only actual loss of control of the well, but preliminary events which indicate that control is likely to be lost, would constitute accidents or occurrences which were likely to give rise to a claim.

There is a comparable provision in clause 19 of the Institute Time Clauses (Hulls),[1] the opening words of which are:

> " In the event of accident whereby loss or damage may result in a claim under this Policy, notice shall be given to the Underwriters prior to survey and also, if the Vessel is abroad, to the nearest Lloyd's Agent so that a surveyor may be appointed to represent the Underwriters should they so desire."

That clause, known as the survey and tender clause, does not oblige the assured to give " immediate " notice, " as soon as practicable." The obligation is to give notice to the insurers " prior to survey," and also, if the ship is abroad, to the nearest Lloyd's agent in sufficient time for a surveyor to be appointed.

G. Arbitration

The cost of control insurance policy may contain an arbitration clause under which a dispute between the assured and the insurers may be resolved. Its wording might not extend to all disputes.

---

[98] s. 55 is entitled " Included and excluded losses."

[99] Policy " A," condition H.

[1] The provision in policy " B," general condition G, is identical except that these words in brackets are added.

For example:

> " In the case the Assured and the Underwriters shall fail to agree as to the, amount of loss [or damage.] the same shall be ascertained by two competent and disinterested appraisers, the Assured and Underwriters each selecting one, and the two so chosen shall first select a competent and disinterested umpire; the appraisers together shall then estimate and appraise the loss, [stating separately the sound values and damage,] and failing to agree, shall submit their differences to the umpire; and the Award in writing of any two shall determine the amount of the loss: the parties hereto shall pay the appraisers respectively selected by them, and shall bear equally the expense of the appraisal and umpire." [2]

"*. . . the amount of loss [or damage]* "

The arbitration clause extends only to disputes as to the amount of the loss or damage.[3] It constitutes an arbitration agreement in respect of the *quantum* of any claim, and not as to whether the assured has a claim. For example, the insurers may contend that the expenses incurred by the assured fell outside the policy, because they were expenses resulting from hostile or warlike action in time of peace or war. If that contention were correct, the claim might be one which was excluded from the cover.[4] If the assured sought to have the matter arbitrated under the arbitration clause, it would seem that the insurers could argue successfully that it was not a matter which fell under the clause. It was not a dispute " as to the amount of loss or damage," but a dispute as to liability. Such a dispute would therefore be one in respect of which the assured would have to find a remedy other than arbitration.

"*. . . two competent and disinterested appraisers, the Assured and Underwriters each selecting one, and the two so chosen shall first select a competent and disinterested umpire . . .*"

The word " appraisers " as contrasted with the word " arbitrators," is used here. So far as their task is limited, as has been pointed out,[5] to an assessment of " the amount of loss," the word used is appropriate. An appraiser is one who is to appraise, that is, to " fix price for; estimate." [6] The fact that the individuals are described as appraisers rather than as arbitrators does not mean that they are any the less arbitrators, or that the clause is any the less an arbitration clause.

The appraisers are to be " competent and disinterested." The first of these adjectives imposes a certain limitation upon the range of person who may be chosen. It is not such a limited or clear definition as that contained

---

[2] Policy " A," condition J. The arbitration provision in policy " B," general condition H, is in identical terms, except that the words in square brackets are omitted.

[3] As to both, in policy " A "; and only as to the loss in policy " B "; but it is doubtful whether the omission of the word " damage " makes any difference. The claim against insurers is for expenses incurred by the assured in regaining control of the well.

[4] See above, p. 408, as to this exclusion.

[5] See this page, above.

[6] *Concise Oxford Dictionary*.

in some arbitration clauses, which may provide, in shipping disputes for example, that the arbitrators must be commercial men, or that they must be members of the Baltic Exchange. The word " competent " does, however, suggest that the appraiser shall be qualified, though not necessarily by means of a professional qualification, to deal with the assessment of the loss. It is not enough that he should be competent in the sense that he is of sound mind, or *compos mentis,* and merely not suffering from one of the defects which have been held to be fundamental bars to the valid appointment of an arbitrator.[7] A person with experience of the work of offshore mobile drilling units, but no legal knowledge, and a person with legal knowledge but with no experience of such work, might both be regarded as competent. So also a person with some experience of the assessment of the measure of losses, such as a loss adjuster, or a quality arbitrator, might be regarded as competent. These should only be regarded as examples, for a person with none of these special skills or, indeed, with no special skill, might well be regarded as competent by virtue of certain qualities of character, or of intelligence, or of both.

The above discussion has proceeded on the assumption that some meaning must be attributed to the word " competent " in this context. It could perhaps be argued that the use of the adjective adds nothing, and that an appraiser, or arbitrator, should in any case be competent, in the sense in which this word has here been defined. Two passages cited in *Russell on Arbitration* [8] are somewhat contradictory in this respect. The first [9] states: " Neither natural nor legal disabilities do hinder any one from being an arbitrator. If they are incompetent judges, the fault is in them that chose them." This suggests that the word " competent," when inserted in an arbitration clause, would add something to the meaning of the clause. The passage in question, however, is dealing with a situation in which the award has been issued, and the arbitrators have been seen to be inefficient. The arbitration clause in the cost of control insurance policy, however, is placing a duty upon the two parties to appoint someone who is competent. The remedy for the aggrieved party, if he believes that the appraiser or arbitrator is not competent, may be for him to seek to have him removed before the two persons proceed to an award.

The second passage states [10]:

> " Touching their sufficiency, such persons are to be elected as have sufficient skill of the matters compromitted, and have neither legal nor natural impediments to give an upright sentence."

According to these words the arbitrators should be skilled in the matters " compromitted," or made the subject of an arbitration, in addition to

---

[7] These have included madness and idiocy; see *Russell on Arbitration* (18th ed., 1970), at pp. 82–83.

[8] (18th ed., 1970), at pp. 82–83.

[9] From Vin.Abr., tit. " Arbitrement," A. 2.

[10] West's *Symboleographie* (1647) Pt. II, tit. " Compromise," s. 23.

being free of legal and natural impediments. If they are to be taken literally, this would mean that the word " competent " in the clause under consideration would be superfluous, as the appraisers should, merely by virtue of being appraisers, or arbitrators, have some skill in the matters in dispute.

It would seem to be more in accordance with the intention of the parties, who have inserted the word " competent," that it should be taken to qualify, and so to add to, the meaning of the word " appraisers." They are to be more than mere appraisers; they must be able to do more than appraise, for they must have a particular competence.

The second adjective used to describe the appraisers is " disinterested," which means [11]: " Not biased by self-seeking, impartial." In this case the word probably does not add anything, as an arbitrator should be a disinterested person.

The clause goes on to say, in the extract quoted above,[12] that the two appraisers chosen by each party " shall first select a competent and disinterested umpire." In the case of an arbitration clause to which the English Arbitration Act 1950 applies, such a step is necessary unless the clause provides to the contrary. Thus section 8 (1) of the Act states:

> " Unless a contrary intention is expressed therein, every arbitration agreement shall, where the reference is to two arbitrators, be designed to include a provision that the two arbitrators shall appoint an umpire immediately after they are themselves appointed."

By section 10 of the Act the High Court has powers in certain cases to " appoint an arbitrator, umpire or third party "; one case in which this power arises is that " where two arbitrators are required to appoint an umpire and do not appoint him." [13]

" . . . *the appraisers together shall then estimate and appraise the loss, and failing to agree, shall submit their differences to the umpire; and the award in writing of any two shall determine the amount of the loss . . .*'

If the appraisers reach agreement as to the amount of the loss they will be able to and should produce a joint award which will bind the parties. This part of the arbitration clause states that in the event of their disagreement they should submit their differences to the umpire. It is at that time, when they submit a written notice of disagreement to the parties or to the umpire, that the umpire enters into the reference. As section 8 (2) of the 1950 Act states:

> " Unless a contrary intention is expressed therein, every arbitration agreement shall, where such a provision is applicable to the reference, be deemed

---

[11] According to the *Concise Oxford Dictionary*. The clause uses the word correctly, though it is often, erroneously, used as a synonym for " uninterested." If that were the case here the arbitrators might not be regarded as competent.

[12] At p. 418.

[13] For further discussion of this problem see *Russell on Arbitration* (18th ed., 1970) at p. 101.

to include a provision that if the arbitrators have delivered to any party to the arbitration agreement, or to the umpire, a notice in writing stating that they cannot agree, the umpire may forthwith enter on the reference in lieu of the arbitrators."

There is a material difference, however, between the wording of this part of the arbitration clause in the cost of control insurance policy and of section 8 (2) of the Act. The clause goes on to state: ". . . and the award in writing of any two shall determine the amount of the loss. . . ." Despite the use of the words " any two," it would seem unlikely that, after disagreement, the two original arbitrators would change their views and agree. The " two " in question would thus be the umpire and one of the arbitrators, who could join in the issuance of an award. Where section 8 (2) of the Act applies, however, the umpire enters on the reference " in lieu of the arbitrators," so that neither of the latter would play any judicial part as members of the tribunal.[14]

Nevertheless, the words " Unless a contrary intention is expressed therein," which are the opening words of section 8 (1), clearly apply to all that is set out in the rest of that subsection. As a result the provision in this arbitration clause that " the award in writing of any two shall determine the amount of the loss " is effective, and the participation by the umpire is not " in lieu " of participation by the arbitrators, one or both of whom may join in the award.

Costs of the arbitration and the award

"*. . . the parties hereon shall pay the appraisers respectively selected by them and shall bear equally the expense of the appraisal and umpire . . .*"

The general rule in English law is that the arbitration tribunal has discretion as to the costs of the proceedings. In the context of that rule these costs comprise (a) the costs of the reference, which may include the costs of lawyers and other expenditure relating to the presentation of their cases by the parties; and (b) the cost of the award, which consists of the fees of the arbitrators and the umpire, and their other expenditure relating to the proceedings, such as the hire of a room for the arbitration.

This general rule is set out in section 18 (1) of the English Arbitration Act 1950:

" Unless a contrary intention is expressed therein, every arbitration agreement shall be deemed to include a provision that the costs of the reference and award shall be in the discretion of the arbitrator or umpire, who may direct to and by whom and in what manner those costs or any part thereof shall be paid, and may tax or settle the amount of costs to be so paid or any part thereof, and may award costs to be paid as between solicitor and client."

---

[14] From the moment of the service of the notice of disagreement they become advocates.

This must be read in conjunction with section 18 (3):

" Any provision in an arbitration agreement to the effect that the parties or any party thereto shall in any event pay their or his own costs of the reference or award or any part thereof shall be void, and this Part of this Act, shall in the case of an arbitration agreement containing any such provision, have effect as if that provision were not contained therein:

Provided that nothing in this subsection shall invalidate such a provision when it is a part of an agreement to submit to arbitration a dispute which has arisen before the making of that agreement."

The arbitration clause in the cost of control insurance policy states, in effect, that each party shall pay (1) the fee of the appraiser or arbitrator appointed by it; (2) one half of the expense, or costs, of " the appraisal and umpire." The first proposition, (1), is one which takes away the discretion which would otherwise be vested in the tribunal by virtue of section 18 (1) of the 1950 Act. The parties, who are the assured and the insurers, are entitled to do this, by virtue of the opening words of section 18 (1), " Unless a contrary intention is expressed therein . . . ," if such an agreement is not otherwise precluded by the Act. We therefore have to look to section 18 (3), where we find that " Any provision . . . that the parties . . . shall in any event pay their . . . own costs of the reference or award or any part thereof shall be void. . . ." Proposition (a), as set out above, is such a provision, because it states that each shall pay its own appraiser's fee. That fee is, as has been explained above,[15] part of the costs of the award. The proviso to subsection (3) would only validate such a provision where the dispute arose before the arbitration agreement, *i.e.* in the case of what is known as an arbitration submission, after a dispute has occurred. As a result the provision that the parties shall pay the appraisers respectively is void under English law.

The second proposition, (2), relates to the expense of " the appraisal and umpire." The expense of the appraisal would seem to consist of the costs of the arbitration, as compared with the cost of the award [16] itself. Those costs consist of lawyers' fees and other expenses incurred by a party so far as they relate to the establishment or rebuttal of the matters in issue in the arbitration. It might be contended that the " expense of the appraisal " should be confined in its application to expense incurred solely in the course of the work carried out by the appraisers so far as their task of appraisal is concerned. It might indeed be argued that an even more narrow definition is correct, in that the expression should relate only to their own expenses during that time, such as the hire of an arbitration room. If, as seems to be the case, the terms " appraisers " and " appraisal " can be regarded as synonymous with " arbitrators " and " arbitration," then the widest of the three interpretations above seems to be correct; as a result the expense of the appraisal must be the same as the costs of the

---

[15] At p. 421.
[16] See p. 421.

arbitration. In English law such costs include both the costs of the reference and the cost of the award.[17] The cost of the award is dealt with by those parts of the provision in question which speak of the payment of the appraisers and the expense of the umpire. We are thus left with the costs of the reference, described here as the expense of the appraisal. This, it is stated, is to be borne equally by the parties.

This provision has, where English law applies, to be interpreted in the light of section 18 (1) and (3) of the Arbitration Act 1950.[18] Such interpretation leads, as in the case of the provision for each party to pay its appraiser,[19] to the conclusion that this provision is void under English law. The only exception is where it is part of an agreement to submit to arbitration a dispute which has arisen before the making of that agreement.[20]

H. Time limit as to claims

Unless an insurance policy provides otherwise, the period of time within which a party may take proceedings or make a claim is governed by the applicable law as to time limits. Where English law applies, such rights of the parties to a contract are governed by the Limitation Act 1939, of which section 2 (1) (*a*) states:

> " The following actions shall not be brought after the expiration of six years from the date on which the cause of action accrued, that is to say:
> (a) actions founded on simple contract or on tort."

The parties, being at liberty to alter the period in question, have done so in the case of certain cost of control insurance policies by such provisions as follows:

> " It is a condition of the Policy that no suit, action or proceeding for the recovery of any claim under this Policy shall be maintainable in any Court of Law or equity unless the same be commenced within the two years and one day after the time a cause of action for the loss accrues, provided, however, that if by the laws of the State shown in the address of the Assured in this Policy such limitation is invalid, then any such claims shall be void unless such action, suit or proceeding be commenced within the shortest limit of time permitted by the laws of such State." [21]

I. Assignment to Insurers

The cost of control insurance policy may contain a clause such as the following:

> " The Underwriters may require from the Assured an assignment of all rights of recovery against any party for loss or damage to the extent that payment therefore is made by the Underwriters." [22]

---

[17] See above, p. 421.
[18] See above, pp. 421 and 422, respectively.
[19] See above, p. 422.
[20] As stated in the proviso to s. 18 (3); see above, p. 422.
[21] Policy " B," general condition J.
[22] Policy " B," general condition J.

This provision gives formal effect to the general rule that an insurer who has settled a loss is entitled to the rights and remedies which the assured may have against any party in respect of that loss. That rule is set out in section 79 of the Marine Insurance Act 1906, so far as policies governed by that Act are concerned.[23]

" (1) Where the insurer pays for a total loss, either of the whole, or in the case of goods of any apportionable part, of the subject-matter insured, he thereupon becomes entitled to take over the interest of the assured in whatever may remain of the subject-matter so paid for, and he is thereby subrogated to all the rights and remedies of the assured in and in respect of that subject-matter as from the time of the casualty causing the loss.

(2) Subject to the foregoing provisions, where the insurer pays for a partial loss, he acquires no title to the subject-matter insured, or such part of it as may remain, but he is thereupon subrogated to all rights and remedies of the assured in and in respect of the subject-matter insured as from the time of the casualty causing the loss, in so far as the assured has been indemnified, according to this Act, by such payment for the loss."

This assignment clause must be read in the light of any provision in the cost of control insurance by which the assured may release other persons from liability.[24] Where the assured has such a right of release, and has exercised or will exercise that right, an assignment of rights of recovery may become less productive for the insurers. The operator in nearly all cases releases the contractor from liability for cost of control expenses, subject to certain restrictions in the case of negligence by the contractor.[25]

J. Release from Liability

The insurers may grant to the assured rights to release persons from their liability, as in the following clause [26]:

" Privilege is granted the Assured to release from liability any person, firm or corporation for whom the Assured is performing operations or who is performing operations for the Assured under contract or otherwise, provided the loss or damage subject to said release and indemnification arises out of or in connection with such operations."

The effect of this important clause is to free from liability, if the assured exercises the privilege thereby granted, persons against whom the assured (or the insurers if the assured had assigned its rights of recovery to them [27]) would otherwise have had a good claim. The clause may be read in conjunction with any provision in the operating contract by which the benefit of its insurance is given by one party to another, as in the words:

" Contractors' insurance shall be endorsed to provide that the underwriters waive their right of recourse against Operator. Operator will, as well, cause its insurer to waive subrogation against Contractor." [28]

---

[23] See Appendix C to this book.
[24] See " Release from Liability," this page, below.
[25] See above.   [26] Policy " B," general condition K.
[27] See above.
[28] Clause 1103, headed " Benefit," in the International Daywork Drilling Contract —Offshore (I.A.D.C.).

K. Cancellation

The cost of control insurance policy usually covers the assured for a period of 12 months,[29] subject to termination upon abandonment or completion of the wells, and subject also to the provision for continuation [30] after the period expires until abandonment or completion of the wells. The policy may also provide for the cancellation of the policy by either party. Such a cancellation clause may state:

> " This Policy may be cancelled by either the Named Assured or Underwriters giving thirty days' notice. Such cancellation shall become effective on the expiry of thirty days from Midnight of the day on which notice of cancellation is issued by or to Underwriters, but shall not apply to the Insurance of any oil or gas well being drilled, tested, deepened, reworked or reconditioned at the effective time of cancellation; such operations being covered hereunder until the total or complete abandonment of the well or the successful completion of the operation. Notice of cancellation may also be given by a Co-Venturer of the Named Assured(s) or Underwriters in accordance with the foregoing clause in respect of that Co-Venturer's interest only, without affecting the insurance afforded hereunder to the Named Assured(s) or to the then Co-Venturers." [31]

This clause contains the following propositions:

1. Either party can cancel by giving 30 days' notice. In the absence of some other provision in the policy that notices should be given in a particular form, as, for example, at the party's office and in writing, a notice of cancellation can be written or oral, and direct or through an agent or other third party.

2. A period of 30 full days begins to run at midnight at the end of the day on which the notice is given. The cancellation comes into effect, and cover ceases, at midnight at the end of the thirtieth full day.

3. This right to cancel does not exist (except of course by mutual agreement) in respect of a well which is being " drilled, tested, deepened, reworked or reconditioned at the effective time of cancellation." The " effective time " is the time at which the cancellation would have come into effect, 30 days having expired, if the right to cancel had not been negatived by this clause. This exception has a direct connection with the continuation clause,[32] by which cover continues while such operations are in progress until the operation has been completed successfully or the well has been completely abandoned. Indeed the cancellation clause provides for cover to continue, in such an event, in words similar to those used in the continuation clause. The cancellation is ineffective where such operations are in progress " at the effective time of cancellation "; this provision has the effect that although they may not be in progress when the notice is given the notice can become ineffective because they have started, or restarted, and are in progress at the end of the 30 days.

---

[29] See above, p. 400.
[31] Policy " B," general condition L.

[30] See below, p. 427.
[32] See below, p. 427.

4. Notice can be given not only by the named assured and the underwriters in respect of each other, but also by a co-venturer of the assured or by the underwriters, in respect of the co-venturer's interest. In such an event the notice will terminate the policy only in respect of that interest and not in respect of the interests of the named assured.

9. *Definitions*

Some cost of control insurance policies provide definitions of the terms used in the clauses which especially concern these terms. Others may contain a separate section devoted to definitions of the most important expressions used. The expressions customarily defined in this manner, with examples of definitions taken from various policies, include:

Well Out of Control [33]

" A well(s) shall be deemed out of control only so long as there is a continuous flow of drilling fluid, oil, gas or water above the surface of the ground which is uncontrollable."

Blowout [34]

" The term ' blowout' shall mean a sudden, accidental, uncontrolled and continuous expulsion from the well and above the surface of the ground of the drilling fluid in an oil or gas well, followed by continuous and uncontrolled flow from the well and above the surface of the ground or oil, gas or water due to encountering subterranean pressures during the drilling or reworking of such well."

Cratering

"The term shall mean a basin-like opening in the earth's surface surrounding a well caused by the erosive and eruptive action of gas, oil or water flowing uncontrolled."

Expenses

(The words which follow constitute an explanation rather than a definition but are sometimes included under the title " Definition of Expense(s).") " In the event the well(s) insured gets out of control the Underwriters will reimburse the Assured for the costs of materials and supplies required, contractors' equipment and services, the services of individuals or firms specialising in controlling wells including directional drilling and similar operations necessary to bring the well(s) under control.

In any circumstances Underwriters' liability for expenses of regaining control of well(s) shall cease when the well(s) is controlled above the surface of the ground or water bottom if located in water."

---

[33] See also above, p. 394.
[34] See also above, p. 412.

10. *Premium*

The provision as to premium may be expressed in the following terms:

" This Insurance is subject to an annual minimum and deposit premium of $ which shall be paid at inception. The actual premium shall be determined at the rates set forth herein, subject always to the earned premium being not less than the minimum and deposit premium stated herein.

The Assured to furnish to
a report over his signature within   days after the end of each   day period of this policy setting forth a statement of the entire operations carried on during the period and shall pay earned premium as determined adding thereto State Tax, if applicable.

The earned premium as determined shall be applied against the minimum and deposit premium until exhausted and thereafter the Assured shall pay the additional premium as indicated."

The provision in the policy for the inspection of the records of the assured [35] is inserted so that the insurers shall have access to the information necessary for premium computation.

11. *Continuation clause*

A continuation clause is a clause which provides that operations begun during the policy period are covered, irrespective of the expiry date of the insurance, until the operation is completed or the well abandoned. One continuation clause states:

" Drilling, testing, deepening, reworking and reconditioning operations which commence during the period of this Policy to be covered hereunder until successful completion of the operation or until completed abandonment of the well irrespective of the expiry date of this Insurance."

To avoid overlapping between successive policies, the policy may also state, as one of its exclusions: " Any wells insured under the Continuation Clause (if any) of the expiring Policy are excluded." [36]

The continuation clause in this policy may be compared with the continuation clause in the Institute Time Clauses (Hulls). Clause 4 thereof states: " Should the Vessel at the expiration of this Policy be at sea or in distress or at a port of refuge or of call, she shall, provided previous notice be given to the Underwriters, be held covered at a pro rata monthly premium to her port of destination." The I.T.C. clause is more strict than the continuation clause in the cost of control insurance in that the prolongation is conditional upon notice being given. Clauses which do not require notice, have, however, sometimes appeared in hull policies.[37]

12. *Relief Wells*

A relief, or directional well, has been defined [38] as " A deviated well

---

[35] See above, p. 413.   [36] See above, p. 412.
[37] As in *Charlesworth* v. *Faber* (1900) 5 Com.Cas. 408.
[38] In *An A–Z of Offshore Oil & Gas* by Whitehead (1976).

drilled into a structure for the purpose of relieving pressure in an adjacent well which has suffered a blowout." [39] A distinction must be made between cover in respect of a relief well and the cost of drilling such a well. So far as cover is concerned, a policy may provide:

> " It is agreed that Relief Wells are automatically held covered hereunder subject to prior advice to Underwriters hereon, except that in the case of Relief Well(s) drilled by the Unit conducting the original drilling operation advice to Underwriters shall be as soon as possible, at an additional premium to be agreed, if any. However, this provision shall not apply in respect of the cost of drilling a Relief Well, coverage for which is as provided elsewhere hereon." [40]

or, more stringently:

> "Absolutely no coverage is provided hereunder on relief well except the cost of drilling a relief well as so provided under this policy." [41]

As for the cost of drilling a relief well, a policy may provide for this in the cover clause itself dealing with the extent of the duty of the underwriters to reimburse the assured for various costs, including the costs of " equipment and services of individuals or firms specialising in controlling wells, including directional drilling, and other operations necessary to bring the well(s) under control." [42]

Another policy contains this last provision, but states also in the section dealing with deductibles: " In the event that a directional or relief well has to be drilled in order to regain control, Assured to bear 25 per cent. of the total claim under the policy for drilling of such directional or relief well."

13. *Areas and Rates*

A cost of control insurance contains, as a schedule to the policy, a list of areas and rates. The areas are relevant not only to the rating but to the deductibles. [72] A typical schedule of areas and rates is as follows, Areas 1 and 2 being omitted here as they are land areas and other areas where offshore mobile drilling units do not operate.

"Area 3

Offshore Gulf of Mexico (except as defined in Area 2 above), Venezuela (excluding Lake Maracaibo), Gulf of Paria.
Drilling rate—Underwater completions:
    per foot drilled (each well up to 10,000 feet)
    per foot drilled (each well 10,000 feet to 17,499 feet)
    per foot drilled (each well 17,500 feet and over)
excluding underwater completions:
    per foot drilled (each well up to 10,000 feet)

---

[39] For a definition of blowout, see above, p. 412.
[40] Policy " B," cl. 13.
[41] Policy " A," cl. 7 (b). See also p. 398, above.
[42] Policy " B," cl. 6 (b).

per foot drilled (each well 10,000 feet to 17,499 feet)
per foot drilled (each well 17,500 feet and over)

Area 4

Offshore elsewhere except North of Arctic Circle and South of Antarctic Circle

per foot drilled (each well up to 10,000 feet)
per foot drilled (each well 10,000 feet to 17,499 feet)
per foot drilled (each well 17,500 feet and over)
—excluding underwater completions.
per foot drilled (each well up to 10,000 feet)
per foot drilled (each well 10,000 feet to 17,499 feet)
per foot drilled (each well 17,500 feet and over)

Rates, Terms and Conditions for Wells North of Arctic Circle and South of Antarctic Circle to be agreed by underwriters hereon.

Reduce above rates by:

25% for Assured insuring in excess of 125,000 feet per annum
30% ,, ,, ,, ,, ,, ,, 250,000 ,, ,, ,,
40% ,, ,, ,, ,, ,, ,, 500,000 ,, ,, ,,
50% ,, ,, ,, ,, ,, ,, 1,000,000 ,, ,, ,,

Such returns to be applied to Areas 1 and 2 and Areas 3 and 4 not to be allowed until requisite footage is at risk, and, in respect of wells North of Arctic Circle or South of Antarctic Circle to be allowed subject to agreement of Underwriters hereon.

Reworking, Reconditioning, Recompletion, Workover Wells:
    75% of drilling rate per foot times completed depth of well.

Deepening Wells: to be rated on basis of final completed depth at above scale.

Producing, Shut in, Plugged, Cemented, Temporarily Abandoned
Wells: 25% of drilling rate per foot times completed depth of well for 12 months' coverage."

Clean-Up and Containment Endorsements

The following endorsement is typical of those used:

" CLEAN-UP AND CONTAINMENT ENDORSEMENT
(for attachment to Cost of Control Policies)

Subject to the terms and conditions hereinafter set forth and in consideration of an additional premium of ... Underwriters shall reimburse the Assured in respect of clean-up and/or containment costs arising from an occurrence covered by the Cost of Control section of this policy. Clean-up and/or containment costs shall mean only those costs of cleaning up and/or containing any oil or gas directly following such occurrence. Coverage hereunder shall be limited to:

1. Costs and expenses incurred for clean-up and/or containment for which the Assured is liable by law.

2. Costs and expenses for clean-up and/or containment other than those mentioned in (1) above incurred by the Assured.

The coverage provided under this endorsement is further subject to all terms conditions and exclusions incorporated under the Cost of Control section of this policy.

No liability shall attach to Underwriters hereunder in respect of any fines or penalties, which shall be deemed to include but not be restricted to punitive or exemplary damages, imposed by law, ordinance, statute, regulation or otherwise.

Where the Assured is, irrespective of this endorsement, covered or protected by insurance against any loss or claim which would otherwise have been paid by Underwriters under this endorsement, there shall be no contribution or participation by Underwriters on the basis of excess, contributing, deficiency, concurrent or double insurance or otherwise.

Upon making payment under this endorsement Underwriters shall be vested with all of the Assured's rights of recovery against any person, corporation, entity, vessel, or other interest and the Assured shall execute and deliver instruments and papers and do whatever is necessary to secure such rights.

The coverage provided under this endorsement shall not extend Underwriters' limit of liability of . . . any one occurrence (reduced by deductible and subject to coinsurance) over both sections of this policy combined."

An operator may, alternatively, and more frequently, instead of taking out a comprehensive seepage pollution and contamination insurance, extend his cost of control insurance to cover liabilities for seepage, etc., and clean-up and containment. The following endorsement is frequently used for this purpose:

" The Underwriters hereon shall reimburse the Assured in respect of clean-up and/or containment costs arising from an occurrence covered by the Cost of Control section of this policy. Clean up and/or containment costs shall mean only those costs of cleaning up and/or containing any oil or gas directly following such occurrence. Coverage hereunder shall be limited to:—

1) Costs and expenses incurred for clean up and/or containment for which the Assured is liable by law.

2) Costs and expenses for clean up and/or containment other than those mentioned in (1) above incurred by the Assured.

The underwriters hereon shall indemnify the Assured for sums which the Assured shall be obligated to pay by reason of the liability imposed upon the Assured by law, or under the terms of any oil lease licence for:—

1) Loss of or damage to property, provided always that this subsection shall apply only to liability for loss, loss of or physical damage to or destruction of tangible property.

2) Damages for bodily injury (fatal or non fatal)

Directly caused by Pollution and Contamination, where such Pollution and Contamination is caused by a sudden unintended and unexpected happening during the period of this insurance and then only if such loss is covered as an insurable loss under the Cost of Control section of this policy.

430

Clean-up and Containment Endorsements

Subject to the terms and conditions hereinafter set forth and in consideration of an additional premium of £ *included* the coverage provided under this section is further subject to all terms conditions and exclusions incorporated under the Cost of Control section of this policy.

No liability shall attach to Underwriters hereunder in respect of any fines or penalties, which shall be deemed to include but not be restricted to punitive or exemplary damages, imposed by law, ordinance, statute, regulation or otherwise.

Where the Assured is, irrespective of this section, covered or protected by insurance against any loss or claim which would otherwise have been paid by Underwriters under this section, there shall be no contribution or participation by Underwriters on the basis of excess, contributing, deficiency, concurrent or double insurance or otherwise.

Upon making payment under this section Underwriters shall be vested with all of the Assured's rights of recovery against any person, corporation, entity, vessel or other interest and the Assured shall execute and deliver instruments and papers and do whatever is necessary to secure such rights.

The coverage provided under this section shall not extend Underwriters' limit of liability of £   any one occurrence (reduced by deductible and subject to coinsurance) over all sections of this policy combined."

LONDON STANDARD DRILLING BARGE FORM

THIS Form, dated March 9, 1972, is discussed in detail in Chapter 3, above.

LONDON STANDARD DRILLING BARGE FORM
ALL RISKS
(except as hereinafter excluded)

1. Assured

2. Period of Insurance
If this insurance expires while an accident or occurrence giving rise to a loss is in progress, Underwriters shall be liable as if the whole loss had occurred during the currency of this insurance.

3. Property insured hereunder
This insurance covers the hull and machinery of the drilling barge(s), as scheduled herein, including all their equipment, tools, machinery, caissons, lifting jacks, materials, supplies, appurtenances, drilling rigs and equipment, derricks, drill stem, casing and tubing while aboard the said drilling barge(s) and/or on barges and/or vessels moored alongside or in the vicinity thereof and used in connection therewith (but not such barges and/or vessels themselves), and including drill stem in the well being drilled, and all such property as scheduled herein, owned by or in the care custody or control of the Assured, except as hereinafter excluded.

SCHEDULE OF PROPERTY INSURED

Description of Drilling Barge	Rate	Insured Value	Hereto Amount

Each deemed to be separately insured.
Any loss paid hereunder shall not reduce the amount of this insurance except in the event of actual or constructive or compromised or arranged total loss.

4. Navigation limits
(a) . . . .
Privilege is granted to be towed within the above Navigation Limits.
Also to cover in port, while going on or off, and while in docks and graving docks and/or wharves, ways gridirons and pontoons, subject to the terms and conditions of this insurance.
(b) This insurance covers up to 25% of the scheduled amount of insurance hereunder on property insured herein (as described in clause 3 above, when separated from the property insured hereunder whilst in temporary storage at, or in local transit to or from, ports or drilling barges within the Navigation Limits provided in Paragraph (a). It is expressly understood and agreed, however, that this extended coverage is included within and shall not increase the total amount of insurance hereunder.

5. Coverage
Subject to its terms, conditions and exclusions this Insurance is against all risks of direct physical loss of or damage to the property insured, provided such

loss or damage has not resulted from want of due diligence by the Assured, the Owners or Managers of the property insured, or any of them.

6. Collision liability

And it is further agreed that:

(a) if the Vessel shall come into collision with any other ship or vessel, and the Assured or the Surety in consequence of the Vessel being at fault shall become liable to pay and shall pay by way of damages to any other person or persons any sum or sums in respect of such collision, the Underwriters will pay the Assured or the Surety, whichever shall have paid, such proportion of such sum or sums so paid as their respective subscriptions hereto bear to the Agreed Value, provided always that their liability in respect to any one such collision shall not exceed their proportionate part of the Agreed Value;

(b) in cases where, with the consent in writing of a majority (in amount) of Hull Underwriters, the liability of the Vessel has been contested, or proceedings have been taken to limit liability, the Underwriters will also pay a like proportion of the costs which the Assured shall thereby incur or be compelled to pay.

When both vessels are to blame, then, unless the liability of the owners or charterers of one or both such vessels becomes limited by law, claims under the Collision Liability clause shall be settled on the principle of Cross-Liabilities as if the owners or charterers of each vessel had been compelled to pay to the owners or charterers of the other of such vessels such one-half or other proportion of the latter's damages as may have been properly allowed in ascertaining the balance or sum payable by or to the Assured in consequence of such collision.

The principles involved in this clause shall apply to the case where both vessels are the property, in part or in whole, of the same owners or charterers, all questions of responsibility and amount of liability as between the two vessels being left to the decision of a single Arbitrator, if the parties can agree upon a single Arbitrator, or failing such agreement, to the decision of Arbitrators, one to be appointed by the Assured and one to be appointed by the majority (in amount) of Hull Underwriters interested; the two Arbitrators chosen to choose a third Arbitrator before entering upon the reference, and the decision of such single Arbitrator, or of any two of such three Arbitrators, appointed as above, to be final and binding.

Provided that this clause shall in no case extend to any sum which the Assured or the Surety may become liable to pay or shall pay in consequence of, or with respect to:

(a) removal or disposal of obstructions, wrecks or their cargoes under statutory powers or otherwise pursuant to law;

(b) injury to real or personal property of every description;

(c) the discharge, spillage, emission or leakage of oil, petroleum products, chemicals or other substances of any kind or description whatsoever;

(d) cargo or other property on or the engagements of the Vessel;

(e) loss of life, personal injury or illness.

Provided further that exclusions (b) and (c) above shall not apply to injury to any other vessel with which the Vessel is in collision or to property on such other vessel except to the extent that such injury arises out of any action taken to avoid, minimise or remove any discharge, spillage, emission or leakage described in (c).

7. Deductible

It is understood and agreed that each claim (including claims under the Sue and Labour Clause and the Collision Liability Clause) shall be reported and adjusted separately and from the amount of each claim the sum of...........

shall be deducted. This clause shall not apply to a claim for actual or constructive or compromised or arranged total loss.

For the purpose of this Clause each occurrence shall be treated separately, but it is agreed that a sequence of losses or damages arising from the same occurrence shall be treated as one occurrence.

8. Exclusions

Notwithstanding anything to the contrary which may be contained in this insurance there shall be no liability under this insurance in respect of:

(a) Loss, damage or expense caused by or attributable to earthquake or volcanic eruption, or fire and/or explosion and/or tidal wave consequent upon earthquake or volcanic eruption.

(b) Loss, damage or expense which arises solely from the intentional sinking of the barge for operational purposes; such sinking shall not constitute a collision, stranding, sinking or grounding within the meaning of this insurance.

(c) Loss, damage or expense caused whilst or resulting from drilling a relief well for the purpose of controlling or attempting to control fire blowout or cratering associated with another drilling barge, platform or unit unless immediate notice be given to Underwriters of said use and additional premium paid if required.

(d) Any claim, be it a Sue Labour Expense or otherwise, for moneys materials or property expended or sacrificed in controlling or attempting to control blowout or cratering or in fighting fire associated with blowout.

(e) Loss, damage or expense caused by or resulting from delay detention or loss of use.

(f) Wear and tear, gradual deterioration, metal fatigue, machinery breakdown, expansion or contraction due to change in temperature, corrosion, rusting, electrolytic action, error in design: nor does this insurance cover the cost of repairing or replacing any part which may be lost, damaged, or condemned by reason of any latent defect therein.

(g) Loss of or damage to dynamos, exciters, lamps, motors, switches and other electrical applicances and devices, caused by electrical injury or disturbance, unless the loss or damage be caused by a peril not excluded hereunder originating outside the electrical equipment specified in this clause. Nevertheless this clause shall not exclude claims for physical loss or damage resulting from fire.

(h) Liabilities to third parties except as specifically covered under the terms of the Collision Liability Clause contained herein.

(i) Claims in connection with the removal of property, material, debris or obstruction, whether such removal be required by law, ordinance, statute, regulation or otherwise.

(j) Loss of or damage to drill stem located underground or underwater unless directly resulting from fire, blowout, cratering, or total loss of the Drilling Barge caused by a peril insured hereunder. There shall be no liability in respect of drill stem left in the well and through which an oil or gas well is completed.

Blowout. The term " Blowout " shall mean a sudden, accidental, uncontrolled and continuous expulsion from a well and above the surface of the ground of the drilling fluid in an oil or gas well, followed by continuous and uncontrolled flow from a well and above the surface of the ground of oil, gas or water due to encountering subterranean pressures.

Cratering. The term " Crater " shall be defined as a basin-like depression in the earth's surface surrounding a well caused by the erosion and eruptive action of oil, gas or water flowing without restriction.

(k) Well(s) and or hole(s) whilst being drilled or otherwise.

(l) Drilling mud cement chemicals and fuel actually in use, and casing and tubing in the well.

(m) Unrefined oil or gas or other crude product.

(n) Blueprints, plans, specifications or records, personal effects of employees or others.

(o) Scraping or painting the bottom of the hull of the drilling barge.

9. Blowout preventer warranty[1]

Warranted that (a) in all drilling operations

(b) in all operations which require the removal of the christmas tree

the well and/or hole will be equipped with a minimum of three pressure operated blowout preventers, which shall be installed and tested immediately after installation. Two of the aforesaid blowout preventers shall be of the pipe ram and blind ram type and the third shall be of the annular full closing type.

10. Limit of liability

In no event, except as provided for in the Sue and Labour Expense Clause and Collision Liability Clause herein, shall the Underwriters' liability arising from any one accident or occurrence exceed the amount insured hereunder as set forth in Clause 3 in respect of the items subject to claim in such accident or occurrence.

In respect of the property insured hereunder Underwriters shall not be liable for more than their proportion of the cost of repairing or replacing the property damaged or lost with materials of like kind and quality to a condition equal to but not superior to or more extensive than its condition prior to the loss; nevertheless in respect of the hull of the Drilling Barge covered hereunder all costs of repair and replacement for which Underwriters may be liable shall be on the basis of new for old with no deduction for depreciation.

In no event shall Underwriters be liable for any increased cost of repair or reconstruction by reason of law, ordinances, regulation, permit or licence regulating construction or repair,

11. Coinsurance

The Assured shall maintain contributing insurance on terms no more restrictive than this insurance on the property insured hereunder of not less than 100% of the new reproductive cost less a reasonable depreciation. Failing to do so, the Assured shall be an insurer to the extent of such deficit and bear such proportionate part of any claim. If this insurance be divided into two or more items the foregoing conditions shall apply to each item separately.

12. Constructive total loss

There shall be no recovery for a Constructive Total Loss hereunder unless the expense of recovering and repairing the insured property shall exceed the actual insured value.

In no case shall Underwriters be liable for unrepaired damage in addition to a subsequent Total Loss sustained during the period covered by this insurance.

13. Sue and labour expense

It is further agreed that should the property insured hereunder suffer loss or damage covered under the terms of this insurance, it shall be lawful and necessary for the Assured, their Factors, Servants and Assigns, to sue, labour and travel for, in and about the Defence, Safeguard and Recovery of the said property, or any part thereof, without prejudice to this insurance, and subject always to the

---

[1] See p. 133 above, as to amendment.

terms conditions limitations and exclusions of this insurance, the charges thereof shall be borne by the Underwriters. And it is especially declared and agreed that no acts of the Underwriters or Assured in recovering, saving or preserving the property insured shall be considered as a waiver or acceptance of abandonment.

The Underwriters' liability for Sue and Labour Expenses shall not exceed 25% of the insured value of the item(s) in the Defence, Safeguard or Recovery of which such expense is incurred.

14. Lay up and cancellation

To return daily pro rata of rates to be agreed by Underwriters for any period of 30 or more consecutive days the vessel may be laid up in port unemployed.

Provided always that:

(a) the location shall be approved by surveyor appointed by Lloyd's Agent or approved by Underwriters.

(b) there shall always be a watchman on board.

(c) no return shall be allowed in the event of the vessel becoming an actual or constructive or compromised or arranged total loss during the currency of this insurance.

(d) there shall be no shifts during the lay up period.

(e) there shall be no movement of legs or variation in buoyancy during the lay up period.

(f) in the event of any amendment of the annual rate, the rates of return shall be adjusted accordingly.

The return for a laid-up period of 30 or more consecutive days which fall on two policies effected for the same Assured shall be apportioned over both policies on a daily pro rata basis.

This insurance may be cancelled:

(a) by the Assured at any time by written notice subject to a return of premium to be agreed;

(b) by Underwriters subject to 30 days written notice, in which event a pro rata daily return of premium shall be payable;

(c) by Underwriters in respect of the perils of strikers locked-out workmen or persons taking part in labour disturbances or riots or civil commotions subject to seven days' written notice without return of premium.

Cancellation by either party is subject to the retention by Underwriters of any minimum premium stipulated in the Policy.

15. Release agreements and waivers of subrogation

The Assured may grant release from liability with respect to loss of or damage to property insured hereunder to any person firm or corporation for whom the Assured is operating under specific contract, provided:

(a) the said release is granted prior to the commencement of the operations;

(b) the loss or damage subject to said release arises out of or in connection with such operations.

Underwriters agree to waive their rights of subrogation against such person firm or corporation having been so released from such liability.

16. Discovery of records

During the currency of this insurance or any time thereafter within the period of the time provided for in Clause 17 for bringing suit against these Underwriters, these Underwriters shall have the right of inspecting the Assured's records pertaining to all matters of cost, repairs, income and expenditures of whatsoever nature relating to the properties insured hereunder, such records to be open to a representative of these Underwriters at all reasonable times.

17. Limitation of action

No suit or action on this insurance for the recovery of any claim shall be sustainable in any court of law or equity unless the Assured shall have complied fully with all the requirements of this insurance, and unless commenced within twenty-four months next after the time a cause of action for the loss accrues, provided, however, that where such limitation of time is prohibited by the law of the State wherein this insurance is issued, then and in that event, no suit or action under this insurance shall be sustained unless commenced within the shortest time limitation permitted under the laws of such State.

18. Loss payable

Loss, if any, (except claims required to be paid to others under the Collision Liability Clause), payable to:...

19. Free of capture and seizure

Notwithstanding anything to the contrary contained in this insurance, there shall be no liability for any claim caused by, resulting from, or incurred as a consequence of:

(a) capture, seizure, arrest, restraint or detainment, or any attempt thereat; or

(b) any taking by requisition or otherwise, whether in time of peace or war and whether lawful or otherwise; or

(c) any mine, bomb, torpedo or other engine of war; or

(d) any weapon of war employing atomic or nuclear fission and/or fusion or other like reaction or radioactive force or matter; or

(e) civil war, revolution, rebellion, insurrection, or civil strife arising therefrom, or piracy; or

(f) (i) the detonation of an explosive

　　(ii) any weapon of war

and caused by any person acting maliciously or from a political motive; or

(g) any act for political or terrorist purposes of any person or persons, whether or not agents of a Sovereign Power, and whether the loss, damage or expense resulting therefrom is accidental or intentional; or

(h) hostilities or warlike operations (whether there be a declaration of war or not) but this subparagraph (h) not to exclude collision or contact with aircraft, rockets or similar missiles, or with any fixed or floating object, or stranding, heavy weather, fire or explosion unless caused directly by a hostile act by or against a belligerent power which act is independent of the nature of the voyage or operation which the vessel concerned, or in the case of a collision or contact, any other vessel involved therein, is performing. As used herein, " power " includes any authority maintaining naval, military or air forces in association with a power.

OFFSHORE DRILLING CONTRACT

THE International Association of Drilling Contractors drafted the "International Daywork Drilling Contract—Offshore," for use by operators and contractors. It is discussed in detail in Chapter 7 where it is usually called, for the sake of brevity, the I.A.D.C. contract. It is set out in full below:

INTERNATIONAL ASSOCIATION OF DRILLING CONTRACTORS

INTERNATIONAL DAYWORK DRILLING CONTRACT—OFFSHORE

THIS AGREEMENT, dated the........................... day of ...., 19......, is made between: ...., a corporation organized under the laws of ...., located at .... (hereinafter called Operator), and
...., a corporation organized under the laws of ...., located at .... (hereinafter called Contractor).

WHEREAS, Operator desires to have offshore wells drilled in the Operating Area and to have performed or carried out all auxiliary operations and services as detailed in the Appendices hereto or as Operator may require; and

WHEREAS, Contractor is willing to furnish the drilling vessel complete with drilling and other equipment, (hereinafter called the "Drilling Unit"), insurances and personnel, all is detailed in the Appendices hereto for the purpose of drilling the said wells and performing the said auxiliary operations and services for Operator.

NOW THEREFORE THIS AGREEMENT WITNESSETH that in consideration of the covenants herein it is agreed as follows:

ARTICLE I—INTERPRETATION

101. Definitions
In this Contract, unless the context otherwise requires:
- **(a)** "**Commencement Date**" means the point in time that the Drilling Unit arrives at the place in or near the Operating Area designated by Operator, or at a mutually agreeable place in or near the Operating Area, or on arrival at the first drilling location, whichever event occurs earliest;
- **(b)** "**Operator's Items**" mean the equipment, material and services which are listed in the Appendices that are to be provided by or at expense of Operator;
- **(c)** "**Contractor's Items**" mean the equipment, material and services which are listed in the Appendices that are to be provided by or at expense of Contractor;
- **(d)** "**Contractor's Personnel**" means the personnel to be provided by Contractor from time to time to conduct operations hereunder as listed in the Appendices;
- **(e)** "**Operating Area**" means those areas of the seabed and subsoil beneath the waters offshore .... in which Operator may from time to time be entitled to conduct drilling operations;

(f) " **Operations Base** " means the place or places on shore designated as such by Operator from time to time.

(g) "**Affiliated Company** " means a company owning 50% or more of the stock of Operator or Contractor, a company in which Operator or Contractor own 50% or more of its stock, or a company 50% or more of whose stock is owned by the same company that owns 50% or more of the stock of Operator or Contractor.

102. Currency

In this Contract, all amounts expressed in dollars are United States dollar amounts.

103. Conflicts

The Appendices hereto are incorporated herein by reference. If any provision of the Appendices conflicts with a provision in the body hereof, the latter shall prevail.

104. Headings

The paragraph headings shall not be considered in interpreting the text of this Contract.

105. Further Assurances

Each party shall perform the acts and execute and deliver the documents and give the assurances necessary to give effect to the provisions of this Contract.

106. Contractor's Status

Contractor in performing its obligations hereunder shall be an independent contractor.

107. Governing Law

This Contract shall be construed and the relations between the parties determined in accordance with the law of ...., not including, however, any of its conflicts of law rules which would direct or refer to the laws of another jurisdiction.

ARTICLE II—TERM

201. Effective Date

The parties shall be bound by this Contract when each of them has executed it.

202. Duration

This Contract shall terminate:

(a) immediately if the Drilling Unit becomes an actual or constructive total loss;

(b) .... months after receipt by Contractor of notice of termination from Operator, but Operator may not give such notice until at least .... months after the Commencement Date, (or, if operations are then being conducted on a well, as soon thereafter as such operations are completed) and the Drilling Unit has arrived at ...., unless some other port is mutually agreed;

(c) on the .... anniversary of the Commencement Date (or, if operations are then being conducted on a well, as soon thereafter as such operations are completed) and the Drilling Unit has arrived at ...., unless some other port is mutually agreed.

439

203. Continuing Obligations

Notwithstanding the termination of this Contract, the parties shall continue to be bound by the provisions of this Contract that reasonably require some action or forbearance after the cessation of the day rates provided for hereinafter.

204. Return of Operator's Items

Upon termination of this Contract, Contractor shall return to Operator any of Operator's Items which are at the time in Contractor's possession.

ARTICLE III—CONTRACTOR'S PERSONNEL

301. Number, Selection, Hours of Labor and Remuneration

Except where herein otherwise provided, the selection, replacement, hours of labor and remuneration of Contractor's personnel shall be determined by Contractor. Such employees shall be the employees solely of Contractor. Contractor represents that its personnel will be competent and efficient.

302. Providing Personnel

Contractor shall have its personnel available at the proper Operations Base or at a mutually agreed place ready to conduct operations hereunder.

303. Contractor's Representative

Contractor shall nominate one of its personnel as Contractor's representative who shall be in charge of the remainder of Contractor's personnel and who shall have full authority to resolve all day-to-day matters which arise between Operator and Contractor.

304. Increase in Contractor's Personnel

Operator may, at any time, with Contractor's approval require Contractor to increase the number of Contractor's personnel and the day rates provided herein shall be adjusted accordingly.

305. Replacement of Contractor's Personnel

Contractor will remove and replace in a reasonable time any of Contractor's personnel if Operator so requests in writing and if Operator can show reasonable grounds for its requirement.

ARTICLE IV—CONTRACTOR'S ITEMS

401. Obligation to Supply

Contractor shall provide Contractor's items and personnel and perform the services to be provided or performed by it according to the Appendices. Operator shall move or pay the cost of moving Contractor's items, personnel and their personal effects between Operations Bases.

402. Maintain Stocks

Contractor shall be responsible, at its cost, for maintaining adequate stock levels of Contractor's items and replenishing as necessary.

403. Maintain and Repair Equipment

Contractor shall, subject to Clause 1001, be responsible for the maintenance and repair of all Contractor's Items and will provide all spare parts and materials required therefor. Contractor shall, if requested by Operator, also maintain or repair, at its cost, any of Operator's Items on board the Drilling Unit which contractor is qualified to and can maintain or repair with Contractor's normal complement of personnel and the equipment on board the Drilling Unit; provided, however, that Operator shall at its cost provide all spare parts and materials required to maintain or repair Operator's Items and the basic responsibility and liability for furnishing and maintaining such items shall remain in Operator.

ARTICLE V—CONTRACTOR'S GENERAL OBLIGATIONS

501. Performance of the Drilling Unit [1]

(a) Contractor represents that the Drilling Unit will be capable of moving from location to location and that the anchoring system will anchor the Drilling Unit for floating drilling, given suitable bottom conditions.

(b) Contractor further represents that the variable deckload of the Drilling Vessel in a floating position is approximately.....................................

502. Contractor's Standard of Performance

Contractor shall carry out all operations hereunder with due diligence, in a safe, workmanlike manner. Contractor shall comply with all current laws covering Contractor's operation of the Drilling Unit hereunder.

503. Operation of Drilling Unit

Contractor shall be solely responsible for the operation of the Drilling Unit, including, without limitation, supervising moving operations, and positioning on drilling locations as required by Operator, as well as such operations on board the Drilling Unit as may be necessary or desirable for the safety of the Drilling Unit. Operations under this Contract will be performed on a 24-hour per day basis.

504. Compliance with Operator's Instructions

Contractor shall comply with all instructions of Operator consistent with the provisions of this Contract including, without limitation, drilling, well control and safety instructions. Such instructions shall, if Contractor so requires, be confirmed in writing by the authorized representative of Operator. However, Operator shall not issue any instructions which would be inconsistent with Contractor's rules, policies or procedures pertaining to the safety of its personnel, equipment or the Drilling Unit.

505. Adverse Weather

Contractor, in consultation with Operator, shall decide when, in the face of impending adverse weather conditions, to institute precautionary measures in order to safeguard the well, the well equipment, the Drilling Unit and personnel to the fullest possible extent. Contractor and Operator shall each ensure that each senior representative for the time being on board will not act unreasonably in the exercise of this Clause.

506. Mud and Casing Program

Contractor shall take all reasonable care to follow the mud and casing program as specified by Operator. Operator shall provide Contractor with these programs reasonably in advance of the spud date of each well to be drilled hereunder.

---

[1] A different clause is suggested for jack-up rigs; see p. 455, below.

507. Cutting/Coring Program
Contractor shall save and identify cuttings and cores according to Operator's instructions and place them in containers furnished by Operator.

508. Records to be Kept by Contractor
Contractor shall keep and furnish to Operator an accurate record of the work performed and formations drilled on the IADC-API Daily Drilling Report Form or other form acceptable to Operator. A legible copy of said form signed by Contractor's representative shall be furnished by Contractor to Operator.

509. Difficulties During Drilling
In the event of any difficulty arising which precludes either drilling ahead under reasonably normal procedures or the performance of any other operations planned for a well, Contractor may suspend the work in progress and shall immediately notify the representative of Operator, in the meantime exerting reasonable effort to overcome the difficulty.

510. Safety Equipment
Contractor shall maintain its well control equipment listed in the Appendices in good condition at all times and shall use all reasonable means to control and prevent fires and blowouts and to protect the hole.

ARTICLE VI—OPERATOR'S OBLIGATIONS

601. Equipment and Personnel
Operator shall at its cost provide Operator's Items and personnel and perform the services to be provided or performed by it according to the Appendices. In addition to providing the initial supply of Operator's Items, Operator shall be responsible, at its cost, for maintaining adequate stock levels and replenishing as necessary. When, at Operator's request and with Contractor's agreement, the Contractor furnishes or subcontracts for certain items which Operator is required herein to provide, for purposes of this Contract said items or services shall be deemed to be Operator furnished items or services, any subcontractors so hired shall be deemed to be Operator's contractor, and Operator shall not be relieved of any of its liabilities in connection therewith; for furnishing said items and services Operator shall reimburse Contractor its entire cost plus............... % for handling.

602. Maintenance and Repair
Operator shall be responsible, at its cost, for the maintenance and repair of all Operator's Items on board the Drilling Unit which Contractor is not qualified to or cannot maintain or repair with Contractor's normal complement of personnel and the equipment on board.

603. Operator's Employees
Operator shall ensure that Operator's personnel on board the Drilling Unit shall be competent and efficient and Contractor may treat Operator's senior representative for the time being on board the Drilling Unit as being in charge of all Operator personnel on board.

604. Replacement of Operator's Personnel
Contractor shall have the right to request in writing Operator to remove and replace any Operator personnel on board the Drilling Unit if Contractor can show reasonable grounds for such request.

605 Operator Representatives

Operator may, from time to time, designate representatives for the purposes of this Contract who shall at all times have access to the Drilling Unit and may, among other things, observe tests, check and control the implementation of the mud program, examine cuttings and cores, inspect the work performed by Contractor or examine the records kept on the Drilling Unit by Contractor.

606. Custom or Excise Duties

Operator shall pay all import or export charges or customs or excise duties including, without limitation, local sales taxes, added value taxes, clearing agent's fees, or other similar taxes or fees that are levied on Contractor's and/or Operator's Items.

607. Drill Site and Access

Operator shall provide Contractor with access to the drilling site as well as any drilling permits, licenses or certificates needed to conduct operations hereunder. The drill site so provided shall be surveyed and marked by Operator and shall be free of obstructions. Notwithstanding any other provision of this Contract, should there be obstructions at or within the anchoring area at the drill site and these obstructions damage the Drilling Unit or the Drilling Unit damages these obstructions, Operator shall reimburse Contractor for such damage to the extent not covered by Contractor's insurance.

608. Taxes

Contractor agrees to prepare and timely file all required income or other tax return or declarations required by the government of the area where the Drilling Unit operates. Upon notification by the Contractor of the amount or amounts of such taxes paid by it which pertain to the performance by Contractor under this Contract, accompanied by copies of each such return or declaration, Operator agrees to reimburse Contractor such amount or amounts less any interest or penalties arising from the fault of Contractor and levied by any of the afore-mentioned governmental bodies. Contractor shall consult with Operator before filing any such tax returns or paying the applicable taxes.

ARTICLE VII—OPERATOR'S INSTRUCTIONS

701. Instructions to Contractor

Operator may, from time to time, through its authorized representative or representatives, issue written or oral instructions to Contractor covering operations hereunder. Operator's instructions may be general or may deal with specific matters relating to operations hereunder including, without limitation, instructions to stop operations, as to safety and well control, and drilling instructions, but Operator may not require Contractor to drill deeper than .... feet unless Contractor agrees.

ARTICLE VIII—RATES OF PAYMENT

801. Payment

Operator shall pay to Contractor during the term of this Contract the amounts from time to time due calculated according to the rates of payment herein set forth and in accordance with the other provisions hereof. No other payment shall be due from Operator unless specifically provided for in this Contract, or agreed to in writing by Operator.

802. Mobilization Fee

Operator shall pay Contractor a mobilization fee of $ .... which shall be payable on the date the Drilling Unit departs for the Operating Area.

803. Demobilization Fee

Operator shall pay Contractor a demobilization fee of $ .... which may be invoiced on the date of termination of this Contract except that no demobilization fee shall be due if this Contract is terminated pursuant to Clause 202 (a) (Duration).

804. Operating Rate [2]

The Operating Rate will be $ .... per 24-hour day and will first become payable from the moment when the Drilling Unit is properly positioned at the first drilling location and ready to commence operations. The Operating Rate shall continue to be payable except as herein otherwise provided.

805. Standby Rate

The Standby Rate will be $ .... per 24-hour day and will be payable:
  (a) during any period of delay when Contractor is unable to proceed because of adverse sea or weather conditions or as a direct result of an act or omission of Operator including, without limitation, the failure of any of Operator's Items, or the failure of Operator to issue instructions, provide Operator Items or furnish services; or
  (b) from the Commencement Date until the moment when the Operating Rate first becomes payable; or
  (c) during any period after Commencement Date that the Drilling Unit is under tow, or under way, provided that if, at the termination of this Contract, the Drilling Unit does not go to .... or the nearest port as agreed, the period shall not exceed the reasonable estimated time required to go to that harbor.

806. Rate During Repair

The Repair Rate will be $ .... per 24-hour day and will be payable for any period in excess of .... days during which operations are suspended to permit necessary replacement, inspection, repair or maintenance of Contractor's Items; provided, however, that should said suspension continue for a period of more than 75 days, Contractor's rate of pay shall after the seventy-fifth day be reduced to .... percent of the Repair Rate. Contractor will use due diligence in effecting such repairs, replacements or inspection in a good workmanlike manner and will use its best efforts to familiarize itself with the location of rentable replacements for Contractor's Items.

807. Force Majeure Rate

The Force Majeure Rate will be $ .... per 24-hour day and will be payable during any period in which operations are not being carried on because of force majeure, other than adverse sea or weather conditions.

808. Additional Payments

Operator shall, in addition, pay to Contractor:
  (a) the cost of any overtime paid by Contractor to Contractor's personnel in respect of the maintenance or repair on board the Drilling Unit of Operator's Items or other overtime required by Operator; and

---

[2] A different clause is suggested for jack-up rigs; see p, 455. below.

(b) Contractor's costs associated with waiting on Operator-furnished transportation or for time in excess of .... hours in transit to or from the Drilling Unit.

809 Variation of Rates

The rates and/or payments herein set forth shall be revised by the actual amount of the change in Contractor's cost if an event as described below occurs or if the cost of any of the items hereinafter listed shall vary by more than the amount indicated below from Contractor's cost thereof on .... or by the same amount after the date of any revision pursuant to this clause:

(a) if labor costs, including all benefits and the cost of foreign income taxes paid by Contractor for its expatriate employees, vary by more than five percent;

(b) if Operator requires Contractor to increase the number of Contractor's personnel;

(c) if it becomes necessary for Contractor to change the work schedule of its personnel or change the location of its operations base;

(d) in the event described in Clause 1202 (Assignment);

(e) if there is any change in legislation (other than Corporate tax legislation) by the country granting Operator the concession in which Contractor is working that alters Contractor's financial burden;

(f) if the cost of insurance premiums varies by more than five per cent;

(g) if the cost of catering varies by more than five per cent;

(h) if Contractor's interest rate varies by more than one-half of one percent;

(i) the rates listed herein shall be increased or decreased for costs other than those listed above on the Commencement Date and at three month intervals thereafter based on changes in the Bureau of Labor Statistics Oilfield Drilling Machinery and Equipment Wholesale Price Index (Code No. 1191–02) as published by the U.S. Department of Labor from that reported for the month of .... Said rates shall be increased or decreased (proportionately and on a pro rata basis) .... % for each change of five percent (5%) in said Index.

ARTICLE IX—INVOICES AND PAYMENTS

901. Monthly Invoices

Contractor shall bill Operator at the end of each month for all daily charges earned by Contractor during the month. Other charges shall be billed as earned. Billings for daily charges will reflect details of the time spent (calculated to the nearest hour) and the rate charged for that time; billings for other charges will be accompanied by invoices supporting costs incurred for Operator or other substantiation as required.

902. Payment

Operator shall pay by telegraphic transfer all billings within thirty days after the receipt thereof except that if Operator disputes an item billed, Operator shall within twenty days after receipt of the bill notify Contractor of the item disputed, specifying the reason therefor, and payment of the disputed item shall be withheld until settlement of the dispute, but payment shall be made of any undisputed portion. Any sums (including amounts ultimately paid with respect to a disputed invoice) not paid within thirty days after receipt of invoice shall bear interest at the rate of .... percent per annum or pro rata thereof from the due date until paid. If Operator refuses to pay undisputed items, Contractor shall have the right to terminate this contract.

903. Manner of Payment

All payments due by Operator to Contractor hereunder shall be made in United States dollars at Contractor's bank which is ....; with the understanding, however, that either Operator or Contractor shall have the right to specify that Operator shall pay Contractor in the currency of the country where the Drilling Unit operates in amounts equal to Contractor's local currency expenditures (including those expenditures incurred locally by Contractor for the account of Operator) and as needed by Contractor. All amounts of local currency so paid Contractor during the month shall be credited against Contractor's U.S. Dollar monthly invoice for that month at the rate of exchange of U.S. Dollars for the local currency in effect on .... as published in the Wall Street Journal.

ARTICLE X—LIABILITY

1001. Liability for Equipment and the Hole

Except as specifically provided herein to the contrary, each party hereto shall at all times be responsible for and shall hold harmless and indemnify the other party from and against damage to or loss of its own items, regardless of the cause of loss including the negligence of such party and despite the fact that a party's items may be under the control of the other party, except that:

(a) Operator shall, to the extent Contractor's insurance does not compensate Contractor therefor, be responsible at all times for damage to or destruction of Contractor's equipment caused by exposure to unusually corrosive or otherwise destructive elements, including those which are introduced into the drilling fluid from subsurface formations or the use of corrosive additives in the fluid.

(b) Operator shall, to the extent Contractor's insurance does not compensate Contractor therefor, be responsible for damage to or loss of Contractor's drill string, as well as Contractor's subsea equipment and subsea mooring gear, and shall reimburse Contractor for such damage or loss at the CIF replacement cost of the item so lost or damaged.

(c) In the event the hole should be lost or damaged, Operator shall be solely responsbile for such damage or loss to the hole, including the casing therein, regardless of whether such loss or damage was caused by the negligence of Contractor, or its employees, agents or subcontractors.

1002. Inspection of Materials Furnished by Operator

Contractor agrees to visually inspect all materials furnished by Operator before using same and to notify Operator of any apparent defects therein. Contractor shall not be liable for any loss or damage resulting from the use of materials furnished by Operator.

1003. Contractor's Personnel

Contractor agrees to protect, defend, indemnify and save Operator harmless from and against all claims, demands, and causes of action of every kind and character, without limit and without regard to the cause or causes thereof or the negligence of any party, arising in connection herewith in favor of Contractor's employees, Contractor's subcontractors or their employees, or Contractor's invitees, on account of bodily injury, death or damage to their property.

---

[3] Different subsections (b) and (c) are suggested for jack-ups; see p. 455, below.

1004. Operator's Personnel

Operator agrees to protect, defend, indemnify and save Contractor harmless from and against all claims, demands and causes of action of every kind and character, without limit and without regard to the cause or causes thereof or the negligence of any party, arising in connection herewith in favor of Operator's employees, Operator's contractors or their employees (other than those identified in Clause 1003 above) or Operator's invitees, on account of bodily injury, death or damage to their property.

1005. Pollution and Contamination

Notwithstanding anything to the contrary contained herein, it is understood and agreed by and between the Contractor and Operator that the responsibility for pollution or contamination shall be as follows:

(a) The Contractor shall assume all responsibility for cleaning up and containing pollution or contamination which originates above the surface of the water from spills of fuels, lubricants, motor oils, normal water base drilling fluid and attendant cuttings, pipe dope, paints, solvents, ballast, bilge and garbage wholly in Contractor's possession and control and directly associated with Contractor's equipment and facilities.

(b) Operator shall assume all responsibility for (including control and removal of the pollutant involved) and shall protect, defend and save the Contractor harmless from and against all claims, demands, and causes of action of every kind and character arising from all pollution or contamination, other than that described in subclause (a) above, which may occur from the negligence of Contractor or otherwise during the term of this Contract or as a result of operations hereunder, including but not limited to, that which may result from fire, blowout, cratering, seepage or any other uncontrolled flow of oil, gas, water or other substance, as well as the use or disposition of oil emulsion, oil base or chemically treated drilling fluids, contaminated cuttings or cavings, lost circulation and fish recovery materials and fluids.

(c) In the event a third party commits an act or omission which results in pollution or contamination for which either the Contractor or Operator, for whom such party is performing work, is held to be legally liable, the responsibility therefor shall be considered, as between the Contractor and Operator, to be the same as if the party for whom the work was performed had performed the same and all of the obligations respecting defense, indemnity, holding harmless and limitation of responsibility and liability, as set forth in (a) and (b) above, shall be specifically applied.

1006. Liability for the Well

Operator shall be liable for the cost of regaining control of any wild well, as well as the cost of removal of debris, and shall indemnify Contractor for any such cost regardless of the cause thereof, including, but not limited to, the negligence of Contractor, its agents, employees or subcontractors.

1007. Liability for Underground Damage

Operator agrees to defend and indemnify Contractor for any and all claims including, but not limited to, claims rising as a result of the negligence of Contractor, its agents, employees or subcontractors against Contractor resulting from operations under this Contract on account of injury to, destruction of, or loss or impairment of any property right in or to oil, gas, or other mineral substance or water, if at the time of the act or omission causing such injury,

447

destruction, loss, or impairment, said substance had not been reduced to physical possession above the seabed, and for any loss or damage to any formation, strata, or reservoir beneath the seabed.

1008. Consequential Damages
Neither party shall be liable to the other for special, indirect or consequential damages resulting from or arising out of this Contract, including, without limitation, loss of profit or business interruptions, however same may be caused.

ARTICLE XI—INSURANCE

1101. Contractor's Insurance
Contractor shall carry and maintain the insurance shown in Appendix B. Contractor may from time to time with the prior approval of Operator change the insurance it carries. Contractor will increase its insurance beyond the limits provided for herein or will change its insurance if required by Operator, but any additional cost will be paid by Operator.

1102. Policies and Receipts
Contractor will furnish Operator, on request, with certificates of all its insurance policies relating to Contractor's operations hereunder.

1103. Benefit
Contractor's insurance hereunder shall be endorsed to provide that the underwriters waive their right of recourse against Operator. Operator will, as well, cause its insurer to waive subrogation against Contractor.

ARTICLE XII—SUBLETTING AND ASSIGNMENT

1201. Subcontracts by Operator
Operator may employ other Contractors to perform any of the operations or services to be provided or performed by it according to Appendix A.

1202. Assignment
Neither party may assign this Contract to anyone other than an affiliated company without the prior written consent of the other, and prompt notice of any such intent to assign shall be given to the other party. In the event of such assignment, the assigning party shall remain liable to the other party as a guarantor of the performance by the assignee of the terms of this Contract. If any assignment is made that alters Contractor's financial burden, Contractor's compensation shall be adjusted to give effect to any increase or decrease in Contractor's operating costs or in taxes in the new operating area.

ARTICLE XIII—NOTICES

1301. Notices
Notices, reports and other communications required or permitted by this Contract to be given or sent by one party to the other shall be delivered by hand, mailed, telexed, or telegraphed to:
Operator's address:

Contractor's address:
as the case may be. Either party may by notice to the other party change its address.

ARTICLE XIV—GENERAL

1401. Confidential information

Upon written request of Operator, all information obtained by Contractor in the conduct of operations hereunder shall be confidential and Contractor will use its best endeavors to ensure that neither Contractor's personnel nor their families divulge any such information.

1402. Arbitration

As between the parties, any claims, disputes or controversies arising under or in connection with this Contract which cannot be adjusted by mutual agreement will be decided by the Courts of .... to whose jurisdiction the parties hereto agree, whatever their domicile may be; provided that either party prior to its having filed a complaint or petition in any court of law, may elect to have any such claim, dispute or controversy referred to arbitration in .... in accordance with the provisions of the .... Arbitration Act or any statutory modifications or reenactment thereof for the time being in force.

1403. Attorney's Fees

If this Contract is placed in the hands of an attorney for collection of any sums due hereunder, or suit is brought on same, or sums due hereunder are collected through bankruptcy or arbitration proceedings, then the Operator agrees that there shall be added to the amount due reasonable attorney's fees and costs.

1404. Force Majeure

Except as otherwise provided in this Clause 1404, each party to this Contract shall be excused from complying with the terms of this Contract, except for the payment of moneys then due, if and for so long as such compliance is hindered or prevented by riots, strikes, wars (declared or undeclared), insurrections, rebellions, terrorist acts, civil disturbances, dispositions or orders of governmental authority, whether such authority be actual or assumed, acts of God (other than adverse sea or weather conditions), inability to obtain equipment, supplies or fuel, or by act or cause which is reasonably beyond the control of such party, such causes being herein sometimes called " Force Majeure." If any failure to comply is occasioned by a governmental law, rule, regulation, disposition or order as aforesaid and the affected party is operating in accordance with good oilfield practice in the area of operations and is making reasonable effort to comply with such law, rule, regulation, disposition or order, the matter shall be deemed beyond the control of the affected party. In the event that either party hereto is rendered unable, wholly or in part, by any of these causes to carry out its obligation under this Contract, it is agreed that such party shall give notice and details of Force Majeure in writing to the other party as promptly as possible after its occurrence. In such cases, the obligations of the party giving the notice shall be suspended during the continuance of any inability so caused except that Operator shall be obligated to pay to Contractor the Force Majeure Rate provided for in Article 807 (Force Majeure Rate).

1405. Right to Audit.

Contractor shall keep proper books records and accounts of operations hereunder and shall permit Operator at all reasonable times to inspect the portions thereof related to any variation of the rates hereunder.

1406. Waivers

It is fully understood and agreed that none of the requirements of this Contract shall be considered as waived by either party unless the same is done in writing, and then only by the persons executing this Contract, or other duly authorized agent or representative of the party.

1407 Entire Agreement

This Contract supersedes and replaces any oral or written communications heretofore made between the parties relating to the subject matter hereof.

1408 Enurement

This Contract shall enure to the benefit of and be binding upon the successors and assigns of the parties.

1409. Expropriation, Confiscation, Nationalisation and War Risks

(a) In the event the Drilling Unit or any or all of Contractor's equipment, spare parts and/or supplies directly associated therewith (i) cannot lawfully be exported from the country in which it was operating following termination of drilling operations under this Contract because Contractor cannot obtain an export license or permit or because of other governmental restrictions; or (ii) are lost to Contractor through confiscation, expropriation, nationalization or governmental seizure; or (iii) are seized or damaged or destroyed as a result of insurrection, terrorist acts, riot or war (declared or undeclared) or other similar occurrences during the term of this Contract, Operator will within sixty (60) days following the occurrence of any such event pay to Contractor the value (as set out in Appendix C) of all such property so restricted, confiscated, expropriated, nationalized, seized, damaged or destroyed, from which value shall be subtracted the total of the following:

(1) any amount paid Contractor by such governmental unit or body;
(2) any amount paid Contractor from insurance;
(3) depreciation in accordance with the schedule attached hereto as Appendix C, but not to exceed 30% of said value. Depreciation shall be computed commencing with the date upon which each component of Contractor's equipment is placed into service under this Contract.

Following the payment by Operator for Contractor's property under the conditions set forth (which shall be made in the currency in which the original purchase thereof was made) and payment of all other moneys then due Contractor, Operator shall have no obligation thereafter to make payments to Contractor and at the time of such payments. Operator shall have the option to require Contractor to immediately assign all of its right, title and interest in the Drilling Unit to Operator.

(b) Should a change of political or other condition occur which would enable Contractor again to assume possession of the Drilling Unit and/or its equipment, spare parts and supplies directly associated therewith, Contractor agrees to repay to Operator such amounts as Operator may have paid to Contractor under this Clause 1409, less such amounts, if any, as may be required to restore the Drilling Unit, equipment, spare parts and supplies directly associated therewith to the same condition they were in at the time of suspension of drilling operations, and also less such amount (to be agreed upon by Operator and Contractor) as shall equitably compensate Contractor for deterioration, and/or depreciation thereof during the period of nonuse resulting from the causes set forth in this Clause 1409. In the event of such resumption of possession of the Drilling Unit by Contractor, if Operator has previously received title to said Drilling Unit.

Operator shall reassign all of its right, title and interest in said Drilling Unit to Contractor as of the time of such resumption of possession.

(c) All costs and other charges provided for in this Clause 1409 are subject to adjustment after audit.

(d) If requested by Operator in writing, Contractor agrees to obtain to the extent then and thereafter available, insurance covering all or such portion of the risks specified in this Clause 1409 as Operator may direct.

Operator shall be named as an additional assured in any such policy or policies of insurance, which shall provide for the payment of losses thereunder in United States dollars. The provisions of such insurance and the cost thereof shall be subject to Operator's approval prior to the issuance thereof.

The cost of such insurance shall be paid by Operator to Contractor within twenty (20) days after invoice from Contractor evidencing the payment by Contractor of the premiums for such specified insurance.

(e) Contractor shall pay to Operator any moneys with respect to such expropriation, etc., which Contractor receives and for which Operator has not already received credit after payment made by Operator to Contractor under Clause 1409.

IN WITNESS WHEREOF, each party has executed this Contract as of the date shown above.

OPERATOR: ....

    By: ....

      Title: ....

CONTRACTOR: ....

    By: ....

      Title: ....

Appendix A[4]

EQUIPMENT, MATERIALS, SERVICES AND PERSONNEL LIST

PART I. CONTRACTOR FURNISHED EQUIPMENT

1. Drilling Vessel	2. Drawworks
3. Mast	4. Traveling Block
5. Hook	6. Swivel
7. Rotary Table	8. Power Equipment
9. Emergency A.C. Alternator	10. Air Compressors and Receivers
11. Pumps	12. Shale Shaker
13. Desander	14. Degasser
15. Mud Tanks and Agitators	16. Pit Level Indicator
17. Mud Mixing Pumps	18. Chemical Mixer
19. Mud Laboratory	20. Distillation Units

---

[4] To the Contract.

21. Cementing Unit	22. Dry Mud and Cement Storage and Transfer System
23. Cranes	24. Weight Indicator
25. Deadline Anchor	26. Drilling Line
27. Sand Line	28. Standpipes and Rotary Hose
29. Kelly Spinner	30. Kelly
31. Drill Pipe	32. Casing Protectors
33. Inside Blowout Preventer	34. Drill Collars
35. Bumper Subs	36. Fishing Tools
37. Handling Tools for Drill Pipe and Collars	38. Casing Handling Tools
39. Wire Line Measuring Unit	40. Deviation Instrument
41. Drilling Rate Recorder	42. Miscellaneous Tools
43. Derrick Substructure	44. Spider Deck Crane
45. Underwater Equipment	46. Choke Manifold
47. Possum Belly Tank	48. Welding Machines
49. Riser Angle Indicator	50. Pitch and Roll Indicator
51. Wind Velocity Indicator	52. Navigation Aids
53. Radios	54. Pipe Straightener
55. Joint Inspection	56. Fire Fighting Equipment
57. Safety Equipment	58 Vent Stack
59. Space for Operator-Furnished Equipment	

PART II—PERSONNEL AND SERVICES TO BE FURNISHED BY CONTRACTOR

1. Marine, land and air transportation other than mentioned under item 5 of Part III, Appendix A, of Contractor's Items, personnel and their families.
2. Transfer onto and from the Drilling Unit of any and all materials, equipment and personnel of Contractor and of Operator.
   Contractor's personnel will only be required to go on board supply vessel in a supervisory capacity, in cases of emergency or when supply vessels will be used for crew change if helicopter unable to fly.
3. Accommodation of Contractor's personnel and their families on shore.
4. All medical services for Contractor's personnel and their families and first aid medical attention for all persons aboard the Drilling Unit.
5. Heated and air conditioned accommodation, housekeeping services and supplies and messing on board the Drilling Unit for Contractor's personnel and for up to .... Operator personnel, Operator visitors, or Operator third party service personnel, such as diving, cementing and electric logging personnel.
   Contractor will furnish, free of charge, board and lodging for up to .... Operator personnel, Operator visitors or Operator third party service personnel; any in excess thereof will be for account of Opertaor at fixed rates per meal or per day as will be mutually agreed upon.
6. Operator toolpusher's office, complete with desk, filing cabinet(s), necessary other furniture.
7. If possible, an Operator petroleum engineer's office with desk, filing cabinet(s), necessary other furniture.
8. Drill pipe inspection in accord with API-IADC classification standards, with Contractor to pay for said inspection in the proportion that the rejected pipe bears to the total pipe inspected.

9. Assistance in all service performed by service companies used in the operations in so far as can be done with Contractor's personnel during the regular working hours, except in the case of emergencies, when the regular working hours will not necessarily be adhered to.
10. Personnel to be furnished by Contractor:

Number Furnished	On Board Drilling Unit

In addition to the above, Contractor will employ the required catering staff on the Drilling Unit and necessary shore-based personnel and labor required.

PART III—EQUIPMENT, MATERIALS AND SERVICES TO BE FURNISHED BY OPERATOR

1. Offshore drilling permit(s).
2. Drilling site, surveyed and marked and cleared of obstructions.
3. Towing services acceptable to Contractor and Operator for towing between locations and from last location to nearest suitable port. Contractor shall have the right to inspect and approve towing contracts with respect to the Drilling Unit.
4. Furnishing of anchor handling vessel(s) and crews for handling mooring and anchors.
5. All marine and air transportation of Contractor's and Operator's Items and personnel between Contractor's and/or Operator's shore base and the Drilling Unit. Means and type of transport at the discretion of Operator.
6. Transfer at Operator's operations base of any and all materials, equipment and personnel of Operator onto and from the marine vessels and air transport.
   Contractor's materials, equipment and personnel will be transferred at Operator's shore base subject to Operator's approval, which approval shall not be unreasonably withheld.
7. Rig positioning, diving, weather forecasting and seabed survey services.
8. All electric well logging services and equipment, including string shot and back-off equipment (but Contractor to provide suitable space for installation of well logging units and for workshop for Operator's electric well logging equipment).
9. All cementing services (but Contractor maintains the cementing unit furnished by Contractor and assists in cementing operations).
10. Mud engineer, if required (but Contractor will carry out routine mud testing and treatment).
11. Mud logging service, if required.
12. Any geological services.
13. Programmed directional drilling service engineer and special equipment.
14. Drilling water, except that Contractor's distillation units can be used in cases of emergency.
15. All bits.
16. All casing, tubing and attachments.
17. All subsea equipment (including related handling tools) not furnished by Contractor, *i.e.*, temporary and permanent guide bases, casing head housings and casing hangers, wellhead housing seat protectors, conductor pipe, corrosion cap, necessary running and retrieving tools for Operator provided items and downhole swabbing equipment.
18. All cement and additives.

19. All mud, chemicals and additives, including pallets if applicable.
20. All diesel fuel for use on the Drilling Unit.
21. Main towing line from Contractor's cables to towing vessel(s) during moves between locations.
22. Well test unit and associated equipment for production testing.
23. Any drill pipe and drill collars, Kellys or subs in addition to those furnished by Contractor under Part I of this Appendix " A."
24. Stabilizers, hole openers, reamers and centralizers.
25. Underwater television, if required.
26. Drill stem testing equipment, if required.
27. All radio and telex equipment other than that to be furnished by Contractor.
28. Shore base with office space and warehouse for Contractor, including basic furnishings.
29. Loading and unloading services at dock site or heliport of all material and equipment of Contractor and Operator.
30. Containers for disposal of refuse and cuttings.
31. Approved safe storage for helicopter fuel.

Appendix B [5]

INSURANCE REQUIREMENTS

A. Insurance for Personnel

Any insurance covering personnel in accordance with the governing law of the jurisdiction where the work is performed or in accordance with applicable laws of other countries, covering those persons employed by Contractor or its subcontractors for work to be performed hereunder whose employment may be subject to such laws, during the period such persons are so engaged.

B. Comprehensive General Liability

Comprehensive General Liability Insurance with the watercraft exclusion deleted covering all operations of Contractor, including, among other risks, the contractual liability herein assumed by Contractor, with a combined single limit of $10,000,000 for bodily injury and property damage liability in any one occurrence. (Protection and Indemnity Insurance may, at Contractor's option, be substituted for this coverage of marine liabilities.)

C. Automobile Liability

Automobile Liability Insurance in accordance with any local legislation on all owned, nonowned, and hired vehicles used in connection with the work hereunder, with limit of US $250,000 for any one occurrence.

D. Marine Insurance on the Drilling Unit and its equipment during all operations under this Contract including moves within the Operating Area.

E. Other

Adequate insurance on Contractor's shore-based property, including housing, offices, stores, materials and equipment, including coverage during transportation of materials and equipment to and from the Drilling Unit.
Should Contractor at any time put in service in connection with these operations any vessels which are either owned by it, or chartered from third parties,

---

[5] To the Contract.

Contractor will carry or require to be carried adequate hull and protection and indemnity insurance on such vessels and will name Operator as an additional insured.

Costs of all insurance as listed above are included in the rates unless specifically stated otherwise in this contract.

Appendix C [6]

DEPRECIATION SCHEDULE CONTRACTOR'S EQUIPMENT

Item	Value as of Commencement Date	Depreciation Rate

REVISED CLAUSES FOR JACK-UP RIG

501. Performance of the Drilling Unit
Contractor represents that the Drilling Unit will be capable of being moved from location to location and performing the work contemplated herein.

804. Operating Rate
The Operating Rate will be $ .... per 24-hour day and will first become payable from the moment when the legs are pinned at the first drilling location and the Unit begins jacking operations. The Operating Rate shall continue to be payable except as herein otherwise provided.

1001. (b) Operator shall, to the extent Contractor's insurance does not compensate Contractor therefor, be responsible for all Contractor's in-hole equipment, including the drill string while in the hole.

    (c) Operator's responsibility for loss of or damage to Contractor's drill string is limited to Contractor's CIF replacement cost less depreciation of 25% per year. Depreciation will be deemed to have commenced on Commencement Date or on date of first use hereunder, whichever is later.

---

[6] To the Contract.

WHETHER INSURANCE OF DRILLING UNIT IS
MARINE INSURANCE

IN this Appendix we discuss whether a contract for the insurance of a drilling unit may be regarded as a contract of marine insurance for the purpose of the English Marine Insurance Act 1906. The drilling unit may be a jack-up, a semi-submersible or submersible unit, or a drilling ship. It may be insured on the London Standard Drilling Barge Form, on the Norwegian Hull Drilling Rig Conditions, or, as is frequently the case with drilling ships, on a policy with Lloyd's Institute Time Clauses or the American Hull Clauses attached. It is of course possible for the policy to provide that the provisions of the 1906 Act should apply; in such a case it would not be necessary to conduct this analysis.

To consider whether a policy for the insurance of the drilling unit itself is a marine insurance policy for the purpose of English law it is necessary to study the opening sections of the Marine Insurance Act 1906:

Section 1, headed " Marine insurance defined," and cited in full, says: " A contract of marine insurance is a contract whereby the insurer undertakes to indemnify the assured, in manner and to the extent thereby agreed, against marine losses, that is to say, the losses incident to marine adventure." [The expression " marine adventure " is described in section 3 (2) of the Act.]

Section 2, headed " Mixed sea and land risks," speaks, at subsection (1), of the possible extension of a contract of marine insurance to protect the assured " against losses on inland waters or on any land risk which may be incidental to any sea voyage." [Section 2 (2) is discussed later.]

Section 3, headed " Marine adventure and maritime perils defined," says:

" (1) Subject to the provisions of this Act, every lawful marine adventure may be the subject of a contract of marine insurance. (2) In particular there is a marine adventure where—(a) Any ship, goods, or other moveables are exposed to maritime perils. Such property is in this Act referred to as ' insurable property '; (b) [This is omitted here as it deals with the insurance of freight, passage money, etc.]; (c) Any liability to a third party may be incurred by the owner of, or other person interested in or responsible for, insurable property, by reason of maritime perils . . . . [There follows a definition of " maritime perils " which is set out below.]

We have two alternatives, the first of which need not detain us for long here. First, the drilling unit may be regarded in law as a ship. The considerations which apply in reaching this decision are discussed elsewhere.[1] If it is a ship for the purpose of the Act then section 3 (2) (a) applies, subject to one proviso, so that we can say that there is a marine adventure.

As for a definition of the word " ship " we do not derive much assistance from Rule 15 of the Rules for Construction of Policy (i.e. a policy in the form set out in the First Schedule to the Act, or in another like form) attached to the Act, but it should be set out here: " The term ' ship ' includes the hull, materials and outfit, stores and provisions for the officers and crew, and, in the case of vessels engaged in a special trade, the ordinary fittings requisite for the trade, and also, in the case of a steamship, the machinery, boilers, and coals and engine stores, if owned by the assured." This Rule deals with the scope of an object which is a ship, and

---

[1] See Chap. 2, above.

does not purport to define a ship. One would therefore rely largely on what the courts have said in other contexts as to the meaning of the word " ship."

As section 1 says, " losses incident to marine adventure " are marine losses, and a contract of marine insurance is a contract for indemnity against such losses. The proviso which has been mentioned is that the ship should be exposed to maritime perils. The term " maritime perils " is defined in section 3, the closing words of which state:

> " ' Maritime perils ' means the perils consequent on, or incidental to, the navigation of the sea, that is to say, perils of the seas, fire, war perils, pirates, rovers, thieves, captures, seizures, restraints, and detainments of princes and peoples, jettisons, barratry, and any other perils, either of the like kind or which may be designated by the policy."

The " ship," as it is assumed to be in the circumstances, is clearly exposed to the perils listed. They are described as being consequent on or incidental to the navigation of the sea. If such a drilling unit has been or is in due course held to be a ship it would follow that she is regarded as an object capable of or engaged in navigation. It would be difficult to argue that the perils were not consequent on or incidental to its navigation of the sea; and they would in any event be incidental to " the navigation " of the sea.

The second alternative is that the drilling unit in question does not constitute a " ship." If it is not a ship does it fall within the words " goods, or other moveables " in section 3 (2) (*a*)? We must first see whether section 90, on " Interpretation of Terms," or the " Rules for Construction of Policy," in the First Schedule, provide any guidance. The term " moveables " is defined in section 90, which states: " ' Moveables ' means any moveable tangible property, other than the ship, and includes money, valuable securities, and other documents."

This definition of " moveables " seems wide enough, in its opening words, to cover self-elevating, submersible and semi-submersible drilling units. Its specific inclusion of " money, valuable securities, and other documents," however, seems to suggest that those drafting the Act had in mind movable objects which were in, on or connected with a ship. It seems probable, particularly in view of the use of the words " the ship " rather than " ship," that these words would not be held to be wide enough to include a drilling unit which had failed to qualify as a " ship " for the purpose of the Act.

Rule 17 of the First Schedule to the Marine Insurance Act 1906 states: " The term ' goods ' means goods in the nature of merchandise, and does not include personal effects or provisions and stores for use on board. In the absence of any usage to the contrary, deck cargo and living animals must be insured specifically, and not under the general denomination of goods."

This definition of goods can be contrasted with the definition in the Sale of Goods Act 1893, at section 62: " ' Goods ' includes all chattels personal other than things in action and money . . . " The definition in rule 17 is more limited, as it (a) restricts the term " goods " to goods in the nature of merchandise, *i.e.* goods which are in fact or would normally be the subject of contracts of sale, hire, or any other transactions by merchants; (b) excludes personal effects and provisions and stores for use on board; and (c) provides for specific and separate insurance of deck cargo and living animals.

It therefore seems, if we may revert to section 3 (2) (*a*), that the word " goods " refers to the cargo, as limited and defined in Rule 17, and the words " other moveables " refer to everything else on a ship, subject to the definition in section 90. It seems most unlikely that drilling units could be regarded as " goods or other moveables " so as to cause the adventure to be a marine adventure. This conclusion is not inconsistent with the use of other similar expressions in the

1906 Act, such as " a policy on goods or other moveables " in section 40 (saying that there is no implied warranty that they are seaworthy) and " a partial loss of goods, merchandise, or other moveables " in section 71 (setting out the measure of indemnity in such a case).

We must consider whether section 2 (2) of the Marine Insurance Act 1906 causes that Act to apply. Section 2 (2) of the Act states:

> " Where a ship in course of building, or the launch of a ship, or any adventure analogous to a marine adventure, is covered by a policy in the form of a marine policy, the provisions of this Act, in so far as applicable, shall apply thereto; but, except as by this section provided, nothing in this Act shall alter or affect any rule of law applicable to any contract of insurance other than a contract of marine insurance as by this Act defined."

Applying this to self-elevating, submersible or semi-submersible drilling units, we can conclude that even if the adventure is not a marine adventure it is analogous to a marine adventure. For something to be analogous to something else it must be " Similar, parallel " [2] to it. We have already seen the definition of a marine adventure in section 3 (2).[3] The establishment in the sea of an installation which, though it is not a ship, can float, can be moved from place to place by sea, spends its working life on the surface of the sea so far as most of its main operating parts are concerned, drills for oil or gas to be obtained from the sea-bed, and carries a crew, can fairly be regarded as an adventure " similar " or " parallel " to a marine adventure.

A question then arises as to whether the adventure " is covered by a policy in the form of a marine policy." There are various forms of policy in respect of the insurance of a drilling unit. If we take the London Standard Drilling Barge Form, as a frequently used form of policy, an examination of its terms shows that it is " in the form of a marine policy." As in the Institute Time Clauses (Hulls), which it so much resembles in some of its wording, there are provisions for collision liability, deductibles (except in the case of actual or constructive total loss), constructive total loss, sue and labour expenses, lay up and cancellation, and a Free of Capture and Seizure Clause.

The closing words of section 2 (2) introduce a safeguard; they may be paraphrased by saying that the Act does not change any legal rule which applies to non-marine insurance contracts, except where section 2 says so. The effect of section 2 (2) appears to be that if the drilling unit is not a ship, and quite apart from the effect of section 3 (2) (*a*), the provisions of the Act apply to a contract for the insurance of drilling units. For the policy to constitute a contract of marine insurance, however, the words of section 2 (2) alone may not be enough. If the adventure is only analogous to a marine adventure, section 2 (2) applies, so that the provisions of the Act apply; but it is possible that the contract is only a " contract of marine insurance " if the specific words and descriptions in section 3 are applicable and the conclusion is drawn that there is a marine adventure.

---

[2] *Concise Oxford Dictionary.*
[3] See p. 456, above.

A NATIONALISATION LAW AND THE DEFINITION OF A SHIP

IN 1976 a minor constitutional crisis in the United Kingdom turned on a dispute as to whether a jack-up drilling unit should be regarded as a ship, though this question arose not in the context of the definition of a ship in public general law, but in the context of the actual definitions contained in the particular Bill. The British Labour government had in 1975 introduced the Aircraft and Shipbuilding Industries Bill to nationalise five separate industries. The Bill was so drafted that neither the Speaker nor the Chairman of the Standing Committee was able to exercise the power, which he otherwise would have had, to order that the Bill be divided into two or more separate Bills. The Bill, which was strongly opposed by the Opposition, listed the companies which were to be nationalised, but it did not include in the list Marathon Shipbuilding (U.K.) Ltd., a subsidiary of Marathon Manufacturing of Houston, Texas. In 1972 the subsidiary had bought the old John Brown shipbuilding yard on the River Clyde. The list included, however, Yarrow Shipbuilding, who were competitors of Marathon. It seems that the omission of Marathon occurred because the then President of the Amalgamated Society of Boilermakers, Shipwrights, Blacksmiths and Structural Workers (also known as the Boilermakers' Union) had given an undertaking before the yard was purchased that a Labour Government would not subsequently nationalise it, though it was never clear on whose authority he gave this undertaking.

The procedural rules of the House of Commons, some of which are embodied in the form of Standing Orders, contemplate four kinds of Bills: Public Bills, Private Bills, Hybrid Bills and Personal Bills. A Public Bill alters the general law, whereas a Private Bill relates to a matter of individual or local interest. The then Speaker of the House of Commons said in 1962 [1]: " A hybrid Bill can be defined as a public Bill which affects a particular private interest in a manner different from the private interests of other persons or bodies of the same category or class . . . I accept the true position to be this, that if it be possible for the view to be taken that this Bill is a hybrid Bill it ought to go to the examiners. There must not be a doubt about it." The procedure in the case of a Hybrid Bill differs from that applicable to a Public Bill, and involves the appointment of a Select Committee to examine petitions and take evidence from interested parties, who may be represented by lawyers.

The Bill defined a ship as a " floating or submersible vessel with an integral hull." This was a definition given in order to limit the scope of the expression " shipbuilding," the nationalisation of which was one object of the Bill. It was not a definition for the many other purposes, such as questions of admiralty jurisdiction and limitation of liability,[2] for which a ship has to be defined. The Bill had received its second Reading, and there had been 58 Standing Committee Sessions, when on May 25, 1976, Mr. Robin Maxwell-Hyslop, the Conservative Member of Parliament for Tiverton, contended, in both oral and written submissions to the Speaker of the House of Commons, that the Bill was a Hybrid Bill, and that as a result it should be submitted to the procedure applicable to such Bills. This, he contended, would waste no time whatsoever, since there was no inherent reason why a Select Committee sitting before the Report Stage but after the Standing Committee stage would take any longer than it would

---

[1] H.C. Deb., Vol. 669, col. 45 (1962–63).
[2] For these and other issues see Chap. 2 (b), above

have taken in its normal interposition between Second Reading and Standing Committee stage.

Mr. Maxwell-Hyslop argued that although Marathon clearly fell within the provisions of the qualifying conditions, being a shipbuilding company, it had been arbitrarily excluded from the Bill, while its competitors, including Yarrow Shipbuilders, had been arbitrarily included: " This arbitrary exclusion," he said, " of one company and the inclusion of another when both companies fall within the same definitions of the schedule endows this Bill with all the characteristics of a Hybrid Bill, and not a public general Bill." In a preliminary response, the Speaker of the House of Commons said that on July 31, 1974, which was the relevant date for the purpose of the Bill, the shipyard, although owned by the company concerned, was being used not for the construction of " ships " but for the manufacture of offshore drilling rigs and the conversion of a ship to a rig. He therefore ruled that the submission did not support the case for hybridity in the Bill. He added, however, that he would make further inquiries.

After the submissions by Mr. Maxwell-Hyslop there had become available certain further facts, which he put to the Speaker by way of an oral point of order in the House of Commons. It appeared that on July 31, 1974, Marathon was engaged in the construction of the *Key Victoria*, a jack-up drilling unit. Upon completion, on October 14, 1974, it was delivered to Key International Drilling Co. Ltd., and later went to work off the coast of Zaire under a charter to Gulf Oil. On October 17, 1974, the American Bureau of Shipping issued a certificate classifying it as a self-elevating drilling unit [3]; its tonnage was put at 3,885 g.r.t. It had a Liberian flag. The Opposition had been unaware of the existence of the *Key Victoria* on the occasion of the first submission. It would appear that the government, for its part, while aware of the *Key Victoria*, had understood that the work thereon involved a conversion from a ship and not a new construction.

The argument that Marathon clearly fell within the qualifying provisions of the Bill depended upon the correctness of the contention that the jack-up drilling unit in question was a ship. Mr. Maxwell-Hyslop said that it was immaterial whether the vessel was also an oil-drilling rig, or whether it dredged the sea floor, drilled holes in the sea floor, or was used to carry goods. He added that it was a vessel within the definition of the Merchant Shipping Act. It seems that it would have been enough that the *Key Victoria* was a ship within the definition of the Bill under consideration, *i.e.* " a floating or submersible vessel with an integral hull." It was not also necessary that it should be a ship within the definition of section 742 of the Merchant Shipping Act 1894, where it is stated: " ' Ship ' includes every description of vessel used in navigation not propelled by oars." [4]

The Speaker made further inquiries and received representations from both sides of the House of Commons. He then reversed his earlier ruling and said that the Bill under discussion was prima facie hybrid. If the usual procedure associated with a Hybrid Bill had then been followed, there would have been consideration, by a select Committee, of the formal petition which by then had been presented by Mr. Maxwell-Hyslop on behalf of a shareholder of Yarrow Shipbuilders, claiming that Marathon met the nationalisation criteria laid down in the Bill.

In the ensuing Parliamentary discussion both the abstract conception of " a ship " and the definition of a ship under the Merchant Shipping Act were considered, whereas it was the definition of a ship under the Bill in question which was material. The Secretary for Industry, with a view to demonstrating that the

---

[3] For the various categories designated by the A.B.S., see Chap. 1, above.

[4] See also the discussion of English decisions on this section in Chap. 2 (c), above.

Key Victoria was not a ship, referred to the description of the *Key Victoria* given by the American Bureau of Shipping, as a " mobile, self-elevating drilling unit." He said that a major part of the structure, namely the drilling legs, was not integral with the platform, which floated only when the platform was being moved from one location to another. He showed a photograph of the unit in its normal operating position, and made copies available to Members of Parliament. He said: " In my view, it is very difficult to construe that structure as a vessel within the natural meaning of the word." He referred to the practice of the Inland Revenue, and indicated that it did not treat self-elevating units as ships for capital allowance purposes. He mentioned also the Industry Act 1975, which distinguished between a ship and an offshore installation for the purpose of eligibility for ship construction grants. The *Key Victoria* had been awarded a construction grant not as a ship but as an offshore installation. Furthermore, he said, Lloyd's Register of Shipping regarded ships and oil platforms as sufficiently different to warrant separate technical staff. It is submitted that it was not the " natural meaning," whatever that might be, nor the Inland Revenue law and practice, nor the definitions in other Acts but the definition contained in the Bill under discussion that was relevant.[5]

One Member of Parliament submitted that the difficulty could be overcome by " a small amendment which defines a ship as a ship and a rig as a rig." Another Member said that shipyard workers were " quite aware of what a ship is [6] and also quite aware of what an oil rig is and they know that an oil rig is an oil rig and a ship is a ship." [7] Yet another Member referred to the words in the definition, " floating or submersible vessel "; the *Key Victoria*, he said, was now drilling off the coast of Zaire, and it must have floated there, whether or not it was towed by other ships.

The government proposed to deal with the problem by obtaining a vote of the House of Commons to suspend the Standing Orders so far as they related to private business. As a result the procedural rules governing Hybrid Bills were suspended and the Bill was able to proceed more expeditiously, as if it had been a Public Bill.

At a later stage (the Report stage) the government altered the definition in the Bill so that oil rigs were excluded from it; but the Bill remained prima facie hybrid, since it was not sent to the Examiners nor re-submitted to the Speaker with a view to his amending his ruling. In accordance with the legislative process the Bill went to the House of Lords,[8] which removed the entire ship-repairing section. The amendments were rejected by the House of Commons. The government reintroduced the Bill in the House of Commons, but after lengthy discussions there, before the Examiners, the Cabinet decided to delete the provision to nationalise the ship-repairing industry. The Bill was eventually passed in its amended form.

---

[5] What is not relevant here is to set out the other arguments which were advanced, as these related to political issues such as the need for nationalisation, unemployment in the shipbuilding industry, and the appropriateness of the certification by the sponsoring departments to the Public Bill Office that the Bill was not hybrid.

[6] For some if the dangers inherent in this approach, see Chap. 2 (a), above.

[7] Some Labour Members of Parliament made this distinction between ships and drilling units; the National Union of Seamen, however, in its campaign to unionise offshore labour and to introduce a closed shop, then regarded the industry as one which was peculiarly appropriate to it and its fellow unions on the National Maritime Board, rather than to the Transport and General Workers' Union. As a result the N.U.S. and other seafarers' unions concluded agreements in 1975 with the owners and managers of the *Dundee Kingsnorth*, a semi-submersible and the first independently owned British offshore mobile drilling unit.

[8] By which time other allegations of hybridity, based on different grounds, had been made; but they were not pursued.

INDEX

Index

OIL INSURANCE LTD.—*cont.*
civil war, and, 372
confiscation, 376
contamination liability, 367–368
contraction, and, 375
cost of control expenses, 363–364
crude oil, and, 374
damage to property, 358–360
design, defects in, 375
deterioration, and, 375
exclusion of ships from basic cover, 368–369
expansion, and, 375
expropriation, 376
failure to save and preserve property, 375–376
fines, 376–377
governments, action by, 369–374
  offshore properties, 369–374
  onshore properties, 374
inherent defect, and, 375
insurable interest, 359
loss of hire, and, 374
material, defects in, 375
minerals *in situ*, and, 374
natural gas, and, 374
nature of indemnity, 358
origin of, 357
penalties, 376–377
physical loss to property, 358–360
piracy, and, 372
pollution liability, 367–368
removal of debris, and, 393
removal of debris expenses, 365–367
seepage liability, 367–368
sue and labour expenses, 360–363
terrorism, and, 372–373
use and occupancy, 376
waste products, and, 376
workmanship, defects in, 375
OPERATING RATE,
drilling contract, and, 286–287
OPERATOR'S GUARANTY, 385–387
effectiveness of, 386–387
OPERATOR'S SURETY BOND, 385 *et seq.*

PENALTIES,
O.I.L. cover, and, 376–377
PERILS,
definition, 164–165
exclusion from insurance policy, 192–195
Norwegian Cover, 231
PERSONAL INJURY,
collision insurance, and, 122
cost of control insurance, and, 407
Norwegian Cover, 225–226, 233–234
protecting and indemnity cover, 209–210
PERSONNEL,
drilling contract, and, 256–258
insurance for, 278–280, 316–317
PIRACY, 40–43
broadcasting, 42–43
definition, 40–41, 372
Geneva Convention on High Seas 1958, 41–42
municipal law, 42
O.I.L. cover, and, 372
PIRATE BROADCASTING, 42–43

POLLUTION, 43–51, 323 *et seq.*
agreement by insured to pay premium, 328
civil liability, international convention on, 45–47
claim under insurance, 338
clean-up clause, 335–336
collision insurance, and, 121
contamination, and, 273–274
cost of preventing substances reaching shore, 337
cost of removal, 335
definition, 334
draft Off-Shore Mobile Craft Convention, 51
drilling contracts, and, 272–275
generally, 323–327
insuring agreements, 327 *et seq.*
International Compensation Fund, 45–47
international conventions, 44 *et seq.*
intervention, international convention on, 47
legal liability, 330–335
  bodily injury, 331
  causation, 333
  property, and, 332
liability for, 323 *et seq.*
obstacles, and, 274–275
offshore operations, and, 49–50
Offshore Pollution Liability Agreement, 377 *et seq. See also* OFFSHORE POLLUTION LIABILITY AGREEMENT.
O.I.L. cover, and, 367–368
operator's insurance, 325–326
prevention of dumping, 47–49
protecting and indemnity cover, 213–214
proviso to cover clause, 338–339
remedial measures, 336
responsibility for, 324–325
sea by oil, of,
  international conventions for prevention, 44–45
seepage, pollution and contamination insurance, 327 *et seq. See also* SEEPAGE, POLLUTION AND CONTAMINATION INSURANCE POLICY.
ships, and,
  international convention, and, 45
statement of underwriters, 328–329
sums and cost in respect of which assured is insured, 329–337
PONTOON,
crane, and, 80–81
damage to, 79–80
seaworthiness, 80
ship, whether, 70–71, 78–81
PORT, IN, 95–96
POSSESSION,
deprivation of, insurance and, 148–150
PROTECTING AND INDEMNITY COVER, 208 *et seq.*
automobile liability, 222
clubs, 208
collisions, 211–212
  ships, with, 211
  objects other than ships, 212–213
  other drilling units, 211–212

470